Community Practice

Community Practice
Theories and Skills for Social Workers

David A. Hardcastle

Stanley Wenocur

Patricia R. Powers

New York   Oxford
Oxford University Press
1997

Oxford University Press

Oxford   New York
Athens   Aukland   Bangkok
Bogota   Bombay   Buenos Aires   Calcutta
Cape Town   Dar es Salaam   Delhi
Florence   Hong Kong   Istanbul   Karachi
Kuala Lumpur   Madras   Melbourne
Mexico City   Nairobi   Paris   Singapore
Taipei   Tokyo   Toronto

and associated companies in

Berlin   Ibadan

Library of Congress Cataloging-in-Publication Data

Hardcastle, David A.
Community practice : theories and skills for social workers
David A. Hardcastle, Stanley Wenocur, Patricia Powers.
p.   cm.   Includes bibliographical references and index.
ISBN 0-19-509352-6
1. Social service.   2. Social workers.
I. Wenocur, Stanley.   II. Powers, Patricia R.   III. Title.
HV40.H289   1996
361.3'2—dc20   95-45038

3 5 7 9 8 6 4 2
Printed in the United States of America
on acid-free paper

Contents

Preface

"I want to do therapy after I graduate." As faculty who read admissions folders, we are mindful of applicants who have decided it is cheaper and easier to obtain an M.S.W. than to obtain a Ph.D. in psychology or an M.D. in psychiatry. As teachers, we notice the growing number of social work students who come to school solely to learn how to do long-term treatment and enticing types of therapies. Usually their vision of professional intervention involves some sort of counseling of "dysfunctional" individual and family clients in an office on a regular schedule of hourly visits over an extended time period. It may also include leading a behavioral change or support group, but the individual is considered paramount.

A commitment to humaneness and helping is essential to good social work practice. Yet, this treatment vision of helping, while important, is incomplete. Certainly any of us may benefit from therapy or counseling and a caring professional at some point during our lives, but we will also benefit from advocacy and professionals who speak up on our behalf. As an academic aspiration, therapy training leaves out the "social" in social work, that part of social work practice that helps individuals and families, as well as groups, organizations, and communities, to address the social environment in order to overcome environmental deficiencies or malfunctions or to take advantage of opportunities. This attention to the interplay of the individual and the social environment is one of social work's great strengths as a profession and a feature that distinguishes it from other kindred helping professions. This expanded view of helping also invites affirmation of social work's historic commitment to serve and advocate for those harmed by modern society. The legitimacy of the social work profession rests on this commitment. In our view, the continuing legitimacy of the social work profession during this time of rampant individualism, a diminishing middle class, demonization of the poor, social retrenchment, and categorical pathologizing of the diversity of human behavior with an expanding *Diagnostic and Statistical Manual* requires this commitment.

When students and teachers get concrete, though, about intervention, some seeming differences in priorities and methodology may disappear. Intervention at the macro level, that is, changing big things, often requires starting with individuals. One advocate may try to influence another individual who can make a decision. This is one-on-one communication and also networking. As a clinical student observed, "To me this seems more similar to counseling than different." Six people may come together to make a change in the community. This is about the same size as a small group that a social worker might facilitate. Thus, social action also builds on interpersonal communication. If six people go to see a commissioner, they do not all talk at once; there is a spokesperson—an individual who must be trained. Both clinical and community social workers want to empower. The graduate student went on to note that "the systems within which we work and operate are really collections of individuals. To me, transforming society isn't a matter of transforming some nebulous structure. It's a matter of changing people."

As we look at the current field of social work, in many ways we seem to be going back to the future. Poverty is on the rise. Ethnic, racial, and social divisiveness is growing. Reactionary forces under the guise of conservatism are destroying the safety net that has undergirded social welfare services for the last 60 years. Our political leaders are touting this as progress and reform. The emerging American design of the market economy is helping large corporations and the top 1 percent of the population to prosper, while socially and economically declining working- and middle-class people experience economic insecurity.

This sounds like the 1920s before the crash. And after the crash, social workers were doubly injured, as they are bound to be in the future, because their own lives and livelihoods, as well as those of their clients, were so directly and harshly affected. What should we do? There are no easy answers, but revitalization of communities and our social connectedness appears to be a critical requisite.

In the 1930s, it was hard to ignore the impact of a malfunctioning social system. While some social workers became politically active and others stayed in the casework trenches, for many in both camps the obvious relationship between private trouble and public issues blurred the distinction between community work and casework. Social workers clearly had to attend to both, and many did. The knowledge and skills of each played a part in the creation of a new system of basic social protections and services. We predict the same will be true in the coming millennium. Our script seems to have been written. It entails struggle—but struggle, of course, with the tools and opportunities that a different era affords, and with the eventual potential for discovering better solutions to old problems and perhaps a different and more humane social order. To the extent that this book enables all social workers to strengthen their community-building skills, we hope to have contributed to the venture.

Our goal has been to provide a comprehensive and integrated text covering community theory and the skills necessary for all social work practitioners and students. It is a foundation textbook for practice. As most students eventually will be direct service practitioners, the book addresses the necessary community theory and community practice skills from the position of the theory, the knowledge of community, and skills required by direct service practitioners—case workers, case managers, and clinicians, including those in or those who anticipate entering proprietary practice—to produce effective social work practitioners. The text does not assume that the students or practitioners are community organizers, but it does assume that community skills are a necessary part of a true foundation for effective direct service practice.

The content addresses community theory and community practice skills, organizational and interorganizational practice theory and skills, and requisite small group theory and skills, as well as theories and skills for professional self-development and intervention. The integrating themes for the book are the theories and skills required for effective direct service practitioners. The book has two parts. Part I covers the ideological, ethical, and theoretical foundation necessary for community practice. We believe professional practice requires an ethical, ideological, and theoretical grounding for the practice skills. Ours is set forth. People and their community are fundamental. The text also reflects our belief that personal fortitude and integrity must accompany the application of practice knowledge and skills.

Part II is devoted to community practice skills. The chapters in this part follow what we believe is a logical order. However, the instructor, the students, and the readers can arrange them to fit their preferences.

We concentrate on the skills, knowledge, personal fortitude, and ethical commitments required of today's social workers if they are to help their clients address the social environment. We call these helping activities and skills *community practice* because the term *community* captures the humanness and interconnectedness among people in a way that *social environment*, *social ecology*, *social systems*, *task environment*, and other physical science terms seem to miss. However, we do use

these theories and concepts, as well as theories and concepts from marketing and other professions, in developing the models of community practice. As social work practice is broad and eclectic and intersects with many other fields, we deliberately use diverse practice examples to illuminate our points. We have featured the difficulties people face individually and collectively in their daily lives, as well as ways that social workers can be of assistance beyond the psychological domain.

The accompanying *Instructor's Manual* contains additional practice exercises so that students can develop and apply, in a simulated fashion, their community practice knowledge and skills. The most recent curriculum policy accreditation requirements of the Council on Social Work Education were reviewed in developing the text.

At various points throughout the book, we have used the specific words of community practitioners to describe their helping practice. Many of these quotes and extracts were taken from interviews conducted by graduate students at the University of Maryland at Baltimore School of Social Work for a project on the experiences, views, and perspectives of social advocates directed by one of the authors. These interviews have been compiled in two monographs, *Stirring People Up* and *Challenging*, which are used in the school's macro or community practice course required for all students as part of their professional foundation. It was that course on communities and social service networks that provided the contours for this textbook. We found that there was a dearth of resources on the development and application of community practice skills by direct service practitioners.

We have, of course, drawn on our own practice experience and on our theoretical and methodological knowledge. Our combined community and social work practice exceeds 90 years and includes community organization and development, social group work, administration, child welfare, aging, disabilities, consumer self-help, mental health, hunger and homelessness, fund-raising, labor organizing, and more. Many of our case examples come from our professional experiences or are composites of our professional experience.

D.A.H.
S.W.
P.R.P.

Baltimore, Maryland
March 1996

Acknowledgments

The authors acknowledge the contributions of their families and friends, whose support made this book possible. We thank Dean Jesse Harris of the School of Social Work, the University of Maryland at Baltimore, for his encouragement and work scheduling flexibility that made our task less onerous. We owe a debt to our colleagues at the School of Social Work, especially our colleagues in the school's Community Organization and Social Administration Concentration and the Community Practice Faculty, for their encouragement, suggestions, and criticisms of the manuscript and their confidence that the project would be completed. Catherine Foster Alter of the School of Social Work, the University of Iowa, is recognized for the insight her casebook provided to our discussion of interorganizational practice and networking.

We expressly thank the students in community practice classes over the past few years for their use and critiques of the material and their patience with us in our revisions of the manuscript drafts. It was their needs and demands for coherence in community practice as a basic skill for all social workers that inspired the book.

Further, we gratefully acknowledge the communities, clients, and practitioners with whom we gained our community practice experience and refined our theories, understanding, and skills. We appreciate the community practitioners, lay and professional, who shared with us their experience in services facilitation and advocacy for people and their communities. Their service and commitment to better neighborhoods and communities as places for people to live informed our discussion of skills building with clients, linkages of clients with support systems, and using skills with communities in forging change. We hope the book will continue their contribution to enhancing community practice and humane communities.

Individually, we wish to thank our families for their patience, empathy, reassurance, and periodic critiques of the work in progress. Without them there for us, there would be no completed work. David Hardcastle particularly thanks his wife, Dr. Cynthia Bisman, of the Graduate School of Social Work and Social Research of Bryn Mawr College, who helped define and elaborate the direct practice applications. She is a persistent helpmate, colleague, consistent supporter, and enduring inspiration. Stan Wenocur adds his special thanks to his wife, Gail, for her constant support and understanding during this project. Patricia Powers thanks her spouse, Tom Harvey, who contributed in so many ways to this book, to nonprofit organizations, and to social causes. We also appreciate the patience and understanding of the staff at Oxford University Press during this process.

We salute the work of the pioneer community theorists and reformers, such as the late Arthur Dunham, who was also concerned with peace and the global village. Arthur was a role model in his personal and professional life. Last, we wish to acknowledge the late Dr. Harry Specht for his constant contribution to community as a central facet of social work practice. His steadfast and clarion call for maintaining community as the central tenet of social work practice, while sometimes discomforting to our profession, has guided our thinking, practice, and instruction. The book reflects our efforts to bring community back into all social work practice. Harry's powerful message remains with us long after his passing, and we trust all social workers will answer his call.

Community Practice

chapter

1

Community Practice: An Introduction

Community practice is basic to all social work and necessary for all social workers, whether generalists, specialists, therapists, or activists. Although usually associated with community organization, social action, social planning (Rothman & Tropman, 1987), and other macro-practice activities, direct service and clinical social workers engage in community practice when they make client referrals, assess community resources, develop client social support systems, and advocate to policymakers for programs to meet clients' needs.

This chapter will present an overview of community practice, explore the conception of community practice as social work practice, review the importance of community practice knowledge and skill for all social workers, describe the generic social work community problem-solving strategy and its use in community practice by clinical and community development social workers, and examine the ethical constraints of community practice. Finally, a cautionary note on the uses and limitations of theories and models for practice is given.

COMMUNITY PRACTICE

Community practice is the application of practice skills to alter the behavioral patterns of community groups, organizations, and institutions or people's relationships and interactions with these entities. Netting and her colleagues (1993) conceive of community practice as part of macro-practice. They define macro-practice as the "professional directed intervention designed to bring about planned change in organizations and communities" (p. 3). Community practice as macro-practice includes the skills associated with community organization and development, social planning and social action, and social administration.

Community organization and the related strategy of community development is the practice of helping a community or part of a community, such as a neighborhood or a group of people with a common interest, to be a more effective, efficient, and supportive social environment for nurturing people and their social relationships. Ross (1967), an early sponsor of bringing community organization into the social work profession, conceived of community organization as

> a process by which a community identifies its needs or objectives, orders (or ranks) these needs or objectives, develops the confidence and will to work at these needs or objectives, finds the resources (internal and/or external) to deal with these needs or objectives, takes action in respect to them, and in so doing extends and develops cooperative and collaborative attitudes and practices in the community. (p. 28)

Social planning, a subset of community organization, addresses the development and coordination of community agencies and services to meet community functions and responsibilities and to provide for its members.

Social action, another subset of community organization, is the development, redistribution, and control of community statuses and resources, including social power, and the alteration of community relations and behavior patterns to promote the development or redistribution of community resources.

But community practice is not limited to macro-oriented practitioners. When a social worker engages in developing, locating, linking with, and managing community resources to help people improve their social functioning and lives, the social worker is engaging in community practice. When a social worker helps clients make better use of the social environment's resources, the social worker is involved in community practice. Social workers seeking licensure protection

for the profession or stronger laws against child abuse from the state legislature are participating in social action.

The macro social worker—the community organizer, planner, and social activist—and the direct service or clinical social worker may differ in perspective. The community organizer assumes that if the community, with its organizations and institutions and behavior patterns, can function more effectively and be responsive to its members, the members of the community will be healthier and happier. In direct service practice, the community is viewed as a supportive or potentially supportive resource for a specific client or a class of clients, and the community change efforts are designed to improve the community for these clients. In attempting to improve the quality of life for individual clients, the social worker may operate from the perspective that if enough individuals can be made healthy, the community will be better for everyone. Both sets of practitioners require knowledge of community structures and behavior and the skills to effect behavior changes in some part of the community. Both sets of social workers generally use a similar problem-solving strategy that will be described later in this chapter. Additionally, social workers often engage in both sets of practices, either simultaneously or sequentially. They work directly with clients and, at the same time, develop community resources. Social work supervisors, adminis-

> Project PLASE (People Lacking Ample Shelter and Employment) . . . [has] been here [for over twenty years]. Our philosophy . . . is advocacy. It's advocacy on the individual level, . . . it's also advocacy if you're getting a law passed. . . . It's like a circle that doesn't have a break in it. (Powers, n.d.)

trators, and social activists often begin their professional careers as direct service social workers.

THE COMMUNITY IN SOCIAL WORK PRACTICE

Communities are the context of social work practice. Communities and community practice have been central to social work's history and development. Understanding, intervening in, and using the client's social environment as part of the helping process are skills consonant with the profession's ecological foundation. Social systems, especially communities, strongly influence the ways people think and act. Communities can be nurturing environments and provide basic social, economic, and emotional supports to individuals and families. Conversely, communities can be hostile places when there are inequities that contribute significantly to individual and family malfunctioning (Anderson & Carter, 1984). One's self-concept, at least in part, is developed through involvement in and identification with social and community groups (Miller & Prentice, 1994).

Communities and Clients

1. Community forces shape, provide opportunities, and limit clients' behavior.
2. Clients need the capacity to assess, access and manage, and alter community resources and forces.
3. Clients need the capacity to contribute to the welfare of their communities.

Community theories explain what a community is and how a community functions. Often the theories offer propositions delineating how communities should func-

tion to serve their members most effectively. Community theories tend to be complex because the concept of community, like many social science concepts, is a slippery, intricate, and multifaceted summary concept covering a range of social phenomena. Cohen (1985) has cataloged more than 90 different definitions of community used in the social sciences literature.

Communities are nonetheless real for most people, although, as we will see in Chapter 4, the concept of community means different things to different people. Community can mean a geographic space, a geopolitical or civic entity, and a place of emotional identity. It is the emotional identity of community that gives it meaning for most people (Bellah, Madsen, Sullivan, Swidler, & Tipton, 1985, 1991; Cohen, 1985; Lasch, 1994).

Cohen (1985) emphasizes the emotional charging, personal identification, and symbolic construction of community by people. He conceives of community as

> a system of values, norms, and moral codes which provoke a sense of identity within a bounded whole to its members.... [S]tructures do not, in themselves, create meaning for people.... [Without meaning] many of the organizations designed to create "community" as palliative to anomie and alienation are doomed to failure. (p. 9)

The community, Cohen continues, is "the arena in which people acquire their most fundamental and most substantial experience of social life outside the confines of the home.... Community, therefore, is where one learns and continues to practice how to 'be social' " (p. 15).

If we accept the importance of the meaning of community to people, the importance of community knowledge and community practice skills as necessary for all social work practitioners follows. Community practice calls on social workers to employ a range of skills and theories to help clients use and contribute to the resources and strengths of their communities. Indeed, postmodernist social work theorists such as Pardeck, Murphy, and Choi (1994) assert that "Social work practice, simply stated, should be community based.... [C]ommunity is not defined in racial, ethnic, demographic, or geographic terms, as is often done. Instead a community is a domain where certain assumptions about reality are acknowledged to have validity" (p. 345).

COMMUNITY PRACTICE SKILLS REQUIRED FOR ALL SOCIAL WORKERS

Community practice as a shared foundation skill of all social workers is rooted in the profession's purpose and mission, its history, the policies of the two major professional social work associations, and the changing environment of social work practice.

Social Work's Purpose and Mission

Gordon (1969), a leading social work theorist until his death in the early 1990s, stated that improvement of the client's social functioning is the cardinal mission of contemporary social work practice. The profession's attention is focused on the transactions between people and their social environment and the management of these transactions. "Transaction is *exchanges in the context of action or activity*" (Gordon, 1969, p. 7).

Polsky (1969) concurred and advocated even more strongly for community knowledge and skills by the practitioner and participation by the client in community change. "Changes in dysfunctioning individuals cannot be effectuated nor sustained unless the system in which they function also under-

goes modification through client efforts" (p. 20).

The importance of the client's community is reflected in social work's dual perspectives of "person in environment," "person and environment," and the "ecological approach" to social casework practice promoted by Bisman (1994), Ewalt (1980), and Germain (1983). Bisman (1983) clarifies the dual perspective and the community's role in social work practice with the following conception:

> What has been called the dual perspective of person and environment actually has three components. Person and environment means the consideration of individuals within the context of the community and its resources, societal policies and regulations and the service delivery of organizations. (p. 27)

Specht and Courtney (1994), in their critique of the contemporary profession, *Unfaithful Angels: How Social Work Has Abandoned Its Mission*, emphatically insist that

> [T]he objective of social work is to help people make use of social resources—family members, friends, neighbors, community organizations and social service agencies, and so forth—to solve their problems.... They (i.e., social workers) deal with social problems, which concern the community, rather than personality problems of individuals. Helping individuals to make use of their social resources is one of the major functions of social work practice. And just as important is the social worker's function of developing and strengthening these resources by bringing people together in groups and organizations, by community education, and by organizational development. (p. 23)

Specht & Courtney (1994), like Gordon (1969), further contend that social workers should examine and facilitate the transaction between clients—indeed, between all people—in the community and inveigh against the social isolation of psychotherapy.

> Social work's mission should be to build a meaning, a purpose, and a sense of obligation for the community. It is only by creating a community that we establish a basis for commitment, obligation, and social support. We must build communities that are excited about their child care systems, that find it exhilarating to care for the mentally ill and frail aged, that make demands upon people to behave, to contribute, and to care for one another. Psychotherapy will not enable us to do that, . . . to give purpose and meaning to people's lives, and enable us to care about and love one another. (p. 27)

Knowledge and skill in community practice are distinguishing attributes that separate the complete social worker from the "wanna be" psychiatrist—a social worker who is only marginally a professional social worker. Without community knowledge and skill, the social worker is limited in the capacity to understand and assist clients in shaping and managing the major forces that affect their lives, and in the ability to help clients empower themselves to develop and manage personal and social resources.

Social Work's History

Community practice skills are and have been an indispensable component of social work's repertoire since the inception of the profession. The recognition of and attention to the community and its influences, the "social" in social work, is one of the properties that has historically distinguished the social work profession and effective social work practice from the profusion of other counseling and therapeutic professions (Doherty, 1995, p. 47).

From its formation as a profession at the beginning of the twentieth century, social

work's central concern has been to improve individual and collective social functioning. Mary Richmond, a pioneer of American social casework, indicated the importance of community theory, the social environment, and community practice skills for social casework in her two books on social casework: *Social Diagnosis* (1917) and *What Is Social Casework?* (1992).

The methodology and techniques of social casework proposed by the 1929 Milford Conference on Social Work went beyond counseling, advice giving, and the modeling and demonstration of behavior to include the community practice skills of information gathering and referrals to other community resources (American Association of Social Workers, 1929). The conference's purpose was to specify social work's professional content and boundaries.

The social casework that Richmond and the Milford Conference championed was not desk bound or introspective counseling, but rather involved confronting the client's problems in the community where the client lived and the problems existed. The Charity Organization Society, for a time Richmond's principal agency and the leading casework agency of the era in Great Britain and the United States, held community work fundamental to casework. Bosanquet, an early leader of the British Charity Organization Society movement, is quoted by Timms (1966) as stating that "Case work which is not handled as an engine of social improvement is not . . . Charity Organization Society work at all" (p. 41).

The profession's often reviewed "cause and function" strain between social action, social change, and reform, on the one hand, and individual treatment and change, on the other hand, poses a spurious dilemma. It is a dilemma only when wrongly framed as an either-or choice between two mutually exclusive activities rather than as two interrelated and complementary social work components. Porter Lee in his 1929 presidential address to the National Conference on Social Welfare, recognized the necessity of both cause and function for the profession (Bruno, 1948). Lee is often credited with conceptualizing the strain in this "cause and function" address. But the speech's title and emphasis were cause *and* function, not cause *or* function (Spano, 1982, p. 7). Lee saw no dichotomy or dilemma, nor is there one. Social work has emphasized and does emphasize individual help, use of the social environment in providing assistance, and social action and reform (Pumphrey, 1980).

National Association of Social Workers and the Council on Social Work Education Policy

The largest social work professional association, the National Association of Social Workers (NASW), and social work education's accrediting body, the Council on Social Work Education (CSWE), recognized the importance of community theory and skills for all social work practitioners. NASW developed and advocates that social caseworkers and social work clinicians use a person-in-environment (P-I-E) diagnostic and classification system. Social environment in the P-I-E schema is defined as "systemic relationships that people have by virtue of being in the same location" (Karls & Wandrei, 1994a, p. 3). The social environment in the P-I-E classification system is essentially the same as the conception of community presented above. The classification system and its manual, *P-I-E Manual: Person-in-Environment System* (Karls & Wandrei, 1994b), underscore the importance of social roles in the community and social conditions that affect clients' social behavior and functioning.

NASW's formulation for clinical social work, the practice methodology claimed by a majority of NASW members, reinforces the importance of community theory and skills. "The perspective of person-in-situation is central to clinical social work practice. Clinical social work includes intervention directed to interpersonal interactions, intrapsychic dynamics, and life-support and management issues" (*NASW Policy Statement 11*, p. 4). Standard 4 of the policy's 11 standards guiding clinical practice requires that "Clinical social workers shall be knowledgeable about the services available in the community and make appropriate referrals for their clients" (*NASW Policy Statement 11*, p. 8).

The Council on Social Work Education, the national accrediting organization for graduate and undergraduate professional social work education, recognized in its foundation curriculum policy accreditation standards the importance of social relations, the community, and community practice skills. Foundation curriculum requirements are the basic knowledge and skills curriculum requirements of all social work students. They are the common base of social work. CSWE's Curriculum Policy for the Master's Degree and Baccalareate Degree Programs in Social Work Education (Commission on Accreditation, 1989) specifications on social work practice, specifications 6.8, 6.11, 7.11, and 7.12, indicate that all social work students should have basic community practice theory and skills as part of their practice foundation curriculum.

Changing Nature of the Social Work Practice Environment

The last quarter of the twentieth century has seen profound changes in the social work practice environment. After the 1960s and 1970s, with their emphasis on federal government involvement and services coordination, we are now seeing federal, state, and lo-

Our Position on Community Practice

Our position, theory, and set of propositions, briefly stated, on the requirement for community practice is that people exist in social ecologies or communities. Behavior is psychosocial and not exclusively biopsychological. It is shaped by interactions, engagements, and exchanges with the social ecology. Personal empowerment requires the capacity to develop and manage the interactions and exchanges with the social ecology. All people, including social work clients, have the capacity to develop and improve their social management skills and functioning. If all people have this capacity and if empowerment is a goal of social work, then all social workers will need to develop knowledge and skill to better enable them to assist people to develop and manage supportive social ecologies or communities.

cal human services policies move toward reduction, competition, divestiture, and privatization of public programs, as well as the rhetoric, if not the reality, of returning power, responsibility, and control to state and local governments, the private sector for welfare and social services, and an increase in personal and family responsibility. The role and responsibilities of the federal government in welfare and human services probably are undergoing their greatest transformation since the New Deal era of the 1930s (Gillespie & Schellhas, 1994; Gingrich, Armey, & the House Republicans, 1994).

The national political landscape has become more conservative. The 1995 congressional elections saw Republicans gain control of both houses of Congress for the first time since 1958, as well as a majority of the governorships up for election and significant gains in state legislatures. While a single election need not indicate a trend, as the 1964 Johnson–Goldwater presidential contest demonstrates, both major political parties appear to have moved to the right in their welfare policies, although the balance of voter registrations for both parties has remained largely unchanged over the past three decades. Voting patterns do not follow political affiliation, as a majority of registered voters remain Democrats. Yesterday's conservatives are today's moderates. Ideological identification, regardless of party, tends to support the thesis that American voters are more conservative than liberal, with 43% of them identifying themselves as conservative, 25% as liberal, and 32% in between in 1988 (Ladd, 1989, p. 17). Coupled with the increasing conservatism of the voters is the declining rate of voting among the young, minorities, and lower-income citizens (Bureau of the Census, 1995, pp. 226–292; Doherty & Etzioni, 1994–95; Ladd, 1989, p. 11; *The New York Times*, November 9, 10, and 13). If these voting and electoral patterns continue, support for a welfare state and public social services will steadily erode (Dowd, 1994; Shapiro & Young, 1989, pp. 61–62).

If the nation moves to privatization of social services and greater local authority, control, and responsibility, greater community practice knowledge and skills will be required by all social workers. Social workers will need to assess local communities for needed resources; to develop resource networks and support systems for themselves and their clients; to advocate for their clients and to broker services; and to engage in social marketing of their services, social ideals, and themselves.

Community practice competence is vital as the social work profession moves out from under the protective umbrellas of public and voluntary, not-for-profit social service agencies into an often harsh, competitive marketplace of proprietary and private practice with its contracts for service, managed care, and the privatization of social services. Increasingly, social work practitioners will be responsible for developing, managing, and marketing their practices. Agencies will not be providing clients, other needed resources, and an employment safety net (Sherraden, 1990; Williams & Hopps, 1990). If social workers have to develop their own resources in a competitive marketplace, clinical skills alone will be insufficient for professional maintenance. With privatization and managed care, social workers unable to market themselves and their services, to get themselves included on managed-care vendor lists, and to access and manage networks will not survive. The trends toward privatization, contract for services, managed care, and proprietary practice by social workers probably will continue. The proprietary practice of social work, either solo, group, or employed by for-profit corporations, either full or part time, involved approximately a fourth of the profession in the early 1990s and by the turn of the century likely will exceed a third of the profession (Gibelman & Schervish, 1993; Hardcastle, 1987).

Advocacy skills are particularly critical for clinical social workers as mental health services under managed care grow; as efficiency becomes the deciding criterion; and where, in the absence of convincing evidence to the contrary, the managed-care representative will seek to cut costs (Asch & Abelson, 1993).

Direct service practitioners, if they are to help their clients, will have to engage in social action in the increasingly fragmented community to develop or protect resources and rights for both clients and social workers. Consider the 1994 Pennsylvania Supreme Court decision that held that an individual cannot be convicted of rape unless the victim struggles and physically resists the attacker. Simply saying "no," regardless of how often and forcefully, is not enough.

Physical resistance must be made. It does not matter that physical resistance may place the rape victim in jeopardy of harm beyond the physical and emotional trauma of the rape itself or that other victims of physical assault do not have to resist. The Pennsylvania Supreme Court argued that its interpretation is compelled by Pennsylvania's rape statutes, which require physical resistance if rape is to be legally considered. A clinician in a rape counseling center and the public, if they wish to reduce the risk to women, will need to engage in social action—lobbying—to change the law so that a clear "no" will suffice as a refusal and life-threatening physical resistance will not be required. Social action to change the law probably will be more effective in sparing women the emotional and physical traumas of rape than rape counseling afterwards. With the growing cutbacks in financial support for programs for children and the elderly, social action appears more productive than counseling in meeting the needs of these populations.

THE NEED FOR REVITALIZATION OF THE COMMUNITY AND THE SOCIAL IN SOCIAL WORK

Although social work has a rich history of community practice, many critics inside and outside the profession hold that the importance of community practice within social work is declining. With this decline, social work's unique professional contribution is also dwindling. In *Unfaithful Angels*, Specht and Courtney (1994) allege that social work has abandoned its historic mission of service, especially service to the poor, in the pursuit of psychotherapies, private practice and autonomy from social agencies, and increased income and status. The therapies used often lack any scientific basis; instead, social workers embrace faddish interventions resting on spiritualism and mysticism. The problem is not so much that individual social workers have abandoned the traditional mission of the profession and, in a sense, the profession, but rather that the profession itself has abandoned its historic service mission, the community, and the community's most needy and vulnerable citizens.[1]

The profession's movement away from community and social concerns is illustrated by NASW's social action and legislative agenda. NASW's major legislative efforts and successes, nationally and by state chapters, over the past two decades have focused on obtaining licensure and public recognition as a profession, as well as the legally mandated capacity to receive third-party vendor payments for therapies (Hardcastle, 1990). Salcido and Seck (1992) concluded, after a survey of the political activity of 52 NASW state chapters, that these chapters

> seemed to act on behalf of goals related to promoting the profession and to a lesser extent on those promoting social services legislation.... These findings imply that the thrust of future chapter political activities may be associated with professionalization and to a lesser degree with political activism on behalf of disadvantaged groups. (p. 564)

Forsaking a mission goes beyond social work's employment auspices and venue. Social workers can pursue the profession's mission or they can renounce it, whether employed by social agencies or engaged in entrepreneurial practice. Social workers can and have often abandoned the historic mission and service calling when practicing under the auspices of public and not-for-profit agencies. When the profession allows the payor to call all the plays—that is, when funding sources and employing agencies unilaterally determine professional functioning and mission—social work forsakes its claim to professionalism. The mission is determined by the strength of the profession's and each professional's service commitment rather than by employment auspices. It is the service commitment that separates professions from occupations (Gustafson, 1982; Lubove, 1977). Without a strong understanding of the impact of the community on individual behavior and opportunities, and the skills necessary for developing and using community resources to enhance the individual's functioning, social work will indeed abandon its mission of service in the pursuit of status.

The assumption of the importance of the social, the community, is emphasized in the profession's name, *social work*. But far too little attention is directed to developing the community practice skills of all social workers compared to the more circumscribed clinical skills. Psychotherapy as therapeutic individualism, Specht and Courtney (1994), Bellah et al. (1985), and Doherty (1994–95) maintain, can be socially amoral, isolating, and at odds with the mandate to strengthen the community and social commitments. Participating in and looking to primary social structures and groups such as the family, church, and neighborhood for guidance has often been replaced by therapy and the therapist. The therapist becomes teacher, spiritual guide, and moral arbiter without a moral base. Therapy is nonjudgmental; it emphasizes looking out for number one and teaches that if it feels right, it is right. While this message may appear liberating, it hardly allows the building of mutual support, a sense of the common good, and a feeling for community.

Social work as a profession exists in and reflects the larger society. The decay of social work's social skills and commitment has accompanied the erosion of America's community spirit and social commitment. It is reflective of the "me-ism," the libertarian, self-centered philosophy presently rampant, and the social isolation and fragmentation of contemporary America (Bellah et al. 1985; Etzioni, 1993; Lasch, 1994).

Communities as unifying social institutions are declining. This decline does not bode well for the future of the individual or the country as a whole. Individual rights and individual well-being are enhanced by strong communities. The 1980s and 1990s—the generation X decades—were an age of anomie and breakdown of social standards with a focus on the self—self-gratification and immediate rewards—with an increase in illegitimacy, public violence, and public and private crime often excused solely on the basis that the opportunity was present or the perpetrator was victimized earlier in life. Our homicide rate and violence levels are unrivaled in any nation with an advanced economy, whether East or West, although post-Communist Russia is approaching us as its economy declines (Gray, 1995). Fewer Americans are involved in civic participation, as reflected by the decline in voting rates, volunteer services, and church participation. Community service has become a penalty imposed by the courts for criminal offenses or an educational requirement in many states (Bellah et al., 1985, 1991; Doherty & Etzioni, 1994–95; Etzioni, 1993; Specht & Courtney, 1994)

Community as a basis of identification is becoming exclusionary rather than inclusionary, socially fragmenting rather than integrating, and resting on a negative rather than a positive base. Support groups focus on negative attributes and separateness rather than on positive traits and ways to integrate their participants more fully into the community. The community has become a means for division rather than integration. In negative communities, the individual is socially isolated and the sense the "person makes of his or her life and the social relationships on which it is based is essentially

an individual task" (Specht & Courtney, 1994, p. 41). Too often the reasons for community participation are individualistic, fragmented, and therapeutic.

Social workers need to integrate clients and constituencies into positive communities. Positive communities are nonutopian, cohesive communities where personal relations are captured by agreed-on communal purposes. The positive community offers the individual a shared structure of meaning, explanation, purpose, and support in both good times and bad (*The Responsive Communitarian Platform*, 1992).

Democratic communities and societies thrive not on the individualistic isolation of their members but on the robust functioning of their intermediate structures such as families, neighborhoods, cooperative efforts, and schools. These are what Berger and Neuhaus (1977) identify as *mediating structures*. Mediating structures serve to counterbalance both individual and state excesses.

The Catholic theologian Hollenbach (1994–95) asserts that both democracy and freedom require dynamic community involvement by its members:

> solitary individuals, especially those motivated solely by self-interest and the protection of their rights to privacy, will be incapable of democratic self-government because democracy requires more. It requires the virtues of mutual cooperation, mutual responsibility, and what Aristotle called friendship, concord, and amity. (p. 20)

THE SOCIAL WORK PROBLEM-SOLVING STRATEGY

The social work general problem-solving strategy is a planned change process that begins with the identification of a problem, a condition that someone wants changed, and terminates with the evaluation of the change effort (Compton & Galaway, 1979, pp. 232–450; Epstein, 1980, pp. 2–5; Hepworth & Larsen, 1986, pp. 25–44; Lippitt, Watson, & Westley, 1958; Netting, Kettner, & McMurtry, 1993, pp. 203–220; Pincus & Minahan, 1973, pp. 90–91.). The strategy, not limited to social work, is a comprehensive and rational approach to problem analysis, resource analysis and aggregation, and intervention. Its social work application is constrained by the profession's values and ethics and usually by the preferences of the client and the client system. The client or client system can be individuals, families and other primary groups, communities, community organizations, and community groups such as neighborhoods or interest groups.

The Social Work Problem-Solving Strategy

1. Recognition of a problem and establishment of the need for change.
2. Information gathering.
3. Assessment and the development of a case theory and plan for change.
4. Intervention and the change effort.
5. Evaluation and termination of the change effort.

---

1. Recognition of a Problem and Establishment of the Need for Change

Problem-solving and change efforts begin with the recognition by an individual or a group, the initiator of the change effort, of a condition perceived as a problem that requires change. The initiator may be the client, a parent, a couple experiencing marital discord, or others such as an individual who fears child abuse or neglect by another person and refers the situation to a protective services agency. A community group may also pinpoint problems of employment, crime, or poor treatment received from public or other social organizations. Implicit, if not explicit, in the identification of the problem and the recognition of the need for change is the outcomes or goals sought. Without some statement of the desired outcomes, data gathering, especially for resources, will be hindered. This phase will be discussed more fully in terms of community interventions in Chapters 3 and 4.

2. Information Gathering

The second phase in the problem-solving process is the gathering of information on the problem and on possible resources for intervention or problem solving. During this phase, the social worker gathers information on the problem in order to develop an intervention plan. The information-gathering phase is guided and limited by the theoretical perspective of those working for the change, on the causes of the problem and the potentially available interventions. This phase includes accumulating information on the problem itself; the client system, including strengths and potential resources useful for intervention; the strengths and limitations of support and potential support systems; and potential constraints on and limitations of any change effort from the target system. Community-based practice models devote more attention to the social ecology, the environment, and the social systems in gathering information on the condition and the potential resources than do psychologically centered problem-solving strategies.

3. Assessment and the Development of a Case Theory and Plan for Change

The third phase is assessment and the development of the case theory or plan for change. The case can be an individual, a group, a community, or part of a community. However, the case in a change effort extends beyond the individual unit to include the ecology, the situation, and the conditions of the unit or the systems outlined above. Case theory, like all theory, involves an explanation of the phenomenon. Case theory (Bisman, 1994) is the theory or coherent explanation of the problem, the specification of desired outcomes, the selection of intervention strategies and methods to change the condition and produce the desired outcomes, and an explanation of why and how the interventions will work. To specify outcomes clearly during this phase, it may be necessary to collect additional information on the availability of potential resources.

Case theory is developed from the data collected in stage 2. The data are assessed and organized according to the change agent's, the social worker's, and social and behavioral theories of choice. Examples of social and behavioral theories include systems theory, exchange theory, operant and social learning theory, and psychodynamic theories. The case theory is the social worker's construction of the problem and the model for the proposed change effort.

In community practice, the concept of assessment is generally preferred over the more limited concept of diagnosis. Gambrill (1983) provides a useful discussion of the distinction between diagnosis and assessment and insight into why assessment is preferred in community practice:

> The term *diagnosis* was borrowed from medicine. . . . Observed behavior is used as a sign of more important underlying processes, typically of a pathological nature. Methodological and conceptual problems connected with the use of diagnosis include frequent low degree of agreement between people in their use of a given diagnosis, and the low degree of association between a diagnosis and indications of what intervention will be most effective. . . .

> Assessment differs in a number of ways from diagnosis. Observable behaviors are not used as signs of something more significant but as important in their own right as *samples* of relevant behaviors. Behavior is considered to be a response to identifiable environmental or personal events. . . . Rather than using behavior as a sign of underlying intrapsychic causes, assessment includes an exploration of how current thoughts, feelings, and environmental events relate to these samples of behavior. (pp. 33–34)

Assessment is a more inclusive and generic concept than *diagnosis*, with a greater emphasis on social and environmental factors.

4. Intervention and the Change Effort

The intervention is the change efforts based on the theory of the case to achieve the desired outcome. While interventions in social work practice can be categorized under casework strategies, clinical approaches, community organization, or environmental and social change, each intervention plan involves a variety of skills, techniques, and tactics; a range of people or systems, either directly or indirectly; and the use of resources. The selection of the specific interventive methodologies and technologies is directed by the theory of the case.

5. Evaluation and Termination of the Change Effort

The last phase of the social work problem-solving strategy is the evaluation of its effectiveness in achieving the stated goals and objectives. Depending on the level of achievement and the stability of the change, the case may be terminated, the process repeated to enhance its effectiveness or to achieve additional objectives, or the case referred to additional service resources. While evaluation is generally presented in the models together with the termination phase, it is a continuous effort and a part of all the phases.

Pincus and Minahan (1973) rightly assert that the intent of the problem-solving process, whether targeted to individual or community change, is to help people, to change people, "not vague abstraction such as the 'community,' 'the organization' or the 'system' " (p. 63). What is changed is the behavior and interaction of the people who constitute the groups, organizations, communities, and systems.

Problem-Solving Systems

The people involved in a social work problem-solving and planned change strategy can be examined, using the system's metaphors, according to what they contribute and how they are affected by the change process (Netting et al., 1993, pp. 224–231; Pincus & Minahan, 1973, pp. 53–64). The system's metaphors represent functions that people fulfill in the change effort. The same people can fulfill more than one function and hence can belong to more than one system in the change process.

1. *Initiator system:* The people or person who first recognize the problem and bring attention to the need for change.

2. *Support system:* The people who have an interest in and will support the proposed change and who may receive secondary benefits from it.

3. *Change agent system:* The people who will work directly to produce the change, including the change agent, the social worker, any social action organizations and groups, and the people who belong to the social worker's agency or who employ the organization working to produce the change.

4. *Client system:* The people who sanction, ask for, or expect to benefit from the change agent's services and who have a working agreement or contract, whether formal or informal, with the change agent.

TABLE 1.1 Systems Typically Involved in the Phases of the Problem-Solving Strategy

Problem-Solving Phase	Systems Typically Involved
1. Recognition of a problem and establishment of the need for change	Initiator and client with change agent
2. Information gathering	Information from initiator, client, and support systems, to change the agent system
3. Assessment and development of a case theory and plan for change	Client, change agent, support, and controlling systems to develop case theory and plan and identify target system
4. Intervention and the change effort	Client, change agent, support, controlling, host, and implementing systems forming the action system to change the target system
5. Evaluation and termination of the change effort	Client, change agent, support, controlling, host and implementing systems

5. *Action system:* The change agent system and the other people the change agent works with and through to achieve the goals and affect the target system. The action system often includes the client as an essential component of the change process.

6. *Controlling system:* The people with the formal authority and capacity to approve and order the implementation of the proposed change strategy.

7. *Host system:* The people responsible for implementing the proposed change strategy.

8. *Implementing system:* A subset of the host system composed of the people with day-to-day responsibility for implementing the change.

9. *Target system:* The people who are the targets of the change effort; the people who need to be changed to accomplish the goals of the change strategy and produce the benefits for the client system. The client may or may not be a part of the target system.

Although some systems and people generally are involved throughout the problem-solving strategy's change process, such as the change agent system and the client system, not all systems need to be involved. The same people at the same or difference phases in the process may be involved in multiple systems, and their involvement may shift as their contributions and their relationship to the change process evolve.

The change agent, that is, the social worker, must anticipate and identify the people who will comprise the various systems involved and perform the change functions in the problem-solving processes. The social worker should recognize that the people or the systems are not static. The membership and importance of a particular system's contributions vary with the phase of the change strategy.

Case Illustration of the Problem-Solving Strategy in Direct Practice: Ms. S.[2]

1. Recognition of a Problem and Establishment of the Need for Change

A working single mother, Ms. S, with two preschool-age children, ages 3 and 4, has difficulty finding a suitable baby sitter. She also recognizes that she is becoming more short-tempered with her children because of the fatigue and stress of working full time and raising the children alone, worries about money, and distress about the baby-sitting arrangements. It is becoming more difficult for Ms. S to maintain her composure when disciplining her children, and she recognizes that if she loses control, she might physically abuse the children.

Ms. S is not sure what to do, as she is very tired at the end of the day after getting up at 5:30 A.M., fixing breakfast for herself and the children, getting the children up, dressed, and fed, taking them to whatever baby sitter is available, and getting to work by 9:00 A.M. After the work day ends, she must first pick up the children, fix dinner, and then put them to bed. She has no time to play with the children or think of herself. Ms. S recognizes that she is starting to resent the children and at times feels she would be better off without them.

Ms. S saw a poster on a bus advertising the child guidance clinic's parent effectiveness training. She goes to the child guidance clinic to obtain help in maintaining her composure when disciplining her children and training to develop better parenting skills. The social worker assigned by the agency to work with Ms. S recognizes that she is under a lot of stress and needs assistance with more than her parenting skills.

Ms. S is the initiator system, as she recognized a problem and perceived a need for change. She and her children are the client system as the beneficiaries of the change effort. The social worker is the change agent and part of the initiator system in recognizing the problem and helping Ms. S define the need for change.

2. Information Gathering

The social worker obtains information about Ms. S, the children, and the children's father, who is regularly employed but pays no support and only occasionally visits the children. The social worker also obtains information on possible resources in Ms. S's neighborhood and other possible social and community supports. She discovers the existence of a public 12-hour day-care center.

Systems most involved in information gathering are the client and the change agent systems. The information is accumulated to define and build the other necessary systems. The necessary information goes beyond describing the client, her problems, and their etiology; it includes information about potential supports for the client and her children, for example, from the absent father, the day care center, and other potential community resources for the client that might be constructed into a support system. These potential resources make up a target system, the people who need to be changed to accomplish the goals of the change strategy and bring about benefits for the client, until they are formed into a support system for the client. The composition of the systems are dynamic over time.

3. Assessment and the Development of a Case Theory and Plan for Change

The social worker and Ms. S review the information to explain why Ms. S is stressed and fatigued and to decide what might be done to change the situation, including greater involvement of and responsibility by the father. The father has stated that he will not pay support until he has regular visitation with the children. Ms. S will not allow visitation until he pays support, thus creating a standoff.

Both the theory and goals are straightforward and direct. Ms. S is exhausted and stressed because she maintains a full-time work schedule in addition to the demands of being a single parent living financially on the edge. She has no social life because of the demands of work and caring for her children, which contribute to her resentment of the children. Her fatigue and resentment place the children at risk. She doesn't know if she can spare the time for parent effectiveness training, although she wants the training and would enjoy the social interaction and support provided by the sessions. The goals are to achieve stable child care, financial and social assistance from the children's father, and the use of any time gained by Ms. S from a stable child-care arrangement and the father's increased responsibility for the children for parent effectiveness training and her own needs.

The client and change agent systems, the social worker and Ms. S, develop a case theory and plan with goals to solve the problem. The plan specifies other needed systems. The father and Ms. S are the target system clients, since the behavior of both must changed. The day-care center is also a target system because Ms. S's children need to be enrolled in the center. If the intervention called for by the plan is successful, the father will ultimately become part of Ms. S's support system. As an agent of the child guidance clinic, the social worker needs approval of the plan by the controlling system, the agency. The court, which must order the support payment, also is part of the controlling system. The agency is the host system, and the social worker is the implementing system. Ms. S, the social worker, and the parent effectiveness trainer are the implementing system, as they are the people "who will have the day-to-day responsibility for carrying out the change" (Netting et al., 1993, p. 228).

4. Intervention and the Change Effort

The intervention plan resulting from the theory of the case is a social intervention. Ms. S is to allow the children's father to have the children for one weekend a month and two evenings a week if he pays child support. A court-ordered support judgment will be obtained for the support and visitation. This should ease Ms. S's financial worries and provide help with parenting responsibilities and some time for herself. The social worker assisted Ms. S in obtaining stable day care from the public neighborhood day-care center. Ms. S will attend the child guidance clinic's parent effectiveness training classes on one of the evenings that the father has the children.

Ms. S, the social worker, the court, and the parent effectiveness trainer form the action system to change the target systems: Ms. S, the father, and the day-care center. As indicated above, if the change effort with the father and the day-care center is successful, they become part of Ms. S's support system for subsequent changes and development.

5. Evaluation and Termination of the Change Effort

At the conclusion of the parent effectiveness training classes, Ms. S, the social worker, and the father, now a part of the problem-solving process, will evaluate the current arrangements.

While evaluation is the final phase, it is also a continuous part of the monitoring of the problem-solving process. The monitoring involves Ms. S, the social worker, and often the support, controlling, host, and implementing systems. The evaluation of a problem-solving strategy before its termination can involve all of these systems, including Ms. S, the social worker, the parent effectiveness trainer, the father, and possibly the child guidance clinic supervisors.

Case Illustration of the Problem-Solving Strategy in Community Development: La Colonia[3]

1. Recognition of a Problem and Establishment of the Need for Change

California's San Joaquin Valley's natural climate is hot and arid for about 8 months of the year. It is very fertile. It ordinarily is a semidesert, with rainfall of between 4 and 12 inches, depending on the location. With the expenditure of millions of federal and state dollars since the 1930s to bring water to the valley's communities and agriculture, the San Joaquin Valley is now the food basket of the nation. However, in the 1960s, there were small rural communities of Chicano, black, and poor white agricultural laborers still without a public water supply. La Colonia was one of these communities.

La Colonia was a small Chicano farm labor village of about 100 families adjacent to a larger agriculturally based community, the Town, with about 5,000 people. La Colonia was a stable unincorporated area with a 90-year history. Its homes were generally owned by its residents. There was no formal government other than a local public utilities district (PUD) with a commission elected by La Colonia's property owners. The PUD provided no utility services because, after its formation and incorporation, it discovered that La Colonia was too small and poor to afford the startup costs of providing public services. Individual La Colonia homes received electric and gas services from the regional gas and electric utility company. The families provided their own sewage service in individual septic tanks or cesspools. Garbage and trash disposal was an individual household responsibility. The PUD and its commission basically serve as a forum to discuss community problems, mediate community disputes, and plan and conduct community events such as the celebrations of Cinco de Mayo and other traditional holidays.

The families obtained their water from individual wells, a significant capital investment for a farm laboring family, by individual agreements with neighbors who had wells, by hauling water from the Town's public water tank taps, or from the irrigation ditches that surrounded La Colonia. Water from the wells was often polluted by septic tank and cesspool seepage. The irrigation canal water contained agricultural field runoff with fertilizer, herbicide, and pesticide contaminants.

The Town's water system was built largely by state and federal community development grants. It delivered abundant potable water to the Town's residents. The water system's mains were located less than a quarter of a mile from La Colonia. A water system connecting each home to the Town's water system could be constructed at a relatively low cost to La Colonia and the Town, as most of the cost would be paid with state and federal funds. However, the Town Council did not want to provide water to communities not incorporated into the Town, regardless of the cost. The Town Council did not want to establish a precedent and risk a possible demand from other rural communities more distant from the Town. The Town Council's policy was to restrict its provision of water to areas incorporated within its boundaries. La Colonia's PUD Commission, La Colonia's nominal leadership, did not want to be annexed to the Town, as they feared La Colonia would lose its identity, would be unable to remain a defined community with its own traditions, would simply become another Town barrio or ethnic neighborhood, and would perhaps incur a Town property tax increase. The Commission simply wanted good, affordable water.

The Commission approached the county's Community Action Agency (CAA), a not-for-profit community development and social action organization, for help with their water problem. After a meeting of the CAA's director and the PUD Commission, the director assigned a Chicano community development worker (CDW) from the Town to work with La Colonia and the Commission to obtain a potable water system.

La Colonia's PUD Commission was the initiator system and the client system. The contract was between the CAA and the Commission. La Colonia was also part of the client system, as the Commission was acting on the community's behalf. The change agents were the CAA director and the CDW. During this phase, the controlling system was the CAA and the Commission. The CAA and the Commission constituted the host system, with the CDW and volunteers from La Colonia composing the implementing system. The client system and the change agent system saw the Town's Council as the target system.

2. Information Gathering

This phase involved the action system—the CDW, La Colonia volunteers, and CAA staff—gathering information on (1) the ability and willingness of La Colonia's residents to pay their share of the water system development costs, hookup cost, and monthly waters bills; (2) grant requirements for state and federal community development funds; (3) the direct costs to the Town beyond La Colonia's costs and the state and federal grants for expanding the water system to serve La Colonia; (4) potential support systems in the Town and County; and (5) procedures for placing the item on the Town Council's agenda.

3. Assessment and Development of a Theory for Change

The initial goals of the planned change strategy were to obtain a stable, cost-effective potable water supply and system for La Colonia. The CAA also had the empowerment goal endemic to community development: to develop La Colonia's capacity as a community to work together to solve its problems and achieve greater cohesion in the process.

The theory for change, the case theory, based on the assessment of the information obtained in phase 2, was rather simple and direct. The problem, the lack of a stable potable water system, was the result of La Colonia's lack of resources and the unwillingness of the Town to connect La Colonia to its water system under mutually tolerable conditions. La Colonia could develop the infrastructure for the water system within its boundaries if a connection with the Town's water system was made. The Town was unwilling to connect the water system for political and economic reasons. Although the Town was ethnically diverse, its Council consisted of the white establishment that largely represented the agricultural interests. There were the fiscal costs of expanding the water system (though minor to serve La Colonia) and the fear of a precedent that would require expansion of the water system to all surrounding rural areas, with ever-increasing, though incremental, costs, accompanying each expansion. Eventually, the Council reasoned, the incremental costs would necessitate a politically unpopular property tax increase, an equally disliked water use fee increase, or both.

The case theory explaining the lack of a stable water system for La Colonia rested on the intransigence of the Town Council and La Colonia's PAC. La Colonia could petition for a property owner's incorporation vote and, if it passed, obtain water as an incorporated area of the Town. The Town could alter its policy against providing water to areas not incorporated into the Town. As La Colonia was the client system, its preferences directed the change strategy to alter the Town's policy.

The information gathered in the assessment phase indicated that (1) one Town Council member had ambitions for higher office as a County Commissioner; (2) several local churches were supporting civil rights efforts in other communities and were eager to do something locally; and (3) farm labor unionizing activity was occurring in the eastern part of the county. The Town and its growers were located in the western part of the county and, as yet, were unaffected by the union organizing activity.

4. Intervention and the Change Effort

The intervention and change effort based on the theory of the case called for a combination of technical assistance to the Town, social action, and political persuasion and support. Its basic strategy was to target certain individuals and groups in the Town—the ministers, church leaders, and politically ambitious council member—to bring them into either the support or the action system. The ministers and leaders were to be brought in by casting the problem as a civil rights issue. La Colonia was a Chicano community. The ministers and leaders were first a target system, with the intent of making them part of the support system. The strategy called for expansion of the action and support systems to induce the politically ambitious Council member to become a sponsor of the proposal to expand the Town's water system to serve La Colonia. In return for this sponsorship, the support system would support her County Commission bid. Additionally, the CAA would assist the Town and La Colonia in developing the proposals for federal and state community development funds. La Colonia leaders would also let it be known that if the proposal did not receive favorable consideration from the Town Council, La Colonia would approach the Farm Labor Union for assistance in developing a water system for La Colonia. This would introduce the farm Labor Union to the west side and provide it with a local sponsor and sanction. When the support and action systems were expanded, the Town Council (the target system) would be addressed. If the proposal to expand the water system was accepted by the Town Council, it would become the controlling system, part of the action system, the host system, and—with the Town's city manager, water department, and CAA—the implementing system to take the final step in La Colonia's water system development.

5. Evaluation and Termination of the Change Effort

Evaluation of the change effort by the client system and the CAA (as part of the action system) of the goal of obtaining a potable water system was direct: the system was obtained. However, evaluation of the community development goals is more complex. Has the community increased its ability to continue its development?

The problem-solving approach of planned change, with its community practice skills of systems identification, community assessment, and developing and linking resources, was important whether the problem-solving strategy was used with a delimited client system such as Ms. S. and her family or a larger client system such as La Colonia.

ETHICS, ADVOCACY, AND COMMUNITY PRACTICE

No discussion of professional practice is complete without attention to a profession's ethics, the values that form the basis for the ethics, and the ethical standards of practice.

Profession as Calling

A profession is more than an occupation; it is a vocation, an avocation, and a calling. The values that constitute the service calling of the profession distinquish professions from occupations. Professions exist and are given public protection and sanction for their benefit to communities, the public, clients, and the common good. Professions require a vision of and a commitment to certain purposes, not just the techniques practiced (Lubove, 1977). Service is not only to the individual clients but to "a larger whole, to a larger good ... of the community" (Gustafson, 1982, p. 512). It is the service to others that provides the inner rewards to the professional and the basic requirements of ethical conduct.

Community practice, whether as a community organizer, planner, social activist, or direct service practitioner, requires adher-

ence to the same high ethical standards of conduct as does any professional social work practice. The NASW provides ethical guidelines for social workers in its Code of Ethics. Many states have adopted the NASW Code of Ethics as part of their legal regulations for social work (Hardcastle, 1990).

The ethical standards grow out of American social work's historical foundations in the social gospel movement (Gustafson, 1982; Lubove, 1977). Social work as a profession, like all professions, is a calling. The essential feature that distinguishes professions from other occupations is not technology but the profession's service mission or calling. This service mission is reflected by the statement of Brother Cyprian Rowe, a faculty member of the School of Social Work, the University of Maryland at Baltimore, and a Marist Brother, on the importance of ethical education for social work students: "I have an awe-filled notion of the meaning of social work. We are, in a sense, the hand's of society conscience. We really minister. . . . [The] people [the social workers] . . . on the line [should be well] prepared to do right and do well by the people they meet" ("Living a Life of Giving," 1994, p. 6).

The service mission to the community supersedes the accrual of personal wealth, the production of particular products or services, or the application of sophisticated techniques. Many occupations have these attributes and even contribute to the public's welfare. But their prime motivation is not service. Although service as a professional motive has been tainted and is often ignored by contemporary professionals, it is embedded in most conceptions of profession. Adherence to the service orientation provides professions and professionals with the community's mandate and authority to be self-regulating (Hardcastle, 1977, 1990; Vollmer & Mills, 1966).

The service calling is both outward to the community and inward for the professional. Gustafson (1982) clarifies the relationship of the outward and inward dimensions of professions:

> the outward is the larger context within which any person's contributions can be seen to have significance. It contributes to the meeting of human needs; it is an element, no matter how small, in the "common good" of the human community. It serves a purpose that is not simply self-referential in the object of its interests. The inward significance is twofold: there is a dignity to one's work that can be affirmed, and thus a dignity to the worker; and there is a sense of fulfillment and meaning that can come from being of service to others and to the common good. (p. 504)

Ethics and Community Practice

Social work's ethics, derived from its more abstract values, are rules to guide the social worker's conduct and behavior. Ethics are prescriptions and proscriptions for professional standards of behavior. Ethics deal with the right, the good, and the correct. Ethics provide the basis for defining professional good guys and bad guys. Professional ethics usually are codified in the profession's code of ethics.

Although NASW's Code of Ethics (*NASW Policy Statement 1*) focuses directly on ethical standards for practice with individual clients, its division titles reflect the Code's relevance for all social workers:

I. The Social Worker's Conduct and Comportment as a Social Worker

II. The Social Worker's Ethical Responsibility to Clients

III. The Social Worker's Ethical Responsibility to Colleagues

IV. The Social Worker's Ethical Responsibility to Employers and Employing Organizations

V. The Social Worker's Ethical Responsibility to the Social Work Profession

VI. The Social Worker's Ethical Responsibility to Society

Section II, while addressing the ethical responsibilities to clients as individuals, the imperatives to serve the client's interests and to protect privacy and informed consent, is equally applicable to community practice when the client is a group or an organization.

Community practice in all its forms does not represent a higher form of practice exempted from ethical constraints. Whether the client is a group, an organization, or a community with the goal of fundamental structural change, the ethical constraints remain. Indeed, community practice may require greater adherence to ethical standards, as the scope of potential change for good or harm is often greater. Teleological arguments that moral and equitable ends can be justified by unethical means explicitly are rejected (Schmidtz, 1991, p. 3). Not only must the ends be ethical and just, but the tactics and behavior used in the pursuit of the ends must withstand the application of ethical and moral criteria. No matter how well-meaning the social worker is in the search of noble ends for the client or community, the ethical constraints of informed consent reflected in The Code of Ethics' standards II.F.6 and 7, and respect for the privacy and rights of clients inherent in standard II.G., as well as the other standards, remain operative even if these ethical standards interfere with the processes of change.

Gilbert and Specht (1976) reinforce the need to guard against the seduction of the teleological position of ends justifying means in client and social advocacy. They also re-inforce the constraints of the ethics. *Advocacy*, simply defined, is representing and support-ing a client, group, organization, or cause to others. The social worker's first responsibil-ity is to the client. The client must not be placed at risk in pursuit of a greater good un-less the client makes that decision. The client should not be placed in harm's way in an-ticipation of producing a subsequently greater social, collective, and institutional good without the client's informed consent. The operative word here is *informed*. The client needs to have information related to the risk, the probability that the risk will pro-duce greater good, the client's personal gains and losses, and the organizational and em-ployment constraints placed on the social worker in the advocacy and change effort. The social worker has a duty not only to warn others of the risk that a client's behavior may pose to them, but also to warn the client of the risks faced in any change effort. In con-

> If I help my client appeal an unfair ruling denying the client services that will be beneficial to the client during this era of fiscal constraints, then I may risk embarrassing my agency, isolate myself in the agency, limit my chances for promotion or raises, or even lose my job and place my family and myself at economic risk.

flict situations, neither the social worker's ideological commitments nor the employer's interests remove the ethical imperatives on the social worker.

While consistent ethical conduct often is difficult for the social worker to achieve, the difficulty generally lies in the conflicts that arise when the social worker pursues prag-matic self-interest over ethical obligations. True ethical dilemmas are rare, although pragmatic dilemmas are frequent. An ethical dilemma occurs when two ethical impera-tives require equal but opposite behavior and the ethical guidelines do not give clear di-rections or indicate clearly which ethical im-perative to follow. Typically, the competing ethical imperatives do not require different and opposite behaviors. Pragmatic consider-ations frequently make ethical behavior ar-duous and professionally or personally risky, but they are not ethical dilemmas.

In terms of self-interest, there are sub-stantial pragmatic dangers involved in both examples presented in the accompanying box, but they are not ethical dilemmas. The conflict is not between two equally com-pelling but opposed ethical imperatives. The apparent conflict between "Ethical Standard IV (The Social Worker's Ethical Respon-sibility to Employers and Employing Organ-izations) and Ethical Standard II (The Social Worker's Ethical Responsibility to Clients) is more apparent than real. Standard IIF pro-vides a solution. It states that "The social worker's primary responsibility is to clients" (*NASW Policy Statement 1*, p. 5). Decisional rules are provided by the ethical standard in its clear statement on where the social worker's primary responsibility lies. The pri-mary responsibility is to the client. The strain, or dilemma, here is between the ethical im-perative to place the client's interest first and the social worker's desire to maintain a job and economic viability for his or her family and self and to retain the employer's good

> Should I as a social worker participate in and adhere to public policies and laws that restrict public services to illegal immigrants, *a consideration of national origin*, and adhere to laws that require service professionals to report illegal immigrant clients to law enforcement officials? If these laws become national policy, my failure to do so may result in loss of employment or being subjected to a civil or criminal penalty.

will. The dilemma is real and important, but it is not an ethical dilemma. The whistle blower usually does not face ethical dilemmas, although whistle blowing does carry with it real personal costs.

The second example presents the risk of criminal and civil penalties to the social worker in addition to the loss of employment.[4] If reporting illegal aliens is the law, doesn't the social worker have to comply? Or are the legal imperatives superseded by the Code of Ethic's standards II.F.3 and VI.P.1.? Both standards state that

> the social worker should not practice, condone, facilitate or collaborate with any form of discrimination on the basis of race, color, sex, sexual orientation, age, religion, *national origin*, marital status, political belief, mental or physical handicap, or other preferences or personal characteristics, condition or status. (Emphasis added).

Standard I.C.2. under professional comportment requires that "the social worker should act to prevent practices that are inhumane or discriminatory against any person or group of persons" (Code of Ethics, p. 4).

Drucker (1974), a social and management theorist, eloquently points out that while the imperative of ethical behavior is not easy, it is not obscure and does not require a formal code of ethics:

> Businessmen, we are told solemnly, should not cheat, lie, bribe, or take bribes. But neither should anyone else. Men and women do not acquire exemption from ordinary rules of personal behavior because of their work or job. . . . The first responsibility of a professional was spelled out clearly, 2,500 years ago, in the Hippocratic oath . . . *primum non nocere*— "Above all, not knowingly do harm." No professional . . . can promise that he will indeed do good for his client. All he can do is try. But he can promise he will not knowingly do harm. And the client, in turn, must be able to trust the professional to not knowingly to do him harm. Otherwise he cannot trust him at all. And *primum non nocere*, "not knowingly to do harm," is the basic rule of professional ethics, the basic rule of ethics of public responsibility. (pp. 366–369)

And any potential risks the client faces as a result of the social worker's intervention are the client's choice under informed consent.

A NOTE ON THE USES AND LIMITATIONS OF THEORIES AND MODELS

Some caveats are in order regarding social science, theories, and models. Firstly, ideology is inherent in the social sciences and in their resultant theories and constructions of reality. This is evident in the current debate between positivism and post-positivism academic social workers such as Fisher (1993) and Tyson (1992). Theories are sets of systematically related propositions or statements used to explain and\or predict phenomena. Theories are developed not only from our observations of nature but also from the paradigms used to guide the observations.

Paradigms, according to the classic work of the science philosopher Kuhn (1970), *The Structure of Scientific Revolutions*, are basic beliefs, or axioms, and contained within the axioms are the methods and approaches for viewing and understanding nature. Paradigms direct and organize theory construction, shape how nature is perceived according to the theories, and direct the ways of finding out about nature. In directing our ways of finding out about nature, including human nature, paradigms constrain our view of nature as we follow their particular rules. Paradigms and their ways of finding out about nature, according to Kuhn, not only have strong value and ideological components, they *are* ideology. Paradigms organize and order our perceptions of nature according to their rules. Theories developed by following the paradigm's rules, when viewed through the ideological lens of the paradigm, appear reasonable to the scientists, scholars, and other devotees. Paradigms and their resultant theories represent certain idea sets, values, and the way things are and ought to be, according to their adherents. They do not appear particularly valid or reasonable to observers who do not follow the paradigm's rules and ideology.

The theories, like all theories, and the skills discussed in this book are models of reality; they are not reality itself. Some of the theories and models are descriptive; others are prescriptive. Some of the theories simply describe certain aspects of nature, of human behavior and interaction. Other theories and models prescribe what should be and what should be done by the social worker. The models are not empirical reality. They are abstractions, simplifications, and sometimes oversimplifications of empirical reality. Models are ideas that try to capture empirical referents, but they are not the referents themselves. If the models are good, they contain the essential elements and structures of realty, enabling the user to gain a better understanding of reality.

The concept of systems used earlier in this chapter and in the practice literature illustrates the notion of a model. A systems model presents a set of elements interacting to achieve a common purpose or fulfill a shared function. However, our use of the systems model in social behavior and social constructions is a metaphor, a way of looking at and organizing reality, but it is our organization of reality, as Anderson and Carter (1984, p. 3) state, not reality itself. Students should take care not to reify the models, that is, to make the models reality. Rather, they should use the models to guide, construct, and understand the complexities of reality.

Our view and construction of reality strongly reflect symbolic interactionism. Blumer (1969), a leading symbolic interactionist theorist, held that symbolic interactionism

> does not regard meaning as emanating from the intrinsic makeup of the thing that has meaning, nor does it see meaning as arising through a coalescence of psychological elements in the person. Instead, it sees meaning as arising in the process of interaction between people. . . . Thus, symbolic interactionism sees meaning as social products, as creations that are formed in and through the defining activities of people as they interact. (pp. 4–5)

Wexler Vigilante (1993) elaborates on the relevance of symbolic interactionism or constructionism in social work practice. She asks us to

> assume that systematic data gathering cannot accurately reflect the complexities of human functioning. The . . . strategy consists of the client and worker successfully framing and reframing the client's story until coherent and shared meanings are achieved. (p. 184)

Symbolic interactionism's emphasis, similar to that of assessment in practice, is on meaning. People tend to define, construct, and give meaning to their world partly as a result of their interactions with others, as will be discussed more fully in Chapter 3. A practitioner needs to understand the meaning of the interactions and the social environment to the client, the client's system, and the other systems of the change process if the practitioner is ever to understand the client's behavior. The client's constructions and meanings of reality, and hence the client's world and opportunities, can be improved with changes in the client's social interactions. A community practice task is to help the client establish new community interactions and hence construct new realities with new meanings (Pozatek, 1994).

THE ORGANIZATION OF THIS BOOK

The book is divided into two parts. Part I, Understanding the Social Environment and Social Interaction, explores the primary theories underlying community practice. This part contains three chapters: Chapter 2: Theories on Community Practice by Direct Service Practitioners, Chapter 3: The Nature of Social and Community Problems, and Chapter 4: The Concept of Community in Social Work Practice.

Part II, Community Practice Skills for Social Workers: Using the Social Environment, examines the skills of community practice. This section is divided into 10 chapters: Chapter 5: Discovering and Documenting the Life of the Community, Chapter 6: Using Assessment in Community Practice, Chapter 7: Using Self in Community Practice: Assertiveness, Chapter 8: Using Your Agency, Chapter 9: Using Work Groups: Committees, Teams, and Boards, Chapter 10: Using Networks and Networking, Chapter 11: Using Social Marketing, Chapter

12: Using the Advocacy Spectrum, and Chapter 13: Case Management as Community and Interorganizational Practice.

A final chapter, Chapter 14, Being "Out There" in Our Practice, explores the demands on the profession for community practice in the 21st century.

THE NASW CODE OF ETHICS[5]

I. The Social Worker's Conduct and Comportment as a Social Worker
   A. Propriety—The Social worker should maintain high standards of personal conduct in the capacity or identity as a social worker.
      1. The private conduct of the social worker is a personal matter to the same degree as is any other person's, except when such conduct compromises the fulfillment of professional responsibilities.
      2. The social worker should not participate in, condone, or be associated with dishonesty, fraud, deceit, or misrepresentation.
      3. The social worker should distinguish clearly between statements and actions made as a private individual and as a representative of the social work profession or any organization or group.
   B. Competence and Professional Development—The social worker should strive to become and maintain proficient in professional practice and the performance of professional functions.
      1. The social worker should accept responsibility or employment only on the basis of existing competence or the intention to acquire the necessary competence.
      2. The social worker should not misrepresent professional qualifica-

tions, education, experience, or affiliations.

C. Service—The social worker should regard as primary the service obligation of the social work profession.

1. The social worker should retain ultimate responsibility for the quality and extent of the service that individual assumes, assigns, or performs.

2. The social worker should act to prevent practices that are inhumane or discriminatory against any person or group of persons.

D. Integrity—The social worker should act in accordance with the highest standards of professional integrity and impartiality.

1. The social worker should be alert to and resist the influences and pressures that interfere with the exercise of professional discretion and impartial judgement required for the performance of professional functions.

2. The social worker should not exploit professional relationships for personal gain.

E. Scholarship and Research—The social worker engaged in study and research should be guided by the conventions of scholarly inquiry.

1. The social worker engaged in research should consider carefully its possible consequences for human beings.

2. The social worker engaged in research should ascertain that the consent of participants in the research is voluntary and informed, without any implied deprivation or penalty for refusal to participate, and with due regard for participants' privacy and dignity.

3. The social worker engaged in research should protect participants from unwarranted physical or mental discomfort, distress, harm, danger, or deprivation.

4. The social worker who engages in the evaluation of services or cases should discuss them only for the professional purposes and only with persons directly and professionally concerned with them.

5. Information obtained about participants in research should be treated as confidential.

6. The social worker should take credit only for work actually done in connection with scholarly and research endeavors and credit contributions made by others.

II. The Social Workers' Ethical Responsibility to Clients

F. Primacy of Clients' Interests—The social worker's primary responsibility is to clients.

1. The social worker should serve clients with devotion, loyalty, determination, and the maximum application of professional skill and competence.

2. The social worker should not exploit relationships with clients for personal advantage.

3. The social worker should not practice, condone, facilitate or collaborate with any form of discrimination on the basis of race, color, sex, sexual orientation, age, religion, national origin, marital status, political belief, mental or physical handicap, or any other preference or personal characteristic, condition, or status.

4. The social worker should avoid relationships or commitments

that conflict with the interests of clients.

5. The social worker should under no circumstances engage in sexual activities with clients.

6. The social worker should provide clients with accurate and complete information regarding the extent and nature of the services available to them.

7. The social worker should apprise clients of their risks, rights, opportunities, and obligations associated with social service to them.

8. The social worker should seek advice and counsel of colleagues and supervisors whenever such consultation is in the best interest of clients.

9. The social worker should terminate service to clients, and professional relationships with them, when such service and relationships are no longer required or no longer serve the clients' needs or interests.

10. The social worker should withdraw services precipitously only under unusual circumstances, giving careful consideration to all factors in the situation and taking care to minimize possible adverse effects.

11. The social worker who anticipates the termination or interruption of service to clients should notify clients promptly and seek the transfer, referral, or continuation of service in relation to the clients' needs and preferences.

G. Rights and Prerogatives of Clients—The social worker should make every effort to foster maximum self-determination on the part of clients.

1. When the social worker must act on behalf of a client who has been adjudged legally incompetent, the social worker should safeguard the interests and rights of that client.

2. When another individual has been legally authorized to act in behalf of a client, the social worker should deal with that person always with the client's best interest in mind.

3. The social worker should not engage in any action that violates or diminishes the civil or legal rights of the client.

H. Confidentiality and Privacy—The social worker should respect the privacy of clients and hold in confidence all information obtained in the course of professional service.

1. The social worker should share with others confidences revealed by clients, without their consent, only for compelling professional reasons.

2. The social worker should inform clients fully about the limits of confidentiality in a given situation, the purposes for which information is obtained, and how it may be used.

3. The social worker should afford clients reasonable access to any official social work records concerning them.

4. When providing clients with access to records, the social worker should take due care to protect the confidences of others contained in those records.

5. The social worker should obtain informed consent of clients before taping, recording, or permitting

third party observation of their activities.

I. Fees—When setting fees, the social worker should ensure that they are fair, reasonable, considerate, and commensurate with the service performed and with due regard for the client's ability to pay.

   1. The social worker should not accept anything of value for making a referral.

III. The Social Worker's Ethical Responsibility to Colleagues

  J. Respect, Fairness, and Courtesy— The social worker should treat colleagues with respect, courtesy, fairness, and good faith.

    1. The social worker should cooperate with colleagues to promote professional interests and concerns.

    2. The social worker should respect confidences shared by colleagues in the course of their professional relationships and transactions.

    3. The social worker should create and maintain conditions of practice that facilitate ethical and competent professional performance by colleagues.

    4. The social worker should treat with respect, and represent accurately and fairly, the qualifications, views, and findings of colleagues and use appropriate channels to express judgements on these matters.

    5. The social worker who replaces or is replaced by a colleague in professional practice should act with consideration for the interest, character, and reputation of that colleague.

    6. The social worker should not exploit a dispute between a colleague and employers to obtain a position or otherwise advance the social worker's interest.

    7. The social worker should seek arbitration or mediation when conflicts with colleagues require resolution for compelling professional reasons.

    8. The social worker should extend to colleagues of other professions the same respect and cooperation that is extended to social work colleagues.

    9. The social worker who serves as an employer, supervisor, or mentor to colleagues should make orderly and explicit arrangements regarding the conditions of their continuing professional relationship.

   10. The social worker who has the responsibility for employing and evaluating the performance of other staff members should fulfill such responsibility in a fair, considerate, and equitable manner, on the basis of clearly enunciated criteria.

   11. The social worker who has the responsibility for evaluating the performance of employees, supervisees, or students should share evaluations with them.

  K. Dealing with Colleagues' Clients— The social worker has the responsibility to relate to the clients of colleagues with full professional consideration.

    1. The social worker should not assume professional responsibility for the clients of another agency or a colleague without appropriate communication with that agency or colleague.

    2. The social worker who serves the clients of colleagues, during a tem-

AN INTRODUCTION29

porary absence or emergency, should serve those clients with the same consideration as that afforded any client.

IV. The Social Worker's Ethical Responsibility to Employers and Employing Organizations

L. Commitments to Employing Organizations—The social worker should adhere to commitments made to the employing organization.

1. The social worker should work to improve the employing agency's policies and procedures, and the efficiency and effectiveness of its services.

2. The social worker should not accept employment or arrange student field placements in an organization which is currently under public sanction by NASW for violating personal standards, or imposing limitations on or penalties for professional actions on behalf of clients.

3. The social worker should act to prevent and eliminate discrimination in the employing organization's work assignments and in its employment policies and practices.

4. The social worker should use with scrupulous regard, and only for the purpose for which they are intended, the resources of the employing organization.

V. The Social Worker's Ethical Responsibility to the Social Work Profession

M. Maintaining the Integrity of the Profession—The social worker should uphold and advance the values, ethics, knowledge, and mission of the profession.

1. The social worker should protect and enhance the dignity and in-

tegrity of the profession and should be responsible and vigorous in discussion and criticism of the profession.

2. The social worker should take action through appropriate channels against unethical conduct by any other member of the profession.

3. The social worker should act to prevent the unauthorized and unqualified practice of social work.

4. The social worker should make no misrepresentation in advertising as to qualifications, competence, service, or results to be achieved.

N. Community Service—The social worker should assist the profession in making social services available to the general public.

1. The social worker should contribute time and professional expertise to activities that promote respect for the utility, the integrity, and the competence of the social work profession.

2. The social worker should support the formulation, development, enactment, and implementation of social policies of concern to the profession.

O. Development of Knowledge—The social worker should take responsibility for identifying, developing, and fully utilizing knowledge for professional practice.

1. The social worker should base practice upon recognized knowledge relevant to social work.

2. The social worker should critically examine and keep current the emerging knowledge relevant to social work.

3. The social worker should contribute to the knowledge base of social work and share research

knowledge and practice wisdom with colleagues.

VI. The Social Worker's Ethical Responsibility to Society

P. Promoting the General Welfare—The social worker should promote the general welfare of society.

1. The social worker should act to prevent and eliminate discrimination against any person or group on the basis of race, color, sex, sexual orientation, age, religion, national origin, marital status, political belief, mental or physical handicap, or any other preference or personal characteristic, condition, or status.

2. The social worker should act to insure that all persons have access to the resources, services, and opportunities which they require.

3. The social worker should act to expand choice and opportunity for all persons, with special regard for disadvantaged or oppressed groups and persons.

4. The social worker should promote conditions that encourage respect for the diversity of cultures which constitute American society.

5. The social worker should provide appropriate professional services in public emergencies.

6. The social worker should advocate changes in policy and legislation to improve social conditions and to promote social justice.

7. The social worker should encourage informed participation by the public in shaping social policies and institutions.

Discussion Exercises

1. Could theories of human behavior and social work intervention be developed and used without a consideration of community influence? If so, would the theories be equally applicable to anyone in the world, without consideration of culture or community?

2. How are interventions and postintervention successes of clients affected by the community? Do the social relations, environment, and networks of a drug user affect drug use? Will drug use be influenced by a "clean" community and a social support network of nonusers?

3. Are there values that are shared by most communities? If so, what are they?

4. What are the social worker's ethical responsibilities to a client and the limits of the social worker's capacity to engage in client advocacy when employed by a social agency? Which ethical codes limit advocacy?

5. Are there limits to client advocacy because of resource scarcity?

6. Are there differences between the legal requirements and ethical obligations in duty to warn, client self-determination, and informed consent?

7. Do the simultaneous obligations to clients, the community, and the employing agency and advocacy of the primacy of the client's interests present practice dilemmas?

8. In "social cause advocacy," does the social work advocate owe primary loyalty to the employing organization, the social cause, or the participants? Is there a client or a client system in social cause advocacy?

9. Can there be a "profession" sanctioned by the community for social reform and social reconstruction? Can reform and social change be professionalized? Can a profession or occupation depen-

dent on and employed by the public sector, either directly or under contract, become a radical change-oriented profession?

10. If the first ethical rule of all professional behavior should be *primum non nocere*—"first of all, do no harm"—what is your position on the question "Should the social worker risk harming an individual client in order to produce social, collective, and institutional change that might result in good for a large number of people?" Defend the position based on the social work profession's Code of Ethics and values.

11. Can affirmative action be defended as ethical by the Code of Ethics? How is affirmative action compatible with the Code of Ethics?

12. Are there ethical canons that allow law and public policy to supersede the Code of Ethics?

Notes

1. For a somewhat different view of social work's need for a common base, see Wakefield (1988). Wakefield distinguishes between "clinical counseling" as social work and "psychotherapy" as lying outside of social work. Wakefield argues for unifying principles derived from John Rawl's conception of minimal distributive justice.

2. This case was provided by a clinical practice colleague.

3. The community development case is based on one of the author's practice experiences. Similar "Colonias" currently dot the southwestern United States.

4. At the time of development of this text, California voters had passed an initiative curtailing the provision of public health, education, and welfare services to illegal immigrants. The U.S. Congress was considering similar restrictions.

5. Copyright 1993, National Association of Social Workers, Inc. Reproduced with permission of NASW, 750 First St., NE, Suite 700, Washington, DC 20002-4241.

References

American Association of Social Workers. (1929). *Social case work: Generic and specific, a report of the Milford Conference.* New York: Author.

Anderson, R. E., & Carter, I. (1984). *Human behavior in the social environment: A social systems approach* (3rd ed.). New York: Aldine.

Asch, A., & Abelson, P. (1993). Serving workers through managed mental health care: The social work role. In P. A. Kurzman & S. H. Akabas (Eds.), *Work and well-being: The occupational social work advantage* (pp. 123–137). Washington, DC: National Association of Social Workers.

Bellah, R. N., Madsen, R., Sullivan, W. M., Swidler, A., & Tipton, S. M. (1985). *Habits of the heart: Individualism and commitment in American life.* New York: Harper & Row.

Bellah, R. N., Madsen, R., Sullivan, W. M., Swidler, A., & Tipton, S. M. (1991). *The good society.* New York: Vintage Books.

Berger, P. L., & Neuhaus, R. J. (1977). *To empower people: The role of mediating structures in public policy.* Washington, DC: American Enterprise Institute.

Bisman, C. D. (1994). *Social work practices: Cases and principles.* Pacific Grove, CA: Brooks/Cole.

Blumer, H. (1969). *Symbolic interactionism: Perspective and method.* Englewood Cliffs, NJ: Prentice-Hall.

Bruno, F. J. (1948). *Trends in social work: As reflected in the proceedings of the National Conference of Social Work, 1874–1946.* New York: Columbia University Press.

Bureau of the Census. (1995). *Statistical abstract of*

the United States; 1994 (114th ed.). Washington, DC: U.S. Government Printing Office.

Chapin, R. K. (1995). Social policy development: The strengths perspective. *Social Work, 50*(4), 506–514.

Cohen, A. P. (1985). *The symbolic construction of community*. New York: Tavistock Publication and Ellis Horwood Limited.

Commission on Accreditation. (1989). *Curriculum policy for the master's degree and baccalaureate degree programs in social work education* (rev. ed.). Washington, DC: Council on Social Work Education.

Compton, B. R., & Galaway, B. (1979). *Social work processes* (rev. ed.). Homewood IL: Dorsey Press.

Doherty, W. (1994–95). Bridging psychotherapy and moral responsibility. *The Responsive Community: Rights and Responsibilities, 5*(1), 41–52.

Doherty, W. (1995). Community considerations in psychotherapy. *The Responsive Community: Rights and Responsibilities, 5*(2), 45–53.

Doherty, W., & Etzioni, A. (1994–95). The commitment gap. *The Responsive Community, 5*(1), 75–77.

Dowd, M. (1994, December 15). Americans like G.O.P. agenda but split on how to reach goals. *The New York Times*, pp. A1, A24.

Drucker, P. F. (1974). *Management: Tasks, responsibilities and practices*. New York: Harper & Row.

Dubin, R. (1978). *Theory building* (rev. ed.). New York: Free Press.

Epstein, L. (1980). *Helping people: The task-centered approach* (2nd ed.). Columbus, OH: Merrill.

Etzioni, A. (1993). *The spirit of community: Rights, responsibility and the communitarian agenda*. New York: Crown.

Ewalt, P. L. (1980). *Toward a definition of clinical social work*. Washington, DC: National Association of Social Workers.

Fisher, J. (1993). Empirically-based practice: The end of ideology? *Journal of Social Service Research, 18*(1/2), 19–64.

Gambrill, E. (1983). *Casework: A competency-based approach*. Englewood Cliffs, NJ: Prentice-Hall.

Germain, C. B. (1983). Using physical and social environments. In A. Rosenblatt & D. Waldfogel (Eds.), *Handbook of clinical social work* (pp. 110–133). New York: Jossey-Bass.

Gibelman, M., & Schervish, P. H. (Eds.). (1993).

Who we are: The social work labor force as reflected in the NASW membership, Washington, DC: National Association of Social Workers Press.

Gilbert, N., & Specht, H. (1976). Advocacy and professional ethics. *Social Work, 21*(4), 288–293.

Gillespie, E., & Schellhas, B. (Eds.). (1994). *Contract with America: The bold plan by Representative Newt Gingrich, Representative Dick Armey, and the House Republicans to change the nation*. New York: Time Books.

Gingrich, N., Armey, D., & the House Republicans. (1994). *Contract with America*. New York: Time Books/Random House.

Gordon, W. E. (1969). Basic construction for an integrative conception of social work. In G. Hearn (Ed.), *The general systems approach: Contributions toward an [sic] holistic conception of social work* (pp. 5–11). New York: Council on Social Work Education.

Gray, J. (1995, January 22). Does democracy have a future? *The New York Times Book Review*, pp. 1, 24–25.

Gustafson, J. A. (1982). Profession as callings. *Social Service Review, 56*(4), 501–505.

Hardcastle, D. A. (1977). Public regulation of social work. *Social Work, 22*(1), 14–20.

Hardcastle, D. A. (1987). *The social work labor force*. Social Work Education Monograph Series. Austin: School of Social Work, University of Texas.

Hardcastle, D. A. (1990). Public regulation of social work. In L. Ginsberg, S. Khinduka, J. A. Hall, F. Ross-Sheriff, & A. Hartman (Eds.), *Encyclopedia of social work* (18th ed., 1990 Supplement, pp. 203–217). Silver Spring, MD: National Association of Social Workers.

Hepworth, D. H., & Larsen, J. A. (1986). *Direct social work practice: Theory and skills* (2nd ed.). Chicago: Dorsey Press.

Hollenbach, D. (1994–95). Civic society: Beyond the public–private dichotomy. *The Responsive Community, 5*(1), 15–23.

How groups divided in the vote for the U.S. House. (1994, November 10). *The New York Times*, p. B4.

Karls, J. M., & Wandrei, K. E. (Eds.). (1994a). *Person-in-environment system: The p-i-e classification system for social functioning problems*. Washington, DC: National Association of Social Workers.

Karls, J. M., & Wandrei, K. E. (Eds.). (1994b). *P-i-e manual, person-in-environment system: The p-i-e classification system for social functioning problems*. Washington, DC: National Association of Social Workers.

Kuhn, T. S. (1970) *The structure of scientific revolutions* (2nd. ed. enlarged). New York: New American Library.

Ladd, E. C. (1989). The 1988 elections: Continuation of the post New Deal system. *Political Science Quarterly, 104*(1), 1–18.

Lasch, C. (1994). *The revolt of the elites and the betrayal of democracy*. New York: W. W. Norton.

Lincoln, Y. S., & Guba, E. G. (1985) *Naturalistic inquiry*. Newbury Park, CA: Sage.

Lippitt, R., Watson, J., & Westley, B. (1958). *The dynamics of planned change*. New York: Harcourt, Brace and World.

Living a life of giving. (1994, February 21–March 7). *The Voice: University of Maryland at Baltimore*, p. 6.

Lubove, R. (1977). *The professional altruist: The emergence of social work as a career, 1880–1938*. New York: Atheneum.

Miller, D. T., & Prentice, D. A. (1994). The self and the collective. *Society for Personality and Social Psychology, 20*(5), 451–453.

National Association of Social Workers. (n.d.). *NASW policy statement 1, code of ethics of the National Association of Social Workers; As adopted by the 1979 NASW Delegate Assembly and revised by the 1990 and 1993 NASW Delegate Assemblies*. Silver Spring, MD: Author.

National Association of Social Workers. (n.d.). *NASW policy statement 11, NASW standards for the practice of clinical social work*. Silver Spring, MD: Author.

Netting, F. E., Kettner, P. M., & McMurtry, S. L. (1993). *Social work macro practice*. New York: Longman.

Olsen, M. E. (1982). *Participatory pluralism: Political participation and influence in the United States and Sweden*. Chicago: Nelson-Hall.

Pardeck, J. T., Murphy, J. W., & Choi, J. M. (1994). Some implications of postmodernism for social work practice. *Social Work, 39*(4), 343–346.

Pincus, A., & Minahan, A. (1973). *Social work practice: Models and methods*. Itasca, IL: F. E. Peacock.

Polsky, H. (1969). System as patient: Client needs and system functions. In G. Hearn (Ed.), *The general systems approach: Contributions toward an [sic] holistic conception of social work* (pp. 12–25). New York: Council on Social Work Education.

Portrait of the electorate: Who voted for whom in the House. (1994, November 13). *The New York Times*, p. 24.

Powers, P. R. (n. d.). *Stirring people up; Interviews with advocates and activists*. Baltimore: School of Social Work monograph.

Pozatek, E. (1994). The problem of certainty: Clinical social work in the postmodern era. *Social Work, 39*(4), 396–403.

Pumphrey, R. E. (1980). Compassion and protection: Dual motivations of social welfare. In F. R. Breul & S. J. Diner (Eds.), *Compassion and responsibility: Readings in the history of social welfare policy in the United States* (pp. 5–13). Chicago: University of Chicago Press.

The responsive communitarian platform: Rights and responsibilities. (1992). Washington, DC: Communitarian Network.

Richmond, M. E. (1917). *Social diagnosis*. New York: Russell Sage Foundation.

Richmond, M. E. (1992). *What is social casework?* New York: Russell Sage Foundation.

Ross, M., with Lappin, B. W. (1967). *Community organization: Theory, principles, and practice*. New York: Harper & Row.

Rothman, J., & Tropman, J. (1987). Models of community organization and macro practice perspectives: Their mixing and phasing. In F. Cox, J. Erlich, J. Rothman, & J. Tropman (Eds.), *Strategies of community organization* (4th ed., pp. 3–26). Itasca, IL: P. E. Peacock.

Salcido, R. M., & Seck, E. T. (1992). *Political participation among social work chapters. Social Work, 37*(6), 563–564.

Schmidtz, D. (1991). *The limits of government: An essay on the public good argument*. Boulder, CO: Westview Press.

Shapiro, R., & Young, J. T. (1989). Public opinion and the welfare state: The United States in comparative perspective. *Political Science Quarterly, 104*(1), 59–89.

Sherraden, M. (1990). The business of social work. In L. Ginsberg, S. Khinduka, J. A. Hall, F. Ross-Sheriff, & A. Hartman (Eds.), *Encyclopedia of social work* (18th ed., 1990 Supplement, pp. 51–59). Silver Spring, MD: National Association of Social Workers.

Social case work: Generic and specific, a report of the Milford Conference. (1929). New York: American Association of Social Workers.

Spano, R. (1982). *The rank and file movement in social work*. Washington, DC: University Press of America.

Specht, H., & Courtney, M. (1994). *Unfaithful an-*

gels: How social work has abandoned its mission. New York: Free Press.

The 1994 elections. (1994, November 9). *The New York Times*, p. B4.

Timms, N. (1966). *Social casework: Principles and practice.* London: Latimer, Trend.

Tyson, K. B. (1992), A new approach to relevant scientific research for practitioners: The heuristic paradigm. *Social Work, 37*(6), 543–556.

Vigilante, F. W. (1993). Work: Its use in assessment and intervention with clients in the workplace. In P. A. Kurzman & S. H. Akabas (Eds.), *Work and well-being: The occupational social work advantage* (pp. 179–199). Washington, DC: National Association of Social Workers.

Vollmer, H. W., & Mills, D. L. (Eds.). (1966). *Professionalization.* Englewood Cliffs, NJ: Prentice-Hall.

Wakefield, J. C. (1988). Psychotherapy, distributive justice, and social work. Part I: Distributive justice as a conceptual framework for social work. *Social Service Review, 62*(2), 187–210.

Williams, L. F., & Hopps, J. G., (1990). The social work labor force: Current perspectives and future trends. In L. Ginsberg, S. Khinduka, J. A. Hall, F. Ross-Sheriff, & A. Hartman (Eds.), *Encyclopedia of social work* (18th ed., 1990 Supplement, pp. 289–306). Silver Spring, MD: National Association of Social Workers.

Part

I

UNDERSTANDING THE SOCIAL ENVIRONMENT AND SOCIAL INTERACTION

chapter
2
Theories for Community Practice by Direct Service Practitioners

A CONCEPTUAL FRAMEWORK FOR PRACTICE

One way professional social work practice differs from nonprofessional practice is that professional practice is guided by behavioral science theories as well as a body of professional values. With theory-based practice, social workers will presumably use similar interventions in similar situations to produce similar results. Under the clearest circumstances, the propositions of practice theory would thus take the form "If X occurs, or under X conditions, do Y," and professional training would primarily involve mastering the theories and their applications. So, for example, a proposition might be: "If you encounter group resistance to a new idea, then identify an opinion leader and try to persuade him or her, outside of the group context, to adopt your idea."

In social work practice, however, situation X is seldom the same as situation Y, and

the complexity of human beings and human relationships is such that behavioral science theories cannot be applied quite so neatly. Nor is there a single, unified master theory of human behavior. So, in the above example, group resistance is not a simple concept; resistance can take many forms and be explained in many different ways. A Freudian would talk about unconscious conflicts; a Skinnerian would consider rewards and punishments. Similarly, persuasion can take many different forms. Therefore, interventions to overcome resistance will vary. Discovering the kind of persuasion that works best for overcoming particular forms of resistance represents a further elaboration of theory, indeed an improvement, but one that still will not yield a simple rule.

In fact, the enormous complexity of social work practice means that we can seldom find a direct correspondence between theory and practice. Behavioral science theory seldom tells us directly exactly what to do, nor could it entirely, since ethical principles also inform professional practice. Should we therefore abandon theory as useless? Not really. Instead, as professional practitioners, we need to develop a conceptual framework for ourselves, namely, a body of related concepts that help us understand and think about the phenomena we are encountering and make decisions about how to intervene. Since (thankfully!) there is no unified grand theory of human behavior, or of social work practice, our conceptual framework will draw on a number of different theories, which will be refined through practice experience. The process of reflecting on our practice experiences in the light of behavioral science theory, and vice versa, and making appropriate modifications in theory and practice as a result (sometimes referred to as *praxis*), helps us to make sense out of our practice world. At the same time, helpful as theory is, we should not overemphasize its importance either, for creative practice draws from many sources. In the words of Rosaldo (1989), as quoted in Saleebey (1994, p. 355):

> Rather than work downward from abstract principles, social critics work outward from an in-depth knowledge of a specific form of life. Informed by such conceptions as social justice, human dignity, and equality, they use their moral imagination to move from the world as it actually is to a locally persuasive version of how it ought to be. (p. 194)

In the sections that follow, we will identify several streams of theory and a number of the concepts and propositions embedded in them in order to suggest useful components of a conceptual framework for community practice. Readers will still have the task of integrating these ideas and organizing their own frameworks.

THE FIELD OF ACTION IN COMMUNITY PRACTICE

For direct service practitioners, practice in the community will often start with understanding cultural and community influences on themselves and their clients as mutual participants in the larger system. Practice interventions may then move to a social system focus, as mentioned in Chapter 1, either to address and resolve system malfunctions (e.g., to replace a local school which has become physically unsafe) or to create development opportunities. In order to do that, we need theories that will help us to understand the behavior of individuals; the behavior of groups and organizations; relationships of power and exchange among individuals, groups, and organizations; and individual and group ideologies (Silver, 1980).

A useful way of conceptualizing community practice, then, is as a series of interventions that take place in a field of action or exchange. The important components of the field include (1) individuals, groups, and organizations or organizational subunits; (2) the main elements that these members exchange, namely, resources and information; and (3) influential aspects of the relationships among the members, namely, power balances and rules of exchange, as well as individual and group ideologies, including values, beliefs, and feelings. For our purposes, keep in mind that resources and information seldom exist apart from the individuals and organizations that control them.

For example, imagine a community practitioner trying to address the problem of the spread of acquired immunodeficiency syndrome (AIDS) among adolescents in a particular community by building a coalition that will mount an AIDS education project. What would this social worker need to consider in order to carry out this task effectively? Seeing the potential elements of the arena in which the interventions will take place, namely, the action field, helps the worker assess the scope of the project. Since the problem is complex, the composition of the action field will also be complicated. Elements in the field will also vary in their importance at different points in the intervention process. Some of the main components of an action field in this case might be the following:

1. adolescents, by no means a monolithic group;
2. parents, also not a monolithic body;
3. groups and organizations serving adolescents, such as high schools, recreation centers, clubs, informal cliques or friendship networks, and so on;
4. public health and social service organizations (non-profit, for-profit, and governmental), such as the health department and the organization you work for, the AIDS outreach service of the health clinic, Planned Parenthood, and the Department of Health and Mental Hygiene of your state;
5. civic and community associations, such as PTAs, sororities and fraternities, neighborhood associations, the Knights of Columbus, and so on;
6. churches and religious organizations;
7. elected officials and governmental bodies such as legislative finance committees;
8. the media;
9. ideologies of the above individuals and groups, including the way they view AIDS and the problem among adolescents, as well as their political, social, professional, and/or religious beliefs or philosophies;

10. relationships of exchange and power differentials that may exist among the members of the field, and the information and resources that the various members may control.

Obviously, just knowing the potential components of the action field does not tell the worker how to go about building an effective coalition. The worker also needs to know something about how the members of the field relate to each other and how they might react to the proposed project. In other words, the worker needs some theories about how this community works in order to decide what to do to accomplish the task. In the next section, we will briefly outline the theories we believe are most pertinent to community practice.

THEORIES FOR UNDERSTANDING THE FIELD OF ACTION

Entire books have been written about each of the theories to be discussed in this section. Our abbreviated presentation here includes ideas, concepts, and propositions that we view as especially pertinent for community-based practice.

Systems Theory and Organizations

A system can be viewed as a whole and its interrelated parts. Its guiding principle is organization. The main assumption underlying systems theory is that a well-integrated, smoothly functioning system is both possible and desirable. Examples of systems are mechanical systems such as computers and automobiles; human or social systems such as the Baltimore Orioles, the Department of Social Services, the AIDS Outreach Service of the health clinic, and Family Services of

America; or, for that matter, any individual human being. To the extent that a system can remain closed—free of outside influences—the assumption that it is well integrated is more tenable. But since systems are seldom entirely closed, and since human or social systems are inherently open, it is more reasonable to suggest that every social system is also inherently messy and that no human system can ever be perfectly integrated.

For a social system to exist, it must be separable from other systems and from its surroundings. It must have boundaries. At the same time, no human system can exist without relating to its environment, a proposition that defines the essence of an open system. Therefore, we could say that every human system is an open system striving for closure. Some degree of closure is necessary for a human system to function and remain intact or coherent. At the same time, every human system must exchange information and resources with other systems and act on that information in order to maintain itself and flourish. In fact, the uniqueness of human systems is that they can process, create, and act on information; they can learn. Thus we can say that every human system must negotiate its environment. Consequently, it must remain open to some degree, and it must manage some degree of uncertainty from external sources. If a human system cannot negotiate its environment, if it cannot process information well enough, then it must either exist in a protected milieu or die.

Social service agencies, like all organizations, can be viewed as open systems striving for closure. They were formed to carry out a particular mission; they are goal oriented. They also attempt to arrange their operations and decision-making rules so as to attain those goals. In short, they attempt to operate rationally. A bureaucracy, in the nonpejorative meaning of the term, represents an attempt to rationalize organizational decision making by locating expertise at the top of the decision-making structure and laying out clear rules and regulations for coordination and decision making by successively lower members in the hierarchy. The organizational chart, depicting the formal structure of authority in the organization, probably best symbolizes the organization as a rational system. This pure form of rational organization works well when the degree of uncertainty that must be managed is fairly low. So, when there is time to make decisions, when information is clear, and when resources are readily available to do the work, it is easier to operate rationally.

A bureaucracy, in the pejorative sense of the term, can be viewed as a nonrational, defensive organization. Our large public social service, health, and educational organizations tend to fall into this category. Required by law to serve or remain open to all who fit within their legislated service categories (current welfare reform proposals may change this mandate) (e.g., all children aged 5–16 who live in Chicago must attend school), yet with insufficient revenues to provide services adequately due to political struggles over the allocation of scarce resources, these public agencies develop red tape, that is, lengthy procedures for decision making and/or other "defensive" features, to stem the tide of unrelenting demand. They try to operate rationally but are overwhelmed by the demands of their environment.

Social service organizations, even nonprofit and proprietary agencies, exist in an increasingly complex, demanding, dynamic, external milieu that poses a great deal of *uncertainty* for them. (It goes without saying that the same is true for social workers and for individual clients.) Due to such factors as the exponential growth of communication and information processing technologies, previously unrelated elements in the environment may link up and bring about unpredictable reactions with far-reaching consequences (Emery & Trist, 1965). Consider, for example, the complexity of the current health care debate and the difficulty of predicting the eventual effects on organizational resources and services, especially for health and mental health agencies. How do new computers and other information system technologies affect an organization's ability to compete for clients, referral sources, and revenue? How will welfare reform affect the demand for services and the availability of funds?

Modern organizations also generate a good deal of internal system uncertainty from a variety of sources, that is, uncertainty that is built into the human differences among the members of the system and the nature of their relationships. Such sources of uncertainty include multiple and conflicting member goals and varying passions, values, interests, needs, and skills, as well as the dynamics of members' interpersonal relationships. So organizations have *informal systems* for making decisions based on the above sorts of nonrational factors, as well as *formal systems* for decision making governed by written rules, job descriptions, and lines of authority.

In this complex and constantly changing environment, organizational decision making can be very difficult. Organizational managers stand at the nexus of political, social, and economic streams of information and relationships, requiring new kinds of management skills (e.g., networking and coalition building), new forms of organizational structure (e.g., problem-solving teams with members from all levels of the organization), and much more familiarity with information processing technologies than ever before. Both organizational managers and community practitioners need to learn who the relevant group and organizational decision makers are for projects they are concerned about, as well as how those systems operate.

In the previous action field example, involving new environmental demands, a public health clinic must now develop an AIDS Outreach Service to deal with a compelling public health threat that is itself enveloped in a political whirlpool. The times require action. Yet, the controversies surrounding AIDS can easily result in confusion and nonaction. The agency cannot design and implement a community education project all by itself if it hopes to be effective. It must build a coalition and learn to work with and through other organizations over which it has little control.

Social Learning Theory

Behavioral approaches to social work practice are usually identified with various forms of individual and group therapy. They are based on the work of a number of important learning theorists such as I. P. Pavlov, B. F. Skinner, Joseph Wolpe, and Albert Bandura. Social learning ideas are also useful in community-based practice, especially in understanding and influencing the behavior of individuals and groups. For example, the development of effective organization leaders, satisfied staff members, and influential social action strategies all benefit from understanding and using social learning concepts and principles.

The basic assumption of social learning theory is that human behavior is learned during interactions with other persons and with the social environment. This is not to deny the presence of biological or psychological processes that produce emotions and thoughts. However, little credence is given to the idea that some sort of internal personality governs behavior. Thus learning theorists are much more interested in observable behaviors and in the factors that produce and modify these behaviors.

A shorthand way of thinking about the factors that produce or modify behavior—that is, the *contingencies* of social learning—is as *cues, cognitions, consequences* (Silver, 1980). In Silver's words:

> To understand social action, social learning looks to cues that occur prior in time, mental processes (cognitions) that mediate them, and rewarding or punishing consequences that follow. There is also feedback from consequences to cuing and thinking for future behavior. All together, these are the social learning *contingencies*. (p. 13)

One major form of learned behavior is called *respondent learning*, sometimes referred to as *classical* or *Pavlovian conditioning*. Examples of respondent behaviors include autonomic nervous system responses such as perspiring, salivating, and flight-or-fight reactions, as well as many fears, anxieties, and phobias. Respondent behavior is essentially learned through prior *cues* that produce an innate or unlearned response, such as the response to a good meal when hungry or to a strong reprimand. When an unconditioned stimulus (one that elicits an innate response) is paired with a neutral stimulus or event, that is, one that evokes little or no response, the neutral stimulus may acquire a similar ability to arouse a pleasurable or painful response. Thus the citizen who speaks at a legislative hearing, which was originally a neutral event, and is strongly attacked by a powerful opponent may be fearful of speaking at or even attending a legislative hearing in the future. This new response is considered a conditioned response, a behavior learned through being paired with an unconditioned stimulus that elicited a painful reaction.

Operant behavior, the other major form of learned behavior, refers to activities that can be consciously controlled, like talking or studying, and is influenced primarily by the positive or negative *consequences* that follow it in time. These consequences are commonly referred to as *rewards* or *punishments*. Behavior that is rewarded, or positively reinforced, usually is maintained or increased, whereas behavior that is punished or not reinforced has a lower probability of being repeated. Praise and attention are common examples of positive reinforcers; disapproval or a physical slap are examples of negative reinforcers or aversive stimuli. The supply of positive and negative reinforcers is endless, although which is which depends a great deal on how the individual thinks or feels about it. That is to say, one's behavior is mediated by one's *cognitions*.

Social learning theory recognizes the importance of cognition in understanding and modifying human behavior. The human capacity to think and feel and to reflect on one's thoughts and perceptions, to believe, to remember the past and anticipate the future, and to develop goals all affect how we behave. Social cognitive theory posits a model of reciprocal causation in which "behavior, cognition and other personal factors, and environmental influences all operate as interacting determinants that influence each other bidirectionally" (Bandura, 1989, p. 2). Thus, if I am a community worker, the manner in which I go about recruiting a prospect to join an AIDS education coalition may be influenced by how competent I think I am as a recruiter (cognition). My success may also be affected by the prospect's prior positive or negative experiences with coalitions (consequences), as well as his or her strong belief in or skepticism about the value of coalitions for addressing a particular problem (cognition). If I succeed in forming the coalition, I will have modified the environment for addressing the AIDS problem, and this, in turn, may influence skeptics to join the effort, which, in turn, may alter my perceptions of my personal competence or self-efficacy, and so on in a continuous interactive causal chain involving behavior, cognition, and the environment.

The concepts of *perceived individual self efficacy* and *collective efficacy* are particularly useful for community practitioners. Perceived individual self-efficacy may be viewed as self-appraisal of one's ability to determine and successfully carry out a goal-oriented course of action (Bandura, 1986). This perception stands between one's actual skills and knowledge and what one does in a given situation. So, for example, while a practitioner's skills may be quite good, his or her self-appraisal of the adequacy of these skills will affect how that worker performs. A practitioner whose perceived self-efficacy is low may often avoid challenges; the worker whose self-appraisal of efficacy is high may take them on.

When individuals give up trying to accomplish a goal because they judge their skills to be inadequate, we can say that they have *low efficacy expectations*. When they feel confident but give up trying because they are up against an unyielding obstacle or unresponsive environment, we can say that they have *low outcome expectations* (Bandura, 1982). In the latter case, this inaction is akin to the concept of *learned helplessness* (Seligman, 1975), a state of mind that comes about after repeated failure to exert influence over the decisions that affect one's life. Still, some people keep on trying even after repeated failure. How can this apparent anomaly be explained?

Abramson, Seligman, and Teasdale's (1978) reformulation of learned helplessness takes a step in this direction by positing the concepts of *personal and universal helplessness*. When individuals believe they cannot work out problems that they should be able to solve—others do solve them—they feel per-

sonally helpless. They themselves are at fault. But when they judge that nobody can solve the problem—it is beyond anyone's control—they experience universal helplessness. Putting the various concepts together (Pecukonis & Wenocur, 1994), if we consider the idea of high perceived self-efficacy and low or high outcome expectancy (the degree of responsiveness of the environment), we can imagine several different states of mind and accompanying action-oriented or political kinds of behavior. Persons whose self-appraisal of efficacy is high and who have been successful in influencing decisions that affect their lives or their external environments develop a sense of *universal hopefulness*. They believe that they can succeed and that others can as well, and so they are willing to take action on behalf of change when needed. Persons with high perceived self-efficacy and low outcome expectations because of an unrewarding or unresponsive environment may develop a sense of *personal hopefulness* if they believe they are not personally responsible for their failures but see that the system is deficient. Such individuals are likely to mistrust the political system and, under certain conditions, will engage in militant protest to change it (Bandura, 1982). Being personally hopeful, they believe they can succeed even if the system tries to stop them. Persons who are angry at political and social injustice and who have a hopeful frame of mind often make excellent leaders in community planning and social advocacy efforts.

Applying the concept of efficacy to group life, *collective efficacy* can be defined as a shared perception (conscious or unconscious) that the members of a group hold about the group's ability to achieve its objectives (Pecukonis & Wenocur, 1994). Collective efficacy includes, but is more than the sum of, the individual members' perceptions of their own efficacy because it is a property that pertains to the group as a whole, like the notion of group solidarity. A positive sense of collective efficacy is shaped by the experiences of the members within the group and by the group's interactions qua group with its external environment. At the same time, these experiences may also contribute greatly to the feeling of personal self-efficacy that each member comes to hold. When the collectivity is a social action group, successful experiences will greatly enhance feelings of personal worth and empowerment. Experiential learning, connecting experiences with knowing about oneself and the world, also create opportunities for political consciousness raising (Gowdy, 1994), an important ingredient in overcoming oppression, which will be discussed later.

Reality Construction

Helping clients gain a greater degree of power over the organizations and institutions that shape their lives is an important goal of social work practice. In the previous section, we proposed that both clients and social workers are more likely to take a step in that direction if they see the world as potentially changeable rather than fixed. To a large extent, this view of the world depends on the meanings that individuals attach to objects and events. In the words of Saleebey (1994):

> Practice is an intersection where the meanings of the worker (theories), the client (stories and narratives), and culture (myths, rituals, and themes) meet. Social workers must open themselves up to clients' constructions of their individual and collective worlds. (p. 351)

But how do we develop our understanding of events and objects that make up everyday life? The theory of reality construction ad-

vanced by Peter Berger and Thomas Luckmann in *The Social Construction of Reality* (1967) suggests that those understandings come about through social processes. Objective facts do not exist apart from the subjective meanings that people attach to them as they are being perceived. "Men (sic) *together* produce a human environment, with the totality of its socio-cultural and psychological formations" (Berger & Luckmann, 1967, p. 51). Therefore, as the book title suggests, the everyday reality that people experience is not simply a confrontation with facts and objects; it is socially constructed. So, for example, in any society people hold different kinds and amounts of riches, but the meaning of "rich"—who is rich and who is poor, what constitutes wealth and poverty—is subjectively experienced, socially defined, incorporated into one's consciousness or internalized through a process of socialization, and eventually taken as truth or reality. This latter process, "the process by which the externalized products of human activity attain the character of objectivity is [called] *objectivation*" (Berger & Luckmann, 1967, p. 60; emphasis added).

The source of the objectivation process is that human beings are by biological necessity social animals. Humans must interact with other humans and with the various elements in their external environments in order to survive and grow, and to do this they need a certain degree of stability or order. This process of ongoing interaction with the external world is called *externalization* (Berger & Luckmann, 1967, p. 56). Social order and interpretations of reality are created through this process as people talk with each other about their experiences and validate their understanding of them, and as they develop established ways of doing things to accomplish their goals. Established behavior patterns and expectations, embodied in the ideas of roles and role behavior, lead, in turn, to the development of institutions, which strongly influence the "meanings" that the members of society take as truth.

For example, the family is an institution whose meaning is very much in flux in American society. Different segments of society are contending for acceptance of their definitions of family and, in fact, for a more inclusive definition of family, based on new and different roles for men and women and changing social and economic conditions. The traditional nuclear family in which Mom stays home with the kids and Dad is the breadwinner, if there ever was such a family, has given way to the recognition of many different kinds of families—families in which both parents work, where one parent is absent, where divorce and remarriage have resulted in "blended" families, where same-sex parents and children constitute a family unit, and so on. And just as the meaning of family is changing, so is the meaning of home and marriage.

The relationship between human beings as the creators of reality and the reality that is the product of the process is a dialectical one. Thus the constructions that human beings produce—for example, the language they use, the meanings they derive, the roles they develop, and the organizations they form—all influence future constructions in a continuous back-and-forth process. "Externalization and objectivation are moments in a continuing dialectical process" (Berger & Luckmann, 1967, p. 61). So, the social order that human existence requires and creates is an order that is constantly being re-created as we negotiate our daily lives together. For community workers who must frequently help their clients as well as themselves to negotiate complicated bureaucratic systems in order to get resources to survive and perform valued social roles, reality is neither predetermined nor fixed for all time. Moreover, it is incumbent on practitioners to validate the

experiences of the individuals and groups with whom they work—their realities.

Symbols, especially language, represent the major currency of social interaction through a body of conventionalized signs and shared rules for their usage. People give meaning and structure to their experiences through language and other symbols, and language, in turn, structures our thinking and beliefs. Feminists, for example, have argued that language is a major source of categorical thinking and helps to sustain the patriarchal order. In this view, "male" is a dominant category and "whatever is *not male* is female" (Sands & Nuccio, 1992, p. 491). Similarly, ethnocentric thinking expressed in census reports has, until recently, treated *whites* as a dominant category, while African-Americans have been defined as *nonwhites*. Thus, language does not merely convey information "but is believed to thoroughly mediate everything that is known" (Pardeck, Murphy, & Choi, 1994, p. 343). Because language can be detached from the here and now, people can use it to record and pass on the past as well as to imagine the future. Language thereby helps to translate individual subjective experiences into objective reality and collective experiences into cultural knowledge. We live in a symbolic universe. Think about the meanings attached to, say, the flag of the United States versus the flag of the Confederacy. Think about the struggle of the United Farm Workers and the role of the Aztec blue eagle in that struggle. Think about the meaning of the "historical truth" so many of us learned in elementary school that Columbus discovered America, despite the obvious fact that a people already lived in America when Columbus arrived.

Human organizations and institutions develop their own cultures and ideologies reflecting the composition of their membership and their most powerful stakeholders. And sometimes institutions become *reified,* that is, they seem to take on a life of their own or to exist as entities apart from their human origins and makeup. "Reification implies that man is capable of forgetting his own authorship of the human world, and further, that the dialectic between man, the producer, and his products is lost to consciousness" (Berger & Luckmann, 1967, p. 89). The expression, "you can't fight City Hall," for example, implies that City Hall exists apart from the politicians and workers who make it up, and that it is something not subject to human influence. Social work's traditional low-income constituents, along with many social workers, often hold this version of reality. Another common example of reification occurs when an organization becomes well established and then begins to lose its vitality because its members assume that the organization can continue to function effectively without their fresh energy, ideas, and leadership. Thus not only do organizations need to continue bringing new members on board, but the newcomers need to be socialized in a manner that values their vigor and creativity.

The "third moment" in the process of reality construction, *internalization*, refers to the incorporation of socially defined meanings into one's own consciousness though a process of socialization. Socialization itself may be defined as "the comprehensive and consistent induction of an individual into the objective world of a society or a segment of it (Berger & Luckmann, 1967, p. 130). Primary socialization occurs early in childhood when the significant persons in a child's life basically teach the child what the world is about and how to behave in it. During this process, the significant others necessarily filter objective reality for the child through the lens of their own selective definitions and personal idiosyncrasies. As the child bonds emotionally with these significant persons, she or he begins to establish an identity that is partially

a reflection of the socializing agents. As a child continues to grow and relate to an expanding and ever more complex universe, secondary socialization into many new "subworlds" proceeds, mainly though the acquisition of role-related knowledge and skills.

The socially constructed realities produced through internalization are stabilized or altered on the micro-level as individuals test their plausibility against the new information and alternative definitions they are constantly receiving. At the macro-level, as new generations arise, the institutional order itself requires explanation and justification, that is, legitimation, as it is tested against changing external conditions and challenged by ideologies that run counter to established beliefs. For example, as medical knowledge and the capacity to sustain premature infants expanded, the belief that life begins at birth was strongly challenged in the 1980s by the counterideology that life begins at conception. Thus will each successive generation have to construct its own complex reality.

Constructionist theory has implications for social work practice. Social phenomena such as health, crime, and normalcy cannot be defined simply in terms of empirical, objective facts. They are embedded in a "web of meanings, created and sustained linguistically" (Pardeck et al., 1994, p. 345), that make up our own and our clients' worlds. Effective social work practice requires skill in communications to understand and enter into the assumptive world of our clients. In this way, the practitioner will be better able to make informed, sensitive assessments of client system problems unhindered by potentially stereotypical and inappropriate diagnostic taxonomies (Pozatek, 1994; Saleebey, 1994). Thus "clients are not merely consulted through the use of individualized treatment plans . . . but supply the interpretive context that is required for determining the nature of a presenting problem, a proper intervention, or a successful treatment outcome. This is true client-centered intervention" (Pardeck et al., 1994, p. 345). From a more macro perspective, a constructionist approach also suggests that social workers help clients understand "the oppressive effects of dominant power institutions" (Saleebey, 1994, p. 358) and tune in to the countervailing knowledge available in their own communities (Reisch, Sherman, & Wenocur, 1981).

Social Exchange Theory and Power

Social exchange theory, associated with theorists such as George C. Homans (1974), Peter M. Blau (1964), and Richard Emerson (1962), forms another conceptual building block for community practice. Built on the operant conditioning aspects of social learning theory and an economic view of human relationships as concerned with maximization of rewards or profits and minimization of punishments or costs, exchange theory underlies such skills as bargaining, negotiating, advocating, networking, and marketing. The part of exchange theory that deals with power and dependency is especially pertinent to community practice.

Earlier we said that community practice takes place in an action or exchange field, and we identified the important elements of the field. In terms of exchange theory, the exchange field represents a market consisting of two or more parties who interact with each other at different points in time and in various combinations in order to exchange desired resources or products. These resources can be tangible or intangible. They can include counseling and community organization services, money (a proxy for other products), information, ideas, political influence, good will, compliant behavior, meanings, and energy. For transactions to occur, the involved parties require information about the products to be exchanged and a desire for the exchange product. Given relevant information and desire, exchange theory holds that parties in a transaction select from all the possible exchanges those that have the greatest ratio of benefits or rewards to costs. In social exchanges, compared to economic exchanges, this calculus is seldom precise. For example, with a contribution to a United Way campaign, the donor is giving dollars, an easily measurable unit, but the products received in return—say, social status, community improvement, and assistance to people in need—are not easily measurable or readily comparable to alternative products for the donor's money.

All the parties in an exchange field do not necessarily have relationships with each other at any given point in time. Two agencies, for example, might not have any transactions, but both might transact business with the same third organization. When Party A in an exchange field, be it an individual, a group, or an organization, can accomplish its goals without relating to Party B, and vice versa, these parties can be said to be *independent* of each other. However, as soon as either party cannot achieve its ends without obtaining some needed product or resource from the other and exchanges begin to occur, they can be considered *interdependent*. Usually interdependent relationships are not perfectly balanced, that is, Party A may need the resources that Party B controls much more than B needs what A has to offer. In fact, B may not need what A can offer at all. In this extremely imbalanced situation, A may be said to be *dependent* on B. This imbalance in exchange relationships sets the stage for relations of power or influence among the members of an exchange field.

Stated most simply, in an exchange relationship *power is a function of the ability to control the resources that another party needs*. To the extent that Party B has control over the resources that Party A must have in order to accomplish its goals, B has power over A. In that relationship, B's position is one of independence. B can, if it so chooses, exercise its power over A by making its exchange of resources with A contingent on A's compliance with certain requirements. A is in a *power-dependent* position with respect to B in their exchange relationship. Consider the relationship between the social worker and the client through this lens (Cowger, 1994). Hearkening back to the contingencies of social learning, favorable exchange is a contingency of A's compliant behavior. If B also wants some of the resources that A controls—and remember that those resources may be tangible or intangible (e.g., money, services, good will)—then the relationship is interdependent, although weighted more in favor of one party than the other. These parties have mutual dependencies, albeit in different degrees.

Suppose, for example, that the local health clinic would like financial support from the United Way for its Aids Outreach Project, and right now that is the clinic's only hope for funding. In that exchange relationship, the United Way has power with respect to the clinic because it controls the resources that the clinic needs. Theoretically, if the United Way chose, it could establish preconditions (contingencies) for obtaining those funds, such as requiring the clinic to coordinate its services with an existing United Way affiliated agency like the Family Services Society. More typical United Way preconditions usually include reporting requirements, a financial audit, and an agreement not to raise funds during the United Way campaign. Now, to the extent, say, that the United Way has been under pressure in the media to become more responsive to community needs, it might view the AIDS Outreach Project as a highly desirable prospect for funding. Therefore the United

Way might be willing to relax its reporting or audit requirements in order to make it easier for the clinic to affiliate.

Parties who need resources that others control can engage in various *power-balancing strategies* in order to bring about more favorable exchanges. For the sake of discussion, let us consider Party A an as "action organization," a community group, that is trying to get resources from Party B, a "target organization," say, a large private university in the area that has resources that A needs. Since A, the community group, is in a dependent position in this situation, B, the university, holds power with respect to A. In order to reduce B's power, A can adopt one of two approaches. Either A can find some way to decrease its dependency on B or A can find some way to increase B's dependency on it. These approaches lend themselves to the following power-balancing strategies: competition, revaluation, reciprocity, coalition, and coercion. Each of these strategies will now be described.

COMPETITION

This strategy requires Party A to find other sources for meeting its goals rather than by making exchanges with Party B. So long as B has a monopoly on the resources that A needs, A will be dependent and B will have power. If A can get needed resources from Parties F and G, B's power will be reduced.

Suppose that A, the community group, would like B, the university, to donate, or sell at a low price, a parcel of land for a community recreation center. So long as A's goal is to build the recreation center and it needs this land, and there is no other place to get it except from B, B has power in relation to A. As a consequence, if both parties are willing to make an exchange, B could potentially force A, for example, to support a piece of controversial legislation before the City Council. If there are other land-holding institutions in the community—say, a couple of churches (F and G) to which A might turn for inexpensive land, then B's power over A will be reduced.

REVALUATION

In this strategy, because of either value or ideological changes, A becomes less interested in the resources that B controls, and B accordingly loses power over A. In situations like this, the target organization, B, may try to maintain A's dependency on it by offering A inducements or new advantages to sustain the exchange relationship.

For example, A, the community group, may lose interest in its goal of building a recreation center because the level of community violence may have increased, causing A to put its energy into a different issue: developing a community policing effort. B, the university, no longer has a resource that A needs, and it cannot use its relationship to get B's support on the controversial legislation it seeks to have enacted. Because B believes it might need A's support in the future, B may offer to contribute money or training to A's community policing effort or to lower the price of the land that A originally wanted for its recreation center.

RECIPROCITY

Here A seeks to find a resource that it controls that Party B would like. If A can thus make itself more attractive to B as a potential trading partner, then the dependent relationship could be transformed into an interdependent one and A could achieve a more equitable balance of power.

Continuing the above illustration, if A, the community group, can gain control over a parcel of land that B, the university, would like for expanded student parking, then A owns a desirable resource. A might be able to use this resource to negotiate a favorable

exchange with B, thereby achieving some balance of power in the relationship.

COALITION

A by itself may not be able to exert much influence over B. The same may also be true of C and D in their exchange relationships with B. But if A can coalesce with C and D, together each may control some portion of what the target organization, B, needs. A and the other parties may thereby reduce their dependency by working out a more even-handed relationship with B.

Let's say that A, C, and D are all community groups that are trying to influence the university's (B's) parking policy in the community. While individually none of these organizations may be able to exert much influence over B, together they may be able to control enough votes on the City Zoning Commission to get B to adopt a more favorable parking policy for the community. These votes may even be important enough to the university to get it to lower the price of the land that A, the coalition leader, wants for the recreation center.

COERCION

Coercion involves the use of force, usually physical force, to compel one party to do what the other party wants. Since threats or actual harm to persons and property are normally illegal and immoral, this strategy falls outside the bounds of professional acceptability. We would distinguish physical coercion from the use of disruptive tactics that are normally legal, such as a sit-in, a rally, a strike, or a media blitz.

In the above illustration, if A were to threaten to do harm to B's personnel or property in an effort to get B to sell its property cheaply, this would constitute an illegal form of coercion. However, if A organized a large demonstration of students and community residents outside of the president's office as a means of pressuring A to change its decision about selling the property by creating unfavorable public opinion, this could be an acceptable strategy. We would consider this a form of reciprocity, namely, gaining control over a resource A needs—favorable public opinion—rather than coercion.

Although the dynamics of power and exchange are important, many transactions in an exchange field do not carry heavy overtones of power. People are constantly relating to one another, exchanging information, and sharing resources without trying to extract advantages from the transaction. In fact, the more people exchange resources with each other, the greater the likelihood that reciprocal obligations will develop and that these will be governed by norms of fairness. As positive relationships develop, exchange partners who each obtain a desirable resource may be attracted to one another and may form cohesive associations such as support groups, networks, new organizations, coalitions, and the like.

In general, within the framework of social exchange theory, it is important to note that exchanges involving power require building relationships among people, making connections where none may have existed previously, and creating interdependencies. Since the potential for building relationships with other people is limitless, the implication is that power is neither limited as a resource nor confined to a set group of people. Rather, power can be viewed as a dynamic resource that is ever expandable. In the words of Lappe and Du Bois (1994):

> Power as it is being lived and learned, is neither fixed nor one-way. It is fluid. Based on relationships, it is dynamic. It changes as the attitudes and behavior of any party change. This understanding of power offers enormous possibilities: it suggests that by conscious attention to the importance of one's own actions, one can change others—even those who, under the old view of power, appear immovable. All this allows us to discover new sources of power within our reach. (p. 54)

Note also that the coalitional power-balancing strategy, in particular, underlies all community organization practice. It suggests that if individuals or groups by themselves do not have sufficient power to influence the decisions that affect their lives, they need to join forces with other people—friends, confederates, others who have power—so that together they can create new sources of influence that alone they did not possess.

Interorganizational Theory

Much community practice involves establishing and managing relationships with other groups and organizations. The selection of theoretical material thus far presented provides the groundwork for many of the ideas that help us understand these interorganizational relations. In this section, we are trying to understand the behavior of groups and organizations rather than individuals, so conceptually in interorganizational relationships, the unit of analysis is the organization or organizational subunit rather than the individual.

The fundamental (by now obvious) idea in interorganizational theory is that every organization is embedded in a larger network of groups and organizations that it must relate to in order to survive and prosper. Within this interorganizational network or exchange field, each organization must carve out a specific *domain*, or sphere of operation. Levine and White (1961), in a study of relations among community health agencies, defined organizational domain as "the claims which an organization stakes out for itself in terms of (1) diseases covered, (2) population served, and (3) services rendered" (p. 597).

To create a better fit for social service agencies and community organizations, we could substitute the phrase "social problems that the organization addresses" for "diseases covered." For example, although there may be overlap, no two organizations serving the homeless will have identical domains. One may serve only men, the other families. One may refuse substance abusers; another may accept all who come but require attendance at a religious sermon. Geographic boundaries may vary. Some organizations may include an advocacy function, others only service.

The domain of an organization identifies the points where it will have to relate to and/or rely on other organizations to fulfill its mission. Mother's Kitchen, which provides hot meals to the needy in South Bostimore, will need serving, eating, and storage facilities, a supply of volunteers, a supply of food, health department approval, and so on. Joe's Van, which supplies coffee and sandwiches on winter weekends to homeless persons in South Bostimore, will need different kinds of volunteers, facilities, and supplies. Depending on an organizations's domain, then, we can readily see that the structure and dynamics of its external environment will have a lot to do with the organizations's ability to achieve its objectives. In some environments, resources are scarce; in others, plentiful. So, volunteers may be relatively easy or hard to find. There may or may not be a "food bank" to draw on for inexpensive staples. Some environments have many competitors or regulations, others few. Complex organizations in dynamic environments may also have specialized positions or even whole departments to assist them in handling environmental transactions—for example, a director of volunteers, a public relations department, and a lobbyist or governmental affairs division.

It is useful to conceptualize the set of external organizations and organizational subunits that a focal organization must deal with to accomplish its goals as a *task environment* (Thompson, 1967). While the concept of *external environment* is somewhat abstract and amorphous, the task environment concept can be delineated quite specifically. The task environment consists of six categories of components (Hasenfeld, 1983, pp. 61–63; Thompson, 1967), which will now be described. For any given organization, some environmental units may fit in more than one category.

1. *Providers of fiscal resources, labor, materials, equipment, and work space.* These may include providers of grants, contributions, fees for products or services, bequests, and so on. Organizations often have multiple sources of funds. Mother's Kitchen may receive federal funds channeled through the local Mayor's Office of Homelessness Services, as well as contributions from a sponsoring church. At the same time, Mother's Kitchen may receive space from a local church, office supplies from a local stationer, and maintenance supplies from a janitorial products company. The school of social work may be an important source of labor via field work interns.

2. *Providers of legitimation and authority.* These may include regulatory bodies, accrediting groups, and individuals or organizations that lend their prestige, support, or authority to the organization. The CSWE accredits schools of social work. A school of social work may lend its support to a local agency's continuing education program. The dean of the school may serve on the board of directors of an agency serving the homeless, along with client representatives from the Homeless Union.

3. *Providers of clients or consumers.* These include those very important individuals and groups who make referrals to the agency, as well as the individuals and families who seek out the organization's services directly. The

Department of Public Welfare may be a major referral source of clients for Mother's Kitchen. Other clients may come on their own as word of mouth passes around on the streets. The South Bostimore Community Association may be a major source of referrals for a new health maintenance organization started by the local university hospital.

4. *Providers of complementary services.* These include other organizations whose products or services are needed by an organization in order to successfully do its job. Mother's Kitchen may use the university medical school for psychiatric consultations and a drug treatment center for substance abuse counseling services. The Welfare Department provides income maintenance for homeless families who may use Mother's Kitchen.

5. *Consumers and recipients of an organization's products or services.* Social service agencies cannot operate without clients; a community organization cannot operate without members; and a school of social work must have students. Clients and consumers are critical to justifying an organization's legitimacy and claims for resources. So the consumers of an agency's services are the clients themselves, voluntarily or involuntarily, together with their social networks. Other organizations may also be consumers of an agency's "products." For example, employers need to be available and willing to hire the graduates of the Welfare Department's employment training programs.

6. *Competitors.* Few organizations operate with a monopoly on consumers or clients and other resources necessary for them to function. With human service organizations, other such agencies are frequently competing for the same clients or for fiscal resources from similar sources. Several schools of social work in the same city may compete for students and will try to carve out unique domains to reach into different markets in order to ensure a flow of applicants. Similarly, private family agencies are competing for clients with social work private practitioners and psychotherapists. Since resources for social services are invariably scarce, the ability to compete successfully is almost always a fact of life for organization managers.

The power and exchange relations discussed in the previous section govern a good deal of interorganizational behavior. This is so because the member units of an organization's task environment represent interdependencies that the organization must establish and manage successfully in order to operate within its domain. Clearly, to the extent that an environmental unit has some of the resources that your organization needs to carry out its business, that unit has power with respect to your organization. Furthermore, if your organization cannot establish the requisite interdependencies—and competitors could make that difficult—it will not be able to carve out a workable domain. Thus Mother's Kitchen cannot operate as a soup kitchen without passing a state health department sanitation inspection and a city fire department safety inspection. Nor will your church be able to establish its homeless shelter without the approval of its neighbors. And a grant agency such as a state department of mental health or a private foundation is usually in a good position to dictate the terms of compliance for the dollars it awards.

Interorganizational relations become truly interesting when we begin to think about the concepts of domain and task environment as dynamic rather than static entities. Imagine an exchange field with multiple individuals, groups, and organizations, each of which has its own domains and task environments but all of which are in some way at least loosely connected, directly and indirectly, as would be the case, for example, in the city of Bostimore's homelessness "sector." Since Bostimore is a city of 650,000 people and since homelessness is a complicated problem, hundreds of organizations provide different kinds of services to, and advocate for, homeless individuals and families. While enough order or consensus exists for these organizations to be able to get the resources they need to function (i.e., there is some level of *domain consensus* among the organizational players), thousands of exchanges are taking place. New organizational relationships are being formed and old ones altered; new needs and new information are emerging; new ideas are being created; available resources are shifting with political and economic developments; new players are entering the scene and old ones exiting; new domains are being carved out in response to new opportunities and constraints; and so on. No organizational domain is static. Modern organizational life, in short, is really interorganizational life, and it involves a continuous process of negotiation in a complex, constantly changing, and highly unpredictable environment (Aldrich, 1979; Emery & Trist, 1965).

Conflict Theory

There is perhaps a natural tendency among human beings to search for social order and organization in their lives. Hence the processes of socialization and social control that support order seem very acceptable, while processes involving social conflict often make us uncomfortable. Yet, as we said earlier, disorder is also a natural and inevitable aspect of human life. Thus the dialectical conflict perspective in sociology, as propounded by theoreticians such as Karl Marx and Ralf Dahrendorf, can further inform social work practice.

Although their images of society differ, Marx and Dahrendorf share some basic assumptions about the nature of society

(Turner, 1978), which help us to see social systems as dynamic entities. Both believe that (1) social systems systematically generate conflict, and therefore conflict is a pervasive feature of society; (2) conflict is generated by the opposed interests that are inevitably part of the social structure of society; (3) opposed interests derive from an unequal distribution of scarce resources and power among dominant and subordinate groups, and hence every society rests on the constraint of some of its members by others; (4) different interests tend to polarize into two conflict groups; (5) conflict is dialectical, that is, the resolution of one conflict creates a new set of opposed interests, which, under certain conditions, spawn further conflict; and (6) as a result of the ongoing conflict, social change is a pervasive feature of society.

For Marx, conflict is rooted in the economic organization of society, especially the ownership of property and the subsequent class structure that evolves. Production, the way that men and women create their daily subsistence, is a central aspect of Marxist thought. It influences cultural values and beliefs, religion, other systems of ideas, social relations, and the formation of a class structure. Under capitalism, the means of production (factories, corporations) are owned by capitalists rather than by the workers. Because workers must now depend on capitalists to be able to earn a living, they are rendered powerless and exploitable. Labor becomes a commodity to be bought and sold, moved and shaped, as the needs of capital dictate. In the modern world, Marx would argue that the movement of corporations to different parts of the United States or to foreign countries to gain tax advantages and find cheap labor are manifestations of the commoditization process. But capitalism also contains the seeds of its own destruction (dialectical materialism). Therefore, as alienation sets in among the workers, a revolutionary class consciousness begins to develop. The workers begin to challenge the decisions of the ruling class, ultimately seeking to overthrow the system and replace capitalism with socialism.

For Dahrendorf (1959), writing a century after Marx, industrial strife in modern capitalist society represents only one important sphere of conflict. Still, conflict is pervasive, having a structural origin in the relations of dominance and submission that accompany social roles in any organized social system from a small group or formal organization to a community or even an entire society. If an authority structure exists, that is, a structure of roles containing power differentials, Dahrendorf calls these social systems *imperatively coordinated associations (ICAs)*. The differing roles in ICAs lead to the differentiation of two "quasi-groups" with opposing latent interests. These quasi-groups are not yet organized, but when they become conscious of their mutual positions, they do organize into manifest interest groups that conflict over power and resources. This conflict eventually leads to change in the structure of social relationships. The nature, rapidity, and depth of the resultant change depend on empirically variable conditions, such as the degree of social mobility in the society and the sanctions that the dominant group can impose.

The transformation of an aggregate of individuals who share a set of common, oppressive conditions into an interest group that will engage in conflict to change the situation is critical for conflict theorists and has relevance for social work advocates and community practitioners. A main ingredient of that transformation seems to be the development of an awareness or consciousness of one's relative state of deprivation and the illegitimate positions of those in power. In a manual on consciousness-raising (CR) groups, for example, the National Organ-

ization for Women (NOW) wrote that "Feminist CR has one basic purpose: it raises the woman's consciousness, increases her complete awareness, of her oppression in a sexist society" (NOW, 1982, p. 3). Thus *political CR* may be defined as the method by which an oppressed group comes to understand its condition and becomes activated politically to change it (Berger, 1976, p. 122). But developing this awareness is not so easy. Marx argued that human beings are victims of a false consciousness born of the exploitive power of the capitalist system. For Gramsci, a neo-Marxist, an alliance of ruling-class fractions maintains hegemony over the subordinate classes by means of *ideology* spread by the state, the media, and other powerful cultural institutions (Hall, 1977):

> This means that the "definitions of reality", favourable to the dominant class fractions, and institutionalized in the spheres of civil life and the state, come to constitute the primary "lived reality" as such for the subordinate classes. . . . This operates, not because the dominant classes can prescribe and proscribe, in detail, the mental content of the lives of subordinate classes (they too "live" in their own ideologies), but because they strive and to a degree succeed in *framing* all competing definitions of reality *within their range*, bringing all alternatives within their horizon of thought. They set the limits—mental and structural—within which subordinate classes "live" and make sense of their subordination in such a way as to sustain the dominance of those ruling over them. (pp. 332–333)

A capitalist system thus finds myriad ways to induce people to believe that happiness lies in the pursuit and achievement of material ends.

Just how and why the transformation into a conflict group takes place is not entirely clear, for many latent interest groups exist under cruel conditions without organizing for change. Both Marx and Dahrendorf, however, do stress the importance of leadership in this process. "For an organized interest group to emerge from a quasi-group, there have to be certain persons who make this organization their business, who carry it out practically and take the lead" (Dahrendorf, 1959, p. 185). In addition, it seems clear that the prospective members of this interest group have to be able to communicate their grievances to each other, that physical proximity helps, and that freedom of association may aid the process, although conflict groups have certainly emerged in totalitarian regimes (Dahrendorf, 1959; Turner, 1978).

Marxist and neo-Marxist theory applied to the role of the state in capitalist society also has special relevance for social workers because many social workers either work directly for government agencies or work in nonprofit organizations in programs funded with state dollars. Unlike conservative political economists, who want to greatly reduce the role of the state in regulating market system activities and its human costs, and unlike liberals, who view the state as a potential leveling force for reducing income disparities and alleviating distress, Marxist analysts view the state in a more complicated fashion. In the long term, they see it as serving the interests of the ruling class by maintaining social harmony (Piven & Cloward, 1971) and preparing a low-wage work force. On an ongoing basis, they argue that the state mirrors the contradictions in the capitalist system, hence it is an arena for ideological and practical struggles over the distribution of income, benefits, and rights (Corrigan & Leonard, 1979). In the words of Fabricant and Burghardt (1992):

> To them, class struggle is not a simplistic "war" between workers and owners, but an ongoing, complex, and contentious relationship among actors in the state, in the economy, and in other social groups struggling over the direction and extent of state intervention. Ultimately, this struggle will either enhance the legitimacy of social services through a combination of expansion and restructuring ... or encourage greater accumulation and unfettered private investment—with the resultant industrialization of social services. . . . (p. 52)

If social workers and managers of social service agencies can become conscious of themselves as actors in this struggle, they can share their awareness and analysis with their clients, and they can resist treating the problems of individual clients only as private troubles rather than as systemic dysfunctions.

Discussion Exercises

1. A number of students have come to Student Health Services in your college or university. On reviewing these cases, the social work staff has found that a majority of the students are women and many are single parents with young children.

(a) Identify some of the stressors that female students who are single parents might be experiencing at your college. Which ones derive from systemic deficiencies in the college and in the larger society? Which are rooted in sexism? How well is the Student Health Service set up to deal with these stressors? Are there any professional ideologies, assumptions, beliefs, and/or practical realities that guide the way social work is practiced in this agency?

(b) As a social worker attuned to the need to address systemic problems to help reduce the stress your clients are encountering, how might you begin to address these problems within Student Health Services? Within the college?

(c) Suppose that the Health Services staff has agreed that the college ought to operate an on-site day-care center for students, staff, and faculty. Identify the components of the potential *field of action* that you might need to consider and work with. Who would you attempt to include in an *action system*? Who would be the potential *target system*? (See Chapter 1, if necessary, for definitions of action system and target system.)

(d) Identify the *domain* and the main elements of the *task environment* of the Student Health Services. Examine the *power and exchange relationships* between task environment members and Student Health Services. How do these relationships affect any potential strategy you might develop for getting the day care center?

(e) What obstacles might you encounter in trying to obtain approval for an on-site day-care center? Which of these might be explained in terms of *conflict theory*?

(f) How might the concepts of *individual self-efficacy* and *collective efficacy* come into play in this project?

(g) Thinking in terms of *reality construction*, can you identify any political ideologies that might be associated with different members of the exchange field and that could be a factor in accomplishing this project? What might be the position of the student Republican organization? The student Democratic club? The student–faculty Feminist Alliance?

(h) Thinking in terms of *conflict theory*, has your own political consciousness been raised through this exercise? In what ways?

References

Abramson, L. V., Seligman, M., & Teasdale, J. D. (1978). Learned helplessness in humans: Critique and reformulation. *Journal of Abnormal Psychology, 87*, 49–74.

Aldrich, H. E. (1979). *Organizations and environments.* Englewood Cliffs, NJ: Prentice-Hall.

Bandura, A. (1982, February). Self-efficacy mechanism in human agency. *American Psychologist, 37*, 122–147

Bandura, A. (1986). *Social foundations of thought and action.* Englewood Cliffs, NJ: Prentice-Hall.

Bandura, A. (1989). Social cognitive theory. *Annals of Child Development, 6*, 1–60.

Berger, P. L. (1976). *Pyramids of sacrifice: Political ethics and social change.* Garden City, N.Y.: Anchor Books.

Berger, P. L., & Luckmann T. (1967). *The social construction of reality.* Garden City, NY: Anchor Books.

Blau, P. M. (1964). *Exchange and power in social life.* New York: Wiley.

Corrigan, P., & Leonard, P. (1979). *Social work practice under capitalism: A Marxist approach.* London: Macmillan.

Cowger, C. D. (1994). Assessing client strengths: Clinical assessment for client empowerment. *Social Work, 39*(3), 262–267.

Dahrendorf, R. (1959). *Class and class conflict in industrial society.* Stanford, CA: Stanford University Press.

Emerson, R. (1962). Power-dependence relations. *American Sociological Review, 17*(27), 31–41.

Emery, F. E., & Trist, E. L. (1965). The causal texture of organizational environments. *Human Relations, 18*, 21–32.

Fabricant, M. B., & Burghardt, S. (1992). *The welfare state crisis and the transformation of social service work.* Armonk, NY: M. E. Sharpe.

Gowdy, E. A. (1994). From technical rationality to participating consciousness. *Social Work, 39*(4), 362–370.

Hall, S. (1977). Culture, the media, and the ideological effect. In J. Curran, M. Gurevitch, & J. Woollacott (Eds.), *Mass communication and society.* London: Edward Arnold.

Hasenfeld, Y. (1983). *Human service organizations.* Englewood Cliffs, NJ: Prentice-Hall.

Homans, G. C. (1974). *Social behavior: Its elementary forms.* New York: Harcourt Brace Jovanovich.

Lappe, F. M., & Du Bois, P. M. (1994). *The quickening of America: Rebuilding our nation, remaking our lives.* San Francisco: Jossey-Bass.

Levine, S., & White, P. E. (1961). Exchange as a

conceptual framework for the study of interorganizational relations. *Administrative Science Quarterly, 5,* 583–610.

National Organization for Women. (1982). *Guidelines to feminist consciousness-raising.* Washington, DC: NOW.

Pardeck, J. T., Murphy, J. W., & Choi, J. M. (1994). Some implications of postmodernism for social work practice. *Social Work, 39*(4), 343–346.

Pecukonis, E., & Wenocur, S. (1994). Perceptions of self and collective efficacy in community organization theory and practice. *Journal of Community Practice, 1*(2), 5–21.

Piven, F. F., & Cloward, R.A. (1971). *Regulating the poor: The functions of public welfare.* New York: Random, Vintage Books.

Pozatek, E. (1994). The problem of certainty: Clinical social work in the Postmodern era. *Social Work, 39*(4), 396–404.

Reisch, M., Sherman, W. R., and Wenocur, S. (1981). Empowerment, conscientization, and animation as core social work skills. *Social Development Issues, 5*(2/3), 106–120.

Rosaldo, R. (1989). *Culture and truth: The remaking of social analysis.* Boston: Beacon Press.

Saleebey, D. (1994). Culture, theory, and narrative: The intersection of meanings in practice. *Social Work. 39*(4), 351–361.

Sands, R. G., & Nuccio, K. (1992). Postmodern feminist theory and social work. *Social Work, 37*(6), 489–494.

Seligman, M. E. P. (1975). *Helplessness: On depression, development, and death.* San Francisco: Freeman.

Silver, M. (1980). *Social infrastructure organizing technology.* Unpublished doctoral dissertation, University of California, Berkeley.

Thompson, J. D. (1967). *Organizations in action.* New York: McGraw-Hill.

Turner, J. H. (1978). *The structure of sociological theory* (rev. ed.). Homewood, IL: Dorsey Press.

chapter
3

The Nature of Social and Community Problems

[C]ompassion . . . encourages people to recognize the value of transcending class barriers, both in their deeds of caring and in their attitudes. . . . [It] creates diffuse connections that bridge the various segmented communities in which we live and reinforces a sense of common membership in the whole society.

R. WUTHNOW (1991, P. 307)

CONCEPTUALIZING A SOCIAL–COMMUNITY PROBLEM

A Viewpoint on Problems and Their Resolution

Communities define which of many social problems they will make their own, just as nations do. We must examine how a condition gets a community's attention in terms of how the community addresses the problem, uses its resources, or changes its behavior. The first tasks are to determine who defines problems and how, the ideology (beliefs and hopes) guiding the definition, and ways to define or recast problems that can tap a wider perception and gather more support for remediation. This chapter will contribute to the social worker's understanding of problems—facilitating more appropriate interventions—and will suggest applications that can lead to mutual construction of problems and solutions and to coalition building. It will emphasize that human variety must be acknowledged and taken into account.

What determines whose definition prevails? Does power or passion play a part?

From whose standpoint is a problem raised and whose worldview is accepted (Lopez, 1994)? Are there service consequences (underutilization, inappropriate interventions) to being oblivious to another group's culture or reality? Are new possibilities conceivable? Can problem solving be used to unite a community? We will explore such questions and rethink the conventional wisdom regarding the nature of social problems, focusing on:

Definition—how problems are conceptualized;

Meaning—how problems are experienced;

Action—how problems are kept in check or solved.

This requires exploring many-sided and fluctuating *realities*. Although reality is not fixed, trying to overcome problems is no quixotic exercise, for there are ways to frame problems and interventions (Chapin, 1995).

Introduction to a Complex Phenomenon

A clinician ordinarily sees but one aspect of individuals who are surrounded and supported by a community of immense complexity. It is as if the professional stands before the open top half of a Dutch door, conversing without seeing the operations of the household or even a single whole person. The same is double true of our view of a social problem, many dimensions of which are veiled. Understanding how specific clients and problems inhabit their social context contributes to problem clarification. We may or may not already be familiar with the problems, those linked with them, or the setting. Suppose a worker is told that a community has problems "related to family breakdown, drug and alcohol abuse, long-term health care, services for the elderly, equal opportunity in employment, and affordable housing"

(Murase, 1995, p. 157). An experienced worker might feel perfectly confident about proceeding. However, if the community is Japanese-American and the worker is not, more information might be needed, for example, about the Issei, Nisei, and Sansei (different generations). The same problems can take different forms within a community and between communities due to cultural variations. Still, problems create common denominators for citizens even while being distinctively experienced.

Human service workers, according to Ginsberg (1994, pp. 45–47), typically will contend with these problems: economic disadvantage, physical illness, mental illness, crime and delinquency, maltreatment, lack of services to special populations, and lack of resources for programs. However, others may not share the professionals' conceptualization of problems.

What is meant by *social problems*? Some scholars are inclusive, connecting social movements and problems. Others are restrictive, limiting problems to what is measurable. *For now, let us view social problems as widespread, intense worries that collectively demand leadership, societal attention, and intervention.* Ginsberg (1994) says it is "the shared belief that the problem represents a serious threat to a community or the larger society which provides people with the will to do something about it" (p. 41).

Distinctions Relevant to Our Profession

A skeptic might ask why social workers need to learn any more about problems since, after all, they work with problem families every day. It is clear that our profession not only assists hard-pressed families but lunges to catch society's "throwaway" citizens. It is less clear whether the problem is these individuals, those who toss them aside, or the circumstances contributing to the "failure" of both. Unemployment and underemployment in an era of global corporate relocation illustrate this complexity. Did blue-collar workers fail to acquire information-age skills, did management focus too much on immediate profits instead of acquiring productive computer-controlled plant machinery, or will corporations always gravitate to cheap labor? How will the problem be defined?

OBJECTIVE AND SUBJECTIVE VIEWS

On a theoretical level, community problems continue to be viewed, in contrasting fashion, as community *conditions* and as community *claims-making activities*—viewpoints referred to as *objective* and *subjective approaches*. Some assume that problems exist in society by themselves, whereas others argue that conditions alone are often ignored; thus, problems are "created" through perception, claims, and action. The *objective view* often means that conceptions of conditions are widely shared. This outlook leads us to the causes, precipitating factors, and prevention of problems, to their seemingly intrinsically harmful nature, to demographic shifts, and to priorities based on severity and occurrence. We also think of possible actions available to the community, such as education (Parsons, Hernandez & Jorgensen, 1988). *From this perspective, "One of the roles of human service workers is to identify and bring to public attention the social problems that they encounter in their daily work"* (Ginsberg, 1994, p. 49). In part, we assume the role of expert.

The *subjective view* is that there are no universally recognized problems. This outlook leads us to the "public designation of social problems" (Blumer, 1971, p. 299), to other injustices competing for attention, conditions unattended to, and mobilization endeavors. There are objective elements to this approach, but changes in problem formulation and success in the competitive "social problems marketplace" (Jenness, 1995, p. 163) are usually linked more closely to sub-

jective elements. *From this perspective, one human service role is to be aware of how affected individuals can help frame social problems.*

Metaphorically, this includes both watching the roller-coaster track of problems and hearing the person who is on the ride.[1] We may play the role of observer-listener or of advocate and power broker.

REACHING OUR OWN UNDERSTANDINGS

When people say to social workers, "Here's a social problem—fix it!," we cannot take either their judgment or their command at face value. Although our offices were created to ameliorate distress and improve conditions (or people's functioning in the situation), problem formulation is too complex for us to proceed blithely (Lopez, 1994). Even when other professionals say, "Here's a social problem—help the victim," analysis still is warranted, for example, to sort out labels and trends (victims of dementia or exhaustion) (see Box 3.1). We may want to come up with our own categories instead of following well-traveled paths. For many reasons, we must not "accept the problem definitions of others" (Glugoski, Reisch, & Rivera, 1994, p. 84). *We must establish our own understandings and agendas— and do so with those affected.*

PERCEIVED INTERNAL VERSUS EXTERNAL ETIOLOGY

Professionals and lay people attribute causes to problems. Since both of these views influence us and others, we should understand these processes. An examination of *how the general public understands problems* helps us acknowledge that not everyone responds as we do. Someone hostile to social welfare goals may read about lack of repairs in public housing and growl "Those people are lucky to have a roof over their heads." Even those sympathetic to human needs will think about problems differently from analysts— for example, believing the conventional wis-

---

BOX 3.1   THREE STRIKES AND YOU'RE IN!

We need to be informed about and wary of changeable norms. Societal practices are unsettling and inconsistent, as policy interaction between politics and incarceration reveals (Gordon, 1994). The same behavior (intoxication) or the same crime (taking a car) may or may not result in a jail term, depending on demographics, the year of the arrest, and availability of holding facilities. The war on drugs of the 1980s promoted sentences for any drug illegalities—regardless of scale or injury to others—until violent street crimes became the federal government's political concern.

Even designations change. In different decades, individuals might be referred to as "habitual offenders," "career criminals" (Kramer, 1982), or "3 strikes, you're out" felons.

---

dom about publicized situations and thinking in either/or ways. The public divides problems between those that *spring from conditions or factors outside the affected individual* (hazardous waste, cataclysms, terrorism) and those that *stem from internal factors* (illness, divorce). "Troublesome behaviors" (a phrase of Spector and Kitsuse, 1987)—such as overdoing (gambling) or lack of impulse control (fire setting, shoplifting)—are viewed as social problems by the lay observer only when there is a perceived cost to society.

Problems can be discussed in *derivation* terms, but the internal–external division may be misleading. When the elderly die in large numbers during extreme heat, is the cause external factors such as weather, crime-ridden streets, or lack of government preparedness or internal factors such as physiology, inertia, or reluctance to spend money on electricity for fans and air conditioners? Does the older person's frugality or poverty reflect internal or external causes? Professionals are trained to look at combinations of cause and accountability and for lessons, so we are less likely to blame city hall. In contrast, *the lay view seldom considers* the following factors:

the complexity of accountability (Box 3.2);

the need for community education; and

BOX 3.2   WHO OR WHAT TO HOLD ACCOUNTABLE

Certain problems are discussed in polarizing ways (e.g., high unemployment among inner-city youth), and an observer's conception of human behavior can produce a continuum of viewpoints. An observer taking a *blame-the-victim* stance might focus all blame for people dying of lung cancer on their smoking habits. This is a philosophy of absolute individual responsibility and no societal-corporate responsibility (no consideration of job conditions, pollution, or relentless cigarette advertising). A milder version uses fact finding (how much did the patient smoke?). An observer taking a *victimization* stance might downplay individual choice by ignoring unwise behavior and blame society totally for subsidizing tobacco interests and not providing preventive health care and free addiction treatment. This is a philosophy of absolute societal responsibility and no individual responsibility. A milder version uses fact finding (was the patient exposed to something that amplified the smoking damage?).

the challenge of finding effective points of prevention or intervention.

Many in the general public follow current events, but, as we shall see, the media reinforce simplified views. Thus, the public may accept, unthinkingly, others' "formulations of complex individual and social problems," which in turn will "re-enforce the prevailing cultural tenet that looks to individual responsibility as the source of institutionally-induced problems" (Glugoski et al., 1994, p. 84).

SUBTLE FORMS OF BLAMING THE VICTIM

Ryan's (1992) blaming-the-victim concept is cited when dress is used as an excuse by rapists or when people with human immunodeficiency virus are blamed for acquiring their disease. *From a blamer's viewpoint,* children who ate lead paint and became ill and their parents, who "obviously" did not exercise proper "surveillance," become the problem, as opposed to manufacturers, landlords, and housing inspectors. Ryan contends that (1) while environmental causes are now accepted as major factors, interventions are directed to individuals, and (2) blaming the victim is "the most characteristic response to contemporary social problems on the part of most citizens, many public leaders, and some social scientists" (Lowry, 1974, p. 32). Social workers and liberals fall into the same trap according to Ryan (also see Kozol, 1995).

Some in society, says Ryan (1991), simply dismiss victims, even in the face of "unalleviated distress," while "kind humanitarians" place blame on the environment, not on individual character (p. 367). Yet, Ryan reproaches the "kind" people who want to be compassionate while (unconsciously) leaving their self or class interests unchallenged—"charitable persons" whose mission is to compensate or change society's victims rather than change society.

> They turn their attention to the victim in his post-victimized state. . . . They explain

what's wrong with the victim in terms of . . . experiences that have left wounds. . . . And they take the cure of these wounds . . . as the first order of business. They want to make the victims less vulnerable, send them back into battle with better weapons, thicker armor, a higher level of morale. (p. 372).

Ryan is thinking of survival battles. Mental health practitioners focus on psychoanalytic explanations and solutions, he suggests, rather than *face with numerous clients* "the pounding day-to-day stresses of life on the bottom rungs that drive so many to drink, dope, and madness" (p. 373).

Parsons, Hernandez, and Jorgensen (1988) add that "society is more willing for social workers to work with these victims than with other components of social problems" (p. 418). Such insights are reason enough to question our assumptions about problem formulation and resolution.

History Allows Us to See Problem Patterns

PERCEPTIONS OF PROBLEMS

An historical perspective involving *youth* can heighten the perception of what was or is viewed as a problem. Conduct and circumstances addressed as social problems in sermons and editorials 100 years ago are still discussed but not regarded in the same way today. These include (Elkin & Handel, 1978; Kett, 1977)

> unregulated spare time;
> masturbation;
> truancy; and
> pilfering from vacant buildings.

Today the public worries about problems involving:

> "innocent" youth, such as victims of kidnapping and child pornography (Best, 1987);
> "troubled" youth, such as those living on the streets or taking and selling illegal drugs; and

"out-of-control" youth, such as children who kill children (Ginsberg, 1994, p. 48), those in gangs, and girls who become pregnant out of wedlock (see Box 3.3).

It is easy to assume our era has found the truth and to forget that *what is deemed a social rather than a personal problem continues to be fluid.* Simons (1988) argued a few years ago that "bearing of unwanted children has been acknowledged as an area of social concern while the inability to bear wanted children has not evoked a similar response" (p. 2). Infertility, frailty, and menopause are recent problem constructions (Greil, 1991; Jones, 1994; Kaufman, 1994; Taylor, 1992; Theisen & Mansfield, 1993).

Proposed *solutions* or timetables may capture our imagination, only to disappoint us later or to make us scoff. Alcohol prohibition—the result of a century of lobbying—was disappointing as a policy *solution.* Facilitated communication with autistic children and recovered memory therapy are current controversial solutions. Homelessness was thought to have quick solutions, but like other problems treated initially as acute rather than chronic and as urgent rather than routine, it has remained for decades, leaving emergency service providers in bad straits (Lipsky & Smith, 1989).

Perceptions of Nonproblems and Nonperception of Problems

PRACTICES NOT CONSIDERED PROBLEMATIC

Less susceptible to notice, but fascinating, is *what has not been labeled a social problem.* For instance, discrimination based on age has rarely been identified as a problem for those in the younger age brackets, except when the voting age was lowered. To give another example, in a democracy, we think of all children as having an even start as opposed to a country with a rigid class system. Yet, children are automatically of the same class as their parents, and the American school experience solidifies that position much in the way that English schools do. As Elkin and Handel (1978) say, "newborns begin their social life by acquiring the status their families have" (p. 119). This is not raised as a problem.

Consider aid to dependent families compared to Aid for Dependent Corporations (Ralph Nader's term). That some low-income families receive long-term welfare is defined as a problem; Aid to Families With Dependent Children totaled $15 billion in 1994. That wealthy families benefit from foundation tax breaks or corporate welfare is *not* defined as a problem; $51 billion in direct subsidies went to business in 1994, including $29.2 billion for agribusiness (Donahue,

| BOX 3.3 | CHANGING PERCEPTIONS OF SOCIAL PROBLEMS |

Spector (1989) captures the historical vagaries of two social problem examples:

People who drink alcohol to excess were thought to be sinners by the temperance movement . . . regarded as criminals by the prohibition movement . . . and as diseased addicts by the medical establishment after 1940. Homosexuality used to be both a crime and a mental disorder [before] the decriminalization

movement and a particularly dramatic official vote by the American Psychiatric Association in December 1973. (p. 779)

Similarly, Gordon (1994) puts the "drug problem" in historic perspective, revealing how often it has been promoted as a problem in this century and in what forms, and showing today's resurrection of the "dangerous classes" construction (p. 225).

1994). Ideology and receptivity affect our conceptions. In Tallman's (1976) words: "An essential element in the problem-solving process is the ability or willingness to recognize that a problem exists. . . . [P]eople will differ in both the kinds of situations they view as problems and the number of situations they are willing to consider to be problems" (p. 151).

SITUATIONS NOT NOTICED OR NOT ACTED ON

Hurtful situations exist that fail to be perceived by those who could intervene. Netting, Kettner, and McMurtry (1993) help us see this by defining a *condition* as a phenomenon present in the community "that has not been formally identified or publicly labeled as a problem" and a *social problem* as a recognized condition that has been "incorporated into a community's or organization's agenda for action" (p. 204). Why is one group's pain noticed rather than another's? Tallman (1976) argues that *problem creation results from human action* (p. 5). The action involves activity to promote a problem and action in response to address the problem.

Kaminer (1992) provides a stark example when she contrasts two very different groups. She points out that Cambodian refugees "who survived torture, starvation, multiple rapes, and internment in concentration camps and witnessed the slaughter of their families" do not use terms like "survivors" and "trauma" loosely and do not "testify" to the distress of their childhoods, as do those who are caught up in "victimization"[2] (pp. 81, 84). Cultural values about silence and resilience characterize this immigrant group. In contrast, articulate and impassioned promotion of recovery and self-help characterize the second group, a diffuse, nationwide network of proselytizers and sincere participants. The persons who *acted* to promote a problem contributed to this outcome: being a child of an alcoholic and many

forms of codependency have become defined and publicized as national "problems," while the needs of Cambodian refugees remain a "condition." (The outcome also was influenced by the fact that millions of persons are involved in self-help programs.) Being a metaphorically "wounded child" has made it onto the media agenda as a problem along with physical abuse. These are now defined problems; as part of the response, programs are being designed and money is being spent to address them.

Sociological Ways to Study Problems

Social problem is a construct, just as *goodness* and *defense mechanisms* are constructs. While we are used to thinking of problems as being revealed by objective indicators and other measurement devices, we have been seeing how difficult it is to rely on "facts" when there are issues of theory versus fact and lack of shared definitions. Sociologists increasingly account for such complexity in their analyses. For example, Rubington and Weinberg (1989) discuss various ways, such as labeling and critical analysis, of looking at social problems (p. 296).

LABELING

Since a single personal behavior or social phenomenon can be called many positive and negative things, those interested in labeling or an interactionist approach are intrigued by the *dynamics of how the naming occurs or prevails, how it changes across time, and how attention and reaction create a problem*. (See Cohen, 1980, and Hardcastle, 1978, for case studies.) Changes in labels are common enough to be mocked in musical theater. For example, the song "Gee, Officer Krupke" from *West Side Story* suggests how members of youth gangs have been characterized by various helping professionals (Bernstein, Laurents, & Sondheim, 1957).

Labeling can be amusing but usually has serious implications. Effects of being labeled "mentally ill" or a "hyperactive child" can be studied. Think what it would be like to say that your child's track in school was the "socially advantaged" track rather than the "honors" track. Consider the difference between being labeled a high school "dropout" and "a dissatisfied preparatory school customer." Social workers specializing in addictions or working in institutions are in a position to ritualize an individual's "reentry into conventional society." Trice and Roman note that someone entering prison is put through elaborate procedures of negative labeling but that on release "no process delabels or relabels him" (in Lowry, 1974, p. 128) in a positive way. There are negative labels from the public such as "ex-con" and "sex offender." Labels are conceptualizations that can create or sustain a problem.

Critical Perspective

A critical approach requires us to step back, examine presumptions, and figure out how maintaining a particular problem (unemployment, vagrancy, conspiracy) furthers the power of whom. *The focus of attention is on the entire social system, in particular on the ruling class.* It encompasses activist inclinations toward *exposing domination and promoting emancipation* (Rubington & Weinberg, 1989, pp. 237–238). *A critical approach asks us to examine societal contradictions.* A contradiction in a program aimed at socialization skills would be to call the program users "members" but then to divide the lunchroom, lounge, and bathrooms into separate member and staff facilities—reserving the preferable rooms for staff (the opposite of other kinds of clubs). Using this approach to problems requires development of "critical consciousness" (Reeser & Leighninger, 1990, p. 73). Judith Lee says that we must learn to question "reality" in order to acquire a criti-

cal perspective (1994, p. 117; see also Real, 1980, p. 258).

Relevance for Practitioners

Since social workers often engage in multidisciplinary work, in team practice, and within a host agency, they must be alert to theoretical perspectives about problems held by other professions. Just as the medical model shapes what should be done, a problem perspective may undergrid the workings of a program with which social workers are associated.

The many *conceptions of problems* outlined in this section reveal that a problem may be promoted on the basis of self-interest or blame. While lay people believe they know a problem when they see it, social workers need to take a larger view. They do not want to disempower by adding to the chorus of those telling their clients that "You are the problem!" As Rose (1990) says poignantly: "Believing in the 'promises' while being constricted by the realities . . . countless people experience themselves as failures, as stupid or inadequate" (p. 42).

DEFINING AND FRAMING A SOCIAL/COMMUNITY PROBLEM

Before confronting community problems, it is important to understand the ways social workers can define and intercede with problems. We seek analysis tools that can make clear the nature of a problem and its potential relationships to its environment and solutions. Such knowledge and understanding will inform our practice interventions.

Problem Definition and Framework Purpose

The elements of social problems can be pulled together into a conceptual framework,

> A social problem is a condition that has been *defined* by a significant group (that has social impact within a population) as being unacceptable and a deviation from or breakdown of social standards that this group believes should be upheld or achieved if human life is to be maintained or have meaning, and that can be redressed or remedied by human action.

the purpose of which is to organize phenomena in a manner that allows the analyst to determine (1) *if* the phenomena or conditions are problematic and, if so, (2) *to whom* they are problematic, (3) *why* they are problematic, and (4) the potential for social *intervention.*

For example, a California initiative (spearheaded by a defining group) bans children who are in this country illegally from attending public schools, among other restrictions on the use of services. The intervention, a voter-initiated referendum, was designed to turn the phenomenon of increasing numbers of Spanish-speaking children into a problem with a remedy in law. While illegal immigrants are the problem to those who launched the initiative, obtaining jobs is the problem to those from Mexico. The initiative group says the immigrants are a problem because they raise taxes, jeopardize a unified, English-speaking society (a standard), and allow unfair job competition. The illegal aliens counter that they pay into Social Security and make work contributions that offset the costs they generate. The voting public accepted the problem as it was defined on the ballot. Now some social service providers and educators may have to enforce rules with which they do not agree. Perhaps this condition of nonservice can be turned into a problem by arguing that denying ed-

ucation and medical care violates American norms and Judeo-Christian values. The problem definition of abortion, and of less controversial issues, also can be traced this way.

Framing a Social/Community Problem

Circumstances often require us to look at a phenomenon in an immediate, rational way. This, in turn, requires a framework that can be used with many situations—pediatric AIDS, use of marijuana, homicide, illiteracy. The framework we utilize here (Hardcastle, 1992) has six elements:

1. definitions of normative behavior;
2. ideology and value configurations involved;
3. views of social causation;
4. scope;
5. social cost; and
6. proposed mode of remediation.

This framework is suited to social work analysis because of the profession's strong normative and ideological emphasis, although as an analytic vehicle the framework strives for ideological neutrality by making ideology explicitly a component. It assists us in understanding how others have come to their conceptualization, how we can come to our own, and how we can position ourselves to address problems.

Before discussing each element, an explanation of *normative* and *deviant behavior* may be helpful. Behavior and circumstances may be regarded as desirable, acceptable, and normal within a group or a community. Then they are normative. However, a situation may be defined as a deviation from the norms of a community, a nation, or another entity. Thus, hunger, homelessness, and mental illness are deviations from community standards. Some standards are manifest; for example, regulations are codified norms, while others are insinuated. Our great-grandparents were openly religious in their speech, letters, and diaries. In today's secular society, similar behavior may be considered deviant by the less religious (touting one's atheism is also not acceptable). To understand why a situation is or can be labeled as deviant, the analyst needs to search for the meaning of a particular deviance to certain community segments. People will have their own outlooks on how things should be.

In the following section, we look at the composition of social problems. We describe six elements of problem analysis and action. After explaining each element, we apply the concept to various conditions (abortion, poverty, etc.). Throughout the discussion, we use unsafe food as a particular illustration since it can affect anyone and has potential manifestations nationwide. We draw our facts from an analysis by a social worker and advocate for preventive measures who works with the American Association of Retired Persons (AARP) to protect older people from harm. In our framework, such a person-organization is called a *defining group*. A condition must be subjected to a problem definition process by defining groups to be *classified* as a problem by an observer. Advocacy was necessary before unsafe/unsanitary food was initially perceived and later reperceived as a problem.

NORMATIVE AND DEVIANT

For a condition to be labeled a problem, it must represent to the defining group an important deviation from an actual or ideal standard or norm. The norm can be statistical and the deviation quantitative, such as poverty based on deviations from standard of living indexes or poverty lines. The norm also can be a model/guideline and the devi-ation qualitative—for example, quality of life standards such as income security or respect. If the group plans to take on an issue and set the stage for successful intervention, the task is to capture the broad range of standards. The community is not homogeneous in its normative conceptions, but the group can figure out what is basically shared, that is, where cooperation or at least toleration is possible. The defining group can anticipate rival depictions.

There is an ideal of wholesome, untainted food. Fears of impurity, adulteration, and contamination have driven reforms (Sinclair, 1906), including creation of the Food and Drug Administration (FDA). Deviations are measured by risk assessment and emergency room visits. Public perceptions of risk and deviation from the worry-free ideal have been associated in recent years with seafood (toxins), apples (alar), hamburger meat in fast-food chains (*Escherichia coli*), chicken (*Salmonella*), pesticides, and dyes. In opposition, the food lobby argues the impossibility of foreign-object-free and risk-free food.

IDEOLOGY AND VALUE CONFIGURATIONS

Ideology means an internally consistent set of values and integrated system of beliefs that form a unit and shape the definer's perceptions. It suggests the ideals that determine how the world should be constructed, (e.g., the United States wants everyone to adopt the work ethic). The term goes beyond limited, formal political beliefs captured by labels like *conservative*, *liberal*, or *right* to encompass the holder's sense of community, community standards and acceptable behavior, belonging, and reciprocal obligations. Ideology is not necessarily controversial, at least within the community where it arises and is articulated. Values range from permissive to punitive on such issues as casual drinking, drug use, and sex. Whether a "deviance" is a problem or is significant depends on perception, which is rooted in ideology. Women's control over their bodies and whether the fetus has human rights are familiar examples. When perceptions are widely held and promoted strongly enough by the defining party, the problem becomes publicly defined.

Underlying the expectation of safe food is the value of human life and protection from fraud and involuntary risk. The well-being of the citizenry includes protection from physical harm. Society is believed to owe members peace of mind concerning purchased food. Note that this is not a right to have food, just to have purchased food be safe and clean. Business argues that regulation limits choice. This pits the deregulation ideology against the regulation ideology. Risks associated with food are a "subject that is loaded with social and emotional meanings" (Kassner, 1990, p. 18).

SOCIAL CAUSATION

The public attributes most problems to social factors. This attribution of cause relates to the definer's perception that the condition is not totally the result of physical or biological forces but also has social roots. It may represent a conflict between the physical or technological and the social, or between social elements within society. Social causation does not mean that problems are exclusively social; they may have strong biological elements. Drought is a function of nature, but emergency supplies are social.

Food decay is natural, but food distribution or the decision to use pesticides is social. Although the effects of unsafe food are biological, and although natural hazards exist within foods, the reasons for unsafe food also include a particular industry's or company's negligent practices or ignorance of the difference between cutting corners and creating hazards. Descriptions of the causes of food contamination (e.g., at processing plants)

make the condition sound plausible as a problem and correctable.

SCOPE

Scope relates to the condition's social nature in terms of the number and proportion of the community affected by the condition. It is reflected in incidence and prevalence. Generally the condition has to affect more than one person. It represents costs to significant portions of the population. These costs, such as restricted choice, are more than one-time costs. If a child falls into a hole or well and is rescued by a huge collective effort, that is *not* a social problem. Thus, the number of persons affected beyond a social worker's individual client or caseload will be relevant. However, if too many are affected, it can be overwhelming, so the deviation's scope should not be overstated by the defining group.

"The Centers for Disease Control (CDC) and the FDA estimate that between 6.5 million and 33 million Americans become ill each year from microorganisms in their food, which constitutes 3 to 14 percent of the population. An estimated 9,000 cases of foodborne illness result in death each year" (Kassner, 1990, p. 12). The public is unaware of the problem's scope, yet, tellingly, the FDA [U.S. Food and Drug Administration] intervened for just two supposedly poisoned Chilean grapes. This suggests that no threat from food contamination is considered permissible, but lack of resources prevents the level of enforcement necessary (which leads us to costs).

SOCIAL COST

Social cost relates to the assumption that the condition, if left unattended, has economic, personal, interpersonal, psychic, physical, or cultural costs. It may be a real cost, an implied cost, or an opportunity cost, the cost compared to what it would be if the conditions were successfully remediated.

There is no assumption that the cost is perceived or carried equally by all members of society. An analytical task is to determine (1) who bears the cost, (2) what is the perceived cost, and (3) what is the perception of its distribution. Defining social costs often propels parts of society toward intervention or remediation. The definitions of social costs also may be a function of affordability. Conditions are defined as problematic as the interventions become affordable. Examples are relative deprivation (the raising or lowering of the poverty line as the wealth of the society increases or decreases) and mental health (expansion of the definition of mental illness as technological gains and society's ability to treat, alter, or address the conditions expand).

Foodborne illnesses have costs; those related to meat alone have personal, medical, and work-absence costs totaling billions of dollars, and the death of children from tainted fast-food hamburgers attracts public concern. People with allergies have physical costs, but it is difficult for unorganized groups to have their condition designated a problem; however, the elderly are organized and do lobby for food safety. Government uses a risk/benefit analysis to determine regulatory costs. It is on grounds other than scientific ones, though, that a defining group usually holds sway. Real business costs are incurred in taking unsafe products *off* the market, voluntarily or involuntarily. But implied liability costs are a big incentive for business to address a condition. There are costs if *confidence* in the nation's food supply is threatened. Opponents say that regulation costs more than harm.

REMEDIATION

For intervention to be considered, there must be a defining party that can turn a condition into a problem and a belief that the condition is alterable and remediable. If there is no belief, there will be no search for possible remediation. The levers of change or those who can affect change cannot be totally out of range for the community. A means of remediation does not have to be known, only the belief that remediation is possible. If a condition is believed to be unalterable or in the natural order of things, the condition may be defined as nonproblematic or as something that must be endured, perhaps with some attention to reducing suffering. One example is how the poor are viewed under the philosophy of Social Darwinism. Combined beliefs about cause and remediation are important in many social work situations. The initial remedial plan can be official or unofficial, and commonly will be changed as interest groups react to it.

Numerous federal laws or amendments regarding food safety and labeling have been passed, which shows remediation is perceived as possible. In recent years, when regulation has been spotlighted rather than food safety, there has been political contention over how vigorous the Food and Drug Administration should be. The U.S. Department of Agriculture under President Clinton seeks to improve meat/poultry inspection, but the Republican party's cost/benefit approach would slow regulation. Although the public supports the idea of ensuring a safe food supply, conservatives want to reframe the problem to accomplish other goals (see the section on Ideology and Value Configurations). Thus, a particular view (and redress that fits with that view), even if supported by results and public opinion, may not last.

Discussion of the Interventive Problem Framework

If we notice that 30 of our clients share a similar condition or circumstance, could this be the start of a problem? Considerations will include our view and others' views of its tractability and whether circumstances (supportive media, public support, etc.) appear favorable for resolution (Mazmanian & Sabatier, 1981). For instance, we can generalize that the less change sought, the more likely it is to happen. On the other hand, if the target group is a majority of the population, the less likely the change will occur. We are not advocating developing a formula for taking immediate action on a perceived problem but rather a means of determining what to do based on a better understanding of what needs fixing and why. Thus, if we intend to "stage" a problem, we figure out the factors that allow us to be most effective as interveners. We determine the norms and deviations of the defining group, compare them with the community's norms and deviations, and, if different, assess whether the condition's deviation can be cast in community norms or whether the community's norms and construction of the situation can be altered. We need to know the problem's scope and the community's costs if the condition remains, compared to those if it is remediated.

This approach thrusts the analyst toward the specification of outcomes without assuming that all of society will benefit equally from any specific outcome or alternative social state. It does not assume that everyone perceives the problem similarly or envisions the same solution. However, a careful use of the framework should enable us to determine to some degree, a priori, to whom certain outcomes will be beneficial and to whom they will be problematic. The framework generally ignores the notion of a fundamental need. Need beyond survival is an elusive concept—highly individualized as well as socially relative; poverty in the United States is not poverty in Haiti. The framework does recognize the social nature of four types of needs or demands—normative, comparative, felt, and expressed. However, it emphasizes the last type, those needs that are translated into expression, since they are more likely to lead to social interventions (Brad-

shaw, 1977; Kettner, Moroney, & Martin, 1990, chap. 3).

Other Models

Other frameworks exist for identifying conditions, distinguishing problems, and moving toward resolution. Two human service books (Kettner, Moroney, & Martin, 1990; Netting, Kettner, & McMurtry, 1993), for example, walk readers through similar processes. Tallman (1976), on the other hand, asserts that "in all social problems" there are three essential and observable elements: "(1) a demand for social change based on moral interpretations of social conditions; (2) overt controversy and conflict between groups over the issues articulated by those seeking change; and (3) an attempt, by at least one of the opposing sides in the conflict, to mobilize support from broader segments of the population" (p. 204). (Think of the earlier example of California's illegal immigrants and citizens with competing claims.)

Tallman's conceptualization is most applicable to a problem where cooperative resolution is not easy. Suppose that boarder babies, some with AIDS, have been abandoned in a hospital, a situation perceived as a problem by social workers who alert the media. A demand for change arises. A group of influential women organizes some volunteers to cuddle the babies and other volunteers who will serve as foster parents once the babies leave. In conventional terms, a problem has been spotted and solved through service provision. Tallman wants us to concentrate on situations involving conflict. If the recruited volunteers were denied entry to the nursery or the babies were quarantined and not allowed to leave the hospital, raising a public uproar, then a problem would be involved. By Tallman's definition, social action—not service—would seem to be the reasonable solution for problems (see Chapter 12 of this volume).

In many cases, social workers are allied with, employed by, or represent the definer of a social problem. The boarder baby example makes it clear why problem study and observation are helpful in our own area of expertise and concern. We must be able to analyze the *domain* encompassed by different definitions of a problem to develop strategies for dealing with it.

GETTING A SOCIAL/COMMUNITY PROBLEM ADDRESSED

Stages, Players, and Techniques of Construction

SOCIAL CONSTRUCTION OF PROBLEMS

Insights related to the construction of problems are often cumulative—a growing realization that a problem is not necessarily one way or the other (males and females view the problem of rape differently) or a recognition that intervention strategies follow from how the problem is defined (Cartwright, 1977). We acquire an understanding of the arbitrariness of any classification scheme and hence of any interpretation from facts. We realize that rather than responding, social workers are obliged to dramatize many problems.

Once a defining group has pinpointed a troubling condition, it must get *itself* in a position to be taken seriously in making a demand. We call this *community organizing* (see Chapter 12). When the group works instead to *position the condition* so that it will be considered a problem and to create an environment in which anyone would be viewed as having a right to make a claim because the condition is so intolerable, we call that *claims-making*. Claims-making is not equivalent to coalition building, where many groups find common ground; it is a competitive process that tends to favor problems with pathetic victims and groups with clout.

Claims-making activities are explicated by Spector and Kitsuse (1987), who are interested in grass-roots efforts and want to show us how we can affect matters. Input is possible since we are dealing with *activities of defining and demanding*.

THE STAGES AND THE CLAIMS PROCESS

Spector and Kitsuse (and others, like Blumer, 1971) help us examine the claims process and how citizens and advocates can make claims. They stress "sequences of events" and "unfolding lines of activity" (1987, p. 158) and see the life of a social issue commonly going through four stages of development and resolution. To them, government responses are key in determining whether social problems become part of society's agenda (p. 155).

- The critical first stage occurs when a public claim is made that a problem exists and should be addressed (at this point, no formal or recognized group may even exist) with an ensuing debate.

- A second stage of getting government engaged will follow if (1) the issue has become public, (2) the claimant has exercised power effectively (see Chapter 4), and (3) the claimant has used the various channels of recourse (such as the government and the media) well. This is the stage in which policymakers (who believe they too have discovered the problem) respond to the claimant and offer official recognition (if the designated agency decides to "own" the program).

- A third stage of renewed claims may follow in which the original conditions, problems, and activities for change reemerge. These may be less of a focus for the claimant than the perceived blocked or ineffective avenues of recourse, discourse, dialogue, and procedural resolution that had seemingly opened in stage two (Spector & Kitsuse, 1987, p. 152).

- Finally, a last stage of return to the community may happen when claimants back away from government agencies, disillusioned with their responses, and develop alternative solutions. The problem might die during or after any of these stages.

Brief examples. Noting the high rate of suicide by the elderly is the first stage of recognition as a problem. Although documented by organizations, scholars, and even the media (*USA Today*, the *New York Times*), elder suicide has not "caught on," as teenage suicide did (Mercer, 1989; Osgood, 1992). In contrast, nursing home reform followed the full course. Applying the stages to concerns about quality care, the development followed this path:

1. abuse documentation;
2. formation of resident and consumer organizations and government response units;
3. ongoing conflicts between advocates and the Health Care Finance Administration; and
4. renewed advocacy at the community-state level.

Another application concerns the deinstitutionalization (following a U.S. Supreme Court decision) of people who were mentally ill but deemed not a danger to themselves or others. This issue is often discussed as if the original advocates or court justices were wrong—because many people ended up in the streets—which implies a first or second stage error. However, Donaldson (1978), the patient/plaintiff in the Supreme Court case, emphasizes *third-stage* stinginess errors: "State legislatures followed up by having thousands of state-hospital patients dumped into the community" (p. 3).

PLAYERS AND STATES OF RESOLUTION

Who and what potentially contribute to recognition of a problem? Blumer (1971)

says that types of action (e.g., agitation and violence) may be factors. He also notes significant types of players: interest groups, political figures, the media, and powerful organizations that may want to "shut off" or "elevate" a problem or both (p. 302). Thus, many groups contribute to problem definition: those suffering from a condition, challenging groups, social movement participants, policymakers, and journalists. Helping professions can be important participants in the process (Spector, 1989, p. 780). Blumer (1971) lumps professionals like social workers with others—such as journalists, the clergy, college presidents, civic groups, and legislators—who have access to "the assembly places of officialdom." We can *legitimate* a problem or a proposed solution through "arenas of public discussion" (p. 303).

In what is essentially a political process, governments "respond to claims that define conditions as social problems by: funding research on solutions to problems; establishing commissions of inquiry; passing new laws, and creating enforcement and treatment bureaucracies" (Spector, 1985, p. 780). In the case of resident maltreatment by some nursing homes, for example, in the discovery stage a Nader report was published that included firsthand accounts by people who had worked undercover in several facilities (Townsend, 1971). The federal government began monitoring more closely, funded reports from the Institute of Medicine, passed the 1987 Nursing Home Quality Reform Act (part of the Omnibus Budget Reconciliation Act), and created the Administration on Aging's Long Term Care Ombudsman Program. (Simultaneously, the nursing home industry has fought hard to keep reform regulations from going into effect.) As one aspect of the response stage, more social workers have been hired by facilities to upgrade quality.[3]

Concurrent with drawing attention to a

condition, claims-makers must interpret it. They must shape public understanding of an emerging social problem, convince the public of its legitimacy, and suggest solutions based on the new consensus and understanding (Best, 1989, pp. xix, xx). This definitional process is often conflictual, as different definitions and the solutions that flow from them compete for public favor and scarce resources[4] (Blumer, 1971).

Extended Examples of Claims-Making Processes

THE RIGHTS OF THE ACCUSED

A criminal justice example will serve as an illustration of simple, straightforward claims-making.

Clarence Gideon as an individual tapped into a social institution (the legal system) and made a claim that injustice was happening and society had a problem it should remedy immediately by paying for lawyers for the indigent in all criminal cases. Gideon was a small-town, middle-aged man who had served time. In 1961, he was unjustly accused of a pool hall robbery in Florida but could not afford a lawyer and had to defend himself. He asked for a lawyer, was denied one, lost his case, and was sent to jail for 5 years. He immediately appealed, though unsuc-

In the morning mail of January 8, 1962, the Supreme Court of the United States received a large envelope from Clarence Earl Gideon, prisoner No. 003826, Florida State Prison. . . . [His documents] were written in pencil. They were done in carefully formed printing, like a schoolboy's, on lined sheets. . . .
Anthony Lewis, *Gideon's Trumpet* (1966, p. 3)

cessfully, to the Florida Supreme Court, wrote the U.S. Supreme Court about the right to counsel, and started a legal revolution that ended with a new system of public defenders in our country. Gideon himself was acquitted at his second trial with the help of a local lawyer. His story was made into a book and a made-for-television movie with Henry Fonda playing Gideon, both called *Gideon's Trumpet* (Collins, 1980; Lewis, 1966). He was an average guy who decided to make a constitutional claim and, in standing up for himself, called attention to a national social problem—the lack of legal representation in noncapital cases. Until then, only poor people facing a death sentence were provided with lawyers.

In the first phase of claims-making, prisoners from many states had petitioned for years to get redress for their perceived injustice. In the second phase, for various internal reasons, the Supreme Court was ready to consider change and therefore accepted Gideon's petition and upheld his claim, which, crucially, had been buttressed by supportive briefs filed by state officials. Claims-making analysis helps us see the important role of the Supreme Court in accepting Gideon's case, providing him, as a pauper, with top-notch lawyers at that level of the legal system, legitimizing the claims of injustice put forward by a convicted felon, and setting the stage for conclusions involving new programs at the state level. Power plays a role in the definition of problems, but so do well-positioned professionals, including social workers. So can the tenacity of one individual.

PROTECTION OF THE INNOCENT

In our second example (Best, 1987), the dramatization of missing *and endangered* children as a major problem and its gradual relegation to back-burner status provides a complex illustration of the claims-making process. In some ways this represents another aspect of the crime and punishment saga, for it is about those who are or fear being victims of major crimes. The public career of this problem started with a number of sensational murders, peaked with milk carton and grocery store sacks printed with pictures of missing children, and continues with the "Have You Seen Us?" cards sent in the mail with the 800 number for the National Center for Missing and Exploited Children.

The designation *missing children* evolved around 1981 and combined into one broad conceptualization what had been three different problems—kidnapping or abduction of children by strangers, kidnapping or child snatching by one parent, and runaway children who were missing but sometimes returned (Best, 1987, p. 104). When they were lumped together, the total number of children involved was higher. The commonly cited incidence figure for missing children became 1.8 million cases per year (inexact estimate), which got attention and led to public hearings but misled almost everyone into thinking that most of these children were abducted by strangers—by far the *least* prevalent circumstance, about "100–200 per year" (Best, 1987, pp. 106–107).[5] By the time the advocacy campaign had lost public interest and some credibility, new organizations were attending to the problem. Many individuals were involved, but more to the point, many advocacy groups and social service organizations were part of the identification, formulation, and promotion of this problem. Parents and child advocates sought to get stolen children returned and to bring flaws in systems to the attention of policymakers and the public.

To highlight aspects of the claims-making process, Best draws on the field of rhetoric (also see Baumann, 1989). This approach helps us see the techniques employed to get this problem on the agenda, such as repeated use of horrific stories ("atrocity tales" and case histories), exaggerated use of sta-

tistics, and frightening parents into having their children fingerprinted. To stage the problem and buttress its need for attention, advocates staked out the claim that no family was exempt, as this problem was not tied to size of locale, income level, or race: "By arguing that anyone might be affected by a problem, a claims-maker can make everyone in the audience feel that they have a vested interest in the problem's solution" (Best, 1987, p. 108). Rationales or justifications for focusing attention on *this* problem were used: the victims were "priceless" and "blameless" (in contrast, say, to drug abusers); even runaways were portrayed as abuse victims who fled, only to face exploitation on the streets (pp. 110, 114). The objectives were to force more sharing and coordination of information between states, and between the FBI—which handles kidnapping cases—and local police, as well as to cut down on the waiting time before children were declared missing so that the official search could begin sooner.

TECHNIQUES USED IN CLAIMS-MAKING

The above descriptions of two claims-making processes that involved individual and collective behavior illustrate ways to make potent arguments and shape perceptions, as we social workers have done and will continue to do as part of our mission. We want to master convincing techniques but should remember that when we make claims, we have the prestige of our field and the combined helping professions to draw on.

Examples and case histories or stories, used so effectively with missing children, are employed with charitable fund-raising (e.g. Jerry Lewis's kids) and other problems. Sexual harassment became identified with Anita Hill after she testified on Capitol Hill in the Clarence Thomas Supreme Court nomination hearings. In shaping perceptions, "welfare advocates focus on the deserving poor, their opponents speak of welfare

THE NATURE OF SOCIAL AND COMMUNITY PROBLEMS

Cadillacs," and both sides find this a convenient "shorthand for describing and typifying complex social conditions" (Best, 1987, p. 114). Of course, examples and buzz words can be overdone to the point where the listener becomes distrustful or desensitized.

To *typify* is to exemplify. "Typification occurs when claims-makers characterize a problem's nature" (Best, 1989, p. xx). Among the forms used are providing an *orientation* or an *example*. Typification through orientation is a device used to position the problem. To illustrate orienting, or steering, think about an organization that wishes to characterize a problem such as kleptomania or prostitution. The organization could characterize it as (pick one) deviance, a crime, a self-esteem problem, evidence that society is being too materialistic, or a woman's problem. Regarding typification through examples, we are all aware of the power of the "typical" case as it is used in politics, from the family unable to pay its medical bills "because" of the Republicans to the rapist who has been paroled "because" of the Democrats.

Social workers can operate with integrity and still provide examples that will withstand scrutiny and reveal why a problem is important. To demonstrate how these two techniques can be employed, we will use an urban scenario. This familiar situation is often commented on but seldom taken seriously. Our choice of who experiences the problem allows us to typify the situation on terms we choose (Box 3.4).

We can aid those who have not had a problem themselves to experience it vicariously through a telling example. Typification tells society about the nature of a problem and implies the advocacy that would be needed to address it. Box 3.4 shows one incident from three points of view, for problems are experienced in many ways. Is the situation justified by saying that there are different perspectives? It is not. As advocates, we must be prepared to use such examples to make a case, which may mean dropping the perspectives of the observer and the taxi driver to emphasize that of the refused customer. Regarding the typification of the problem in Box 3.4, the person featured in the example (a professor of religion at a prestigious university and a best-selling author) cannot be discounted, and the objected-to behavior is given the *orientation*, or spin, of being antidemocratic and unlawful, a violation

---

BOX 3.4	AN EXAMPLE REGARDING PERSPECTIVE

Cornel West has allowed plenty of time to make an important appointment, but he must catch a cab and none will stop for him in downtown New York City. West, a theology professor from Princeton, New Jersey, is dressed in a suit and tie. He is on the way to have his picture taken for the book cover of what will become his best-seller, named, appropriately, *Race Matters*. However, the taxis drivers do not know any of this and drive by West to pick up white passengers, only yards beyond him, instead. Ten cabs refuse him. West becomes angrier and angrier.

The observer would see this as an example of discrimination. Taxi drivers would highlight their fear not of West in his suit but of his destination. To the refused passenger, the unfairness goes deeper than the fact that the drivers—whatever their race—are violating their own regulations. The experience negates democracy, the "basic humanness and Americanness of each of us," as West puts it (1994, p. 8), and causes achievement stories to seem like a mockery. To West, the increasing nihilism of minority groups results not from doctrine but from lived experience (pp. xv, 22).

of core societal values. West's interpretation hints, moreover, at risks if such practices continue. The incident could also be used to typify differential power and subordinate groups (Wilson, 1973). Those fortunate enough to obtain the cab instead of West are not even conscious of their "white privilege."

PROBABILITIES AND PRECONDITIONS

If problem creation results from an organized human response, then we should be interested in the inducements for and indicators of that action. In collective action and social movements, terms such as *critical mass* are used. Gitlin (1991) speaks of "critical social thought, oppositional energy," and "a vision of social change." Goldberg (1991) talks about an "energizing event" (p. 14). Netting et al. (1993) think that "a condition becomes a problem when it receives enough attention that it can no longer be ignored by community leaders, or when one or more leaders declare a condition unacceptable and decide that something must be done" (p. 210). Is there a *threshold* that must be met or a *trigger* that puts a condition over the top? Must a critical mass experience the problem or get involved in promoting a solution? Netting et al. argue against a threshold notion because they see no precision "in terms of time of appearance, size, or severity" (p. 210). (They still believe that such factors, along with urgency and duration, should be analyzed.)

The number of those having a condition is not sufficient because those affected may not act and because other factors may be involved—perceived costs and who bears them. For example, numerous people have sarcoidosis, a disease that does not spread and threaten public health and that is more common in African-Americans, a less influential group in medical circles. Consequently little research money is spent on this somewhat mysterious, incurable—albeit rarely fatal—condition. *Intensity of effects*, or the suffering, of many individuals, is also not a criterion; lupus and arthritis are not

treated as problems. Even the *death* of many individuals annually may be treated as just a condition. We can contrast the relative lack of action regarding the safety of space heaters, despite many deaths, with decisive action on lawn darts, on the basis of two deaths, due to the efforts of the determined father of a child who died. Many women died from breast cancer before attention was paid. We can identify the process of organizing a response, factors (as in the missing-children example), and techniques, but there is no one precipitant.

THE MEDIA AND SOCIAL PROBLEM FORMULATION

A century-long debate has been waged concerning

- the amount and form of influence the media have on society (e.g., effects on how much children read);
- media sway or leverage in politics (e.g., negative coverage in elections);
- media responsibility for creating social problems (e.g., effects of television violence); and
- media potential to resolve social problems (e.g., documentation of police violence or the promotion of safe sexual practices or birth control).

Today we believe the media have cumulative influence through their ability to set or stall an agenda and their reality-shaping capacity.[6] We need to know about short- and longer-term media effects and how to use the media to advance an agenda regarding individual and social problems. We also must devise means to counter the way the media reinforce destructive individual and societal tendencies.

One role played by the media today is to introduce us to a parade of issues or problems until we are saturated. Humorist Art

Buchwald once compared this process to the Miss America pageant—with its Miss Georgia, Miss South Dakota, and so on. Every year issues such as Miss Radon, Miss English-Only, and Miss Pollution compete for attention until one is crowned. We have a multiyear hit parade of social problem favorites: "Here she comes," Miss Hunger in America. "Here she comes" Miss Global Warming, Miss Failure of the Public Schools, Miss Domestic Violence. "There she goes" is the accompanying verity. This hypothetical competition comes to life, in a political context, as we think about problems first ladies have selected as projects, such as mental illness, drug addiction, illiteracy, and lack of health care and insurance coverage, as well as problem solutions that spouses of vice-presidents have promoted, such as emergency preparedness and mental health coverage. Lucky the problem that wins the contest or receives a sponsor!

Wrap-up. Thus, we discover a hidden challenge in social work: how to avoid being pressured or dominated by others who would define problems for us. The better able we are to follow the amorphous nature of problem development, the more we can influence the process for professional ends. We need to have as many perspectives as possible; one person's judgment cannot be automatically preferred because it is limited in perspective and knowledge. To be relevant and consumer-centered (Tower, 1994) regarding social problems requires flexibility. As Castex (1993) says, "An awareness of the occasional arbitrariness of one's assumptions should lead to an openness about altering those assumptions in new situations or when more information is supplied" (p. 687).

To recapitulate, we can analyze the nature of a social problem by

- knowing our own minds and ideas and learning how clients or consumers of ser-

vices think regarding the problem's implications for them;

- figuring out which significant actors or community segments can potentially provide resources;

- on any issue, finding out our profession's stance, reading in other disciplines and studying the media, and reviewing past and present general views regarding solutions, as well as conservative/liberal positions; and

- discovering the collective definition process this problem has undergone to date and an appropriate role, if any, for our agency. If we plan to intervene, we must also look at what others have done and consider what we can do.

CONCEPTUALIZING THE WORLD IN WHICH A PROBLEM EXITS

Effective problem solving requires not only an examination of pertinent elements but also a recognition of mental processes. Our natural thought process takes us through stages of preparation, incubation, illumination, and verification (Wallas, 1926, pp. 80–81). The cerebral aspects of social work are much influenced by our pictures of the world, as Hartman discussed in "Many Ways of Knowing" (1990) and "Words Create Worlds" (1991).

Social Workers and Reality Conceptions

The process of defining social problems collectively, covered earlier, is a subset of a larger process called the *social construction of reality* (see Chapter 2). *Reality* and *meaning* concepts encompass ideas from philosophy, anthropology, and constructivist thinking in many disciplines. Our field's emphasis has been on the potential for shared meaning with clients (Saari, 1991, p. 187). Becoming

A journalist met with five teenaged boys, wards of the state of Illinois, to hear their stories but became lost in trying to understand the world of a former gang member. "He tried to explain the economy to me, the drugs and the colors and the beepers. He got me so confused I felt like I was in history class in the seventh grade, unable to even raise my hand to ask a question because I didn't quite know what the words meant. It occurred to me, then, just how remote those of us in Medialand are from our neighbors. So many realms of reality" (Laskas, 1994, p. 6).

aware of systems of meaning and different realities contributes to heightened competence for practitioners. We can have more confidence in later actions if we explore multiple conceptualizations first.

Substitute "social services" for "Medialand" and this anecdote illustrates why we must come to know intimately the communities and realities of our clients if we want to be relevant in interventions and to establish a shared reality.[7] We strive for these goals realizing that personal "frames of reference and personal worldviews will always be at best partial—they can never be absolute" (Castex, 1993, p. 687).

MULTIPLE, NOT SINGULAR, REALITY

Due to their training in human variation, social workers are better positioned than other professionals to accept the notion of a forged reality. Those interested in social action feel freed by the notion of reality as fluid, because they already conceive of it in these terms, as something that can be at least partially shaped or transformed. Those interested in psychology are accustomed to thinking of multiple realities at the level of personality types and states of mind. For in-

stance, cultural and religious beliefs about the nature of reality may skew the results of standard psychological tests. If so, this would illustrate that "normalcy" is a construct, not an independent truth (Pardeck, Murphy, & Choi, 1994, pp. 343–344). If we take differing realities as a given in our practice, we can explore what concepts such as *normalcy* and *psychosis* mean to a particular group. We can inquire whether alternative or conflicting concepts exist for health and illness such as "energy balance and imbalance."

Inside Our Heads and Our Universities

Two intellectual currents are relevant to our flexibility as community practitioners. One asks us to look at multilayered consciousness, reexamine taken-for-granted assumptions, and engage in critical self-reflexivity. The other centers on a process whereby one paradigm accepted as appropriate and central by the scientific or scholarly community gives way gradually to another; the new or revised paradigm, which has been struggling to be heard, consolidates at some point. (While both currents seem to reveal society in the throes of pulling apart, they can also be viewed as modes of recentering or regrouping.) To see the connections to social problem contexts and our practice, we must understand reality constructions, thought structures, paradigms, and conceptual frameworks.

SOCIAL REALITY

"What is recognized as social reality," according to Pardeck et al. (1994), "is a matter of definition and conceptualization" (p. 343). As a perfect example, most Americans know the non-Western world from photographs in *The National Geographic*. Yet, its pictures have 'rarely cried out for change" (Lutz & Collins, 1993, p. 280) even if they were about South African mine workers during apartheid (p. 279). As another illustration, negative images of troubled neighborhoods "populated by needy, problematic and deficient people" in our own country "are not regarded as part of the truth; they are regarded as the whole truth" (Kretzmann & McKnight, 1993, p. 2). *This is not to say that everything is relative and nothing is understood in common.* Kaminer (1992) asserts that "Americans of different races, ethnicities, religions, genders, degrees of physical ablement, and socioeconomic classes may be affected by the same cultural phenomenon, such as television, celebrity journalism, confessional autobiographies, consumerism" (p. 4). We look for differing realities within our common culture.

Not everyone imagines exactly the same color when "red" is mentioned. Red is seen from the inside. Therefore real communication requires people to construct a shared color reality. If "New Year" is mentioned by a client, coworker, or community resident, we should not assume that the reference is to January. The new year also has accounting connotations, but even in a holiday context different dates apply for the Jewish, Chinese, and Vietnamese New Year. Everybody nods on reading examples like these and yet, in the bustle of daily life, we unconsciously assume that the "others" have a grayer, less red, less real picture of the world, or we halfway believe that their holiday is less important than ours. When we elevate our reality, we forget that there "is no privileged position, no absolute perspective" (Rabinow & Sullivan 1987, p. 8). We who serve others must stay open to their ideas and to multiple possibilities (Jaffe, 1983).

If red can be experienced diversely, imagine the multiple interpretations and experiences of being a patient (Sacks, 1984) or a "crip" (Milam, 1993) or of shame or fear. Social workers and clients cannot presume to understand each other—another reason for checking

things out. However, that may not work until a common vocabulary develops. "It is imperative that social workers ensure that their manner of speaking is similar enough to the client's manner of speaking so as to be part of a shared discourse" (Pozatek, 1994, p. 399). This entails careful listening, building trust, and verifying whether key ideas are comprehended. In addition, different knowledge bases create miscommunication at a basic interactional level. As Wells (1993) points out regarding emergency rooms, "Choice of words is an important consideration when dealing with a patient's family. Excessive use of medical terminology [such as intubated] may escalate anxiety" (p. 339).

Pozatek (1994) takes another angle, arguing that "human beings experience multiple, and often conflicting, realities" (p. 398). For instance, most experience "push-pull" and "stay-flee" feelings in relationships, jobs, and school. A person may experience, internally, differing realities regarding a relationship with her partner (e.g., good breadwinner, bad temper). Consequently practitioners can misinterpret or clients can miscommunicate intentions to leave an erratic spouse.

SOCIETAL THOUGHT STRUCTURES

The way we (and clients) conceive problems and solutions depends on *thought structures*, that is, systematic ways of thinking and frames of reference. *Thought structures can set limits and shape whether and/or how we see something.* (A similar idea was broached earlier regarding conditions that escape notice or never become defined problems.)

If we have no way to place something mentally or lack a cognitive structure to which we can tie our thought, X is seldom considered. For instance, a columnist pointed out (in jest) that in one fell swoop, *our nation could nearly eliminate crime, teenage pregnancy, and drug abuse* by "sequestering," or putting on "reservations," all males "between the ages of 15 and 29" (Allen, 1995). Something may be unable to be considered because we lack the framework to formulate it in our minds. In most cultures, for instance, *abolition of inheritance is unfathomable.* We may avoid thinking something that offends those in power. To combat ideological unthinkability, contending groups use bumper stickers as a tactic to shift perceptions. The Movement for Economic Justice once used the slogan "Robin Hood Was Right." Something can be unthinkable because it violates our values. Centuries ago, Swift realized that our minds recoil from what we cannot accept (eating babies) but tolerate what we can accept (letting people starve). Angry about England's indifference to Irish suffering and Ireland's lack of initiative, the great satirist wrote an ironic letter of advice from a supposed public-minded citizen. Entitled "A Modest Proposal for Preventing the Children of the Poor People in Ireland from Being a Burden to Their Parents or Country, and for Making Them Beneficial to Their Public," it said that *poor parents could sell their children as food to the rich.*

Thought structures relate to one's country. In the United States, we incline toward libertarian author Ayn Rand's views on money ("In $ we trust"). New thoughts about money are entertained by most Americans only after exposure to ideologies other than capitalism, to cultural configurations other than those of the Western developed world, and to utopian novels and communities. However, *even a little exposure to a contending thought structure* can *put new possibilities on the table,* although people can become defensive about their current frames of reference and realities.

Why does any of this matter in direct practice? First, we must start from the premise that we have certain cognitive blinders. Second, if a way of thinking is unfamiliar—or even a bad idea or based on error—a social worker still must understand it and be able to

stand in the shoes of those who use it. For example, a practitioner who discounts collectivism will fail to see the pluses when a religious or immigrant community pools its capital and decides who will use it in which order for what. We may have heard of immigrant burial societies, but we may be unaware that "savings and credit associations are common to many cultures" (Sun, 1995, p. 22) and that money pools, which make payouts based on need or a lottery, operate for practical and social bonding reasons. Ethiopians call this arrangement an *ekub*, Bolivians refer to it as *pasanaqu*, Cambodians as *tong-tine*, and Koreans as *keh* (pp. 1, 22). Suppose family money is held in common, yet the practitioner urges the young adults to become independent and use their savings to buy a house for themselves, their spouse, and child. Reciprocal obligation and the family safety net are being ignored. The mainstream American worldview puts the *individual* at the center, with "family, community, and society as the environmental context"; many immigrants and refugees, however, operate out of a worldview "in which the family, community, or society, not the individual, is central" (Glugoski, Reisch, & Rivera, 1994, p. 83).

Thought structures affect how we look at phenomena. *Feminists warn against looking at problems one by one, at relationships couple by couple, and at violence culture by culture, since it is the gestalt, the persistence of patterns in many times and places, that is important.* In Saudi Arabia, female citizens are forbidden to drive cars even today and feminism is in the formative stage, so thought structures are culture specific and yet some concerns seem universal. The award-winning films *Because You Are a Woman* (Kim, 1990) and *The Accused* (Kaplan, 1988) raise similar issues about rape and judicial systems in Korea and the United States, respectively.

While we often attempt to see the total picture, we rarely attempt to *propose* a different picture. Brandwein (1985) does just that by outlining the feminist thought structure that currently contends with the dominant Western white male thought structure. The dominant structure is rational and materialistic, while one of the feminist constructs places value on emotional and intuitive knowing (p. 177). Instead of asserting a strictly gender-based conflict, Brandwein juxtaposes two philosophies and ways of seeing the world or thinking—for example, contrasting feminism's "both/and" with the dominant "either/or" and feminism's "collaborative" with the dominant "competitive." Brandwein argues that true change comes only when a new thought structure is introduced and gains acceptance and ascendancy (p. 174). She is adamant that most movements, although "advocating social and economic justice," stay stuck in old thought patterns, that is, adhere to "the dominant thought-structure in our society" (p. 169).

Thus, thought structures can be contested. Those in critical legal studies (a critical approach to law) ask whether it makes sense to continually take a "rights" approach to law reform or social change. Yet, allegiance to individual rights goes so deep that it is hard for us to conceive of alternatives. In social work, the gay/lesbian movement (Tully, 1994; Warner, 1993) has challenged the way we teach normal human behavior and development and couples counseling.

PARADIGM SHIFTS

Our notions of problems are affected most of all by paradigm shifts. The concepts of *thought structures* and *paradigms* can be combined (as Brandwein does), but we separate them here for maximum understanding. In social work, education, and business, *paradigm* is a trendy term often used as synonymous with major ideas within a field or individual (as opposed to shifts of suppositions in metapatterns of thought). *Paradigm shift* is used here in the sense of a societal fault line where dominant ideas are reconfigured

and reconsolidated—for example, the impossibility of black rule in South Africa.

One classic paradigm shift was from the belief that the world was flat and ended somewhere to the belief that it was round and continuous. Another was the shift from the belief in the innate inferiority of indigenous people to a realization that it was in white people's self-interest to hold such a belief. Possibly the next shift will be to a transcultural worldview (Gould, 1995). Like the changing status of women, these are global and s-l-o-w shifts. Debates over "pay equity" do not take place so long as women are deemed to be possessions—whether as slave or wife.

Paradigms affect our actions. "God's in his heaven and all's right with the world" wrote the poet Pope. If such is the societal orientation, then for us to presume to fix something is wrong—ipso facto perverse. Today the orientation might be "If there is a higher power, She or He is absent because nothing seems to be going right. So, folks, if we don't fix it, who will? Still, whatever will be, will be."

CONCEPTUAL INVIGORATION

Even though intellectual constructs are seldom at the metalevel of thought structures and paradigms, abstract thinking is important in social work. We must understand the conceptual frameworks and premises with which we approach challenges. For instance, Martin (1992) has discussed "bridging the gap" between research and practice. At a conference, Meyer posed a query that Martin believes is a challenge to our entire field: "What if what was needed was not a bridge at all but a tunnel under the river or a ferry to cross the river?" Such flexibility in our thinking and even in our metaphors enhances problem solving. As another example, Van Soest and Bryant (1995) call for a shift in the profession's thinking about violence from a focus on domestic, interpersonal violence to the complex ways in which it is embedded in U.S. culture through omission, repression, and alienation (p. 550).

Models of Reality in a Cultural Context

Having looked at the ways in which our thoughts are filtered, we turn to other filters. "Because we are each a product of our culture(s), culture provides the filters through which we each interpret reality," explain Kavanagh and Kennedy (1992, p. 23), but they add that approaches flowing from many cultures can have merit. Saari (1991) says that "the clinical social worker needs to know about both culture and the environment" but primarily hears about the environment (p. 49). She adds that "culture has often been referred to as if it were a singular and static thing. It is not" (p. 52). Nor is it solely about language and racial differences.

WAYS OF THINKING ABOUT CULTURE

House of culture
- *culture* as an underpinning, a substructure;
- *(multi)cultural* social units as a manifestation, many rooms; and
- *Culture* as another manifestation, a front parlor.

We will discuss culture, as Real (1980) does, as "a system with subsystems and multiple layers of meaning" (p. 257). Above are three different and interrelated ways in which the concept of culture is employed; social workers should be familiar with all of them. Most of us participate in all three forms of culture simultaneously. Only Culture involves literacy, at least enough to be familiar with some of the Torah, Koran, or Bible.

Paradoxically, high Culture—"being cultured"—can be acquired by anyone, yet it establishes class boundaries and is labeled as special by those with influence. (It is often shown off by a people, as a front parlor may be by a family, but it can be used as a common room that all can share.)

A society is made up of many collective entities that can be identified even though they all share a common culture. These overlays or ways of life make some groups distinct enough that they label, or others label, this (sub)culture by some characteristic such as race, region, or religion (e.g., Amish). Our multicultural communities offer opportunities to learn and share—music, dance, literature, rituals, religion, and medicines. (Like house mates or family members, the members are not always in perfect accord.)

Underlying both Culture and subculture is *culture*, knowledge that enables us to interpret and act coherently in our environment. Those things that seem to come instinctively or intuitively and in which we have the most confidence may create strains when service users have equally strong tendencies in nearly opposite directions flowing from their own distinct cultural heritage. This is our received culture, which we seldom question. (People experience culture without conscious thought, just as a family counts on the foundation to support the rooms above it.) (See Box 3.5.)

EXPECTATIONS REGARDING
CULTURAL AWARENESS
Social workers are expected to acquire multicultural awareness and cultural competence in dealing with discoverable differences, such as godparents as a resource in many Hispanic families (Vidal, 1988). We also must acquire interpretive abilities regarding less apparent differences. To grasp the hidden, a social worker, like an ethnographer, must search for the "meaning of

BOX 3.5	CULTURE: A REVIEW (SAME WORD, THREE MEANINGS)

The U.S. president's wife and the Russian president's wife attend a performance at the Kennedy Center by the modern dance choreographer Twyla Tharp. Two Muslim, Iranian-American women, one with her head covered and the other wearing blue jeans, walk down a public street in the United States speaking Farsi. A 2-year-old in the Rockies or the Smokies makes a transition from diapers and proudly shows off his "big boy" pants.

1. *Culture*, in the liberal arts sense, essential to the development of a refined and knowledgeable person, includes etiquette and respect for antiquities. Knowing Culture means knowing when to clap during a ballet or orchestral performance, knowing the first line of the novel *Moby Dick*, and knowing to stand for the Hallelujah Chorus during a performance of Handel's "Messiah." Sometimes Culture is discussed in terms of the national character or culture (e.g., knowing to stand for the seventh-inning stretch in baseball). It is defined and controlled by the elite and image makers of a country and by the custodians of culture but is often international in scope (e.g., the plays of Shakespeare). It is so well known that a shorthand develops: the BBC, the Met, $E = mc^2$. It can be written up à la Bloom's cultural literacy lists or the Great Books programs. Most residents of a country know some literate Culture—which is obvious and explicit—through school and the media, so it provides unity to help balance diversity.

2. *Multiculture* is used in the pluralistic societal sense and the focused studies sense (Asian-American, Indigenous, Latino Studies) of many distinct cultures within a country or community (e.g., gay and lesbian). While sociologists use the term *subcultures*, anthropologists and social workers avoid it because it seems to imply "lesser." Each such culture has its own knowledge, preferences, values, and (at least superficial) identities. Thus, exchanges between them are cross-cultural, just like those between countries. Looked at this way, middle-class or mainstream culture becomes another variant, but its political dominance must be acknowledged—for example, its dialect becomes the gauge (Standard English). Residents of the country will not know about each of its cultures. Only those who are part of a particular culture feel ownership. Cultural differences can be observed in overt behavior, dress, names, lifestyles, hairstyles, festivals, and food (e.g., "keeping kosher").[8] *Multiculture* is used broadly—it is not necessarily race, religion, ethnicity, or region based. Social work has enough of a culture that comedians can mock it ("I *feel* . . ."), and "active listening" skills are known to all members. Much variety exists within a culture (e.g., generational differences are often significant). At a global level, similar distinctions are drawn between Western, Eastern, and Islamic cultures.

3. *culture* is used in the anthropological sense of near-universality within a country. It is "that which makes us a stranger when we are away from home" (Caughey, 1984) and provides most of the unity for the national community. This system is the foundation underlying both Culture and (sub)cultures. It includes worldviews, meanings, ideas/customs (e.g., beliefs about death and rituals at the time of death), deeper identities, and so on. It is used to judge others on matters such as arrival time or posture (e.g., "Stand up straight"). We "read" people on the basis of how they sit in chairs, or if they do. The members of society internalize this culture and its rituals (e.g., people of every variety get flowers or a gift for Mother's Day if they are acculturated Americans). Yet, anyone fully immersed finds the understood aspects of the culture hard to articulate. How to tie a shoe is explicit knowledge to youngsters, their parents, and teachers; how to greet others in an elevator and winking or coughing behavior is tacit knowledge for adults. We overlook culture.

things" that a full participant in a separate culture "knows but doesn't know he knows" (Spradley & McCurdy, 1972, p. 34). Cultural participants have a tacit understanding, for instance, of the conventions and values associated with public speaking. Conklin and Lourie (1983) point out that not all speeches use the form taught in school of previews, reviews, summaries, and evaluations. An alternative form is topic chaining, shifting from one topic to the next. Moreover, Native Americans "offer all known facts, regardless of how they apply to their own personal opinions" (p. 274):

> The interactional goals of Anglo-Americans and American Indians—the one to convince the listeners, the other to submit information for their private deliberation—lead to two radically different oratorical structures. (p. 274)

As professionals, we must know our biases, how we see the world, and how we take the measure of others. Do we grasp our own ethnocentrism (Castex, 1993) regarding what constitutes an effective speech, an appropriate-acceptable human body, or the best way to eat a formal meal? Ethnocentrism makes us feel that our way is right because it is what we know, even though facts can give us a broader view (e.g., Americans hold silverware differently than most other Westerners do). To a person learning a new culture, it is clearer that multiple ways are acceptable. Cao O is Chinese, born in Vietnam. Now a social worker in the United States, he describes his transition as his family became more American, acquiring new habits and new wants such as privacy.

> Now what I use to eat with depends on who I am eating with. . . . At home we don't use the small rice bowls any more. We use the American soup bowls to eat with. Yet my family would use chopsticks to go with that. We don't pick up the bowl anymore. . . . Before my family all lived and slept in one big room. Now I have to have my own room. (Lee, 1992, p. 104)

It sometimes takes a jarring twist for us to notice either *different practices* (e.g., when people do not smile) or *competing perspectives* (e.g., when members of the mainstream are asked to think of themselves as "temporarily able-bodied" rather than thinking of some of their fellow citizens as "mobility impaired" or "handicapped"). Oliver (1990) describes a survey of adults with disabling conditions that included questions such as "Can you tell me what is *wrong* with you?" and "Does your health problem/disability mean that you *need* to live with relatives or someone else who can help *look after* you?" (emphasis added).

> the interviewer visits the disabled person at home and asks many structured questions. . . . It is in the nature of the interview process that the interviewer presents as expert and the disabled person as an isolated individual inexperienced in research, and thus unable to reformulate the questions [which never focus on the environment, just the person]. (pp. 7–8)

No matter how pleasant the interviewer is, niceties cannot overcome his or her built-in power and control, yet the professional may not think of this or the competing realities. A *disabled identity* that affects the thinking of everyone with every degree of ableness, in Oliver's view, is constructed through medicalization, dependency expectations, and "externally imposed" images of disability (p. 77). In thinking of those with severe disabilities—perhaps institutionalized—who are unable to advocate for themselves, it is easy to forget how many do take care of themselves and are compelling advocates for others similarly situated. Society has not made up its mind about parenting from a wheelchair and other facets of independent living. There are dominant and subordinate cultural realities.

MULTIPLE WORLDS

Geographically and politically, as well as culturally, humans live and function in different worlds, yet also coexist within other overarching worlds. This becomes obvious when we think of nation-states and the global community. It may seem less obvious domestically until we think of a specific community. Many of Flint, Michigan's, neighborhoods were devastated by factory layoffs while residents of other neighborhoods stayed involved in country clubs and theater outings (Moore, 1989).

Multiple worlds and identities are dramatically juxtaposed in Crown Heights (a small world subdivided into even smaller ones), within Brooklyn (a larger world), New York. This rich but strained mix is dramatically and effectively illustrated by a remarkable book and film called *Fires in the Mirror* (Smith, 1993), which portray several dozen responses to and understandings of the intertwined deaths of a Guyanese-American (black) child and a young Lubavitcher Hasidic (Jewish, Australian) scholar. The criminal and civil rights laws of New York State and the United States, along with the national media, constitute part of the overarching world that affects Crown Heights, Brooklyn, as does U.S. and world history. The problem is racism; the problem is anti-Semitism; the problem is riots: competing realities. Community workers trying to ease tensions in Crown Heights needed to be aware of and had to facilitate communication across many social boundaries. They also had to explain behavior based on little-understood community norms to the media. According to Pozatek (1994), such a task is no longer unusual: "An awareness of the many layers of culture—global, hemispheric,

national, racial, ethnic, religious, political, gender, economic, local, and subjective—is essential to post-modern social work" (p. 399). We come from different worlds, and that creates issues for defining and prioritizing problems and sharing our subjective experience in the process.

PRACTITIONERS AND CULTURE

The concept of communitarianism, discussed earlier, helps us avoid getting stuck in tribalism, balkanism, victimization, and martyrdom so that we can avoid replays of Crown Heights. However, differences and history cannot be ignored, whether one is working in a military community, with its tendency to reject "homosexuals," or in a "gay" (even the language is different) community where the 1978 murder of San Francisco city supervisor Harvey Milk and the 1969 Stonewall battle in Greenwich Village still have meaning (Duberman, 1993; Simon, 1994, p. 150). A caseworker takes a social history; a community worker digs out a social history. A practitioner involved with the community in capacities such as adoptions of babies needs to know personal and communal social histories and their accompanying worldviews.

We can best communicate across social boundaries when we realize that ours is not the only reality (Green, 1982, p. 7). Service users and community residents have stories they can tell if they realize that we know something about their world. If a sixth grader in a self-esteem group says that she sleeps in the same bed as a parent, we do not presume incest when the problem may be poverty and she wants to share her dream of a canopy bed of her own. Greif (1994) speaks candidly to that example when he discloses that "working with these parents [from public housing] has taught me to rethink many of my basic assumptions about therapy with poor families and African-American families. Twenty years ago I had been trained, for example, that parents should never share a bed with children. Yet these mothers have little choice" (p. 207). Awareness of multiple realities keeps us from making premature assessments. Feminist standpoint theory takes a similar position. "Members of each group must work to understand the standpoint of others to construct views of our shared reality that are less partial," says Swigonski (1994, p. 392). For direct and indirect practice, the "[k]ey to successful intervention is communicative competence" (Pardeck et al., 1994, p. 344).

REALITIES TIED TO INCOME STATUS

Saari (1991) asserts that "members of traditionally disadvantaged minority groups are by no means the only persons in society who must participate in more than one culture. . . . In a complex society, the individual normally participates in a number of somewhat different cultures or shared meaning systems in the course of an average day" (pp. 53–54). Some of these cultures or systems are more deeply experienced than others. Class differences, for example, may be underestimated if the focus is solely on race and ethnicity.

Those who are more privileged and better educated, with certain tastes, have the idea that they see things as they really are and are sure that Others lag, without drive, stuck in their provincial or limited realities and behaviors. Less privileged and less educated people of the same heritage, with certain tastes, consider themselves down-to-earth people who see things as they really are but view Others as fixated on striving and appearances, uptight and stuck-up, limited by snobbish realities and behaviors. Each view is ethnocentric. These views are internalized quite young; children know about subtle distinctions, as this telling story shows: a little girl was shown a card depicting five bears who looked exactly alike, but one bear was being shunned by the other four. When she was asked what was hap-

pening in the picture, her quick reply was, "He's not our kind of bear."

INSIDER/OUTSIDER PERSPECTIVES ON REALITY

Children gain cultural knowledge from a variety of sources ranging from parental commands ("leave your nose alone") to peer teaching. They also develop a perspective of their own. Sixth-grade girls can "distinguish nearly one hundred ways to *fool around*," including *"bugging other kids, playing with food, and doodling"* (Spradley & McCurdy, 1972, pp. 18–19). Adults have a different perspective on such activities.

We must be aware of how experience is viewed by the other person. "The effective communicator learns to acquire and to understand, to the greatest extent possible, both insider (emic) and outsider (etic) perspectives" (Kavanagh & Kennedy, 1992, pp. 45–46). *Etic analysis*, which is observer oriented, gives us the ability to see similarities and differences and to compare or find commonalities across systems. Such a level of analysis might further a communitarian view by pointing out categories that all humans relate to, such as "kinship." In social work, planners and organizers build on such a perspective. In contrast, *emic analysis*, which is actor oriented, allows us to become immersed in a worldview or lifestyle and its minutiae as a participant or a participant-observer. Emic analysis takes us into a collective, culture-specific mindset. Kavanagh and Kennedy (1992) see trade-offs; "the emic view provides the subjective experience but limits objectivity, whereas the etic perspective is more objective, but is farther from actual experience of the phenomenon" (p. 23). These perspectives—not tied to conventional diversity differences—can be discerned in the example in Box 3.6.

UNITING WITH CLIENTS

Often it seems as if there is a client–community–cause world and a social worker

BOX 3.6	ETIC–EMIC DISTINCTION

Let's distinguish *etic* (a global, abstract perspective from outside the culture under scrutiny) and *emic* (a localized, group-specific perspective from inside the culture under scrutiny) forms of analysis.

Suppose that, pad and pen in hand, a student asks everyone he sees in the dormitory on Sunday morning: "Were you drinking last night?" We can ask a person operating from an etic point of view, such as the student's research supervisor, "What do you see the student doing?" We can ask a person operating from an emic point of view, such as someone being questioned, the same thing. The supervisor's (etic) response could be: The student is "categorizing behavior and experience" or "taking a survey." The (emic) responses from a student questioned, however, might be vastly different. One might think: "Maybe he's a religious nut who is going to ask me to go to church." Another might think: "Know that mf's writing a paper for Professor So and So. I tell everybody not to take her—she sucks."

Observer and observed each has a language of his own ("categorizing" and "sucks"), academic versus colloquial, formal versus profane. If they got together, the research supervisor and the dormitory residents might talk past each other about this experience because they do not ordinarily "hang with" each other (as a student would say), just as social workers and their clients cannot always "cross social boundaries" (as a professor would say).

If this does not seem like a true insider–outsider situation—since the questioner and answerer are both students—convert the scenario into the student researcher asking skid row alcoholics: "Were you drinking last night?" Or imagine a question-asking scene where a police officer or a social worker is trying to figure out if someone lying on the sidewalk is drunk or has overdosed; the crowd may not assume that one is there to help rather than to arrest.

(See Spradley, 1970; Spradley & McCurdy, 1972; Spradley, 1979.)

world, while for practice purposes the ideal is a joint one. Three key ideas to derive from the etic–emic discussion are as follows:

- *Those experiencing the social problem have an emic or insider view.* Therefore, "Instead of asking, '*What do I see these people doing?*' we must ask, '*What do these people see themselves doing?*'" (Spradley & McCurdy, 1972, p. 9). Kavanagh and Kennedy (1992) urge that we "assess from the client's perspective what the most appropriate goals are in a given situation" (p. 24).

- *Social workers and clients may not share the same context or realities during an interaction.* What we say may not be what clients hear and vice versa. "It is essential," writes Pozatek (1994), "for practitioners to be

aware of this phenomenon, and to socially construct, through dialogue with the client, a shared reality that they agree is a representation of their interaction" (p. 399).

- *Clients have reasons for what they do or decide.* We must individualize. Green (1982) warns that if social workers view intervention modes as having universal applicability, such thinking constitutes applied ethnocentrism.

One area where we want to build a shared reality is in constructing *the story of the problem* as it is told by individuals, families, groups, or community residents (Saleebey, 1994). We may be the experts on resources and options, but our clients are the experts on their own needs and problems

(Hartman, 1992). We must convert the question "What can I as a social worker do to help out those poor people?" to a question to mull over: "What are they saying to me?"

The second area in which we want to build a shared reality is through *mutual hope, mutual expectation, and a shared sense of efficacy.* Saleebey (1994) sees narrative and the building of hope as connected. If only negative tales are being told (e.g., by residents in public housing), then *counter* stories of success or "grace under pressure" might be spread and "scenarios of possibility" might be opened up (pp. 356–357). Most individuals and advocates have such stories to tell. Since "meaning . . . can inspire or oppress," suggests Saleebey, "why not take the time to work with individuals to articulate those meanings, those stories, those possible narratives that elevate spirit and promote action?" (p. 357).

In terms of self-efficacy, we can "help make possible different stories that clients . . . tell about themselves" (Saleebey, 1994, p. 357) and we can approach our work in new ways. Clinicians can allow clients to "direct their therapy" (Pardeck et al., p. 343). At the macro level, we should make an equally strong commitment to those directly involved: their interpretations should determine the agenda of community development (or it could be a joint venture). Symbolic interactionists might call this a "community of perspectives"; postmodernists might speak of a community based on mutually acknowledged "assumptions about reality," and community organizers might see it as "getting the people who are most affected by the change involved in the process."

If we have an etic view while simultaneously trying to gain an emic perspective, what is our role? We should not give ourselves short shrift, especially since we have resources and options. As practitioners, we have much to offer. We take our own reality for granted and forget how much we know that our ser-

vice users do not know about how systems work or the ways certain aspects of the community function. We know how to manipulate our own and other organizations to get them to serve clients better. Our function at times is to connect one world to another. As a shelter and employment director for chronically mentally ill adults puts it, "There are all these homeless people who have fallen out of the larger system. They almost can't get back without someone to be a bridge and to help them access all those systems and services that they may be able to get." This social worker does not operate from a superior position—she talks of "kinship" with her clients—but rather from another reality, with different knowledge, where both perspectives are validated. She believes that success for a social worker is predicated on "being somebody that can deal with diversity of backgrounds and *functioning* levels and cultures, if you will."[9]

SOLVING A SOCIAL/COMMUNITY PROBLEM

The emphasis placed on professional understanding and appropriate reaction does not mean that we should or can stop there. Social workers and clients are sociopolitical actors in the physical and cognitive environment we have described.

Myths Must Be Confronted

The first component of problem solving, in Tallman's (1976) view, is "perception," and the second is "action" (p. 29). What sometimes stops us from taking personal or collective action is uncertainty or lethargy induced by beliefs or myths. Myths are of two types—myths of facts (vs. illusions) and myths of construction. We concentrate on the latter. Lowry (1974) says that many in society see problems as "accidents and inevitable," "as a result of evil," or "as a result of imperfections in the victims" (pp. 24–25). Lowry cites Claiborne, who said that such myths and "schlock" research lead to the following conclusions (p. 40), which harken back to social causation:

• Nothing can be done about the problem; it is an inherent aspect of humanity and nature.

• Nothing needs to be done about the problem; things aren't that bad; enjoy things as best you can.

• Nothing much needs to be done; a little cosmetic reform of the system will suffice.

Here is a starting point for our profession, which has firsthand experience with the personal pain and social costs involved in these supposedly inconsequential problems. We can renounce such myths and bear witness to the need for a community-based system of social care (Specht & Courtney, 1994). We can make sure that the burdened and oppressed reject such myths and do not get tricked into adopting positions that are in conflict with their own self-interests. We can play a role in community education.

We must not skip past clients' attitudes. How do those we work with view themselves and life? Success frequently follows when community residents make a simple adjustment in their thinking, a cognitive action equivalent to cleaning one's glasses. While many want to see change, they cannot imagine it happening or themselves being involved in the process. A community activist makes this point quite eloquently:

> The initial problem that any community organizer has to overcome is a sense among people that (1) there's nothing I can do to make a difference on the way things are, or (2) even if I tried, I wouldn't be successful. It's what a lot of people call apathy. I don't think it is apathy. A lot of folks haven't re-

ally looked at their environment with a goal of changing it. It's a new idea for many people. Quite a few people go through life thinking that *life is happening to them*. What you do in organizing is help people see that life isn't something that necessarily happens to you, it's something that you can change as a group. The trick in the beginning is having enough hope in people's hearts that doing something will work.[10]

The phrase "making a difference" became a personal mantra for advocates, a successful volunteer and activist recruitment pitch, and a popular advertising theme because most people hunger for meaning and quietly hope that their lives indeed count for something. Freire (1994) says poetically, "I do not understand human existence, and the struggle needed to improve it, apart from hope and dream. . . . Hopelessness is but hope that has lost its bearings, and become a distortion of that ontological need" (p. 8).

Since we know how much problems have to do with our own view of them, perhaps we can say this: the nature of social problems is such that they initially seem overwhelming but, with engagement, emerge as fairly resolvable. Personal passivity can change to action before or after this perceptual conversion. Therefore, those who are affected by a social problem can get angry about how they are being treated and can be motivated to face the problem squarely. They may even try to recruit us as an ally once they have moved from a feeling of futility to one of self-efficacy.

Problem Solvers Must Be Supported

Problem solvers are those who identify, develop, and accelerate the reaction to social problems (Tallman, 1976). They include citizens in social distress, the many "players" in problem solving, and those local heroes—professionals and community leaders alike—who stay engaged in problem solving for decades, often taking on one problem after another. The lucky ones engage out of choice or professional commitment, but as Tallman (1976) points out, "others are forced to take action either by circumstances or by confrontations which they cannot avoid" (p. 150). It is outside our scope to discuss the many influences that give individuals the capacity to act, but Tallman's emphasis on vision and values is noteworthy: "One of the most important elements influencing the development of social-problem solvers is the expectations they hold for how society should treat its members" (p. 172).

Problem solving also involves the emotions of those who initiate action and those who respond. Most people like to hear about "imminent possibility and triumph grounded in real circumstances," states Saleebey (1994):

> Tales of the quest for respect, relief, or redemption or the creation and reviving of symbols that unite hopes with action have moved people and have encouraged them to alter or defy their circumstances. . . . So stories and myths and narratives can be the instruments of empowerment—individual and collective. (p. 354)

Those of conviction who are already empowered clearly can help empower others. Still, those out in front pushing on for the rest of society must be supported in their quest to provide solutions to social problems. Their intensity of emotion should engender some reciprocal passion in us (Tallman, 1976, p. 6).

Problems Must Be Approached Intelligently

Taking into account the multifaceted nature of problems, we can identify and approach them in a logical fashion. Even in a tiny community, social problems that are defined and identified locally, that is, accepted as community problems, will be evident if we look at human service agencies and who they currently serve. For instance, Williamson, West Virginia, has only six or seven agencies (including the Red Cross, the Salvation Army, the Scouts, and the Armed Services U.S.O.), but one of them provides shelter for victims of domestic violence. When we first start to work out conceptualizations of social problems, the more local or community oriented they are, the better. The more broadly a problem is conceptualized, the harder it is to sell. The right to health care, the right to shelter, and international human rights are beyond the purview of most practitioners. Ironically, local manifestations of larger social problems, such as inadequate health care for the uninsured, homelessness, and refugees tortured so badly that they cannot work, exist in part because the rights to health care and shelter go unadopted and human rights go unenforced. When labeled community problems, they must be dealt with by those in human services. Until we are experienced, we should keep a local focus—for practical and tactical reasons, not because unsolved national and international problems are irrelevant.

Small-scale versions of national problems like domestic violence are easier for beginners to analyze. Spector and Kitsuse (1987) suggest a rudimentary approach to analysis and action: cut out community newspaper clippings; put down fundamental ideas and your own beginning knowledge regarding a situation that should be addressed for personal or professional reasons. The requisite activities are these:

Describe a condition;
Describe why it is annoying, disturbing, harmful, unethical, destructive, or unwholesome;

Identify what causes the condition;

Describe what should be done about it; and

Explain how one would begin to accomplish this. (pp. 161–162)

Once we or those we work with get started, we are not eager to take time out to do this type of analysis. Emotions can take over. Also, simply because *we* have finally defined a condition as a problem does not mean that others have done so. We have to look for support or mutual understanding in the wider world, and we have to think logically about the elements of problems so that our emotions and actions will be purposeful and successful. To start, we need to find out how many people are morally indignant (Tallman, 1976). How many hold our point of view or see a situation our way? One of the first impulses after recognizing and discussing the seriousness of a problem is an intuitive attempt at "often ill-advised" reform, which Broussard calls the "Well, let's do something, folks" stage (Spector & Kitsuse, 1987, p. 138). However, doing just anything to satisfy others' or our own sense of frustration is unprofessional and fruitless.

Our problem framework components relate to intervention as much as to definition. Concepts such as *ideology* and *labeling*, discussed earlier, may become relevant again as applications to community problems are discussed. We must consciously work toward a shared construction of a problem. The way a group's purpose is characterized will expand or narrow the number and variety of people who will join the action. It has become clear, for example, that "right to life" was successful as a recruitment and umbrella term for diverse constituencies, while "antiabortion" was more limiting. In the same way, "proabortion" was not something many wanted to endorse compared to the idea of "pro-choice." If we are clear that we will be working with people of many minds, our appeals can be better directed to reach a broad group. The same holds true as we try to build an action coalition. To lobby with the community requires us to find core beliefs that unify.

CONCLUSION

We must build community and link with communities. Most of this text focuses on how to bring people together to improve the community and promote the well-being of its residents. Fellow inhabitants of a place will not have the same realities, perspectives, or cultural beliefs, although they can mutually engage in the process of problem remediation. Therefore, human variety must be respected before true unity will occur and a community can be forged or maintained. In addition, columnist William Raspberry (1995), quoting Amitai Etzioni, urges us to attend to "the encompassing whole," that is, to the "community of communities," and the connecting "glue" of our societal "mosaic" (p. A28).

Many of us became or are becoming social workers in order to eradicate certain social problems, specific objective conditions. It is therefore disconcerting to discover that such problems are not as definite or fixed as we had supposed. At the same time, it is rejuvenating to realize that we can help shape the action agenda and that we now know how to resist being molded ourselves. Society is ever changing, so it redefines problems in response to new *data* (e.g., computers allow many employees with restricted mobility to work at home), *demands* (e.g., how to view sexual orientation), and *power bases* (e.g., the Latino community). This means that social workers, as part of the "early warning system for social problems" (Ginsberg, 1994, p. 49), can provide data, make proposals, wield influence, and work for the acceptance of constructs they favor in the arena of social problem definition.

Practitioners must combine ideas of fluidity, uncertainty, and shifting realities and paradigms with the ideals of service, justice, and caring and the lessons of experience. We must seek a holistic view while knowing that we see only in part. We also need to *become conscious* (Gowdy, 1994, p. 364) and to find a new angle of vision on the outer world. As social workers, we know we cannot

work properly without understanding our own consciousness, but ordinarily we take this to mean various psychological or emotional states—the inner world. We need to expand our awareness to those facets of consciousness that can free us from a fixed or frozen viewpoint and lead to personal empowerment. As professionals, in cooperation with those we serve, we can use this new mental flexibility to further collective self-determination and perhaps cognitive liberation.

Discussion Exercises

1. Did you disagree with any of the premises or arguments set forth in this chapter? Over which sections do you think you and your parents or you and your neighbors would have the most disagreement?

2. On what basis should social workers take action regarding social problems?

3. Regarding alternative realities, watch the movie *Rashomon* or *Six Degrees of Separation*. *Rashomon* is a classic Japanese movie about a lady, a gentleman, and a bandit, with segments from each of their points of view about the question of whether there was a sexual assault and about virtues such as bravery. *Six Degrees* concerns a college-age African-American male who pretends to be the son of Sidney Poitier, the responses to him during and after the deception, and the permanent influence he has on one society matron. How can we take differing realities into consideration without losing

confidence about whether there is any solid ground on which we can stand to practice?

4. Discuss similarities and differences in societal perspectives over time regarding honor and respect. Think about deaths resulting from "being dissed" (disrespected) and from dueling.

5. What types of privilege does your group (individual reader) take for granted? One example of white privilege is having "flesh"-colored bandages that more or less match one's skin color.

6. The documentary *Hoop Dreams*, about two high school basketball players and their families, was highly praised (Angell, 1995). Apply Ryan's distinction between *people who won't help* and *helpers who hurt* to high-caliber schools that offer scholarships to promising basketball stars. Poor parents are required to pay half of the private school tuition. Debate this issue.

Notes

1. Regarding the roller coaster rider, Gowdy (1994) quotes an intriguing statement by a consumer: "Throw away the textbooks and let me teach you about being mentally ill. I have a PhD in mental illness!" (p. 362).

2. Empowerment expert Simon (1994) discusses "healer" and "survivor" as *positive* client metaphors (chap. 1). By contrast, victimization cultivates a "sense of resignation" rather than a desire to act (Kaminer, 1992, p. 158; see also Peele, 1989).

Regarding dysfunctionality as a defense, see Mauro (1994).

3. Most social work jobs are a result of a problem creation process. Think of positions in houses for battered women or mental health centers.

4. The National Association of Social Workers and the National Rifle Association made competing claims during the 1994 Omnibus Crime Bill debate. See the articles in *NASW News* for September and October 1994 (Vol. 39).

5. During the 6 years of the creation of the missing children problem, some of those missing turned up murdered, but most stayed missing although not necessarily in danger. Today claims about the number of people murdered at work and the percentage of homosexuals in the population are alleged to be inflated. Interest groups (and we are all part of at least one) making claims use statistics to arouse passions and raise money. Opponents downplay numbers.

6. For an overview, see McQuail (1994). See the Glossary in Lull (1995). On controlling the agenda, psychological abuse of any group is hard to sell as a problem to market-driven television because there is nothing to see, just as in the women's movement, consciousness raising was not observable (Tuchman, 1978, p. 139). Regarding culture–media connections, see Schiller (1989) and Stevenson (1995).

7. Pozatek (1994) provides an illuminating example of traditional Hispanic differences and realities (p. 397).

8. Regarding food, culture, and social work practice, see recent articles by Melvin Delgado.

9. Mary Slicher, executive director of Project PLASE (People Lacking Ample Shelter and Employment), in *Stirring People Up* (interviewed by Sally Dailey).

10. Susan Esty of the American Federation of State, County, and Municipal Employees in a videotape by Bell and Garcia, University of Maryland at Baltimore School of Social Work, entitled "Action Adventures in Our Own Backyard." A separate interview with Esty by Rebecca Smith appears in *Stirring People Up.*

References

Allen, J. T. (1995, February 19). Throw away the key: Locking up every young guy (for a while) can save America. *The Washington Post*, p. C5.

Angell, R. (1995, March 13). Two dreams. *New Yorker*, pp. 6–7.

Baumann, E. A. (1989). Research rhetoric and the social construction of elder abuse. In J. Best (Ed.), *Images of issues: Typifying contemporary social problems* (pp. 55–74). New York: Aldine De Gruyter.

Bernstein, L., Laurents, A., & Sondheim, S. (1957). Gee officer Krupke! In *West Side Story* [song].

Best, J. (1987). Rhetoric in claims-making: Constructing the missing children problem. *Social Problems, 34*(2), 101–121.

Best, J. (Ed.). (1989). *Images of issues: Typifying contemporary social problems.* New York: Aldine De Gruyter.

Blumer, H. (1971). Social problems as collective behavior. *Social Problems, 18*, 298–306.

Bradshaw, J. (1977). The concept of social need. In N. Gilbert & H. Specht (Eds.), *Planning for social welfare: Issues, models and tasks* (pp. 290–296). Englewood Cliffs, NJ: Prentice-Hall.

Brandwein, R. A. (1985). Feminist thought-structure: An alternative paradigm of social change for social justice. In D. G. Gill & E. A. Gill (Eds.), *Toward social and economic justice: A conference in search of social change* (pp. 169–181). Cambridge, MA: Schenkman.

Cartwright, T. J. (1977). Problems, solutions and strategies: A contribution to the theory and practice of planning. In N. Gilbert & H. Specht (Eds.), *Planning for social welfare: Issues, models and tasks* (pp. 119–132). Englewood Cliffs, NJ: Prentice-Hall.

Castex, G. M. (1993). The effects of ethnocentric map projections on professional practice. *Social Work, 38*(6), 685–693.

Caughey, J. L. (1984). *Imaginary social worlds: A cultural approach.* Lincoln: University of Nebraska Press.

Chapin, R. K. (1995). Social policy development:

The strengths perspective. *Social Work 40*(4), 506–514.

Cohen, S. (1980). *Folk devils and moral panics.* New York: St. Martin's Press.

Collins, R. (Director). (1980). *Gideon's Trumpet* [film].

Conklin, N. F., & Lourie, M. A. (1983). *A host of tongues: Language communities in the United States.* New York: Free Press.

Donahue, J. (1994, March 6). The fat cat freeloaders: When American big business bellys up to the public trough. *The Washington Post*, p. C1.

Donaldson, K. (1978). *Don't jump on the flypaper: Re the specter of mental illness in senior citizens.* (Available from Pat Powers, 4001 Montpelier Rd., Rockville, MD 20853.)

Duberman, M. (1993). *Stonewall.* New York: Dutton.

Elkin, F., & Handel, G. (1978). *The child and society: The process of socialization.* New York: Random House.

Freire, P. (1994). *Pedagogy of hope: Reliving pedagogy of the oppressed.* New York: Continuum Books.

Garvin, C. D., & Cox, F. M. (1995). A history of community organizing since the Civil War with special reference to oppressed communities. In J. Rothman, J. L. Erlich, & J. E. Tropman with F. M. Cox (Eds.), *Strategies of community organization* (5th ed., pp. 64–98). Itasca, IL: F. E. Peacock.

Ginsberg, L. (1994). *Understanding social problems, policies, and programs.* Columbia: University of South Carolina Press.

Gitlin, T. (1991). The politics of communication and the communication of politics. In J. Curran & M. Gurevitch (Eds.), *Mass media and society* (pp. 329–341). New York: Edward Arnold.

Glugoski, G., Reisch, M., & Rivera, F. G. (1994). A wholistic ethno-cultural paradigm: A new model for community organization teaching and practice. *Journal of Community Practice, 1*(1), 81–98.

Goldberg, R. A. (1991). *Grassroots resistance: Social movements in twentieth century America.* Belmont, CA: Wadsworth.

Gordon, D. R. (1994). *The return of the dangerous classes.* New York: W. W. Norton.

Gould, K. H. (1995). The misconstruing of multiculturalism: The Stanford debate and social work. *Social Work, 40*(2), 198–205.

Gowdy, E. A. (1994). From technical rationality to participating consciousness. *Social Work, 39*(4), 362–370.

Green, J. W. (1982). *Cultural awareness in the human services.* Englewood Cliffs, NJ: Prentice-Hall.

Greif, G. L. (1994). Using family therapy ideas with parenting groups in schools. *Journal of Family Therapy, 16*(2), 199–208.

Greil, A. L. (1991). *Not yet pregnant: Infertile couples in contemporary America.* New Brunswick, NJ: Rutgers University Press.

Hardcastle, D. A. (1978). Negative label attribution: A community study. *Arete, 5*(7), 117–127.

Hardcastle, D. A. (1992). *SOWK 631: Social work practice with communities and social service networks: A manual of readings, concepts and exercises.* Baltimore, MD.

Hartman, A. (1990). Many ways of knowing. *Social Work, 35*(1), 3–4.

Hartman, A. (1991). Words create worlds. *Social Work, 36*(4), 275–276.

Hartman, A. (1992). In search of subjugated knowledge. *Social Work, 37*(6), 483–484.

Jaffe, S. (Director). (1983). *Without a Trace* [film].

Jenness, V. (1995). Social movement growth, domain expansion, and framing processes: The gay/lesbian movement and violence against gays and lesbians as a social problem. *Social Problems, 42*(1), 145–170.

Jones, J. (1994). Embodied meaning: Menopause and the change of life. *Social Work in Health Care, 19*(3/4), 43–65.

Kaminer, W. (1992). *I'm dysfunctional, you're dysfunctional: The recovery movement and other self-help fashions.* Reading, MA: Addison-Wesley.

Kaplan, J. (Director). (1988). *The accused* [film].

Kassner, E. (1990). *Regulation, risk and food: Issues related to health and safety.* Washington, DC: American Association of Retired Persons.

Kaufman, S. R. (1994). The social construction of frailty: An anthropological perspective. *Journal of Aging Studies, 8*(1), 45–58.

Kavanagh, K. H., & Kennedy, P. H. (1992). *Promoting cultural diversity: Strategies for health care professionals.* Newbury Park, CA: Sage.

Kett, J. F. (1977). *Rites of passage: Adolescence in America, 1790 to the present.* New York: Basic Books.

Kettner, P. M., Moroney, R. M., & Martin, L. L. (1990). *Designing and managing programs: An effectiveness-based approach.* Newbury Park, CA: Sage.

Kim, Y-J (Director). (1990). *Because you are a woman* [film].

Kozol, J. (1995). *Amazing grace: The lives of chil-*

dren and the conscience of a nation. New York: Crown.

Kramer, R. C. (1982). From "habitual offenders" to "career criminals": The historical construction and development of criminal categories. *Law and Human Behavior, 6*(3/4), 273–293.

Kretzmann, J. P., & McKnight, J. L. (1993). *Building communities from the inside out: A path toward finding and mobilizing a community's assets.* Evanston, IL: Northwestern University Press.

Laskas, J. M. (1994, July 17). Cut from the chase. *The Washington Post Magazine,* p. 5.

Lee, J. A. B. (1994). *The empowerment approach to social work practice.* New York: Columbia University Press.

Lee, J. F. J. (1992). *Asian Americans: Oral histories of first to fourth generation Americans from China, the Philippines, Japan, India, the Pacific Islands, Vietnam and Cambodia.* New York: New Press.

Lewis, A. (1966). *Gideon's trumpet.* New York: Vintage Books.

Lipsky, M., & Smith, S. G. (1989). When social problems are treated as emergencies. *Social Service Review, 63*(1), 5–25.

Lopez, S. (1994). *Third and Indiana.* New York: Viking Press.

Lowry, R. P. (1974). *Social problems: A critical analysis of theories and public policy.* Lexington, MA: D. C. Heath.

Lull, J. (1995). *Media, communication, culture: A global approach.* New York: Columbia University Press.

Lutz, C. A., & Collins, J. L. (1993). *Reading National Geographic.* Chicago: University of Chicago Press.

Martin, M. (1992). Assessment: A response to Meyer. *Research on Social Work Practice, 2*(3), 306–310.

Mauro, T. (1994, January 31). Victimization proves best defense in an increasing number of trials. *USA Today,* p. 2A.

Mazmanian, D. A., & Sabatier, P. A. (1981). The implementation of public policy: A framework of analysis. In D. A. Mazmanian & P. A. Sabatier (Eds.), *Effective policy implementation* (pp. 3–35). Lexington, MA: Lexington Books.

McQuail, D. (1994). *Mass communication theory.* Newbury Park, CA: Sage.

Mercer, S. O. (1989). *Elder suicide: A national survey of prevention and intervention programs.* Washington, DC: American Association of Retired Persons.

Milam, L. W. (1993). *CripZen: A manual for survival.* San Diego, CA: MHO Works.

Moore, M. (Director). (1989). *Roger and me* [film].

Morris, R. (1986). *Rethinking social welfare: Why care for the stranger.* New York: Longman.

Murase, K. (1995). Organizing in the Japanese-American community. In F. G. Rivera & J. L. Erlich (Eds.), *Community organizing in a diverse society* (2nd ed., pp. 143–160). Boston: Allyn & Bacon.

Netting, F. E., Kettner, P. M., & McMurtry, S. L. (1993). *Social work macro practice.* New York: Longman.

Oliver, M. (1990). *The politics of disablement.* New York: St. Martin's Press.

Osgood, N. J. (1992). *Suicide in later life: Recognizing the warning signs.* New York: Lexington Books.

Pardeck, J. T., Murphy, J. W., & Choi, J. M. (1994). Some implications of postmodernism for social work practice. *Social Work, 39*(4), 343–346.

Parsons, R. J., Hernandez, S. H., & Jorgensen, J. O. (1988). Integrated practice: A framework for problem solving. *Social Work, 33*(5), 417–421.

Peele, S. (1989). *Diseasing of America: Addiction treatment out of control.* Boston: Houghton Mifflin.

Pozatek, E. (1994). The problem of certainty: Clinical social work in the postmodern era. *Social Work, 39*(4), 396–403.

Rabinow, P., & Sullivan, W. M. (Eds.). (1987). *Interpretive social science: A second look.* Berkeley: University of California Press.

Raspberry, W. (1995, December 8). Between assimilation and tribalism. *The Washington Post,* p. A28.

Real, M. (1980). Media theory: Contributions to an understanding of American mass communications. *American Quarterly* (Bib. Issue), *3,* 238–258.

Reeser, L. C., & Leighninger, L. (1990). Back to our roots: Toward a specialization in social justice. *Journal of Sociology and Social Welfare, 17*(2), 69–87.

Rose, S. M. (1990). Advocacy/empowerment: An approach to clinical practice for social work. *Journal of Sociology and Social Welfare, 17*(2), 41–51.

Rubington, E., & Weinberg, M. S. (1989). *The study of social problems: Six perspectives* (4th ed.). New York: Oxford University Press.

Ryan, W. (1992). Blaming the victim. In P. S. Rothenberg (Ed.), *Race, class and gender in the United States: An integrated study* (pp. 364–373). New York: St. Martin's Press.

Saari, C. (1991). *The creation of meaning in clinical social work.* New York: Guilford Press.

Sacks, O. (1984). *A leg to stand on.* New York: Harper & Row.

Saleebey, D. (1994). Culture, theory, and narrative: The intersection of meanings in practice. *Social Work, 39*(4), 351–359.

Schiller, H. I. (1989). *Culture Inc.: The corporate takeover of public expression.* New York: Oxford University Press.

Simon, B. L. (1994). *The empowerment tradition in American social work: A history.* New York: Columbia University Press.

Simons, H. F. (1988, May). *RESOLVE, Inc.: Advocacy within a mutual support organization.* Unpublished doctoral dissertation, Brandeis University, Waltham, MA.

Sinclair, U. (1906). *The jungle.* New York: New American Library.

Smith, A. D. (1993). *Fires in the mirror.* New York: Doubleday.

Specht, H., & Courtney, M. E. (1994). *Unfaithful angels: How social work has abandoned its mission.* New York: Free Press.

Spector, M. (1985). Social problems. In A. Kuper & J. Kuper (Eds.), *The social science encyclopedia* (pp. 779–780). New York: Routledge.

Spector, M., & Kitsuse, J. I. (1987). *Constructing social problems.* New York: Aldine De Gruyter.

Spradley, J. P. (1970). *You owe yourself a drunk.* Boston: Little, Brown.

Spradley, J. P. (1979). *The ethnographic interview.* New York: Holt, Rinehart & Winston.

Spradley, J. P., & McCurdy, D. W. (1972). *The cultural experience: Ethnography in complex society.* Chicago: Science Research.

Stevenson, N. (1995). *Understanding media cultures: Social theory and mass communication.* Thousand Oaks, CA: Sage.

Stirring People Up. (1993). University of Maryland at Baltimore School of Social Work monograph. Edited by P. Powers.

Sun, L. H. (1995, February 17). Traditional money pools buoy immigrants' hopes. *The Washington Post,* pp. 1, 22.

Swigonski, M. E. (1994). The logic of feminist standpoint: Theory for social work research. *Social Work, 39*(4), 387–393.

Tallman, I. (1976). *Passion, action, and politics: A perspective on social problems and social problem solving.* San Francisco: W. H. Freeman.

Taylor, B. C. (1992). Elderly identity in conversation: Producing fraility. *Communication Research, 19*(4), 493–515.

Theisen, S. C., & Mansfield, P. K. (1993). Menopause: Social construction or biological destiny? *Journal of Health Education, 24*(4), 209–213.

Tower, K. D. (1994). Consumer-centered social work practice: Restoring client self-determination. *Social Work, 39*(2), 191–196.

Townsend, C. (1971). *Old age: The last segregation: Ralph Nader's study group report on nursing homes.* New York: Grossman.

Tuchman, G. (1978). *Making news: A study in the construction of reality.* New York: Free Press.

Tully, C. T. (1994). To boldly go where no one has gone before: The legalization of lesbian and gay marriages. *Journal of Gay and Lesbian Social Services, 1*(1), 73–87.

Van Soest, D., & Bryant, S. (1995). Violence reconceptualized for social work: The urban dilemma. *Social Work, 40*(4), 549–557.

Vidal, C. (1988). Godparenting among Hispanic Americans. *Child Welfare, 67*(5), 453–458.

Wallace, A. F. C. (1956, April). Revitalization movements. *American Anthropologist, 58,* 264–281.

Wallas, G. (1926). *The art of thought.* London: Jonathan Cape.

Warner, M. (Ed.). (1993). *Fear of a queer planet: Queer politics and social theory.* Minneapolis: University of Minnesota Press.

Wells, P. J. (1993). Preparing for sudden death: Social work in the emergency room. *Social Work, 38*(3), 339–342.

West, C. (1994). *Race matters.* New York: Vintage Books.

Wilson, W. J. (1973). *Power, racism, and privilege: Race relations in theoretical and sociohistorical perspectives.* New York: Free Press.

Wuthnow, R. (1991). *Acts of compassion: Caring for others and helping ourselves.* Princeton, NJ: Princeton University Press.

chapter
4

The Concept of Community
in Social Work Practice

It is hard to imagine a more elusive concept than the idea of community. Fraught with meaning, community conjures up memories of places where we grew up and where we now live and work, physical structures and spaces—cities, towns, neighborhoods, buildings, stores, roads, streets. It evokes memories of people and relationships—families, friends and neighbors, organizations, associations of all kinds: congregations, PTAs, clubs, teams, neighborhood groups, town meetings. It evokes special events and rituals—Fourth of July fireworks, weddings, funerals, parades, the first day of school. It evokes sounds and smells and feelings—warmth, companionship, nostalgia, and sometimes fear, anxiety, and conflict as well. We all grew up somewhere; we all live in communities somewhere; we all desire human associations, some degree of belonging to a human community; we all carry around some sense of community within us (Box 4.1).

From Box 4.1, you may have already

surmised that the elusiveness of the concept of community derives from its multidimensionality. Accordingly, for this book, we have adopted Fellin's (1987) formal definition of communities as

> social units with one or more of the following three dimensions:
> 1. a functional spatial unit meeting sustenance needs
> 2. a unit of patterned interaction
> 3. a symbolic unit of collective identification. (p. 1)

This definition is akin to Hillery's (1955) earlier finding that the common elements in sociological definitions of community are geographic area, social interaction, and common ties. However, while connection to a territorial base is frequent, so that neighborhoods, villages, or cities fit the definition, in Fellin's version functional and cultural communities or "communities of interest," without a clear

97

BOX 4.1	MR. BIRTHDAY MAKES HIS ROUNDS by Steve Twomey

On the morrow, she will turn 7. On every birthday of her life, she has awakened to find a festooned sign planted in her front yard and signed at the bottom, "Mr. and Mrs. Jerry Engert." Annie has no blood tie to Mr. Engert. Nor do Johanna and Greta Pemberton, nor Robert and Emma Speiser, nor Wendy and Lisa Bauman, nor any of the 18 neighborhood kids whose names and birth dates appear in a 3-by-5 index file in Mr. Engert's basement. But each gets a lawn sign every year, individually crafted and bearing a bag of goodies. . . .

What Mr. Engert does, though, isn't only about birthdays. It's about neighborhood. . . . Mr. Engert lives on Luzerne Avenue, a shaded lane of delightful bungalows in North Woodside, not far from downtown Silver Spring. . . . On Easter in North Woodside, there's an egg hunt. On Mother's Day, a softball game. On Labor Day, Luzerne has a block party. And all year long, Luzerne has birthday signs.

Source: © 1995. The Washington Post. *Reprinted with permission.*

geographic base, such as the social work community or the Chicano community or the gay and lesbian community, may also be included.

Most of us have connections to several communities, partly because we are geographically mobile and increasingly tied together though electronic and other media, and partly because the smaller communities we affiliate with are usually embedded in larger communities that also affect our lives. As social workers, we need to understand the multiple communities of our clients as well as our own communities. Communities provide us with a rich social and personal life. They shape the way we think and act. They surround us with values and norms of behavior, explicit laws, and unwritten rules of conduct. They furnish us with meanings and interpretations of reality, with assumptions about the world. They provide resources and opportunities, albeit unevenly—places to work, to learn, to grow, to buy and sell, to worship, to hang out, to find diversion and respite, to be cared for. They confront us with traumas and problems; they intrude on our lives, and they hold out the possibilities for solutions. In keeping with the social work ecological model's emphasis on person in environment, communities must be the object of social work intervention as much as individuals, families, and groups. As stated earlier, by using some of the skills of community organization and development, social workers can help expand community resources and opportunities and can strengthen the capacity of community members to solve community problems and to reform the institutions that affect their lives.

THE CHANGING AMERICAN COMMUNITY

To understand the modern community as a context for social work practice, we will briefly review some important changes in American life that have occurred over the last 50 years. Not that change is a new phenomenon for Americans. In a country with vast resources, Americans have always been an ambitious people with the freedom and energy to invent, to explore, to develop, to challenge, and thereby to unleash great forces for change.

Although we have not always felt in control of the forces for change, in the 20th century, especially after World War II, America seemed to be in control of national and world events. The economy was booming. We seemed clear about the constellation of the good family, hopeful about being able to buy a new house, and sure that a college education would bring the rewards of a better life. World peace again seemed to be on the horizon. Yet by 1959, with America already deeply involved in the cold war, it was apparent to some observers that the future as history could no longer be predicted, that Americans, "accustomed by our historical training to expect mastery over events," could no longer remain uncritically optimistic about the future (Heilbroner, 1960, p. 208).

The social movements of the 1960s— civil rights, community action, women's liberation, peace—together with the Vietnam War did much to shake America out of its complacency. However, the conservatism of the 1970s and 1980s was arguably as much a reaction to the extremes of the previous decade as it was to the decline in the American economy nationally and internationally. The necessity for two earners to support a family; the burgeoning cost of health care; the expansion of unemployment, welfare rolls, homelessness, and crime; and the growing disparity in income between the wealthy and the poor and middle classes all bespeak complex forces at work in American society unresponsive to an easy fix, whether politically conservative, liberal, or populist. Let us now consider some of these important forces and trends in order to deepen our understanding of social work practice in the mid-1990s. The changes mentioned in the following paragraphs reflect the authors' views of what seems significant. The order of presentation, however, does not represent a statement of priority or importance.

1. More Americans now live in 39 metropolitan areas (Metropolitan Statistical Areas, or MSAs) of 1 million people or more than in smaller cities or rural communities.

Reflecting the shift from a manufacturing and farming economy to a service economy, urban areas in the nation's interior have generally experienced a decline or only modest growth, while urban coastal centers and those in the Southwest have grown substantially. In all, 90% of the largest metropolitan centers gained population during the 1980s. However, most of that growth was in the suburbs and exurbs beyond the suburbs, not in central cities. "Newer cities are mostly southwestern and southeastern. They have a 'suburban' style of life, which is automobile-dependent, home-owning, private. They also have a base in newer manufacturing industries . . . as well as regional and national services. . . . [T]hey provide the sort of middle-class life that people identify with the American Dream" (Zukin, 1991, p. 259). It is worth noting, too, that while the population of metropolitan areas has been growing, no system of metropolitan government exists to coordinate the activities of the multiple jurisdictions within the MSAs. Probably the greatest resistance to such arrangements has come from suburbanites who do not want to mingle their public amenities and tax resources with the neighboring core cities in the MSAs (Warren, 1978).

2. By contrast, the extensive loss of higher-paying, stable manufacturing jobs and the growth of lower-paying service jobs have greatly exacerbated the decline in older northeastern and midwestern central cities. One result has been high and persistent rates of unemployment and underemployment among older industrial workers and unskilled minority group men and women of all ages. Despite advances in civil rights, in particular, African-Americans in urban areas with large black populations have remained highly segregated, creating significant barriers to upward social mobility (Massey, 1994). Poverty among women and children has also been increasing since the 1960s. Single par-

ent, female-headed families now make up nearly half of the households living below the poverty line. Forty-four percent of these are black families, and most live in central cities due to historic, still extant patterns of racial segregation and economic entrapment.

3. During the 1980s, federal support to the cities for social programs, housing, education, employment, and physical infrastructure repairs was severely cut back. These cutbacks generated crises in city services, necessitating programs of fiscal austerity as well as struggles to increase the cities' tax base. Unfortunately, efforts by city and business leaders to improve the urban real estate tax base contributed to the population decline in many cities. Slum clearance, reconstruction, government subsidies, and tax breaks have had some success, but not enough for a tax revenue breakthrough that can meet the demand for services and attack social ills. The rush for corporate center redevelopment generally paid little attention to the social costs and benefits for poor and working-class residents of inner-city neighborhoods. Gentrification increased overcrowding in some neighborhoods and, in others, forced families out of the city due to escalating rents and property values. The population of many older central cities is now heavily weighted toward poor and working-class whites and minorities and wealthy young professionals (Zukin, 1991). A growing cadre of Hispanic and African-American mayors and city council members have painfully won the authority to govern fiscally marginal operations.

4. In the 1980s and 1990s, immigration from Latin America and Asia greatly increased, raising the questions again, as it did in the 1920s, about immigration quotas, limits to benefits, and adding a requirement that English be the primary language taught in schools and used in the workplace. At the same time, the continuing struggle for civil rights has both heightened sensitivity to cultural diversity and increased fears of social and political fragmentation.

5. A number of studies over the past 20 years have indicated that Americans have developed a strong belief in individual rights and entitlements from the government without an equally strong regard for individual responsibilities to the local community and the nation. In the 1990s a communitarian movement began to emerge with the goal of redefining American civic culture. In general, communitarianism stresses the responsibilities of the good citizen to participate actively in civic life and to balance the protection of individual rights with a commensurate fulfillment of responsibility to the community (Bellah, Madsen, Sullivan, Swidler, & Tipton, 1985; Etzioni, 1993; Lappe & Du Bois, 1994).

6. The growth of an aging population between 65 and 85 and a frail elderly population over 85 has become a significant factor in human service and health care planning and delivery in the United States and will continue to be so in the future. The frail elderly, in particular, are likely to require costly in-home and institutional support, as well as more complex and expensive medical care, and many have incomes below the poverty line (Ginsberg, 1990). In addition, the growing number of middle-class, active retirees has made the elderly a potent political force leading to higher pension benefits and lower rates of poverty compared with other dependent population groups. The disparity in poverty rates and benefits in the United States between the elderly and children has raised politically sensitive issues of generational equity (Pampel & Adams, 1992).

7. On the national political scene, the Reagan and Bush election victories of the 1980s ruptured traditional working-class and southern support for the Democratic party. However, Republican gains were not sustained in congressional elections until the rev-

olutionary shift from Democratic to Republican congressional control in November 1994. In the late 1980s and early 1990s, as politics became more expensive and rancorous, a sense of congressional gridlock seemed to prevail. Whether the new Republican leadership in Congress can unfreeze federal decision making remains to be seen.

In the November 1994 elections, Republicans also made significant gains at the state and local levels. Through proposals for welfare reform coupled with bloc grants to the states, a constitutional amendment to balance the federal budget, and significant federal de-regulation, an alliance of governors and Republican leaders in Congress could dismantle the welfare state as we have known it since the New Deal and reinstate a form of federalism reminiscent of an earlier period in American governance.

8. The world of work has changed significantly over the last 50 years. Foreign competition in American markets has increased dramatically, and American companies faced with aging manufacturing plants, high taxes, and comparatively expensive labor have not been able to compete successfully. Many American companies responded by selling out, shutting down their plants, and/or moving large parts of their operations to foreign countries to take advantage of cheap labor and low tax rates. These factors contributed heavily to a loss of some 39% of the U.S. manufacturing jobs that existed in 1969 (Fabricant & Burghardt, 1992). As the number of manufacturing jobs plummeted by more than 40% since the 1950s, service and financial sector jobs more than doubled over the same time period, marking a major shift from a manufacturing to a service economy. This deindustrialization process, in turn, has had widespread ramifications for American workers, including a steep drop in labor union membership, a serious decline in income for the average worker, the growth of

a largely black, urban underclass, a concomitant expansion of two-earner families to try to make up for lost earnings, and a shrinking tax base (Fabricant & Burghardt, 1992; Ginsberg, 1990; U.S. Bureau of the Census, 1992; Wolfe, 1991).

9. The proportion of two-earner families has been growing in the United States (by nearly 15% from 1980 to 1990), whether by necessity to maintain a decent standard of living or by choice as women continue to redefine their roles and status in American society. As a consequence, family patterns of interaction and childrearing have changed greatly. Families spend less time eating and playing together and more time negotiating arrangements to get through the day. With extended families often unavailable to help out, day care for infants and children has become a fast-growing industry, and services for "latch-key" kids have begun to appear, ranging from hot lines to after-school transportation. Social scientists have yet to determine definitively whether the newly required independence for children is a positive or a harmful development or somewhere in between, depending on other factors. In any event, families are frequently no longer the primary provider of basic social protection. As a society, we are more dependent on government, nonprofit associations, and for-profit organizations to meet basic human needs. This means more time spent in negotiations with bureaucratic organizations such as school systems, health maintenance organizations (HMOs), welfare agencies, and employers.

10. American society is in the midst of a rapidly spiraling, totally pervasive, unbounded technological revolution. The widespread increase in the use of computers and other communication equipment for information access, data processing, and communication has electronically (and magically) decreased the space between people, organi-

zations, and communities. In the midst of a reengagement with issues of pluralism and diversity, we are simultaneously becoming a more national community, served by national franchises, shaped by national media, and well on the way to being connected up nationally and internationally by a high-tech information superhighway. Computers are also forcing us to learn new ways of gathering and sorting information and to consider new issues of privacy. In politics, not only do we have television campaigns and sound bites, but we are also on the verge of a new form of participatory democracy with interactive TV, electronic town hall meetings, and home balloting. In business, through computers, modems, and fax machines, we are developing the capacity for home-based production and new cottage industries, as well as for home shopping with electronic payments. In recreation, game simulation is reaching the point of virtual reality, with crossovers to scientific modeling and basic research. No aspect of life in America is unaffected, nor can we predict the short- or long-term implications for the way we live and work.

11. Finally, it is more true than ever that change in America, now and in the future, will be as much a function of global shifts as of internal forces. The local American community cannot escape the effects of extranational policies and practices, whether on jobs and the economy, or military service, or cheaper products, or immigration. American wealth, corporate versatility, and military power make us influential players in a newly evolving political and economic world order, although one in which our once dominant role is modulating. Remote as the idea may seem right now, the development of *planetary* political, social, and economic institutions will be the challenge of the next 1,000 years. The cooperative space station venture between America, Russia, Canada, Japan, and

several other European countries may well be the first step in that direction.

THEORETICAL GUIDES FOR PRACTICE

Taking into consideration the changes going on in the American community and the definition of community presented at the beginning of this chapter, we will consider two theoretical perspectives on the community to guide social work practice: the community as *a social system* and the community as *an arena of conflict*. As social workers become involved in developing new programs and services and redesigning old ones, as they provide community education and client advocacy and help structure support networks, these models suggest the kinds of information, contacts, and activities we should consider in our practice. One additional basic approach to understanding the community also bears brief attention, namely, the community as *people* (Warren, 1978), a sociodemographic view. In proposing these approaches, we are mindful that the literature offers many others, such as the community as a system of interaction (Kaufman, 1959), as a system of human ecology (Fellin, 1987; Poplin, 1979), as shared institutions and values (Warren, 1978), and as an ecology of games (Long, 1958).

The Community as People: A Sociodemographic View

The U.S. Bureau of the Census collects, compiles, and distributes a huge quantity of information about the characteristics of the American people and their activities. The annual *Statistical Abstract of the United States*, for example, contains aggregate information about the numbers of people, births, deaths, homeownership, occupations, income and expenditures, labor force, employment and earnings, health and nutrition, business enterprise, manufacturing, and more. In addition, the Census Bureau disaggregates information by census tract, its smallest spatial unit at the local level. The local municipal or county planning department and local libraries usually have census tract information that reveals a good deal about the composition and character of the local community. Thus one can learn about the ages, nationalities, average income, and educational levels of people in different local areas, for example, and the data are available for comparative purposes across census tracts and municipalities. Comparisons can also be made for geographic areas over time, so that community changes can be examined. Social indicators of the relative well-being of a community can be developed, for example, by tracking crime statistics, infant mortality rates and various other health statistics, and so on. The utility of socio-demographic information for social planning purposes and to understand the community is readily apparent.

The Community as a Social System

The community as a social system is essentially a view of the community as a system of interrelated systems that perform important functions for their members. What differentiates the community as a system from an organization that may also be construed as a system of systems is that a community's subsystems are not rationally organized by a centralized authority and coordinated with each other to achieve a common goal. Even if we think of the American community as a political jurisdiction, like a city with a mayor and a city council, there are important subsystems that are not subject to central control, such as the nonprofit sector or the economic sector where multiple business firms produce and distrib-

ute necessary goods and services. Intentional communities may be conceived to operate more rationally, but these do not typify communities in America.

Following Warren's system analysis of the American community (1978, p. 9), we may view the community as "that combination of social units and systems that perform the major social functions having locality relevance." In other words, *community* means an organization of social activities that provides people with access to the resources they need to live on a day-to-day basis. A community, in this definition, has a locality but no well-defined geographic boundaries. Communities can be loosely compared along the following dimensions: (1) the relative degree of dependence of the community on extracommunity institutions and organizations to perform its locality-relevant functions (autonomy); (2) "the extent to which the service areas of local units (stores, churches, schools, and so on) coincide or fail to coincide"; (3) "the extent of psychological identification with a common locality"; and (4) the relative strength of the relationships between the local units (horizontal pattern) (Warren, 1978, pp. 12, 13).

The critical locality-relevant functions that Warren proposes are:

1. production-distribution-consumption;
2. socialization;
3. social control;
4. social participation; and
5. mutual support.

These functions do not have to be performed by formal organizations; they could be done by informal associations and groups. Also, the same social unit may perform more than one function—for example, a school that provides for socialization and potentially all of the other functions as well, evolving into a total community service center. More important, the units that do provide these functions may have a local physical site but are not necessarily controlled by the members of the community. For example, a supermarket may serve several different communities and belong to a regional or national supermarket chain where decisions are based partly on regional or national interests. A child protective service unit may serve several local neighborhoods, but the number of workers it can hire to meet the need may be controlled by the state's child welfare department.

Production-distribution-consumption functions refer to the process of creating, distributing, and using the basic material goods and services that we require for daily living, especially food, clothing, and shelter. Many different types of organizations and institutions carry out this function. A realty agency may rent housing units, and a local church may build and sponsor housing for the elderly; a department store as well as a consumer coop may sell clothing.

Socialization refers to the process by which individuals learn the knowledge, values, and behavior patterns of the society and its constituent social units. Every social unit—family, group, organization, community—teaches its members, directly and largely indirectly, the information they need to get along. The family and the school are major institutions for socializing children, but socialization is a lifelong process.

Social control refers to the process by which a group obtains its members' compliance with its social roles, norms, and rules. Social control has two aspects: the internal controls developed through socialization and the external controls imposed by the group to ensure conformity. The government, through the authority it exercises, is a major agency of social control. The police department and the sheriff's office are typical local agents of social control. Other important institutions also exercise social control functions, such as the child protective services department and the local school system.

Social participation refers to the process of taking part in the various social groups and organizations to which the community provides access. These include, but are not limited to, the groups that perform the other community functions, whether informal associations or formal organizations. Examples are family and kinship groups, religious organizations, neighborhood associations, social clubs, business firms, and planning bodies. Social interaction is the glue that builds the community and holds it together.

Mutual support refers to the process of caring for the well-being of other members of the local community. Primary groups—family, neighbors, friends—traditionally provide the first line of social support and protection. As communities have become more complex, many secondary groups have developed to also perform these functions, such as governmental, for-profit and nonprofit health and welfare agencies, other proprietary organizations such as insurance companies and daycare centers, and a host of voluntary, nonprofit organizations such as burial societies, credit unions, and child care coops.

If we think of the community as a complex web of interrelated systems or units that perform locality-relevant functions, is there some useful way to conceptualize the relationships among these units? Warren suggests thinking of these relationships along *vertical and horizontal axes*. That is, local units usually have relationships with other local units (horizontal), as well as with extracommunity units (vertical). For example, a local elementary school will usually have relationships with a local PTA, with other elementary and middle schools, possibly with a local health clinic, a local child protective services department, and a group of community service volunteers. At the same time, the elementary school will relate to a city or county school board and a superintendent's office, a citywide school social work department, a state board of education that sets educational standards, and the U.S. Department of Agriculture, which is responsible for providing surplus food for its school breakfast program. Even local families will have both horizontal and vertical ties—for example, to a local church and at the same time culturally to a nationality group of great significance for its values and patterns of relationships.

More formally, the community's *vertical pattern of relationships* is "the structural and functional relation of its various social units and subsystems to extracommunity systems." The community's *horizontal pattern of relationships* is "the structural and functional relation of its various social units and subsystems to each other" (Warren, 1978, pp. 163, 164). As has already been noted, social units have both horizontal and vertical relationships; however, the nature of those relationships tends to be rather different. Horizontal relationships occur among community units at approximately the same hierarchical level, that is, within the local community with similar levels of authority and with a locus of decision-making at that community level. These relations are often informal, personal, and face-to-face. Vertical relationships, by contrast, involve transactions of local community units with extracommunity structures at higher hierarchical levels of authority, such as regional, state, national, or even international bodies. These relations tend to be task-oriented, instrumental, impersonal, and formal.

Warren's main thesis, consistent with the changes in the American community identified earlier, is that communities over the last several decades have shifted along their axes. They have changed from horizontal communities emphasizing primary and holistic relationships and responsibilities to vertical communities based on more explicit social contracts, a greater and more specialized division of labor, and secondary relationships. The local community is where people live and get their basic needs met. But the members of the community have less and less control over the decisions that affect their lives because these decisions are being made by outside institutions whose interests are very different. The local bank, for example, is increasingly unlikely to be owned by local residents; rather, it is probably a branch of a much larger regional or national corporation, whose offices are located across the country and whose decisions are ultimately governed by national and international economic concerns. Similarly, national media, which cannot be easily ignored but whose corporate decisions cannot easily be influenced at a local level, bring potentially uncomfortable values into every household. The results of this shift in orientation are less civic responsibility, greater alienation, greater dependence on but more mistrust in government and large bureaucracies, more fragmented community decision making, and loss of a sense of community. The remedies, in simplified fashion, are more emphasis on community organization and development to foster community citizenship and self-reliance, local social and economic development, and greater community control over significant community institutions (Box 4.2).

The Community as an Arena of Conflict

Viewing the community as a social system has some built-in biases that make it insufficient by itself to serve as a framework for social work practice in the community. The basic bias is that the systems perspective assumes a set of integrated subsystems working together for the benefit of the whole. But what happens when there is disagreement between powerful groups in different sub-

BOX 4.2	BUILDING COMMUNITY

We worked in ever-widening circles and spent many months building relationships and developing the kinds of feelings that are important to getting people to work together.

By trust, I am talking not just about honesty, but respect for each other's intelligence and perceptions. I liken it sometimes to two people sitting on two ends of a long couch facing a window. They see different although overlapping views. It is necessary to develop the kind of trust in each other that when you say to me, "I see a menace outside the window," and I don't see it, I won't say to you, "you must be mistaken," but that I realize that if you say you see that out the window, then it is real. I've got to believe you and help you deal with that menace even though I may not be able to see it,

Source: *Ruth Wolf Rehfeld, a community organizer in a changing neighborhood in Baltimore* (Challenging, 1994).[1]

systems or when the whole and some of its subsystems disagree? We know, for example, that this is often the case when there are minority groups whose fundamental interests are not being acknowledged or taken adequately into account by the majority group. The good of the system as a whole—that is, the inclusive community—does not necessarily mean the good of all of its subsystems. How is the conflict perceived, and how should it be resolved (Warren, 1978)? The perspective of the community as an arena of conflict suggests that conflict and change are characteristic of American communities, and that the process of determining the public interest therefore involves conflict and negotiation as much as it does rational planning, collaboration, and coordination. Whereas issues of power do not seem to enter into the systems perspective, viewing the community as an arena of conflict brings power and politics to the fore. We are forced to ask a variety of questions. What does it mean to say that the community has a collective identity? How do we take into account community differences in values and beliefs, goals, and interests? Does the community have an overriding public interest, and, if so, how is that public interest determined? Who is influential? Is the public interest synonymous with

the interests of the most powerful people in the community? To answer these questions, we must turn to *conceptions of power and power structure.*

Most definitions of power stem from the Weberian notion that power is "the chance of a man or of a number of men to realize their own will in a communal action even against the resistance of others who are participating in the action" (Gerth & Mills, 1958, p. 180). In other words, power is the ability to get what you want when you want it, despite the opposition of other people, and in this case the "you" is a decidedly masculine pronoun. Dennis Wrong's (1979) review of the literature on power through 1979 comes up with a somewhat similar definition, namely, that "power is the capacity of some persons to produce intended and foreseen effects on others" (p. 2). Some social scientists use the term *influence* rather than *power* in order to shade the definition toward the use of persuasion rather than coercion, but the essential concept remains the same. Even for very powerful individuals and groups, however, power is seldom unlimited. Some authors therefore suggest that power can be usefully viewed as a medium of exchange, a commodity that can be invested or consumed depending upon gains or losses (Banfield, 1961).

Jean Baker Miller (1983) offers a more feminist conception of power. She defines power as

> *the capacity to produce a change*—that is, to move anything from point A or state A to point B or state B. This can include even moving one's own thoughts or emotions, sometimes a very powerful act. It can also include acting to create movement in an interpersonal field as well as acting in larger realms such as economic, social, or political arenas. (p. 4)

In this view, fostering another's growth or increasing another's resources, capabilities, and effectiveness to act involve exercises of power. Thus people who perform nurturing, socialization, and educational roles—parents, teachers, social workers—hold and often exercise a great deal of power. This is quite different from a masculine conception of power that often involves limiting or controlling the behavior of others (Box 4.3).

Most theorists also distinguish power from *authority*, along the lines proposed by Max Weber, defining authority as legitimated power. It is power that has been legally or voluntarily granted to the holder of a particular position, such as the CEO of an organization. In the U.S. form of democracy, authority is granted to various elected officials to enact laws, to the executive to carry out the business of the state, and to the courts to interpret, arbitrate, and enforce the laws in a tripartite system of balanced powers. The distinction between authority and power notes that while authority is a form of power, not all persons in authority are powerful and powerful persons exist alongside of authorities in any social system. Other than formal authority, the sources of power are multiple, including access to and control of strategic information, economic resources, connections to other powerful people, charisma, intelligence, wisdom, age, and more.

Finally, some theorists distinguish between *reputed or potential power* and actual power. The argument here is that power does not exist, except potentially, until it is exercised successfully. However, potential power may itself be powerful in that the threat to exercise it may serve to constrain the actions of others. The classic example is the labor union, which has the power to strike. The potential for a strike often acts as a stimulus to negotiation and the resolution of differences. The actual strike, should it occur, is some-

---

BOX 4.3	FACETS OF POWER IN OUR WORK

Power is the ability to control one's own destiny and the ability to form support systems that affect one's life. Power has three dimensions: personal, interpersonal, and political. The work of psychologist Robert White [enhances] an understanding of personal power . . . [He] has suggested that all human beings have a basic drive, which he calls the *effectuance drive*, a drive to experience oneself as a cause, to interact effectively with the environment—in other words, to experience oneself as having power.

Interpersonal power is closely related to personal power because it carries it into the social domain. [Inter]personal power is the ability to influence the human surround, and it is dependent upon social competence, on the ability to interact effectively with others. Political power is the ability to alter systems, to bring about some change in social structure or organization, to redistribute resources.

Source: *Speech excerpts by Ann Hartman, then editor of* Social Work, *from a speech at the University of Iowa, 1990.*

times difficult to sustain and is often costly, so in this case the threat may be more potent than the reality.

Turning now to the matter of public interest, the question of whether there is such a thing as community decisions and who makes them is complicated. The closest we come in our democratic market economy are the public policy processes of our elected governments. Always operating under conditions of resource scarcity, government (or the state, small "s") partially regulates economic, social, and political life, provides social protections and services, and furnishes opportunities for investment and community improvement. Because communities can seldom express a clear and overwhelming public interest and because resources are limited, the public policy process invariably favors some interests over others. The question, though, is: "Does the process always favor the same interests?" Or, stated differently, "Is power distributed unevenly and in such a way that the outcomes of the public policy process are essentially predetermined?"

The literature on power structure, which developed in the 1950s and 1960s in the United States, proposed two principal theories on the distribution of power: *elitism* and *pluralism*. Without identifying current variations at this point, the chief early proponents of elitist theory were Floyd Hunter (1953), William Domhoff (1967, 1974, 1990), and C. Wright Mills (1956). Some of the main early proponents of pluralist theory were Robert Dahl (1961), Edward Banfield (1961), Nelson Polsby (1980), and David Riesman (1951). The essential issues raised by these theories still generate discussion and elaboration.

The gist of *elitist theory* is that community life is dominated by a small group of people with sufficient economic and political power to control public decision making in their own interests. Citizen participation, in this conception, is limited and/or ineffectual.

Still under contention by current theorists are the questions of whether, in fact, an upper-class elite dominates the state, whether this group constitutes a ruling capitalist class, and whether the state has a special position and a logic of its own above the promotion of purely class interests (Domhoff, 1990, p. 14).

Mills (1956) offers a slightly different version of elitism. He contends that the structure of power in the United States resembles a pyramid with three levels (Kornhauser, 1968). At the top is the *power elite*, a group composed of the leaders of (1) giant corporations, (2) the executive branch of the federal government, and (3) the military. This group controls large national and multinational corporations and their corresponding public organizations. They control the means of political power, production, and destruction. They are the men (almost exclusively male and white) who make the big decisions, especially in economic and foreign policy, and they have the power, through the control of dominant institutions, to manipulate public opinion and ensure that the rest of the society accepts their decisions. Although this group is not an economic class in the traditional Marxist sense (membership is not strictly based on the ownership of property), it does share, values, interests, and experiences and does comprise a ruling class. The need for America to project itself as a world power and the absence of competing elites makes this group indisposable. Surrounding this power elite is a circle of people who are advisers, technical experts, powerful politicians, regional and local upper classes, and celebrities, some of whom may be elevated to the top level.

The second tier of the pyramid, at a middle level of power, consists of a variety of special interest groups, such as labor unions, professional associations, and farm organizations, that struggle with modest influence within the parameters established by the power elite. Unorganized mass society falls into the bottom level of the pyramid—the majority of the populace, who have little power over the decision makers at the top and to whom the top leaders send orders, information, and interpretations of events. From an elitist perspective, top leaders determine the fundamental direction of public policy and shape the public interest to coincide with their own general interest.

A number of studies using *reputational methods*, especially Floyd Hunter's (1953) seminal work, have found evidence of an elitist power structure in both smaller and larger communities, although the makeup of these structures does not strictly follow Mills's conception. Numerous studies have also found the members of this group to be related by social class (Domhoff, 1967, 1974, 1990). The reputational method essentially involves asking many people who are in a position to know who they think the top community leaders are. Names that frequently recur are selected as the top leaders. Then, through interviews and further community investigation, the researcher begins to sort out the extent of these leaders' influence, how they exercise power in the community, and their patterns of interaction with each other.

A variation of the reputational approach, the *positional method*, has also been used in studying community power structures. This approach identifies power in terms of the positions that various people hold in the community. Essentially the researcher identifies the major organizations active in the different sectors of community life, then identifies the occupants of the top positions in these organizations, and finally checks for overlap to pinpoint the most powerful individuals (Meenaghan, Washington, & Ryan, 1982).

Pluralist theorists have strongly criticized the elitists along three lines. First, they argue that the basic premise of an ordered system of power in every human institution is faulty. Researchers who begin their studies with the question "Who runs this community"? are asking a loaded question. The question assumes that there is a particular structure of power, and therefore that the researchers are sure to find it. Second, they argue that the power structure is not stable over time, as elitists suggest, but rather is tied to issues that can be transitory or persistent. Therefore the assumption of a stable coalition or set of coalitions in the community is inaccurate. Third, they contend that the elitists wrongly equate reputed (and positional) power with actual power. Power does not exist until it is actually exercised successfully.

In contrast to the elitists, the *pluralists* propose that power is distributed among many different organized groups, with control shifting depending on the issues. Citizens participate in the public policy process through a variety of interest groups. Because individuals potentially have the freedom to organize a group and compete in the policy arena, differences can be resolved amicably. The political system therefore operates much more democratically than the elitists would have us believe, the public interest being whatever comes out of the pluralistic melting pot after the process is completed.

If we compare David Riesman (1951) as a pluralistic thinker with Mills (Kornhauser, 1968), Riesman would argue that the power structure pyramid has only two levels, corresponding roughly to Mills's bottom two tiers. There is no power elite. "The upper level of the Riesman's pyramid consists of 'veto groups': a diversified and balanced body of interest groups" (Kornhauser, 1968, pp. 39–40). Each of these groups mainly wants to protect its own power and prerogatives by blocking the efforts of other competing groups. There is no dominant ruling group. Instead there are multiple power centers, thereby creating a much more amorphous structure of power. The lowest level of the pyramid, as with Mills, consists of an unorganized mass public, but in this case the public is pursued as an ally rather than dominated by interest groups in their struggles for power (Kornhauser, 1968). Therefore pluralist power figures are potentially more responsive and accountable to the majority of citizens than are elitist power holders.

Elitist theories imply that democracy is at best a weak institution or at worst a sham altogether because the public interest is basically determined by a relatively small (though not necessarily conspiratorial) group of powerful leaders. Pluralist theories, such as Riesman's, on the other hand, suggest that the political process is complex and increasingly remote due to the large number of interest groups protecting their turf and struggling for power. Because it is so hard to get anything done, leadership is weakened and political alienation begins to set in. Where an issue involves the community (or the country) as a whole, no individual or group leadership is likely to be very effective due to the presence of entrenched veto groups. Consider, for example, the battles to enact health care legislation during the Clinton administration. For Banfield (1961) this struggle leads to public decision making that is seldom the result of deliberate planning. For Lindblom (1959) it leads to "disjointed incrementalism."

In order to demonstrate how power is exercised in the community and by whom, pluralist theorists turn to the analysis of concrete issues under lively contention (*issue analysis method*). Thus the pluralist researcher goes about the investigation by (1) selecting a number of key as opposed to routine political decisions to study; (2) identifying the people who took an active part in the decision-making process; (3) obtaining an ac-

count of their actual behavior while the policy conflict was being settled; and (4) analyzing the outcomes of the conflict to determine who won.

There are several lines of criticism of the pluralistic approach. One main criticism is that the pluralists present a rather idealized version of the political process. Since interest groups cannot be easily organized and sustained without many resources, a large part of the community cannot participate. Furthermore, the notion that the pluralist process operates amicably and effectively by a set of institutionalized political rules does not conform to the experience of challenging groups who have succeeded primarily by using norm-violating, disruptive tactics (Gamson, 1990).

Another main line of criticism is that pluralist theory does not recognize a hidden face of power (Bachrach & Baratz, 1962, 1963, 1970). That is, by assuming that power is played out solely in relation to concrete issues, pluralists omit the possibility that in any given community there may be a group capable of preventing contests from arising on issues that it considers important. Power may well be at work in maintaining the directions of current policy, limiting the parameters of public discourse to fairly safe issues—in short, preventing some items from ever reaching the community agenda and becoming issues. Moreover, since the pluralist methodology offers no criteria for adequately distinguishing between routine and key political decisions, by accepting the idea that in any community there are significant, visible issues, the researcher is only accepting what are *reputed* to be issues. Hence the pluralists are guilty of the same criticism they level at the elitists.

Although both elitist and pluralist theories talk about groups in the political policy process, most of the early theories tended to focus on powerful individuals rather than powerful organizations. But if power is exercised over large and heterogeneous areas of community life, it would seem that no small group of persons could command enough personal resources to be able to influence the outcome of a range of issues. In keeping with the tremendous growth of powerful corporations in American society and their need to maintain a stable business market, and consistent with the growing power of government in American life, recent power structure theorists have focused on networks of organizations as sources of widespread and enduring power (Perruci & Pilisuk, 1970; Perrucci & Potter, 1989). Through such arrangements as interlocking boards of directors and government–corporation executive exchanges, Interorganizational (IO) leaders can mobilize the resources of a network of organizations (including governmental units) to influence the public policy agenda. These sorts of IO arrangements operate as much at the local level as they do at state and national levels. In the final analysis, it is not so much the specific persons who occupy the organizational linking roles (the persons change) as it is the shape of the IO network that represents the enduring structure of power in the community.

Mediating Structures and Community-Sensitive Social Work Practice

This chapter has suggested that there is value in strengthening the local community in the face of an onslaught from larger forces outside of its control. But since community is an elusive concept, just what is it that we should be strengthening? Berger and Neuhaus (1977) propose that we focus on mediating structures, which have great value for empowering ordinary people.

Mediating structures are "those institutions standing between individuals in their private lives and the larger institutions of public life" (Berger and Neuhaus, 1977, p. 2). The main public institutions that order modern life are the state and its huge public bureaucracies—education, health, welfare—as well as major corporations and big labor. Mediating structures include family, churches, schools, neighborhoods, and a host of voluntary associations, such as social service agencies, labor unions, advocacy groups, support groups, credit unions, and cultural groups. Mediating structures help people relate to and gain protection from the large, impersonal institutions of public life. They generate and maintain community values, a function that would be filled by megastructures in the absence of mediating agencies. They foster participatory democracy and in the process empower people by helping them gain more control over their lives. Collectively people live their public lives through mediating structures. Without them the individual is relatively powerless compared to the megastructures of government and commerce.

Mediating structures need the same degree of continuity as megastructures. However, care must be taken to maintain their personal quality and scale, for as mediating structures develop over time, they themselves risk becoming impersonal and imposing hierarchies, like labor unions, political parties, and large voluntary associations.

Berger and Neuhaus (1977) argue that "public policy should protect and foster mediating structures and wherever possible, public policy should utilize mediating structures for the realization of social purposes" (p. 6). In general, we support these propositions. But neither of them is simple to fulfill. As always, we have to find a balance between individual rights and community rights and between the protective functions of the state and the defensive functions of the mediating structures. It is easy to imagine, for example, that some public social services might be better received and more effectively utilized if local religious and voluntary associations were involved in the service delivery. We already have good examples of community-based psychosocial programs and living arrangements for former mental patients and retarded citizens. The latter, however, developed largely because the state, under pressure from legal rights organizations, deinstitutionalized its mental health facilities and enforced fair-housing laws, to the chagrin of many local neighborhood leaders. It is also harder to decide whether a neighborhood is right in preventing a church-sponsored homeless shelter from locating in its midst. We can say, though, that the community has a legitimate claim to being involved in the location decision. A fair process is at least a step toward democratic decision making.

It is also not hard to imagine that mediating structures themselves, due to size and patterns of decision making that are not truly participatory, may have difficulty building a strong sense of community among their participants. In a recent study of the black community in Baltimore, Harold McDougall (1993) made a potent argument for the need for even smaller, informal community building blocks called *base communities*.

> Mediating institutions, such as churches, schools, and community organizations, are essential to this task [of community strengthening, institution building, and networking], but small base communities of one or two dozen people, spun off from mediating institutions or growing independently, are essential to counterbalance the tendency of mediating institutions to mirror the hierarchical character of the public and private bureaucracies with which they contend. (pp. 186–187)

CONCLUSION

The assumption of this chapter has been that for social workers to be effective, we need to understand how community affects the lives of the people we work with, ourselves included. While we are all touched by regional and national developments beyond our immediate control, we live and work and play in multiple, overlapping local communities of different kinds. These communities are often culturally diverse and potentially quite different from the communities where we ourselves grew up and now live. The importance of community calls for a community-based social work practice, which is re-emerging in many current practice settings (see Chapter 14). Some examples of how community may bear on practice will help clarify this idea.

Consider the social worker employed by a church-sponsored nonprofit social work agency. In her practice she has begun to see more and more clients who are HIV positive or who have AIDS. How should she deal with this problem? Suppose that the church has strong anti-gay sentiments and sees AIDS as a gay problem. Suppose that the church reflects values that are prevalent in the community. What kinds of services can be provided for these new clients? How do the clients themselves feel about their circumstances, given the community's values? What kinds of services are needed in the community? How might the social worker begin to address that need? (Obviously many other kinds of problems might raise similar questions, such as homelessness, substance abuse, and teenage pregnancy.)

To take another example, suppose that you are a school social worker and you have encountered a child who appears to have been abused. You are obligated to involve Child Protective Services (CPS). Do you need to know how the community views CPS workers or the nature of the relationship between the school and the community? How will the situation be handled if the police become involved? How do the school authorities feel about CPS and potential disruptions of the school day? How would you approach the family and the child? How can you get CPS to work with you to manage the situation in the most helpful fashion for all parties involved?

To take a third example, suppose that you are a social worker with the department of family medicine of a large university hospital. You suspect that the children in the family you are seeing have been poisoned by lead paint from their substandard apartment house. How can you prevent further damage? What about the children who live in other units in that building? Might there be legal or political issues that you should know about? What are some of the different professional roles you might have to play to help your clients and their neighbors?

There are no simple answers to the questions posed in all of these illustrations. Hopefully this book contains enough information to show the reader a way of proceeding.

Discussion Exercises

1. How have vertical and horizontal changes in community functions affected social work practice? Give examples.

2. Select a client and describe the institutions and organizations in that client's life that are used to fulfill the five locality-relevant functions. How much do the organizations coincide in terms of service areas? What is the locus of decision making for the organizations? Repeat the exercise for yourself. How many of the structures are the same for yourself as for your client.

3. In a small group discussion, consider the examples and questions posed in the Conclusion and try to answer them. Identify the role of mediating structures in your answer.

4. Identify an issue in your community relevant to the provision of social services and try to follow it through a public policy process. Identify the stakeholders for various sides and facets of the issue. What is the role of the media in this process? Of elected officials? Of public agency representatives? Of leaders from voluntary associations? Of corporate leaders? Is the process democratic? Who has power? Who is left out? Is there a "hidden face of power" influencing the process?

Note

1. Ruth Rehfeld worked for many years as a community organizer and director of the Northwest Baltimore Corporation in Baltimore, Maryland. She was interviewed for *Challenging* by Michael K. Oppenheim, a graduate student at the University of Maryland, School of Social Work, on April 21, 1993.

References

Bachrach, P., & Baratz, M. S. (1962). The two faces of power. *American Political Science Review, 56,* 947–952.

Bachrach, P., & Baratz, M. S. (1963). Decisions and nondecisions: An analytical framework. *American Political Science Review, 57,* 641–651.

Bachrach, P., & Baratz, M. S. (1970). *Power and poverty: Theory and practice.* New York: Oxford University.

Banfield, E. (1961). *Political influence.* New York: Free Press.

Bellah, R. N., Madsen, R., Sullivan, W. M., Swidler, A., & Tipton, S. M. (1985). *Habits of the heart: Individualism and commitment in American life.* Berkeley: University of California Press.

Berger, P. L., & Neuhaus, R. J. (1977). *To empower people: The role of mediating structures in public policy.* Washington, DC: American Enterprise Institute.

Challenging. (1994). *Interviews with advocates and activists. University of Maryland at Baltimore, School of Social Work.* Monograph, ed. by P. Powers.

Dahl, R. A. (1961). *Who governs?* New Haven, CT: Yale University Press.

Domhoff, W. G. (1967). *Who rules America?* Englewood Cliffs, NJ: Prentice-Hall.

Domhoff, W. G. (1974). *The Bohemian Grove and other retreats.* New York: Harper and Row.

Domhoff, W. G. (1990). *The power elite and the state: How policy is made in America.* New York: Aldine de Gruyter.

Etzioni, A. (1993). *The spirit of community: Rights, responsibilities, and the communitarian agenda.* New York: Crown.

Fabricant, M. B., & Burghardt, S. (1992). *The welfare state crisis and the transformation of social service work.* Armonk, NY: M. E. Sharpe.

Fellin, P. (1987). *The community and the social worker.* Itasca, IL: F. E. Peacock.

Gamson, W. (1990). *The strategy of social protest.* Belmont, CA: Wadsworth.

Gerth, H. H., & Mills, C. W. (1958). *From Max Weber: Essays in sociology.* New York: Oxford University.

Ginsberg, L. (1990). Selected statistical review. *Supplement, Encyclopedia of social work* (18th ed., pp. 283–285). Silver Spring, MD: National Association of Social Workers.

Hartman, A. (1990). Transcript of a speech (unpublished). University of Iowa.

Heilbroner, R. L. (1960). *The future as history.* New York: Harper Torchbooks.

Hillery, G. A., Jr. (1955, June). Definition of community: Areas of agreement. *Rural Sociology, 20,* 111–123.

Hunter, F. (1953). *Community power structure.* Chapel Hill: University of North Carolina Press.

Kaufman, H. F. (1959). Toward an interactional conception of community. *Social Forces, 38*(1), 9–17.

Kornhauser, W. (1968). "Power elite" or "veto groups"? In W. G. Domhoff & H. B. Ballard (Eds.), *C. Wright Mills and the power elite* (pp. 37–59). Boston: Beacon Press.

Lappe, F. M., & Du Bois, P. M. (1994). *The quickening of America: Rebuilding our nation, reworking our lives.* San Francisco: Jossey-Bass.

Lindblom, C. E. (1959). The science of "muddling through." *Public Administration Review, 19,* 79–88.

Long, N. E. (1958). The local community as an ecology of games. *American Journal of Sociology, 64,* 251–261.

Massey, D. S. (1994). America's apartheid and the urban underclass. *Social Service Review, 68*(4), 471–487.

McDougall, H. A. (1993). *Black Baltimore: A new theory of community.* Philadelphia: Temple University Press.

Meenaghan, T. M., Washington, R. O., & Ryan, R. M. (1981). *Macro practice in the human services.* New York: Free Press.

Miller, J. B. (1983). Women and power. *Social Policy, 13*(4), 3–6.

Mills, C. W. (1956). *The power elite.* New York: Oxford University Press.

Pampel, F. C., & Adams, P. (1992). The effects of demographic change and political structure on family allowance expenditures. *Social Service Review, 66*(4), 524–546.

Perrucci, R., & Pilisuk, M. (1970). Leaders and ruling elites: The interorganizational bases of community power. *American Sociological Review, 35,* 1040–1057.

Perrucci, R., & Potter, H. R. (Eds.). (1989). *Networks of power: Organizational actors at the national, corporate, and community levels.* New York: Aldine de Gruyter.

Polsby, N. (1980). *Community power and political theory*. New Haven, CT: Yale University Press.

Poplin, D. E. (1979). *Communities: A survey of theories and methods of research*. New York: Macmillan.

Riesman, D., Denny, R., & Glazer, N. (1951). *The lonely crowd*. New Haven, CT: Yale University Press.

Twomey, S. (1995, June 19). Mr. Birthday makes his rounds. *The Washington Post*, p. B1.

U.S. Bureau of the Census. (1992). *Statistical abstract of the United States* (112th ed.). Washington, DC: U.S. Department of Commerce, Bureau of the Census.

Warren, R. L. (1978). *The community in America*. Chicago: Rand McNally.

Wolfe, A. (Ed.). (1991). *America at century's end*. Berkeley: University of California Press.

Wrong, D. H. (1979). *Power: Its forms, bases, and uses*. New York: Harper Colophon Books.

Zukin, S. (1991). The hollow center: U.S. cities in the global era. In A. Wolfe (Ed.), *America at century's end* (pp. 245–261). Berkeley: University of California Press.

Part
II

COMMUNITY PRACTICE SKILLS FOR SOCIAL WORKERS: USING THE SOCIAL ENVIRONMENT

chapter

5

Discovering and Documenting the Life of a Community

The "inner life" of communities is bubbling away all the time.

J. ARMSTRONG AND P. HENDERSON (1992, P. 189)

One of our psychiatrists was wandering about the neighborhood one day in order to become better acquainted with it and to explore what sort of crises and problems our neighborhood program must be prepared to serve beyond those we already anticipated. . . .

E. H. AUERSWALD (1968, P. 207)

No matter what their position, social workers must reckon with their communities. This can be as enjoyable as discovering their communities while documenting information needed to be more effective with clients—as employees of a neighborhood health service in a disadvantaged community (Auerswald, 1968, p. 206), like the aforementioned psychiatrist, or as professionals in family agencies. This chapter situates the community concept in interdisciplinary and human ser-

vices contexts, describes four ways that communities are often studied, and gives practitioners guidance on conducting and finding complete or mini versions of such studies.

A community's size and location help shape the form that problems take and the response to them. In a rural town, the current concern of the planning board may be whether sidewalks should be added downtown. In a rural area, local law enforcement's announced anti-drug program may consist of asking residents to write down the names of suspected users and dealers and sliding the paper under the town hall door (R. V. Demaree, personal communication, January 2, 1995). Such details are as important for those servicing that area to know as the formal plans of a big county or the dozen drug programs coordinated by a city.

MULTIDISCIPLINARY APPROACHES

Many facets of *place* (shared territory) and *nonplace* (other common ties) communities have been explored in ways that practitioners can build on. In its most sweeping terms, the *status* of community in contemporary life has been closely examined,[1] with themes emerging such as "community lost," "community saved," and, more recently, "community liberated," that is, from a focus only on neighborhood (Wellman & Leighton, 1979). For instance, in *The Eclipse of Community*, Stein (1972)—reviewing anthropological, psychoanalytic, and sociological perspectives on modern community—makes a distinction that is relevant to our concerns between "generalized social processes and their concrete embodiments in specific communities" (p. 6). As professionals, we must be familiar with social processes and factors[2] affecting community life. We want to "know why" (Henderson & Thomas, 1987, p. 25).

However, the ability to spot and contend with the embodiment of social processes in particular places is of more practical importance to social work. An excellent example from community development pertains to the embodiment of racism in a Bristol, England, neighborhood. A changing neighborhood composition led to the challenge of integrating elderly Asian and black persons into a resistant all-white community center. Discrimination had to be confronted by community workers (Gilchrist, 1992). Com-

munities as an abstraction or entity subjected to social forces and national trends constitute one focus of study; individual communities in all their variety constitute another.

Particular communities—of many sizes —as well as their inhabitants or members and neighborhoods have been scrutinized and portrayed in creative ways by many disciplines through case studies, investigative research, studies of influentials and decision makers, and other approaches. The explorations range from longitudinal and broad studies to short-term, focused studies of a block, a senior center, or the comprehensive needs of a scattered population. Some are deliberately inclusive, while others examine limited facets of community such as power, architecture, or attitudes. Approaches have included *autobiography* (Addams, 1910), *social history* (Davis, 1992; Duberman, 1972), *planning critiques and frameworks* (Goodman & Goodman, 1947), *sociological descriptive studies* (Lynd & Lynd, 1929), *sociological explorations of specific phenomenon such as disaster* (Erikson, 1976), *political science empirical regional studies* (Gaventa, 1980), and *ethnographies with a concentration on particular populations* (Edgerton, 1967; Liebow, 1967; Myerhoff, 1980). Such studies help us know about community (Henderson & Thomas, 1987, p. 25).

Practical and prosaic reasons also lead to analysis of community, such as using the concept politically, engaging citizens, or naming and classifying geographic areas. Examples from politics, social work, and social demography illustrate these pursuits.

At a *policy* level, "community" and "grass roots" have had a certain currency; they have become buzz words in *politics* and have been of interest to the ideological left and right.[3] However, they seem to have generated more rhetoric and slogans than original methodologies and objective, systematic academic study. For instance, think of community enterprise and empowerment zones, community control and participation, and community partnerships.

Social work brings *citizen involvement and participation emphasis* (Gamble & Weil, 1995), with a strategies perspective, to the investigation of community.[4] Our scholars often study community in order to generate or cope with social change and, hence, bring an *action* perspective. Social work contributions to the literature on community are frequently process oriented, "how-to" works (Mondros & Wilson, 1994), such as how to build capacity.

- One aspect of process-oriented works is how to meet the needs of individuals and families by understanding their environment more clearly. "Communities have lives of their own," point out Henderson and Thomas (1987), who add, "Social workers have to recognize this [complexity], not keep it at a distance with a passing nod of recognition" (p. 8). Social workers might write about how to best provide community-based services or how to form community-based teams, taking such differences into consideration.

- Another aspect is how to help people organize and "take action for the benefit of a wider constituency" (Henderson & Thomas, 1987, p. 7). Social work has contributed books and articles on how to organize and mobilize—as well as plan for/with—large numbers of people. (see Chapter 12).

- A third aspect concerns how to size up and study a community. Bracht and Kingsbury (1990), for example, suggest stages of organizing in communities, the first of which is community analysis—the focus of this chapter (p. 74).

Social work literature offers intervention ideas. Henderson and Thomas (1987) note a craving for "know how" materials ranging from how to enter and get to know an area through how to leave the locale (p. 26).

Before we can act, we must figure out the right level of intervention. Therefore, we want to have a sense of the geographic areas, regions, districts, catchment areas, or blocks served by our organizations and agencies, which are the contexts for our work and/or the lives of our members or service users. To obtain and best use the many documents available to us, we must utilize *sociodemographic* reports and master Census Bureau terms such as *metropolitan*, *nonmetropolitan*, *urban*, *rural*, and *urbanized area*.

In summary, to study the phenomenon called community, we should read widely and learn the lingo of multiple fields. In a social work context, Fellin (1995) provides an in-depth discussion and definition of community and neighborhood. While community was defined formally in Chapters 1 and 4 of this text, here we can distinguish between communities and neighborhoods informally: *community* suggests people with social ties who at least partially share an identity and a social system, while *neighborhood* suggests places where face-to-face relationships are feasible.[5] However, since they can overlap, the two terms are often used interchangeably in social work.

Learning about communities and engaging in a communitywide study or an in-depth study in one sector are intellectual challenges. However, as the rest of this chapter will show, it is also a satisfying challenge.

FOUR TYPES OF COMMUNITY STUDIES

This next section presents four types of community studies—two broad and two narrow—and the relevant history, values, variables, and methodologies associated with each. Since social workers may well end up conducting or contributing to one of these studies, we also cover the broad topic areas usually included, distinct knowledge sought, and available sources.

From among many varieties of broad community studies, we will consider the (1) *fieldwork study* (original research), (2) *community power structure study* (original research, compared with a previous study of community power if available), (3) *community analysis study* (secondary sources plus original data from informal interviews and observation), and (4) *problems and services study* (secondary sources plus input from meetings, interaction with service providers and users, and surveys). All of these studies help us learn more about community settings, structures, processes, and functions.

Sociologists, anthropologists, and political scientists favor the first two studies, which focus on geographic area or place communities; elements of both are utilized by social workers as well. Journalists appreciate the third study because it provides useful information for a broad audience. The last two varieties, which permit investigation of a place or nonplace community, are commonly used by social workers. In fact, social workers sometimes move too swiftly into the fourth type of exploration. Readers may be more familiar with problems and services studies than with the other three types, but keeping an open mind and paying close attention to all four options permits us to make more informed judgments about applicability.

Learning about community studies will assuredly be helpful to macro practitioners and organizers, who will likely *initiate* comparable projects. Those in direct service are more likely to *help* with such studies, but they still need to be familiar with all the ways to learn more about who and what is out there in their localities. Practitioners should inquire whether such community studies have

been completed by others and are available locally. Such knowledge can be useful in situations like these:

- In the hospital outpatient clinic where he works, Jason notices that different health beliefs create communication problems between staff and patients. He wonders if anyone has studied the culture of the immigrant patients or made meaningful contacts in the surrounding neighborhoods, and he decides to seek out field studies that can help inform the work of his department (Daley & Wong, 1994; Mowry, 1994).

- Elsa heads an interagency project to recruit and train spouses of local corporate leaders to be board members for service and advocacy organizations ranging from mentoring programs to food kitchens. She wonders how to attain the names of such people and hopes that someone has already done a community power structure study.

- Chandra is to supervise two AmeriCorps volunteers (Brown, 1993), from another area and with no rural experience, assigned for a year to her outreach agency. She will find out if any type of community profile has been completed—say, for a grant application. Otherwise she and the volunteers might do a community analysis together to give them an overview so that they can be of more use much sooner.

- A church in a working-class neighborhood proposes to start an after-school program. The minister calls Charlie's child welfare department for advice. Delegated to work with the church, Charlie wants to track down recent studies about current/needed neighborhood services.

Since we believe students and practitioners benefit from experiential as well as intellectual understanding, we have also included a number of suggested ways to appraise your area firsthand. There is an old expression about people being from many "walks of life." We want you to come to appreciate your community in all the diversity that this phrase implies, not just as an abstract system, and to understand what holds it together.

Community Field Studies

DEFINITION

A community field study is a case study with a holistic perspective that uses methods such as informal interviewing and observation to describe from firsthand acquaintance a particular locality, culture, or network. Out of a concern with society and with individual identity, the investigator interacts face-to-face with a group of people (informants) over time in order to understand life from their perspective.

HISTORY

Such studies are closely linked with an interest in being "where the action is" and a willingness to meet people where they are in both a geographic and cultural sense. To illustrate, the purpose may be to record and interpret "lower class life of ordinary people, on their grounds and on their terms" (Liebow, 1967, p. 10) or to study the "network of relationships that make up [the] general human surround" (Erikson, 1976, p. 187). Field study trailblazer Robert Park's broad background familiarized him with many aspects of city life. He believed his "tramping about" helped him gain "a conception of the city, the community and the region, not as a geographical phenomenon merely but as a kind of social organism" (Bulmer, 1984, p. 90).[6]

The first such studies conducted in Chicago employed a multimethod approach, using newspapers as a source to study "certain types of public behavior" and using participant observation—"following Park's injunction to get the seat of one's pants dirty with *real* research" (Bulmer, 1984, p. 108). These sociologists valued the subjects or informants and their environment and attempted to explain each to outsiders, which is one way social workers employ such studies today. Along with the *Middletown* study by Robert and Helen Lynd (1929) and the *Street Corner Society* study in 1943 by William Foote Whyte (1993), the Chicago studies set parameters for the in-depth study of a community, neighborhood, or sector of the population (Ritzer 1992; Stein, 1972). While the Lynds studied people in general in Muncie, Indiana, plus the leading family in town, Whyte looked at particular people and situations and the social structure of an Italian slum.

TERMINOLOGY

The anthropological field study approach—which we connect with scholars like Margaret Mead—has been of interest lately, in part because of its effectiveness in making us aware of our own ethnocentrism and cognizant of the logic and wholeness of others' cultural perspectives (Spradley & McCurdy, 1972, p. vii). This approach of experiencing another culture, or racial/ethnic/age group, from its own viewpoint is labeled *ethnography* (cultural description). It also uses participant observation methods. Elliot Liebow (1967) and James Spradley and David McCurdy (1972) pioneered in applying methods originally used in places outside our borders to groups within our nation. The goal is to acquire exhaustive knowledge of a group—its inner experience. Recent studies of relevance include one on the homeless as a community (Wagner, 1993), another on a continuing-care retirement community (Dorfman, 1994), and a shorter one about social workers—professional and eligibility workers—and unions (Burton, 1991). Social workers and nurses, as well as anthropologists, conduct ethnographies today (Brandriet, 1994). Rachelle Dorfman, for example, is a clinical social worker specializing in gerontology who included an examination of psychotherapy with the elderly as part of her community study. She moved into the retirement community she studied for 3 months (*immersion*).

Sometimes such qualitative work is referred to as *naturalistic inquiry* (Rodwell, 1987), and sometimes grounded theory is used instead of ethnographic theory (Brandriet, 1994). Regardless of the label, these approaches to field studies entail a humanistic approach and an empathetic stance, as advocated by Emilia Martinez-Brawley (1990):

> Practitioners need to understand the tangible and intangible factors that shape the character of their communities. They need to be skilled applied ethnographers . . . able to see the world and assess its problems as members of their constituencies would, not necessarily to agree with them, but to define clearly the practitioner's point of view in the sociocultural mosaic. (p. 13)

METHODOLOGY

Those who study the community this way have willingly shared their methods (e.g., listening, keeping careful notes on details of daily life, and forming relationships with insiders). While any member or resident is a potential informant, this method relies on those willing to initiate us into their world. Green (1995) calls them "cultural guides" (p. 102). *Key respondents or informants* are well-positioned insiders who can and will act as interpreters for the outsider. Not necessarily indigenous or elected leaders or professional observers such as newspaper reporters, they may be amateur historians, people with con-

nections, or "networkers" who do everything from matchmaking to transporting people to vote. If we can establish a working relationship with key informants, they are potentially valuable because they can "act as . . . de facto observer[s] for the investigator; provide a unique inside perspective on events . . . serve as a 'sounding board' for insights, propositions, and hypotheses developed by the investigator; open otherwise closed doors and avenues to situations and persons" (Denzin, 1970, p. 202). They sometimes read and comment on a draft study report to help maintain insider input.

According to Whyte (1993), the first question his key informant Doc asked him was: "Do you want to see the high life or the low life?" (p. 291).[7] Social workers familiarizing themselves with a place should ask to see both facets of the community, for they need to understand both the X-rated moviegoer and the churchgoer. We need to keep in mind that one common insider reaction is to put a good face on things and another is to try to deliberately "freak out" the outsider. If we begin to understand a culture well enough, we can interpret aspects of it for others. Circumstances often require social workers to make a case for client or citizen participation in decision making or for hiring a paraprofessional from the community. The more we understand and can convey the worldview of another class or culture, the more logical it will seem to have that viewpoint represented. Social workers are also asked to explain the behavior of community residents. Since we want to do so from their perspective as much as possible, it is helpful if we learn to write what has been called *thick description*.[8]

EXAMPLES

To illustrate field studies and give the flavor of the study process, we look at the physical and social worlds of two groups as depicted by a planner and an anthropologist. They describe their first looks at a place and a people and the means they used to conduct their studies. Joseph Howell, the planner, portrays life on an urban block he calls Clay Street. His study of the blue-collar community opens with a long list of details he noticed including

> old cars jacked up on cinder blocks . . . the number of dogs and "beware of dogs" signs . . . the chain link fences . . . the small gardens . . . old folks rocking on their porches . . . a few old, shabby houses, with excessive amounts of debris and junk out front—old toys, bedsprings, tires, and old cars. In one of these houses lived the Shackelfords. . . . (1973, p. 8)

Later, documenting lifestyles, Howell discusses this family's relationship with helpers. He noted that on April 20

> Bobbi had her first visit from the caseworker. When she had been notified that the caseworker was coming to visit, she became very excited. She spent the preceding day cleaning and straightening the house, and when the caseworker arrived, Bobbi was ready. Everything was picked up and the house was very clean. (pp. 125–126)

As these two excerpts show, behavior and values are revealed to be complex. We cannot presume or assume after seeing one piece of the picture, like the yard. Howell assesses coping patterns and, eschewing stereotyping, distinguishes between "hard living" and "settled living" residents. He lets us hear directly from those in the area through reconstructed scenes and dialogue, which makes us care about those on the street. Such an orientation to a particular place makes us curious, rather than judgmental, about the Shackelford family and their "intense, episodic, and uninhibited" ap-

proach to life (p. 6). Thus, one purpose of a community study has been achieved—to highlight the lifeways and values of a group. Of special interest to us, this study pinpoints how family "events, crises and problems" can "fall outside the orbit of community service systems and how service systems are often insensitive to life situations of those they seek to serve" (p. xi). This represents a different way of examining service adequacy. Field studies demonstrate that knowing more completely even a few families helps us better understand a community.

Barbara Myerhoff, the anthropologist, studied a community within a community— a neighborhood in Venice, California, populated with Eastern European Jewish immigrants, many concentration camp survivors of advanced age. The focal point for the residents was the cultural community connected with a senior citizen center which she introduces by noting that "the front window was entirely covered by hand-lettered signs in Yiddish and English announcing current events" (Myerhoff, 1980, pp.12–13; see next page).

Rather than looking at a community in terms of demographics or 5-year plans, we look through the eyes of particular individuals. The words of encouragement on the signs say a good deal about those being beckoned. Social workers can use this method too and learn by looking at details that accrue to become the physical environment and cultural life of those with whom they work.

Regarding methodology, Howell (1973) believes that participant observation consists of making friends, being where the action is, writing it all down, and pulling it all together.

> I had three things going for me. I lived in the neighborhood. I had a southern accent, and I had a family. . . . The approach I decided to follow consisted of . . . involvement with families on my block and . . . with com-

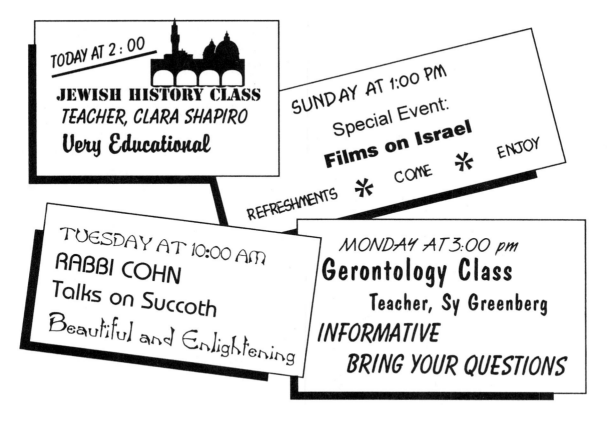

munity groups and community activities. (pp. 367, 372)

Like Howell, Myerhoff (1980) worked with individuals and an area. She knew 80 center members and spent time with 36. She describes her method, with the reminder that there is no definitive way to "cut up the pie of social reality."

> I tape recorded extensive interviews ... ranging from two to sixteen hours, visited nearly all in their homes, took trips with them from time to time outside the neighborhood—to doctors, social workers, shopping, funerals, visiting their friends in old age homes and hospitals. ... I concentrated on the Center and its external extensions, the benches, boardwalk, and hotel and apartment lobbies where they congregated. (p. 29)

Immersed in their lives, Myerhoff spent time in nursing homes and hospitals and at funerals or memorial services. She probed for their viewpoint, asking questions such as "Do you think that being a Jew makes the life of a retired person easier or harder in any way?" Box 5.1 gives typical field study questions.

Howell and Myerhoff focus more on interpersonal ties and solidarity sentiments and activities than on locality (Wellman & Leighton, 1979); both use key informants (Warren & Warren, 1984). This naturalistic inquiry "does not assume the separation between the observer and the observed" (Rodwell, 1987, p. 238). We are learners, not experts coming in; we and our informants will share, affecting each other and the process, so there is emphasis on interchange,

BOX 5.1	REPRESENTATIVE QUESTIONS FOR FIELD STUDIES

- Would you show me around your _____ (town, neighborhood, school)?
- Tell me about your typical day.
- What do you mean? (as a response)
- What's the best way around here to do so and so? (rent a cheap room, get a free meal, a truck, a _____)

- What kind of neighborhood would you say this is?
- If I needed a _____ (passport, green card, a box at the opera), what would I have to do to get one?
- Describe the sort of things I shouldn't do at this meeting.

"mutual learning," and "respect" (Daley & Wong, 1994, p. 18).

APPLICATIONS TO OUR OWN WORK

Inquiry conducted in a natural setting introduces us to groups and individuals who help us see the larger context of our practice and life in subcommunities with new eyes. The experience teaches us how to avoid being irrelevant or condescending. Such studies may assist us in speaking the same language as our involuntary clients or give us a clearer sense of their worlds. They allow us to see the lack of fit between one of our clients and his or her culture. Abbreviated versions of such studies may be appropriate in work with marginalized populations or before doing outreach to new communities. Because social scientists are more likely to conduct surveys to learn about community ideas, even modest face-to-face studies can be a valuable counterbalance. Few of us can move into a neighborhood or retirement community or spend years hanging around a service center, but faster ways exist to enhance our understanding of neighbors, fellow citizens, and service users. We can seek out anyone who has conducted such studies in our area and ask for a briefing. We can borrow from field methods, such as observation, listening, and ethnographic interviewing, and embrace accepting attitudes. Those of us working in

agencies outside of our own neighborhoods can peek around the corner and develop our own impressions (not necessarily the conventional wisdom) of the agency environs, even if we cannot move into the neighborhood or the local homeless shelter. We can get to know local residents on our staff, where we eat lunch, or at our parking lots or bus stops. We can become more a part of our clients' lives. Social workers already deeply involved in low-income areas and fully conversant with their subcultures can move in the other direction and meet a cluster of higher-income community residents.

When we develop a deep understanding of communities, we bring fresh insights to counseling, case management, and other interactions. More important, engaging in such studies makes us want to keep working, to do more, because the rich pastiche we discover is so intriguing and the individuals we meet are so reassuring (Box 5.2).

Community Power Structure Studies

DEFINITION

If field studies give us the essence and variety of a community, power studies help us identify those who exert influence, "can produce intended effects," and affect community decision making in the political, economic, or communications sphere (Dye,

BOX 5.2	TRAMPING ABOUT—A COMMUNITY WALK, DRIVE, JAUNT

The goals are to discover people, places, and rituals, build relationships with informants, and talk with persons often avoided. Exploring alleys and byways on foot or bicycle takes time, but main thoroughfares can be covered in several hours; stroll through an area again and again. *Learn* via speaking with, sitting with, and accompanying those encountered: mail carriers, shopkeepers, delivery drivers, individuals sitting on stoops. Ask them about their communities; listen to the tales. What generalizations do residents make about themselves? Learn their names. Traffic court, public benefit office waiting rooms, and blood banks can be used for resting and observing. Riding the subway in new directions makes sense; riding a bus provides an opportunity to ask passengers natural questions; someone in a wheelchair might take an excursion through a barrier-free retirement community, spending time with many residents.

Write-ups of such outings (*field notes*) include particulars, observations, inferences and might start as follows:

I live in a popular neighborhood. When I take my child to day care, I walk past Rafael's Cuban restaurant—supposedly owned by militant exiles (scuttlebutt says its neon sign was used years ago to signal clandestine meetings), the grocery store, the apartment building with the circular drive, and the park. When we walk home at 6, I always notice which parents and children are at the playground. In the mornings, I've noticed three men in the opposite corner of the park. Maybe I am seeing in new ways, because recently I observed them washing in the fountain and today I realized that they are living in the park.

1993, p. 4). A community power structure study—using surveys, interviews, and library investigation methods—explores the configuration and dynamics of the system of influence at the local level and the characteristics of dominant individuals; it results in a list of names and rankings of persons who are perceived to exercise power in the locality where they live or work. As discussed earlier, this power may be exercised by a small circle or by different and sometimes competing blocs or interest groups.

HISTORY

The beginning of the *community power structure* study as a methodology is usually linked to a 1953 book of that title by Floyd Hunter, a social worker in Atlanta. Critical of Hunter's approach, in 1961 Robert Dahl, a political scientist, did a famous study of the role of power in community decision making in New Haven. These pioneering books came up with different models of local power systems or types of power constellations: *elite* (business community) in Hunter's study and *pluralistic* in Dahl's study. Much of that original debate concerning the structural findings and the methods used to obtain such findings continues,[9] and different models continue to be proposed (Olsen & Marger, 1993; see Chapter 4, this volume).

TERMINOLOGY

The concepts of power and social class tend to intermingle. One book suggests that the following class groups exist in the United States: very poor, poor, working class, middle class, upper-middle class, upper class, ruling class, and mixed class (Mogil & Slepian, 1992, pp. 160–161). The very poor, poor, and working classes have no power except in numbers; they have been called everything from the *underclass* to the *silent majority*, depending on their income level.

Nevertheless, others in society are very interested in the leaders of these groups. Most individuals and families who are in positions of power or who can exert power are currently upper middle, upper, or ruling class, regardless of their original background and social standing.

Who do we want to locate? The terms *the powerful*, *dominants*, *influentials*, and *elite* are used fairly interchangeably to describe individuals who exercise power or are widely regarded by perceptive people as having that option. (In describing studies, we will employ the researcher's language.) The terms *power actors* or *power brokers* may be used for those who appear to be within the circle of influence but are not part of its core or those whose exact role in decision making is unclear. For instance, we may observe local power actors with pull in the local arts world, or those who are "players" due to corporate charitable contributions or lobbying, or who own valuable land. Full-fledged community elites and influentials, fewer in number, exert considerable to complete influence over important local institutions—which can be documented through a study of key decisions—or have the potential to do so. Occasionally, the term *influential* is used in a commonplace sense to describe a person who is viewed by others as effectual, instrumental, and carrying weight with others.

Questions to the public are worded this way since many other terms are not understood; responses tell us, through their context, if and how this influence is limited—to a religious or another group, for example. Box 5.3 suggests questions to direct to knowledgeable citizens to learn more about the powerful.

Admittedly, such questions as those in Box 5.3 may not elicit information about the power elite in the community; the upper class is not necessarily the ruling class. To determine those who are at the *core* of the entire community power structure, we need access to formal power structure reports.

We should also distinguish between a community-level power elite and an American elite. Those who constitute the core of community power are rarely part of a national ruling social class (described by Mills and Domhoff as *dominating America*) and seldom part of the new social elite and meritocracy described by Lasch (1995), even if these individuals are quite privileged, influential in a regional area, or in control of a city. At the community level, social workers may wish they had access to the powerful person's Rolodex, lunch partners, and golf buddies, but those community elites would think the same about national elites, who would think the same about international elites. The last are more Internetters than jet setters, with the ability to influence areas like inter-

---

BOX 5.3	REPRESENTATIVE QUESTIONS FOR POWER STUDIES

- Who runs this city? Who are the most economically powerful persons?
- Who controls the resources?
- Who determines local taxes such as real estate taxes? Who benefits?
- Tell me about the power brokers in this county that everyone knows about. Is there anyone operating behind the scenes?

- Does anyone with connections at the county or state level live in your subdivision, neighborhood, or town?
- Who is influential due to the high regard people have for them or because of their clout with politicians?
- Do you know any family that sends their children to an excellent boarding school?

national banking or another part of the financial system. Celebrities and those who are useful for publicity purposes or for swaying elected officials on a one- or two-time basis, and who thus might be viewed by the general public as having significant influence, are rarely true elites or influentials.

METHODOLOGY

Different approaches for studying the powerful include reputational, positional, and decisional (sometimes called *issue analysis* or *event analysis*) studies. These studies ask "Is this person perceived to be powerful, occupying a position that confers authority and power, or actually involved in specific decision making?" Frequently two of the three approaches are combined to enhance the chances of identifying either a tight-knit inner circle or various leading groups. If all three are employed, a social worker can feel assured that those leaders whose names reappear often are "likely to exert influence in an array of decisions and in a variety of areas" (Martinez-Brawley, 1990, p. 75).

Although full-blown studies using any approach may take a year, modest exploratory or shortcut studies can be completed in 2 months, especially if an earlier study is available. Newspaper offices and political science, economics, or sociology departments at colleges or universities are starting places to unearth such a study.

EXAMPLES

Our first example shows how a nonscientific newspaper study of local power can be useful to our field. A journalist conducted a survey of 27 community leaders, often called a *panel* in power structure literature, to elicit names of "folks with real clout" in a large, mostly metropolitan county (Sullivan, 1994). The leaders were asked to name "influential individuals . . . not necessarily those with the big jobs or titles, but the 10 people they would

want on their side if they were trying to get something big accomplished."

The "runaway winner" in the survey turned out to be fairly similar to county influentials in other informal studies, who are often concerned with growth, because he was a developer. His family connections also fit the picture—a father who had been acting governor and a grandfather who had run a political dynasty in the county. That the winner was also a political columnist and cable TV host illustrates a newer route to influence. The school superintendent, county executive, and a U.S. representative ranked second through fourth. Public service does not equate automatically with power; in this study, not one of 9 county council members was in the top 10. Influence can also be wielded by those who serve the community outside of office; the former president of the National Association for the Advancement of Colored People (NAACP) ranked eighth.

To the surprise of many, including the reporter responsible for the survey, the person ranked fifth most influential in the county was not a household name and was active in social service causes. The newspaper described him as "a Presbyterian minister who devotes his life to outreach programs for the poor and hungry, through the Community Ministry." As the reporter quipped, "That's hardly a Boss Tweed formula for power and influence, but [he] makes the list hands down." Probes used to locate influentials, as shown here and in Chapter 4, range from interorganizational network studies of corporate heads to snapshots of who is, at a particular point in time, well regarded by leaders. The results are useful in different ways. In this instance, the reporter did not know the minister but planned to call on him in the future for opinions, which had the unusual result of putting a social service type into the mass communications loop (K. Sullivan, classroom presentation, April 25,

1994). Social work managers and practitioners must also reach out to someone like that, who is positioned to know the thinking of the least and most powerful, both as a key informant and for help with needs assessment and planning.

The survey method used by the reporter was reputational. However, the key question—"Who do you want on your side to accomplish something big"—had a decision-oriented focus. Since this study focused as much on issue resolution as on economic clout, some captains of industry and county business community leaders were ignored, a weakness of this particular survey. For social work purposes, however, such wording may reveal a good cross section of influentials or at least powerful actors to whom we probably will have access through acquaintances.

Inclusion of "one of us" on the list of county influentials is astonishing to social service students or practitioners. Yet, almost invariably when the results of local power studies are in, to our surprise we know, an acquaintance knows, or someone in our family knows an individual on the long list, if not the top 10 list, fairly well. Reading community power studies makes it clear that we have more access to influentials than we realize.

Even if studies are already available, it may still be worthwhile to do a study of one's own. *Our second example illustrates steps in the process and the payoffs for learners when they conduct the study themselves.* Our first example was from an urban county and our next concerns a rural county; in either place, social workers need to figure out who to go to for what, who to hold accountable on various issues, and who to approach as decision makers in a community. Such objectives were pursued as a class project by undergraduate social work students located in a low-density area encompassing a city of 25,000. The students divided into two teams, each with a

graduate student mentor. Since the teams used different approaches, both will be described, along with a brief report on the integrated results of the studies. These class project results were then compared and contrasted with an existing newspaper study. Some names were predictable; others on both lists evoked surprise. The student findings and the daily newspaper findings overlapped for 21 people. In a medium-sized community, knowing the names of that many decision makers is extremely useful to our profession. How did the students locate those significant to our field?

One team (1T), using a *positional* approach, sought to identify decision makers in public affairs and the human services field. It searched for a list of city and county boards, committees, and appointed citizen panels; found out which members were appointed and which were volunteers; obtained the names of members on each board and committee; and compiled a comprehensive list. This step took longer than expected, about a month. By asking questions, 1T informally determined which boards or committees were considered most important in city and county affairs (e.g., zoning, the airport, land and water resources, and natural resources were important to businesspeople).

Unlike investigators in other disciplines, these social work students also included the names of government service boards and committees affecting social services and low-income citizens, such as the community planning and development committee, human services board, community action board, and law enforcement advisory board. (1T could also have added influential voluntary sector boards such as United Way's board of directors.) Even if many were not countywide influentials, they were power actors in the social service world.

With the results in hand, 1T noted the

names of those who served on multiple committees and those with the same last names. 1T also talked with long-time residents, who pointed out other family connections the team would have missed. This method of looking at those in authority can reveal an elite or pluralistic power structure.

Throughout the 2-month process, students on this team learned about city and county government operations, the appointments process, board volunteer possibilities, the types of citizens who do and do not participate in civic activities, the individuals and families who are extremely involved in such activities, professionals in the social service community with government connections, and finally, those in the client community who serve on one or more boards. This represents quite an informational payoff, apart from the way the findings may help.

The second team (2T) employed a modified *reputational* approach, with the aim of identifying those in power behind the scenes. This approach requires nominations and meeting with those nominated. The students wondered if anyone would talk with them, but they learned that busy, powerful people open their doors when they learn that others consider them to be influential, perhaps because they hope to discover who nominated them, if nothing else, although the students did not disclose that information. As a starting point, 2T asked their field supervisors for names of community influentials; since this was a town of 25,000 with mostly local service providers, the field instructors had more community knowledge than might be true elsewhere. 2T compiled a list, and those persons mentioned most frequently were interviewed and asked for additional names. All this was accomplished in less than a month.

As another way of seeking local elites, 2T checked traditional places where those with money and position might be identified: at the university for evidence of founders and large donors (names of buildings) and at town banks for the plaques that listed the founders and the current directors. 2T noted any family names of local funds and charities and obtained the names of current chamber of commerce officers. There were no country clubs; however, country club presidents could be used elsewhere. In cities, the boards of prestigious hospitals might be important (Ollove, 1991). Finally, 2T obtained the names of the largest employers (factory owners) in the city, county, and region. 2T compiled a larger list from its three sources: those nominated early on, those suggested by influentials (who were interviewed after they were nominated), and names culled from other places.

Throughout this process, this second group of students interacted personally with several people considered important in the area and thus made contacts. The team also enjoyed sleuthing to find the monied families in a town where none were obvious. They did not conduct library research; in a bigger locale, such research might save time while making findings more reliable and would teach different skills (Warren & Warren, 1984).

To finish up, the names from 1T and 2T were combined and compared with those appearing in a reputational study published in the local newspaper of the 50 most influential people in the city. Neither the student city/county study nor the newspaper city study was scientific, but they provided leads to influentials and to power actors with the potential to exert influence, who were certainly the right people to contact for many purposes (Martinez-Brawley 1990). *For social work purposes, the longer the list the better. Our purpose is not to prove who is on top but to involve as many influential people as possible in our work.*

Every student researcher turned out to know someone who was considered influential. In one instance, this information proved useful for lobbying purposes; at the request of an advocate, an influential arranged and attended a meeting with a state representative. Before the study, the advocate was unaware that this person, well known to the advocate, had broad influence.

We profit from doing power studies, which introduce social workers to important community figures and to people with resources who might help with community assessment and other tasks. Regardless of the controversies surrounding the validity of different power structure approaches and outcomes, we can use our studies for advocacy or exposé purposes, or for assessment or administrative purposes. Thus we benefit, and so do our constituents.

Our final example suggests additional ways to use power studies to further an organization's self-interest. Learning the names of powerful persons behind the scenes and influentials at the city and neighborhood levels can be useful for your own agency's board of directors

recruitment process and for resource development. If power studies are being undertaken for direct, obvious agency purposes such as fund-raising, they probably should be contracted out and conducted by a consulting group or university—not directly by the agency—to put some distance between the requests for information and the later use of that information. Advocacy groups could do the studies themselves.

Emenhiser (1991) writes convincingly about how we can make fund-raising approaches to the influential, spot long-term corporate mentors who can assist nonprofit organizations, and link power structure members to a low-power population in a mutually beneficial way. This is why we need to identify the powerful by name. Emenhiser gives a clear explanation of how to do this (Box 5.4).

Who is or is not an elite or influential continues to be debated, but among those who are usually *not* part of the power structure, according to Emenhiser, are politicians,

---

BOX 5.4	**FUND-RAISERS HAD BETTER KNOW ABOUT ELITE POWER STRUCTURES A REPUTATIONAL STUDY METHOD**

Emenhiser (1991) describes a reputational method in simpler fashion than most authors. He conducted a study in Indianapolis to identify and rank influentials by following these steps:

1. *Put together a base list of potential influentials* (from research on the corporate 5% club, banks, etc.).

2. *Ask seven or eight respected members of the community to review the list, to rank order the 30 most influential names on the base list, and to add names* (these experts must be well connected or positioned to know).

3. *Compile a new list, weight the names according to the ranks given, and reorder them.*

4. *Interview the 30–40 on the final list, asking these questions:*

 • If a project were before the community that required decisions by a group of leaders, which 10 leaders could obtain its approval?
 • Place in rank order, 1 through 10 with 1 being the most influential, those individuals who in your opinion are the most influential in the city—influential from the point of view of their ability to lead others.

5. *Weight and compile the rankings by interviewees to get the names of the 7–12 persons at the top.*

Source: *Based on Emenhiser (1991), pp. 9–14. Copyright 1991. NSFRE Journal. Used with permission; all rights reserved.*

plant managers, women and minorities, professionals (except for lawyers from large firms), university presidents, civic association executives, media executives, and ministers (p. 11).

APPLICATIONS TO OUR OWN WORK

Why do we concern ourselves with something that seems so remote from casework and group work? The type of decision making dominant in a community has implications for practice. If there is equilibrium among competing groups, then social workers want to become part of the field of exchange and be able to influence local policy through bargaining. If there is centralization of power and local government responds to a set of elites with a shared set of interests, then social workers need to bargain with elites, get elites to propose policy alternatives, and keep elites from controlling the public, which, after all, has distinct and dissimilar interests from the elites. Finally, social workers can look for common interests in the community and try to link groups to expand their influence.

The type of decision maker dominant in a community also has implications for practice. A remote circle of people unknown to social workers presents less of an opportunity than known influentials whom workers have direct or indirect means of contacting. Either way, specific names are helpful. If key decision makers turn out to be generally hostile to social services, we can still find out which influential has a personal situation that may open a door. According to Martinez-Brawley (1990), "a thorough knowledge of people and structures that promote or interfere with community decision-making is essential to [social workers'] understanding of community units and to their professional functioning" (p. 52).

We kid ourselves if we think that some social workers can avoid dealing with power.

Even private practitioners may be confronted by the discretionary authority of local power players who control zoning restrictions on such matters as placing business signs in front of homes or establishing inequitable tax rates (Barlett & Steele, 1994). It is imperative for everyone in our field to know who is on the board of directors of the agency with which we are associated, as well as any parent organization, what each person's background is, and why he or she was chosen. Those working in a government agency should be similarly aware of citizen advisory boards or other influentials who might be swayed by staff concerns.

As in field studies, conducting and discussing local power structure studies turns out to be an antidote to burnout. Instead of discouraging social workers, as national power elite studies tend to do, community power studies seem to heighten our desire to critique results and methodology and to pursue new leads because they activate our juices and kindle our curiosity (Box 5.5).

Community Analyses

DEFINITION

Community analysis can be a task, an orientation method, and a particular type of report write-up. To illustrate, Haglund, Weisbrod and Bracht (1990) look on analysis as a "critical first step" before any intervention, a way of "adapting implementation plans to unique community characteristics," and a "profile [that] includes a community's image of itself and its goals, its past history and current civic changes, and its current resources, readiness, and capacity for [activity]" (p. 91). A community analysis will be discussed here as a broad interpretive study based on factual documents, interviews with officials and natural leaders, observation, and search methods; a once-over-lightly examination of many aspects of a particular

BOX 5.5	THE POWERS THAT BE—A COMMUNITY WALK, DRIVE, JAUNT

The goal is to identify old, monied, or revered families in the area. Drive around the oldest and best-kept cemeteries, stopping by the mausoleums and largest stones to record the names (this doesn't work for all religions). Find the oldest building or the administration building at any college or university, look for the wall that lists the institutional founders, and record names. See if there is a foundation center in town and find out which families, if any, have their own foundations; otherwise, seek out planning offices or multi-million-dollar real estate sellers (often promoted in newspapers and on office windows) who are likely to know about land holdings; ask the chamber of commerce about family enterprises that have continued for more than 100 years. In a small town or suburban community, track down the town historian and see if any historical or genealogical books have been published on the area. For a swift walk, go straight to the public or university library and seek help in identifying big law firms and banks in town. In cities, look at the *Social Register*, if available. Review available telephone books and other directories.

area or group; and a process of refining initial impressions.

Community or neighborhood analyses have many forms but often combine elements of field and community power structure studies—without going as deeply into either—with factual information about social conditions and statistical indicators and with practical tools such as maps that facilitate exploration. While the analysis helps us differentiate, comprehend, and respond to a certain population or neighborhood and determine who generally runs things in town, it is also designed to grasp intangibles such as ethos, morale, spirit, energy, and enthusiasm. Although it may sound more ambitious, traditionally this type of analysis is done in fleet fashion as a preliminary procedure. "Neighborhoods are different," assert Warren and Warren (1984), who state: "Identifying the sources of this uniqueness is the first step in designing effective outreach programs and organizing for citizen action" (p. 27). And, we would add, a first step in determining whether your agency does the job it is supposed to in aiding the community.

HISTORY AND TERMINOLOGY

This type of study has a less definite history. Robert Lamb's 1952 widely used shortcuts to gain a comprehensive picture of the life of one's "Hometown" and Roland Warren's 1965 book on studying the community may be the progenitors; their suggestions have been employed by practitioners ranging from salespersons to organizers. Compared to the first two, this type of study is less well defined, in part because of its many names and descriptions. It is viewed alternatively as getting the pulse of community life, profiling one's community setting (Spradley, 1990), doing a first approximation of an official community survey, gaining enough knowledge to allow one to function effectively in a community, and sizing up a situation. We believe *community analysis* is an appropriate designator.

Journalistic community profiles published over many decades are the closest popular equivalent. These include in-depth examinations of places published in the housing section or Sunday supplement of a large newspaper, city magazines such as *Pittsburgh*, or national publications such as

The New Yorker. Such pieces, historical or current, are worth reading, if available, because they provide names of centrally important individuals and thoughtful analysis of economic ups and downs, of civic strengths and problems. Such articles help orient us to a community, but it will be our task to add assessments of a social work nature. For example, a magazine featuring the fishing past and picturesque present of a small town will not note a dearth of hospitals, clinics, and physicians within its borders, which requires residents to drive 30 minutes to the next larger town.

METHODOLOGY

While a field study often starts with certain individuals and families, and through their lives and activities works up to the city level, analyses start with countywide and citywide institutions and then move down to the neighborhood, suburban, or smaller unit level. Thus, one might start with city librarians and the census and later interview the corner druggist and the head of the elementary school PTA. Among the reasons for starting with a wide focus are that maps usually portray a broad geographic area, many planning studies look at a region, and histories are seldom written on small residential enclaves. Cook County and Chicago are too huge to analyze, but if we want to put the area around the University of Chicago, called Hyde Park, in perspective, then statistics and demographics for the whole area can be used as a basis of comparison for data on Hyde Park. Sometimes the opposite is true: a village is too small to study in a vacuum because data are collected at the county or consolidated school district level.

Obtaining an introduction to a town can be accomplished with brief stops at the most conspicuous gas station and most noticeable church, the real estate office, pizza parlor, and elementary school. At this point, we do not need to speak with business owners, principals, or ministers; anyone working in the establishment who has time will do fine. In fact, sometimes others will be better initial guides to the area. Every place is different, so the social worker has to explore. In Carlinville, Illinois, a key person to contact would be a school janitor who has been around for 14 years and knows many families. He is also "a city alderman . . . a volunteer fireman, deputy coroner, a member of the Macoupin County Historical Society, American Legion and the Elks" (Browning, 1995). Of course, we would not know any of that, but if one of our stops is an elementary school, we might be lucky enough to run into him (or someone like him in another town) outside the building. Although the community itself will take a long time to know, newcomers can quickly start familiarizing themselves with the town. What does one say at such stops besides "I'm interested in this area"? See Box 5.6 for typical questions asked at this and later stages of the analysis.

Exactly what are we talking about here in terms of a community analysis process and product? A social work study of an inner-city area conducted one summer covered these topics: sociodemographics, history, political life, drugs–crime–law enforcement, the revitalization process, community impressions, and notable community programs. Appendices in the report included a list of contacts, a community survey by another university, a "community-building" report from another organization, census tract data, crime statistics, and descriptions of three social agencies involved with the community.

How do we begin such an analysis? Lamb (1977) recommends these first steps for analyzing a town: buy a map, including a street directory; look up local history; review *Rand-McNally's Banker's Register, Moody's Banks,* and *Standard and Poors' Directory of Directors* at the library to obtain the names of

BOX 5.6	REPRESENTATIVE QUESTIONS FOR A COMMUNITY ANALYSIS

- What are the boundaries of this area or community? What do you call it? Do old-timers call it something else?
- Where do people stop to chat, hang out, or relax around here?
- Have you ever seen anything written up about this area? Should I read it?
- What are the good and bad points about living here?

- What special problems or central issues does your (network, area, neighborhood, community of common interest) have?
- Who are important civic leaders in your community and why?
- Who are the chronic gripers in the area? What is their complaint?

local bank and corporate manufacturing directors (today we might also look at the names of the directors of the largest service and information businesses); and read census data and area studies by social workers detailing the citywide distribution of types of cases and social problems. To study a neighborhood, Warren and Warren (1984) suggest the following process: the observer should first walk around city hall or central government buildings, pick up pamphlets on city services, and visit the central business district; obtain maps, the telephone book, and local newspapers; go by the library and chamber of commerce to get a list of community organizations and their contact persons; and then drive and walk around the neighborhood, chat with people on the street, and ask them to define the boundaries of the area. After getting more settled, the observer should precisely identify key informants and various networks and generally figure out "how the neighborhood operates" (p. 34). See Box 5.6 for questions that might be asked.

Cox (1977) adds his voice to the chorus emphasizing that practitioners "must get a grip on the needs of the communities they will serve" (p. 15). By and large, the tasks needed to do so are easily completed, but time must be set aside to reflect on them; otherwise, says Cox:

practice is apt to be governed entirely by preconceived ideas, expedience, past habits of work, stereotyped attitudes, the insistent demands of a vocal minority, and accidental encounters with atypical situations. . . . There is no real substitute for firsthand knowledge of people and their problems, their needs and hopes. (pp. 15–16)

Why do we, as professionals, begin such an analysis? A sound reason is given above; a blunter one is this: an analysis helps us get our bearings and avoid false starts in our practice. Warren and Warren (1984) put it extremely simply: "When you first arrive in a community, it's a good idea to spend a short time getting a feel for the city *as a whole*" (p. 27; emphasis added). Since we want to root ourselves in the social fabric, we must go beyond the "Welcome Wagon" plane of information for ourselves and those we serve— for example, by attending some city council or town hall meetings or watching the cable television channel that covers civic meetings. The next steps in analyzing a community, even if easy, may not be as obvious or apparent as they first seem.

EXAMPLES

Perhaps our clients come from many different neighborhoods; however, many may live in a few areas that we could visit, and we all meet in a certain place—where the office is located. Without much effort, we can walk to different places for lunch and use new routes to drive to and from work until we have seen the 10-square-block area surrounding our urban office or the 10-mile radius surrounding a rural office. If our agency has satellite offices or scattered service delivery sites, we can visit each of them and, where possible, again move out in concentric circles to get the lay of the land.

We should pinpoint the central area of the suburbs or towns or neighborhoods from which the majority of our service users come and pick a central point, such as a key street corner, to make some instant but ongoing observations. These may not be surprising "snapshots" but rather written observations that prove useful regarding such subjects as who might need what services. Here are notes from one student who observed in a gentrified section of a large city:

> *Tuesday, 11 a.m.* Many walking by are elderly (counted 9 older people in five minutes I stood here). I also noted 5 women pushing baby carriages—a couple looked like young mothers; the rest looked older and may have been babysitters. I saw a group of Hispanic women waiting for the bus but not any black people. I saw a handful of people, casually dressed, coming up out of the subway. *Tuesday, 6 p.m.* People with briefcases and wearing running shoes pour out of subway exits—in five minutes at least 50—almost everyone white adults. Bumper to bumper traffic. *Saturday, 2:30 p.m.* From same vantage point, I saw large numbers of couples with small children, but very few older people. Again, almost everyone was white. The bus stop by the 7-11 appeared to be a meeting place for young people hanging out.[10]

A number of possibilities can be explored if further observation reveals similar patterns. Among these are (1) potential needs of the el-derly, and of house cleaners and babysitters who come into the area such as day care for their children (or for residents' children), (2) whether play space is safe and adequate, and (3) possible discrimination in housing in the area, which could be checked out by "testers."

Observers can be surprised by what they see while observing more closely than usual. For example, students noticed a number of Asian-American families grocery shopping in a suburban area that was thought to have a homogeneous population (Box 5.7). Their finding might have program development implications.

Noticing newspaper stories about incidents in one's community of interest is another way to be observant. The idea here is to check things out: What does the community think about this incident? What is a problem for them? For example, one student read about a hate crime in which two young white men doused an African-American woman with lighter fluid and tried to set her on fire. She began interviews to learn more about the suburban area where it happened and to determine whether this event indicated that skinheads or other organized groups had moved into the neighborhood. Here is part of her report:

> According to police who attended a meeting to discuss the incident, this neighborhood does not have a greater propensity for this type of violence than others, and every person I interviewed felt that this was an isolated incident. However, I got an interesting perspective from G, a black man who works in the shopping center. He was not surprised and felt that if the woman had been lit on fire, the whole area would have exploded. He feels relations between blacks and whites are strained. He added that there were more media at the neighborhood rally than participants, and as far as he could see, there were no civic leaders in attendance.[11]

BOX 5.7	GETTING IN SYNC OR SWIM—A COMMUNITY WALK, DRIVE, JAUNT

Speedily discover if an area is heterogeneous. Look through the telephone book (as many named Kim as Kelly, Nguyen as Nash?), stop by unisex hair cutting places in neighborhood shopping areas and by the motor vehicle center in your immediate vicinity—and take the answer into consideration in planning a walk. The goal is to identify small worlds within the geographic area.

A walk just beyond an urban university campus and a few blocks around the environs might reveal multiple communities of a sort: the campus, ranging from professors to security guards, a yuppie neighborhood, a public housing project, and an enclave of medical-related residential services flanking a hospital (e.g., a Ronald McDonald House). Find specific places where people congregate in a locale. Explore neighborhoods and walk in or around local centers of activity like these: pool hall, video arcade, casino, skating rink or good roller blading areas, bingo hall, swimming pool, coffee shop, jazz or other night spot, bowling alley, karaoke bar, the Royal Bakery downtown, Hot Shoppes at the suburban mall, the Country Store at the crossroads, the small town Dairy Queen. Look for other places where residents interact, such as a central bus stop, the high school, the lobby of the post office, the corner where day laborers are picked up, a storefront check-cashing place, or the farm implement store. Record who (in a demographic sense) is found where and at what time. How are you greeted along the way?

It would be foolish to rely on scattered interviews for truth, but ordinarily we get only one version of reality, while a community analysis reports on multiple versions and perceptions.

What we observe or fail to observe can also tell us about the larger society. Even that alert, intelligent student who looked into the meaning of the hate crime might not have thought to follow up on the rape of a woman of any color or the death of a battered wife because those by now are taken as normal events and not highlighted in the newspaper.

Ways to dig deeper exist that can take us beyond observations and a few interviews. To assist in such a process, Meenaghan, Washington, and Ryan (1982) suggest six methodological approaches to delineating and apprehending communities: a rural method; corporate and statistical area methods; social area analysis (census data, etc); the interactional approach; a systems approach; and locality development and social action (we discuss systems in Chapter 4, locality and action in Chapter 12). These authors believe, as we do, that such methods can help us "move into the ethos of an area in a relatively quick manner." (p. 96). If we are interested in examining our community as a place where functions occur (see Chapter 4), we could employ the rural method. If we want to understand "the population characteristics of people who inhabit the land," social area analysis can be used. If we want to study our community as a "place within defined boundaries," corporate and statistical methods are appropriate (Meenaghan et al., 1982, p. 104).

The *rural method*, which Meenaghan et al. recommend for large areas with scattered populations, nicely fits our notion of a community analysis. The mechanics of the study (starting with a map, identifying major institutions, contacting longtime residents from many sectors who are "relevant and representative organizational people") remind us of the earlier tips from Lamb. The rural method's emphasis on getting the "qualitative flavor of the community" and the interest in learning how the informants "see and define the area, its needs, and possible strengths" characterize solid but manageable community studies (Meenaghan et al., 1982, pp. 98–101). We particularly like the emphasis of Meenaghan et al. on figuring out "smaller social worlds within the larger arbitrary unit" to be served by entities such as multicounty community mental health programs, hospital planning boards, or rural legal services (p. 99).

Identifying *social networks* (Maguire & Biegel, 1982; see also Chapter 10 in this volume) is another aspect of analyzing a small or large community. A town can be so divided by religion or length of residence that networks become more obvious. In some cities, gangs (often another way of saying youth or immigrant networks) may create and enforce divisions. Finding networks in average communities is more of a challenge.

To take the suburbs as an example, the *interactional approach* operates from the premise that place does not necessarily dominate the lives of those living in such communities (Meenaghan et al., 1982). In this interactional model, to look for *isolates*, who are not part of the community, we can note the person who drives alone to work in the city and goes to the same bar most nights; we can observe at the unemployment center; or we can inquire at beauty shops about patrons who seldom venture out except to get their hair done. To search out *neighbors*, we can research car pools into the city, or to and from day-care centers or schools or lessons on weekends, or we can track down ongoing poker games; these may be the start of at least "weak-tie" social networks (Flanagan, 1993, p. 22). To seek *key actors* in the suburbs, we can obtain the names of those who started the Neighborhood Watch group, as well as those who serve as block captains and those who started the children's soccer league or the adult softball league, along with current coaches.

Remember, these are suggestions for detecting social networks—not family networks or community leadership; none of this activity will detect networks of deviates or locate volunteers for the agency. We are attempting to meet a portion of the community. Any good social worker will also stay in contact with social service networks, but here we are trying to figure out a given community.

We began our community analysis by seeking out logical resources. We finish by writing a report and having it double checked by our key informants.

1. A sample of topics to cover in a community analysis

   Geographic, corporate, jurisdictional boundaries
   Demographics, statistics, subgroups
   History, community strengths today
   Political structure, governance
   Economic structure, major or key employers
   Social services structure
   Mutual aid, community action organizations
   Potential/actual civic and service problems
   Power relations

2. A sample of approaches to use in a community analysis

   Interviewing, "hearing" the community in new ways
   Observing, analyzing
   Collecting illuminating anecdotes, stories
   Following methods used by social scientists
   Providing orientation materials (map, photographs)
   Being aware of personal bias, limits of analysis

Sometimes an innocuous topic such as transportation or community boundaries, or a basic step such as identifying those boundaries, turns out to be difficult, rewarding to capture on paper, and quite helpful for practice purposes. Meenaghan et al. (1982) describe the *"corporate" approach* and suggest the types of administrative entities, as well as government boundaries, that should be noted, such as "a unified school district, a metropolitan parks district, a library district, or a water treatment district" (p. 102). One student determined which political ward his community was in and located the names and telephone numbers of political block captains and neighborhood advisory board members. As part of a study of an affluent subdivision, another student examined schools and the boundaries that dictated which children went to what school. She learned that the influential subdivision's elementary school prevailed more often in school politics than a buffeted-around elementary school (that received the children nobody wanted) located quite close by in a noninfluential neighborhood. The student said that seeing how physically close to each other these schools were opened her eyes to power, influence, and class.

APPLICATIONS TO OUR OWN WORK

Agencies and organizations need the information contained in a community analysis. If we cannot conduct one ourselves, we should ask librarians and newspaper editors if they know of a community profile that has been published recently; an economic development office might also be a place to check. By doing it ourselves, we will learn more, target it more precisely to our concerns, and become known to significant people in the process. We will be on top of things and in a position to make better judgments about social service/justice interventions.

Once we have successfully conducted a community analysis, we will be ready for the day the mayor calls to ask our advice or the day we need a detailed understanding of several elements in our town or city or county. This type of study also generates many ideas that allow us to do our jobs better and more easily.

At a more mundane level, we are wise to keep abreast of even simple community developments—if only to avoid embarrassment. Suppose that a therapist working downtown gets a ride to work with his wife but pays no attention: Will he give accurate and easy directions to clients on how to reach the office and where to park nearby? Be aware that clients may be late due to a parade, baseball traffic, or a political demonstration (not to resistance)? Realize when the buses or subway go on strike? Know when the school holidays occur? Know where clients with modest incomes can purchase cheaper medicine? The more specific we can be about resources and the more knowledgeable we are about how systems work, the easier we can make life for the users of our services.

Problems and Services Studies

DEFINITION

After studying the social environment, we turn to community concerns and resources. This focus in discovering and documenting the community is epitomized by the title of an article—"The Ecology of Child Maltreatment: Identifying and Characterizing High-Risk Neighborhoods" (Zuravin & Taylor 1987). Social problems and services/programs can be studied separately or in combination. We will call a *problems study* the kind needed to determine the extent and severity of specific problems or to give an overall diagnosis of the range of problems; we will call a *services/programs study* one that looks at provision and utilization of services (affordability, suitability, effectiveness) Both fall under our umbrella term *problems and services studies*, the fourth type of community study.

Many professionals conduct such research, including social demographers, health economists, policy analysts, and social workers. Clients and residents contribute to them as well. According to Siegel, Attkisson and Carson (1987), anyone living or working in a community "forms impressions" about human service needs; thus, we want to obtain community residents' perspectives on "the accessibility, availability, acceptability, and organization of services" because their reactions give us "indispensable clues about the human service needs of the community as a whole" (pp. 86–87). (See Box 5.8 for questions that might be asked in such studies.)

HISTORY

Power and influence studies look at one dimension of community—structure—while social welfare studies emphasize the values facet of community; that is, meeting common needs, caring for others, troubles and difficulties, communality, obligation, justice (Morris, 1986; Wuthnow, 1991). Sociologists are more likely to take a problem slant—what is breaking down society? (see Chapter 3 regarding problems)—and social workers usually take a services slant—what can reintegrate society?

Because subject matter is so varied, problems and services studies have evolved differently in each discipline. In our field, some of the earliest social work endeavors included this type of community study or social survey—obtaining necessary facts for planning and for documenting the link between poor sanitation and disease, the numbers of child laborers, and other social conditions or problems (Garvin & Cox, 1995). We still debate the trade-offs of in-depth versus quick and superficial community needs assessment studies (Slaght & Schopler, 1994).

TERMINOLOGY

The most common approach used by helping professions when they undertake a community inquiry is to spotlight a "target population" (Netting, Kettner, & McMurtry, 1993) or "targets for change" or a "population at risk" (Meenaghan et al., 1992). Some of this language starts with funding sources (Neuber, Atkins, Jacobson, & Reuterman, 1980, p. 14). Also mentioned are related service delivery problems, the responsiveness of the community to the target or at-risk pop-

---

| BOX 5.8 | REPRESENTATIVE QUESTIONS ASKED IN SERVICES STUDIES |

- How do you get here? How many buses or transfers does it take?
- What types of needs go unaddressed in your community?
- What are some differences between your group and others in the community? Are those differences a problem for any of you?
- Who are the various players who are trying to solve these problems and meet these needs? If the community is not being responsive, what do you think is the reason?

- Have you received mail, telephone calls, or in-person calls about _____ (how you obtain dental care, etc.)?
- Please answer the following about your child care arrangements: [from a questionnaire with open- or closed-ended questions]
- Have any social or health indicator analyses or surveys been conducted for this area? [asked of planners or officials]

ulation, and its capacity to respond (Menolascino & Potter, 1989). Less common but connected are a concentration on a "solution environment" (Rothman, 1984), a "problem solving community" (Spradley, 1990), a "human services system" (Netting et al., 1993), or even players, procedures, and linkages affecting human services (Hahn, 1994). These studies help bridge the gap between community and agency analysis.

Such investigations may be utilized when an organization has to prove to others that a problem exists, believes some problems are unaddressed, or resolves to move toward community-based services. Or an agency might be concerned with factors impinging on the lives of all stakeholders in its enterprise (community residents, agency donors, directors, staff, service users and their families) rather than with the community as a whole; one example of this type of study is a marketing study (see Chapter 11).

Our agency can originate a study, but first we should locate relevant studies conducted in our locale or in similar communities—in order to discover the variables that define problems and their solutions. We are looking for multidimensional and systematic studies of (1) social problems, (2) private and public sector programs addressing problems (that have been field tested) and other solutions for these problems, and (3) implementation critiques (issues, cost/benefit analyses, evidence of consumer satisfaction or uninterest).

Many national studies to assess solutions can be replicated easily on the local level. When we hear of new programs that are supposedly *the* solution to old problems, we might consider an *exploratory* study to appraise the application of the idea to our community or an *evaluation* study to determine whether the program accomplishes what it is touted to do. One modest follow-up study in the field of aging, for example, examined popular, low-cost utility *gatekeeper* programs

that train meter readers in outreach, referral, and crisis intervention to help link frail customers with appropriate service agencies to see how they were faring several years after inception. The programs were well received, yet referrals were few and not of the type anticipated (Hexter, 1989). The questions in that study were directed to program managers.

In many community-oriented versions of problems and services studies, such as general population or target population surveys, the perspectives of citizens and participants in the service delivery system must be solicited and valued equally with the advice of peers, funders, professionals, and service providers (Meenaghan et al., 1982). Potential and actual service users have opinions on the types of services they want and can suggest priorities for skills they desire.

METHODOLOGY

Netting et al. (1993) illustrate how to deliberately narrow the parameters of a community study to social problems and human service systems of interest to social workers. Unlike the field study, with its focus on cohesion and shared purpose, their approach highlights distinctions rather than commonalities. These authors lay out a detailed set of tasks and questions for conceptualizing community (pp. 91–92). To obtain the big picture, we must identify target populations, determine community characteristics, recognize differences, and identify structures. More precisely, Netting et al. counsel us to

> understand the characteristics of target population members;
> identify community boundaries;
> profile social problems;
> understand dominant values;
> identify formal and covert mechanisms of oppression;
> identify evidence of discrimination;
> recognize locations of power;

determine resource availability; and identify patterns of resource control and service delivery. (pp. 68–89)

The field and power structure studies described earlier should make clearer to us what is meant by "understand[ing] dominant values" or "recogniz[ing] locations of power." Our fourth type of study focuses on profiling social problems, determining resource availability, and identifying resource delivery.

Since developing a profile of a social problem may involve survey research, practitioners may need to consult with colleagues who excel in that area of practice. Specific types of problems and services studies, and many of the "how to's" for conducting this type of community study, are discussed in the next chapter.

EXAMPLES

Since our professional lives are made up of problems and programs, why does a particular problem/service study first come to mind? In terms of *identifying new problems*, staffers may remark on *patterns* that seem to call for community education if the situation is widespread. For example, in an office serving the aged, staffers may focus on older people who have saved all their lives for their old age but will not now spend to maintain their well-being. After such a discussion, other service providers could be contacted to check out such patterns. Eventually, a survey of providers could be conducted or a focus group with the very old could be held to get ideas on how to grapple with this problem.

A problem can be spotted from within a social service agency or externally in the community, or both. For example, a senior services center may receive consistent suggestions from family members of elderly clients, from their own experiences with the elderly, and/or from advocacy groups on the

need to address a particular phenomenon, such as suicide among the elderly. Inter-organizational coordination would probably be required to undertake this sort of study properly. A working group comprised of a social worker, physician, nursing home professional, someone knowledgeable about elderly persons who live alone, and a psychologist might begin to refine the objectives and questions.

In formulating a study to explore a particular problem or solution or program, we may try to cover too many topics as everyone in the office jumps on the survey bandwagon. A modest study of alcohol use can expand to a study of caffeine, nicotine, and illegal drugs. Some problems and services studies have an appropriately narrow focus. Suppose that someone working in the employee assistance program (EAP) of a huge corporation has determined the annual number of cases of alcohol abuse that come to the attention of his EAP office; he now *wants to put those numbers in perspective* by looking at a community study on alcoholism, particularly among employed individuals. If such a study does not exist, the social worker can propose one and coordinate it with other agencies in the addictions field. Regardless of the host agency, before undertaking a community alcohol education program targeted at white-collar workers or pregnant women or the elderly, it would help to have a community study on the topic, since the findings could sharpen the message. If the study is done well and the results are reliable, the information will generally be of use to the agency and the larger community.

Keep in mind, though, that formulating sensitive study questions, gaining access to study participants, interpreting results, and ensuring reliable findings can be difficult. *Even seemingly cut-and-dried problems and services studies sponsored by human service agencies are affected by community and cultural dy-*

namics. If the agency has conducted a prior field study or community analysis, these steps will be easier to take. Members of the target population—who may or may not know us already—often are affiliated with a number of subgroups, some of which are wary of us as researchers or service providers.

> Disempowered consumers view providers through the prisms of history, contemporary inequities and their previous experiences with health and other human service providers—often negative. . . . Part of diversity competence with disempowered people is anticipating distrust, accepting it, and knowing how to build trust. (Rauch, North, Rowe, & Risley-Curtis, 1993, p. 23)

To address such multiple interwoven concerns, social workers may benefit from combining qualitative research methods, ethnographic approaches, and ethnocultural awareness with the conventional quantitative methods usually employed in problems and services studies. A *qualitative approach* is especially useful in exploratory studies, in follow-up studies that bring to life existing data on the incidence and prevalence of a disease or social problem, and in studies to design and promote services for special populations (Delgado, 1979; Rounds, Weil, & Bishop, 1994). For example, Rauch and her colleagues believe that learning about genetic illnesses requires sensitive questioning about personal issues surrounding health and genetic inheritance. Using open-ended kinds of questions, as in conducting a careful social history, they find they can probe a family's experiences with an inherited disorder much more deeply than with typical survey questions. Furthermore, the qualitative approach enables the researcher to enlist the cooperation of the study participants who are coping with the illness (hence the real authorities). Without this cooperation and without

exploring solutions acceptable to the consumers, research findings would be much less reliable and services designed to respond to the problem would be of little value.

APPLICATIONS TO OUR OWN WORK

Many federal agencies collect data on social problems and utilization, and even on the quality of services, but by necessity most such studies are quantitative. We social workers must be familiar with the ongoing studies conducted in our field of interest. We also have an obligation to stay informed on events at the local level, consulting with planners and interagency task forces that prepare relevant reports. If we are unable to do studies of our own, we can seek them from hospitals, the United Way, government planning departments, urban or rural centers that specialize in social demography, and universities or colleges that do social problem or program evaluation studies. Our special role is our commitment to involving clients, service users, and the general public. We seek input less for magnanimous reasons and more because of our growing awareness of being insufficient alone and needing input from consumers, other providers, demographers, and other experts (Box 5.9).

As we shift our emphasis from broad study to focused assessment (Cox, 1995), the problems and services theme will continue to be addressed in the next chapter.

INTEGRATING METHODS TO SUIT THE PROJECT

When practitioners wish to get to know their clients' worlds better, or when program development or another course of action is underway, several of the studies discussed here can be combined or elements of all four can be mixed to fit the situation. For instance, in health promotion, the key elements of a

BOX 5.9	WALKING IN THEIR SHOES—A SUGGESTED COMMUNITY WALK, DRIVE, FORAY

Choose a population (teenage parents, dually di-agnosed (MR/MI) adults in group homes, Haitian immigrants) in the area that is underserved. Arrange to spend the day with a member of that group. Someone who has work that takes him through the *residential or place community* of this population (if one exists), such as a pizza deliv-erer, meter reader, pest control employee, local transit worker, or activities director, would be a good choice. If this is a *scattered or nonplace community*, ferret out members of this population whose work takes them on rounds involving this group, such as a public health worker, job coach, English as a second language tutor, or Head Start outreach worker. Better yet, on a weekend, take a walk with two clients or community residents. This may be easier and more natural for case man-agers and community-based practitioners than for clinicians, but it would be useful for all to better understand relationships; obtain basic information on errands, shopping, transportation, and missing resources; and solicit opinions informally about service adequacy and other delivery dimensions. (Avoid being intrusive, be humble, and make clear your desire to understand.)

community analysis, according to Bracht and Kingsbury (1990), are defining the commu-nity, collecting data, assessing community capacity, assessing community barriers, as-sessing readiness for change, synthesizing data, and setting priorities. All of our study methods could contribute to attaining such knowledge. The ability to figure out "community-oriented prevention/treatment approaches" can be crucial in assisting eth-nic communities (Edwards & Edwards, 1990, p. 290). Again, this chapter provides both a framework and concrete tools.

Readers should be advised that we have oversimplified the four types of studies to il-luminate their distinctions and stress their feasibility. In practice, the study design may be far more complex. For instance, in order to identify problems, opportunities, and re-sources before engaging in any health pro-motion intervention, Haglund, Weisbrod and Bracht (1990) recommend putting to-gether at least six components: a general so-cioeconomic community profile; a health risk profile; a health wellness outcomes profile; a survey of current health promotion pro-grams; special studies (target groups, etc); and a study of community leadership. These authors mix methods, drawing on both quan-titative and qualitative data. Coulton (1995) speaks similarly about her work in Ohio:

> [W]e learned that community studies can-not be done using either quantitative or qual-itative methods alone. We have combined epidemiological, survey, and ethnographic methods, all of which were necessary to un-derstand internal processes as well as met-ropolitan trends. Multiple methods will be a hallmark of effective social work research in the community. (p. 438)

CONCLUSION: UNPRETENTIOUS BUT NECESSARY OUTINGS

We conclude this overview of how to study and size up communities and the day-to-day realities of residents and members with these summarizing points:

- In order to be aware of local mores and clients' assumptions about reality, we must involve ourselves as much as possible in their worlds with the aim of gaining cognitive and affective knowledge.

- There are many ways to recognize and analyze communities; therefore, one must decide on appropriate variables (you can't find it if you don't look for it) and methodologies (how to find it).

- Practitioners can learn more about any of the four approaches described by exploring their particular area. We suggest that readers review the suggestions for the four walks—designed to capture the flavor and other aspects of each type of study. If you are still not sure of what to look for, think of yourself as a film maker depicting aspects of your community that you are discovering and want to document or share with your office.

- We also suggest that readers review carefully the possible questions to ask community residents or clients. Those who anticipate conducting a study should think of additional relevant questions and then recruit a small focus group of individuals from the community to help refine suggested questions and additions.

- Even if inexperienced practitioners use such unpretentious methods as looking, asking questions, and listening, they can be more relevant and helpful in their future work.

Ultimately, we must look beyond needs and differences to see what pulls a community together. Residents of rural Arcadia, Indiana, for instance, came together to throw a farewell party for the United Parcel Service driver when he retired. Each store in town had hand-made signs inviting the public to a potluck dinner held in his honor. He had been a link between various communities.

Discussion Exercises

1. How oriented are you to the place where you live? To the place where your clients live?

2. Has your field agency conducted a neighborhood or community study? The community study might be of the larger metropolitan area or of a particular population (e.g., the gay community or the drug community). If so, determine whether it fits one of these types. (Needs assessments are covered in Chapter 6.)

3. It is incumbent on practitioners in small communities to know about the "local," the person who has always resided in the town and is respected as an authority by other locals. Martinez-Brawley (1990) puts it this way: "The community-oriented social worker needs to know a great deal about these residents and their unique claims, not only because they are often part of the power structure, but because they are also part of the community's fibers" (p. 222). Referring to three of the methods presented in the chapter, discuss how you would go about identifying such locals.

4. Do you know the names of the newspapers in each community you serve, especially the weekly ones?

5. How do movies and television shows steer our interest toward meeting the need of a single individual rather than all members of a group? What mechanisms in print and broadcast media (e.g., personalization) make us identity with an individual rather than a group or neighborhood? Link your answer to the premises in Specht and Courtney's *Unfaithful Angels* about our field's embrace of psychotherapy for the few rather than social care for the many.

6. What are the advantages of quantitative studies that examine problem incidence rates and other social indicators? (see Zuravin & Taylor, 1987).

Notes

1. See Jacobs (1961), *The Death and Life of Great American Cities*; Berger and Neuhaus (1977), *To Empower People*; Berger, Berger, and Kellner (1973), *The Homeless Mind*; and Bellah, Madsen, Sullivan, Swidler, and Tipton (1985), *Habits of the Heart*.

2. Urbanization, dislocation, industrialization, bureaucratization, development, environmental hazards, and ethnocultural and other factors affect community life.

3. The American Enterprise Institute and the Center for Community Change—both D.C. based—promoted very different political ideas of community.

4. For example, Coulton (1995) states: "The community needs to become a partner in our applied research, action research, policy research, and practice research" (p. 438).

5. Community is more than local space, especially in urban areas. Flanagan (1993), says: "People sleep in their neighborhood, they identify with it to a greater or lesser extent as being their own special place in the city, but they live their daily social lives within a spatially diffuse and more heterogeneous social network . . . It is appropriate to picture a very highly interconnected web of relationships among [rural] residents. In the city, it is rare for all of one person's friends, acquaintances, and other contacts to know and be in regular contact with one another" (p. 21).

6. The beginnings of the community study, as a vehicle for firsthand inquiry and as a research methodology, are linked to the Chicago school of sociology. The reports of that 1920s era, such as, *The Unadjusted Girl* and *The City*, were descriptive and ethnographic, utilized personal observation and documentary sources, and built on an urban ecology model. Diverse and marginal groups—homeless men, waitresses, department store saleswomen, gangs, African-Americans—were studied by researchers.

7. The appendix to the enlarged versions of *Street Corner Society* (especially from p. 288 to the end) gives a wonderful introduction to street work and field work. The latest edition includes materials on controversies over the original portrait of Boston's North End.

8. See Clifford Geertz in Rabinow and Sullivan (1987); Spradley and McCurdy (1972); and Rodwell (1987).

9. Domhoff (1983) analyzes both the Hunter and Dahl studies and redoes aspects of Dahl's study in order to refute its conclusions on pluralism (pp. 184–196).

10. From a community analysis by Faith Little.

11. From a community analysis by Michele Feder.

References

Addams, J. (1910). *Twenty years at Hull House: With autobiographical notes* (Introduction and Notes by J. Hurt, 1990). Urbana: University of Illinois Press.

Armstrong, J., & Henderson, P. (1992). Putting the Community Into Community Care. *Community Development Journal, 27,* 189.

Auerswald, E. H. (1968). Interdisciplinary versus Ecological Approach. *Family Process, 7,* 207.

Barlett, D. L., & Steele, J. B. (1994). *America: Who really pays the taxes.* New York: Simon & Schuster.

Bellah, R. N., Madsen, R., Sullivan, W. M., Swidler, A., & Tipton, S. M. (1985). *Habits of the heart: Individualism and commitment in American life.* New York: Harper & Row.

Berger, P., Berger, B., & Kellner, H. (1973). *The homeless mind: Modernization and consciousness.* New York: Vintage Books.

Berger, P. L., & Neuhaus, R. J. (1977). *To empower*

people: The role of mediating structures in public policy. Washington, DC: American Enterprise Institute.

Bracht, N., & Kingsbury, L. (1990). Community organization principles in health promotion: A five-stage model. In N. Bracht (Ed.), *Health promotion at the community level* (pp. 66–88). Newbury Park, CA: Sage.

Brandriet, L. M. (1994, July). Gerontological nursing: Application of ethnography and grounded theory. *Journal of Gerontological Nursing, 20*(7), 33–40.

Brown, M. J. (1993). Summer of service, 1963. *Social Policy, 24*(2), 17–20.

Browning, T. (1995, February 28). For the children. *The State Journal-Register* (Springfield, IL), p. 9.

Bulmer, M. (1984). *The Chicago school of sociology: Institutionalization, diversity, and the rise of sociological research*. Chicago: University of Chicago Press.

Burton, A. (1991). Dividing up the struggle: The consequences of "split" welfare work for union activism. In M. Burawoy, A. Burton, A. A. Ferguson, et al. (Eds.), *Ethnography Unbound: Power and resistance in the modern metropolis*. Berkeley: University of California Press.

Coulton, C. J. (1995). Riding the pendulum of the 1990s: Building a community context for social work research. *Social Work, 40*(4), 437–439.

Cox, F. M. (1977). What's going on: Addressing the situation. In F. M. Cox, J. L. Erlich, J. Rothman, & J. E. Tropman (Eds.), *Tactics and techniques of community practice* (pp. 15–16). Itasca, IL: F. E. Peacock.

Cox, F. M. (1995). Community problem solving: A guide to practice with comments. In J. Rothman, J. L. Erlich, & J. E. Tropman with F. M. Cox (Eds.), *Strategies of community organization: Macro practice* (5th ed., pp. 146–162). Itasca, IL: F. E. Peacock.

Dahl, R. A. (1961). *Who governs? Democracy and power in an American city*. New Haven, CT: Yale University Press.

Daley, J. M., & Wong, P. (1994). Community development with emerging ethnic communities. *Journal of Community Practice, 1*(1), 9–24.

Davis, M. (1992). *City of quartz*. New York: Vintage Books.

Delgado, M. (1979, Summer/Fall). Health care and Puerto Ricans: A consultation and educational program. *Patient Counseling and Health Education, 1*(1), 164–168.

Denzin, N. K. (1970). *The research act: A theoretical introduction to sociological methods*. Chicago: Aldine.

Domhoff, G. W. (1983). *Who rules America now: A view for the '80s*. New York: Simon & Schuster.

Dorfman, R. A. (1994). *Aging into the 21st century: The exploration of aspirations and values*. New York: Brunner/Mazel.

Duberman, M. (1972). *Black Mountain: An exploration in community*. New York: E. P. Dutton.

Dye, T. R. (1993). *Power and society: An introduction to the social sciences*. Belmont, CA: Wadsworth.

Edgerton, R. B. (1967). *The cloak of competence: Stigma in the lives of the mentally retarded*. Berkeley: University of California Press.

Edwards, E. D., & Egbert-Edwards, M. (1990). American Indian adolescents: Combating problems of substance use and abuse through a community model. In A. R. Stiffman & L. E. Davis (Eds.), *Ethnic issues in adolescent mental health* (pp. 285–302). Newbury Park, CA: Sage.

Emenhiser, D. (1991, Spring). Power influence and contributions. *National Society of Fundraising Executives Journal*, pp. 9–14.

Erikson, K. T. (1976). *Everything in its path*. New York: Simon & Schuster.

Fellin, P. (1995). Understanding American communities. In J. Rothman, J. L. Erlich, & J. E. Tropman with F. M. Cox (Eds.), *Strategies of community organization: Macro practice* (5th ed., pp. 114–128). Itasca, IL: F. E. Peacock.

Flanagan, W. G. (1993). *Contemporary urban sociology*. New York: Cambridge University Press.

Gamble, D. N., & Weil, M. O. (1995). Citizen participation. In R. Edwards (Ed.-in-Chief), *Encyclopedia of Social Work* (19th ed., pp. 483–494). Washington, DC: National Association of Social Workers.

Garvin, C. D., & Cox, F. M. (1995). A history of community organizing since the Civil War with special reference to oppressed communities. In J. Rothman, J. L. Erlich, & J. E. Tropman with Fred M. Cox (Eds.), *Strategies of community organization* (5th ed., pp. 64–99). Itasca, IL: F. E. Peacock.

Gaventa, J. (1980). *Power and powerlessness: Quiescence and rebellion in an Appalachian valley*. Urbana: University of Illinois Press.

Geertz, C. (1987). Deep play: Notes on the Balinese cockfight. In P. Rabinow & W. M. Sullivan (Eds.), *Interpretive social science: A second look*. Berkeley: University of California Press.

Gilchrist, A. (1992). Grey matters: Struggles for

new thinking and new respect. *Community Development Journal, 17*(2), 175–181.

Goodman, P., & Goodman, P. (1947). *Communitas.* New York: Vintage Books.

Green, J. W. (1995). *Cultural awareness in the human services: A multi-ethnic approach* (2nd ed). Boston: Allyn & Bacon.

Hagland, B., Weisbrod, R. R., & Bracht, N. (1990). Assessing the community: Its services, needs, leadership, and readiness. In N. Bracht (Ed.), *Health promotion at the community level* (pp. 91–108). Newbury Park, CA: Sage.

Hahn, A. J. (1994). *The politics of caring: Human services at the local level.* Boulder, CO: Westview.

Henderson, P., & Thomas, D. N. (1987). *Skills in Neighbourhood.* London: Allen & Unwin.

Hexter, K. W. (1989). *Private sector services to aid older Americans: A survey of gatekeeper programs and other programs sponsored by utility companies.* Washington, DC: American Association of Retired Persons.

Howell, J. T. (1973). *Hard living on Clay Street: Portraits of blue-collar families.* Garden City, NY: Anchor Books.

Hunter, F. (1953). *Community power structure.* Chapel Hill: University of North Carolina Press.

Jacobs, J. (1961). *The death and life of great American cities.* New York: Vintage Books.

Lamb, R. K. (1977). Community life: How to get its pulse: Suggestions for a study of your hometown. In F. M. Cox, J. L. Erlich, J. Rothman, & J. E. Tropman (Eds.), *Tactics and techniques of community practice* (pp. 17–23). Itasca, IL: F. E. Peacock.

Lasch, C. (1995). *The revolt of the elites and the betrayal of democracy.* New York: W. W. Norton.

Liebow, E. (1967). *Tally's corner.* Boston: Little, Brown.

Lynd, R., & Lynd, H. (1929). *Middletown.* New York: Harcourt Brace.

Maguire, L., & Biegel, D. (1982). The use of social networks in social welfare. In *Social Welfare Forum, 1981* (pp. 140–159). New York: Columbia University Press.

Martinez-Brawley, E. E. (1990). *Perspectives on the small community: Humanistic views for practitioners.* Washington, DC: National Association of Social Work Press.

Meenaghan, T. M., Washington, R. O., & Ryan, R. M. (1982). *Macro practice in the human services.* New York: Free Press.

Menolascino, F. J., & Potter, J. F. (1989). Delivery of services in rural settings to the mentally retarded-mentally ill. *International Journal of Aging and Human Development, 28*(4), 261–275.

Mogil, C., & Slepian, A. with P. Woodrow. (1992). *We gave away a fortune: Stories of people who have devoted themselves and their wealth to peace, justice and a healthy environment.* Philadelphia: New Society.

Mondros, J. B., & Wilson, S. M. (1994). *Organizing for power and empowerment.* New York: Columbia University Press.

Morris, R. (1986). *Rethinking social welfare: Why care for the stranger.* New York: Longman.

Mowry, D. D. (1994). Mentoring the Hmong: A practice outlet for teaching faculty and a possible community development tool. *Journal of Community Practice, 1*(1), 107–112.

Myerhoff, B. (1980). *Number our days.* New York: Simon & Schuster.

Netting, F. E., Kettner, P. M., & McMurtry, S. L. (1993). *Social work macro practice.* New York: Longman.

Neuber, K. A., Atkins, W. T., Jacobson, J. A., & Reuterman, N. A. (1980). *Needs assessment: A model for community planning.* Newbury Park, CA: Sage.

Ollove, M. (1991, February 17). Johns Hopkins Hospital: The board to be on. *The Baltimore Sun,* Sunday magazine, p. 8.

Olsen, M. E., & Marger, M. N. (Eds.). (1993). *Power in modern societies.* Boulder, CO: Westview.

Rauch, J. B., North, C., Rowe, C. L., & Risley-Curtis, C. (1993). *Diversity competence: A learning guide.* Baltimore: University of Maryland at Baltimore School of Social Work.

Ritzer, G. (1992). *Contemporary sociological theory* (3rd ed.). New York: McGraw-Hill.

Rodwell, M. K. (1987). Naturalistic inquiry: An alternative model for social work assessment. *Social Service Review, 61*(2), 231–246.

Rothman, J. (1984). Assessment and option selection (introduction to part one). In F. M. Cox, J. L. Erlich, J. Rothman, & J. E. Tropman (Eds.), *Tactics and techniques of community practice* (2nd ed., pp. 7–13). Itaska, IL: F. E. Peacock.

Rounds, K. A., Weil, M., & Bishop, K. K. (1994). Practice with culturally diverse families of young children with disabilities. *Families in Society, 75*(1), 3–15.

Siegel, L. M., Attkisson, C. C., & Carson, L. G. (1987). Need identification and program planning in the community. In F. M. Cox, J. L. Erlich, J. Rothman, & J. E. Tropman (Eds.), *Strategies of* community organization: Macro practice (4th ed., pp. 71–97). Itasca, IL: F. E. Peacock.

Slaght, E., & Schopler, J. (1994). Quick and dirty community needs assessments: Debate 10. In M. J. Austen, & J. I. Lowe (Eds.), Controversial issues in communities and organizations (pp. 142–157). Needham Heights, MA: Allyn & Bacon.

Specht, H., & Courtney, M. (1994). Unfaithful angels: How social work has abandoned its mission. New York: Free Press.

Spradley, B. W. (1990). Community health nursing: Concepts and practice (3rd ed). Glenview, IL: Scott, Foresman.

Spradley, J. P., & McCurdy, D. W. (1972). The cultural experience: Ethnography in complex society. Chicago: Science Research.

Stein, M. R. (1972). The eclipse of community. Princeton, NJ: Princeton University Press.

Sullivan, K. (1994, April 14). The power people: Government, corporate, community and media figures who stand out. The Washington Post, Maryland section, pp. 1, 8.

Wagner, D. (1993). Checkerboard square: Culture and resistance in a homeless community. Boulder, CO: Westview.

Warren, R. B., & Warren, D. I. (1984). How to diagnose a neighborhood. In F. M. Cox, J. L. Erlich, J. Rothman, & J. E. Tropman (Eds.), Tactics and techniques of community practice (2nd. ed., pp. 27–40). Itaska, IL: F. E. Peacock.

Warren, R. L. (1977). The community in America (3rd ed.). Chicago: Rand McNally.

Wellman, B., & Leighton, B. (1979). Networks, neighborhoods and communities: Approaches to the study of the community question. Urban Affairs Quarterly, 14(3), 363–390.

Whyte, W. F. (1993). Street corner society: The social structure of an Italian slum (4th ed). Chicago: University of Chicago Press.

Wuthnow, R. (1991). Acts of compassion: Caring for others and helping ourselves. Princeton, NJ: Princeton University Press.

Zuravin, S. J., & Taylor, R. (1987). The ecology of child maltreatment: Identifying and characterizing high-risk neighborhoods. Child Welfare, 66(5), 497–506.

chapter

6

Using Assessment in Community Practice

Although it generally is understood that people live in complex social milieus that dramatically affect them, assessment rarely takes into account larger social variables.

A. WEICK, C. RAPP, W. P. SULLIVAN, AND W. KISTHARDT (1989, P. 351)

ASSESSMENT AS A BASIC SOCIAL WORK PROCESS

We must know how to include community factors in any case assessment and analyze the community itself. Assessment frameworks can serve as a means of planning or inquiry, as a vehicle for information exchange, as part of formal problem solving, and as a way to determine which services are needed by whom. This chapter includes types, philosophies, and methods of assessment; reflection on assessment; and a look at the transition to action. It is meant to be a guide to *preparation* for client assistance, program development, and community-based services.

Overview of Assessment as a Process

B.D.: *Still* no full disability. They want to further "assess" my condition. . . . Remind me to get sick with a brand-name disease next time, Boopsie—Gulf War Syndrome doesn't seem to cut it. . . . (Trudeau, 1995)

To *assess* an individual such as Doonesbury comic strip character B.D. or a health problem is to analyze (not assume); to interpret data, phenomena, and written or oral reports; and to appraise in preparation for intervention and/or evaluation. Assessment considers the "interacting personal, environmental, and cultural factors involved" (Germain & Gitterman, 1995, p. 816).[1] All three are involved in Agent Orange and Gulf War Syndrome.

Used at every level of practice, in organizational and community settings, assessment involves ongoing surveillance of people, situations, and environments, as well as immediate analysis. We can assess an individual, a family, or a neighborhood ecosystem including informal networks, mediating structures, and formal organizations. *Assessment* serves as an umbrella term for a sequence of stages. One way to view the process is depicted in Box 6.1, which uses an arbitrary but informative breakdown of important aspects of assessment. It gives us a look at the conscious use of self (see Chapter 7) inherent in assessment and summarizes guidelines for doing *community assessment*.

The process can have a wide or narrow, general or targeted focus. Communitywide study methodologies can be employed to research, classify, map, and assess *any* community, anywhere, anytime (see Chapter 5). Assessment also indicates a cognitive process used with particular clients, situations, or problems (All, 1994), *which pays attention to uniqueness* (Meyer, 1993, p. 9; Stiffman & Davis, 1990). In line with this thinking, Johnson (1995) views assessment in broad terms, as including

> social study analysis and understanding;
> resource-oriented needs assessment.

More narrowly, Johnson views it in the sense of:

> fitting the pieces together for particular individuals or systems.

The Ethics and Impact of Assessment

Forster's 1910 novel *Howards End* centers on a cavalier assessment, based on community rumors and thirdhand information about an individual's situation, that destroys a man.

BOX 6.1	**THE A'S OF ASSESSMENT: A SOCIAL WORKER (SW) CONDUCTS AN ASSESSMENT**

Awareness—SW becomes alerted to an aspect of a problem in the community

Abeyance—SW suspends judgment about the situation but delves into it

Abstraction—SW thinks beyond the immediate situation to theory and in gestalt terms

Accumulation—SW gathers information, opinions, and knowledge about assets and concerns

Affiliation—SW uses collaboration and other means to involve the community

Analysis—SW dissects, synthesizes variables, and draws inferences

Apprehension—SW interprets, grasps meaning, and tries to understand community perspective(s)

Appraisal—SW (with others) designs and formulates a plan, uses own judgment, and makes decisions

Application—SW moves to intervention

Activation—SW engages others in implementing the assessment plan

Amelioration—SW joins in the collective effort to address the situation

Ascertainment—SW (with others) evaluates the effort, figures out the next steps, or wraps things up

Wanting to assist a promising but nearly penniless insurance clerk, Leonard Bast, two sisters put his situation to knowledgeable people of means who are quick with their assessments. Mr. Wilcox, a millionaire familiar with the business world, says:

> My dear Miss Schlegel. . . . My only contribution is this: let your young friend clear out of the Porphyrion Fire Insurance Company with all possible speed. . . . It'll be in the receiver's hands before Christmas. (p. 105)

With his erroneous advice taken and Bast destitute, Wilcox proves to have an "undeveloped heart" (p. ix).

Certain principles flow from this cautionary tale:

- assessment should inform, not force, action;
- advice should take into consideration the social environment *and* the individual;
- hasty judgments can bring harm or ruin; and
- people bear responsibility for conclusions they reach unilaterally that affect another's future.

Caution and caring: *"Only connect,"* Forster suggests. Disconnection, not bad advice, is his concern. Meaningful interaction requires risk, hope, trust (p. xiii), and objective, yet *attached*, assessment.

The Multiple Meanings of Assessment

Assessment connotes professionalism. In plain language, conducting assessments keeps us from indulging in knee-jerk reactions or off-the-cuff pronouncements of the type illustrated by the all-knowing but myopic Mr. Wilcox. Certainly some assessments have to be instantaneous, even though a sys-tematic approach is preferable, but reflective wisdom must inform our hunches (Scott, 1990).

Assessment is a product such as a report or an answer to a question; a process such as a study, inquiry, or evaluation; and a rational skill central to practice. Unlike our fictional bad example, assessment is also a participatory process, whether involving an "appropriate care plan" (Martinez-Brawley & Delevan, 1993, p. 171) or "collective community needs" (Netting, Kettner, & McMurtry, 1993, p. 95).

VARYING EMPHASES IN DIFFERENT CONCENTRATIONS

Assessment is used throughout social work with differing emphases and terminology. Practice literature equates assessment with diagnosis, evaluation, judgment, understanding, and fact gathering. In community work, it is one of a complex of preparatory activities such as gaining entry, developing rapport, building credibility, and problem solving. In direct service, it is considered to be both the process of gathering social history-type information[2] and the *judgments* based on what is learned. Clinicians might base judgments on DSM-IV or person-in-environment (P-I-E) classifications. Jansson (1990) describes another type of judgment. He uses assessment in the *evaluation-argument* sense and believes that a fundamental logic makes policy and clinical assessment similar:

> Policy assessment . . . forces us to ask, How (if at all) is the external world different because a specific policy exists, and what (if any) difference would it make if we removed, deleted, or modified the policy? . . . Direct-service practitioners who examine their work in a critical fashion often wonder, Will such-and-such an intervention improve the well-being of specific clients—or will it be counterproductive—or has the sum total of our

interventions over a specific time period led to improvement in their well-being? (p. 415).

Jansson thinks assessment occurs at the start and end of a process, but to Lauffer (1984), assessment and evaluation are "conceptually distinct" because assessment focuses on "the examination of what is, on what is likely to be, or on what ought to be" (p. 60).

Until recently, we spoke of "diagnosing" individuals and neighborhoods, that is, looking for what is amiss. Today we say "assessment," whatever the unit of attention (Cowger, 1994, p. 267; Meyer, 1995). Thus, for insight into a community, we shift from an emphasis on a "need-deficiency-problem" assessment to one on "asset-capacity-problem-solving" (Kretzmann & McKnight, 1993, p. 1), that is, to "strength assessment" (Rosenthal & Cairns, 1994, p. 58). This, in turn, leads us to pay more attention to mapping and inventorying—for example, relevant relationships, and resources (Johnson, 1995; Miley, O'Melia, & DuBois, 1995).

FORMAL ASSESSMENT

Auspices and context. When we assess X (e.g., the adequacy and effectiveness of a given program), the question becomes, from whose point of view? Are we a consultant for the subsystem in question, do we represent an advocacy group, or are we a disinterested party? Do we share affinities and perspectives with those who are being assessed? We should keep in mind our predispositions toward individual cases and programs. Basic decisions underlie *any* assessment. Who do we listen to? Who will we trust? How will we decide? Whose views count most? Answers can be influenced by the auspices under which we proceed—be it a county government, a nonprofit organization, a credentialing body, a university, or an agency.

Frameworks. It is valuable to understand the methods commonly used to assess service and advocacy needs (Moxley & Freddolino, 1994). Whether examining the situations of clients or of community residents, we first must identify relevant variables. Then assessment can serve as "a way to bring order out of the chaos of a melange of disconnected variables" (Meyer, 1993, p. 3). Meyer describes a process that takes practitioners from *exploration and study*, to *inference*, to *evaluation*, to *problem definition*, along with a realistic appraisal of what is doable, to *intervention or planning* (1993, chap. 2). Hepworth and Larsen (1993) refer to these dimensions of assessment: the *nature of the problems*, the *coping capacities* of those involved, the *relevant systems* involved, the *available or needed resources*, and the *motivation* to resolve problems (p. 192). While these authors concentrate on the course of individual cases that include ecological factors, the processes they mention are transferable to community cases that include individual factors. We will apply these ideas where the community is a likely starting point for discovery (Miley et al., 1995). See Box 6.2.

LINK BETWEEN ASSESSMENT AND MODELS OF PRACTICE

The type of assessment just illustrated fits well with task-centered, education-oriented, and ecological models of practice and with the concepts of reciprocality and connection. For example, Freeman (1990) advocates a social health approach that stresses a coping model (p. 253). Maluccio (1979) urges educators to teach students "a more active orientation toward the environment" (p. 199) and urges students to continue the process through client education. Approaches that emphasize the basics—resources and concrete services—will "help clients to make their environment more nurturing and more conducive to their growth

BOX 6.2	WHAT IS OUT THERE?

School social worker Chris is aware of a child with a facial disfigurement who is teased callously by classmates behind the teacher's back and by neighborhood children whose parents apparently never intervene.

A practitioner must take account of the negative affects of this community and simultaneously explore it as a positive resource. *Ponder how you would approach this if you were Chris.* In doing so,

1. Keep in mind this *definition*: "Assessment involves synthesizing relevant factors into a working hypothesis about the nature of problems and their contributory causes" (Hepworth & Larsen, 1993, p. 277).

2. Follow these *guidelines*:

- "Move the assessment toward personal and environmental strengths" (Cowger, 1994, p. 265).
- Think in terms of "a particular person:environment relationship, whether it is positive, negative, or neutral" (Germain & Gitterman, 1995, p. 816).

3. Consider ways to *link* the child to resources.

You will start with the child's definition of the problem so that you can mutually shape the assessment (Rodwell, 1987). You will make factual inquiries. You will discover the history of the child's family with the school. You will assess child and parent attitudes. However, before settling on discipline for the teasers, support for the teased, or anything else, you must assess both the intensity of the teasing and the neighborhood. Are other children being derisive or merely turning away from what makes them uncomfortable? Does this child experience normal grade school teasing as torment due to unresolved feelings about the disfigurement? Or are the playground, hallway, and journey to and from home a living hell by anyone's estimate? A janitor or playground aide might shed light on this issue. Until you know more about the situation, you do not know whether "strengthening the client" will work.

Is the child's condition correctable? Could the child's appearance be improved by plastic surgery? What are the family's religious beliefs regarding medicine? Does the family have insurance? If not, are you aware of public and private resources if the child wants medical intervention? While we must always consider whether it is possible to eliminate a problem, practitioners who aim solely for a medical solution, even if successful, may not solve the problem. If the child is being scapegoated due to a neighborhood situation, the harassment might be aimed at something else if the disfigurement disappeared. What resources within the child, family, and environment do we draw on in that eventuality? Who might mediate?

What information do you want about the neighborhood before seeking allies there? Is the family out of step with the community? Perhaps the family is hated for some reason (e.g., responsible for the death of someone on the block) and the child is a scapegoat. How might this situation be related to the values and traditions of the community? Perhaps the family and/or neighbors view deformities as punishment for religious or cultural reasons. To which neighborhood leaders do young people listen?

Regardless of the origin of the teasing, what might you do to stop it or, failing that, to balance it? Besides talking to the teacher, finding out which children from the same neighborhood might be reasoned with, and checking to see if a priest, scout or band leader, or relative can be helpful, you can assess larger systems. Does the principal realize that individuals with disfigurements are protected under disability discrimination laws? Are the parents part of an informal network (a food coop, people who go fishing together) or a formal organization (Masons or a labor union) that can be tapped? For instance, if the parents participate in folk dancing, the child

BOX 6.2   (Continued)

could go with them and master a skill in a friendlier environment. What talents does the child possess?

How can school and community assets be used? What might the principal do to place the child in a more positive light? Is there a coveted student role (e.g., making announcements over the loudspeaker) that this child could assume, becoming known in a new way? What community programs might fit? Are there individuals in town who could be role models? Do disability or veterans groups know of adults who coped with similar problems in their youth and might share their stories?

Chris has been assessing individual and social factors and making inferences and can now make

a formal assessment. Let us assume that neighborhood conflict was apparent. A concise, focused individual assessment report should be shared with the child, the family, and the teacher. The community assessment may be in the form of a memo to colleagues in the school or to a neighborhood civic association. It should share observations and recommendations while protecting confidentiality, although privacy is admittedly difficult to maintain in this particular example.

The community provides resources to its members and social workers. Discovering not only the clients' internal strengths but also their "external strengths"—networks, organizations, institutions with resources—is "central to assessment" (Cowger, 1994, p. 266).

and self-fulfillment" (Maluccio, 1979, p. 189). He urges social work to give "more weight to nonclinical activities such as advocacy, situational intervention, and environmental manipulation." (p. 189). The more we can integrate information about a community system into direct practice, the more useful to groups and individuals we will be (Box 6.3).

Wrap-up. Assessments help us organize our work and engage in activities of most significance to a client. Environmental factors play a part in assessing individuals and groups. Before we can assess our communities as entities, we must be able to identify community elements in case and group work.

FORMS OF COMMUNITY ASSESSMENT

Over the past decades, many localities were asked by state planners to engage in futurist studies to prepare for the next century. That is one form of community assessment. Here four different types of more immediate

community assessments will be introduced and described briefly. Then special attention will be given to problem-oriented and subsystem types, including a discussion of what they require of professionals. Resource and collaborative assessments are also discussed in this section.

One Assessment Typology

Barbara Spradley (1990) categorizes community assessments by their purview as

1. *comprehensive* assessments;
2. assessments of a *familiarization* nature;
3. *problem-oriented* assessments; and
4. *subsystem* assessments. (p. 388)

COMPREHENSIVE ASSESSMENT
Assessments can be comprehensive in the sense of *encompassing the entire community, being methodologically thorough, and generating original data.* To Martinez-Brawley (1990), assessment starts with abstract ques-

tions of a high order such as "How does the community rate in terms of cohesiveness, engagement and interdependence among its members?" (p. 23). Such questions require in-depth examination. Field and power structure studies (Chapter 5) are methodologies for conducting comprehensive assessments. What reason would we have to assess something as large as a community? Think of someone who organizes migrant farm workers—someone who has many locations from which to choose to begin work, since the workers need help wherever they live. An assessment would help to select a community where townspeople and media outlets are somewhat sympathetic; other occupations have a history of collective bargaining; unemployment is relatively low; interaction among minority groups is positive; and numerous residents speak the migrants' language.

FAMILIARIZATION ASSESSMENT

Some community assessments, based on available data with some firsthand data added, entail a more cursory *examination of the entire community, with the goal of achieving a general understanding*. An abbreviated version of community analysis (Chapter 5) falls

into this category. The vignette about Chris, the school social worker, illustrates the start of a neighborhood familiarization process. Another example could flow from acquainting oneself with community and client concerns, such as by inviting those with similar problems to come together for a speak-out session. For instance, those from rural areas who must travel to receive radiation therapy or dialysis might share their needs and frustrations about their care or transportation. These patients could provide a more complete picture of the adequacy of their hometown supports. Follow-up assessments of rural towns could be of this type.

PROBLEM-ORIENTED ASSESSMENT

Problem-oriented assessments *involve the entire community but center on one problem*, such as the uninsured or child protection. Practitioners write such assessments as part of grant proposals (in "The Problem" or "Contributing Factors" sections). An interdisciplinary team might be motivated to undertake such an assessment to better coordinate programs and cases (Lenherr, Haase, & Motz, 1988, p. 216). Or a community foundation might coordinate a fresh look at vio-

---

| BOX 6.3 | NOTING COMMUNITY INFLUENCE |

One aspect of community assessment involves consideration of the role the larger community plays in the lives of program participants. An outing for young teenagers to an indoor ice skating rink, for instance, can provide an opportunity for a social worker to observe community influences. Suppose that the members of the group belong to the same youth group and are all of the same race and religion, yet come from different areas in a town. The worker notices that group members divide into cliques based on their prior attendance at First or Third Ward elementary schools. Today no one will be a partner with a South Side boy who is considered "smelly" by the others, so he skates alone. Parents who came along as drivers don't skate with him either, although they skate with other teenagers, because, they mutter, his hands are dirty. Adults and youth have brought their community with them into the activity. Group dynamics are being influenced by community dynamics; both require assessment. The worker must deal with the exclusion of the one group member.

lence in the home and assess how services to combat abuse against children, women, and elders could be better integrated under a family umbrella. Kettner, Moroney, and Martin (1990) astutely observe that problem analysis includes "analysis of the political environment, an assessment of a community's readiness to deal with the problem, and a measure of the resources the community is willing to commit to its solution" (p. 41). This topic will be described in more detail below.

SUBSYSTEM ASSESSMENT

Assessing a subsystem means *examining a single facet of community life*, such as the business sector or religious organizations (Spradley, 1990, p. 388). Such assessments might (1) focus on those who live in manufactured housing/mobile homes, (2) consider the local corrections system, ranging from jails to halfway houses, or (3) examine Jewish social services. A subsystem has a structure that must be demarcated and should be diagrammed. To illustrate, board and care homes are one of many subsystems on which clients rely. These care facilities are part of a multilevel provider–regulator subsystem (which is part of the long-term care system, which, in turn, is part of the health care system). Box 6.4 depicts a *formal* local system—the many offices with which we must be familiar, from zoning to the fire marshall—and an *informal* system (Dobkin, 1989). Depictions of subsystems look dauntingly detailed but provide essential yet scarce information.

Until the complexity of a subsystem is internalized, any assessment aiming at change is premature. This topic will be discussed in more detail below.

Problem-Oriented Community Assessments

Assessment of problems and responses to them can be further explicated through practice examples such as our responses to political requests and community responses to the social problem of rape.

SCOPE, REQUEST INITIATOR, AND PRACTITIONER ROLE

Social workers ought to be able to conduct full-blown, long-term problem assessments and quick ones. We can expect to receive *targeted questions from journalists and public officials*. We might be asked: "Who will use public toilets if they are installed along sidewalks in our city, and what is the prediction for nontraditional use?" or "What is the capacity of our community and its service network to absorb more refugees?" Although the requests may be unexpected, assessing the coping capacities of a client and of a social service network have much in common (see Box 6.1). Public officials like to involve those with firsthand experience. A group set up to assess the portable potty issue could be comprised of those providing direct services to the homeless; a Travelers Aid-type organization; a Women, Infants and Children program representative; someone from a methadone clinic; and officials from the city's tourist bureau and police and sanitation departments. The refugee question could be addressed to church sponsors, job placement and housing location groups, public welfare staff, civic leaders, and representatives of (and translators for) the refugee/immigrant community already in the area.

We must organize our knowledge in a form that can be pulled together and used by others. As Covey (1991) says, "Decision makers need to see a balanced picture and to receive information in user-friendly ways" (p. 229). The journalist or politician comes to the front-line worker neither for statistics nor diatribes, but rather for cases and insights that make sense of statistics. They also want easily remembered points on both sides of the question. To illustrate: if refugee wives and

BOX 6.4   A SERVICE SUBSYSTEM, INCLUDING ITS REGULATION

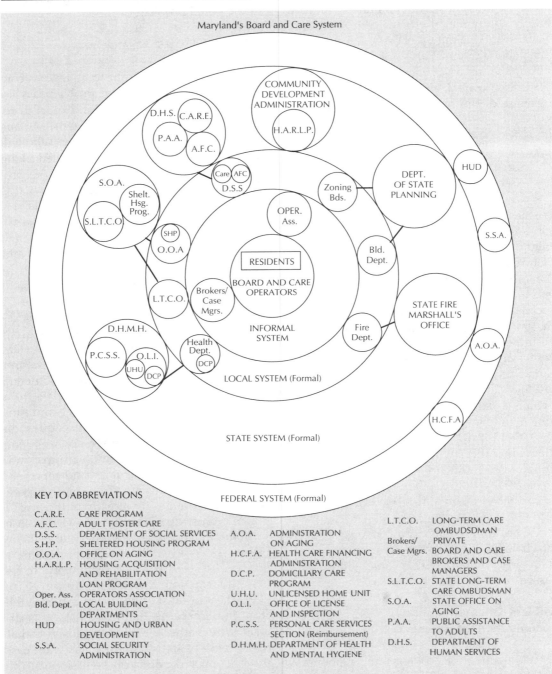

Maryland's Board and Care System

KEY TO ABBREVIATIONS

C.A.R.E.	CARE PROGRAM		
A.F.C.	ADULT FOSTER CARE		L.T.C.O.	LONG-TERM CARE OMBUDSDMAN
D.S.S.	DEPARTMENT OF SOCIAL SERVICES	A.O.A.	ADMINISTRATION ON AGING
S.H.P.	SHELTERED HOUSING PROGRAM		H.C.F.A.	HEALTH CARE FINANCING ADMINISTRATION
O.O.A.	OFFICE ON AGING		D.C.P.	DOMICILIARY CARE PROGRAM
H.A.R.L.P.	HOUSING ACQUISITION AND REHABILITATION LOAN PROGRAM	U.H.U.	UNLICENSED HOME UNIT
Oper. Ass.	OPERATORS ASSOCIATION	O.L.I.	OFFICE OF LICENSE AND INSPECTION
Bld. Dept.	LOCAL BUILDING DEPARTMENTS	P.C.S.S.	PERSONAL CARE SERVICES SECTION (Reimbursement)
HUD	HOUSING AND URBAN DEVELOPMENT	D.H.M.H.	DEPARTMENT OF HEALTH AND MENTAL HYGIENE
S.S.A.	SOCIAL SECURITY ADMINISTRATION		

(Key, continued)

L.T.C.O.	LONG-TERM CARE OMBUDSDMAN
Brokers/ Case Mgrs.	PRIVATE BOARD AND CARE BROKERS AND CASE MANAGERS
S.L.T.C.O.	STATE LONG-TERM CARE OMBUDSMAN
S.O.A.	STATE OFFICE ON AGING
P.A.A.	PUBLIC ASSISTANCE TO ADULTS
D.H.S.	DEPARTMENT OF HUMAN SERVICES

parents can join men already here, there might be less crime and alcoholism, but as housing in the community for large families is in short supply and there is a waiting list, tensions could be heightened if refugees are given preference. While this may seem mere common sense, it is our role to inject common sense, facts, and ethics into political decision making.

A Beginning Point for Analysis

A social problem can be a starting point to learn more about community responsiveness and how different systems interrelate. We can examine problems and responses to them (1) from a flow chart perspective, tracing those entities involved after the fact to those involved before the fact, or vice versa, and (2) from an overview of the "quality and comprehensiveness of local services" for a problem (Koss & Harvey, 1991, p. 115). Box 6.5 illustrates resources a community may or may not have to respond to rape.

This simple resource inventory can be used to assess local services, give guidance on a range of community actions that can be taken, and look for gaps or problems. (However, each community problem will require a different list.) Assessment helps with more than research, planning, and evaluation; it gives us a quick look at areas of difficulty within the system.

Monitoring and Listening

Koss and Harvey (1991) analyze rape as a community problem and discuss "the interrelationships that exist among community attitudes, community services, and the psychological experience of the woman raped" (p. 92). Task-centered social work recommends keeping a focus on client-articulated problems. Moreover, we want to learn about our own mistakes and to hear about systemic problems. To cite one notable example, it was victims and advocates who made those concerned about violence against women per-

ceive the unhelpful reaction of individual officers and the unfairness of police/court procedures regarding rape and family violence. An individual crisis can signal a community crisis. Rape is a problem that shows how casework, group work, community intervention, and social reform efforts can function as an integrated whole. Still, unless providers, advocates, and evaluators take responsibility for monitoring the progress of different community elements, individuals may fare no better. Thus, problem assessment must be an ongoing process.

Assessments of Community Subsystems

We will now explicate subsystem assessments using education, housing, and disability examples.

Figuring Out Subsystem Dynamics

Portrayed schematically (as in Box 6.4), a subsystem may seem static and easily manageable, but assessment takes into account subsystem dynamics. Wiseman (1968, 1994), the documentary filmmaker, has captured such dynamics in portrayals of multiple subsystems. Twice he has filmed high schools as a way of learning about communities. He is famous for examining without judging. We too must initially set aside preconceived ideas to become attuned to those affiliated with whatever slice of the community we are examining (Weiner, 1996). We want to be able to show the operations of a subsystem from both the participants' and our viewpoints. Eventually, if appropriate, we can make judgments (e.g., for advocacy purposes).

Advocacy-Oriented Subsystem Assessments

Subsystem assessments can be fairly complex, especially if intended to hold institutions accountable. Think of a community's financial system. Community development advocates have held lending institutions

BOX 6.5   ASSESSING A COMMUNITY'S RESPONSE TO RAPE

Service Component	Criteria				
	Availability	Accessibility	Quantity	Quality	Legitimacy
Victim Services					
Crisis					
1. Hot line	_____	_____	_____	_____	_____
2. Counseling	_____	_____	_____	_____	_____
3. Hospital accompaniment	_____	_____	_____	_____	_____
Hospital care					
1. Emergency	_____	_____	_____	_____	_____
2. Follow-up	_____	_____	_____	_____	_____
Police services					
1. Rape unit	_____	_____	_____	_____	_____
2. Investigatory procedures	_____	_____	_____	_____	_____
District attorney's office/ court procedures					
1. Rape unit	_____	_____	_____	_____	_____
2. Victim advocacy	_____	_____	_____	_____	_____
3. Court accompaniment	_____	_____	_____	_____	_____
Mental health/social service					
1. Short-term	_____	_____	_____	_____	_____
2. Long-term	_____	_____	_____	_____	_____
3. Special services	_____	_____	_____	_____	_____
Offenders					
Police and district attorney					
1. Investigation	_____	_____	_____	_____	_____
2. Arrest	_____	_____	_____	_____	_____
3. Prosecution	_____	_____	_____	_____	_____
Court systems					
1. Trial practice	_____	_____	_____	_____	_____
2. Sentencing by judges	_____	_____	_____	_____	_____
Alternative treatment					
1. Juvenile	_____	_____	_____	_____	_____
2. Adult	_____	_____	_____	_____	_____
Community Intervention					
Social action					
1. Victim advocacy	_____	_____	_____	_____	_____
2. Law and policy reform	_____	_____	_____	_____	_____
Community education					
1. Avoidance	_____	_____	_____	_____	_____
2. Prevention	_____	_____	_____	_____	_____

Note: For availability: Y = Yes; N = No.
For other measures, use 1–5 rating scale (1 = Excellent; 5 = Poor) for individual services and categories of service.

Source: *Koss and Harvey (1991),* p. 116. Copyright © 1991 by Sage Publications, Inc. Reprinted by permission of Sage Publications, Inc.

(banks and savings and loan institutions) accountable by monitoring their compliance with the Community Reinvestment Act and reporting to regulators. Such advocates often follow a three-stage process on behalf of communities in need of investment: (1) assess the community's credit needs; (2) assess and evaluate the lender's record of meeting those needs; (3) work with lenders to meet neighborhood needs (Center for Community Change, 1987). The assessment process stays much the same even though the purposes differ.

SERVICE-ORIENTED SUBSYSTEM ASSESSMENTS

Assessments of community subsystems often involve direct service practitioners. In one city, for example, a huge public housing complex was to be entirely rebuilt; therefore, residents had to relocate to other sites in town for 2 to 3 years. Part of the overall analysis of residents' needs included questionnaires and planning sessions with social workers and housing officials to identify services and programs wanted by residents in their temporary location and in their remodeled housing complex. The degree of importance of each option—from mentoring programs to General Equivalency Diploma (GED) classes—was examined. An assessment of relevant service providers and other civic entities was also made to identify programs already in place at the new sites, services that could be transferred with the resi-

dents, and gaps that existed. All of this involved an elaborate assessment of organizations serving low-income people.

However, a separate survey of residents revealed worries not just about the continuity and predictability of services but also about the transition itself—how they would be accepted in the receiving neighborhoods. This meant that (1) the overall assessment needed to encompass residents as well as agencies, and (2) neighborhood civic associations also needed to be contacted as part of the assessment. See also Box 6.6.

Resource Assessments

Looking at types of assessments from another angle, resources and collaboration are important. (See Chapter 13.)

KNOWING COMMUNITY RESOURCES

To be comprehensive, a social worker can examine the "four realms of resources that are available in a community: power, expertise, funding, and service" (Whitworth, Lanier, & Haase, 1988, p. 574). The type of assessment we wish to examine focuses on service resources. To grasp a *human service system*, Netting et al. (1993) would have us inspect three types of "service-delivery units"—informal, mediating, and formal—and identify the sponsoring organizations or auspices for each. (Self- or mutual-help groups and associations are examples of me-

---

Suppose that a mother calls about her daughter who is in college in your town and needs immediate and effective help but is not getting it at school. In the last year, her boyfriend back home has been murdered and two dorm acquaintances have been arrested for drug use. The daughter has handled these traumas by drinking so much that her grades are falling. The resource network for college students is outside your field, but you either must be able to refer the mother to the right person or do a quick assessment of this subsystem of services. Community assessments are not designed for crisis intervention. You recognize that you would be better off if you already knew about services for young adults and groups for problem drinkers, and about gaps, so that you do not make exaggerated claims to the mother about what is available.

| BOX 6.6 | A SUBSYSTEM ASSESSMENT VIGNETTE |

To comprehend a subcommunity or network, we often must increase our knowledge of that entity. We may need to particularize our assessments as well.

> A social worker in a speech and hearing clinic is about to meet with the deaf parents of a preschooler with a profound hearing loss who are coming in to talk about the child's schooling needs.

We will use this vignette to look at a subsystem. This is an opportunity to study a system and, as a by-product, our preconceptions (reflexive assessment).

- Assessment of supportive service systems will be influenced by how professionals conceptualize persons with differences. Assessment of the educational needs of this child will be influenced by whether the worker views a "disability" as a personal tragedy, a variable to consider, something culturally produced by society, or a target of social oppression (Oliver, 1990, chap. 1).
- Cultural diversity (ethnic and other cultures viewed as existing at the periphery of our society) must be factored into the design and implementation of assessment.
- Examination of past change efforts and perceptions of the problem by others significant in the arena or subsystem will be important (Cox, 1995).

Many assessment variables exist at the societal level, where there are competing views. Talk of multiple perspectives may strike us merely as semantics or rhetoric until we apply the idea in this case and confront the debate as to whether deafness is (1) a medical condition causing social isolation compensated for with signing, "a poor substitute for language," or with mainstreaming or (2) a fact conveying one into a special culture that communicates with a different but equally rich

mode of language expressed by the hands and face instead of the tongue and throat (Dolnick, 1993, p. 40; Sacks, 1989, p. ix). Some in the self-identified Deaf community see themselves as "a linguistic minority (speaking American Sign Language) and no more in need of a cure for their condition than are Haitians or Hispanics" (Dolnick, 1993, p. 37). Describing the controversy, Dolnick points out *dis*similarities to such ethnic minorities, since "90 percent of all deaf children are born to hearing parents" (p. 38). These various splits illustrate why assessments must consider social context, current "theories" (Cox, 1995, p. 155), and various tensions beneath the surface.

Many challenges come to the fore in a subsystem analysis. When we learn that our taken-for-granted assumptions are in question, we have no easy answers, but we can list pros and cons. The *implications of these differing perspectives* for treatment, schooling, and living arrangements, for intervention or nonintervention, for identity and reality, are heightened by the fact that a decision about a baby's first language needs to be made very early. Having so much at stake in making the best decision makes the situation more pressing. One camp alleges that Deaf culture has an "anti-book bias" and that without reading skills, dead-end jobs are common; the other camp argues that signing introduces children to language much earlier (Dolnick, 1993, pp. 46, 51; Sacks, 1989, p. x).

An educational assessment must take note of these differing philosophies. What did the parents decide to do with their baby? How far have they gone down a certain path? Do they want to turn back or continue? How do they view their child's *degree of hearing loss*: (1) as a personal problem (e.g., child's temperament), (2) as a social problem (e.g., child's future), (3) as no problem at all (e.g., child can communicate satisfactorily), or (4) as affecting a decision to be made (e.g., education in this instance is more significant than a public vs. private school decision, but it is comparable)?

BOX 6.6	(Continued)

Luey, Glass, and Elliott (1995) warn that "social workers must look at the complicated and inter-related dimensions of hearing, language, culture, and politics" (p. 178). Social workers may be dealing with the emotional upset of hearing parents who have a deaf child or the disappointment of deaf parents who have a hearing child).[3] Just as likely, they may need to gain acceptance for a particular child or for the Deaf community. Thus, this social worker must establish the family's self-definitions, listen to the *experiencer* (Oliver Sacks's word—the child in this case), and weigh community and societal factors. Practically, the community and the world beyond must be assessed for resources; the family may decide to move to a community with a public school sys-tem featuring mainstreaming, decide on a particular bilingual approach, or find the local Deaf community and move in a different direction. The worker also must figure out what the agency has to offer. Linking this family with community organizations may be as therapeutic as personal counseling. If the problem for the child is acceptance and the clinic does not engage in advocacy, then the worker must join with those who do on the family's behalf.

An assessment process should attune us to the realities of a given subsystem. Did the worker arrange for someone to sign/interpret when the deaf parents come in to talk over options? Is that service wanted by the consumer (McEntee, 1995)?

diating delivery units.) These authors believe that an "astute practitioner will carefully assess all avenues of service delivery to the target population" (p. 102). Narrower resource assessments can be undertaken before or at time of need. We can conduct such assessments ourselves or stay aware of others who make them and learn to interpret their conclusions. At any time, we may face a situation that requires knowledge of previously unexplored facets of the community.

ENSURING GOOD REFERRAL MATCHES

Role. Most practitioners engage in *brokerage* or *linkage* activities. When the focus is on the *individual*, tasks include "locating appropriate community resources; connecting the consumer to the resource; and evaluating the effectiveness of the resource in relation to the consumer's needs" (Anderson, 1981, p. 42). However, if the focus is less on "a clear statement of the consumer's need" and more on "an investigation of the nature, operations, and quality of available resources" (1981, pp. 42–43), then we are engaged in *community* assessment. To give the best advice to the student's mother, Netting et al. (1993) would say, we must know not only what agencies are available but also how well they work together and if they make the linkages they should—"whether these interacting units truly comprise a system that is responsive to multiple needs" (p. 110).

Tasks. Kettner et al. (1990) suggest developing resource inventories for subpopulations (pp. 61–64); an example was shown in Box 6.5. We survey other providers to obtain an understanding of

- what actual services are available;
- which services are most often utilized and why (location, quality, staff attitudes?); and
- different uses of key terminology (Kettner et al., 1990, p. 63).

Assessing service integration and utilization for a population, such as HIV/AIDS-related services, can do more than ensure good matches; it can lead to new agency directories, service coordination, and community empowerment (Mancoske & Hunzeker, 1994). To do such tasks, we must be organized (see Box 6.7).

Collaborative Assessments

So far, we have looked at the scope, purpose, and multidimensionality of assessment from the perspective of professionals acting generally on their own. In contrast, assessments can be made of the community or in the community in conjunction with service users and community residents, or even by residents alone. Rothman (1984) reminds us that whatever the form or method, one of the first decisions to make is who will do the community assessment and where:

> Assessment can be a fairly technical and solitary professional activity carried out in an office surrounded by computer printouts and area maps. On the other hand, it can be conducted on a collaborative basis in neigh-borhood clubs, and meeting halls, with the professional and the constituency taking joint responsibility as partners. (p. 8)

ASSESSMENTS OF, IN, AND BY THE COMMUNITY

Community participants can be involved as full partners most easily when community assessment is the first stage of a funded project, as illustrated by a project in Richmond, California, where community members of an informal planning group not only helped plan surveys and field observations but even hired the project coordinator (Hunkeler, Davis, McNeil, Powell, & Polen, 1990). Participation continued from analysis through the design initiation and implementation phases. In Eagle Pass, Texas, program staff ran seven focus groups to learn about grass-roots health concerns. Five involved members of the community and two were with "prominent figures" who could influence the community (Amezcua, McAlister, Ramirez, & Espinoza, 1990, p. 259).

BOX 6.7   VALUABLE OFFICE RESOURCES

The information and referral directory lying around the office is invariably out-of-date, requiring practitioners to supplement it. City, county, and neighborhood telephone directories provide telephone numbers such as those of housing inspectors, polling places, elected officials, blood banks, and police–community relations offices. Some localities also have specialized directories listing such organizations as mutual help (e.g., grief) or neighborhood self-help groups (e.g., recycling or mural painting) or resources for a particular population. A resourceful practitioner keeps a number of handy references and lists. These include the basics—emergency numbers pasted on the telephone and a tickler file of con-tact people and key deadlines or time frames. As the Rolodex grows, the professional adds the names of individual and organizational contacts (which can be contacted about the soup kitchen, etc.). The practitioner should also *obtain organization charts for state and city governments and for key agencies*; without the precise name of the agency with jurisdiction, a telephone book will be less useful. Big organizations often have a (more or less) permanent chart with division names and job titles and a parallel (constantly changing) chart with the names of those who currently occupy those slots. They readily provide the former and often send outdated copies of the latter. Be persistent.

Wrap-up. Community assessments can take many forms. Before launching one, we should consider such elements as collaboration, scope, focus, and purpose.

PHILOSOPHIES BEHIND ASSESSMENT

An initial assessment interaction with an individual or a community should be guided by a listening, learning, exploring style and philosophy.

Attitude of the Professional

Our philosophy of assessment matters because assessment is a first step in establishing our relationship with a community. The stance taken at the beginning will affect all of the operations that come later. Underpinning these efforts must be the belief that we have the capacity to assist individuals and groups (and that they, in turn, have the same capacity) and that we can solve social problems (Huber & Orlando, 1993). Otherwise, there is little point—besides complying with paperwork requirements—in doing assessments at any level. We also must believe in the potential of the community as a living system to nourish, to grow, and to change.

ANALYZING A GROUP OR CLASS

Typical individual assessments cover "information about physical status, economic resources, ethnicity, social class, education, past help-seeking behavior, and available social supports" (Saari, 1991, p. 89). Sullivan (1992) states that "the manner in which assessment is conducted and the choice of data gathered set the tone for future intervention" (p. 205). Using the mentally challenged as an example, he stresses how workers describe, assess, and work for this population.[4] He is quite persuasive

about the negative ramifications of an assessment process that requires clients "exclusively to recount previous hospitalizations [and] illness episodes" (p. 206). *Even if it requires modification of current assessment tools used by agencies*, he believes, workers must also ask about

> abilities, interests and past accomplishments.... Information should be gathered on client interests and aspirations; resources currently or previously used; and needs in various life domains including living arrangements, employment, leisure-time activity, and health. (p. 206)

We want to avoid simply asking people if they are taking their medicine. We establish a different relationship with a person if we ask: "What place were you born? Reared?" "Do you ever go back there?" "What have been important events during your life?" "Do you have any special interests, skills, hobbies, interesting possessions?" (Jackson, 1987, p. 35).

ANALYZING COMMUNITY NEEDS
AND RESILIENCE

We must avoid self-fulfilling prophecies. By focusing on weaknesses, social work and other professions may inadvertently create a *client neighborhood*. Human services, urban studies, and community development too often have had "deficiency-oriented policies and programs" responses. Consequently:

> many lower income urban neighborhoods are now environments of service where behaviors are affected because residents come to believe that their well-being depends upon being a client. They begin to see themselves as people with special needs that can only be met by outsiders.... Consumers of services focus vast amounts of creativity and intelli-

gence on the survival-motivated challenge of outwitting the "system," or on finding ways—in the informal or even illegal economy—to bypass the system entirely. (Kretzmann & McKnight, 1993, p. 2)

We must discern what each party can contribute (Delgado, in press). Meyer (1993) would ask why assessment is limited to "what is the matter," in an individual or community situation, when it should also include *how people are doing* with what is the matter (p. 36).

Practitioners are urged to identify the capacities of local individuals, citizen associations, and institutions and to build connections and strong ties with and among them. This method of assessment looks for *problem solvers*, not problems. Embodying affirmative community assessment, Kretzmann and McKnight depict the same community as it

looks on paper mapped by assets in contrast to needs (see Box 6.8).

Values, Preferences, and Mutuality of Interest

AGENCY, COMMUNITY VALUE DIFFERENCES

Assessment involves more than points of view (e.g., a strengths perspective) and how we behold things. It involves values and variation. Given differing perspectives, an agency and a community may not share philosophies or opinions about behavior. Yet, as workers we easily forget this fact because we take so much for granted—things like what mental health is and how it should be maintained. We value self-insight, facing up to adversity, and talking things over, for instance. Atkinson, Morten, and Sue (1993) provide good suggestions for clinicians on

---

BOX 6.8   ALTERNATIVE PERCEPTIONS

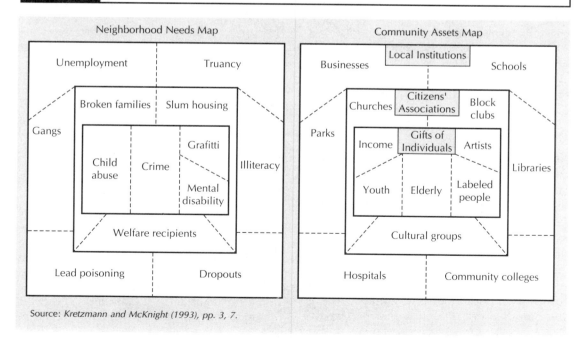

Source: *Kretzmann and McKnight (1993), pp. 3, 7.*

how to "hear" clients with beliefs about mental health different from their own. For example, some Asian-Americans believe that mental health is "maintained by the avoidance of morbid thoughts" (p. 212). Clients who put off treatment would not regard themselves—as some workers might—as hiding their heads in the sand, but rather as being appropriately stoic about a family member's condition. Thus, we note knowledge and philosophical differences that might affect outcomes because being oblivious can lead to an unstated conflict that could hamper mutual assessment.

We may assess situations one way and the public another—for example, interdependence and commonality versus independence and individuality. We providers usually value progress for those in our programs over the desire of townspeople for the neighborhood to be the way it used to be. Job Corps staff have a different sense of self-interest and public interest from community merchants and residents who live near the urban center. Being oblivious here can lead to overt political conflict or even the closing of the center.

Awareness may not suffice. The hardest situations are those in which our professional values are in conflict with those of most community residents. Such situations require decisions about when and where to substitute professional values for the values of the community, when to adhere to the community's values, and when to strive for compromise or consensus. A subcommunity or the town as a whole may feel imposed on or affronted by our program, whether it distributes condoms in schools or clean needles on the streets; arranges for Norplant birth control implants; or makes controversial recommendations regarding releases from mental hospitals. We must develop means of finding out where residents and potential users of services stand and judging the intensity of feelings, opposition, and resistance. Such facts could determine whether we would be better off going public (on talk shows, for instance), in order to educate and give our point of view, or lying low.

RESPECT AND RESPONSIVENESS

We will follow this principle: respect community residents enough to seek and listen to their views on the subject at hand. In the previous chapter, we grounded ourselves in social science approaches as a means of understanding. Here we highlight tapping current and potential service users and others in our network as sources of information and insight. Along with doing or reading formal studies, we must integrate intelligence gathered from our environments into our operations.

How might we do this? We must know who and what to ask. As one form of inquiry, Mitroff and Linstone (1993) urge us to list all *stakeholders* connected with our organization, that is, "any individual, group, organization, institution that can affect as well as be affected by [our] policy or policies" (p. 141). Then, after discovering through interaction all the assumptions each player has about the nature of the problem at hand, we mutually analyze the fundamental differences in our assumptions. (Also see the discussion of multiple realities in Chapter 3.) Moving further out in our environment, Greever (1983) defines *intelligence* as what we need to know in advance of an action and as "gathering broad pieces of information (Military Intelligence calls them 'EEIs—Essential Elements of Information') and working with them until some sort of pattern emerges" (p. 1). In our context, intelligence can also involve keeping an ear to the ground regarding client concerns.

Circulate. Peters (1987) gives an example of a Lutheran minister in a small

Pennsylvania town who built relationships through his philosophy of "Ministry by Wandering Around" and was the "first minister in over *twenty years* to stop by the corner coffee shop to sit down and have coffee with the local farmers" (p. 148). Peters believes that listening and being receptive to customers are fundamental guidelines. This philosophy underlies current business preoccupations with quality and management innovation (Moore & Kelly, 1996). We could wander around our waiting rooms, checking out the ambience to see if we have humanized our organizational presentation. We can ask those who have used our services: "How are we doing? What did you think?" We can reach out to those in our vicinity: "Do you know who we are? Where we are located? Are our hours convenient for you?" This is no public relations game. We must assess who we are serving well and who we are not because social workers are accountable to community residents and clients (Maluccio, 1979, p. 199) and can learn from them in the same way that the minister in Peters's story learned from the farmers at the coffee shop.

Listening to Feedback

Feedback will figure heavily in this learning process. Agencies can experiment with anonymous satisfaction-with-services evaluations, on-premise suggestion boxes, a newsletter written and controlled by clients to be read by practitioners, formal evaluation by users of services through an outside evaluator, and serious analysis of any complaints received. *Services* is used here in a broad sense since feedback can be given on training, group therapy, oversight of homemaker services, psychodrama, and many other activities.

Colleagues. Although we will concentrate on feedback from those outside our programs, we should not forget coworkers with

community ties who receive few opportunities to give feedback. When asked, staffers such as receptionists, cooks, house parents, drivers, aides, and work crew leaders can provide valuable information on service users. They can also provide feedback on program functioning and *community reactions*—yet professionals rarely ask them for such information.

People working in organizations of all types—businesses, government agencies, nonprofits—should "use every listening post [they] can find" (Peters, 1987, p. 152). We identify three possible ones here. First, we should encourage *case managers* to give honest performance feedback—based on client statements with due regard to confidentiality—to each office on quality of services and responsiveness of personnel. They can tell us about desired new programs as well. Case managers focused on client strengths may be particularly attuned to agency limitations (Sullivan & Fisher, 1994). Second, since *self-help and mutual support meetings* are places where grievances against professionals are aired regularly, we should ask groups related to the work of our office to give us summaries of common complaints. Third, we should identify *service providers, entrenched in the community* and plugged into different networks, who will be blunt with us.

Independent Assessments from Service Users

Accepting Formal Service Critiques

More surprising perhaps, we want to encourage formal critiques and legitimize the consumer's voice. Our organizations should have consumer advisory boards, democratically selected, whose advice is carefully heeded during strategic planning and at other times. We must welcome the presence of advocates—for example, for the mentally challenged and their families (who often have different viewpoints from each other)—and others who question our actions as a professional group or with particular clients. This questioning may be verbal or written. Our worries about accreditation, funding sources, and staying out of trouble with bureaucracies cause us to avoid collecting potentially negative documents. There is a trend, however, toward the legitimacy of *independent* service user evaluation. Consumers can now complain to state occupational licensing boards about practitioners such as physicians and social workers; information about physicians is gathered from malpractice insurance claims and disciplinary actions and fed into the National Practitioner Data Bank. Moreover, the government is beginning to require the input of users; for example, federal law requires nursing home inspectors to talk to residents, not just staff and management. It is natural for us to be excited about citizen efforts to assess

another institution but threatened if the target is our own agency. However, we should still listen. See Box 6.9.

ADVOCACY RECOMMENDATIONS

Our assessment philosophy must embrace openness and willingness to integrate input from many sources because it is of critical importance to learn what people want from service providers and their communities.

- We can encourage individuals and advocacy groups to explain, face to face, how the environment can become more responsive to their needs.

- We can also seek out state and national publications with relevant recommendations about our area of work. Advocacy publications may be sophisticated guides to citizen involvement or one-page flyers.

BOX 6.9	TWO TYPES OF ASSESSMENT

Brief descriptions of two consumer critiques will illustrate (1) how the public can be informed about availability and quality of services in a form they can easily utilize and (2) how providers can get valuable input from independent assessors. Two different groups rated long-term care facilities and made the results available to the public in simple formats. A metropolitan area and an entire (different) state were studied.

The *metropolitan advocacy group* visited each facility but relied more on official reports about nursing homes and board and care homes. The group compiled the results of local fire, state health, state social services, and federal Medicare inspections over a period of time. Their report showed clearly which homes were always, sometimes, or never in compliance with various regulations (e.g., the most luxurious nursing home had

been noncompliant). Facilities had preferred to keep such information hidden, but now the compliance information was public.

In the *statewide survey*, an interdisciplinary team, composed of a nurse and students of social work and gerontology, asked questions of administrators designed to help families understand the variety of services available in different facilities. While in the facility, they also made careful note of such things as odor, morale, and treatment of residents. In the end, whether or not the administrators agreed with the final guide, the facilities did learn how people representing service users would compare them with their competitors. Detached consumer advocates had provided an assessment from which the providers could take suggestions. Such rare events should be welcomed rather than resisted.

Consumer-oriented assessments of problems and their discussions of appropriate responses deserve our attention. Such discussions may focus on (1) how community life affects particular sectors or groups, (2) practical tips that might be implemented within a reasonable length of time, and (3) citizen participation or rights. For instance, older people and their advocates have suggested that communities *assess their liveability* and make traveling easier. They argue for traffic lights to be set to allow sufficient time for pedestrians to cross the street. They point out that bells or other sounds permit those with visual impairments to know when it is safe to cross. They also suggest the creation of large, separate paths to accommodate safely those walking, along with those using conventional two-wheel bicycles and three-wheel electric vehicles (Parker, Edmonds, & Robinson, 1989, p. 8). This illustrates how community assessments by citizen advocates may differ in emphasis from those prepared by professionals.

Wrap-up. An assessment philosophy establishes our attitudes, organizes our approach, and directs many of our applications. It even dictates whether assessment should be a two-way process. Information gathering provides a foundation for more elaborate assessment and research.

TRADITIONAL ASSESSMENT: INFORMATION-GATHERING METHODS

Disciplines usually evolve a few specialized assessment methods but adapt most of their methods from common sources such as sociology, political science, or planning. In community health, for instance, surveys and descriptive epidemiological studies are common methods used to carry out an assessment (Spradley, 1990, p. 382), just as needs identification and assessment methods, including surveys, are common in social work. Having discussed nontraditional ways to learn from and be more interactive with the public, we now turn to established methods used to assess community or client needs, launch program development, and update strategic plans. Focus groups, public meetings, needs assessment, and outreach methods can bring results helpful to providers and to those who will ultimately be served. Since focus groups and public meetings are more narrowly defined than needs assessment and outreach, we will look at them first.

Focus Group Methods

PROTOCOL AND PARTICIPANT SELECTION

Agencies can conduct focus groups for assessment purposes on their own or with assistance. A *focus group* is a qualitative data collection process in which a small number of individuals meet together with a trained facilitator to discuss a narrow topic in a detailed, guided way. Sometimes this is done with a written, predetermined agenda or set of questions. The point is not to reach a consensus but to air many ideas; members of the group react to each other, and the process builds to refinement of opinions. The session may be recorded for later study. Broadcast and print media use this form of opinion gathering during political campaigns; a heterogeneous group of 8–12 people is generally shown reacting to a debate or commenting on issues. Any results must be qualified because we cannot generalize from small samples.

We will describe focus groups made up of strangers, although social service personnel or acquaintances can be used (Martinez-Brawley & Delevan, 1993, p. 177). A cross section of the community is sought in terms of income, race, education, and other factors unless a particular segment, such as women or teenagers, is targeted. The more targeted the group, the more expensive the process of finding a representative sample through telephone solicitation.

Ideally, several groups are run in different parts of the community. Most focus group sessions meet one time only for about 2 hours. Working people find it hard to arrive early in the evening. Older people prefer daytime hours and are more likely to expect to have transportation or taxi money provided. Sometimes participants are given a modest sum; more often, they are provided with a meal or refreshments because they are volunteering their time.

The goal of bringing people together in this way is to encourage them to give their candid opinions. If we interrogate them or ask them questions calling for a yes or no answer, we will learn little. We are trying to create the atmosphere of a study group, not a courtroom or research laboratory.

PURPOSE: TO PROVIDE VALUABLE INFORMATION

Individual and group reactions provide insights into issues of comprehension, suitability, and acceptable phrasing. (Thus, politicians test campaign themes on focus groups.) Let us explore focus group methodology by understanding how a group can serve as a test audience. In the recent past, federal regulators and the apparel industry were considering voluntary warnings for sleepwear. A focus group of middle-aged and older participants was asked their preferences regarding flame-resistant fabric and/or warning labels to protect themselves or frail, older parents with cognitive or physical limitations. (Older people have high mortality rates associated with fires involving apparel, especially nightwear.) The meeting opened with a videotape documenting a burn hazard. The group then examined and discussed several proposed wordings for a cautionary label in sleepwear. Participants

examined handouts of alternative warnings, which were also printed on big signs and displayed at the front of the room. The discussion that followed made clear a common misconception among the participants: that a labeled product must be more dangerous than an unlabeled product. Without more education, honesty might backfire in the marketplace. The advocates involved had failed in many ways to anticipate how members of the public would react, *which is precisely why focus groups can be helpful.*

PURPOSE: TO "TEST THE WATERS"

This flexible methodology also can be applied in clinical settings. A social worker at a sexual assault center wants to start a group for males who experienced sexual abuse as children. Uncertain about how to reach prospective members, he sends letters to potential referral sources and places free advertisements in community newspapers. After receiving five responses, the worker asks if these individuals would be willing to come in and discuss perceived needs and how to reach others. Since this is not a randomly selected group—which would have been impossible in this case—the worker has to note ways in which the group may be atypical (e.g., race, sexual orientation).

Instead of using an outside facilitator, the worker moderates the session himself and explores topics such as where and how to reach out, wording of the invitation, appropriateness of the agency location and hours, and the most effective descriptors for a group. Because the participants have experience with this problem, they can share (1) their personal states of mind about seeking help (embarrassed, relieved); (2) what they had responded to and what others might want (opportunity to talk? get help? pursue redress?); (3) how they regard themselves or identifiers they find acceptable ("incest victims"? "sexual assault victims"? "abused children"? "adults struggling with childhood traumas"?); and (4) what type of outreach slogans they might best respond to ("angry today about what happened yesterday?" "never talked about it before?") During the focus group meeting, the social worker listens for themes and key words that can be used in outreach and as a basis for the therapeutic group. Having taped the session with permission, he has a coworker listen because he admits to himself that he already has notions about the best means of reaching out to this group. The professionals then reassess the original plan for the group.

PURPOSE: SPECIALIZED ASSESSMENT

Our planning should take into account the subject matter, the task to pursue, and the literacy level of the population. To assess what types of sensory devices Deaf and Hard of Hearing (D/HH) people would like developed, Gallaudet University used focus groups

> because both mail and telephone communication would require reading and writing. A survey involving prelingually D/HH would be biased toward those who had excellent reading and writing skills. Among D/HH persons with marginal literacy, it would be difficult to ascertain whether the questions were understood. . . . [Also] the subjects were required to think creatively about communication problems and possible technological solutions. . . . Probing on the part of the researcher is needed to bring out this thought process, something which would be extremely difficult to do by mail or by telephone. (Harkins & Jensema, 1987, p. 2)

Society's increased use of intercoms was one communication problem that surfaced: "Repeated mentions were made of difficulty in using the drive-through service in fast-food restaurants. Secure buildings which require a visitor to use the security system's

phone also present problems" (p. 7). Details such as this, along with a process that allows other participants to jump in and say "me too" (instant, albeit limited, confirmation), make focus groups with facilitators popular assessment tools.

Methods of Data Gathering from Community Events

PUBLIC PARTICIPATION

The title says it all: "Taking the Pulse: A Community Exchange to Gather Information About _____ Needs in _____ County." Our profession supports civic involvement, open government, and public participation in decision making. We can learn through community meetings and events. Realistically, few participants at such an event will read the write-up of the recommendations, but they have the opportunity to talk, to hear the options, and (later) to read the report. Today many open meetings are mandated public hearings (Kettner et al., 1990, p. 69). In various fields, for obligatory and democratic reasons, individuals are allowed more say. A citizen could travel from forums about cable television rate hikes to sound-off meetings about animal control. The current competition for everyone's time must be kept in mind as our agency plans opportunities for participation.

Community residents often take these meetings more seriously than we do. Current and potential service users envision something tangible coming out of such interchanges and expect their recommendations to be taken seriously. To be credible and ethical, we must not falsely raise expectations, and we should want input if we ask for it. (Regarding doing it right through planned town meetings, see Alcorn and Morrison, 1994.) Town meetings must be accessible (transit, building, audio loops, interpreters, etc.) too.

MEETING PROTOCOL

Suggestions for running any meeting are covered in Chapter 9. The warnings here involve only those matters that may color or cloud the assessment process. The trend to give more "say" to the community means that meetings can be taken over by a group with an especially obdurate agenda—such as those on either side of abortion, capital punishment, gun control, or immigration issues. A group can also be taken off the agenda by one smooth-talking person. This requires being alert but open. For example, a meeting to discuss the perceived need for more day care might be attended by parents who oppose day care, prefer after-school care, or want help in coordinating relief time for families teaching their children at home. Genuine needs may exist, making it inappropriate to tell these parents that they came to the wrong meeting. We may not agree with or like everyone who comes to public meetings, but worthwhile information can often be found in the unexpected or the unreasonable.

To avoid disruption, some people who run meetings make a show of letting everyone take part but actually controlling the process tightly to reject unwanted input. We should anticipate that community people will organize and try to control meetings; this is part of the process. We want to be sure that in small gatherings each person present is offered equal time and that in big gatherings access to the microphone is handled fairly. Moderators can set time limits and establish ground rules ("Avoid arguing with someone else's statement; just make your own") without squelching participants. It is common for sensible ideas to appear garbled or self-serving in their delivery; therefore, input is properly measured by the usefulness of the suggestion, not the speaking skills and demeanor of proponents or their stance on issues.

FOLLOW-UP ANALYSIS AFTER THE MEETINGS

During a forum, an agency staffer and someone who lives in the community should take notes on each point made and who said it. They can then organize the notes, using tentative headings, and have the moderator check them for errors. We must sort out what we heard using these notes and our own memory or, better yet, listening to a tape and noting the intensity of feelings expressed on given topics—from represented groups in particular. Next, we must separate needs from preferences and gripes, not by how participants characterized what they were saying but by customary use of the following terms:

Need: essential, necessity, requirement;
Desire/wish/preference: want, choice, longing;
Complaint: gripe, grievance, objection, protest.

Despite a focus on the need for day care, complaints may have poured out about a particular caseworker or about how a current program is being run because constituents may mix needs, desires, and gripes. Perhaps there should be a period of time in which participants can air complaints and preferences before beginning constructive discussion about agency mission and community needs.

OTHER WAYS TO LISTEN TO THE COMMUNITY

To gather *community impressions*, practitioners can go to those sectors believed to have the most intense needs—whether served, underserved, or unserved to date—interview key informants, and use the target group to validate objective data (Siegel, Attkisson, & Carson, 1987, p. 93). Newer possibilities involve electronic networks and interactive media. Those interested in needs and preferences can monitor sectors of a community via community computer bulletin boards.

Although practitioners and managers must know how to put on successful forums, they may be better off attending already scheduled community events than holding their own. We may hear better from the back rather than the front of the room when we do not have to be in charge. Getting out into the swim of things is something we know we should do, but we often lack time. Professionals neglect communitywide celebrations and specialized events where they can gain information and exposure: Hispanic International Day, Strawberry Festival, Ice Carnival. We must look for opportunities to interact with the public and other providers. For example, if it is our turn to oversee our office's booth at the mall, then we should visit every other organization's table to gather information (to check service gaps and overlaps) and renew contacts.

Informal Need Assessment Processes

Assessment occurs regularly as we discuss the needs of our locality. Informal problem solution assessment takes place each time a vague concern is thrown at an agency—for example, "You must do something about those 'crack kids' [born to ad-dicted mothers] who are reaching school age." Everyone has an immediate opinion about the problem, the solution, and the perfect program, but this is reaction, not need analysis. Is there a problem regarding "crack kids," or is a phrase being thrown around? What is social work's role in this interdisciplinary area? Whom do we target (teachers, school counselors, the children, their mothers)? And for what purpose—training to sensitize regular and special education teachers, screening programs in preschool or through medical facilities, family support? Should the community identify crack babies at birth and follow them so that they do not disappear? What has been done to date? What, ideally, should happen? Who should have responsibility? Or should we do none of this because we are labeling children, which could cause them to be tracked in a counterproductive way? We must sort out the basics of a target problem or system and an action system before we can say that we have identified a need (see Chapters 1 and 3). See Box 6.10 on the first steps in case sorting.

Need assessment also happens informally because it is interwoven with the skills of identification (size of the problem or population) and intervention (Whitman, Graves, & Accardo, 1987). As Box 6.10 illustrates,

---

BOX 6.10   CONSTRUING THE SITUATION

When a problem or case is brought to your official notice, you must decide how narrowly or broadly to interpret it. For example, Rosenthal and Levine (1980, p. 401) point out that an individual complaint about discrimination in a local government's handling of a job promotion might be investigated as follows:

• An individual complaint only: Did the government agency discriminate against this person?

• A class complaint: Does the government agency discriminate against all persons in certain categories?

• A broadly construed class complaint: Does the entire government discriminate against all persons in certain categories?

need is an elastic concept, so we must review each situation.

Formal Need Assessment Processes

Need studies can be designed to show us the *big picture of need* in the community. For instance, communities forced to undergo economic conversion from military to other economic endeavors must plan and reevaluate. Their need assessments provide an example of a big-picture look and macro-level involvement (Mary, 1994). Here we examine, instead, assessments undertaken to provide tailored guidance to an agency or a multi-agency team whose scope of work is already fairly well determined but could change in the future (Whitworth et al., 1988; Witkin & Altschuld, 1995).

COMMUNICATION ABOUT NEED

Social workers, as people with research knowledge, must ask themselves what constituents could benefit from, and what would be required in terms of data or input to come up with indicators and answers. To oversimplify, if a neighborhood group says "We need better housing," a worker might hypothesize that they live in substandard housing and would want to know whether that is true. If we look up census figures to learn how many homes in the area lack running water or indoor toilets and find that the answer is none, that information redirects our assessment. Are there multiple housing violations in apartments? What is the average rent people are paying, and what percentage of their income does that represent? Is the problem housing or security? The worker returns to the group with questions that show interest, concern, and some knowledge.

Neuber, Atkins, Jacobson, & Reuterman (1980) define *need assessment* as "a communication medium between consumers and service providers," which can affect "the planning and evaluation of the various services to be delivered to the community and consumers" (pp. 62–63). Need assessments may be *client-oriented* (population at risk) or *service-oriented* (addressing gaps and fit). To give an example of the latter, a graduate student thinks she has identified a need. Her dream is to start her own agency after she leaves school to provide housing for post–high-school-age youth. She wishes to find a niche in the transitional housing market and has several communities in mind, but she wants to find out if such a service is essential, in the opinion of local practitioners, and desired by decision makers in the area. Thayer (1977) would say that she would benefit by finding out what circumstances would be altered through her new services. The student believes a service-oriented need assessment will help her to determine in which locality there will be a positive fit and where her plan will most likely succeed.

IDENTIFICATION AND ASSESSMENT

The terms *need identification* and *need assessment* often are used interchangeably. We find Siegel et al.'s (1987) distinction helpful: *need identification*, they state, is a process that "describes health and social service requirements in a geographic or social area," whereas *need assessment* is "aimed at estimating the relative importance of these needs" as well as "an environmental monitoring system" (pp. 71, 75). Need assessment is also an ongoing process that involves the community in a form of continuous quality improvement (D. Menefee, personal communication, June 1995). With any engagement-with-needs process, one objective is to help develop the residents' ability to solve problems for themselves so that social workers will not be needed at some point.

Multiple Approaches

Assessment processes involve compiling available information, developing new information, or integrating relevant new information with the old. Neuber and associates urge us to obtain data from *demographic-statistical profiles*, *key informants*, and *random community members* in order to define needed services, develop programs, enhance interagency cooperation, and improve accountability. Among the traditional methods used to do this are *indicator* approaches, *social area survey* approaches, and *community group* approaches (Siegel et al., 1987, pp. 76–77). While it is beyond the scope of this book to explain all these methods fully, in general social indicator approaches are oriented to available data, while surveys gather new data. Both are quantitative in nature (Jacob & Willits, 1994), while the community approaches are more qualitative. The community approaches include forums and community impressions, the Delphi technique (Raskin, 1994), and the nominal group technique (Alcorn & Morrison, 1994).

As we have seen, need assessment methods involving the community are used to obtain ideas from current and potential service users. *Forums* may be attended by social service practitioners, but the community approaches focus primarily on people with a direct stake in any outcome(s) of the information-gathering, planning, and priority-setting process. Community representatives are asked what is and is not working, what they are satisfied with, proud of, and afraid of concerning the future of their community.

In contrast, the *Delphi method* involves input from experts—more detached and not usually directly affected by the outcomes of the process—who refine and synthesize ideas on a topic. "It is axiomatic with the Delphi method that the respondents need not be a random sample of the population" (Molnar & Kammerud, 1977, p. 325). When an *environmental impact study* is done, for instance, decision makers want to hear from those who study similar situations, have informed judgments, and can suggest new options, rather than merely support or oppose what is on the table. Johnson

(1995) describes a parallel *social impact assessment* (p. 275).[5] Typically, with this method, a question is put to a panel. The Delphi process involves several "rounds" in which anonymous experts look at each other's ideas (or the range as summarized) in writing. It is an "inquiry system" for moving toward "agreement or consensus" (Mitroff & Linstone, 1993, p. 29)

A *nominal group* is a structured exercise in which each participant works silently alongside other individuals and then answers questions when called on until the meeting is opened to free discussion. A moderator might pose a question and ask each participant to list ideas. Each would give one answer from these lists when it is her or his turn until each participant has reported each response. Thus, 8 to 10 people sit in a group but talk in rotation as a facilitator records all ideas; eventually these will be discussed and may be ranked. The initial round-robin sharing format prevents individuals from taking over the brainstorming session (Siegel et al., pp. 88–90) and gives equal voice to usually reticent members (Alcorn & Morrison, 1994, p. 36). This technique can help avoid disruption—for example, when groups holding different stakes in a particular question, such as rent control reforms, are together. Nominal group meetings can also be held consecutively; landlords could give their opinions in one group and tenants in another at an earlier or later time.

Survey Options

Common types of social or community surveys include citizen surveys (Siegel et al., 1987) or general population surveys, target population surveys, and service provider surveys (Meenaghan et al., 1982). The time and expense involved can discourage our use of any of these formats, but we can learn to use and interpret others' surveys. A practitioner wanting to supplement a huge survey with some special questions or to do a limited survey should contact a trained researcher, survey expert, or pollster. Such people can usually be found in a city or county planning office or a local college. Some public service agencies have such experts in-house.

Our information needs may be simple and our target easy to reach. Suppose that an adolescent unit wanted to find out the literacy level of parents of adolescent clients, that is, the families of current service users. Case records could be examined to discover how long adults currently in the household attended school, but that does not necessarily reflect literacy. We would need to determine whether a telephone or face-to-face survey of parents would get the fullest results at the least cost. *Alternatively, our information goals may be less clear and our target harder to reach.* We may start with service providers to reach potential service users. For example, one study wanted to determine the needs of mentally challenged adults and their children. The directors used an *agency informant method* to identify individuals in the target group and then interviewed a subset of them. Since the "actual prevalence of intellectually limited parents is unknown," Whitman et al. (1987) instead "attempted to identify those retarded parents in a large metropolitan area who had come to agency attention and to survey a sample of these parents in order to determine their perceived service needs" (p. 636).

We may decide that we can benefit from any information about certain potential service users' needs/preferences or their knowledge of available services. Let us say that the target group is women whose lives are threatened by their weight—a small number compared to the many women who would potentially be noticed or experience rejection due to their size (Wiley, 1994). A physician survey will run into confidentiality issues and miss women who avoid doctors. A questionnaire can be designed to be administered on a given Saturday in front of department stores, factory outlets, and shops selling large-size women's fashions. The challenge would be to get the stores'

cooperation; they may want to screen the questions for potential offensiveness. Surveyors would have to be trained. Results could serve as a pretest, since responses would help us design a more relevant (and perhaps less fatphobic) questionnaire that could be administered outside diet stores, the clothing stores again, and so on. Shoppers are not a random group, and obese women who stay at home (of whom there are probably many) will be missed, which is one reason why such a survey would be unscientific.

However, surveys can have a value that goes far beyond their scientific validity. For assessment purposes, they are often revealing no matter how limited they are in sophistication, subject, or sample, as the following letter (sent to the Gray Panthers) shows:

Sir/Madam:

   My name is Troy Moore. I am in the 4th grade. I am doing a project on older people.

   I recorded some answers on older people. I got some answers from children in my school. My results were that old people have gray hair and wrinkle skin, are mean, are unhealthy and are smart. We want to know if they are true. Do you have information about old people? Would you please send me information?

Sincerely,

Troy Moore
c/o Mrs. Beeson
1415 29th Street East
Palmetto, FL 34221

Note: If you have ideas or information to help Troy, please write to him at the above address.

The letter reveals how some people regard the older population. (The responsiveness of the organization to these questions undercuts the writer's findings about "mean[ness].")

One group of students practiced the skills listed in Box 6.11 and may have benefitted the community by conducting a quick survey for an urban community association. The goal/larger objective was to find out about problems, use of public services (e.g., the local recreation center), and so on. The study population consisted of residents of an older, racially and ethnically mixed area of about 1000 households in the north-central/western part of the city. The immediate objective was to complete 100 household interviews in order to provide information on concerns and some sociodemographics. The students designed the survey instrument and cleared it with the association. Using a large city planning map, they randomly divided the neighborhood into quadrants, then streets, then select houses. They organized into teams. After they completed 118 face-to-face interviews, the data were processed and the frequency distributions, along with anecdotal information, were reported to the director of the association. The results gave direction for action. Elderly residents were afraid to go out and were trapped in houses they could not sell because the market value was going down. Drug dealers were moving into the area; residents identified particular crack houses.

Outreach Methods

Outreach and assessment intertwine in two ways. Community assessment may help determine the best means of outreach. Assessment can be made possible through outreach to less well known segments of the population.

A BROAD DEFINITION

Typically, *outreach* involves systematically contacting isolated people in their homes or wherever they reside (institutions, streets), or in the neighborhoods where they congregate, and linking them to services and financial programs for which they are believed to be eligible. Outreach involves efforts to include those often left out (such as absent fathers). Directories can be part of outreach, as can 800 or 888 telephone numbers. Outreach is also used to expand an agency's program (1) into new settings and communities, thus making a service or resource immediately and more widely available; (2) into new time periods to reach a target group, as has been done with midnight basketball; and (3) into client "linkage" with institutions, the community, or other clients to enhance "peer support" (Wells, Schachter, Little, Whylie, & Balogh, 1993).

Sometimes we fail to recognize the *information gathering and assessment potential* of outreach efforts or programs because we think of them as a satellite operation, a cus-

---

| **BOX 6.11** | **HOW TO RUN A SMALL SURVEY** |

1. Determine the objectives.
2. Define the study population.
3. Determine data to be collected.
4. Select the sampling unit.
5. Select the contact method.

6. Develop the instrument.
7. Organize and conduct the survey.
8. Process and analyze the data.
9. Report the results.

Source: *Based on Dever in Spradley (1990, pp. 382–383).*

tomer recruitment strategy, or an obligation. We should be aware that outreach involves an interesting mix of giving and *getting* knowledge.

VARIETIES AND METHODS

Outreach methods vary. Some government agencies are mandated to alert potential service users or beneficiaries—for instance, regarding food stamps or Supplemental Security Income (Brandon, Plotnick, & Stockman, 1994). They often perform outreach through public service announcements, although even door-to-door canvassing has also been done. In contrast, around 10 P.M., homeless shelter director Mitch Snyder used to take hamburgers and blankets out to individuals who chose to stay on the streets rather than come in from the cold. While distributing the food and blankets, he gained intelligence from those on heat grates about specific fears people had about coming indoors and who on the streets were the sickest or most violent. A continuing education program on mental health, on the other hand, employed more conventional but equally important ways of reaching out to older people: selecting *accessible community sites*, allowing registration at the first class so that frail people did not have to make an extra trip, and printing materials in large type (Blackwell & Hunt, 1980). Telephone *hotlines* offering legal assistance to the poor or elderly have been tried in several localities as a way to make information more available, as well as a means to collect information on the types of requests received over time. The University of Maryland at Baltimore has a Social Work Community Outreach Service that links university resources with community groups and residents. *Support groups* can be initiated, in either a public or a circumspect manner (Anderson & Shaw, 1994), as a form of outreach.

As shown, methods of outreach can be direct or indirect, expected or unexpected.

> If sky-writing in Spanish were the best way to identify a service and encourage its use for a particular target group, and resources were not at issue, then it would be an appropriate mechanism. Direct, personal outreach ... must, of course, be made as non-threatening and non-disruptive as possible. (National Public Law Training Center, 1981)

Successful outreach through direct contacts in a Texas program revealed some specific, nonthreatening steps that can be taken to serve a previously unserved group (Watkins & Gonzales, 1982). The plan sounded easy enough: a Mexican-American counselor was hired to spend time in an isolated neighborhood and in homes, gaining trust, and later to provide mental health counseling. However, much assessment of, and with, the community went on concurrently with hiring and initial outreach. *Research was studied* and community leaders and referral sources were contacted regarding the perceived need for services by the target group, the compatibility between counselor and client regarding culture and decision making, and the best site for services. Initially, counseling was done in homes. Later, it was done at a community center in the barrio. In addition, an original play in Spanish was performed to facilitate discussion of pressing issues. Interaction was key to assessment and action. The agency saw more of a need for marriage counseling services than did militant community leaders, who wanted economically oriented help. The leaders ended up being more accepting of the services than they anticipated, and the services rendered were more resource and advocacy oriented than the agency had anticipated. This variety of outreach can overlap with case finding. Auerswald (1968) describes case recruitment—in contrast to acceptance of referrals—as part of an inte-grated services approach to a "so-called dis-advantaged community" (p. 206).

The philosophy is to meet people where they are in every way we can—through their own language or their own stores (e.g., botanical shops in Puerto Rican communi-ties), accommodating them in their own en-vironment and in ours (getting rid of barri-ers such as stairs), providing services or programs in a way and at a time that is convenient, and conveying messages at an appropriate level of comprehension. It is im-portant to assess the informational require-ments of the public. We can be creative in community education: comic books, for in-stance, are part of adult education and ad-vocacy efforts. (See the discussion of read-ability in Chapter 11). A mental health handbook could use pictorial graphics to di-rect less educated readers to the right ser-vices. It could contain pertinent information on emergency psychiatric evaluation, desig-nated government agencies, community re-habilitation services, resident grievance sys-tems in psychiatric hospitals, and related assistance such as pharmacy programs. Sullivan (1992) believes that personal com-mitment also is required: "Helpers can best assist mentally challenged individuals in re-claiming the community through daily work on the street and in the community" (p. 208).

Wrap-up. The idea behind the methods discussed is to look for practical ways to fa-cilitate our discovery of who and what is out there and to identify what we may have to offer that others in the community can use.

THOUGHTFUL ASSESSMENT

The act of assessment covers an aston-ishingly wide range of activities, from tech-nical analyses, to preparation for massive programmatic intervention in a community, to judgments about a society itself. We must be familiar with methods and prescriptive rules. However, it would be a pity if the pur-poses of our profession were submerged by the practical. We must also heed the evoca-tive in the assessment process—that is, what is indicative of what—and consider values. We will benefit from imaginative explo-ration, a willingness to face complexity, an ability to contemplate that which is not seen or heard yet still applies, and an awareness of our own mental processes.

An Allegorical Aside

How do we include self-reflection in community-based research (Murphy & Pilotta, 1983)? What frame of mind is needed to as-sess a family or community? Such an assign-ment requires a detached but caring attitude and a nonjudgmental but certainly not value-free stance. How do we pick our field of vi-sion and action? *It requires confidence that we can understand the gestalt well enough to deter-mine at what level assessment should be aimed (individual, societal?).* A task so nuanced, yet so audacious, is hard to describe. Therefore we draw on the imagery of Edward Bellamy's *Looking Backward* (1960), and on Ursula K. Le Guin's short story "The Ones Who Walk Away from Omelas" with its de-scription of an imaginary place called Omelas (1975).

Bellamy and Le Guin provide us with so-cietal extremes to consider. Bellamy, writing a novel in 1888 about the year 2000, made no pretense about neutral observation. He wrote about his vision of the perfect society of the future, contrasting it with the war and poverty of his era. In a famous comparison, Bellamy likened our society to a "prodigious coach which the masses of humanity were harnessed to," with hunger as the driver, while the rich had the seats up on top, where they could "critically describe the merits of the straining team."

> Naturally such places were in great demand and the competition for them was keen, every one seeking as the first end in life to secure a seat on the coach for himself and to leave it to his child after him. . . . For all that they were so easy, the seats were very insecure, and at every sudden jolt of the coach persons were slipping out of them and falling to the ground, where they were instantly compelled to take hold of the rope. . . . [C]ommiseration was frequently expressed by those who rode for those who had to pull the coach. . . . [I]t was a pity but it could not be helped. (pp. 27–28)

Various explanations were developed to explain why society had to operate the way it did (the innate abilities of the pullers and the pulled, etc.).[6]

Most notions of better societies are built on the idea that we know what is right but must take the next steps to do it. Bellamy's assessment was that inhumanity grew out of failure to even comprehend what could be. Le Guin helps us look at the constant trade-offs. In her story, Le Guin paints a related but prettier picture than Bellamy. See Box 6.12.

Sometimes when the macro level and the collective good are stressed, practitioners worry that the individual will get lost. Le Guin's story is one reason that social work must never lose sight of the good of the individual. Bellamy's coach metaphor reminds us, though, that if we look only at individuals pulling the coach, or at those inside it or those on top of it, we may miss the big picture, the connections. We hope social workers can believe in happiness and festivals, and not look compulsively for what is in the closet or cellar, but that they will do something when misery is found. Our ethics tell us that the happiness of the many must never come at the expense of even one, but if we blithely condemn the people of Omelas for their Faustian bargain, we condemn ourselves.[7] Finally, it is to our benefit that the "narratives of humanists discuss a variety of communal, social, and psychological dilemmas" (Martinez-Brawley, 1990, p. xxiv).

Wrap-up. We not only assess at the individual and communal levels. We also care about the states of existence of persons and classes of persons.

MOVING FROM ASSESSMENT TO ACTION

In a community, as in a clinical situation, practitioners may be exploring and formulating a number of problems simultaneously to make an overarching assessment (Reid, 1992, p. 5), which is eventually acted on. We move into the middle phase of the task-centered model when we act in the community on the basis of study, information gathering, and assessment gained in the initial phase.[8] As we make the transition from assessment to problem solving and developing task strategies, we can ask what *integrates* the process of assessment → application → re-assessment? Perhaps the answer would be the same in most fields that engage in such processes: open-minded inquiry combined with purposeful proceeding.

Making Inferences and Moving On

It is hard to pinpoint when we have seen enough to stop assessing, draw inferences, and start action. A clearer challenge as we wind up an assessment is organizing what we now know. What has come to our attention? What should come to the forefront? Meyer (1993) talks of "advancing from the presenting request to the presenting problem" (p. 46). For example, the presenting request to the school social worker from the

---

BOX 6.12   **A FANTASTIC FICTION?**

Someone arriving to do an assessment of Omelas would find a picturesque world without our woes—a land of bright towers and bells, meadows and dance, and "faint sweetness of the air." If the visitor looked for social problems, he or she would find that the people lead full lives of prosperity, beauty, and delight. If the residents were analyzed, they would be found to be not simple but happy, content. No class of people in Omelas struggles in the dust and mud pulling the rich up on a coach. The residents are appreciative of what they have. The visitor will realize how rare it is elsewhere to observe "mature, intelligent, passionate adults whose lives [a]re not wretched." Le Guin asks "Do you believe? Do you accept the festival, the city, the joy?"

An observer would soon learn about a small locked room in which a "feeble minded" child of about 10 is kept, fed but uncared for, miserable, whining but unanswered, alone most of the time. A professional doing a diagnosis would say: "Aha, the negative side of the community finally shows through." And it is true that the child is a scapegoat or sacrifice, for if this pitiful being receives as much as one kind word, then all the ordinary woes of mortal life, infirmity, fatal disease, and cruelty will be inflicted on all the citizens and the beauty, wisdom, and abundance of the harvest will disappear from Omelas. Is the child hidden? No, all children are brought to encounter the child when they are between 8 and 12. The knowledge of this child's existence rips into each citizen who experiences feelings of outrage and impotence, who weighs the suffering of the many against the suffering of the one, and who fears throwing away the "happiness of thousands for the chance of the happiness of one." The citizens of Omelas un-derstand the terms of this world. Moreover, theirs is "no vapid, irresponsible happiness. . . . It is because of the child that they are so gentle with children." Le Guin predicts that those in Omelas will appear more believable to us as soon as we know about the "wretched one."

What does this have to do with assessment? If positives are focused on exclusively, the distress will never be revealed. If positives are ignored in the search for negatives, then the story ends with the discovery that the community is letting a child suffer. Instead, a full assessment might compare this imperfect community with other imperfect communities. The unusually limited amount of suffering would be remarked on, as well as the fact that every single citizen acknowledges human suffering. Even when we are most horrified during an assessment, we do not ignore positives; we persevere, trying to understand more. Le Guin ends her story with a reference to exceptions. "At times one of the adolescent girls or boys who go to see the child does not go home to weep or rage. . . . Sometimes also a man or woman much older falls silent for a day of two, and then leaves home. . . . They leave Omelas, they walk ahead into the darkness, and they do not come back" (p. 356). They will not agree to the terms, those who walk away from Omelas; each one goes alone. An assessment of this community will include what keeps the system in place, what permits individuals to fortify their resolve and give up their community ties to adhere to different values, and what keeps collective protest from taking place. This material gives us a warning: if we come to assessment with a single view of what we will measure, we prejudge the question and miss complex meanings.

---

teacher in Box 6.2 about the teased child might have been for assistance in dealing with the child's acting out in the classroom after recess, and the presenting request from the child might have been to keep his or her parents from being called to school again. The presenting *requests* were individual and family oriented, but the presenting *problem* turned out to involve the larger neighborhood system.

There are so many wants and preferences and survival needs in a community that doing an assessment to prioritize them, even when taking one's agency limits and capacities into consideration, is a formidable task. A public hearing epitomizes a situation where we typically face myriad desires, preferences, and perceived needs (e.g., a public hearing to discuss community development or social service block grant priorities and disbursements). After allowing interest groups to speak and make proposals at the hearing, a social worker must integrate this oral input with studies. This process provides a good community-level example of the assessment issue just mentioned: moving from the presenting requests (from interest groups) to the presenting problem (e.g., the issue that jumps out as cross-cutting and unaddressed). We also must stay in communication with the community groups who came to the hearing. All the tools of logic and techniques of assessment that we have been discussing will be useless without community participation in the problem-solving process.

Problem Solving and Intervention[9]

MANAGING COMPLEXITY

Activation of citizens and amelioration of problems can be an outgrowth of the community assessment process. The overriding task of the community practitioner is to help groups respond to the vicissitudes of life while keeping long term community welfare on the agenda. A need for community problem solving usually exists when:

- there are many individuals or a class of people involved, with problems that are viewed as being large or serious enough to pose some threat, real or imagined, to the well-being of the community; or
- the community experiences pressure due to problems in the operation of a system,

such as problems in communication or socialization (see Chapter 4).

The practitioner intervenes, on behalf of an agency or organization or as part of a coalition, in the workings of the community system and its parts. Since the magnitude, complexity, and responsibility of the task of addressing either type of problem are almost overwhelming, what is needed is a way to think about the job. A guide that points up difficulties and charts ways of overcoming obstacles is helpful.

Community problem solving. Here are 10 "ideal steps" that seek to explicate the thinking and behavior of a community practitioner engaging in problem solving:

1. Problem intake (identification, delineation of a social problem);
2. Selection of potential problem-solving actors (construction, location of the action group or system);
3. Determination of desired goals and potential consensus;
4. Specification of types of action outcome (e.g., alleviate condition, control, rehabilitate, prevent, innovate);
5. Analysis of the facets of the anticipated intervention;
6. Inventory and evaluation of resources;
7. Specification of means/actions to attain goals;
8. Selection of priorities (among problems, needs, and services);
9. Implementation of decisions made to reach solutions (allocation of resources);
10. Evaluation (ongoing and feedback).

With the exception of step 6, which we discussed earlier, the focus of these steps is more on intervention than on assessment. The process could be applied to the problem of the "crack kids" who may need supportive services, but it would be even more helpful for a contested issue such as obtaining investment credit from local lenders or trying to integrate the families of prisoners into the community where a correctional facility is located.[10] Just as we looked to agency stakeholders for *insight intelligence*, we must identify community people who have a stake in a problem and its solution for *action intelligence*.

Community problems, public concern for those problems, and the authority to do something about them cross institutional, geographic, and special interest boundaries (Turner, 1963). This makes community work and problem solving interesting and challenging. There are no clearly detailed road maps; worse, there is an absence of well-marked roads and the existence of many potholes. Any guide simply specifies the points of the compass that we need to chart our daily practice excursions.

Based on community problem-solving steps (see Chapters 1 and 3), the emphasis may seem to be on all head and no heart. However, that view overlooks the emphasis on spirit found in actual practice. Belief in a cause and commitment are necessary because, in the final analysis, we must recognize that disturbances of the status quo are inherent in community organizing and planning. Resistance is to be expected. A second aspect of spirit requires that the practitioner learn to be comfortable with uncertainty. This is the companion of change and development. A third requirement is for the practitioner to master *feasibility management*. Practitioners must work with what is feasible at the moment they need to take action. Thus, the task of the community problem-solving practitioner is to constantly stretch the parameters of what is feasible and determine the moment for action. This, then, is the spirit of purpose and determination.

TAKING INFORMED ACTION

The knowledge gained from the activities described so far helps us to better understand all sectors and to comprehend the stated and unstated needs of our community; enables us to be better "curbstone caseworkers" (Ecklein & Lauffer, 1972, p. 133); and allows us to do a better job in handling our regular tasks. It helps us determine how much and how well our organization is in touch with the community. This is essential if community-based programs are to be established. For example: Are materials available in each language extensively used in the area? Is the agency knowledgeable about issues concerning ethnic diversity yet still requiring adoptive mothers to stay home for the baby's first 2 years in a working- or middle-class area? Martinez-Brawley (1990) reminds us that community-oriented services are "as much an attitude as a collection of techniques" (p. 239).

What will be the outcome of all this self-scrutiny, community examination, and assessment? Using the data, insights, and community contacts gained from study and assessment, appropriate steps become more apparent. Possible action plans include:

- finding community connections for service users;
- mobilizing community resources for clients;
- selecting appropriate community interventions (development, problem reduction, education, sector mobilization, prevention, promotion); and
- organizing sectors of the community around an issue.

Decisions must be made about whether to gear projects to a target audience/area or the community at large. Some believe that it is misleading for an agency to say it has a community-based program unless it has a large reach (Rakowski, 1992). A satellite office does not necessarily mean a community emphasis.

A CONTINUOUS CYCLE

Community-based interventions are of many types. For an example of intervention and reassessment at the end of a program effort, see Box 6.13. It summarizes results from a survey of community AIDS projects funded by the Robert Wood Johnson Foundation during the 1980s. The projects' employees were asked about their preventive work on behalf of people not yet infected with HIV and about their service work or activities with people who were HIV positive. Operational and problematic issues that surfaced are also shown in this box.

Regarding reevaluation, if we lack the money to evaluate our projects as systematically as this, we can look to evaluation results of projects comparable to ours for guidance.

Assessment, problem solving, and intervention processes flow together. Resources, once identified, must be channeled. As a prime example, Bracht and Kingsbury (1990) conceive of community organizing in five overlapping stages:

Community analysis;
Design and initiation;
Implementation;
Maintenance and consolidation; and
Dissemination and reassessment. (pp. 66, 74)

While Bracht and Kingsbury's interest is in activating or "mobilizing citizens and communities for health action," these stages are reminders of processes such as program development that are followed in agency-based or community-based settings.

Box 6.14 also illustrates the cycle of assessment, intervention, and reassessment. It provides an example of the use of a community-oriented viewpoint in planning a specific program. Note how closely the steps correspond to the fundamentals emphasized in this chapter.

This section has sketched the later phases of the assessment process. Additional forms of intervention will be addressed in subsequent chapters.

Community Reengagement

In Chapters 3–6, we have urged commitment to community study, analysis, and interaction. Certainly a "single social worker cannot implement community-oriented social work" (Martinez-Brawley & Delevan, 1993, p. 27), but we end this unit with hopeful signs that activation of residents and professionals is increasing, which may result in more widespread use of community assessment and community social work.

HITTING THE BRICKS, PICKING A PATCH

Certain trends are appearing, such as home visits by some physicians and a requirement of community service at public/private high schools. Bloomfield College in New Jersey requires students to take "a course called Social Responsibility and another called Society and Culture, as well as complete at least 30 hours of community service" (Sanchez, 1995). Nationwide, professors and students are being urged to become more engaged in the community around the campus, whether through work in new empowerment zones, outreach, or new partnerships (Ruffolo & Miller, 1994). Political and community pressures drive some administrators in that direction. A sense of obligation to assist and interact with "have-nots" motivates some professors. Idealists want students to face the stark needs of other human beings and the unfair aspects of society; to explore community service, public service work, and projects addressing societal problems; to develop their ethical sense; and to

BOX 6.13 **COMMUNITY INTERVENTIONS REGARDING AIDS**

Program Results

Prevention Projects	%	Service Projects	%
Project activities rated as most effective by projects using that activity			
Small group discussions	61	Case management	44
Outreach to high-risk populations	28	Testing for HIV	33
Train peers/volunteers	23	Counseling	30
Provide safer-sex kits	22	Advocacy services to HIV+	25
Large group discussions	22	Medical care	25
Support groups	21	Small group discussions	20
Individual counseling	20	Crisis intervention	20
		Homecare services for HIV+	20
		Hospice care	20
Project reports of "problematic" issues for participants			
Reluctance to be involved with AIDS issues	27	Reluctance to be involved with AIDS issues	28
Transportation	10	Getting clients needed services	28
Recruitment	8	Transportation	16
Geographic problems	8	Recruitment	12
Retention	8	Geographic problems	8
Financial problems	6	Retention	4
Staff-related problems			
Too much work	38	Too much work	44
Burnout	25	Rapid organizational growth	28
Retention/turnover	22	Retention/turnover	20
Rapid organizational growth	16	Staff communication	20
Staff communication	8	Different staff/manager goals	20
Different staff/manager goals	8	Burnout	16
Recruitment	8	Recruitment	16
Morale	8	Concern with risk to personal health	16
Concern with risk to personal health	3	Morale	12
Project reports of "problematic" community-/client-related issues			
General community awareness	21	General community awareness	32
Media awareness	17	General fears about contracting AIDS*	28
Target population's awareness	14	Media awareness	24
General community acceptance	14	Target population's awareness	24
Other AIDS organizations' acceptance	11	Media acceptance	20
Non-AIDS organizations' acceptance	11	Other AIDS organizations' acceptance	8
Media acceptance	8	Non-AIDS organizations' acceptance	4

*This response option was available only for service projects.
Source: Robert Wood Johnson Foundation Report Making Connections: AIDS and Communities.

| BOX 6.14 | STEPS TO ESTABLISHING SUCCESSFUL WORK SITE HEALTH PROMOTION PROGRAMS |

1. Build community support.
   (a) Assess community norms, culture, and activities.
   (b) Establish community advisory board.
2. Assess work-site culture and social norms.
   (a) Capitalize on opportunities to facilitate the program.
   (b) Identify and modify existing barriers.
3. Solicit top management and union support.
4. Use employee input in planning.

   (a) Conduct employee surveys.
   (b) Appoint employee steering committee.
   (c) Appoint work-site liaison.
5. Provide ongoing programming with environmental and social supports.
6. Conduct periodic program evaluation.

Source: *Sorensen, Glasgow, and Corbett (1990, p. 160).*

promote societal unity (Swarthmore, 1994). This "hitting the bricks" philosophy tries to ensure that the real listening and responsiveness, which can be by-products of concrete experience, will inform future assessments made by sensitized citizens as well as present assessments made by professionals.

Different fields are taking a second look at their relationship with the communities they serve and at new modes of direct assessment. As one facet of an aging-in-place community support program in California (Cullinane, 1993),

> a social worker walks a "beat" in an inner city neighborhood. Through her contacts with merchants, bankers, pharmacists, and barbers, the social worker and the resources she represents become known to the community. In turn, she gains the confidence of the merchants, who refer their customers who need her assistance in maintaining independence. (p. 135)

Community policing requires officers who usually react to individual incidents and complaints to become "proactive in resolving community problems," to use a problem-and-prevention approach, and to work more closely with community residents (Greene & Mastrofski, 1988, p. xii). The idea is to get out from behind a desk, even if on a part-time basis, and interact with citizens, update one's sense of the place, and experience the area's problems and struggles but also its strong points and vitality. In community nursing, the focus is on the needs of populations rather than on individual psyches or ailments. Since social work has already had community programs, this trend may not seem relevant, except that we know that we, like the police, are spending more and more time indoors, in relative calm and safety, avoiding "bad weather" on the "beat."

Professions add a community component to the individual component in order to further the goal of "promoting the common welfare" (Greene & Mastrofski, 1988) or to express their fundamental concern for the "collective good" (Spradley, 1990). Current providers of community-based services and community care are already out on the front lines, as is now being advocated for others. However, some are struggling to make a niche for themselves, so they are working more closely with community associations.

Domestic and international programs can provide models for our engagement and service delivery efforts in this direction. For instance, we can learn from the *patch* system, a community intervention concept imported from England. With its field workers, it is a decentralized but unified way of providing personal social services to people in an immediate geographic area. It makes use of natural helpers. This model has a "single-door" orientation, which resonates with those in human services here who have always wanted service centers and "one-stop shopping" for service users. A locality-based patch is not as small as it sounds, since it includes 4,000 to 20,000 people (Martinez-Brawley & Delevan, 1993, pp. 171, 181). The patch can be general or specialized and focused on a particular clientele or broad-based (p. 9).

This system, which has been experimented with in Iowa and Pennsylvania, is somewhat parallel to community policing and community/public health work. *Community-oriented social work* is viewed in the British model as an approach that

> uses local networks, teamwork by professionals, integrated service delivery systems, and *user* involvement . . . concerned with responding to need but also with preventing future problems. . . . It attempts to expand the vision of . . . workers beyond the individual and the family to the community as a center of networks. (Martinez-Brawley & Delevan, 1993, pp. 193–194)

England has additional community-based programs that make legal and counseling help and review more readily available through the use of volunteers. Social benefit tribunals, dominated by lay people, are one example. Citizen Advice Bureaus, which are lay advisory agencies, are another. Rural and isolated areas are less well served by these mechanisms (Levine, 1990), but England's programs, including patch programs, point up that social work can tune in to the community.

Discussion Exercises

1. Despite the many different parts of your community, what are the ties that bind? (a sports team, a widespread love of the outdoors, or a tendency to be stoical)?

2. Who or what do you view as the best source of information about community needs and why?

3. How might we give something back to a community (written observations, volunteer help, etc.) as part of any study in which we take the time of residents and leaders?

4. Compare (a) the teased child with a disfigurement and (b) the teenage "dirty" boy at the ice skating party with (c) Le Guin's fictional child in the cellar in terms of societal responses, both individual and programmatic.

5. What role, if any, do you think IQ plays in *justifying* who pulls the coach of society (à la Bellamy)? How do values and assessment fit together?

6. Discuss program accountability and assessment.

7. Using Box 6.4 as a model, represent a subsystem relevant to your agency. This will require many telephone calls and much consultation with old-timers in the field.

8. Using Box 6.5 as a model, draw up a similar chart to evaluate the quality and comprehensiveness of social services for a social problem of your choice.

9. Using Box 6.8 as an example, evaluate the needs and strengths of the area where you currently reside or where a parent or grandparent resides.

Notes

1. Regarding ecological practice, see Hepworth and Larsen (1993, pp. 15–17); Johnson (1995, pp. 413–414); and Levine & Perkins (1987, chap. 3).

2. Lee (1994) suggests these topics: basic information, life transitions, health and mental health, interpersonal patterns, physical and socioeconomic environment, manifestations of oppression, areas of powerlessness or inadequate power, strengths, the weighing/assessing process, the working agreement, and next steps in intervention (pp. 143–144).

3. In the documentary *The Land of the Deaf*, a sign language teacher and deaf rights crusader refers to his hearing daughter and sighs, "I had dreamt of having a deaf child—communication would be easier. But I love her all the same" (review by Richard Harrington, *Washington Post*, October 7, 1994, p. B7).

4. Shifting our lexicon helps shift professional and communal attitudes: "The potential benefit of shifting the focus from deficits and inabilities to strengths and abilities can be illustrated by a consideration of changing views of physically challenged people" (Sullivan, 1992, p. 205).

5. Johnson (1995) gives an example of a social impact statement: the local office of the human services department is closing, so a social worker decides to "determine the impact of such a change" (p. 276). See the Susskind profile in Kolb (1994, p. 317) on the impact of assessment, citizen participation, and public disputes.

6. Ironically, in our own era, conservatives often succeed in convincing the middle class that it is the poor (the have-nots) who sit on top of the coach snapping the whip—because of all the programs designed for them—while hard-working capitalists (the haves) strain to pay their benefits and pull them along. See Saleebey (1994, p. 357) on values.

7. "The Ones Who Walk Away from Omelas," copyright © 1973 by Ursula K. Le Guin; from the author's collection, *The Wind's Twelve Quarters*; first appeared in *New Dimensions 3*; used by permission of the author and the author's agent, Virginia Kidd.

8. The terminal phase, not covered here, might involve termination, program evaluation, or intervention research.

9. This section is based on work by Hardcastle (1992) and Turner (1963).

10. Analysis of facets of anticipated intervention (No. 5) is similar to the strategy chart analysis designed by the Midwest Academy and familiar to organizers.

References

Alcorn, S., & Morrison, J. D. (1994). Community planning that is "caught" and "taught": Experiential learning from town meetings. *Journal of Community Practice, 1*(4), 27–43.

All, A. C. (1994). A literature review: Assessment and intervention in elder abuse. *Journal of Gerontological Nursing, 20*(7), 25–32.

Amezcua, C., McAlister, A., Ramirez, A., &

Espinoza, R. (1990). *A su salud*: Health promotion in a Mexican-American border community. In N. Bracht (Ed.), *Health promotion at the community level.* (pp. 257–277). Newbury Park, CA: Sage.

Anderson, D. B., & Shaw, S. L. (1994). Starting a support group for families and partners of people with HIV/AIDS in a rural setting. *Social Work, 39*(1), 135–138.

Anderson, J. (1981). *Social work methods and processes.* Belmont, CA: Wadsworth.

Atkinson, D. R., Morten, G., & Sue, D. W. (1993). *Counseling American minorities: A cross cultural perspective.* Dubuque, IA: Wm. C. Brown.

Auerswald, E. H. (1968). Interdisciplinary versus ecological approach. *Family Process 7*, 202–215.

Bellamy, E. (1960). *Looking backward.* New York: New American Library. (Original 1888)

Blackwell, D., & Hunt, S. (1980). Mental health services reaching out to older persons. *Journal of Gerontological Social Work, 2*(4), 281–288.

Bracht, N., & Kingsbury, L. (1990). Assessing the community: Its services, needs, leadership, and readiness. In N. Bracht (Ed.), *Health promotion at the community level* (pp. 66–88). Newbury Park, CA: Sage.

Brandon, R. N., Plotnick, R. D., & Stockman, K. (1994). Outreach for entitlement programs: Lessons from food stamp outreach in Washington State. *Social Services Review, 68*(1), 61–80.

Center for Community Change. (1987). *The community reinvestment act: A citizen's action guide.* Washington, DC: Author.

Covey, S. R. (1991). *Principle-centered leadership.* NY: Summit.

Cowger, C. D. (1994). Assessing client strengths: Clinical assessment for client empowerment. *Social Work, 39*(3), 262–268.

Cox, F. M. (1995). Community problem solving: A guide to practice with comments. In J. Rothman, J. L. Erlich, & J. E. Tropman with F. M. Cox (Eds.), *Strategies of community organization: Macro practice* (5th ed., pp. 146–162). Itasca, IL: F. E. Peacock.

Cullinane, P. (1993). Neighborhoods that make sense: Community allies for elders aging in place. In J. J. Callahan, Jr. (Ed.), *Aging in place* (pp. 133–138). Amityville, NY: Baywood.

Delgado, M. (in press). Puerto Rican food establishments as social service organizations: Results of an asset assessment. *Journal of Community Practice.*

Dobkin, L. (1989). *The board and care system: A regulatory jungle.* Washington, DC: American Association of Retired Persons.

Dolnick, E. (1993, September). "Deafness as culture." *The Atlantic Monthly*, pp. 37–40, 46–53.

Ecklein, J. L., & Lauffer, A. A. (1972). *Community organizers and social planners.* New York: Wiley & Sons, and the Council on Social Work Education.

Forster, E. M. (1985). *Howards End.* New York: Bantam. (Original 1910)

Freeman, E. M. (1990). Social competence as a framework for addressing ethnicity and teenage alcohol problems. In A. R. Stiffman & L. E. Davis (Eds.), *Ethnic issues in adolescent mental health* (pp. 247–266). Newbury Park, CA: Sage.

Germain, C. B., & Gitterman, A. (1995). Ecological perspective. In R. Edwards (Ed.-in-chief), *Encyclopedia of social work* (19th ed., pp. 816–824). Washington, DC: National Association of Social Workers.

Greene, J. R., & Mastrofski, S. D. (1988). *Community policing: Rhetoric or reality.* New York: Praeger.

Greever, B. (1983). Tactical investigations for peoples' struggles (c. 1971). Reprinted in *Advocacy and the new federalism.* Washington, DC: National Public Law Training Center.

Hardcastle, D. A. (1992). *Social problems, needs and social policy: A conceptual review.* Baltimore: University of Maryland at Baltimore School of Social Work.

Harkins, J. E., & Jensema, C. J. (1987). *Focus-group discussions with deaf and severely hard of hearing people on needs for sensory devices.* Washington, DC: Gallaudet University.

Hepworth, D. H., & Larsen, J. A. (1993). *Direct social work practice.* Pacific Grove, CA: Brooks/Cole.

Huber, R., & Orlando, B. P. (1993). Macro assignment: Think big. *Journal of Social Work Education, 29*(1), 19–25.

Hunkeler, E. F., Davis E. M., McNeil, B., Powell, J. W., & Polen, M. R. (1990). Richmond quits smoking: A minority community fights for health. In N. Bracht (Ed.), *Health promotion at the community level* (pp. 278–303). Newbury Park, CA: Sage.

Jackson, B. (1987). *Fieldwork.* Chicago: University of Illinois Press.

Jacob, S. G., & Willits, F. K. (1994). Objective and subjective indicators of community evaluation: A Pennsylvania assessment. *Social Indicators Research, 32*(2), 161–177.

Jansson, B. S. (1990). *Social welfare policy: From theory to practice.* Belmont, CA: Wadsworth.

Johnson, L. C. (1995). *Social work practice: A generalist approach* (5th ed.). Boston: Allyn & Bacon.

Kettner, P. M., Moroney, R. M., & Martin, L. L. (1990). *Designing and managing programs: An effectiveness-based approach.* Newbury Park, CA: Sage.

Kolb, D. (1994). *When talk works: Profiles of mediators.* San Francisco: Jossey-Bass.

Koss, M. P., & Harvey, M. R. (1991). *The rape victim: Clinical and community interventions* (2nd ed.). Newbury Park, CA: Sage.

Kretzmann, J. P., & McKnight, J. L. (1993). *Building communities from the inside out: A path toward finding and mobilizing a community's assets.* Evanston, IL: Northwestern University Press.

Lauffer, A. (1984). Assessment and program development. In F. M. Cox, J. L. Erlich, J. Rothman, & J. E. Tropman (Eds.), *Tactics and techniques of community practice* (2nd ed., pp. 60–75). Itasca, IL: F. E. Peacock.

Lee, J. A. B. (1994). *The empowerment approach to social work practice.* New York: Columbia University Press.

Le Guin, U. K. (1973). The ones who walk away from Omelas. In U. K. Le Guin, *The wind's twelve quarters* (pp. 345–357). New York: HarperCollins.

Lenherr, M. R., Haase, C. C., & Motz, J. K. (1988). Program and case coordination. In D. C. Bross, R. D. Krugman, M. R. Lenherr, D. A. Rosenberg, & B. D. Schmitt (Eds), *The new child protection team handbook,* (pp. 215–286). New York: Garland.

Levine, M., & Perkins, D. V. (1987). *Principles of community psychology: Perspectives and applications.* New York: Oxford University Press.

Levine, M. L. (1990). Beyond legal services: Promoting justice for the elderly into the next century. In P. R. Powers & K. Klingensmith (Eds.), *Aging and the law* (pp. 55–79). Washington, DC: American Association of Retired Persons.

Luey, H. S., Glass, L., & Elliott, H. (1995). Hard-of-hearing or deaf: Issues of ears, language, culture, and identity. *Social Work, 40*(2), 177–182.

Maluccio, A. N. (1979). *Learning from clients: Interpersonal helping as viewed by clients and social workers.* New York: Free Press.

Mancoske, R. J., & Hunzeker, J. M. (1994). Advocating for community services coordination: An empowerment perspective for planning AIDS services. *Journal of Community Practice, 1*(3), 49–58.

Martinez-Brawley, E. E. (1990). *Perspectives on the small community: Humanistic views for practitioners.* Washington, DC: National Association of Social Workers Press.

Martinez-Brawley, E. E., & Delevan, S. M. (1993). *Transferring technology in the personal social services.* Washington, DC: National Association of Social Workers Press.

Mary, N. L. (1994). Social work, economic conversion, and community practice: Where are the social workers? *Journal of Community Practice, 1*(4), 7–25.

McEntee, M. K. (1995). Deaf and hard-of-hearing clients: Some legal implications. *Social Work, 40*(2), 183–187.

Meenaghan, T. M., Washington, R. O., & Ryan, R. M. (1982). *Macro practice in the human services.* New York: Free Press.

Meyer, C. H. (1993). *Assessment in social work practice.* New York: Columbia University Press.

Meyer, C. H. (1995). Assessment. In R. L. Edwards (Ed.-in-chief), *Encyclopedia of social work* (19th ed., pp 260–270). Washington, DC: National Association of Social Workers.

Miley, K. K., O'Melia, M., & DuBois, B. L. (1995). *Generalist social work practice: An empowering approach.* Needham Heights, MA: Allyn & Bacon.

Mitroff, I. I., & Linstone, H. A. (1993). *The unbounded mind: Breaking the chains of traditional business thinking.* New York: Oxford University Press.

Molnar, D., & Kammerud, M. (1977). Developing priorities for improving the social environment: Use of Delphi. In N. Gilbert & H. Specht (Eds.), *Planning for social welfare: Issues, models, and tasks* (pp. 324–332). Englewood Cliffs, NJ: Prentice-Hall.

Moore, S. T., & Kelly, M. J. (1996). Quality now: Moving human services organizations toward a consumer orientation to service quality. *Social Work, 41*(1), 33–40.

Moxley, D. P., & Freddolino, P. P. (1994). Client-driven advocacy and psychiatric disability: A model for social work practice. *Journal of Sociology and Social Welfare, 21*(2), 91–108.

Murphy, J. W., & Pilotta, J. J. (1983). Community-based evaluation for criminal justice planning. *Social Service Review, 57*(3), 465–476.

National Public Law Training Center. (1981). *The advocacy spectrum training manual.* Washington, DC: Author.

Netting, F. E., Kettner, P. M., & McMurtry, S. L. (1993). *Social work macro practice.* New York: Longman.

Neuber, K. A., with W. T. Atkins, J. A. Jacobson, &

N. A. Reuterman, (1980). *Needs assessment: A model for community planning.* Newbury Park, CA: Sage.

Oliver, M. (1990). *The politics of disablement.* New York: St. Martin's Press.

Parker, V., Edmonds, S., & Robinson, V. (1989). *A change for the better: How to make communities more responsive to older residents.* Washington, DC: American Association of Retired Persons.

Parsons, R. J., Hernandez, S. H., and Jorgensen, J. D. (1988). Integrated practice: A framework for problem solving. *Social Work, 33*(5), 417–421.

Peters, T. (1987). *Thriving on chaos: Handbook for a management revolution.* New York: Alfred A. Knopf.

Rakowski, W. (1992). Disease prevention and health promotion with older adults. In M. G. Ory, R. P. Abeles, & P. Darby (Eds.), *Aging, health, and behavior* (pp. 239–275). Newbury Park, CA: Sage.

Raskin, M. S. (1994). The Delphi study in field instruction revisited: Expert consensus on issues and research priorities. *Journal of Social Work Education, 30*(1), 75–89.

Reid, W. J. (1992). *Task strategies: An empirical approach to clinical social work.* New York: Columbia University Press.

Rodwell, M. K. (1987). Naturalistic inquiry: An alternative model for social work assessment. *Social Service Review, 61*(2), 231–246.

Rosenthal, S. J., & Cairns, J. M. (1994). Child abuse prevention: The community as co-worker. *Journal of Community Practice, 1*(4), 45–61.

Rosenthal, S. R., & Levine, E. S. (1980). Case management and policy implementation. *Public Policy, 28*(4), 381–413.

Rothman, J. (1984). Assessment and option selection [intro to part one]. In F. M. Cox, J. L. Erlich, J. Rothman, & J. E. Tropman (Eds.), *Tactics and techniques of community practice* (2nd ed., pp. 7–13). Itasca, IL: F. E. Peacock.

Ruffolo, M. C., & Miller, P. (1994). An advocacy/empowerment model of organizing: Developing university–agency partnerships. *Journal of Social Work Education, 30*(3), 310–316.

Saari, C. (1991). *The creation of meaning in clinical social work.* New York: Guilford Press.

Sacks, O. (1989). *Seeing voices: A journey into the world of the deaf.* Berkeley: University of California Press.

Saleebey, D. (1994). Culture, theory, and narrative: The intersection of meanings in practice. *Social Work, 39*(4), 351–359.

Sanchez, R. (1995, March 15). Western studies no longer sufficient: More colleges requiring education in other cultures. *The Washington Post,* pp. A1, 12.

Scott, D. (1990). Practice wisdom: The neglected source of practice research. *Social Work, 35*(6), 564–568.

Siegel, L. M., Attkisson, C. C., & Carson, L. G. (1987). Need identification and program planning in the community. In F. M. Cox, J. L. Erlich, J. Rothman, & J. E. Tropman (Eds.), *Strategies of community organization: Macro practice* (4th ed., pp. 71–97). Itasca, IL: F. E. Peacock.

Sorensen, G., Glasgow, R. E., & Corbett, K. (1990). Involving work sites and other organizations. In N. Bracht (Ed.), *Health promotion at the community level* (pp. 158–184). Newbury Park, CA: Sage.

Spradley, B. W. (1990). *Community health nursing: Concepts and practice* (3rd ed.). Glenview, IL: Scott, Foresman.

Stiffman, A. R., & Davis, L. E. (Eds.). (1990). *Ethnic issues in adolescent mental health.* Newbury Park, CA: Sage.

Stirring People Up. (1993). Interviews with advocates and activists. Monograph ed. by P. Powers. Baltimore: University of Maryland at Baltimore School of Social Work.

Sullivan, W. P. (1992). Reclaiming the community: The strengths perspective and deinstitutionalization. *Social Work, 37*(3), 204–209.

Sullivan, W. P., & Fisher, B. J. (1994). Intervening for success: Strengths-based case management and successful aging. *Journal of Gerontological Social Work, 22*(1–2), 61–74.

Swarthmore College. (1994, June). *The Garnet Letter.* (Available from the college, Swarthmore, PA).

Thayer, R. (1977). Measuring need in the social services. In N. Gilbert & H. Specht (Eds.), *Planning for social welfare: Issues, models and tasks* (pp. 297–310). Englewood Cliffs, NJ: Prentice-Hall.

Trudeau, Garry. (1995, July 2). Sunday edition, Doonesbury strip.

Turner, J. B. (1963, February). *Guidelines to a search for a theory of priority determination.* Paper presented at the Inter-Community Staff Conference, Case Western Reserve University, Cleveland, OH.

Turner, J. B. (1963, May). *The continuing debate: Community organization or community planning?* Paper presented at workshop on planning, group work, and recreation. Cleveland, OH.

Watkins, T. R., & Gonzales, R. (1982). Outreach to Mexican Americans. *Social Work, 27*(1), 68–73.

Weick, A., Rapp, C., Sullivan, W. P., & Kisthardt, W. (1989). A strengths perspective for social work practice. *Social Work, 34*(4), 350–354.

Weiner, A. (1996). Understanding the social needs of street walking prostitutes. *Social Work, 41*(1), 97–105.

Wells, L. M., Schachter, B., Little, S., Whylie, B., & Balogh, P. A.. (1993). Enhancing rehabilitation through mutual aid: Outreach to people with recent amputations. *Health and Social Work, 18*(3), 221–229.

Whitman, B. Y., Graves, B., & Accardo, P. (1987). Mentally retarded parents in the community: Identification method and needs assessment survey. *American Journal of Mental Deficiency, 91*(6), 636–638.

Whitworth, J. M., Lanier, M. W., & Haase, C. C. (1988). The influence of child protection teams on the development of community resources. In D. C. Bross, R. D. Krugman, M. R. Lenherr, D. A. Rosenberg, & B. D. Schmitt (Eds.), *The new child protection handbook* (pp. 571–583). New York: Garland.

Wiley, C. (Ed.). (1994). *Journeys to self-acceptance: Fat women speak*. Freedom, CA: Crossing Press.

Wiseman, F. (director). (1968). High school [film].

Wiseman, F. (director). (1994). *High school II* [film].

Witkin, B. R., & Altschuld, J. W. (1995). *Planning and conducting needs assessment*. Thousand Oaks, CA: Sage.

chapter
7

Using Self in Community Practice: Assertiveness

When people see that you can get things done, they line up behind you.

L. THOMPSON (1990, QUOTING D. KESSLER, P. 11)

Tiny steps . . . contribute to the making of the 'hardy spirit.'

S. PHELPS AND N. AUSTIN (1987, P. 227)

USE OF SELF[1]

This chapter briefly discusses competency in social work and then focuses on assertiveness as a pivotal skill.

Effective Use of Self

CORRESPONDING SKILLS
Consider how dancers and social workers are alike. Both respect highly developed use-of-self abilities that contribute to professional accomplishments and benefits for others. Initiative and persistence also are basic

to any success. While ballet and modern dance both require the same mastery over the body and an ability to relate to an audience, each requires specialized abilities; similarly, clinical work and community work draw on the same aptitudes while requiring the refinement of specific proficiencies.

The fact that we can draw on the same core skills means that elements of practice learned in one social work job—such as casework—are easily transferred to quite different employment settings—such as community organizations. Interviewing and information gathering, for example, are used in innumerable types of social work. Direct service workers might use these skills to elicit knowledge to improve a client's condition or to run a group more effectively, while community practitioners might synthesize information from interviews to undergird an exposé as part of social justice work. Dealing with an upset patient or community resident by telephone requires corresponding skills.

Social workers develop competence in relating to a variety of people and build on that competence in different aspects of practice. Coordination and advocacy are as basic to community practice as active listening and counseling are to clinical practice; assertiveness is vital to both. All five of those skills—coordination, advocacy, active listening, counseling, and assertiveness—involve communication. Social workers also attempt to heighten their self-awareness, that is, to become aware of personal skills and limitations in shifting settings (Burghardt, 1982, p. 51). Direct service practitioners can apply their interpersonal skills (e.g., awareness of others'

feelings, body language, and attentiveness) in their community work.

More basically, "use of self" implies that we must be able to perform solo because we may be the only person on the scene who can and will act. Principal dancers are thrown roses or presented with a bouquet at the end of a performance. Nobody brings roses to social workers at the end of a job; even so, we know when we have used our minds, hearts, and training to change lives. See Box 7.1.

SKILLS FOR CLIENTS AND COMMUNITIES

We integrate our abilities and experiences and apply them as needed. This is not just self-knowledge and development for its own sake. Social workers are engaged with individuals and with the larger community. Would a ballet be meaningful if the dancers simply performed the steps without regard to creative interpretation or audience appeal? Community connections are integral to our practice, as is making the community itself a better place. To do this effectively, practi-

---

BOX 7.1   DRAWING ON RESOURCES, INCLUDING OURSELVES

At a respite center for parents of totally dependent children, one child was deaf, mute, mentally challenged, and in a wheelchair because of cerebral palsy. Rick's mother communicated with him through story boards. He communicated with others through squeals and jerky arm movements. A social worker drawn to this eager youth attempted to find ways in which Rick could play and express himself. Wooden puzzles were tried successfully. As Rick mastered difficult ones, the worker began to suspect that he had more cognitive ability than had been detected during years of testing and residential programs. She contacted Hospital School, which he had attended, and the public schools for guidance—but to no avail. She spoke to the founder of the respite center and recommended,

based on her observation and assessment, that a special education tutor be found for Rick. Her advice was followed. Within a year, the "retarded" child was reading.

The worker found other ways to open up Rick's world. At home, he often sat on the porch and waved to the traffic. He was particularly pleased when a driver for Pepsi began waving back. The mother and worker contacted the company to thank the driver and ask if he would be allowed to stop and see Rick. The driver not only came to call but brought a miniature company truck and tiny cases of bottles that fit on the wheelchair tray. Thereafter, Rick whooped and waved his truck whenever the Pepsi truck passed his corner.

tioners need certain attitudes and a broad array of abilities. Attitudinally, community social work practice calls for a vision of communal life and the collective good. It also requires knowledge of human and social problems, of the social forces that keep many of them in place, and of the interventions needed to address them. The decision to *consider the community* and to draw on all facets of our field does not mean a lessening of interest in or commitment to individuals such as Rick. After all, all good social work must connect the personal to the social, and vice versa (anonymous reviewer letter; Weiss, 1993). Considering community does mean getting a better sense of who we are serving and which of their needs we have not addressed, as well as discovering who we are not serving and why and forming new partnerships for service delivery and advocacy. It requires a set of skills, which will be covered in this and subsequent chapters, ranging from assertiveness to case management.

We want to be able to follow a concern rising out of our work wherever it leads us, confident that our skills are flexible enough to meet most of the challenges of venturing into new professional territory. We want to be able to follow clients and community residents into facets of their lives outside social services. We need to hear their pride: "It was me and Jack that stopped the train"! See Box 7.2.

Expansion of Self

NEW ROUTINES—POLITICAL ASPECTS

Problems call us into the community if we allow ourselves to hear them. Ann Hartman (1990), former editor of *Social Work*, worries that we will use "psychic numbing to protect ourselves from the pain of seeing what is going on around us" (p. 4). She is concerned that we can tune in to one youth like Rick but cannot deal with a junior high school where many students are on drugs. Yet, to tune out is to tune out the community, and we have trained our emotions, minds, and beings for a public purpose.

Dancers who have mastered floor work must still learn to jump and soar to be professionals. To some social workers, becoming proficient in larger systems may seem like "leaps" into the stratosphere; for them, a fear of falling/failing hampers their ability to address more complex problems head on. However, the transition for many social workers should be uncomplicated. Building on superior skills in relating, interacting, and listening, we can move on readily to collective interaction, political talk, and citizen action.

BOX 7.2	WANTED: MORE THAN REHABILITATION

Jack lost his legs from a slate fall in the mines. . . . [At the hospital] they were trying to rehabilitate him. . . . [W]hen the disabled miners first went out on strike with the active miners, Jack was out there in his wheelchair on the picket line. The disabled miners was out to get their hospital cards and their pensions. . . . It was me and Jack that stopped the train during the strike. We didn't have a twelve-gauge shotgun like some folks say. . . . We had a sign with us that said *Hospital and Pension Card* on it. And we just held it up. We was beside the tracks, over on the edge, we didn't really block the train. But they saw our sign and they stopped the [coal] train. They pulled it back into the company's yard.

Source: *Della Mae Smith in Kahn (1973, pp. 40–43).*

Social workers must enter the political world of civic and community participation, of self-governance and responsiveness to larger problems.[2] In this regard, Barber (1984) urges universal participation in public action, politics, and the "realm of we." He believes that most Americans see "politics as a thing or a place or a set of institutions—as, at best, something done by others," which means that we undervalue "the degree to which action entails activity, energy, work, and participation" (pp. 122–123).

Achieving true community and strong democracy requires a kind of talking and listening to which social workers can uniquely contribute. Barber (1984) believes that the talk on which democracy builds "involves listening as well as speaking, feeling as well as thinking, and acting as well as reflecting" (p. 178)—principles totally compatible with social work. He wants us to understand the political functions of "talk" for democratic and community-strengthening processes. Barber lists "features of talking and listening in public," that is, an inventory of civic interactions and obligations:

1. The articulation of interests; bargaining and exchange;
2. Persuasion;
3. Agenda-setting;
4. Exploring mutuality;
5. Affiliation and affection;
6. Maintaining autonomy;
7. Witness and self-expression;
8. Reformulation and reconceptualization;
9. Community-building as the creation of public interests, common goods, and active citizens. (pp. 178–179)

Strong democratic *talk*, according to Barber, involves "deliberation, agenda-setting, listening, [and] empathy," while strong democratic *action* involves "common work, community action, [and] citizen service" (p. 266).

We single out Barber's basic community activities and political talk because they seem more within our reach than legislative advocacy or getting an initiative on a ballot, but also because such civic engagement is a moral imperative. If we do not have the confidence and willingness to engage as citizens, then it is more difficult for any course of training to transform us into strong professionals.

Neither dancers nor social workers can stay in the wings and watch. To develop one's capacities and yet be afraid to get out on the stage of life would be a sad waste of ability, which—fortunately—seldom happens. However, some social workers are reluctant to "go on tour," to perform away from their home base.

NEW ROUTINES—PERSONAL ASPECTS

Some practitioners have not yet experienced using themselves in a way other than that demanded by the direct service part of their jobs, so they are untested in macropractice tasks. Too often, apprehension or inexperience restrain them from making the contributions they are capable of making at the board, association, service delivery system, neighborhood, or city level.

Since social workers have core aptitudes and solid competence in skills that are transferable, why are some of them uneasy about moving outside their current sphere of work? Like the ballet dancer who joins a modern dance troupe, clinicians face discomforts when easing into collective endeavors. Confidence was established within a particular niche, and new proficiencies will have to be developed. To make the best use of one's professional self is difficult at any time, but especially when engaging in new aspects of social work.

In addition, the clinician may be uncomfortable utilizing new types of assessment or with the manner in which work in the community commonly is discussed. For example, a person accustomed to determining diagnoses using a manual and personal intuition and experience may be uncomfortable switching to weighing and calculating variables. Some persons making such a transition in practice express discomfort with the analytical language of "trade-offs," "bottom lines," "bargaining chips," and "best practices" because they say they value openness, empathy, and doing the right thing for its own sake. Yet, social work's very emphasis on genuineness, authenticity, and getting in touch with feelings may lead us to simplify ideas and follow impulses too easily at the community level. Mastering a full repertoire of skills will make us more thoughtful and confident practitioners.

Although we often have an uneven sense of our power and competence as practitioners, we see ourselves as capable of effective action. The question is "What action?" We may stick closely to what we have done, the familiar, and resist areas where we anticipate failure. Yet, by analyzing our anxieties and watching our behavior, we can deal with our attitudes and improve our performance. "Knowing how to work with one's personal and emotional capacities is a fundamental skill in social work practice," states Burghardt (1982, p. 49). Assertiveness can help.

ASSERTIVENESS OVERVIEW

Background and Orientation

How does assertion fit into social work? Wakefield (1988) views it as "properly within social work's natural domain" (p. 361). A psychological or professional trait—like self-respect, confidence, problem-solving and social skills—assertion facilitates the fulfillment of our "intentions" (p. 361). Obstacles are external as well as internal:

Clearly, not all obstacles to minimally effective goal-oriented activity originate within the person. Environmental obstacles, especially in difficult environments where a person does not possess great power or social connections, can be a constant source of frustration and despair. Some degree of assertiveness is necessary in dealing with these obstacles, or actions would rarely be carried to completion. (p. 365)

The history, theory, and practice of assertiveness are linked with the *human potential movement, encounter groups,* and *sensitivity training* (Back, 1972; Peterson, 1971); *the women's movement and consciousness raising* (Bloom, Coburn, & Pearlman, 1975; Enns, 1992); *business success ideas* (Siress, 1994); and *behavior therapy and social learning theory* (see Chapter 2). Although different terms—"taking charge," "sticking up for yourself" (Kaufman & Raphael, 1990), or "empowering oneself" (Harris & Harris, 1993)—may now be utilized, ideas about assertiveness have entered into both the popular culture and the specialized training of professionals.

Assertiveness is a learned social skill (Hepler, 1995) and a communication style frequently discussed in terms of three response patterns: passive/nonassertive, aggressive, and assertive. Before discussing these frameworks, we will examine assertiveness in a more personalized way.

The Psychology of Assertion

ASSERTIVENESS STARTS WITH US

Competent involvement in the processes of conflict and change, which lie at the heart of the social work enterprise, begins with articulation, with the overcoming of apprehension, with assertion. *Assertion* "is the act of standing up for one's own basic human rights without violating the basic human rights of others" (Kelly, 1979) in an "interpersonal context in which there is some risk of a negative reaction by the recipient" (Rakos, 1991, p. 10). See Box 7.3.

From childhood, human beings engage in a process of sorting out the right to refuse from stubborn resistance, the desire to please from passive acquiescence, tact from timidity, circumspection from cowardice, and assertion from aggression. They learn to understand their motivations and behavior in this realm and to interpret signals and signs from family, acquaintances, and strangers. With difficulty, people learn to stand up for themselves and others and to deal with the consequences. To be a mature, assertive person means taking risks. The story in Box 7.3 speaks to a universal challenge: standing up to adults as a child (Sears 1990, 1993).

A related predicament for adults is standing up when one feels like a child. In adulthood, Bower and Bower (1991) say, "lack of assertiveness makes millions of people feel uneasy and inadequate" (p. 2). Thus, assertiveness has been recommended for anxiety reduction (Cotler & Guerra, 1976, p. 3). Although circumstances may require anything from saying no to curbing abuse, the essence is similar: "When you assert yourself, you communicate your positive or negative feelings honestly and directly" (Zuker, 1983, p. 12). See Box 7.4.

FACING THE DRAGON

What should we do? Such elemental emotions and basic quandaries remind us of archetypes for stances people take in such situations. Pearson (1989) writes about six archetypes or ways of seeing the world that we live by: the innocent, orphan, wanderer, warrior, martyr, and magician. Each is appropriate sometimes as part of human development and life's quests. In professional life, we are no longer innocents, but the other archetypes remind us of states of assertion and nonassertion. In response to a dragon, the orphan "denies it exists or waits for rescue"; the martyr "appeases or sacrifices self to save others"; the wanderer "flees"; the warrior "slays"; and the magician "incorporates and affirms" (Pearson, 1989, p. 20).

Each of these reactions makes sense as we think about the varying responses one could have to the chaotic scene in the wait-

---

BOX 7.3	WORKING UP NERVE: CHILD

Grace said we had to go get a chicken for dinner. [She] walked around in the yard, looking at all the birds, and finally spied one she liked. She chased it until she caught both the wings flat, with the chicken squawking the whole time. . . .

I didn't never think on killing nothing to eat and didn't want to do it. . . . Now Grace wanted me to kill the chicken and I didn't want to, so I tried to back away, only she said, "I know you are strong enough to do this, Jodi."

She stuck out the handle to the hatchet, but I couldn't take it. *I shook my head no and said, real quiet, "I don't want to, ma'am"* [emphasis added].

. . . I ran into the barn. I climbed the ladder and went behind some hay and pulled it all over me till nobody could see me and stayed real quiet. I sucked in air and didn't give it back. Grace came and called out, "Jodi, I'm sorry if I scared you. It's all right if you don't want to help. Jodi? You don't have to hide. It's all right."

But *I was thinking on how I told a grown-up no and didn't do what she said* [emphasis added]. I knew I was going to get whipped. Paul and Grace would send me and Brother back because I was bad.

. . . I watched Grace real good the rest of the time before bed, but she never said nothing about the chicken or me not being good. She never said nothing about it ever again.

Source: *Vickie Sears, "Grace" in Simple Songs. Firebrand Books, Ithaca, NY. Copyright © 1990 by Vickie Sears.*

BOX 7.4	WORKING UP NERVE: ADULT

Midnight. You sit in a hospital waiting room with someone who called you in a suicidal state and needs a consult and probably a prescription. The police arrive with a woman, high on drugs, who twists to get away. They handcuff her to a leg of the couch near you. She shrieks and tries to free herself. One officer slaps and kicks her. "Shut-up," he yells. She makes a scene—cursing and ripping off her blouse—as the receptionist routinely goes over paperwork with the other officer. As the policeman stands over her, you are silent, sickened. You are concerned for the woman but also about the effects of all this on your client. You know things like this go on but a part of you wants "out of there"—you are not, after all, the woman's advocate. You try to make sense of the situation. You consider: waiting things out, covering the woman up with your jacket, pointing out to the policeman that she is defenseless even though behaving obnoxiously, going outdoors with your client, telling off the "brutal cop," appealing to the receptionist, and asking the other officer to simmer things down.

"There are five key steps in assessing a situation and becoming aware of what you intend to do: your sensations, interpretations, feelings, desires, and intentions," says Zuker (1983, p. 56). Thus, I see → I think → I feel → I want → I will. However, we need not act on everything we become aware of.

ing room. *Looking at archetypes* (in simplified fashion) *purely from the dimension of how threats are met*, we suggest that the passive person approaches life as an orphan, martyr, or wanderer; the aggressive person approaches life as a warrior; and the assertive person approaches life as a magician. (A wanderer's independence also might allow assertion.) The assertive person, the magician, visualizes what he or she wants, develops tools, and takes action to make it happen while keeping all elements in balance.

Assertiveness involves a rational approach to occurrences usually dominated by uneasiness, if not fear. Depending on the person, becoming more assertive may require reevaluating a lifelong stance (e.g., martyr, warrior) or simply learning new scripts for specific situations. Ordinarily assertion, even assertion involving potential conflict, as in Box 7.4, is *not* as "dangerously risky," as nonassertive people are prone to think (Rakos, 1991, p. 66). We tend to make the other person into a dragon, as shown in Box 7.3. Training allows us to face realistic "negative consequences" while knowing that the probability is that "appropriate" assertion will actually lessen risks (Rakos, 1991, 66).

The Boundaries of Assertion

COMMUNICATION RESPONSE STYLES

Alberti and Emmons (1990) believe that *assertive behavior* "promotes equality in human relationships" (p. 26). Those acting assertively, according to Drury (1984), "make clear, direct, nonapologetic statements" about expectations and feelings and criticize in "a descriptive rather than a judgmental way" (p. 3)—for example, "I'd like you to hear me out." They describe their own reactions to a situation. We can see that this would be important to act effectively in the waiting room incident. Assertiveness is a strong, steady style, not a formula for automatic success.

When assertive people meet resistance, Drury says they persist in "following through on issues"; they also negotiate, compromise, and listen to others respectfully (p. 3). They are accountable and responsible for their behavior. Such a style is illustrated by *The One Minute Manager*, which urges getting to the point, truth telling rather than wounding, and not using feedback as an excuse to tell someone off (Blanchard & Johnson, 1982).

Basic assertiveness includes such non-verbal behaviors as animation, maintaining appropriate eye contact and an upright stance, and verbal behaviors such as using "I" rather than "you" messages (e.g., "I am uncomfortable that we have not reached a decision"). This does not mean that the word "you" is forbidden but rather that the response is not an attack. Phelps and Austin (1987) illustrate a request for information:

> Boss: I want those reports to be more efficient and better looking next time.
> You: What specifically do you mean...? Can you show me an example or describe a report? (p. 227)

More advanced assertiveness might include "working a room" during a huge meeting reception (RoAne, 1988).

Nonassertive or passive behavior can result from being overly deferential to authorities or those established and well positioned in society. In the waiting room incident, nonassertion could involve doing nothing. Or a comment could be prefaced by "I know none of this is any of my business, but . . ." Eberhardt (1994) provides two examples of this style:

> "I'm sorry to take up so much of your time."
> "It doesn't matter, whatever you want to do." (p. 133)

A *person's real position* may be hidden by nonassertive behavior when expressions like "I guess," "I wonder if you could, maybe," "it's not really important," and "maybe I'm wrong" are used. Such expressions aim to disarm the recipient by presenting a weakened picture of the speaker or writer. Tannen (1994) gives another motive: "Many people (especially women) *try to avoid seeming presumptuous* by prefacing their statements with a disclaimer such as, 'I don't know if this will work, but . . .' " (p. 279; emphasis added). Nonverbal passive responses resulting in the same effect include "don't hurt me" stances, downcast eyes, shifting of weight, a slouched body, whining, hand wringing, a childish tone of voice, and the poor-me seduction of others. Both passive and aggressive responses can be manipulative.

Aggression appears in many forms. In the waiting room, it could take the form of a shouting match or speaking to the police officers as villains without acknowledging the drug reaction with which they are contending. Aggressive people, interested in winning and dominating, may want to prove themselves to the client and fail to check out the client's feelings in this situation. Aggressive behavior can go so far as to injure, demean, or diminish another person through words with an implied threat such as "you'd better" and through behavior such as using a raised, haughty, snickering, or snarling tone of voice or pointing. Some white collar aggression is layered under propriety or disguised by parliamentary procedure. Such "indirect aggressiveness" or passive aggressiveness is often mentioned as another communication style (Phelps & Austin, 1987, p. 25) or "flavor" (Life Would Be Easy, 1995).

ACTORS AND APPLICATIONS

Situations calling for assertion permeate all facets of practice and personal life. We need assertion skills, and so do those with whom we work (e.g., welfare recipients who are seeking jobs). The prospective users of assertiveness will differ greatly.

Assertiveness and Behavior

ACTING ASSERTIVELY

The basics of assertiveness, to Phelps and Austin (1987), are "saying no, expressing anger, recognizing the Compassion Trap, shedding the need for approval, giving up excessive apology" (pp. 1–2). (For example, we may, out of compassion, feel that we must always be on call or helpful.) Even though conflict is more commonly discussed, Rakos (1991) points out that "assertiveness comprises interpersonal expressiveness in both positive and negative contexts." A literature review by Schroeder, Rakos, and Moe delineated seven categories of assertive responses: admitting personal shortcomings, giving and receiving compliments, initiating and maintaining interactions, expressing positive feelings, expressing unpopular or different opinions, requesting behavior changes by other people, and refusing unreasonable requests (Rakos, 1991, p. 15). For many people, the first hurdle is handling praise and criticism, not conflict. Therefore, in assertiveness groups—as in encounter groups—individuals learn to accept "strokes" and to give positive and negative opinions or reactions.

An assertive act may be quite simple:

- You ask questions of a lecturer.
- A colleague says you are good with protective service clients, and you respond with a "thank you" instead of disclaimers, false modesty, or a return compliment.
- Your coordinator asks you to review a paper. You thoughtfully mark up the draft to suggest reorganization.

Or an assertive act may be tricky to perform:

- Parents of a medically fragile infant feel they are not getting straight answers on home care options/risks and want you to force the doctor to spend time with them.

TAKING THE LEAD

Assertiveness is not, at heart, simply a matter of demeanor, accepting praise, or adroit handling of social predicaments. It is *self-advocacy*:

- A social worker with seniority on an interdisciplinary team suggests that team leadership rotate, rather than having only the psychiatric staff be leaders.
- Parents of seriously emotionally disturbed children raise the point that they need respite care, not a proposed party, during the holidays.
- A frail person says to a volunteer, "Let me hold on to you instead of you holding on to me," thus asserting a modicum of control over her life.

Assertiveness is a *tool* to use in our work lives. It enables a quiet staffer to ask a vocal colleague to stop talking over him at staff meetings. It helps a social worker to sell her project to the rest of the staff at a meeting. It helps supervisors. Drury (1984) asks what an appropriate assertive statement would be under these circumstances: "The group has just spent 15 minutes of a 1-hour staff meeting complaining about clients, the agency, and the newspapers. Four items need to be discussed at the meeting." Drury suggests saying, "I'm concerned because we have four items we need to discuss at this meeting. I would like to move on" (pp. 171–172).

Assertiveness can be expected of us. Suppose that the head of your section asks you, as a lower-level manager, to arrive at a staff retreat prepared to discuss your unit's strengths and weaknesses, opportunities and threats, and future plans. Modesty and rigorous self-scrutiny seldom carry the day in a public forum; they also can lower subordinates' morale. You need to draft forceful comments about the positives and give con-

> We present technically complex information, that is easily understood by nonexperts and the media, in interviews and through fact sheets and issue briefs.

vincing specifics regarding what works in your unit, such as:
Taking the lead or spelling out capabilities may be hard for people conditioned not to boast (Tannen, 1990, pp. 218–224; 1994, pp. 38–39), but internal agency success can have benefits for the community.

Assertiveness and Gender

There is no formula for assertiveness. Still, some people are listened to more than others—and it is important to be heard.[3] Two people can say the same thing quite differently (Tannen, 1994):

> They may speak with or without a disclaimer, loudly or softly, in a self-deprecating or declamatory way, briefly or at length, and tentatively or with apparent certainty. They may initiate ideas or support or argue against ideas raised by others. When dissenting, they may adopt a conciliatory tone, mitigating the disagreement, or an adversarial one, emphasizing it. (p. 280)

Tannen's quote is descriptive, not prescriptive. Assertion experts would call those whose behavior consistently and noticeably fits an extreme form of those patterns "passive" or "aggressive."

More than communication skill can be involved. Tannen's communication research reveals differences by gender, race, culture, and context. Rakos, summarizing assertiveness research, concurs that content and style of communication will vary "according to situational, social, and cultural norms and values" (1991, p. 18). Regarding context, our behavior as individuals varies according to the situation (e.g., are we at the office picnic or a meeting?). Regarding diversity, there will be a continuum of assertive behavior for those of similar background or those of the same gender and striking differences between various groups. For example, one small study of faculty meetings found that men speak more often and longer than women. Tannen says that women are more likely to "speak at a lower volume, and try to be succinct so as not to take up more meeting time than necessary." In the study, the "longest contribution by a woman was still shorter than the shortest contribution by a man" (1994, pp. 279–280). There is no ideal length of time to talk, so long as everyone is getting a turn. "There is no *a priori* correct assertive response, though there are general behavioral guidelines for effective expression of feelings and desires," explains Rakos (1991, p. 24).

In another study, personnel officers listened to tapes of prospective female employees—half with "unassertive speech features." Those *without* such features were "described as more likely to succeed in the workplace, more likely to be chosen for management positions, and more likely to be respected by coworkers" (Knotts, 1991). Examples of "powerless language" that makes speakers seem indecisive, tentative, and lacking in authority are:

Tag questions	"John is here, isn't he?"
Hedges	"I'd kind of like to go."
Hesitations	"well"
Intensifiers	"really"

Men also are perceived negatively when they use "unassertive speech features." Drawing from other studies, Knotts states that "men use speech to report, to compete, to gain attention, and to maintain their position in a social hierarchy," while "women use speech to gain rapport, maintain relationships, and reflect a sense of community" (pp. 1–32).

Tannen (1990) makes an intriguing, controversial contention along these lines: "Sensitivity training [and therapy] judges men by women's standards, trying to get them to talk more like women. Assertiveness training judges women by men's standards and tries to get them to talk more like men." She believes that learning each other's strategies and habits increases our flexibility as communicators (p. 297). The authors of this text take the position that both men and women in social work can benefit from increasing their assertiveness. Assertiveness in its basic form, Phelps and Austin (1987) remind us, was never gender specific but rather a way of pushing past blocks or "confronting the unpleasant or difficult without getting squashed (or squashing others) in the process" (p. 80).

Assertiveness and Class/Minority Status

Analysis or assessment of assertive behavior requires an awareness of individual, gender, and cultural differences. *Differences in what constitutes assertiveness* speak to the emic (culturally specific) nature of assertion, according to Marianne Yoshioka (1995). She studied differences in styles and values associated with assertiveness in African-American, Caucasian, and Hispanic (mostly Mexican) *low-income* women living in north Florida. (Contrary to expectations, the Hispanic women were found to be the most assertive by conventional and Hispanic criteria.)

Yoshioka makes a number of useful observations:

1. Besides linguistic differences, there may be value differences between cultures.

"Mainstream" assertiveness rests on rights, individualism, personal control, and self-reliance—values not necessarily equally endorsed by other cultural communities. There are differences regarding an individual's connections and obligations to others.

> When a request or demand must be made of a friend, Hispanics in the study were more likely to preface their assertiveness with a positive affirmation of the friendship.

2. The basic message of a response must be identified apart from the language chosen to convey it. Responses may differ in word construction and intensity of language from the way a practitioner speaks but may still be considered a culturally appropriate, assertive response within the community.

> Language such as "Anytime, you push on me, I'm going to push you right on back" is viewed as assertive, not aggressive, by African-Americans in the study. Hispanics placed more emphasis on correctly addressing the other party and using good manners. Caucasians and African-Americans more often referred to consequences or obligations to elicit compliance from the other party.

3. There are differences within a population, just as there are between racial and ethnic groups.

4. People from varied backgrounds differ in where they place the boundaries between passivity, assertiveness, and aggressiveness.

Individual Caucasian reactions in one role play in the study went from inability to formulate a response to threats to kill. Individual African-Americans had fewer types of aggressive acts but used behaviors that other groups defined as aggressive. They were more direct and forthright in their strategies than Caucasians and Hispanics.

Each group of women in the study could stand up for themselves, but they acted according to different notions of appropriate personal conduct. This was particularly true when the other party in the role play mistreated them. Would they accept an apology? Shove back?

Even if other studies find different particulars about these cultures, Yoshioka's conclusion is germane: understanding specific ways a culturally different client may approach a given situation could enhance social work effectiveness.

Assertiveness and Being

Regardless of our background, for assertiveness or self-advocacy to be effective, we must learn to manage situations and ourselves. Shoma Morita posits three principles (developed from Zen Buddhism) that appear relevant to effective assertive behavior:

- Know your purpose: know what you want to accomplish, as (perhaps) distinct from what others want you to accomplish or what you want others to believe (i.e., you simply want to get through the meeting or encounter looking as though you care, not

communicating information or having others adopt your position).

- Accept your feelings: accept being angry, scared, and so on, but recognize that while you are not responsible for feelings, you are responsible for how you manage them and your behavior.

- Do what needs to be done: put your energy into developing and using the skills needed to deal with a situation, not avoiding or being anxious over it. Actively choose the strategy for managing the situation (Clifton & Dahms, 1993, pp. 164–165).

PURPOSES AND BENEFITS OF ASSERTIVENESS IN SOCIAL WORK

Philosophy and Character

ASSERTION—A FLEXIBLE VEHICLE

To Hartman (1990), "there is no effective way of intervention that does not cut across all levels of possible resources and possible places of intervention" (p. 4). She envisions a social worker as "one who moves with competence across system boundaries and who follows the problem wherever it leads" (p. 1). Assertiveness is a particularly useful skill for such integrated practice since it is applicable in expressive therapies, casework, group work, administration, community work, and social reform. It also relates to other key concepts—empowerment, personal power, advocacy, client self-determination, behavior modification, personal comfort level, and ethics. Those in human services see applications in specialized areas ranging from corrections to rehabilitation (Lange & Jakubowski, 1976, p. 241) and in the community. Alberti and Emmons (1974) discuss helping youth leaders apply assertiveness principles in working with young people in camp programs and as part of leadership training for community organizations (p. 87).

Social workers have a reason to acquire assertiveness skills, too. Sometimes sticking up for our own place of work (e.g., family planning center) requires assertion due to the opposition's force. It is fairly common today for social service agencies to be rebuked publicly in front of elected officials by neighbors resistant to group homes. Assertive comebacks may need to be practiced for such moments. Equally important, we want to be able to promote public interests as well. A social worker may feel an obligation to argue for a teen center in an isolated hamlet even during a time of budget cutbacks. In such situations, though, as Rakos (1991) says, "assertive behavior is only one option for coping with difficult or problematic circumstances" (p. 5).

A MEANS TO IMPORTANT ENDS

Assertiveness is critical for effective social work practice and may well be a prerequisite for working in the community, an experience that almost immediately requires us to interact with strangers, officials, and competitive organizations. *Assertiveness* is used in social work as an umbrella term for many positive attributes: initiative, persistence, poise, spunk, alertness, responsiveness, and the ability to defend oneself. It can be viewed as a means to an end—usually discussed as a skill or tool—and as an end in itself—usually discussed as self-development, a coping device, a positive outcome, or being at the top of one's form. The development of assertiveness is meant to enable the social worker to:

- identify, be in command of, and be comfortable with personal power and the assertion of basic human rights;
- provide a model for and teach assertiveness to the client and the client/citizen sys-

tem, and help them realize and use their power; and

- use personal power appropriately in advocacy and other interpersonal, organizational, and political situations.

Although the emphasis is usually on *personal* assertion, the importance of examining *political* assertion (i.e., being the squeaky wheel that gets greased) has been urged as well. Alberti and Emmons (1990) believe that if we become "expressive enough, governments usually respond":

> The growth and successes of assertive citizen lobbies—minority/homeless/children's/gay and other rights movements, Common Cause (for political reform), AARP and Grey Panthers (for older Americans), the various tax reform movements—are powerful evidence: assertion does work! And there may be no more important arena for its application than overcoming the sense of "What's the use? I can't make a difference." (p. 15)

DISTINCTIVE NATURE OF ASSERTION IN SOCIAL WORK

Being personally or professionally assertive is viewed in human services as a respectful act, one implying that the other person can be (at least somewhat) trusted to behave responsibly, not to retaliate, and to remain open to a closer relationship. Lange and Jakubowski (1976) add two other aspects: respect for oneself and for the other person's needs and rights (pp. 7–8). The more difficult implementation of this philosophy focuses on interactions with involuntary clients, where respect and an awareness of clients' strengths are important but where issues of control and structure play a part in most communication transactions (Cowger, 1994, p. 263).

Professions that countenance tougher behavior, such as law and journalism, do not discuss "assertive" behaviors by that designation, with the exception of business management. Assertive, persistent business people are expected to "raise the muscle level when necessary" (Drury, 1984, p. 76). Moreover, few occupations outside human services emphasize respect as part of assertiveness. Good will does not necessarily underlie assertive transactions as they are defined and practiced in business. Other professions deemphasize authenticity and use assertiveness to obtain clients, information, or tactical advantages. Trial lawyers must be persuasive (Simons, 1976) and assertive—but not "boorish" (Magladry & Macpherson, 1994).

Why Are Assertiveness Skills Important for Social Workers?

The query "What is the point of learning to be more assertive?" must be addressed before the practical problem of how to learn this mindset and skill is outlined. We have just seen one reason—we have to be able to deal effectively with persons from other fields. There are even more important reasons. Assertiveness employed by those in our field can contribute to

the interests of clients and citizens;
the social worker's mental health;
the social worker's physical safety;
the social worker's success rate; and
the voicing of social work values.

CLIENTS AND CITIZENS

Increased assertiveness benefits more than individual social workers. Those with whom we interact and those we assist (directly or indirectly) also benefit. When we are stronger, there is a valuable ripple effect. In addition, assertive people are more likely to speak up to government and nongovernment operations that have an obligation to serve citizens. After mastering assertiveness principles and skills themselves, some clinicians will engage in training with community groups, as well as assertiveness therapy with individuals and groups with special needs.

SAYING "NO" TO PROTECT STAFF AND SERVICE USERS

Angel and Petronko (1983) discuss such consequences as danger, "inferior patient care and consumer complaints" when nurses fail to say no (p. 142). Sherman and Wenocur (1983) relate the social worker's ability to say "no" to high-quality casework. One reason, then, to increase our assertiveness involves our concern for clients; our workload and professional autonomy affect them. Another reason, pure and simple, is *mental self-preservation*, managing our own attitude and stress level by establishing fair but firm limits.

BALANCING SAFETY AND SERVICE

Learning to be more assertive can also contribute to *physical self-preservation*. Self-defense calls for decisive acts—running out into the street, for instance, or stopping a passing stranger. Practitioners are becoming increasingly worried about their personal safety in dealing with clients and the community. In response to this concern, one state program on violence and practice included sessions on "Street Smarts for Social Workers" and "The Intimate Terrorist" (NASW, 1995). The *Encyclopedia of Social Work* includes an entry on "Social Worker and Agency Safety" (Griffin, 1995). A recent study found that social work students are more likely to be exposed to verbal or physical violence *within* the agency than outside (Tully, Kropf, & Price, 1993, p. 195). As more students come from suburbia, with little experience of urban life, their personal sense of danger in field placements and on the job may be heightened. Increased confidence and competence will help quell irrational fears (Box 7.5).

BOX 7.5   PERSONAL SAFETY IN THE FIELD

A thoughtful student responded to the dilemma of serving the neediest while exercising caution by taking hold of the situation:

"I feel strongly that social workers (and doctors and lawyers and . . .) have an obligation to work where our clients are. If I am unwilling to visit an elderly, homebound woman because I fear her neighborhood, how can I be comfortable, as her social worker, if she continues to live in such a dangerous place? For home visiting, I take several commonsense, precautionary steps. These include:

- bringing a second person along when I feel a need for additional support. (One older woman took her labrador retriever along for the ride.)
- always telling someone exactly where I'm going, how to reach me (if there is a phone), who I'll be meeting, and when I'll be back.

- if possible, having the client or another known person watch for my arrival and even come out to escort me into the apartment/house.
- limiting visits to daytime hours, preferably mornings.
- driving to appointments, so I can park close to the place I'm going and control when I leave. (I went through a . . . period without a car, and felt more vulnerable, although nothing actually happened.)

There is recognition in the surrounding area that we are a place worth having around. Our clients are a part of the overall organization, and they are also our neighbors. My sense is that we are protected by our reputation and our role in the community."

Source: *Sara Cartmill.*

From the District of Columbia to Hawaii, people feel or are in peril; therefore, professionals must develop "peacemaking" skills to deal with potential violence (Colburn, 1994, p. 399). Social work training allows us to help protect *others* from danger—for example, in the workplace, where we can plan ahead using threat assessment teams (Masi, 1994, p. 23). Assertiveness is needed to implement precautions, as well as to continue working effectively when precautions are not possible.

INCREASING SUCCESSES

Becoming more assertive in our outreach to the community includes believing that we are worth listening to, as the following experience reveals:

I was invited to a dinner of the Board of the Department of Social Services, and I was the last agenda item. The president an-

nounced that we would be finished in time for the football game. I thought by the time they got to me I'd have ten minutes. I spoke about the local jurisdiction putting an extra fee on the cost of issuing a marriage license and using that fee to help fund domestic violence programs. By providing them with this information, I got their attention. They stayed past 9:00 and that was the vehicle they ended up using. . . . That was the beginning of a community effort and we also established a rape crisis center, so it all worked out well. (Heisner in *Challenging*)[4]

Because she resisted the impulse to cut short her remarks, this social worker helped create a new funding stream to support two additional community services.

Success may follow the discomfort associated with being invited to speak to a large or important group. Advocates can be asked to speak on their area of expertise and still be unnerved by short notice, the type of audience (highly visible leaders or unfriendly participants), or fear of failure. Many individuals dread being the center of attention. To overcome stage fright, we need to go beyond mere speaking to assertively making a case for action—or inaction.

For those of us who help with charity auctions, annual and capital-giving campaigns, and phone-a-thons, a third difficult area could be asking others to volunteer or to give money; yet, success is vital to our organizational survival. Resource development requires networking and meeting with contacts, and is highly reliant on using assertiveness skills.

IMPLEMENTING VALUES

Being assertive allows us to implement values in many spheres—from how our office should operate to how society should operate. We think of organizers as being assertive on behalf of a community; however, psychiatric social workers, group workers, and other direct service practitioners do this too. A few years ago, in a conservative western state, community mental health services were being denied to the populace of one county because a few individuals did not want "crazy people to move to Happy Valley." Thus, although millions of federal dollars were available, the region had only two private psychiatrists and no services for low- or moderate-income people until the local NASW chapter worked with planners to write a grant and successfully crusaded to get county officials to approve the development of a mental health center. Once underway, that center served hundreds of local people through the services of social workers with bachelor's and master's degrees, among others.

Operationalizing our values continues to require assertive stances. A church decides to feed the hungry, and neighbors object vigorously. To match the voting power of objectors, social workers associated with shelters and subsidized housing have had to learn to articulate the needs and reasons for their work. "Not in my backyard!" or "We have enough of those here already!" must be met with caring but persuasive counterarguments that property values are not negatively affected by nonprofit and community projects. We must protect individual citizens who are being humiliated and programs that are being discredited while dealing fairly with neighbors and listening to them (Gilbert, 1993; Plotkin, 1990).

A Skill to Use on Whose Behalf?

Our focus is not on assertiveness for a business payoff—although those in private practice assuredly need such skills—but as a way to free practitioners and empower them to make their maximum professional contributions. Assertiveness is often thought of as an individual skill, not collective by nature, and as a way to market oneself, but it also can be a resource for building collective and community endeavors. We can use our assertive strengths to raise new ideas, despite resistance from outside and inside our field. Assertiveness can facilitate our functioning as advocates by allowing us to present clients' cases more effectively to others (see Chapters 12 and 14) and by enhancing our relationship with our clients. It can also be a gift to ourselves by stimulating our "commitment to break out of somebody else's idea of what you should be so you can go and be who you want" (Phelps & Austin, 1987, pp. 21–22). Thus, when put to use, competent assertion benefits the practitioner, the profession, and the population at risk.

ASSERTIVENESS TRAINING

Attention to assertiveness is part of human services research and practice—in particular, cognitive-behavioral intervention, interpersonal helping, feminist practice, and time-limited intervention models or training programs. Researchers and clinicians often use increased assertiveness—inside and/or outside a counseling or workshop setting—as an indicator of positive change. Related changes in thinking or behavior are cited as measures of successful intervention. Increased assertiveness is applauded, whether or not assertiveness was taught during the program.

Characteristic Instruction

Beliefs concerning who will benefit from assertiveness training (AT) and who should become assertive vary according to the type of practice. In direct practice, assertiveness is viewed primarily as a social skill tool to be taught to service users, often in a group context. There is less focus on a professional need for assertiveness or on serving as models for service users (Cotler & Guerra, 1976). In management and conflict resolution, emphasis is placed on the professional's ability to use assertiveness.

WORKING WITH AN AT INSTRUCTOR

AT is taught through workshops and counseling as part of educational and therapeutic intervention and through self-help. AT instructors commonly review various spurs and blocks to assertion—inhibitors and other psychological and sociological factors, as well as reasons for being assertive and not being assertive (Angel & Petronko, 1983; Phelps & Austin, 1987). Much of the discussion of inhibitors focuses on *perceptual and cognitive obstacles* (Alberti & Emmons, 1990, p. 13; Rakos, 1991). Hepworth and Larsen (1986) suggest that feeling *overly* obligated to others, *overly* concerned with pleasing or impressing others, and *overly* fearful about negative reactions to being assertive are ways in which our irrational beliefs stymie action (1986, p. 445).[5]

In teaching how to push past obstacles, instructors explain that trainees will be taught new ways of expressing theselves, often using practice scripts (Smith, 1991) that will seem extreme to them initially. Instructors also acknowledge that hard-nosed assertiveness rules and normal conversational traditions are at odds. At one time, AT was more simplistic and prescriptive regarding what counted as true assertion, but the trend has been toward a less narrow approach to instruction (Rakos, 1991, p. 31).

The AT approach uses conceptual schooling (chalk talk) combined with worksheets and practice exercises (rehearsal). Few AT methods are dictated by the type of audience. Rose (1997) describes separate groups, composed of young adults, older people, women, and social workers, that followed similar programs involving modeling, coaching, overt behavioral rehearsal, covert rehearsal, group feedback, buddy contacts, selected readings, homework assignments, and contingency contracts. Additional elements of AT program "packages" may include instruction, contingent feedback, observation of performance through audio or video, self-instruction training, booster sessions, cognitive restructuring, covert modeling, problem solving, social perception skills, and self-regulation training (Rakos, 1991, chapter 7). Contingent feedback involves coaching, positive reinforcement, and self-evaluation. Cognitive restructuring involves changing misconceptions and stopping self-defeating thoughts.

Exercises are designed and used to:

- change cognition (e.g., modify thoughts—ending patterns of always expecting the worst—and attitudes;
- pinpoint areas in need of upgrading (e.g., dealing with difficult people or handling put-downs); and

- practice new behaviors (e.g., refuse an unreasonable request or respond to criticism).

Following an exercise, coaches give positive or constructive feedback to participants. Lange and Jakubowski (1976) say that coaches

- describe the behavior;

- offer a possible way of improvement (in a tentative manner); and

- ask for a reaction to the suggestions. (p. 195)

For examples, see Alberti and Emmons (1990), Hepworth and Larsen (1993, chapters 14 and 15), and Spolin (1983, p. 28).

One methodology for change involves keeping a log of situations and recording the types of behavior usually employed (Bower & Bower, 1991, pp. 64–65), then practicing the recommended assertive behavior until it becomes an available response for the situation. Logging helps us focus on the behaviors and words, not imputed motives, of the other party; one examines what, not why. For this to work, we must examine behavior concretely in terms of the specific time, place, frequency, and situation.

SELF-HELP INSTRUCTION

A good deal of instruction in AT is not face-to-face, although workshops have been popular for decades. Books for a general audience include simple tests that allow readers to ascertain how assertive they are; how-to-do-it programs; and messages of personal growth, hope, and emancipation. The popular literature stresses remedies for specific personal weaknesses—for example, learning "how to avoid speech patterns that make you seem like a lightweight" (Siress, 1994, p. 49). A telling example is "This may be a dumb question, but . . ." The increasingly assertive person, this literature suggests, masters specific behaviors, such as making requests and eliminating mannerisms (Bower & Bower, 1991, p. 176); gives up particular behaviors, such as "gunnysacking," that is, saving up anger and frustration (Drury, 1984, p. 24); overcomes inhibitions (Phelps & Austin 1987, p. 229); and gains inner strength and hopeful attitudes toward life's possibilities.

AT for Clients and the General Population

In seeking to enhance social functioning and self-esteem, a typical intervention program combines AT with several other skills. These usually are *problem solving, communication, stress reduction, coping, relaxation,* and *changing thought patterns* (Hardy, 1989; Hawkins, Catalano, & Wells, 1986; Smith, 1991). Less often, a social skill such as *networking* or a personal release skill such as *improvisation* (Spolin, 1983) or *humor* (Ventis, 1987) will be combined with AT. Persons in many different age, income, and cultural groups have taken AT (Engels, 1991; Hsu, 1992; Planells-Bloom, 1992; Sue, Sue, & Ino, 1990; Wood & Mallinckrodt, 1990).

The diversity of groups with which AT has been tried is striking. A distinction is sometimes made between standard training for a general (Dow, 1994) population concerned primarily with self-presentation and AT for those with clinical disorders, adjustment problems, or special needs. Compared to a general audience, training and evaluation for special groups may place less emphasis on immediate successful mastery of techniques and more on transferability of skills and persistent use after treatment. The most important outcomes of social skills training, Hepler (1995) maintains, are "long-term generalization of learned skills in the community" and "meaningful change for individuals in their social environment" (p. 2202).

Professionals often view AT as a resource that can benefit clients. For instance, skill-focused activities, including assertiveness, are often employed by groups dealing with the aftermath of sexual abuse (Cohen & Mannarino, 1993), sexual assault and rape trauma, incest, and spousal abuse. Interestingly, assertiveness is recommended for both victims of abuse and abusers. Some would argue that batterers can learn to handle the outside world better through AT and hence take frustrations out less often on their partners. Other client groups that have received benefits include chronic pain patients (Subramanian & Rose, 1988), developmentally disabled adults (Bregman, 1985), mothers (Wayne & Fine, 1986), pregnant teenagers (Vardi, 1992), maltreated children (Howing, Wodarski, Kurtz, & Gaudin, 1990), and alcoholics (Orosz, 1982).

Many clients face daunting challenges. Kaysen (1993) tells of steps she took to leave a mental hospital after 2 years:

> The hospital had an address . . . to provide some cover. . . . It gave about as much protection as 1600 Pennsylvania Avenue would have. . . . Applying for a job, leasing an apartment, getting a driver's license: all problematic. The driver's-license application even asked, Have you ever been hospitalized for mental illness? "You're living at One fifteen Mill Street?" asked a . . . person who ran a sewing-notions shop in Harvard Square where I was trying to get a job. . . . "I guess you haven't been working for a while?" (p. 123)

Vague or sarcastic responses do not work in such circumstances. An assertiveness technique called *fogging* (Smith, 1975)—agreeing with what we can without letting the jab get to us emotionally—may protect the client emotionally while she summons up a firm response about her qualifications for the job. A fogging response would be "You are correct," followed by the assertion, "I would do well at this job, however, because I have had time to practice many sewing techniques that I could teach to others." (See the Exercises at the end of the chapter.) AT attempts to strengthen coping skills for those at a disadvantage in society (Glueckhauf & Quittner, 1992).

Hepworth and Larsen (1986) sum up AT as an educational and treatment resource this way:

> As a clinical training or treatment approach, assertiveness training has been applied to almost every major diagnostic classification or behavioral disorder and has been conducted in a wide variety of settings by paraprofessionals and practitioners of all mental health disciplines. (p. 441)

A few authors caution (1) that AT was evaluated as only moderately effective in a particular case (Nezu, Nezu, & Arean, 1991; Pfost, Stevens, & Parker, 1992); (2) that when overdone, AT has some negative associations in the public's mind that must be addressed (Ruben & Ruben, 1989); and (3) that AT can sometimes be faked by compliant individuals who go along by "acting" assertive (Kern & Karten, 1991).

AT for Professionals

Assertiveness also is targeted to service providers, who must be able to confront and speak to the point (Schulman, 1974, pp. 176–178). Police and correctional staff and counselors—pastoral, youth group, and crisis types—are among those who have been trained in assertiveness. Providers may want to enhance their professional skills, but in some cases they are learning it to help their client group. For instance, rehabilitation counselors have led groups for the differently abled, focusing on how to "deal assertively with persons who treat them in an overly protective or solicitous manner" (Lange & Jakubowski, 1976, p. 241). A consensus among helping professionals is that "The positive nature of assertion training and its focus on maintaining personal strengths and improving less effective qualities leaves many participants with a greater sense of self-worth" (p. 241).

Assertiveness in practitioners is often presumed but not mentioned in social work. For instance, in the strategic family therapy approach, for a "directive" or "pretend technique" to be effective, a clinician must be able to make requests and talk in a precise manner with a minimum of passive or aggressive distractions. Otherwise, intervention will be clouded (Madanes, 1991). The parallels with community work, where representatives must be able to make requests and talk precisely with county officials, are evident. In sessions, practitioners must be able to say "no," set limits, and relate assertively to clients by making requests and giving directives ("Will you please turn your chair . . ."), maintaining focus and managing interruptions, interrupting dysfunctional processes, and "leaning into" clients' anger (Hepworth & Larsen, 1993, pp. 131–135). A specialized AT workshop would be helpful. Angel and Petronko (1983) and Drury (1984) provide useful discussions on implementing assertiveness on the job after completing AT.

AT for Students

Standard social work education alone apparently does not guarantee increased assertiveness (Pardeck, Anderson, Gianino, Miller, Mothershead, & Smith, 1991), which is our rationale for including this topic. Several authors address the need for students to receive AT (Healey, Havens, & Chin, 1990). Cournoyer (1983) argues that "professional social work practice requires assertive self-expression skills of a high order" (p. 24). Hardina (1995) provides rationales for expanded skills in this realm:

> Social workers may not be adequately prepared either to advocate on their own behalf or to improve access to services for consumers. . . . Without confrontation, it may not be possible to develop the power resources necessary to fight for social change that will benefit members of oppressed groups. Assertiveness training for social work students is an essential component of such education. . . . (p. 13)

AT is equally appropriate for clinical and macro practice students. Since clinical applications of assertiveness have been the focus thus far, we turn briefly to its advocacy, administrative, and community applications, which highlight the theme of breaking free of conventionality and "can't-do" thinking.

Cummerton (1980) works with students to establish positive expectations because "an assumption of a negative response from the target system" undermines our confidence:

> Expecting a "no" we act on this assumption and get the response we expect. . . . To get practice in reversing this negative chain of events, students were asked to reach out in a positive way to people they ordinarily viewed in a negative way, in order to create a "yes" climate and develop ability to deal positively with a potential adversary. (pp. 4–5)

She asks students to think about a coworker they have been avoiding and then arrange a meeting or encounter with that person. (See Richan and Mendelsohn, 1973, for similar exercises.)

Garvin and Gruber (1978) note that as students enter a community, they are "quite concerned about rejection of themselves and their ideas: this can lead to presenting one's position in either an overly aggressive or timid manner" (p. 5). They describe an exercise in which students involved in community organizing "identify organizing situations in which they experienced difficulty in expressing their positions" and role play these many times until they feel able to handle them in the field (p. 10). This type of training teaches students to think on their feet, according to Hardina (1995).

BROADER CONCEPTIONS OF ASSERTIVENESS

An Assertive Orientation

Assertiveness is competent communication and more. Beyond learning new techniques, we want to increase our own competence and that of those we serve, as well as elevating our aspirations and theirs.

Becoming More Hopeful

Jansson (1990) links assertiveness with power and winning. He argues that assertiveness is "undermined" by fatalism and a victim mentality, which deny individual potency. These ideas are similar to the *irrational* beliefs that AT tries to overcome, such as that 'one's past dictates one's future' (Lange & Jakubowski, 1976, p. 135). Fatalism contributes to societal cynicism and to personal passivity and submission. Jansson (1990) says it well:

> The effective use of power requires people to decide in the first instance that they possess power resources, that they can use them effectively, and that they want to use them. The word *assertiveness* describes this proclivity to test the waters rather than to be excessively fatalistic. (p. 154)

To illustrate an assertive orientation to power *within* an agency, Jansson gives the example of a hospital social work administrator who learned to make successive requests for increased funds, even though a number of her entreaties were fruitless. Her justifications educated the decision makers and sent a signal of confidence. "Unlike departments with more timid executives, her department gained in size and stature as she assertively sought resources for her department," points out Jansson (1990, p. 155). Expectancy can replace fatalism, a sense of potency can replace a sense of victimization, and hopefulness can replace helplessness (see Chapter 2). An assertive orientation to power *outside* of an agency might involve governmental funding. Social workers must make regular personal contact with policymakers and test the waters by assertively stating what problems should receive priority attention, what services should receive full funding, and what cuts should be made in other sectors of the economy to protect social service resources. Here, as elsewhere, we must guard against fatalism, that is, thinking that our efforts are useless.

Phelps and Austin (1987) believe that "broad scale social issues . . . [cruelty to animals, drunk driving] can be influenced with assertive attention" (p. 243). They encourage such action but add a realistic caution.

> Public and social issues are amenable to change through assertive action. It's also important not to regard assertion as a cure-all for every social ill or as a simplistic way to achieve personal strength and self-worth. Real problems are stubborn and significant change requires patience and power. Speaking out on a subject you believe in will invite criticism or even censure—it is not easy. (p. 244)

BECOMING A CLIENT ALLY

While empowering ourselves, we can work together with service users to increase their options. Within health care settings, for instance, assertive people will "perform a valuable function" if they acknowledge, support, and protect patients' rights (Angel & Petronko, 1983, p. 94; Knee & Vourlekis, 1995). Providers such as social workers can actively aid and abet patients in getting their rights in the concrete ways outlined by Angel and Petronko (1983):

- Educate patients in the knowledge that they have—both basic human rights and more specific rights as health care consumers;

- Provide written information;

- Help patients to evaluate the advantages and disadvantages of asserting their rights;

- Assist patients in planning for successful assertion;

- Promise and deliver support if patients decide to exercise their rights;

- If required, help the patient to navigate through the complaint process;

- When necessary, assist the patient in enlisting the help of an ombudsman or consumer group. (p. 95)

Becoming Open to Challenge

Another arena for assertiveness involves the relationship of service users to the experts in their lives. This is especially important, says Weiner (1990) (in discussing Ivan Illich), during this "age of disabling professions," where too little emphasis is put on "people's energy to do for themselves" (pp. 40–41). Angel and Petronko (1983), for example, suggest that nurses should apply their assertiveness to patients' rights, organizational and societal change, and new directions to influence the future. According to these authors, assertive skills can be part of "changing nursing's public image, influencing leg-

islation, and influencing the health care system" (p. 233).

During the last few decades, advocates have worked to demystify law and medicine and to highlight the right to challenge lawyers, psychiatrists, and other traditional authority figures in a respectful, polite, and cordial manner. At a behavioral level, if a patient-consumer goes to another physician to get a second opinion without telling the first, that shows independence of mind and constitutes an *indirect challenge* (Haug & Lavin, 1983), but patient-consumers who are able to tell the original physician they are seeking a second opinion are assertive and capable of *direct challenge*. Assertiveness comes into play because the patient has a goal or agenda that should not have to be subordinated to the physician's personality or expectations. Those who become preoccupied with the doctor's feelings or get trapped by timidity may never get that second opinion; here nonassertiveness can have life-and-death consequences.

This trend has relevance in our field for three reasons. First, social workers are the beneficiaries of a new relationship between professions, and between consumers and professionals, that support us as equal players on an intervention team. Second, however, we must stay alert to ways in which our service users are "consumers" and treat them the way we like to be treated by the professionals in our personal lives (Tower, 1994). Third and most important, we should encourage service users and citizens with whom we work to be assertive with *us*, not just with others; we need to be strong enough to engage in mutual participation, with initiative coming from either party (Gutierrez, 1990; Simon, 1990; Smith, 1975, chapter 7, on prompting criticism). As a logical outgrowth, some social workers encourage the formation of client, resident, or user groups to play a watchdog role.

BECOMING BOLDER

Those who care about professional ethics may face situations that precipitate *voicing* or *exiting*. *Voicing* is another term or vehicle for being assertive.[6] A social worker cannot function effectively as a client advocate, a legislative advocate, or a community advocate without standing up for what is necessary in the circumstance. *Most books emphasize an individual's right to be assertive without discussing the responsibility to be assertive*, although integrity and responsibility while being assertive have been discussed (Angel & Petronko, 1983; Rakos, 1991, p. 8). See Box 7.6.

Communities often hide the existence as well as the nature of problems. Close examination is necessary to deal with this and to find out what actions can be taken to eliminate the problems. Social workers may have a duty to be impolite when politeness is keeping a social misery in place. Politeness can be a tool used by the powerful to evade challenges or hide venal purposes. An investigative reporting text includes skills to overcome secrecy and hostility. The author calls for guts and warns against gullibility. (He does not discuss psychological barriers or behavior modification techniques—common subjects in human services.) The focus is on *will* and willingness. The text gives permission to go against societal norms to accomplish professional goals (Williams, 1978):

> If you are afraid to argue, if you dread being shoved around, if you hate to go back after your polite requests for information have been refused—then you probably will not be a successful investigative reporter. If you believe something is true simply because a person in authority says it is true, you are in trouble. (p. 8)

You probably will not be successful in our field either, although we may too easily permit passiveness in providers, consumers, and citizens. Then, when advocacy is required, not even the first step—assertiveness—has been mastered.

Even popular magazines are beginning to reflect a broader view of bold assertiveness. Box 7.7 gives pointers on having "moxie."

| **BOX 7.6** | **IN PRAISE OF GIRAFFES** |

Dressing for success to establish authority or employing proper communication skills means little unless, when it counts, those who care about people come forward and voice. For instance, chancing rejection and embarrassment, a staffer for World Vision went up to a conservative member of Congress from Virginia who was making a campaign stop in a mall. She recruited him, on the spot, to take a trip to a famine site across the globe. This trip permanently committed him to eradication of hunger and misery (Harden, 1995). Many individuals risk far more, and their valor is honored by activists of different types.

- *Aging:* The Gray Panthers have presented "giraffe" awards to those who stick out their necks to change society.
- *Brave stands:* The Giraffe Project, a small nonprofit project in Langley, Washington, honors with certificates people who "stick their necks out and stand tall for what they believe in" and who face what scares them (Shulman, 1995, p. 16). A Jewish publication described these "giraffes" as "individuals who stick their necks out for the common good (i.e., Tzedakah-Tzedek . . . plus an element of risk)" (Ziv Tzedakeh Fund, 1994).

BOX 7.7	IT IS NOT ALL RIGHT WITH ME!

- Stating your needs unequivocally, with the sense that you have a right to state them, is half the battle.
- Sometimes, the truth hurts. Get used to it.
- You can be blunt without being a tactless cretin.
- When necessary, be just as ballsy on behalf of others as you are [on behalf] of yourself.
- Standing up for what you believe in isn't convenient? Sorry, you gotta do it anyway.

- Pick your fights carefully.
- Being assertive with people who can't fight back isn't being assertive, it's being a bully.
- If you're trying to make a stand just for the sake of making a stand, it'll be particularly obvious.

Source: *Excerpts from "Assertiveness Training" by comedian Rosie O'Donnell (Know-How, 1995, p. 62).*

THE CONTEXT AND THE SETTING FOR ASSERTIVE BEHAVIOR

Immediate Situation

A professional considers the immediate conditions. The necessity to "step up to the plate" occurs in varied ways. What would be considered aggressive physical behavior in ordinary circumstances could be quite appropriate in an emergency. Suppose that a social worker accompanies an adolescent to a medical appointment and the individual suddenly blacks out in the waiting room. This is hardly the time to wait one's turn or to be assertive with the receptionist—but it is a time for calling out. *Overcoming one's hesitancy* is a type of assertiveness that goes beyond *expressing one's opinion and desires*, as this and the next example show. A mental hospital in St. Louis had a fire requiring the evacuation of all patients to the auditorium, even those unwilling to leave their rooms. Social workers helped attendants and nurses to get downstairs individuals who, up to that time, had not left their floor in years and did not want to go. Holding the hands of the terrified patients and whispering consolation, the assertive social workers pushed and tugged dozens of hysterical residents to a safe location.

The Other Party

A professional is alert to potential misunderstandings. Is assertiveness appropriate to the circumstances? Forgoing assertive expression can be a matter of safety. Think about the protective services worker who is overseeing an office visit between a child and the parent who did not get custody. There are times when we should not try to have our way through assertiveness, particularly if the other person is going to feel disrespected or manipulated. We have to consider how our behavior will be interpreted and what other people's life experiences teach them to expect. As one advocate put it:

There is the risk of being misunderstood by people with whom you're trying to be in partnership. A lot of bruised and hurting people don't have the advantage of meeting, what we call, "authentic persons." So, the first shot they get, they're gonna take you because they have to react to somebody, and they react many times with violence. Or they not only act out on you all of these latent pains, but seek to beguile you . . . test you out. They've got a street keenness. They deal with you from their learnings, and their learnings are always "people do you in, so you do them in before they do you." (Dobson in *Challenging*)[7]

Limitations Rather Than Universality

A professional distinguishes legal rights from preferences. Although assertive rights can and have been stated, these do not have the force of law, as do the rights of airline passengers in our country to smoke-free flights. Our "rights" are culture and nation bound, (e.g., an American can request but not require someone in Spain to stop smoking in a restaurant). Typical AT stresses rights as if they should be available everywhere, but it may not acknowledge that our assertive requests will be *denied* more frequently the further we get from our own social circles. A related criticism is that even within our own networks, some AT professionals do not caution trainees and fail to "alert them to and/or prepare them for the possibility of retaliation or other highly negative reactions from others" (Alberti & Emmons, 1990, Appendix C).

Internal Reactions to Situation

A professional considers interpersonal factors. The willingness to use assertion, and the resulting success of having used it, are usually situation or person specific. Think back to the child trying to stand up to her foster mother, Grace, over killing a chicken (Box 7.3). One professional can be appropriately directive with the cranky office receptionist but not with the kindly consulting psychologist. A support group facilitator handles the most difficult group members but turns obsequious around the church officials who grant the group free space. Social workers who have mastered most aspects of their life successfully may nevertheless doubt their ability to handle particular difficulties or demands: insurance companies refusing to honor certain bills, conflicts with suite mates over the use of space, negotiations with a client's landlord, responding to an angry community improvement association, or appearing on television to explain the death of someone in their agency's care. Some of us appear totally unassertive with peers yet are fearless on behalf of clients and causes. Because of human and cultural variation, we will be more successful in some circumstances than others and should be comfortable with this fact in advance. We can continue to expand our competency.

Power Nuances to Consider

A professional considers political/sociological factors. Success in assertiveness does not depend solely on personality characteristics; gender, race, and social status play a role too. Assertiveness is more likely to be "accepted from those who have traditionally had power, while it may not be accepted from those who have not had power" (Drury, 1984, p. 133). Thus, assertiveness is more easily mastered by those who are part of the dominant culture. In fact, Yoshioka (1995) argues, "assertiveness as it has been defined is reflective only of the dominant sociocultural group." Put another way, assertive behavior—as usually described—is largely a white, upper-class, well-educated mode of expressing one's preferences (Rakos, 1991, p. 78). Still, assertiveness is something that is readily acquired, unlike power, which could be described similarly. Transactions with persons from different backgrounds require us to be adaptable, considerate of the way their preferences are expressed, and aware of power differentials between us.

For practical reasons, Rakos (1991) suggests, many minorities will need and want to be biculturally assertive. They will benefit from knowing (1) what is considered assertive in two distinct worlds, (2) how to function effectively in the dominant system, and (3) what norms will be violated in their (sub)culture if standard assertiveness is applied without adaptation. Rakos also exhorts *trainers* to plan and "consider relevant cultural, ethnic, and religious variables" when they train people with distinctive backgrounds or work with special populations (p. 89).

Nuances to Consider

A professional considers the uniqueness of those with whom he or she will work. This topic was discussed more narrowly earlier, but it is worth reiterating that while we are all one extended community, unless differences are accommodated, true communication and bonding rarely happen. For example, if group A speaks in a subdued way and emphasizes correct enunciation, and group B speaks with force and emotion and incorporates more slang, then B language may be perceived as inappropriate by listeners from the A group (Yoshioka, 1995). Certain religious, ethnic, racial, or urban subcultures are freer in expression, and their members may argue, interrupt, criticize, or laugh loudly. They are viewed as aggressive by those from other regions or backgrounds in our society. Conceivably, it may be more difficult to "tone down" to be acceptable—if that is desired—than to "speak up."

Salcido (1993) describes culturally insensitive behavior that will alienate many who reside in Latino barrios, such as violations of preferred protocol; interviews with Mexican-American social workers suggest that an emphasis "towards a task orientation, urgency, and lack of courtesies can lead toward cultural misunderstandings." The act of cutting off someone is fraught with possible misunderstanding, anger, and withdrawal in many cultures. An Anglo feminist who has finally learned to speak up to men may have to readjust once more in a home visit involving Latino men, at least in an initial interview. Part of the bicultural challenge involves negotiating new conceptual and behavioral parameters for assertiveness in any bicultural interchange.

The physically challenged and other differently abled individuals frequently are assumed to be passive; therefore, they are ignored in conversations or decision making as if they were invisible. Or they may be condescended to, whether they are service users, citizens, or peers. Busy professionals trying to be expeditious may not take time to listen to a slow-speaking person with cerebral palsy or a developmental disability who is making an assertive point.

Age, gender, and other factors affect the perceptions of those served by social workers, so we must be alert to what will be considered appropriate assertiveness. An older service user or volunteer may respond more to a commanding "presence" or be more attuned to civil but declarative sentences than to direct, firm "I" messages. We need to pay attention to how others communicate as we observe service users, volunteers, community residents, and institutional residents. Apologizing is especially common among older women who grew up in another era—tentativeness, overreliance on experts, and meekness may mask a strong personality underneath—and older men may feel expected or obligated to steer the conversation. Assertive attitudes and skills of our own, and awareness of the forms assertiveness can take in others, allow us to be more proficient and mindful practitioners.

MODES OF ASSERTIVE COMMUNICATION

Being Assertive in Writing

WRITTEN EXAMPLES: EVALUATIONS

Although AT literature emphasizes *verbal* communication, assertive writing should be employed too (e.g., in letters, reports, and performance evaluations). Participant evaluations of workshops provide one illustration, but such critiques sometimes address weaknesses obliquely or heartlessly. Assertion does not always mean being positive; sometimes an occasion calls for assertive criticism. Jan, a new community education instructor, had nervously but unconsciously clicked a ballpoint pen throughout a lecture. One participant wrote on the evaluation form, "Lose the pen." Jan laughed and appreciated this feedback. More oblique references, such as "The speaker was nice but had distracting habits," are less concrete and usable while still creating discomfort. A hostile comment such as "The points were completely lost because Jan kept clicking that stupid pen" might be ignored or might damage confidence.

If the evaluator does not know the speaker or has high expectations, evaluations usually will be tougher than when the evaluator is asked to comment on a peer or classmate. In the latter case, silent, unconscious pacts often undercut the spirit of constructive criticism: "I will be generous to you when it is your turn if you will be nice to me." Training and community education programs call for assertiveness with integrity by both speaker and listener.

WRITTEN EXAMPLES: TESTIMONY

Written or public testimony, in legislative and regulatory forums, provides a notable instance in which assertiveness is structurally built into the form of the communication and is less dependent on the writer's attitudes and skills. A shortened version of testimony is often read, and a longer version is submitted for the record; those reading testimony stick to the script. No matter how timid the writer or deliverer, by tradition the opening and closing paragraphs of testimony are strong. (Testimony starkly contrasts to the traditions of other kinds of presentations. Classroom presentations often start inappropriately with an apology or an expression of nervousness from the student.) No matter how angry the testimony writer or presenter, the language is civil and respectful.

Testimony usually starts with an introduction of the group being represented and its organizational position on the issue at hand, such as this:

> Mr. Chairman, and members of the committee, I am Mrs. Alice Willer, President of L.R. Vincent Homes for Children, Inc. The L.R. Vincent Homes is a nonprofit service offering substitute care for children, organized by a statewide federation of local agencies, each of which is guided by a citizens' board of directors. We thank you for giving us this opportunity to present our views on House Bill 5293.
>
> The member agencies of L.R. Vincent Homes across the state strongly oppose in principle the practice of surrogate parenthood and strongly oppose the Surrogate Parenthood Bill. (Flynn, 1985, p. 270)

Because testimony is time limited, those testifying are compelled to make a point and skip unassertive asides.

Weasel words and phrases, such as "unscheduled event" or "therapeutic misadventure" (Walton, 1989, p. 164), and tentative or wishy-washy opinions are out of place in public testimony. Testimony does not hedge or bully. The tone and the choice of words are expected to be assertive, as the following excerpt illustrates:

> On behalf of the American Association of Retired Persons (AARP), thank you for this opportunity to offer our recommendations regarding reauthorization of the Low Income Home Energy Assistance Program (LIHEAP). LIHEAP is extremely important to low income older persons who are excep-

tionally vulnerable to extremes in weather conditions. The Association strongly supports both LIHEAP reauthorization and certain modifications that we believe will improve program administration and funding security. [testimony March 25, 1990]

Writing as spare and slangy as "lose the pen" would be used in different situations but could be as assertive as robust phrases such as "exceptionally vulnerable" and "strongly supports."

Being Assertive in Speaking

SOME ARE ALREADY ASSERTIVE

By the time we train for a professional career, we have had many life experiences and have attended many workshops, perhaps even ones on assertiveness, so it is not surprising that a high percentage of students are good with people and often able to stand their ground professionally. While some professionals-in-training are aware of their shyness or timidity, others view themselves as "mouthy" or quite professional already. The latter sometime believe they are as assertive as they will ever need to be. However, confidence in attitude is not always matched by competence in skills.

OTHERS CAN LEARN THROUGH ROLE PLAYING

Role play can highlight assertion strengths and weaknesses. Directions frequently stipulate that one person must present a claim or request an action for the other person to perform. Lange and Jakubowski (1976) emphasize that it is "OK for people to make reasonable requests and it is also OK to refuse them" (p. 102). Asking for a pay raise is a simulation with universal relevance and appeal. (In "real life," a busy employer often appreciates directness.)

A FOR-PROFIT SOCIAL SERVICE AGENCY

Employee: Thanks for seeing me.
Boss: Now what do you want?
Employee: I am here to ask for a $2,000 raise.
Boss: No one is getting one. Money is tight.
Employee: I am entitled to more money next year because of my recent contributions to the company.
Boss: We applaud your efforts. Maybe we can talk about salary in the future.
Employee: That's your call, but I'd like to talk about it now.
Boss: You still fall asleep at your desk. On the other hand, your suggestion did save the firm thousands of dollars.
Employee: Yes, that's correct.
Boss: OK, I'll take it under advisement.
Employee: That's great. I appreciate your considering the raise. When might you make a decision or contact me for further discussion?

Wrap-up. Assertiveness is a skill available to micro and macro practitioners. A switch hitter in baseball is able to adapt batting skills to match left- or right-handed pitchers. We may not think about it, but as was discussed earlier, social workers also acquire skills that can be adapted to most levels and places of intervention. However, it takes practice.

PUTTING ONESELF TO THE TEST

Illustrative Examples

Example 1

Introducing oneself can reveal any of the three basic communication styles. Imagine yourself knocking on the door of the building manager to resolve a problem for a member of your organization. Imagine walking in, shaking hands, and saying: "My name is _____ . I am from _____ agency. I am Mrs. Brown's advocate. She lives in your building." Your knock, walk, handshake, voice, and demeanor will convey passive, aggressive, or assertive attitudes.

Example 2

Here are varying responses to a comment. Read them all and then devise your own assertive response.

Speaker One: I don't think family preservation programs work. Earlier positive research findings haven't held up.

Possible Responses from Speaker Two

Assertive response

1. "I think the results are mixed but tell me your thoughts on the subject."
2. Write one of your own: _____

Nonassertive or passive response

1. [disagreeing but not saying so]
2. "Usually we agree, but not this time. I don't mean to make you mad, but I think family preservation is the way to go—not that I know the research."

Aggressive response

1. "That shows how little you've read about it."

Example 3

You'll find this example more demanding. Read the two questions and four types of responses.

- The head of your community advisory board says: *"How do 'you people'* [fill in "African-Americans," "Jews," "Asian-Americans"] *celebrate this holiday anyhow?"*
- An exasperated person says: *"Why is it that 'you people'* [fill in "men," "women," "secretaries," "cleaning staff"] *always mess up our lunch room?"*

Possible Responses

Assertive responses

1. (Deliberately) "Well, first, let's find a better phrase than 'you people.' I'd suggest _____."
2. (Pleasantly) "I won't respond to that" [re the lunch room].
3. [You decide that the person is naive or sincere, not hostile, and you answer the question in that spirit.]

Nonassertive or passive responses

1. "Don't generalize now . . ." (smilingly changes the subject).
2. Answers content of question while ignoring its form or tone. "It strikes me that the important thing about what you are asking is . . . ," etc.
3. "*Not that I care* about political correctness, but don't you think some people might react negatively to 'you _____ are always'? I *admit* that it bothers me."

Aggressive responses

1. (Coldly) "I don't appreciate your tone."
2. "Some people around here think they can ask anything [or control everything]."
3. "Well, you people are worse. (swear word)."

Passive-aggressive responses

1. "What's with you? Did you have burned toast for breakfast?"
2. (Turns back on questioner and mutters to peer) "I get so *frustrated* with this song and dance."

Techniques and Structured Exercises

DECLARATIVE STATEMENTS

Gamble and Gamble (1990) suggest that we stop "automatically asking permission to speak, think or behave" and "substitute declarative statements for permission requests." They would say, "I'd like to know" such and such instead of asking, "Do you mind if I ask to have this point clarified?" (p. 222). As social workers, we need to be able to state our case firmly. Yet, a recent trend toward ending sentences with a raised inflection when the person is *not* asking a question makes it even more challenging to speak in a manner that does not sound tentative. Examples 1 and 4 include declarative statements and ones said without explanation or justifications.

Example 4

Advocate: *I want to look at the campaign finance records for the mayor's race.*

City Hall employee: Who are you? Why do you want to see them?

[*Nonassertive response:* "I'm just a student. But can't I see them anyway? I'm writing a paper."]

Advocate: *The report of contributions to each candidate's campaign is to be filed here. Are the reports kept in this office?*

City Hall employee: Yes, but we can't show them to just anyone.

Advocate: *As you know, it is public information. I would like to see the reports.*

City Hall employee: Are you with the media?

Advocate: *Please direct me to a place where I can read the reports or bring them to me. Thank you.*

[The advocate could give a legal citation that gives the public access.]

BROKEN RECORD TECHNIQUE

AT has specialized techniques. One of these, "broken record" (Smith 1975), is an accepted and easily understood idea of persistent, calm repetition so that one's point cannot be ignored. Sometimes people feel odd practicing it because they normally do not talk that way, but exaggeration and repetition allows them to internalize this technique. The example 5 script can be *read aloud* by two individuals while a third critiques how assertive the "advocate" role player is in regard to tone of voice and ability to convey resolve.

Example 5

Social worker: I need to speak to the principal about the Jones brothers he dismissed from school on Friday morning.

Receptionist: Mr. Markman is busy right now. Why don't you go down the hall and speak to those boys' classroom teachers?

Social worker: Thank you, but it is the principal I need to see. Here is my card. I represent the Department of Children and Family Services.

Receptionist: Maybe the guidance counselor is around this morning. She is usually pretty busy on Mondays, but I can try to find her for you.

SW: Thank you for your offer. However, I must speak to Mr. Markman himself.

R: You should have made an appointment. He never sees anyone "off the street."

SW: I can appreciate that policy. I did call repeatedly Friday afternoon and was never put through to him. I'll wait until he has a break in his schedule.

R: Those boys were causing everyone headaches. I know why they were suspended indefinitely.

SW: Would you please call the principal and let him know their caseworker is here?

R: I couldn't bother him during a staff meeting.

SW: When will it be over?

R: In about five minutes, but he has other things after that.

SW: Please give him my card. I will wait over here until I can get ten minutes of his time.

Left to their own devices, some would change the tone drastically. They would make friends with the receptionist and say something like this:

Social worker: Aren't you nice to suggest that? I bet you've been with the school for years and have seen everything. So you are probably familiar with our agency and what we need. Maybe I can sit with you and wait.

An ingratiating approach feels right but (1) risks getting caught in stalling, (2) drops the broken record strategy, and (3) loses the high ground—the emphasis on the right of the children to be in school and of the worker to deal directly with the decision maker.

Assertiveness comes into play when we have a goal or agenda, such as getting the boys back into school, and we adapt our behavior to that goal rather than to another person's personality or expectations. *Aggressiveness* arises when we subordinate the goal to a desire to respond forcefully to another person, such as the receptionist or principal. *Passivity* occurs when we allow the goal to be overridden by intimidating signals (internal or as received from another person).

Selective Ignoring and Fogging

Selective ignoring means that we do not have to respond to every element or nuance of a remark made to us. *Fogging* is another technique. "Like a fog bank, you remain impenetrable. You offer no resistance or hard striking surfaces" (Zuker, 1983, pp. 134–135). If those in Ian's car pool tease him about losing his hair, he may tell them to "knock it off." But there are times when we must listen calmly to annoying comments and criticism—say, from a state trooper giving us a ticket. Lange and Jakubowski (1976) call fogging and selective ignoring "protective skills" to use in response to "nagging" (p. 115). A fogging *rejoinder* to a crack like "Ian, you're about as bald as they get, aren't you?" is designed to dampen potential confrontation. Ian can say lightly, without affect, "I probably am" or "You could say that." Assertion is about self-control more than controlling others. See example 6.

Mentioned by Smith (1975), fogging is criticized by Cotler and Guerra (1976), who view it as passive-aggressive in psychological situations. Drury (1984) uses it at work to prevent arguments: "You [agree] with the criticism in principle without necessarily agreeing with the implied judgment." But she limits its use: "The technique stops communication and interaction rather than uncovering and solving problems. Humor, ignoring, and fogging are all techniques that should be used only for responding to teasing or attempts to start an argument, not for cases in which someone is criticizing to solve a problem" (p. 227).

WHEN FOGGING IS APPROPRIATE

Example 6

Client's boss: You are wearing an earring.
Client: Yes, I am. (not "So what?")
Boss: Why would ya do that? You know what people are going to think. I bet your parents are upset.
Client: It's possible they are.
Boss: I don't think men should pierce their ears.
Client: _____

[Act as a coach. What should your client say here?] What was selectively ignored? What was fogged?

WHEN FOGGING MAY BE USEFUL

This script can be read by two people, with a third person giving feedback. Notice that the social worker does not give in and does not make matters worse.

Example 7

Social worker: Hello. This is Community Action.
Hostile caller: Is this Erin (Aaron) Wallace?
SW: Speaking.
H caller: Are you the person who has been out looking for housing deficiencies?
SW: Who is calling, please?
H caller: I happen to be a property owner in this community.
SW: And your name, sir?
H caller: Name's Ross Gibson. But never mind that. I wanted you to know that we landlords don't appreciate your actions.
SW: I see. Do you care to be more specific?*
H caller: You're stirring up trouble with the county for no reason without talking with me first.
SW: I could have contacted you personally.†

*Taking the call seriously, not sure what the problem is.

†Starts fogging because the caller wants to ventilate, not communicate.

H caller: That group of yours is against free enterprise, you're trying to help a bunch of low lifes, and you're going about it all wrong.

SW: Perhaps you're right.

H caller: I checked up on you and found out you're just a student. I bet that school of yours does not even realize what you are up to.

SW: I am a graduate student; you're correct.

H caller: I have been checking with my lawyer, and I think we can get you jailed for disturbing the peace with some of your activities.

Social worker: _____

_____

Read the script until the end and then invent a fogging style response (which does not involve your supervisor, who is working under a deadline).

The caller is not a client and need not be treated in the same way. The idea is to not take the bait, to let Gibson "run down," and to get off the phone without getting an immediate return call from Gibson.

ASSERTIVE RESPONSE OPTIONS

Standard assertiveness is a firm come back without explanation or apology. "Assertions that contain explanations, acknowledgement of feelings, compromises and praise have been termed *empathic assertions*" (Rakos 1991, p. 31; Lange & Jakubowski, 1976, pp. 14–15). See example 8.

HANDLING A POWER IMBALANCE SITUATION

Example 8: The Intern and the Doctor

The head of your interdisciplinary health team says: "You social workers always think you know better than physicians when the patient is ready to leave the hospital. Where did you study medicine?"

Possible Responses

[*Empathic assertion—contains an explanation*]
- "There's more than a medical dimension to knowing when a patient is ready to leave."

[*Standard Assertion*]
- "You seem to like to give me a hard time, Dr. ___ ___"

[*Fogging response*]
- "It's true that social workers have professional opinions about diagnostic related groups and the length-of-stay issue."

[*Timid response*]
- "Dr., I don't know what to say. Maybe my supervisor should explain social work's concern to you."

[*Hostile response*]
- Looking up from your notes, ask, "How do you spell anal-retentive?" [clever, but say goodbye to your internship]

Your response: _____

Example 9

[*More elaborate role play*]

You work as a development director for a religious group that sponsors nonprofit institutions. You have been asked to be on the board of one retirement center. At the first meeting, you notice that there are no residents on the board and are told that there is no interest on their part. Later, you learn that the Residents Council has no real decision-making powers and functions as a social club. What will you say at the next board meeting?

Remember, if you voice your concerns, you are being assertive—even if you cannot phrase everything in perfect assertive fashion.

Discussion Exercises

1. Assume that you will be working temporarily with a health service delivery system on Native American land. Besides learning about tribal and federal leadership systems, you want to know this tribe's customs before you challenge anyone in your standard assertive manner. You once read a

parable about a Native American who wanted to be on equal terms with every person he encountered, so he either brought individuals up to or down to his level, depending on their station in life. How can outsiders learn what is myth or reality regarding assertion beliefs for Native people or members of any other culture unfamiliar to us?

2. Our work lives are saturated with phrases about impotence: "falling through the cracks," "bogged down in the bureaucracy," "a half loaf is better than none." What is our field's equivalent to "going for" the gold (sports), the moon (astronomy), the cure (medicine), the scoop (journalism), or the Nobel Prize (science)?

Notes

1. Conscious *use of self* refers to honing and maximizing practice skills and being aware of matters that could cloud judgment. As one social worker put it, "Probably the most important thing they teach you in social work school is the conscious use of self; that will serve you extremely well as an administrator and as a community organizer. Whether it's with your staff, your community support, or with policy-makers, you have to pose your language in ways to bring about the outcome that you want. . . . If you can put what you want them to know in ways that they are able to hear, you have a much better chance of getting them to do what you want them to do" (Judith Vaughan-Prather, executive director of the Montgomery County Women's Commission, in *Challenging*). Regarding women's use of self in leadership roles, see Healey, Havens, and Chin (1990). Spolin (1983) described how to use oneself (e.g., "physicalization," (p. 15).

2. A full skill repertoire includes the ability not only to perform but also to sustain our performance by securing needed resources. Those in the arts and in

social welfare have to be concerned with national politics in regard to government funding.

3. Attitudes of the sender and receiver influence whether someone is listened to, but we focus on the sender. Status differences and differences between social work and other professions echo gender differences. Some have no desire to move toward their opposite and defend noncompetitive stances.

4. Linda Heisner, director of the Office of Family and Children's Services (D.H.R., Maryland). From an interview by Cathy Raab in *Challenging* (1994).

5. These are irrational, at least in western culture. See Yoshioka (1995) and Rakos (1991).

6. *Voice* and *exit* are terms used by Hirschman to illustrate two responses to a perceived wrong. Laura Nader (1980) applies them to the way we deal with complaints and small injustices.

7. Rev. Vernon Dobson discussing people in and out of the justice system. From an interview by Paul Collinson Streng in *Challenging* (1994).

References

Alberti, R. E., & Emmons, M. L. (1974). *Your perfect right: A guide to assertive behavior* (2nd ed.). San Luis Obispo, CA: Impact.

Alberti, R. E., & Emmons, M. L. (1990). *Your perfect right: A guide to assertive behavior* (6th prof. ed.). San Luis Obispo, CA: Impact.

Angel, G., & Petronko, D. K. (1983). *Developing the new assertive nurse: Essentials for advancement.* New York: Springer.

Back, K. W. (1972). *Beyond words: The story of sensitivity training and the encounter movement.* New York: Russell Sage Foundation.

Barber, B. (1984). *Strong democracy: Participatory politics for a new age.* Berkeley: University of California Press.

Blanchard, K., & Johnson, S. (1982). *The one minute manager: The quickest way to increase your own prosperity.* New York: Berkley.

Bloom, L. Z., Coburn, K., & Pearlman, J. (1975). *The new assertive woman.* New York: Dell.

Bower, S. A., & Bower, G. H. (1991). *Asserting your self: A practical guide for positive change* (updated ed.). Reading, MA: Addison-Wesley.

Bregman, S. (1985). Assertiveness training for mentally retarded adults. *Psychiatric Aspects of Mental Retardation Reviews, 4*(1), 43–48.

Burghardt, S. (1982). *The other side of organizing.* Cambridge, MA: Schenkman.

Challenging (1994). *Interviews with Advocates and Activists.* University of Maryland at Baltimore School of Social Work monograph. Edited by P. Powers.

Clifton, R. L., & Dahms, A. M. (1993). *Grassroots organizations: A resource book for directors, staff, and volunteers of small, community-based nonprofit agencies,* (2nd ed.). Prospect Heights, IL: Waveland.

Cohen, J. A., & Mannarino, A. P. (1993). Sexual abuse. In R. T. Ammerman, C. G. Last, & M. Herson (Eds.), *Handbook of prescriptive treatments for children and adolescents* (pp. 347–366). Boston: Allyn & Bacon.

Colburn, L. (1994). On-the-spot mediation in a public housing project. In D. M. Kolb (Ed.), *When talk works: Profiles of mediators* (pp. 395–425). San Francisco: Jossey-Bass.

Cotler, S. B., & Guerra, J. J. (1976). *Assertion training: A humanistic-behavioral guide to self-dignity.* Champaign, IL: Research.

Cournoyer, B. R. (1983). Assertiveness among MSW students. *Journal of Education for Social Work, 19*(1), 24–30.

Cowger, C. D. (1994). Assessing client strengths: Clinical assessment for client empowerment. *Social Work, 39*(3), 262–268.

Cummerton, J. M. (1980, March). *Empowerment begins with me.* Paper presented at Council on Social Work Education meeting, Los Angeles.

Dow, M. G. (1994). Social inadequacy and social skill. In L. W. Craighead, W. E. Craighead, A. E. Kazdin, & M. J. Mahoney (Eds.), *Cognitive and behavioral interventions: An empirical approach to mental health problems* (pp. 123–140). Boston: Allyn & Bacon.

Drury, S. S. (1984). *Assertive supervision: Building involved teamwork.* Champaign, IL: Research.

Eberhardt, L. Y. (1994). *Working with woman's groups: Structured exercises in: Consciousness raising, self-discovery, assertiveness training.* Duluth, MN: Whole Person Associates.

Engels, M. L. (1991). The promotion of positive social interaction through social skills training. In P. A. Wisocki (Ed.), *Handbook of clinical behavior therapy with the elderly client: Applied clinical psychology* (pp. 185–202). New York: Plenum.

Enns, C. Z. (1992). Self-esteem groups: A synthesis of consciousness raising and assertiveness training. *Journal of Counseling and Development, 71*(1), 7–13.

Flynn, J. P. (1985). *Social agency policy: Analysis and presentation for community practice.* Chicago: Nelson-Hall.

Gamble, T. K., & Gamble, M. (1990). *Communication works* (3rd ed.). New York: McGraw-Hill.

Garvin, C., & Gruber, M. (1978, February). *Raising the consciousness of community organization students: The personal and professional identity issues for an organizer in the 1980's.* Paper presented at Council on Social Work Education meeting, New Orleans.

Gilbert, D. (1993). Not in my backyard. *Social Work, 39*(1), 7–8.

Glueckhauf, R. L., & Quittner, A. L. (1992). Assertiveness training for disabled adults in wheelchairs: Self-report, role-play, and activity pattern outcomes. *Journal of Consulting and Clinical Psychology, 60*(3), 419–425.

Griffin, W. V. (1995). Social worker and agency safety. In R. Edwards (Ed.-in-Chief), *Encyclopedia of Social Work* (19th ed., pp. 2293–2305). Washington, DC: National Association of Social Workers Press.

Gutierrez, L. M. (1990). Working with women of color: An empowerment perspective. *Social Work, 35*(2), 149–152.

Harden, B. (1995, July 16). A one-man human-rights crusade. *The Washington Post,* pp. B1, B6.

Hardina, D. (1995, March). *Teaching confrontation tactics to social work students.* Paper presented at Council on Social Work Education meeting, San Diego, CA.

Hardy, A. (1989). In vivo desensitization: Action and talking therapy. In C. Lindemann (Ed.), *Handbook of phobia therapy: Rapid symptom relief in anxiety disorders* (pp. 261–267). Northvale, NJ: Jason Aronson.

Harris, C. C., & Harris, D. R. (1993). *Self-empowerment: Reclaim your personal power.* Carmel, CA: Carmel Highlands.

Hartman, A. (1990). *Family-based strategies for empowering families.* Paper presented at the School of Social Work meeting, University of Iowa.

Haug, M. R., & Lavin, B. (1983). *Consumerism in medicine: Challenging physician authority.* Beverly Hills, CA: Sage.

Hawkins, J. D., Catalano, R. F., & Wells, E. A. (1986). Measuring effects of a skills training intervention for drug abusers. *Journal of Consulting and Clinical Psychology, 54*(5), 661–664.

Healey, L. M., Havens, C. M., & Chin, A. (1990). Preparing women for human services administration. *Administration in Social Work, 14*(2), 29–94.

Hepler, J. B. (1995). Social skills training. In R. Edwards (Ed.-in-Chief), *Encyclopedia of Social Work* (19th ed., pp. 2196–2205). Washington, DC: National Association of Social Workers Press.

Hepworth, D. H., & Larsen, J. A. (1986). *Direct social work practice* (2nd ed.). Pacific Grove, CA: Brooks/Cole.

Hepworth, D. H., & Larsen, J. A. (1993). *Direct social work practice* (4th ed.). Pacific Grove, CA: Brooks/Cole.

Howing, P. T., Wodarski, J. S., Kurtz, P. J., & Gaudin, J. M. (1990). The empirical base for the implementation of social skills training with maltreated children. *Social Work, 35*(5), 460–467.

Hsu, C. J. (1992). Assertiveness issues for Asian Americans. In I. G. Fodor (Ed.), *Adolescent assertiveness and social skills training: A clinical handbook* (pp. 99–112). New York: Springer.

Jansson, B. S. (1990). *Social welfare policy: From theory to practice.* Belmont, CA: Wadsworth.

Kahn, K. (1973). *Hillbilly women.* New York: Avon.

Kaufman, G., & Raphael, L. (1990). *Stick up for yourself: Every kid's guide to personal power and positive self esteem.* Minneapolis: Free Spirit.

Kaysen, S. (1993). *Girl interrupted.* New York: Vintage Books.

Kelly, C. (1979). *Assertion training.* La Jolla, CA: University Associates.

Kern, J. M., & Karten, S. J. (1991). Fakability of two different role play methodologies for assessing assertion. *Psychological Reports, 69,* 467–470.

Knee, R., & Vourlekis, B. (1995). Patient rights. In R. Edwards (Ed.-in-Chief), *Encyclopedia of Social Work* (19th ed., pp. 1802–1810). Washington, DC: National Association of Social Workers Press.

Knotts, L. S. (1991). *Characteristics of "women's language" and their relationship to personnel decisions.* Paper presented for departmental honors in psychology, Hood College, Frederick, MD.

Lange, A. J., & Jakubowski, P. (1976). *Responsible assertive behavior: Cognitive/behavioral procedures for trainers.* Champaign, IL: Research.

Life would be easy if it weren't for other people (1995). *Trial, 31*(1), 82.

Madanes, C. (1991). *Strategic family therapy.* San Francisco: Jossey-Bass.

Magladry, J., & Macpherson, J. E. (1994). Now cut that out! Extremes of boorish behavior. *Trial, 30*(7), 43.

Masi, D. A. (1994). Violence in the workplace: The EAP perspective. *EAP Digest, 14*(3), 23.

Nader, L. (1980). *No access to law.* New York: Academic Press.

National Association of Social Workers—MD Chapter. (1995, March). *Violence—caught in the crossfire—Implications for social work practice.* Program meeting.

Nezu, C., Nezu, A. M., & Arean, P. (1991). Assertiveness and problem-solving training for mildly mentally retarded persons with dual diagnoses. *Research in Developmental Disabilities, 12*(4), 371–386.

O'Donnell, R. (with J. Newman). (1995, Summer). Assertiveness training with Rosie O'Donnell. *Know How, 5*(2), 60–63, 101.

Orosz, S. B. (1982). Assertiveness in recovery. *Social Work with Groups, 5,* 25–31.

Pardeck, J. T., Anderson, C., Gianino, E. A., Miller, B., Mothershead, M. S., & Smith, S. A. (1991). Assertiveness of social work students. *Psychological Reports, 69*(2), 589–590.

Pearson, C. S. (1989). *The hero within: Six archetypes we live by.* New York: HarperCollins.

Peterson, S. (1971). *A catalog of the ways people grow.* New York: Balantine.

Pfost, K. S., Stevens, M. J., & Parker, J. C. (1992). The influence of assertion training on three aspects of assertiveness in alcoholics. *Journal of Clinical Psychology, 48*(2), 262–268.

Phelps, S., & Austin, N. (1987). *The assertive woman: A new look* (2nd ed.). San Luis Obispo, CA: Impact.

Planells-Bloom, D. (1992). Latino cultures: Framework for understanding the Latina adolescent and assertive behavior. In I. G. Fodor (Ed.), *Adolescent assertiveness and social skills training: A clinical handbook* (pp. 113–128). New York: Springer.

Plotkin, S. (1990). Enclave consciousness and neighborhood activism. In J. M. Kling & P. S. Posner (Eds.), *Dilemmas of activism* (pp. 218–239). Philadelphia: Temple University Press.

Rakos, R. F. (1991). *Assertive behavior.* New York: Routledge.

Richan, W. C., & Mendelsohn, A. R. (1973). *Social work: The unloved profession.* New York: New Viewpoints.

RoAne, S. (1988). *How to work a room: Learn the strategies of savvy socializing—for business and personal success.* New York: Warner Books.

Rose, S. D. (1977). Assertive training in groups: Research in clinical setting. *Scandinavian Journal of Behavior Therapy, 6*(2), 61–86.

Ruben, D. H., & Ruben, M. J. (1989). Why assertiveness training programs fail. *Small Group Behavior, 20*(3), 367–380.

Salcido, R. M. (1993, February). *A cross cultural approach for understanding Latino barrio needs: A macro practice model.* Paper presented at Council on Social Work Education meeting, New York.

Schulman, E. D. (1974). *Intervention in human services.* St. Louis, MO: C. V. Mosby.

Sears, V. (1990). Grace. In *Simple Songs* (pp. 139–159). Ithaca, NY: Firebrand Books.

Sears, V. L. (1993). Grace. In P. Riley (Ed.), *Growing up Native American* (pp. 279–298). New York: William Morrow.

Sherman, W., & Wenocur, S. (1983). Empowering public welfare workers through mutual support. *Social Work, 28*(5), 375–379.

Shulman, S. (1995, September 17). They hunt for heroes. *Parade Magazine,* p. 16.

Simon, B. L. (1990). Rethinking empowerment. *Journal of Progressive Human Services, 1*(1), 27–39.

Simons, H. W. (1976). *Persuasion: Understanding, practice and analysis.* Reading, MA: Addison-Wesley.

Siress, R. H., with C. Riddle, & D. Shouse. (1994). *Working woman's communications survival guide: How to present your ideas with impact, clarity and power and get the recognition you deserve.* Englewood Cliffs, NJ: Prentice Hall.

Smith, J. C. (1991). *Stress scripting: A guide to stress management.* New York: Praeger.

Smith, M. J. (1975). *When I say no, I feel guilty.* New York: Dial.

Spolin, V. (1983). *Improvisation for the theater: A handbook of teaching and directing techniques.* Evanston, IL: Northwestern University Press.

Subramanian, K., & Rose, S. D. (1988). Social work

and the treatment of chronic pain. *Health and Social Work, 13*(1), 49–60.

Sue, D., Sue, D. M., & Ino, S. (1990). Assertiveness and social anxiety in Chinese-American women. *Journal of Psychology, 124*(2), 155–163.

Tannen, D. (1990). *You just don't understand: Women and men in conversation.* New York: William Morrow.

Tannen, D. (1994). *Talking from 9 to 5: How women's and men's conversational styles affect who gets heard, who gets credit, and what gets done at work.* New York: William Morrow.

Thompson, L. (1990, November 20). Finally, a new chief for the FDA. *The Washington Post* (health section), pp. 11–12.

Tower, K. D. (1994). Consumer-centered social work practice: Restoring client self-determination. *Social Work, 39*(2), 191–196.

Tully, C. C., Kropf, N. P., & Price, J. L. (1993). Is the field a hard hat area? A study of violence in field placements. *Journal of Social Work Education, 29*(2), 191–199.

Vardi, D. (1992). Assertiveness training for pregnant and parenting high school teenagers. In I. G. Fodor (Ed.), *Adolescent assertiveness and social skills training: A clinical handbook* (pp. 249–268). New York: Springer.

Ventis, W. L. (1987). Humor and laughter in behavior therapy. In W. F. Fry, Jr., & W. A. Salameh (Eds.), *Handbook of humor and psychotherapy: Advances in the clinical use of humor* (pp. 149–169). Sarasota, FL: Professional Resource Exchange.

Wakefield, J. C. (1988, September). Part 2: Psychotherapy and the pursuit of justice. *Social Service Review 62*(2), 353–382.

Walton, D. (1989). *Are you communicating? You can't manage without it.* New York: McGraw-Hill.

Wayne, J., & Fine, S. B. (1986). Group work with retarded mothers. *Social Casework, 67*(4), 195–202.

Weiner, M. E. (1990). *Human services management: Analysis and applications* (2nd ed.). Belmont, CA: Wadsworth.

Weiss, J. O. (1993). Genetic disorders: Support groups and advocacy. *Families in Society: The Journal of Contemporary Human Services, 74*(4), 213–220.

Williams, P. N. (1978). *Investigative reporting and editing.* Englewood Cliffs, NJ: Prentice-Hall.

Wood, P. S., & Mallinckrodt, B. (1990). Culturally sensitive assertiveness training for ethnic minority clients. *Professional Psychology: Research and Practice, 21*(1), 208–214.

Yoshioka, M. (1995, March 5). *Measuring the assertiveness of low income, minority women: Implications for culturally competent practice.* Paper presented at Council on Social Work Education meeting, San Diego, CA.

Ziv Tzedakah Fund, Inc. (1994, April 1). *Ziv.* Annual report. (Available from Ziv Tzedakah Fund, 263 Congressional Lane, Rockville, MD.)

Zuker, E. (1983). *The assertive manager: Positive skills at work for you.* New York: Amacom.

chapter

8

Using Your Agency

[O]rganizations are necessary and important because they enable people to accomplish *collectively* what cannot be accomplished by individuals acting on their own. The maintenance of complex industrial societies is inconceivable without the existence of large-scale organizations, together with a great number of very small organizations.

H. E. ALDRICH, *ORGANIZATIONS AND ENVIRONMENTS* (1979, P. 3)

As social workers, we spend our professional lives practicing in human service organizations—governmental (public) or nonprofit agencies in most cases and proprietary organizations in a few instances. These organizations profoundly affect our personal and professional well-being. Regardless of our talents and skills, organizational structure, culture, and management strongly influence how well and in what manner we are able to deliver services, that is, how well we are able to do the professional work for which we were trained. At the same time, our work or-

ganizations affect our self-image, our livelihoods, and our sense of accomplishment and worth as human beings. For these reasons, understanding how organizations operate is not simply an abstract exercise. We need that knowledge to be able to create a personally and professionally more satisfying work environment.

This chapter is written from the perspective of the direct service worker rather than the supervisor or manager. It deals with human service organizations in general first, and then with the formal and informal aspects of organizational life that workers should know about to understand the forces that impinge on them and the opportunities for intervention. We also remind the reader of the interorganizational context of organizational life because external economic, political, and institutional forces strongly affect *intra*organizational behavior. Throughout the chapter, we try to regard workers as organizational actors intervening on their own behalf and on behalf of their clients. As a prelude to this chapter, we encourage the reader to review the material on systems theory, exchange theory, and interorganizational theory in Chapter 2.

THE ATTRIBUTES OF HUMAN SERVICE AGENCIES

Social workers practice in a very broad array of human service organizations. Although these agencies vary in such characteristics as size, complexity, auspices, domain, and whether or not social work is the dominant profession in the agency—and more, as a class of organizations—they are also alike in many ways. These similarities help to explain the organizational problems and opportunities that human service workers and service users often encounter. In briefly reviewing these shared attributes, we shall draw on Hasenfeld's (1992b) work on the nature of human service organizations.

Human service organizations are *people processing and people changing* agencies in that "the core activities of the organization are structured to process, sustain, or change people who come under its jurisdiction" (Hasenfeld, 1992b, pp. 4–5). Some organizational examples are job placement, information, and referral (processing); Social Security, long-term nursing home care (sustaining); counseling, school (changing). (Social action, planning, and fund-raising or-

ganizations that do not offer a direct service fit this description less comfortably.) However, since service users are not necessarily passive participants in organizational transactions, the outcomes of professional intervention are difficult to control and standardize. To maximize compliance, and hence control, human service workers must win their clients' cooperation and trust. This relationship is vulnerable to deliberate or unwitting abuse, since workers typically control some of the resources that clients need. Moreover, control and standardization of the services that are delivered are difficult to achieve because services, the products of professional intervention, are intangible and "inextricably bound to the person and personality of the producer" (Larson, 1977, p. 14; Wenocur & Reisch, 1989, pp. 9–11). Since human service "technologies" (modes of intervention) are variable and hard to reproduce (though greater reliability is the object of professional training), and since the outcomes of intervention are hard to measure and not clearly visible, human service organizations, not surprisingly, have difficulty gaining support for their work.

In a market economy, human service organizations are unique in that their primary funding sources are largely governmental tax dollars and philanthropic contributions. (For-profit human service organizations are exceptions.) One implication of this is that, for the most part, the service users are not the same people as the service funders. Therefore, unlike the situation of a company selling products in the marketplace, an increase in the numbers of clients and corresponding services does not automatically result in increased revenues. In addition, since service users are not funders, they lack a major source of power over the operations of the organizations that serve them. Nevertheless, service users are valuable assets for human service organizations—no clients, no organization—and as such, agencies often see them as objects of interagency competition or interagency exchanges (Greenley & Kirk, 1973).

The sources of funding for human service organizations make them dependent on an uncertain, competitive, often turbulent political and institutional environment for legitimacy and resources. Consequently, the legitimacy of and funding for human service agencies wax and wane with changes in political administrations and the currency of new ideas that happen to be in vogue. Human service managers, by the same token, usually have their political antennae up and their political hats close at hand.

Human service work is often stressful, not only because of inadequate resources, but also because it is both "moral work" and "gendered work" (Hasenfeld, 1992b). It is moral work in the sense that workers inevitably are involved in making value-laden decisions, often painful ones, that render moral judgments about the social worth of an individual or a family—for example, whether or not to make one more attempt to reach a difficult client, whether or not to cut off a service or separate a child from a family, or what kind of diagnostic label to attach. In the all too common situation where resources are scarce and clients' needs are strong, if not overwhelming, workers often agonize over requirements to ration services. In organizational settings where stress levels are constant and high, workers may burn out and leave or stay and find a functional or dysfunctional mode of accommodation. In public welfare agencies, such accommodations may include (1) finding a special niche in the organization that removes the worker from the firing line, (2) capitulating to agency demands to serve only "deserving" clients, (3) openly resisting agency demands, and (4) adopting a victim mentality by overidentifying with the clients (Sherman & Wenocur, 1983).

Human service work is "gendered work." Women make up the majority of the direct service workers in human service organizations, while men tend to hold positions of authority. Although this pattern is slowly changing, a study of members of the NASW (Gibelman & Schervish, 1993, p. 95) recently found that 74.8% of the more than 80,000 respondents were women and more than 72% of these women held direct service positions compared to 57.1% of men. With regard to administration, although more women held these positions than men in absolute numbers (7,991 vs. 5,330), the percentage of men in administration was twice the percentage of women (25.6% vs. 12.9%). This skewed gender distribution potentially generates stressful dissonance between the workers' "feminine value orientation" of altruism, caring, and nurturing that requires nonroutine activities and the formal organizations's "masculine value orientation" that requires routine and standardization for the sake of efficiency (Dressel, 1992; Hasenfeld, 1992b). This conflict, coupled with the lower pay attached to female-dominated occupations and industries and the fact that many of the clients of human service agencies are poor women and other "undeserving" poor, devalues human service work and demeans all human service workers. And since devalued human services attract inadequate financial resources, it is difficult to have the impact on complex social problems that might change the pattern of allocations significantly in the future (Hasenfeld, 1992, pp. 8–9).

Organizational Auspices

Having discussed some of the similarities among human service organizations, we should also attend to some of the differences, as these also will have a strong bearing on service delivery and worker satisfaction. In particular, this section will consider the differences between public, nonprofit, and for-profit human service agencies. According to the previously mentioned study of NASW membership conducted in 1991 (Gibelman & Schervish, 1993), 38.7% (39,686) of the 102,617 respondents identified their primary auspice of employment as a public organization (federal, state, local, or military). This percentage is down from the 41.6% who identified public organizations as their primary work site in 1988. The percentages for the nonprofit sector for 1991 and 1988 were, respectively, 39.1% and 39.9%. Only the for-profit sector showed an increase in 1991 over 1988, 22.2% compared to 18.5%. (We should note that not all professional social workers belong to NASW, so a survey of all social workers, could it be done, might turn up different results.)

The terms *public* or *governmental* organizations refer to human service organizations that are established by federal, state, or local governmental regulations and supported by tax revenues. Examples include the Department of Health and Human Services, a department of public welfare, a community mental health center, and a local high school. Since public organizations are established by government, the top of the governance structure is often a politically appointed executive officer (titles may vary), such as the secretary of a department of health and mental hygiene appointed by the governor or the executive director of the local department of public welfare appointed by the mayor or county executive. Other top-level administrators may also be political appointees. Below the top echelons, federal, state, and local governmental employees are hired and fired in accordance with civil service regulations that provide job classifications, salary levels, criteria, and procedures for meritorious appointments and promotions and procedures for termination.

Some public agencies have governing boards that make major policy decisions and hire the organization's chief executive officer(s). Examples include an elected local school board, a library board, or the board of regents of a state university, which is appointed by the governor and which, in turn, appoints the university president or chancellor. Some public organizations utilize advisory boards to assist with guiding policy and making top-level appointments and decisions, but advisory boards do not have the legal authority to make the final decisions.

In this text, the terms *voluntary*, *private*, and *nonprofit* organizations refer to human service organizations that are legally incorporated in their state as nonprofit corporations and thereby subject to state charitable laws. In addition, nonprofit organizations have been granted tax exemption by the Internal Revenue Service (IRS), which means that they do not have to pay federal taxes on their corporate income. Usually nonprofit organizations are exempt from state and local taxes as well, although some financially strapped municipalities are currently reconsidering this policy. The IRS has at least 26 categories of tax-exempt organizations, but most human service agencies have been granted tax exemption as 501 (c) (3) organizations, a category reserved for religious, charitable, and educational organizations. Clearly this sector covers a very broad range of organizations, from huge hospital corporations such as Johns Hopkins, to family service associations, to small church-sponsored soup kitchens and everything in between.

Nonprofit organizations receive significant funding from private philanthropy (individual, corporate, and foundation donations and grants). They may also receive significant governmental funding through purchase of service contracts, grants, and governmental insurance payments such as Medicaid. In addition, nonprofits frequently earn revenue from fees for services of various kinds, including third-party private insurance payments, direct fees for a service or product, and income from other related business activities, such as the operation of a health spa by a YMCA or a blood testing lab by a medical school. Hence the source of funding does not clearly distinguish nonprofit agencies from governmental and for-profit organizations.

The key feature distinguishing nonprofits from public agencies is that nonprofits are self-governed. That is, they are governed by an all-volunteer board of directors to whom the executive officer is responsible. The voluntary board is a legal requirement of incorporation as a charitable organization.

Although nonprofits cannot earn a profit to be distributed to shareholders and board members, they can generate surplus income to be saved for a rainy day or to be reinvested in agency programs. Nevertheless, *the feature that most clearly distinguishes nonprofits from for-profit organizations is that in nonprofits, payment for services rendered does not cover the full costs of production plus an amount for profit.* Profit is not part of the calculus. Nonprofits use charitable dollars to help subsidize their services.

The presence of a large nonprofit sector supports pluralistic democratic values. Nonprofits represent the essence of voluntary action by citizens to provide the services they need and want, services that government and private corporations cannot provide legally or fail to provide because they are not politically or economically viable. So, for example, many nonprofits are sponsored by sectarian and culturally distinct groups, such as a Korean Community Center, a Jewish Family Services agency, a Black Mental Health Alliance, an Associated Catholic Charities, or a Hispanic Community Council. Moreover, because nonprofits are voluntary, self-governing bodies, they can challenge the

policies and practices of private corporations and governmental agencies. Most of our important social reforms came about through nonprofit activities—child welfare, civil rights, environmental protection, women's rights, workplace safety (Salamon, 1992).

Nonprofit organizations usually provide a very different work environment from governmental agencies, one that is potentially less formal and more flexible and varied. When large and complex, both types of organizations can operate quite bureaucratically, with many policies and rules to follow, a hierarchical system of decision making, and a clearly differentiated division of labor. However, many nonprofit human service organizations are not very large. A study of the Baltimore area nonprofit sector, for example (Salamon, Altschuler, & Myllyluoma, 1990), found that in 1987 72% of the nonprofits had expenditures of less than $500,000. Even when they are large, nonprofits have the capacity to make decisions more quickly and to operate more flexibly than their governmental counterparts. In part, this is a function of their system of self-governance; the executive, with the approval of the board, has great leeway to make program and policy changes. In part, it is also a function of their ability to choose whom they will serve and the nature of the services they will provide. If the market is there, a nonprofit agency could decide to provide therapy only to people with three nostrils. If the market is too large, they can decide to limit their services even further or expand if they want. Governmental organizations have no such flexibility. Legally they are mandated to serve all who are eligible according to the legislation that established the organization, regardless of the numbers. For example, a child welfare agency must serve all abused and neglected children in its geographic service area, ultimately an indeterminate number, and additional staffing is subject to political competition for scarce resources. (As this book goes to press, current welfare reform proposals may change the legal mandate of entitlement services by placing a budgetary cap on services and benefits. Thus, if the budget runs out, some eligible clients would go unserved.)

For-profit or *proprietary* organizations are a growing segment of the human service field. Some examples are hospitals, home health care agencies, solo or group counseling practices, residential treatment facilities, and nursing homes. These organizations are incorporated in a state as businesses, and they pay local, state, and federal corporate income taxes. They are required to have a board of directors with a minimum of three members, who are the main administrative officers of the company. Other board members may be added because of stock ownership or the special connections and expertise they may bring. The chairperson is frequently the chief executive officer of the corporation. For-profit board members expect to be paid for their services (Houle, 1989). Proprietary organizations sell their services or products at a price sufficient to cover the cost of production plus an amount for profit. The profit that is not reinvested in the organization is divided among the owners.

For-profit organizations must be extremely sensitive to the marketplace, much more so than public or voluntary organizations. This necessity brings advantages and disadvantages. The advantages, some would argue, are that services are more flexible, efficient, client-friendly, and more likely to be in tune with the latest trends and knowledge. Social workers or other human service professionals in small firms, like a solo or group professional practice, are likely to have greater leeway to exercise professional judgment without bureaucratic constraints. The disadvantages are that for-profit services may not be responsive to the needs of poor and working-class people who cannot afford to pay the fees directly or through insurance coverage. Related to this, some observers claim that human service for-profits ignore the advocacy and social reform responsibilities of the social work profession. In addition, professionals in solo or group practices must operate as entrepreneurs generating business, so that the flexibility gained in one aspect of practice may be offset by the time requirements of marketing and business management in another. Large for-profit human service organizations, like their counterparts in other fields of business or government, may evolve complex bureaucratic organizations with a highly differentiated division of labor and specialized work roles, such as marketing and public relations departments, various departments of professional services, a governmental affairs department, and so on. Small private practice firms are more likely to involve professional staff in a variety of organizational roles.

PERSPECTIVES ON HOW ORGANIZATIONS FUNCTION: A BRIEF REVIEW

Intraorganizational Systems

The whole point of establishing an organization such as a social work agency or a private business is that an individual or, more commonly, a group of people has a complicated goal in mind that requires the joint efforts of many persons to accomplish efficiently and effectively. The aim might be to deliver an intangible product, such as mental health services, to a needy population or to produce a tangible product, such as the all-famous widget, for an enormous market of widgetarians. In any event, the organizational founders logically set up systematic rules for organizing the work in order to accomplish their aims and then put their plans into action. In a word, they create an organization. Frequently, if the founders know what they are doing, these plans work out fairly well—but seldom exactly as intended, because there are too many variables and unknowns to contend with. Some clients do not neatly fit the image projected; some staff members do not get along with each other; some sources of funding are unexpectedly cut off; and so on. All of this is to say, as we did in Chapter 2, that organizations are open systems striving for closure. That is, by definition, organizations always try to operate rationally, but they never can do so completely because of multiple uncertainties deriving from internal organizational sources and the external political and institutional environments that they are part of and must relate to (Thompson, 1967).

Internally, uncertainty creeps into organizations through at least three different paths: structural complexity, technological indeterminateness, and human variability. When organizations are set up to serve a large, heterogeneous population that has many complicated needs, these agencies themselves necessarily become complex systems. As mentioned previously, organizational directors and managers will usually divide the work of running the organization and producing its products or services into smaller subdivisions, some of which may become quite specialized. For example, a nonprofit antihunger organization with a $3 million dollar budget might have an emergency services department; a feeding program; a public policy unit; a community organizing and advocacy division; a resource development unit that includes fund-raising and public relations; a general administration unit that includes building maintenance, purchasing, and bookkeeping; and a management division that includes planning, personnel, volunteer oversight, and training. Even small nonprofits are likely to have sub-

divisions; large governmental or for-profit organizations can be infinitely more complex. The more differentiated the organization, the greater the difficulty in coordinating the work of the various subsystems to produce products and services efficiently and effectively. Interestingly, at various times, both greater organizational centralization and greater decentralization have been proposed as ways to improve coordination in the interests of organizational efficiency and effectiveness. However, there is no simple answer. The structural solution that works best depends on the goals, needs, and managerial capacities of the particular organization (Webber, 1979), as well as the organization's technology and conditions in the external environment.

Technological uncertainty in human service organizations comes from several sources. First, we are not always sure about how best to intervene to help deal with certain problems. What is the best approach to deal with the alcoholic, for example, or with the high incidence of alcoholism in the larger society? How about a client who is both alcoholic and mentally ill? How about the low-income, multiproblem family? In addition, many different technologies and belief systems may exist simultaneously in the same organization. A psychiatric hospital employs nurses, psychiatrists, psychologists, social workers, recreational therapists, and so on, each of whom may approach the patients quite differently. And even within the individual disciplines, professionals may have contrary intervention practices—for example, behaviorists versus psychodynamically oriented psychologists. Second, to provide assistance effectively, we often have to rely on the cooperation of other agencies and service providers over whom we have little control. And finally, since our service users are reactive, individual human beings, not inert physical materials, our interventions depend on feedback from our clients, and we cannot always predict their responses. In effect, we have to use individually customized rather than standardized technologies (Thompson, 1967) in situations, incidentally, where the external world often seems to be demanding mass solutions to widespread problems, such as crime or substance abuse.

Human variability, of course, also enters the organization through its employees, managers, and directors, all the people who make up the organization. They differ in personalities, beliefs and values, needs, goals, ideas, knowledge and skills, life experiences, cultural identity, and so on. They also tend to form groups and subgroups that strongly influence employee and managerial behavior and that can differ greatly, for example, on goals, status, and expectations. As various interest groups form based on shared values, norms, and predilections, some authors view the process of reaching agreements on goals and activities as an ongoing negotiation and the organization in essence as a "negotiated order," constantly in flux, rather than fixed and determinate (Cyert & March, 1963; Strauss, Schatzman, Ehrlich, & Bucher, 1963).

One consequence of the unique characteristics of human service organizations is that they tend to be structured internally as *loosely coupled systems* (as opposed to tightly coupled systems). In essence, this means that the hierarchical structure of authority and clear lines of communication that one might associate with a strictly rational system of organization do not work well in human service organizations. Instead, (1) strict top-down authority is likely to be weak and dispersed in multiple authority units; (2) various subunits are likely to maintain a considerable degree of autonomy and identity, and their tasks and activities tend to be weakly coordinated; and (3) there is "a weak system of control over staff activities" (Hasenfeld, 1983, p. 150). Imagine a school

system with administrators (principals), teachers, social workers, guidance counselors, psychologists, and various other specialists. Despite directives from above, ultimately the teacher runs the classroom autonomously, and necessarily so, because of the great variations among students and teaching styles. Evaluation of effective teaching performance is difficult. Evaluation of succesful counseling and social work intervention is even more difficult, since these activities are carried out even more autonomously than teaching. Moreover, while the principal exerts authority over the social workers, the social workers also report to the head of the school's social work department, so the principal's authority is dissipated. A similar pattern exists with guidance and psychology, adding to coordination problems between all of the different units. Without the ability to hold staff accountable for their performance through monitoring and evaluation—and unionization and civil service requirements may add to these difficulties—the administrator's authority is further weakened. One result of loose coupling is a potentially fragmented, disjointed service delivery system. At the same time, this arrangement may serve important functions for the organization, such as creating more potential for a flexible response to changes in the environment and buffering the organization from failures in any particular unit (Hasenfeld, 1983).

Interorganizational Systems

In Chapter 2 we discussed two concepts central to understanding interorganizational relations, *domain* and *task environment*. For social service agencies and community organizations, we said that organizational domain represents the territory that an organization has carved out in terms of social problems it will address, populations it will serve, and types of advocacy or services it will provide. Two points relevant to interorganizational relations flow from this concept. The first is that since every other organization also makes domain claims, "turf battles" and competition often crop up, particularly when resources are scarce, a condition sometimes referred to as *domain dissensus*. Over time, conflict and negotiation may lead to some resolution, a state of *domain consensus*, where the different actors have basically worked out agreements about boundaries and overlaps and expectations about what each actor will and will not do (Thompson, 1967). The second point is that an organization's domain determines what other organizations and individuals it will have to relate to or pay attention to in order to fulfill its mission. This network of organizations, organizational subunits, and individuals forms the focal organization's *task environment*.

The task environment is a convenient way of conceptualizing the immediate external environment with which an organization must transact business. It consists of the following categories of actors: (1) suppliers of fiscal resources, (2) suppliers of nonfiscal resources, (3) consumers and clients and their suppliers, (4) competitors, (5) collaborators or complementary service providers, and (6) suppliers of legitimation and authority. These are not necessarily exclusive categories; organizations may be represented in more than one category at the same time. For example, a prestigious foundation that supplies funds in the form of a grant also supplies legitimacy by lending its name to the work of the organization.

An organization's external environment inevitably poses uncertainty for the organization because it contains needed resources and information that the organization cannot fully control or even, in some cases, perceive. Human service organizations, for example, depend on having clients or members in order to obtain resources and legitimacy. While this is usually not a problem in public agencies, it can be a severe problem in nonprofit and for-profit organizations as needs change, populations shift, or new competitors enter the field.

For any given organization, not only its task environment but also the structure and dynamics of the larger environment surrounding the task environment may affect organizational functioning. Structurally, the larger environment may be relatively simple or complex, or resource rich or poor, for example. Therefore the options and opportunities for finding clients and funds are quite different for rural as opposed to urban or suburban agencies. Dynamically the larger environment may be relatively stable or constantly changing and therefore highly unpredictable. Organizations providing health care seem to be in a rapidly changing, uncertain environment due to political, economic, organizational, and technological developments. Changes in health care, in turn, may have a ripple effect on many other human service organizations. Health care trends may be still easier to anticipate than other distant political or economic changes that can have local short- and long-term ramifications. Foreign policy in relation to Southeast Asia, for example, has led to an influx of Asians from many different nations and their dispersal to American communities often totally unprepared to serve persons of with such diverse backgrounds and languages.

Uncertainty and Power

In the section on exchange and power in Chapter 2, we noted that the ability to control resources that another party needs is a major source of power in an interdependent relationship. Since any organization depends on satisfactory exchanges with the members of its task environment in order to accomplish its goals, at various points in time members of the task environment may hold a certain amount of power over the organization. This idea is most clearly illustrated with funding sources. Grant-making organizations usually stipulate the requirements that an organization must meet in order to receive funds. In market-based organizations, individual customers have power because the organization needs them to purchase its products or services. Customers who form a consumer organization can wield even greater influence over a target organization. Similarly, since organizations need workers to produce products or provide services, when workers form labor organizations, they too gain power over their employing organization.

Relating the concept of uncertainty to power and exchange we could say that the *in*ability to control the elements that an organization needs to accomplish its goals creates organizational uncertainty. In today's much more competitive climate for charitable dollars, for example, nonprofit human service organizations experience increasingly greater uncertainty about their funding sources. In this formulation, then, within an organization, power accrues to those individuals or groups that can resolve uncertainties for the organization (Crozier, 1964). These uncertainties may stem from internal or external environmental sources. Thus, in a human service organization that needs the capacity to process a great deal of information rapidly, employees with computer-based information-management skills may have a great deal of influence and command high salaries. The employee who can get the system up when it crashes may be the most powerful of all.

In view of the pervasive uncertainty that permeates modern organizational life, ad-ministration involves an ongoing struggle to manage internal and external environmental uncertainty while keeping the organization on the path to accomplishing its goals. To succeed at this complex task, administrators and professional staff members must be able to obtain and process strategic information about every aspect of organizational life, particularly environmental trends and opportunties. A recent study by Menefee and Thompson (1994, p. 14) comparing management competencies of the early 1980s with requirements for the 1990s found a dramatic shift from roles and skills, such as supervising and direct practice, "focused primarily on internal operations to one(s) that (are) strategically oriented," such as boundary spanning and futuring, aimed at managing a complex external environment. Thompson (1967) likens this idea of *opportunistic surveillance* to natural curiosity in the individual, defining this search activity as "monitoring behavior which scans the environment for opportunities—which does not have to be activated by a problem and which does not therefore stop when a problem solution has been found" (p. 151).

Opportunistic search roles take many different forms and involve both regular staff members and managers. Because they help the organization manage environmental uncertainties, they may also carry special status and influence. One important role set focuses on *strategic planning*. Strategic planning activities engage the organization in (1) systematically scanning its internal and external environments to identify organizational strengths and weaknesses in relation to short- and long-range trends, opportunities, and threats and (2) formulating stategies to manage the issues confronting the organization and developing a vision for the future (Bryson, 1989, p. 48). Management, staff, and volunteers may all carry out strategic planning activities. In some larger organizations, strategic planning is the ongoing business of an organizational planning department.

Boundary-spanning roles encompass a large range of activities carried out by managers and staff persons, sometimes alone and often as parts of specialized departments, such as a public relations division, a government affairs office, an admissions department, and a discharge-planning unit. The strategic planning activities mentioned above are also boundary-spanning functions. *Boundary spanning* refers to transactions that enable the organization to manage (environmental) "constraints and contingencies not controlled by the organization" (Thompson, 1967, p. 67). Boundary-spanning roles typically involve networking skills, the ability to develop relationships with a broad array of individuals and groups in order to exchange resources and information of value to the organization. The social worker in a hospital doing discharge planning is performing a boundary-spanning role. She enables the organization to respond to the constraints placed on it by the insurance companies for length of inpatient stay. She must learn about and develop relationships with a variety of external organizations, such as home health care agencies and different types of nursing homes, in order to help patients continue their recovery after hospitalization. The job is a sensitive one, and a powerful one if no one else can perform this function effectively, because the hospital is under pressure to discharge patients but, at the same time, to ensure that the planning is sound so that patients recover appropriately and are satisfied with the services they have received. In one hospital where the number of non-English-speaking patients increased, a social worker developed a network of interpreters by scanning the community and reaching out to a host of immigrant groups, who were then linked to the hospital to lend their special assistance. An agency's government relations department speaks to an organizationally recognized need to be able to identify, promulgate, and influence legislation that affects the organization's ability to fulfill its mission.

Boundary spanners may develop a good deal of power in their organizations if they help the organization manage environmental contingencies that are important to it and if others cannot easily do the job (Thompson, 1967). Organizational fund-raisers or resource developers, for example, can often bargain for much higher salaries than other staff members. In the growing culturally diverse environment of many social agencies, social workers who have skills in working with diverse populations will potentially gain leverage. Boundary-spanning roles in organizations facing complex, competitive, and highly dynamic external environments are likely to require the exercise of a great deal of personal discretion. If handled well, these positions are likely to bring influence and high compensation. In homogeneous and more stable environments where boundary-spanning roles can be routinized, influence will be correspondingly less.

EXAMINING THE FORMAL STRUCTURE AND OPERATIONS

Organizational Mandates, Mission, and Goals

In order to understand the workings of an organization, we need to examine both the rational and nonrational aspects of organizational life. On the rational side, we can begin by trying to understand the purpose for which the organization was formed, the mandates under which it is operating, and its operative goals. Straightforward as this may sound, such an examination usually moves us quickly onto the road of organizational complexity.

Organizational *mandates* indicate what the organization is required to do according to its charter or articles of incorporation or, in the case of a public agency, as codified in laws and ordinances (Bryson, 1989). A department of child protective services, for example, may be required by statute to investigate all cases reported to it of child abuse and neglect in a particular locality. A nonprofit agency may require, in its articles of incorporation, that the organization serve the poorest families in the county. Organizations may exceed their mandates and provide additional services, so any search for organizational purposes should not stop with mandates.

The organizational *mission* usually flows from the organization's mandate. An organization's mission statement "delineates the organization's reason for existing, usually in a short paragraph capturing the essence of what the organization is attempting to do" (Fisher, Schoenfeldt, & Shaw, 1990, p. 691). Two examples of mission statements are presented in Box 8.1. Such statements often appear in annual reports, agency brochures, and newsletters and provide a basis for the organization to acquire needed legitimacy and support in the community.

Mandates and mission statements represent the *official goals* of an organization. These are relatively easy to discover and may be essential to understand for purposes of evaluating agency effectiveness, holding it accountable, and comprehending the underlying beliefs and values about human nature guiding the organization (Hasenfeld, 1983). However, they also tend to be rather general or vague and do not really tell us what the organization spends its energy and resources actually doing in the face of multiple or competing interests and pressures generated from both internal and external environmental sources.

Instead, to really understand an organization, according to Perrow (1961), we need to try to uncover the organizations *operative goals.* "Operative goals designate the ends sought through the actual operating policies of the organization; they tell us what the organization is actually trying to do regardless of what the official goals say are the aims" (p. 856). A corrections unit may include rehabilitation as one of its main aims, but if lit-

---

| BOX 8.1 | TWO MISSION STATEMENTS |

THE CHESAPEAKE FOUNDATION FOR HUMAN DEVELOPMENT, INC.

The purpose of the Chesapeake Foundation for Human Development is to provide education and training opportunities for youth in an effort to foster positive relationships and the personal development that leads to satisfying and appropriate ways of living. Of particular interest to the Foundation are those youngsters at risk who have the greatest needs—those youth who are growing up without the benefit of adequate supervision and guidance and without a nurturing family and healthy neighborhood environment.

THE DOOR

The Baltimore Urban Leadership Foundation trading as the Door is organized and shall be operated exclusively for social, economic, educational, physical, spiritual, and charitable purposes by providing resource services and fund raising support to urban and multi-cultural community-based organizations and ministries for the purpose of promoting racial reconciliation, urban leadership development and community renewal in neighborhoods with minority and poverty concentrations.

tle of its budget goes into staff to provide rehabilitative services, we would have to conclude that its primary function was custodial. Hasenfeld's (1983) report of his study of community action agencies found that whereas the official goals stressed aims such as "linking low income people to critical resources" and "developing in and among the poor the capacity for leadership," the centers actually functioned more like welfare departments and seemed to serve primarily "to provide jobs to the poverty workers themselves rather than to their clients" (pp. 86–87).

Operative goals are much more difficult to discern than official goals. First, any complex organization is likely to have multiple and sometimes conflicting goals. Second, organizations are dynamic systems. Therefore goals are not necessarily fixed for all time; they shift as the organization loses and gains staff and board members and as the environment produces new threats or opportunities. How, then, might we determine what an organization's goals are? Hasenfeld (1983) provides one approach in his description of what he did to learn about the goals of community action centers. His data-gathering strategy included participant observation, analysis of a sample of client case files, observations of client–staff transactions, and formal interviews with numerous staff members. Perrow (1961) indicates that if we know something about how the organization accomplishes its major tasks of acquiring resources and legitimacy, the skills that it marshals to deliver its services, and how the staff and clients and other external agencies are coordinated, and if we learn about the characteristics of the the organization's "controlling elites," we can develop a pretty fair idea of an organization's operative goals. First, this means observations and interviews with key people in the organization, those in high positions of formal authority as well as pow-

erful informal leaders. To this we would add analysis of the agency's budget to see where resources are allocated. Much of this information is available to organizational insiders, namely, staff members, if pursued thoughtfully and systematically.

Authority and Structure

Organizational authority is an important form of organizational power, though not the only form as we have seen. It derives from the constitution of the organization, which legitimates the power ascribed to positions of authority by its laws. It may be supported as well by tradition, expertise, and the charismatic leadership of the authority holders. The exercise of authority depends partly on the strength of the sanctions that can be applied to produce compliance. In the final analysis, however, authority rests on the consent of the governed. Persons in positions of authority who exceed their limits or whose dictates are considered unfair may breed subtle forms of noncompliance, sabotage, or even open mutiny.

Every organization has a hierarchical structure of authority that delineates a chain of command for decision making and a span of control for all of the organization's participants. This *formal organizational structure* can be depicted graphically in an organization chart, as shown in Box 8.2. The logic of this arrangement is that "it establishes clear lines of responsibility and accountability" for decision making, "it provides for a system of controls to ensure staff compliance," and "it enables the coordination of various tasks by means of hierarchical centers of responsibility" (Hasenfeld, 1983, p. 161). Under the assumption of organizational rationality, the higher the level of authority, the correspondingly greater degree of knowledge and competence of the authority holder.

BOX 8.2   ORGANIZATION CHART OF A STATEWIDE ANTIHUNGER AGENCY

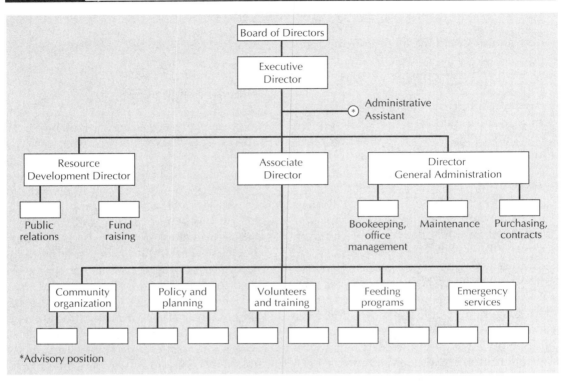

*Advisory position

As we know from our previous discussion, rational assumptions do not hold true for human service organizations. First, these tend to dissipate authority due to the autonomy required of the service delivery staff and the many different forms of uncertainty that pervade these systems. Thus authority seldom operates in a straight-line fashion. Second, in complex organizations, authority and expertise seldom come together in single individuals well enough to be able to make the most effective decisions. For example, the director of the antihunger organization in Box 8.2 may understand hunger policy and legislation quite well and have strong planning skills, but she may know relatively little about the whole area of resource development. To the extent that effective organizational decision making requires the unification of knowledge and authority, a collective decision-making process will be necessary. Third, in order to operate effectively in a turbulent external environment, organizations are finding that they need more flexibility than a rigid hierarchical system allows. One way of gaining this flexibility is by using temporary structures. "Through independent, limited-life project, product, problem, or venture teams, specialists necessary to accomplish a mission are brought together for as long as necessary, but no longer" (Webber, 1979, p. 383). Box 8.3 illustrates a project team put together by the antihunger organization in Box 8.2 to take advantage of a grant opportunity for a voter registration project.

BOX 8.3 ANTIHUNGER ORGANIZATION PROJECT TEAM

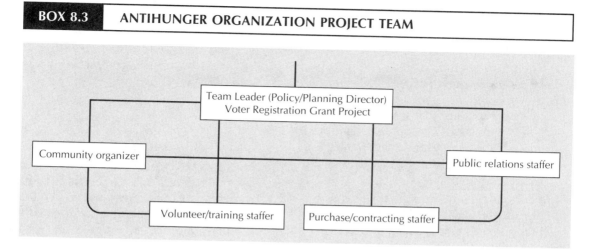

Boards of Directors

This section concerns the boards of public and nonprofit organizations where the bulk of social workers are employed. (Boards of for-profit companies may operate somewhat differently.) In these organizations, the ultimate authority for decision making about the direction of the organization rests with the board of directors or trustees, hereafter referred to as a *governing board* (Houle, 1989). Rather than flaunt this authority, the governing board normally works in partnership with the executive who oversees the operation of the organization on a daily basis and with the staff who daily carry out the actual work of the agency. The popular notion that boards establish policy and executives and staff carry it out does not work out that way in practice for a variety of practical reasons. Board members serve only on a part-time basis and seldom have the professional expertise in the organization's service area or the necessary staff of their own to be able to make operating and even long-range policies. They are not in a good position to dictate policy from on high. If the board and the executive have developed a good working relationship, then, more typically, the execu-

tive will generate policy, fiscal, and programmatic recommendations for the board to consider and act on in a timely fashion. Usually these deal with general policies and large fiscal expenditures or programmatic changes, and an understanding of the meaning of *general* and *large* will need to be worked out between the parties involved.

The above does not imply that power struggles between executives and boards never arise, that executives may not keep their boards properly informed, or that boards never try to micro-manage their organizations (Kramer, 1965). In fact, in the early stages of organizational development, when an agency is starting out, board members may commonly exercise a great deal of authority over the daily affairs of the organization (Mathiasen, 1990). As the organization matures, however, governing boards evolve that recognize the need to shift from specific to general oversight.

Borrowing from Cyril O. Houle (1989, pp. 90–94), the functions of governing boards can be described briefly as follows:

1. The board should make sure that the organization remains true to its mission.
2. The board should make sure that the or-

ganization engages in long-range planning and should approve such plans when developed.

3. The board should "oversee the program of the institution to assure itself that objectives are being achieved in the best fashion possible." This means that that board will need to become sophisticated enough about programs, with the help of the executive and staff to be able to make informed judgments.

4. The board should hire the chief executive officer and establish the conditions for that person's employment.

5. The board should "work closely and interactively with the executive and, through him, with the staff." While the executive has responsibility for administering the agency, and therefore for such functions as recruitment and deployment of staff, developing personnel policies, participatory decision making, conflict resolution, and developing effective fiscal control measures, the board is ultimately responsible for making sure that these functions are carried out effectively.

6. The board should "serve as arbiter in conflicts between staff members on appeal from the decision of the executive and in conflicts between the executive and the staff." Usually the executive sees to it that such conflicts are resolved within the staff, but occasionally the board must serve as the court of last resort.

7. The board should establish broad policies governing the organization's program within which the executive and staff can function. These policies may originate with the board, executive, and/or staff. As mentioned earlier, usually such policies are drafted by the staff and executive in the form of recommendations to the board, and the board may adopt, modify, or reject them after due consideration.

8. The board "should assure itself that its basic legal and ethical responsibilities are fulfilled."

9. The board "must accept responsibility for securing and managing adequate financial resources." This is tantamount to saying that the board must secure funding for its policy decisions. The board, for example, should not decide that the organization should move into a new area of programming without attending to the resources needed to operate that program. While securing resources is not just a board responsibility, it is one of its most important functions.

10. The board should help the organization promote a positive image with the public and with the other institutions with which the organization must transact business. The board is one of the organization's main links to the larger community. These links are very important in helping the organization establish legitimacy and find the resources it needs to operate.

11. The board should evaluate its performance and composition. "It should do everything in its power to keep its membership able, broadly representative, and active." It should assess its own processes and its ability to help the organization achieve its mission.

THE INFORMAL STRUCTURE: WHAT'S NOT ON THE ORGANIZATION CHART

A transitional shelter for homeless men has a formal policy of not serving drug addicts. To check on their clients, a random system of urine testing is carried out, and if the test is positive, the client is supposed to be asked to leave the shelter. A new social worker tries to follow this policy with one of his clients but is overruled by his supervisor. Why? Unknown to the new staff member, the social work staff has developed an informal system for rating drug-addicted clients, so that some are given second and third chances after positive test results. He did not yet know the system; it was not part of any official agency policy. Analyzing why this unofficial policy developed and how it operates would provide a lot of insight into the workings of this particular organization.

This example and our own experiences in organizations, if we think about them for a moment, remind us that the formal aspects of organizational life do not tell the whole story of how organizations function. A more complete understanding requires examination of the *informal structure* as well, that is, the associations among members of the organization that are not part of the formal organizational chart (Scott, 1973, pp. 105–106). The members of any organization form relationships with each other for many different reasons—physical proximity on or off the job, mutual interests, personal attractiveness, similar job responsibilities, shared values, social class, status, income or other social characteristics, or because of some special issue that arises. Informal associations may take on a small group life of their own with unique status and communication systems, leaders, membership requirements, and norms for behavior that associational members are expected to follow. If formal relationships provide a skeletal structure for an organization, informal relationships are the glue that holds an organization together and makes it work.

Informal associations can strongly influence organizational culture and behavior. From a management perspective, they can tie up an organization in open conflict over a new policy or program, or subtley sabotage it, or make it work well. Since such associations always develop, management would seem to do well to work with the informal organization. This involves "not threatening its existence unnecessarily, listening to opinions expressed for the group by the leader, allowing group participation in decision-making situations, and controlling the grapevine by prompt release of accurate information" (Scott, 1973, p. 107).

Nonmanagerial members of an organization also will benefit from an understanding of the informal structure. The formal structure tells you who has the authority to make decisions; but when that authority is remote, the informal structure suggests who communicates with whom, who has influence with the decision makers, and how to gain access to them. The informal system reveals alternative sources of power in the organization. In addition, the informal system often serves as the repository of organizational tradition and history, oral history actually, because much of organizational life is left unrecorded. Since formal and informal values and practices do not always agree, sometimes organizational members are faced with conflicting demands that are difficult to resolve. Better understanding of the informal system and some attention to organizational history may help an individual avoid these situations.

Communication is the lifeblood of any organization. Within the informal structure, communication tends to be oral rather than written. If the memo is the symbol of bureaucratic communication, the rumor could be considered the symbol of informal communication. "A rumor is an unconfirmed message transmitted along interpersonal channels" (Rogers & Agarwala-Rogers, 1976, p. 82). Since anyone can talk to someone else in the organization, rumors spread quickly through the grapevine winding under, over, and around official communication pathways. Rumors often have some truth to them, a characteristic that tends to make them credible (p. 82).

In studying organizations, the organizational chart gives us some idea of the formal structure of communications. But how do we uncover informal communication structures? Communication in organizations generally can be studied through network analysis, a *network* referring to "a number of individuals (or other units) who persistently interact with one another in accordance with established patterns" (Rogers & Agarwala-Rogers, 1976, p. 109). The basis for the interaction may be common work tasks, common attraction or liking for one another (sociometric dimension), or a topic of mutual interest. "Each network is a small pocket of people who communicate a great deal with each other, or a multitude of such pockets that are linked by communication flows" (p. 110). Informal analysis might involve observations of who spends time in whose offices, which groups eat together, regularly sit with each other at general meetings, and the like. Through careful observation it should be possible to identify cliques, opinion leaders, and individuals who seem to be able to bridge different formal and informal groupings (liaisons). Further systematic analysis is more complicated, involving the collection of sociometric and other kinds of data through surveys of the members of an organization or a subsystem therein.

"WORKING THE SYSTEM"

Formal decision-making processes in organizations are necessary for action on major policies, organizational goals, and large expenditures of resources. However, within the formal structure of goals and policies, staff members and managers must make daily operative decisions using their own discretion on a wide array of significant and insignificant but necessary matters. Some of these operative decisions fall solely within one's own jurisdiction; many also involve someone else's purview. A letter has to get out right away, but the secretary you share with several other workers has a backlog of work to finish; documents must be copied to complete an important client referral; a client in crisis needs immediate attention and an exception to policy to take care of it. How do you get around the rules or get the rules bent or priorities rearranged to make the organization work better for yourself and your clients? In other words, how do you "work the system" to accomplish what you need to get done on your own behalf or on behalf of a client? We will consider this question in the present section, recognizing that some of the requirements for working the system also apply to broader efforts to change agency policies and priorities that will be discussed in the next section.

In considering the question of working the system and/or changing agency policy, let us first note our assumption that the worker is an active organizational participant, not merely a passive recipient and implementer of orders from above. As a professional social worker, you are called on to exercise judgment in your practice in accordance with the values of the profession, not merely to act out of loyalty to the organization. Sometimes this means working the system. Sometimes it means trying to change agency policy and practices altogether. Second, the question of working the system implies that organizational flexibility is necessary and desirable in the face of the myriad uncertainties that every human service organization encounters.

Both working the system and changing the agency require the worker to understand formal processes for decision making, formal and informal sources of power, and formal and informal agency rules that guide decisions. This means the worker needs to understand how decision are made, who makes them, and who influences the decision-making process, since persons in authority seldom act alone without input from various subordinates or others connected with the organization (Patti & Resnick, 1972). In order to work the system, the worker will then have to decide whether a formal decision is necessary to pursue the particular course of action in mind, or whether the course of action merely involves some organizational tinkering (Pawlak, 1976) that can be handled informally or by exercising personal discretion. If you are new in the organization, if you have not yet established your own legitimacy and influence, or if the course of action you want to take violates a basic policy or organizational tradition, you may be wise not to act without first seeking a formal decision or the approval of an administrator.

Types and Sources of Organizational Power[1]

Expert power: the power of knowledge
Referrent power: charisma, the power to attract others or to inspire special loyalty and enthusiasm
Reward power: the capacity to provide inducements
Coercive power: the capacity to punish or apply sanctions
Legitimate power: the power to use the authority invested in one's position in the organization

---

Formal and informal organizational rules beg to be tinkered with. The reason is that "rules vary in specificity, in their inherent demand for compliance, in the manner in which compliance is monitored, and in their sanctions for a lack of compliance" (Pawlak, 1976, p. 377). Therefore workers can bend or get around the rules by exercising discretion in the case of an ambiguous or general rule or by the interpretation of the rule that they choose to make. For example, an agency rule for referring homeless persons for emergency health care can be interpreted strictly or liberally. In some cases, a sound knowledge of the rules may enable a worker to challenge an interpretation of a rule with another contradictory rule or to find the exceptions that can be used to justify one's decision. Workers also need to exercise caution in asking their superiors to interpret a rule, rather than using their own judgment, lest the authority render an unfavorable decision that must then be complied with.

In working the system and/or trying to change it, we can increase the success rate of our efforts as advocates and change agents by developing our own "social capital" or influence in the organization (Brager & Holloway, 1977). This involves two approaches: (1) establishing positive exchange relationships with other members of the organization and (2) establishing personal legitimacy. In the former case, by offering support, assistance, approval, and/or favors, the worker creates an obligation to reciprocate on the part of others, hence building potential political or social indebtedness. In a reciprocal relationship, the debt that you are owed may be used to obtain assistance, reorder priorities, or take care of a problem that you need to solve—for example, getting your letter typed right away by a busy secretary or getting some inside information. As these exchanges are made, of course, you may incur debts in turn.

In order to strengthen one's legitimacy in the organization, the worker seeks to establish competence and expertise to deal with a particular problem area. Thereby, the worker gains influence in decisions affecting the problematic area. Remember, power in an organization is a function of controlling resources others need or the ability to resolve uncertainties that the organization cannot tolerate. Competence in one area may help the worker to establish a reputation for competence in other areas, thereby gradually enlarging his or her sphere of influence. Building up one's social capital is a major practice task preceding a worker's attempts at organizational change.

CHANGING THE AGENCY FROM WITHIN

Sometimes agency rules, policies, or even entire programs need to be changed in order to prevent or correct an injustice or to improve agency programs and services. For a variety of reasons, these changes may not be initiated from the top down. Line workers and middle managers often have to act as agency change agents in their own interests or in the interests of their clients and for the good of the agency. For example, a new staff member in a community mental health cen-

ter found, in following up with clients, that many former mental patients were living in group homes near the agency that were little more than human warehouses. When she suggested to her supervisor that some group services might be extended to these homes, she was met with a negative response: "Our agency has no funds for outreach services of that sort." Should the matter end here? From our point of view, no. The worker, as an advocate for her clients, should try to find some way of getting them needed services, and her own agency is a reasonable place to begin. Can the worker do anything to help move the agency in a different direction? Potentially, yes. How might a worker go about acting as an agency change agent, whether in this instance or in the numerous other situations that arise?

Viewing the agency here as the client system, let us consider the change process for a moment. As in other forms of professional social work practice, change, as we are considering it here, is purposeful change. That is, it is change that results from a deliberate process of intervention by the worker. Using

| BOX 8.4 | RULES OF THUMB FOR WORKING THE SYSTEM |

1. Learn the decision-making process in the agency and for the particular course of action you are interested in.

2. Learn who has formal authority for making decisions, as well as who has informal influence with decision makers and in the organization or department generally.

3. Build your social capital in the organization by developing positive exchange relationships with other members of the organization and with organizational decision makers.

4. Build up your social capital by establishing your expertise and competence to manage a particular problem area.

5. Learn as much as you can about the rules that will be bent or avoided by your course of action.

6. Search for loopholes, contradictory rules, or cases where exceptions were made previously as support for your action.

7. Decide whether your course of action requires a formal decision or whether you are better off exercising personal discretion or handling the matter informally.

8. Use the informal system to get necessary information and compare notes.

9. If necessary, draw on your social capital to accomplish your objective.

a traditional problem-solving framework, then, the worker would first *study* the problem and learn as much as possible about the agency, with special attention to how power is exercised, who exercises it, and how decisions are made. Next, the worker would *assess* what needs to be done in order to bring about a change based on the information that has been generated, and a specific change goal or goals would be developed. Third, the worker would *develop intervention strategies*, or strategies for changing the client system, and implement them. And finally, the worker would *evaluate* progress or lack thereof toward achieving the goal(s) and make necessary adjustments.

While the internal agency change process mirrors other client change processes, the position of the worker in this process differs. Since the client system, in this case the agency, did not request assistance from the worker, and since the worker is an employee of the agency and therefore in a reduced position of power vis-à-vis the client system, the worker may be vulnerable to punitive sanctions. The risk of such sanctions depends on a variety of factors, such as the nature of the change that is being sought, the culture surrounding agency decision making, the change strategies that are selected, and the relative power of the change agent.

The worker's potential vulnerability suggests two practical steps. First, the worker, as an internal change agent, must *assess the risk of punitive sanctions* and take these into consideration in planning a change strategy. A new worker who is still on probation must obviously operate more cautiously than a worker with civil service longevity or long-standing influence in the agency. Strategies and tactics that are apt to provoke a strong response from the administration should be weighed carefully. Second, the worker should try not to act alone; that is, the change agent should really be a change agent sys-

tem. This means that the worker must utilize knowledge of the informal system to *identify allies* who share his or her concerns and think strategically about involving influentials in the change effort. Connections to sources of power outside of the agency may also help the decrease one's vulnerability to sanctions.

In order to operate as an internal agency change agent it is useful, even necessary, to have a mental image of the organization as a dynamic system. (If you don't see the system as changeable, you're not likely to try to make any changes.) Kurt Lewin's (1951) *field theory* helps to provide that image. Lewin looks at organizational systems as fields of countervailing forces. Imagine a system made up of different kinds of forces pushing, with varying degrees of intensity, both in the direction of system change (driving forces) and in the direction of resistance to change (restraining forces). Forces include variables ranging from external environmental factors, such as access to resources, to internal organizational factors, such as rivalries for influence or any other of the myriad variables of organizational life. When these forces are in balance, the status quo is maintained; but when the forces are out of balance, the resulting stress creates a period of disequilibrium until the forces are realigned and a new dynamic equilibrium is reestablished. With respect to a specific change, if driving forces are increased or restraining forces are reduced, or some combination thereto, then change will take place (Brager & Holloway, 1978).

After studying the problem (in this case, the problem is in the agency but the framework could be applied to an individual, a family, a group, or a community), collecting the necessary information about the agency mentioned previously, finding allies, and taking account of the workers' potential risk, a worker can systematically analyze the force field to develop a strategy for organizational

BOX 8.5

CHANGING AN AGENCY FROM WITHIN
Chainie Scott[2]

Quiet and attractive, Chainie Scott is an MSW with the foster care system in the District of Columbia. In 1990 she took part in a sustained effort within the agency to draw attention to huge caseloads and subsequent neglect by the system of children entitled by law to receive help from the city. First a foot soldier going to meetings and sharing her horror stories, Ms. Scott gradually became more involved and was eventually one of only two agency workers to testify against the system in the case the American Civil Liberties Union brought against the city. As a result of her leadership and as part of their change tactics, Ms. Scott was featured in several stories in the Washington Post *(see Chapter 12). The social action in which Ms. Scott participated resulted in mandates for new policies for the foster care system. (In 1995, the courts placed the system in receivership.)*

The whole process we went through, myself and other social workers, I don't think we put a title to it in any set category of social activism or anything. It was a reaction of professionals. The kind of thing you do for your clients all the time, we needed to do for ourselves. It was a natural progression of events. The situations we faced were so difficult: large volume of cases, inability to visit clients, lack of basic resources like cars, and telephones that didn't work.

I had gone to meetings, had voiced concerns, but I didn't spearhead the action that went on. I was a soldier rather than a leader, which was good because everyone needed to play their role. Working with the agency for about three years, I was very frustrated; 99 percent of the people were feeling frustration. I had reached the point where I decided it didn't matter—there wasn't anything they could do to me. It didn't seem fair, because I thought I deserved better than this as a professional. I have a graduate degree, and so I assume I should have a better working environment. Most importantly, it didn't seem fair to the children. It

seemed like such a lie. Here we are, an agency that is suppposed to protect and serve children, and we weren't doing either. To see the kind of suffering that happened. There was a lot of hesitancy on my part. I figured, "What the hell, what do I have to lose?" [Jokingly] Fire me! Fire me! . . .

Q: Can you describe the social action involved in confronting the injustices in the foster care system?

A: There was definitely a plan. There were social workers who spearheaded the whole thing. Everyone else made their contribution either by comments or by coming to meetings or helping draft memos that would be sent upstairs. There was fear, too. No one wanted to risk their job, or their reputation, or their career or whatever. We tried to go through the chain of command. All the memos went to the right people. All the meetings were checked with the right people. The newspaper. . . . Everything started gradually.

There were some studies going on by the Child Welfare League looking at foster homes. The climate for foster children in the District of Columbia was such that they were not being provided the services mandated by Public Law 2-22. How not to run a child welfare system! The American Civil Liberties Union became involved. From reviewing records, they focused on the cases of Leshawn A, a child in foster care, and seven other plaintiffs, all foster children. The ACLU also began to see the problems that the system was having.

It was, for me, a feeling like somebody had to do something. There was a meeting with an ACLU attorney. The word was out that this person from the ACLU needed to talk with line-level social workers to see what's going on. I went to the meeting. I listened. There were a couple of people there, and they were saying things that didn't hit home. They weren't getting at the meat of it. So, I just started talking.

BOX 8.5 (Continued)

I said, "Wait a second, what about this? What about that?" They, I don't know, I guess they were impressed. They kind of said, "Oh, yeah, she'd be good. Get her." [Laughing]

They asked if I wanted to do it. I said no at first. Then after some thought, I said, "Okay, I'll do it."

As a result, the ACLU decided it was appropriate to bring suit against the District of Columbia on behalf of Leshawn A and seven other foster care children. The suit talked about the lack of continuity of care for the children, children remaining in homes that were inappropriate, children who didn't have appropriate permanency plans. The suit named all the defendants: the mayor, a director of human services, the commissioner, the administrator, and the family services division chief. We had to go to court.

It was scary! There was only two of us who gave testimony in Federal Court, Judge Hogan's courtroom. It was just matter-of-fact questions, but it was someone who was on the front line answering those questions with answers that you wouldn't get from the administration. The order came down from Judge Hogan that our child welfare system is unconstitutional to the children. After the Leshawn hearing ended and the ruling came down, we did interviews for the radio. That was still a part of the process.

I'm not sure what the process is going to be in the post-Leshawn days. I don't know how active I'll be. I'll be there, but I may not be in the front. We said early on we should be part of the remedy for change. It never happened. I read through the plan, and it's a good plan. But I think it could have had a different tilt to it had line-level social workers been involved. There's this callousness beyond the line-level social worker. Maybe as you move up and become more of the policy part of it, you're so far removed you don't feel it—because you don't see it. That's why we're having so many problems now with the plan.

That's been real difficult. Here we are now, 2 years later, and people are still leaving. The big thing our agency keeps talking about now is, we have hired 90 new social workers. I say you need to ask how many have left and why did they leave? I can bet you, they left for the same reasons that came out at the court hearing—lack of cars, lack of support, lack of resources, lack of direction, too many cases, overwhelmed. They're leaving for the precise reasons that folks like myself and all the others have been complaining about and crying and screaming and saying, "Hey, help us!" Nothing has changed for it! How could that possibly be?

Now that the lawsuit has been won and reforms are slowly underway, Ms. Scott has had time to reflect on the process and the outcome.

Professionally I say the court win was good. Personally, I say I don't think it really made a difference. Professionally it was good because it was something you have to do as a social worker. You have to be the one that says, "Oh, wait a second, this is wrong, this is not right, we're not doing this right." You have to not allow yourself to get brainwashed by your system, whatever that system is—private or government. If it's not right, then you have to say something or do something to make it different. Personally, I don't think it made a big difference because I just don't think our administration has the stomach for it, the courage, or the commitment to do it. They talk good talk, but they're not walking the walk.

When I started in 1987, we were getting cases on our unit, mommy on crack, mommy selling food stamps, mommy leaving child alone, leaving child with unwilling caretaker, child left alone, electricity about to be cut off, mother facing eviction. Every single case. Now somewhere along that line, somebody in a position of policy, of administration, should have said, "Now what kind of cases are we getting? What's going on here? Is there a trend going on out there?" There was no

BOX 8.5	(Continued)

forecasting, no planning, no sense of how the population changes or what kinds of things we are seeing. It didn't have to get as bad as it was. What could have qualified as social action is if one of the administrators had said, "Wait a second. We have a problem here. Let's stop this." If commitment was there, why are we still where we are? I don't want to hear that it takes a while to turn the system around. I know it takes a while to turn the system around. How did it get this way? Why didn't someone do something, rather than taking the posture of business as usual?

I feel real changed by what happened in that I'm not afraid. I was afraid of them. It was like treading on water. But now, I think I have a better sense of the process. When you speak out, and if you have the commitment, you have to figure, "What can they do?" If they do something, what difference does it make so long as the change that you want comes about?

Inside themselves, social activists have to know where their commitment lies. They need to know what that battle is for them; if they have the resolve to do it; if they end up becoming a sacrificial lamb, whether that's okay with them. This is something you have to go through and not feel bitter about in the end. In the classroom you have to learn what it is to organize, how to communicate what those concerns are that you're dealing with

and how you want to see those issues resolved. You certainly have to have a frame of reference. You need to understand why people didn't want to change. You bring all your knowledge together. In the process of change, you have to continue to be part of the remedy. You just can't bring it on. You have to be there to help devise the rules.

[Laughing] It was a fun process. You get all psyched up! "Yes, let's go! Oh, yeah, that's what you want to do? Grrr!" It's very exciting! I have no regrets about anything I did. As a matter of fact, I feel proud of myself. I have a sense of principle. I thought testifying, etc., was the right thing to do. Now, I want to leave district government. I can make a much more positive impact outside of a system that's restrictive and bureaucratic and censorized. So, while I'm still feeling some of those frustrations that led to wanting to change the foster care system, I made my mark when it was appropriate for me to make my mark. I don't want to continue being on the front line anymore. I have enough experience and ammunition and that thing that gets in you when you've been through a lot—that "we can't let this happen again because I've lived through it." It would be a natural progression to do advocacy for a group. I always find myself looking at this big picture. I see myself staying in social action in some capacity or another.

---

change. The material that follows provides a practical set of steps for conducting a *force field analysis* leading to a potential organizational change strategy. Follow these steps, using the accompanying Force Field Analysis Inventory. We have partially completed the inventory using the example of the deinstitutionalized mental patients warehoused in group homes. See if you can complete it or try your own situation.

Changing the agency from within, as we

have presented it here, views the organization as a target of change (a target system). This perspective does not assume cooperation from management at the outset, although it by no means eliminates that possibility. In fact, to the extent that collaborative strategies, such as joint planning sessions, can be used to help change the organization, these are almost always preferable to conflict-oriented strategies. They are most appropriate in situations where the action

FORCE FIELD ANALYSIS STEPS*

Step 1

Describe the problem or need succinctly. This is the situation you want to change. Record this on the Force Field Inventory.

Step 2

Specify the goal or objective to be reached. In doing this, you begin to break the problem down into smaller parts. Be as operationally specific as possible. Your goal or objective should be stated so that it can be measured. Record your goal on the Force Field Inventory.

Step 3

Identify all the restraining forces—those that contribute to the problem or prevent goal achievement. Record these forces on the Force Field Inventory.

Step 4

Identify all the main driving forces—those that currently or potentially support the change goal. Record these forces on the Force Field Inventory.

Step 5

Estimate the amenability to change of each force. Designate each as H (high), L (low), or U (uncer-

tain). Place the appropriate letter in the column to the left of the restraining forces and to the right of the driving forces.

Step 6

Identify the critical actors and facilitators whom you feel will be best able to influence the forces you have identified as amenable to change. Record these names on the Force Field Inventory.

Step 7

List the driving and restraining forces that are amenable to change and identify the actors who can influence these forces. Record them on the Force Field Inventory.

Step 8

Select two or more restraining forces from your diagram and outline a strategy for reducing their potency. Record your plan on your Force Field Inventory.

Step 9

Select two or more driving forces from your diagram and outline a strategy for increasing their potency. Record your plan on your Force Field Inventory.

system and the target system have good communication, and where they basically agree that a change needs to be made and that the direction of the proposed change is desirable (Brager, Specht, & Torczyner, 1987).

When the change agent is an outside consultant brought into the agency by management to help solve an agency problem or to create a particular change, such as more

receptivity to an emerging client population, the organization in this context can be viewed as a client system. The agency, in effect, is the management consultant's client. Many management consultants use *organization development (OD)* strategies, which are always "cooperative, collaborative, and consensus building in nature" (Resnick & Menefee, 1993, p. 440), to achieve their aims.

FORCE FIELD ANALYSIS INVENTORY*

Definition of Terms

Critical Actors: These are the individuals or groups who have the power to make a change. Their support or approval is necessary in order for your goal to be achieved.

Facilitators: These persons are of two types: (1) those whose approval must be obtained before the problem can be brought to the attention of the critical actor(s) and (2) those whose approval, disapproval, or neutrality may have a decisive impact on the critical actor(s).

Driving Forces: Forces that, when increased, change behavior in a desired or planned manner.

Restraining Forces: Forces that, when increased or stay the same, reinforce the status quo or support a condition that is the antithesis of the change goal.

Amenability to Change or Influence: Refers to the potential of a force to be modified, for example, the ability to increase a driving force or decrease a restraining force.

Problem Situation or Need	Goal or Objective
Group services needed for former mental patients in group homes	Develop a socialization group by Jan. 30, 19xx, for residents of the Green Street group home

Rate	Restraining Forces	Driving Forces	Rate
H, L, U	(against change)	(for change)	H, L, U
L	tight budget	sw intern available	H
L	prof'l tunnel vision	new progr. director	H
L	high caseloads	law re least restraining	
		environment	U
U	new to agency	media story on ware-	
		housing mental patients.	H

Critical Actors and Facilitators

1. program director CA

2. field work coordinator CA

3. supervisor F

4.

5.

Forces Amenable to Change and Critical/Facilitator Individuals

1.

2.

3.

4.

Change Strategies

Strategy to reduce restraining forces

Strategy to increase driving forces

*Force Field Analysis Steps and Force Field Analysis Inventory format, with minor modifications, from Lauffer (1982) and Salus, Ragan, and DePanfilis (1986). See also Brager and Holloway (1978).

The interventions that are part of this discipline include such methods as "team building, intergroup activities, survey feedback, education and training, technostructural activities, process consultation, grid organization development, third-party peacemaking, coaching and counseling, life and career planning, planning and goal setting, and strategic management" (Resnick & Menefee, 1993, p. 439). Staff members who are acting as change agents and who have had some organization development training may also use OD methods of intervention when collaborative strategies are appropriate.

When the action system and the target system agree that a problem exists but disagree strongly on what should be done about it, change agents may have to use campaign tactics to influence the organization (Warren, 1969). "Campaign tactics include political maneuvering, bargaining and negotiation, and mild coercion" (Brager et al., 1987, p. 353). Political maneuvering is involved in all sorts of internal (and external) change efforts. It takes many forms,

from persuading uninvolved agency or outside influentials to join the change effort to trading "bargaining chips." However, once a campaign moves to formulating demands as the basis for bargaining and negotiation, this approach, as well as more disruptive, conflict-oriented strategies and tactics, require a well-organized action system, intensive, careful planning, and a strong commitment to the end purpose. It goes without say that such strategies are usually time-consuming and are more than likely to provoke angry, hostile responses from management. For these and other reasons, staff rebellions occur relatively infrequently, though they may be necessary when important values are at stake. On the other hand, successful bargaining and negotiation commonly does take place when a staff is unionized. Social workers have a long history of participation in the union movement, past and present (Alexander, 1987; Wenocur & Reisch, 1989), so that unionization still remains as a viable option for disgruntled social workers.

Notes

1. Derived from J. R. P. French and B. H. Raven, "The Bases of Social Power", in D. Cartwright and A. Zander (Eds.), *Group Dynamics*. Evanston, IL: Row, Peterson, 1960.

2. Chainie Scott was interviewed on November 6, 1992, by Brenda Kunkel, a graduate student at the University of Maryland School of Social Work for "Challenging: Interviews with Advocates and Activists," a project directed by Dr. Patricia Powers.

References

Alexander, L. B. (1987). Unions: social work. *Encyclopedia of social work* (Vol. 2, 18th ed., pp. 793–798). Silver Spring, MD: National Association of Social Workers.

Brager, G., & Holloway, S. (1977). A process model for changing organizations from within. *Administration in Social Work*, 1(4), 349–358.

Brager, G., & Holloway, S. (1978). *Changing hu-*

man service organizations: Politics and practice. New York: Free Press.

Brager, G., Specht, H., & Torczyner, J. L. (1987). *Community organizing* (3rd ed.). New York: Columbia University Press.

Bryson, J. M. (1989). *Strategic planning for public and nonprofit organizations.* San Francisco: Jossey-Bass.

Challenging. (1994). Interviews with advocates and activists. University of Maryland at Baltimore, School of Social Work. Monograph, ed. by P. Powers.

Chesapeake Foundation for Human Development, Inc. (1993). *Annual Report.* Baltimore, MD 21225.

Crozier, M. (1964). *The bureaucratic phenomenon.* Chicago: University of Chicago Press.

Cyert, R. M., & March, J. G. (1963). *A behavioral theory of the firm.* Englewood Cliffs, NJ: Prentice-Hall.

The Door. (1992). *Annual Report.* Baltimore, MD 21231.

Dressel, P. L. (1992). Patriarchy and social welfare work. In Y. Hasenfeld (Ed.), *Human services as complex organizations* (pp. 205–233). Newbury Park, CA: Sage.

Fisher, C. D., Schoenfeldt, L. F., & Shaw, J. B. (1990). *Human resource management.* Boston: Houghton Mifflin.

Gibelman, M., & Schervish, P. H. (1993). *Who we are: The social work labor force as reflected in NASW membership.* Washington, DC: National Association of Social Workers.

Greenley, J. R., & Kirk, S. A. (1973). Organizational characteristics of agencies and the distribution of services to applicants. *Journal of Health and Social Behavior, 14,* 70–79.

Hasenfeld, Y. (1983). *Human service organizations.* Englewood Cliffs, NJ: Prentice-Hall.

Hasenfeld, Y. (Ed.). (1992a). *Human services as complex organizations.* Newbury Park, CA: Sage.

Hasenfeld, Y. (1992b). The nature of human service organizations. In Y. Hasenfeld (Ed.), *Human services as complex organizations* (pp. 3–23). Newbury Park, CA: Sage.

Houle, C. O. (1989). *Governing boards: Their nature and nurture.* San Francisco: Jossey-Bass.

Kramer, R. M. (1965). Ideology, status, and power in board–executive relationships. *Social Work, 10,* 108–114.

Larson, M. S. (1977). *The rise of professionalism.* Berkeley: University of California Press.

Lauffer, A. (1982). May the force be with you: Using force field analysis. In A. Lauffer, *Assessment tools for practitioners, managers, and trainers.* Beverly Hills, CA: Sage.

Lewin, K. (1951). *Field theory in social science.* New York: Harper & Row.

Mathiasen, K. (1990). *Board passages: Three key stages in a nonprofit board's life cycle.* Governance Series Paper. Washington, DC: National Center for Nonprofit Boards.

Menefee, D. T., & Thompson, J. J. 1994). Identifying and comparing competencies for social work management: A practice driven approach. *Administration in Social Work, 18*(3), 1–25.

Patti, R. J., & Resnick, H. (1972). Changing the agency from within. *Social Work, 17*(4), 48–57.

Pawlak, E. J. (1976). Organizational tinkering. *Social Work, 21*(5), 376–380.

Perrow, C. (1961). The analysis of goals in complex organizations. *American Sociological Review, 26,* 854–866.

Resnick, H., & Menefee, D. (1993). A comparative analysis of organization development and social work, with suggestions for what organization development can do for social work. *Journal of Applied Behavioral Science, 29*(4), 432–445.

Rogers, E. M., & Agarwala-Rogers, R. (1976). *Communication in organizations.* New York: Free Press.

Salamon, L. M. (1992). *America's nonprofit sector: A primer.* New York: Foundation Center.

Salamon, L. M., Altshuler, D. M., & Myllyluoma, J. (1990). *More than just charity: The Baltimore area nonprofit sector in a time of change.* Baltimore: Johns Hopkins University, Institute for Policy Studies.

Salus, M., Ragan, C., & DePanfilis, D. (1986). *Supervision in child protective services.* New York: Child Protective Services Training Academy.

Scott, W. G. (1973). Organization theory: An overview and appraisal. In F. Baker (Ed.), *Organizational systems: General systems approaches to complex organizations* (pp. 99–119). Homewood, IL: Richard D. Irwin.

Sherman, W. R., & Wenocur, S. (1983). Empowering public welfare workers through mutual support. *Social Work, 28*(5), 375–379.

Strauss, A., Schatzman, L., Ehrlich, D., & Bucher, R. (1963). The hospital and its negotiated order. In E. Freidson (Ed.), *The hospital in modern society* (pp. 147–169). Glencoe, IL: Free Press.

Thompson, J. D. (1967). *Organizations in action.* New York: McGraw-Hill.

Warren, R. L. (1969). Types of purposive social change at the community level. In R. M. Kramer & H. Specht (Eds.), *Readings in community organization practice* (pp. 205–222). Englewood Cliffs, NJ: Prentice-Hall.

Webber, R. A. (1979). *Managing organizations.* Homewood, IL; Richard D. Irwin.

Wenocur, S., & Reisch, M. (1989). *From charity to enterprise: The development of American social work in a market economy.* Urbana: University of Illinois Press.

chapter
9

Using Work Groups: Committees, Teams, and Boards

Sometimes it seems that all social workers ever do is go to meetings! There are staff meetings to clarify agency policies, team meetings to coordinate treatment plans, interagency meetings to work out service agreements, board committee meetings to plan a fund-raising event, NASW committee meetings to do conference planning. None of these meetings involve direct group work with clients—for example, running a treatment group for sexually abused girls, or a parenting group for new mothers, or a socialization group for senior citizens. Yet all of these meetings are necessary for direct service work to go forward. All of these meetings involve work with task groups of some kind—committees, task forces, boards, teams, coalitions, planning bodies, and the like. Ephross and Vassil (1988) identify task groups as working groups

> that do not aim at changing the attitudes or behaviors of their members, but rather form to accomplish some purpose, produce a prod-

uct such as a plan or budget, develop policies, or participate in decision-making processes. It is the focus on producing or influencing something external to the group itself that defines the essence of a working group. (p. 1)

Effective work with task groups, an important aspect of all social work practice is essential for community practice because the task group is one of the main vehicles through which community practice is carried out. Organizing groups and committees and participating as chair, member, or facilitator of these bodies are the means by which social advocacy, interagency and interprofessional planning and coordination, and community development are accomplished. Although we often participate as members of a task group, in this chapter the role of the social worker will be conceived predominantly as leader, chair, or staff member.

Like other parts of professional social work, social work practice with task groups involves a deliberate process of intervention to accomplish a goal. Just as direct service workers interact purposefully during interviews with their clients, social workers use themselves consciously and deliberately in meetings to further the aims of the task group. *No social worker participating in a task group, whether as staff, leader, or regular member, should approach a meeting unprepared.* The task group, in that sense, almost becomes the client system for the social worker. The "almost" is meant to convey the caution that the members of a task group usually participate as citizens, and sometimes as colleagues, who have not sought the social worker's help with an interpersonal or intrapsychic problem. Even when the task group is composed of agency clients, the aim of the group, as a working group, is external, not internal.

On the other hand, as with a client system, the worker does develop a contractual relationship with the group. Sometimes the contract is explicit: the agency board hires a social worker to coordinate its fund-raising efforts or the agency staff hires a consultant to help them improve their skill in serving a population with special needs. A written job description may form the basis for a working contract, and direct negotiation about roles and boundaries will usually take place before any substantive work begins. Frequently the contract is implicit, as with the school social worker who organizes a parents group to develop a mentoring program. Here the worker's and members' understanding of their respective roles and responsibilities will evolve out of their shared interaction and out of the worker's explanations or interpretations of the roles of the different parties in the group.

GROUP DEVELOPMENT AND THE ROLE OF THE SOCIAL WORKER

Task and Process

Professional practice with task groups requires good listening skills and keen ob-

servation of behavior. The worker is truly a participant-observer, but what should the worker attend to? The answer is that all group interactions have a *task* and a *process* dimension, and *task groups of all kinds must attend to both in order to succeed.*

The *task dimension* of the group refers to the subject or content of the group's interactions. For example, when parent volunteers begin to meet with a school social worker to plan a mentoring program for their children's school, the different ideas they discuss about mentoring programs and how they should be established represent the task dimension of that interaction. In the course of the meetings, the worker will listen to alternative proposals and help the group to assess clarity, see connections between ideas, consider their merits, determine what information may still be needed, and make decisions that will eventually lead to agreement on a plan and its implementation.

The *process dimension* of group interaction deals with the nature and dynamics of the relationships that develop in the group. In the words of Philip Hanson, (1972):

> process is concerned with what is happening between and to group members while the group is working. Group process, or dynamics, deals with such items as morale, feeling tone, atmosphere, influence, participation, styles of influence, leadership struggles, conflict, competition, cooperation, etc. (p. 21)

When the members of the mentoring group become angry at Mrs. Smith, who monopolizes the meetings, and arguments begin to break out and attendance begins to wane, these are manifestations of the process dimension of the group. In observing a group, the items that Hanson mentions above suggest questions for a worker to think about, such as: What signs of feeling do I see in the group members? How do the members feel about each other? Are there any cliques that seem to be forming? What's the energy level of the group? Are all the members getting a chance to participate? How does the group make decisions? In the course of the meetings, the worker will try to facilitate interaction that strengthens the members' bonds to each other and their commitment to the group as a whole. The worker, of course, is also mindful of keeping the group on task.

Having made a distinction between the task and process dimensions of group interaction, it is important to note that many interactions contain elements of both. In the above example, where Mrs. Smith arouses the ire of the other group members, the arguments that take place may well be about the proposals someone has offered or the procedures for reaching a decision. So, both content and process issues emerge at the same time. Or suppose that a member asks the group to review how a particular decision was made, that is, to consider the process that the group went through. For analytical purposes, we can generally assign interactions around issues of communication to the process dimension and interactions around issues of goal implementation to the task dimension. The category that one assigns interaction to, however, is less important than sensitivity to both dimensions of group life in dealing with a group.

When Is a Group a Group? Stages of Group Development

People who meet for the first time in order to do some work together, whether as a committee or a team or planning body, will vary greatly in the amount of energy they want to invest in the task and in their commitment to working with other people to do it. Yet they have come together because the task is either too complex or too difficult to do alone; it will take a group to do it. This tension between *differentiation* (going it alone, doing it my own way) and *integration* (col-

laborating with others, giving up some of my autonomy) captures the essence of the struggle involved in forming a group (Heap, 1977). *Until that collection of autonomous individuals begins to feel some allegiance to the collectivity and finds some way to work together on a common goal, a group has not yet fully formed.* Clearly, group formation is a process that takes place over time, and according to numerous students of group life over the past 35 years, it is also a process that takes place in stages.[1]

Stage theories of group development exhibit a remarkable degree of similarity despite variations in the number and names of the stages. They are useful for at least two reasons. First, they reinforce the simple but important idea of *development over time*, that is, that one should not expect groups in the early stages of development to be as efficient or effective as groups that have had the time to mature.

Second, they indicate the kinds of behaviors and accomplishments that one might expect at different points in the course of group formation. This knowledge gives workers a frame of reference for their interventions in the group and helps them to set realistic objectives for group meetings.

A few cautions are in order before we consider the stages of group development in more detail. First, the stages of group development, presented discretely in theory, cannot be neatly separated from each other in the real world. One phase runs into another; groups take two steps forward and one step backward; and so on. Nor can we define an exact length of time for a given phase. We cannot say, for example, that it takes a group three meetings or 3 hours to get through the formative stage. Nor does the notion of stages make group life as predictable as it might seem. In the same way that each of us is unique even though we all pass through similar stages of growth and development, groups are unique. The dynamics of any group are influenced by many different variables—size, purpose, sponsorship, context, composition, nature of the task (complexity, emotionality, etc.), time frame, and more. Therefore, as Ephross and Vassil (1988) point out, practitioners working with any group should always ask themselves three questions:

1. What do I know about groups in general that leads me to expect certain things to happen in this particular group?
2. What do I know about groups of this type that leads me to expect certain things about this particular group?
3. What do I know about this particular group that leads me to hold particular expectancies for this group? (p. 60)

These questions indicate that behavior in the group is not simply a function of the group's stage of development.

With these cautions in mind, we can now review the stages of group development. Tuckman (1965) synthesized a great deal of research on small groups into a developmental model that links group task (instrumental) and process (socioemotional) dimensions with stages of development. His easy-to-remember stages are *forming, storming, norming,* and *performing.* He later added a fifth stage, *adjournment* (Tuckman & Jensen, 1977), which we prefer to call *terminating.* Table 9.1 presents a comparison of the main features of each stage, the characteristic behaviors one might expect along the task and process dimensions, and the role of the worker. We have augmented Tuckman's ideas with information from other models and practice experience.

1. *Forming:* In this stage, the prospective members of the group are trying to determine what the group is all about. They are trying to get oriented. They are wondering what the group will be like, what will be expected of them, whether they will be accepted, and whether or not to make a commitment. They are rather dependent on the leader, organizer, or chair to provide an orientation. They will ask orienting questions and sometimes exhibit "testing" behaviors and ambivalence about commitment, as in an unwillingness to volunteer for tasks, joking around, and irregular attendance. In this formative phase, the worker, either directly if there is no chairperson or working through the chairperson if there is one, helps to establish the group climate (accepting, businesslike, formal, informal, open, etc.). He or she also helps the group to clarify its goals, develop some ground rules for interaction, and work through issues of dependency by accepting responsibility for the group's functioning, all of which is part of the development of a working contract.

2. *Storming:* As the group members begin to invest their emotions and energy in the group, they initiate a stage of development often characterized by conflict and struggles for power and control. The newness of the group has worn off. Emotions may run high; disagreements over substance and procedure arise. Although conflicts may be difficult to manage, the fact that they are going on indicates that a group is beginning to form. The members care enough about the group to fight over it. This is a crucial period in the life of the group. The group members are moving toward some resolution of the tension between differentiation and integration, between having one's way and giving in to the requirements of the group. The worker or leader must help the group to resolve conflicts in a constructive manner and to foster a democratic structure for decision making. Alternatively, the group is at risk of developing an authoritarian structure or of falling apart.

3. *Norming:* Having found a workable resolution to the conflicts created in the previous stage, the group begins to gel. A

TABLE 9.1 Stages of Group Development

Stage of Development	Main Features	Task Dimension	Process Dimension	Role of Worker
Forming	Ambivalence about commitment; disbandment	Orientation to task and context; search for ground	Testing behaviors; irregularity in performance due to ambivalence about commitment	Orienting members; contracting; setting goals and rules, working through dependency issues
Storming	Conflict; struggles for power; development of structure	Disagreements with content or substance Procedural conflicts	Heightened emotions; hostility; struggles for control; resistance to work	Constructive conflict resolution; foster democratic participation and structure
Norming	Development of group cohesion; harmony	Open exchange of opinions	Acceptance of the members and their idiosyncracies; development of a "we" feeling, unity	Keep group focused on task; discourage age oversocializing;
Performing	Structure is an instrument for task accomplishment	Task completion; emergence of solutions	Functional role relatedness; interpersonal issues temporarily set aside	Structure work to lead to outcomes; evaluate efforts celebrate success; develop new leadership
Terminating	Regression to earlier patterns of behavior	Disagreements over decisions	Reappearance of emotionality; resistance to completion of work; other regressive behaviors	Discuss winding down of group; plan closing events; orient members toward a future beyond the group

sense of cohesion emerges, characterized by greater acceptance of the unique traits of each member and a willingness to express one's views openly. The members feel comfortable with each other and begin to get down to doing the work necessary to accomplish the group's goals. The worker's role is to help the group avoid too much socializing and to keep the group on task.

4. *Performing:* In this stage, the interpersonal structure that has developed becomes the functional instrument for dealing with task activities. Roles become flexible and functional, and group energy is channeled into task completion. Structural issues have been resolved (e.g., who plays what role, rules for decision making), so that the structure can now support task performance. The group can make decisions efficiently. This is a period characterized by the emergence of solutions. The worker helps to structure the work of the group in order to lead to outcomes, and helps the group to evaluate and celebrate its accomplishments. The worker may also help new leadership to emerge or, if the group's mission has been completed, to prepare for adjournment.

5. *Terminating:* As the group begins to recognize that its work is reaching a conclusion, members often feel ambivalent about ending—pleased about accomplishments, sad about ending relationships and coming to a conclusion. During this period, groups often express their ambivalence by regressing to earlier forms of nonconstructive behavior and patterns of relating. Meetings may be missed; emotions may run high again; old conflicts may break out. The worker needs to help the group reach a successful conclusion, usually by encouraging the members to talk openly about the ending and express their feelings; by planning for group-appropriate closing rituals or events such as parties, testimonial dinners, and the like; and by focusing on future plans and life beyond the group.

EFFECTIVE MEETINGS

How many times have you gone to a meeting and left with the feeling that it was a waste of time? Nothing was accomplished. When this happens, frequently it is because whoever was responsible for running the meeting did not think through the specific decisions to be made at the meeting or could not facilitate the decision-making process effectively. *Task group meetings all share a common purpose: making decisions or completing a task.* Whatever the larger purpose of the group, when a task group holds a meeting, it does so in order to make decisions that will help the group move toward achievement of its goals. The fact that meetings may also provide opportunities for socialization, networking, and education does not alter their decision-making function. Therefore effective meetings require both planning and chairperson skills. (Members of a group who are not chairing a meeting also have responsibility for advance planning and for helping a meeting accomplish its tasks by their interventions, both verbal and nonverbal.) Let us look at the planning aspect first.

Meeting Planning: "Footwork and Headwork"

The main point to realize about effective meetings is that *a meeting is the culmination of a prior planning process* (Tropman, 1980). The planning process begins before the first meeting and occurs thereafter with the follow-up work after the meeting, thereby beginning the premeeting planning process for the next meeting. When the meeting takes place, enough attention should have been paid to administrative chores and decision-making requirements ahead of time so that effective decisions can result. Since there are many different kinds of task groups (e.g., staff groups, coalitions, treatment planning teams, boards), and since meetings range in their degree of formality, premeeting planning activities will vary as well, but in all cases premeeting planning should go on. In advance of a meeting, the chair (and the staff member for the group, if assigned) should have thought about the following:

1. the dynamics of the group in light of its development;
2. task and process objectives;
3. decisions that need to be made at the meeting;
4. information the group must have in order to make decisions;
5. the various roles of the participants and how the work of the group might be carried out;
6. the actual meeting agenda.

In formalized groups, such as a social service agency team meeting or a board meeting, or a neighborhood association community meeting, or a working coalition strategy session, typically the chair, and possibly some other members, plan the agenda and consider the decision-making process for the meeting far enough in advance so that the members can get the agenda and meeting materials early enough to review them before the meeting takes place. If the group has a staff member assigned, such as with a board of directors or with a community group that a social worker is forming (e.g., to do a neighborhood needs assessment), then the worker and the chair and/or other members would meet and plan in advance of the meeting. If a group is meeting monthly, the members should receive the agenda and materials at least a week in advance of the meeting. Every item on a meeting agenda will not necessarily lead to a decision, as for example, with progress reports of a committee or subcommittee or an informational briefing by an expert in a particular substantive area. Getting member input and feedback about the business of the group and its process is important. Also, some agenda items may take more than one meeting to complete. However, for every task group meeting that is scheduled, the worker and chair (and members too) should be asking themselves what decisions should be made at the meeting that will advance the purpose of the group. The agenda should reflect these prospective decision items.

In planning the agenda, the worker and chair will also want to consider how various agenda items will be disposed of during the meeting in light of the group's needs and dynamics. For example, to foster group participation, preplanning may include asking particular members to take responsibility for reporting on or handling an agenda item. If members have been doing work in preparation for a meeting, they must be given the opportunity to report back. Otherwise you will discourage future voluntary action. Many prospective agenda items will emerge during a meeting with insufficient information for the group to make a decision. Usually these items need to be assigned to an existing committee for work outside the meeting, leading to recommendations for group action in the future. Of course, sometimes the best-laid meeting plans may be interrupted by a critical but unplanned issue that suddenly arises in a meeting. In this situation, modifying the agenda may be a necessary and appropriate course of action. However, these issues also will often have to be assigned to an existing or newly formed committee in order to bring them to resolution at a later meeting.

The worker and chair must also pay attention to the process or socioemotional dimension of the group in meeting planning. Members who make an emotional investment in a group seldom go through the group experience without being aroused by the way a decision is handled, or the way some members behave, or the lack of opportunity to present their own points of view. For example, observations of unexpressed or expressed anger may be cues for follow-up phone contact to help members manage their feelings and/or find a way to express them constructively at the next meeting. Other pre-meeting contacts may be important for any number of reasons, such as to encourage participation, to bridge communication gaps, to lend support, or to try to understand a member's reactions. In addition, groups have the wonderful capacity to be able to reflect on their own process. If emotions are running high, a chair may need to plan for some time in a meeting for the group to look at its process and take corrective action.

Finally, administrative chores that need to be taken care of before a meeting include these:

1. preparing meeting minutes;
2. getting out meeting notices;
3. reproducing agendas and other informational materials and getting them to members in advance of the meeting;
4. arranging for and setting up meeting space; and
5. arranging for refreshments.

Usually staff handles these chores, as well as helping the chair prepare for the meeting. Obviously a leader, chair, or member will need to take care of these details if there is no staff. Inattention to these details can throw any meeting off course.

The Meeting Itself

Members usually come to meetings of a working group to do business during some specified time period, usually between 1 and 2 hours. Effectiveness tends to diminish if the meetings last longer than 2 hours. Although there is no guarantee that members will come to a meeting properly prepared, *if* the agenda and other materials have reached them in advance and *if* the meeting stays on track so that the agenda is dealt with in the allotted time and decision are made, the probability for meeting effectiveness increases (Tropman, 1980). The "ifs" are important.

Staying on track means beginning and ending a meeting on time and covering the items on the agenda. If meetings begin late, members will start to arrive late. Soon the time for conducting the group's business will be reduced, and meetings will begin to run over the agreed-on time of closing. Inevitably some members will arrive late, so it is usually a good idea to begin the meeting with the lighter part of the agenda, such as approving minutes and making announcements. Save roughly the middle third of the meeting for the weightiest agenda items, when the members' attention is most focused and everybody is ready to get down to business. The final portion of the meeting can then be more relaxed. This is a good time to generate new agenda items, talk about the process and progress of the group, pull together the decisions that have been made, and remind the group of the next meeting date (Tropman, 1980).

The structure for decision making that task groups adopt varies on a continuum from formal to informal. Many groups fall somewhere in between. At the formal end of the continuum, the group adopt formal rules and procedures for reaching decisions based on a vote. Usually this process is guided by *parliamentary procedure*, a fair and orderly process for reaching decisions that follows *Roberts' Rules of Order*. Developed over a hundred years ago, *Roberts' Rules* is used extensively by chairpersons to preside over meetings. Revised editions are available in any bookstore or library, and short versions are published regularly. (For a useful shortened version, see Zastrow (1985, chapter 12). Any social worker regularly involved in task group work should become familiar with the basics of parliamentary procedure.

A formal structure for decision making can be very useful when the group is too large for easy decision making (e.g., a meeting with 25 or more community members compared to a committee of 8–10 people). The bigger the group, the more important the procedures for reaching decisions. Formal decision rules, such as those of parliamentary procedure, have the advantages of preventing a minority from controlling the group and ensuring that group decisions have been clearly ratified. On the disadvantage side, discussions may easily become bogged down in rules and in competitive parliamentary strategizing to gain advantage; a minority group can be abused; and the procedures can be handled so rigidly and mechanically that the process dimension of group life is totally ignored.

An informal decision-making structure, at the other end of the continuum, usually involves a consensus-seeking process, which can but often does not culminate in a vote. Consensus-seeking behavior tends to emphasize careful listening, the broad expression of different viewpoints, constructive conflict over ideas, and a search for creative solutions that have wide member input and approval. It places a premium on process. An informal structure tends to be most useful when the group is fairly small, when member trust is high, when creative problem solving is needed, and when time for reaching decisions is not a problem. On the disadvan-

tage side, consensus seeking can be a time-consuming, overly complicated, frustrating process in which a minority can potentially control the group.

As we stated earlier, many task groups fall somewhere along the formality–informality continuum. Many groups use a modified version of parliamentary procedure to formally consider an agenda item and reach a decision through voting; at the same meeting, some decisions will be reached by consensus—a nod of the head from the participants, signifying agreement. Some meetings benefit from the best of both worlds: strict parliamentary procedure with an allotted period of consensus-building time within the meeting. For example, very formal meetings may also set aside time for a brainstorming session on a difficult agenda item, with no censorship of ideas—in fact, encouragement of even the wildest notions—and a conscious attempt to avoid reaching any decision. There are no explicit rules on how task group meetings must be run. Much depends on the leader's and staff's assessment of a particular group's task and process needs and their skills in these roles.

Chairing Meetings

A well-chaired meeting is no easy feat because the chairperson's role is complex. Meetings represent a public space in that whatever happens at a meeting is available to all of its participants. If a participant is treated unfairly, for example, by being insulted or cut off prematurely, all the other participants also observe and experience that treatment in some way. For meetings to be effective, therefore, it is incumbent on the chair to act as a neutral, objective arbiter of the group's business and to insist on sensitivity and fair play. The chair sets the tone for the meetings. If the chair has very strong feelings or opinions about an issue and wants to express them, he or she usually asks some-one else to preside until that agenda item is resolved.

Issues of distance arise in other ways as well. In general, the chair must be involved enough in the substance and process of a meeting to be able to engage with the ideas and the people, and yet must be uninvolved enough to be able to step back and guide the interchange to fruitful decisions. In that sense, *the chair operates with a split vision or dual consciousness, one aimed at understanding the ideas being expressed and the meaning of the interaction, the other aimed at using the group process to help the group members make sound decisions in which they are also invested.* This duality comes together in the various roles that the chairperson plays in a group meeting. We have identified these as *presider, facilitator,* and *administrator.*

PRESIDER

In this role, the chair makes sure that the business of the meeting is accomplished in a democratic fashion. The chair is in the position of controlling the flow of interaction in a meeting so that the agenda is dealt with effectively. The chair convenes the meeting, calls on the members to start the work (calls the meeting to order), and closes the meeting at its conclusion. Between the start and the finish, the chair regulates the discussion by calling on people to express their feelings and viewpoints. By summarizing, clarifying, repeating, and reminding the participants of the topic under discussion and the time available, the chair keeps the meeting agenda on track. The chair often synthesizes ideas for the group and determines when the group is ready to make a decision. When the group is ready to act, the chair clarifies the decision that is being made and ratifies the action by taking a vote or a reading of the degree of consensus. (Group members, of course, may also help to keep meetings on track, synthe-

size ideas, and clarify decisions. These roles are by no means limited to the chair, nor would you want them to be.)

FACILITATOR

As group facilitator, the chair must observe and interpret the way relationships are developing among the members and the development of the group as a whole. In addition, the chair must intervene so that the group process supports the group's task objectives. This involves the chair in many different kinds of interventions. Four important types of intervention are the following:

1. *Providing support* (e.g., "That's really an interesting idea") helps to create a positive "climate for expressing ideas and opinions, including unpopular and unusual points of view," and to "reinforce positive forms of behavior" (Sampson & Marthas, 1981, p. 258).

2. *Mediating conflict* (e.g., "Let's see if we can get to the bottom of this disagreement") helps the group members communicate more openly and directly with each other to relieve tension and to reduce disruptive behavior.

3. *Probing and questioning* (e.g., "I wonder if that idea could be enlarged") helps the group "expand a point that may have been left incomplete" and "invites members to explore their ideas in greater detail" (Sampson & Marthas, 1981, p. 259).

4. *Reflecting feelings* (e.g., "The group seems to be having a very hard time coming to grips with that decision") "orients members to the feelings that may lie behind what is being said or done" (Sampson & Marthas, 1981, p. 259).

(Perhaps it should be stated again here that group members can and should also help to facilitate the group process. The role is not limited to the chair.)

ADMINISTRATOR

In the absence of staff support, the chair, as administrator, basically coordinates the work of the group before, during, and after meetings. The chair, for example, attends to many of the premeeting tasks mentioned earlier, such as ensuring that information the group needs for making decisions is available in a timely manner. Before and during the meetings, with the help of other group members, the chair generates agenda items for future meetings. During the meeting, the chair usually assigns tasks and delegates responsibilities—for example, assigning a particular agenda item to a committee or subcommittee for follow-up work. Obviously, the chair would make sure that the particular agenda item was then brought back to the group at an appropriate future date. The chair also serves as spokesperson for the group when the group needs to be represented (Tropman, 1980).

Staffing a Task Group

Many social workers provide staff support to task groups, as with boards of directors or board committees, community development associations, interagency teams, planning bodies, and long-term coalitions. In these instances, the role of the professional is to enable the group to function effectively by providing assistance to the group, mainly through the chair, in handling administrative tasks and coordination, preparing for meetings, and serving as process consultant and, in some cases, as strategy and substantive expert. The main point here is that the professional staff person plays a critical, but *behind-the-scenes*, role, assisting the leaders of the group (the chair and various other members who accept responsibilities) to perform

their functions effectively. The staff person thus primarily carries out a *leadership development* role.

Although the paid staff person clearly has responsibility for the group, he or she is normally not a voting member of the group. In many cases, the staff person is directly hired and fired by the group. In many other instances, the employment relationship with the task group is much more indirect, although the group still has influence over a staff member's status. A direct service worker who is organizing a community group to sponsor a health fair would serve as staff to the health fair steering committee and would not typically be a voting member of that body. Or, for example, in an organization such as United Way, the staff person is a member of a larger professional staff responsible to the organization's executive director. This professional staff works with a host of volunteer planning and fund-raising committees but is not a voting member. The executive is responsible to the board of directors and serves as its professional staff. The executive here is usually an ex-officio board member, a board member by virtue of the office held, but again without a vote.

In working with chairpersons and other group leaders, staff will have to gauge their experience and sophistication and adapt the assistance they provide accordingly. In general, staff should help a chair prepare for meetings by jointly developing and reviewing the agenda, tasks to be accomplished, and a plan for accomplishing them. The plan may include preparing some group members for roles they might play in the meeting; planning for how to break down a complicated agenda item into smaller decisions; considering process snags and how to handle them; and, in some cases, considering how to reach an acceptable decision in the face of the political machinations of various subgroup factions. Inexperienced chairs may need help in role-playing parts of a meeting. More so-phisticated chairs may need other forms of assistance, such as sensitization to process concerns.

At meetings, professional staff are, of course, visible and have a good opportunity to talk to the group members and get to know them better, and vice versa. Once the meeting begins, though, staff members should take a back seat to the chair, who is directing the meeting. Since the staff member has already had input into the meeting by virtue of premeeting preparations with the chair, during the meeting the staff person should be carefully observing the group process as well as following the substance of the discourse. Sitting beside the chair, the staff person can then share comments, suggestions, and observations discreetly with the chair. This is not to say that the staff member must be totally silent. Sometimes the chair or a member will ask the staff person directly for observations or suggestions. Sometimes a meeting may be getting out of hand or straying too far off course, and the staff person may judiciously make a corrective comment or ask a question. Sometimes it may be apparent that the chair does not know how to handle a particular situation, and the staff member may have to help out. *The principle to keep in mind, however, if leadership and group development are staff goals, is that the staff should neither usurp nor outshine the chair.*

Since professional staff members tend to spend more time on the business of a task group than do the chair or other leaders, they often tend to take over a group or at least to dominate it. Sometimes this is not even a conscious decision; staff members just find it easier to act for the group than to work through the group. The problem with this approach is that group leadership and the group as a whole have difficulty developing fully. Yet presumably, forming a group was necessary to reach some specified set of goals. The bottom line is that the *members of the group have to own the group if it is to succeed.* For ownership to occur, staff members have to enable the group members to make their own decisions about the nature and direction of the group and to take responsibility for its work. Enabling involves a delicate balance between holding back advice and hands-on assistance and offering them at various critical points to guide a group over a rough spot. There are no simple guidelines for managing the balance, but if a group does not seem to be developing, staff members at least need to ask themselves whether they have done too much for the group. Perhaps more holding back would be appropriate.

DEALING WITH GROUP PROBLEMS

All groups experience problems; these come with the territory. For example, task groups commonly experience difficulties getting started, handling conflict, reaching decisions, dealing with disruptive behavior by an individual member (the meeting monopolizer, the angry challenger, etc.) or by a subgroup (negative bloc voting), and more. Common as these and other group problems may be, however, there is no standard recipe for how best to deal with them. Because groups differ in so many ways and because the circumstances surrounding any problem are unique, in working with groups, just as in social work with individuals, families, or communities, we prefer a general approach to problem solving rather than a set of fixed solutions. Let's look at the framework first and then apply it to some group problems one might encounter.

A Problem-solving Framework

The now familiar problem-solving framework used in this book has four steps:

(1) study, (2) assessment, (3) treatment or intervention, and *(4) evaluation or reassessment.* (See also Sampson & Marthas, 1981). This framework provides a useful guide, a kind of mindset, for dealing with group task and process problems. The time frame involved in these steps can range from instantaneous to prolonged. As a problem arises in the group, the social worker as leader, member, or staff person may respond then and there, based on observations and some conclusions about the meaning of the behavior. Alternatively, the social worker may choose not to intervene, but to continue to observe and consider the nature of the problem and what to do about it, saving the intervention for some later date. (Remember that since a group is a public space for all the participants, nonintervention may sometimes be a form of intervention, depending on how this is interpreted.) Whenever the intervention has occurred, the social worker should assess its effect and make a decision about whether to respond further and what kind of intervention to make, again at that particular moment or at some later date. The transition from thought to action and back to reflection, sometimes referred to as *praxis*, can be seamless or spaced out.

STUDY

The study section of the problem-solving framework, then, is the period for defining and clarifying the nature and extent of the problem in the group. When a problem arises, therefore, we need to ask ourselves the following questions: What is the actual problem? What are the observable behaviors indicating that there is a problem? How is the group affected? How serious is the problem?

ASSESSMENT

Here we want to clarify what we think is the cause of the problem or what it means. We connect our observations to our theoretical knowledge in order to intervene effectively. Therefore we ask ourselves questions like the following: Why is this problem occurring? What's going on outside the group and/or in the group that may be contributing to this problem? Am I contributing to the problem in some way? Where is the group developmentally? What role do subgroups or factions play in this problem? What part do the individual needs and personalities of the participants play in this problem? Is there any pattern to the behavior I am observing? What is my understanding of the problem?

INTERVENTION

This is the point of action. The worker needs to say or do something in the group, or sometimes outside of the group, to help the group deal with the problem. When intervening, the worker may think about the following kinds of questions: How can I get the group to start to handle the problem? How will my reaction to an individual member or to the group as a whole facilitate the group process and keep the group on course? How will my intervention be perceived by the group? Are there specific techniques I can use to affect the problem?

EVALUATION

Having intervened to try to deal with the problem, the worker now needs to observe the impact of that intervention. The main questions, then, are as follows: What effect did my action have on the group? What effect did my intervention have on specific individuals and/or subgroups? Does my diagnosis seem to be correct, or do I need to modify my understanding of the problem? Do I need to take any follow-up action?

Three Common Group Problems

As we turn to some examples of problems and interventions, we should keep in mind, once again, that the responsibility for dealing with problems does not rest with the leader/chair or staff person alone. All members of a group share responsibility for helping the group to function effectively, and any member may be instrumental in helping the group address problematic behavior. Since this chapter is written from the perspective of the chairperson or leader and staff person, and since these individuals often do intervene to deal with group problems, we shall adopt that stance in the illustrations that follow. As we go through these examples, consider your own analysis of the problem and possible interventions.

THE MEETING MONOPOLIZER

Scenario. Imagine the third meeting of a treatment planning team of staff members on an acute illness unit of a large psychiatric hospital. The unit leader, who is a social worker with many years of seniority, is also the team leader. The other members of the team include a psychiatrist, a head nurse, a nursing assistant, a psychologist, an occupational therapist, and a recreational therapist. Team planning on the unit is not new, but this particular team, with three new members, represents a new team configuration. The team meets weekly. The newcomers are the psychiatrist, the head nurse, and the nursing assistant. Although the social worker, Karen Jones, chairs the meetings, the meetings have increasingly been dominated by the psychiatrist, Dr. Matthew Freud (no relation), who has a lot to say about each case before the group. Other team members have had difficulty interjecting their ideas. Some group members are beginning to grumble outside the group about their inability to be heard, and it is becoming difficult to arrive at treatment plans that everyone can accept. So far, the team leader has taken a laissez-faire approach to chairing the group, but now

the time has come to intervene more directly. In this third meeting, when the second case is put before the group for discussion, Dr. Freud immediately takes the lead in explaining the nature of the patient's illness. How might the chair intervene?

Study. At each meeting, Dr. Freud monopolizes the discussion of the cases. He usually does a lot of "teaching" about the nature of the illness and reviews current research before getting to his own recommendations. While the information is interesting, other members are forced to sit and listen passively. The doctor is not good at picking up cues that others want to contribute their observations. He does not maintain good eye contact with other group members. He also discounts input from other disciplines. Group members have begun to resist coming to agreement on treatment plans and are often restless. Two members have come late to the third team meeting and have expressed some resentment to the leader outside the meeting. Dr. Freud's behavior is threatening the effectiveness of team planning.

Assessment. A number of factors may be contributing to this problem. The team leader has not dealt with the fact that the team has several new members who may not be familiar with the ground rules the old team had established. Her laissez-faire approach thus has not provided the group with a sufficient orientation to the team's expectations and norms. The psychiatrist is new and is trying to find his niche in the group. Other new members have a similar challenge, while older members are used to their particular format for team meetings. Dr. Freud's previous experiences as team leader himself may have led him to adopt a dominant leadership-teaching pattern. His behavior may reflect discomfort with his status on the unit and in the group. Also, Dr. Freud appears not to be a good listener, at least as far as the staff is concerned.

Intervention. The group leader has a number of options. Some possibilities include the following:

1. She could confront Dr. Freud directly about his behavior. "Dr. Freud [firmly until she has his attention], you seem to have an awful lot to say about each case before the group. Although your points are informative, I'd like to stop your discourse at this point so that other members have a chance to express their views on the case. Thank you."

2. She could reflect the group's behavior back to the group and solicit their feedback. After Dr. Freud finishes his discourse, or after politely interrupting, the leader might say, "I'd like to stop the discussion of cases for a few minutes to consider our process. As I look around the group, I see a lot of restlessness and dissatisfaction. I wonder if we could talk about what's going on."

3. She could reflect back her own behavior to the group as a means of inviting clarification of ground rules. After Dr. Freud finishes his discourse or after interrupting him politely, the leader might say, "Before Dr. Freud finishes his explanation, I need to interrupt the group for a few minutes to take care of some important business that I realize I neglected. As I've been observing the group, it seems that I never took the time to orient this team from the outset about expectations for team functioning. Since we have three new team members, maybe we could take some time now to make some decisions together about how we want to handle our cases in the group meeting."

Evaluation

1. The first intervention offers Dr. Freud some support but also lets him know directly that his behavior is not acceptable, sets limits on it, and lets the other team members know that their participation is valued. Other group members may also feel freer to interrupt Dr. Freud in the future. Dr. Freud, however, may find the confrontation surprising and irritating, laboring under the notion that he was doing what he was supposed to do as team psychiatrist. He may feel that he has lost face in the group.

2. The second intervention potentially allows the group to express their dissatisfaction with Dr. Freud's monopolistic behavior, as well as their own expectations for participation. Since this is only the third team meeting, the members may not be willing to take Dr. Freud on. If they are willing, the leader risks a session that deteriorates into an attack on the psychiatrist.

3. The third intervention recognizes the group's formative stage of development, directs some of the group's anger back to the leader rather than the psychiatrist, and opens the way for the team to establish its ground rules in a constructive fashion. Once the members have negotiated the rules of the game, monopolization will be less likely to occur and easier for the team leader and other members to limit, since the group has guidelines for participation.

GROUP CONFLICT

Scenario. You are serving in your first year as associate director of a moderate-sized nonprofit family services agency. Your responsibilities include supervising the professional staff and chairing monthly agency staff meetings. Along with a director and an associate director, the agency staff consists of 12 professional social workers, 2 immigrant resettlement workers, and 4 case aides. The agency is departmentalized into four divisions: family and children's (six social workers), single adults (two social workers), senior adults (two social workers), and immigrant services (two social workers and two resettlement workers). One case aide works in each division, handling arrangements for in-home services, transportation, respite care, and the like. Staff turnover in the agency is generally low, so that these staff members know each other quite well. Half of the professional staff members have been with the agency for more than 10 years.

During a midyear staff meeting, the agency has been trying to work out a policy on home visiting. Currently the only staff who regularly make home visits are the nonprofessional workers and the two social workers handling adoptions in the family and children's division. The associate director, Bill Green, has proposed the policy that every client seen by the agency should have a home visit, with the exception of single adults unless there is severe contagious illness. The professional staff has split on the policy, with one faction, led by Molly Black, the head of the family and children's division and a senior staff member, adamantly opposed and the other faction, led by Jane White, head of immigration services and also a senior staffer, strongly in favor. The nonprofessional staff, feeling caught in the middle, have tried to stay out of the line of fire. After going round and round for nearly an hour and making no headway, rational discourse has deteriorated into simmering anger. How might the chair intervene to begin a process of constructive conflict resolution?

Study. Groups frequently experience conflict, especially as part of their develop-

ment. The task is to manage the conflict effectively so that group cohesion can be enhanced rather than destroyed. When the group has a strong sense of trust and commitment to group goals, when the conflicts represent substantive disagreements over ideas, procedures, or priorities, and when the group has a history of productive problem solving, constructive resolutions are easier to achieve. When conflicts erupt due to struggles in the group over status and power, when attacks become personalized and hostile, when there is a win/lose competitive atmosphere and the members begin to take sides, the group may be involved in destructive conflict. Constructive resolution is much harder to achieve.

In the family services staff group, conflict seems to have taken a destructive turn. The group has not been able to make any progress on coming up with an acceptable policy. Anger is running high. The professional staff has polarized into two factions. The nonprofessional staff are not participating so as not to be subjected to personal attacks or retribution from more powerful group members. The atmosphere has degenerated into a win/lose situation.

Assessment. A number of factors may be contributing to this destructive climate. The members of the family and children's division under Molly Black see themselves as highly professional "therapists" who have neither the time nor the resources to do extensive home visiting. In addition, Molly wanted but did not get the associate director's job. Instead, an outsider was hired for the position. Bill Green is aware that Molly was a candidate for his position, but as her supervisor, he has never discussed this matter with her.

Jane White, also a senior professional staff member in charge of immigration services, already spends a lot of time seeing immigrant families in their homes. She believes the proposed policy will eventually generate more resources for her department. A number of other staff members do as well, and they maintain that prevention, social support, and resocialization should represent the major professional goals of the agency.

The nonprofessional staff have mixed feelings about the policy. Some believe that if all members of the professional staff did home visits, the contribution of the nonprofessionals would be recognized and more greatly appreciated. Others fear that if all staff members do home visits, there will be less need for their services, potentially leading to cutbacks in nonprofessional positions. Thus a shift in agency policy could upset the existing group equilibrium.

The associate director is being tested. His honeymoon period as a new staff member is over; staff members no longer feel they have to be polite. They can take more risks in expressing their feelings and ideas and find out how the new group leader/authority figure will react and what the limits are. Will he understand them? How does he deal with anger and internal competition?

The associate director did not recognize the potential ramifications of his proposal and therefore made no moves before the meeting to get feedback on his idea and to reduce the anxiety that often accompanies change. Had he recognized the potential for conflict ahead of time, he might have prepared the staff for his proposal more effectively before the meeting. He also has been avoiding dealing with Molly's competitive feelings about the associate director's job.

Intervention. The following are some possible interventions:

1. The chair tries to legitimate differences of opinion and defuse the situation a bit. Ideally he will recognize that he is being tested and will not overreact. He does not want a win/lose solution; he would like a win/win solution that still deals with the task, that is, the proposed policy change. "After an hour of hot and heavy debate, let's recognize that there are legitimate differences of opinion. I don't think there is any 'right' or 'wrong' solution here. Why don't we think about the policy and come back to it next month with some ideas about how to blend the different positions."

2. The chair recognizes that more is evidently at stake than a substantive difference over a policy option. He tries to get at the underlying anger and fear by reflecting back the group's behavior. "After listening and watching the interchange about this policy, I've noticed that several people have not said anything for almost an hour, while the rest seem to have decided to take sides and do battle without listening to each other. I'd really like to understand what's going on."

3. The chair recognizes that the conflict goes deeper than the policy itself and tries to get at this by reflecting back the group's feelings. "I think we need to stop for a minute and try to understand the anger and fear that this policy suggestion seems to have aroused. I don't think we'll make much progress if we're this tense about the proposal, and I would like to make some progress."

4. The chair tries to defuse the conflict by adopting a structural approach (Ephross & Vassil, 1988). "We seem to have hit an impasse on this policy for now. One group is strongly opposed, one group is strongly for, and another contingent seems stuck in the middle. I'm going to ask two members from each subgroup to meet during the week and see if they can work out a compromise proposal that everyone can live

with. I'll meet with the group afterward to see what has been worked out, and we'll discuss it at the next staff meeting."

Evaluation. Not every conflict that a group experiences has to be processed by the group. Otherwise, the group might spend all of its time doing that and nothing else. When a conflict has destructive qualities, as was the case in this scenario, the group probably does need to look at it in more depth. Nor are these responses necessarily mutually exclusive. For example, the fourth alternative, or something like it, might well follow a discussion generated by the second or third alternatives. The interventions identified above also are not the only possible responses. Sometimes a group may even need the assistance of an outside facilitator to get at their difficulties and resolve them.

1. In the first response, the chair perhaps recognizes that the group is tired and has gone as far as it can that day. Legitimizing differences is generally a constructive approach, and allowing for a cooling-off period may be helpful. He also wants to set a tone of calm acceptance, in contrast to the group's turmoil. In this situation, it seems unlikely that the group will come up with a compromise policy on its own without some specific structure in place for doing the work. Since the conflict has some destructive properties, the chair needs to be sure that the situation will not be dropped, lest it fester and surface again and again in different ways. Before the next meeting, the chair might find an opportunity to talk with Molly and other staff members individually to get a clearer sense of their feelings and concerns. He should then be more prepared to lead a discussion of the policy at the next staff meeting.

2. In the second intervention, the chair feeds his observations of the group's behavior

back to the group. In effect, he holds up a mirror and shows them how their behavior appears, with the aim of opening up the discussion about their underlying concerns and feelings in a manner that can lead to some resolution. Again, his tone is calm and accepting.

3. In the third intervention, the chair openly recognizes the strong feelings that the proposal has aroused and legitimates discussion of feelings and concerns. Again, the aim is to move beyond the policy itself because the staff's anger and fear are blocking effective progress.

4. In the fourth alternative, the chair tries to defuse the staff's anger by taking time to deal with the policy outside the group. This is like the first alternative except that here, the chair sets up a structure for working on the compromise. He still has work to do between meetings in eliciting the staff's feelings and concerns.

GROUP SILENCE OR NONPARTICIPATION

Scenario. The six-member steering committee of a local homeless service provider coalition is meeting to decide on an activity that will mobilize support for a bill requiring the city to provide 24-hour mobile emergency aid teams to reach out to the homeless on cold days. The mayor has come out publicly against the proposal due to budgetary constraints. The group has met six times, and the members generally know each other because of their common work with the homeless population in the city. The discussion, chaired by the organizer/leader, has gone on for about an hour, without much enthusiasm or focus. The members don't seem to be able to come up with viable ideas or to take hold of the issue. Finally, the group leader, Mary Brown, enthusiastically proposes a dramatic activity to get media coverage on the issue—

a demonstration in front of the mayor's private home. Nobody responds. There is an uncomfortable silence (Sampson & Marthas, 1981, p. 271).

Study. The group has shown signs of apathy throughout the meeting. The discussion has been unenthusiastic and unproductive. The feeling tone of the meeting has been apathetic. The leader has tended to carry the discussion, until finally her last proposal has been met with silence.

Assessment. There are many reasons why a group may behave apathetically or withhold participation. Some common reasons may apply to this group. Among the first possibilities a group leader must consider are reasons related personally to the leader. The leader may be out of tune with the interests and experiences of the members. Or the leader may have been monopolizing the group, creating a dependent relationship in which the members' level of participation is low. In this case, we have a group of service providers who may not be accustomed to social action. Social action is outside their professional experience but not outside of the leader's interests and experience. The leader is out of step with her group.

Some of the members' reluctant participation may be due to a variety of unspoken fears. As homeless service providers, each member's organization receives some funding from the city. They are afraid that political action may result in funding cutbacks to their agencies. In this light, the proposal to challenge the mayor is particularly threatening.

Some members do not believe that social action is the purpose for the group's formation. Their primary interest is in better service coordination and networking with other providers. The group has never discussed its goals and arrived at a consensus on the group's purpose.

The task of mobilizing support for passage of a bill in the city council may be too daunting. The providers are up to their ears in work just to keep their services operating. Even if they are interested, they may not have the time or energy to devote to this sort of project.

The leader herself is a highly respected, long-time advocate for the homeless. Some group members are uncomfortable about opposing her openly.

Intervention. Again, a variety of interventions are possible, depending in part on the leader's diagnosis of the problem.

1. If the leader has had a flash of insight about being out of step with the group, she might say: "Judging from the unenthusiastic discussion over the last hour and your silence, maybe I've been pushing for social action too hard. What do you think?"

2. The leader might tune in to the lack of clarity about the group's purpose. "I can see there is not too much excitement about a campaign to pass the city council bill. I guess this is pretty different than the other work the group has done. Maybe we should go around the room and check on what we see as the purposes of the group. John, could you start us off?"

3. The leader might open up further discussion about the group's purposes by zeroing in on the underlying fears of the members. "Since nobody is saying anything, I'm guessing that the idea of going after the mayor is pretty scary. How do you all feel about our coalition getting involved in social action?"

Evaluation

1. In the first intervention, the leader reflects back the behavior of the group and

tries to solicit feedback, starting with responses to the direction of her own leadership.

2. In the second intervention, the leader is fairly direct about starting the feedback process. She is also beginning a process of negotiating a contract that did not take place previously.

3. Here the leader tunes in to the feelings of inadequacy about a social action campaign that she senses in the members. This approach can also lead to further clarification of the group's purposes and negotiation of the group's contract. With some expression of feelings on the table and a chance to look at the project, the group might be more ready to engage in action, but something appropriate to their level of experience and available time.

CONCLUSION

The group problems and interventions we have illustrated in this chapter are only a few of the many typical and atypical problems and challenges that task groups encounter. As should be apparent, although task groups are about decision making, group behavior and feelings sometimes interfere with the best laid plans and require a leader to facilitate the group process. In this chapter, we have advocated a systematic approach to problem solving that is transferable to all kinds of group practice situations you may encounter. We have also suggested that a self-critical approach to practice is highly desirable. Whether as member, leader, chair, organizer, or staff, social workers invariably participate in task groups and, just as in other aspects of professional practice, they need to be able to use themselves consciously to enable a group to achieve its goals.

Discussion Exercises

1. The director of the state's foster care review board has appointed you to chair an interagency foster care review team of eight members. You are preparing for the first meeting. The team reviews cases of children placed in foster care by the city child protective services agency to be sure that the placements are appropriate.

(a) Identify your process and task goals for the meeting.
(b) Write out an agenda for the meeting.
(c) Identify the tasks you will attend to before the group convenes.
(d) Explain how you would start the meeting and how you would end it.

2. The foster care review team is having its fifth meeting. In a carryover discussion from the previous month's meeting, the group has gotten bogged down in figuring out how to handle the large volume of cases most efficiently. Two main proposals

have been identified: adding extra meetings and dividing up the cases between two subcommittees. At this point, one of the committee members, Connie Williams, who missed the previous meeting, introduces a third alternative: adding more members to the committee. Mae Harris supports this new proposal. The other members get upset.

(a) Explain what may be going on in terms of your knowledge of group development.
(b) Indicate what you would do in this situation.

3. This is the first meeting of a group of seven representatives from local public and private agencies who are trying to develop a citywide referral system. The staff person from the department of social services has worked hard in pregroup contacts and discussions to help develop an acceptable agenda and get the group going. She is chairing the meeting. About halfway through the meeting, a re-

spected agency director asserts loudly, "This meeting isn't getting anywhere and I have to leave. I sure hope the next meeting is more productive!" And with that, he packs up and walks out. The members look a bit stunned and turn to you for the next move.

    (a) How would you explain what is going on?

    (b) What would you do?

4.   Near the end of the first meeting of the above group, someone suggests that the group appoint a chair to conduct the meetings. The idea is received enthusiastically. When you ask for nominations, no one responds.

    (a) How would you explain what is going on?

    (b) What would you do?

5.   It is the fourth meeting of a planning committee in an agency. One staff person comes in 15 minutes late. Although she has done this before, no one says anything about it, including the chairperson of the group. The late arrival is also the highest-status member of the group, representing a large department in the agency.

    (a) How would you explain what is going on?

    (b) What would you do?

6.   The fifth meeting of the above agency planning committee begins with silence. Although the agenda has been prepared and members received it in advance, no one says anything. It is beginning to seem that the silence might continue for some time.

    (a) How would you explain what is going on?

    (b) What would you do?

Note

1. An alternative model of group development for task forces has been suggested by Gersick (1988). Task forces are viewed as a special subset of working groups that are action-oriented, time-limited, and formed administratively to deal with problems that cannot be solved by routine methods (Johnson, 1994). Their particular nature, it is argued, make them prone to a development pattern of "punctuated equilibrium" whereby the group alternates between fairly long periods of inertia and bursts of creative energy, rather than developing gradually, as proposed in most group development models.

References

Ephross, P. H., & Vassil, T. V. (1988). *Groups that work: Structure and process.* New York: Columbia University Press.

Gersick, C. G. (1988). Time and transition in work teams: Toward a new model of group development. *Academy of Management Journal, 31,* 9–41.

Hanson, P. G. (1972). What to look for in groups. In J. W. Pfeiffer & J. J. Jones (Eds.), *The 1972 annual handbook for group facilitators* (pp. 21–24). La Jolla, CA: University Associates.

Heap, K. (1977). *Group theory for social workers: An introduction.* New York: Pergamon Press.

Johnson, A. K. (1994). Teaching students the task force approach: A policy-practice course. *Journal of Social Work Education, 30*(3), 336–347.

Sampson, E. E., & Marthas, M. (1981). *Group process for the health professions* (2nd ed.). New York: Wiley.

Tropman, J. E. (1980). *Effective meetings: Improving group decision-making.* Beverly Hills, CA: Sage.

Tuckman, B. W. (1965). Developmental sequence in small groups. *Psychological Bulletin, 63,* 384–399.

Tuckman, B. W., & Jensen, M. A. C. (1977). Stages of small group development revisited. *Group and Organizational Studies, 2*(1), 419–427.

Zastrow, C. (1985). *Social work with groups.* Chicago: Nelson-Hall.

chapter

10

Using Networks and Networking

WHAT IS A NETWORK? WHAT IS NETWORKING

Clients with multiple problems and needs are increasing. An abusive mother may require income assistance, job training, day care, psychosocial therapy, parenting education and skills, and social supports in order to change her behavior. If the father is present, family therapy may be needed. If not, she may need assistance in obtaining absent parent financial and social supports.

Rarely are all needed services available from a single agency; usually they must be obtained from many autonomous organizations. The social worker and the client will need to construct and manage a service network. Social networks and networking are the integral building blocks and skills of social work practice. Social workers network when they refer clients to other agencies, help clients develop social supports, and

work with social action coalitions. While *networking* has become a buzz word of the 1980s and 1990s, it is an essential social work skill. Networks and networking are inherent in social work's emphasis on the client's social ecology, service coordination, and the holism of social work's person-in-environment (P-I-E) perspective. Networking occurs when people seek others who can or may be able to help them or whom they may be able to help. Networking involves building and maintaining social relationships with others. Networks are support systems in that they provide a structure for social exchanges. Networks can affect worker and client morale in the change effort, resources for task completion, and community cohesion and individual alienation.

This chapter will review social network theory and its underlying social theories, the dimensions of social networks, client social supports as networks, and the application to social work practice.

Social networks are social systems composed of people, groups, or organizations that interact and engage in exchanges to achieve objectives or fulfill a shared purpose. For a discussion of the system's model in a variety of social contexts, see Anderson and Carter (1984, pp. 1–23), Churchman (1965, pp. 29–33), Hearn (1969), Leighninger (1978), and Martin and O'Connor (1989), among others. Networks can be personal, professional, and organizational; networking can be interpersonal between individuals and interorganizational between organizations and agencies. Networking is interorganizational when the people in the network bring the resources of their organizations to the network rather than only their personal resources. The network links the resources of organizations. Client referral systems between agencies and service coordination between two or more agencies are examples of interorganizational networks. McIntyre (1986) argues that networks and support systems exist in any situation involving an exchange of resources. The resources exchanged can be tangible, such as money and clients, or intangible, such as information and status.

Networks and networking exist, although often temporary and small, when social workers make and accept client referral. Networking and coordination between agencies and between social workers are necessary, as client needs do not always coincide with a single agency's packages of services. The sheer number of agencies and services generates greater management complexity for the individual client and social worker and demand commensurate network management skills. Not only do multiple-problem clients need the services of a network of social agencies and social resources, but even single-problem clients often require interorganizational networks if they need long-term or continuous care. The client's immediate need may be addressed by a single agency, but if the client requires ongoing aftercare, monitoring, periodic reassessment, or long-term support, additional agencies likely will be involved. The former offender released to a probation worker and the elderly man discharged from the hospital and linked to a homemaker service have something in common: they need continuity of service and a network that takes an indeterminate rather than a limited interest in them.

FACTORS AFFECTING NETWORKS AND NETWORKING

Network involvement for an agency or an individual means potential loss of autonomy and the necessity to invest some resources in developing and maintaining the network. Why then do agencies expend resources and give up some freedom to cooperate with other agencies that are, actually or potentially, its resource competitors? Agencies become involved in networks because they expect to make gains over the expenditures of resources sufficient to compensate for the loss of autonomy. Research (Galaskiewicz & Wasserman, 1990; Woodard & Doreion, 1994) indicates that networks can develop and be maintained under the following conditions:

"We developed an ecumenical committee with many influential members of the community and a real variety of people. We invited the governor to speak at a banquet and, as a result, got two million dollars for school lunches. . . . This is what I mean by developing a critical mass: bringing together a variety of people."
Founder of a food action committee (Powers, n.d.)

- Agencies need other agencies for the resources to fulfill their functions and achieve their goals. The network provides a structure, that is, a marketplace, for exchanging resources.

- Agencies need other agencies to respond to an external problem, opportunity, or mandate because the resources necessary to respond are available only through networking. The network provides a structure for aggregating resources and for coordinating domains politically and functionally.

- Agencies that share similar and overlapping domains—human problem or need, population or clientele, technology, treatment and service methods, geographic or catchment area, and sources of fiscal and nonfiscal resources—may need to regulate competition and conflict. The network provides a structure and mechanism for politically regulating competition, negotiating domain consensus and legitimating the domains of network members, and managing conflict between network members.

As indicated above, personal, professional, and organizational network understanding, construction, and management are rooted in an understanding of an organization's political economy and exchange theory.

POLITICAL ECONOMY

Organizations and social agencies generally exist in a competitive task environment. Survival in a competitive task environment depends on the agency's ability to establish recognition of and to maintain a domain and link with resource providers in the task environment. Political economy theory assumes that an organization must have a flow of resources. It also assumes that organizations change when there are alterations in the resources and in the exchanges and linkages an organization must make with its task environment (Wernet, 1994; Zald, 1970). For a review of domain theory, see Chapter 2. The seminal work on domain theory was done by Levine and White (1961, 1963). The primary concepts in domain theory are *domain*, *task environment*, and *social exchange*.

Domain

An agency's *domain* is the claim for resources the agency stakes out for itself based on its purpose and objectives. The claim from the task environment is for some combination of (1) human problem or need, (2) population or clientele, (3) technology or treatment methods, (4) geographic or catchment area, and (5) sources of fiscal and nonfiscal resources. While some of the domain may be shared and other parts may be in dispute, all parts cannot be shared or be in dispute if the agency is to maintain itself as a separate entity.

Task Environment

Every organization exists in an environment composed of other organizations similar to it, as well as a host of other entities that may be sources of resources or competitors for the resources the agency needs to achieve its objectives. These organizations represent the resource set. They are not a system until united or linked to fulfill a shared objective (Evan, 1963). The *task environment* is the specific set of organizations, agencies, groups, and individuals with which the agency may exchange resources and services and with which it establishes specific modes of interaction, either competitive or cooperative, to achieve its goals and fulfill its mission. It is the part of the environment that can positively or negatively affect the agency's functioning and survival.

The task environment does not include everything in the agency's physical environment. The concept is limited to those things in the environment, the ecology, that can add to or detract from the agency's well-being. While not including everything in the general environment, the task environment is influenced by the general environment's level of resources and richness, the competition for the resources by all alternative demands, the social ideology and philosophy of need meeting, and the socioeconomic demographics of the population: age distribution, family composition, income distribution, economic base, and so forth. The resources in the task environment do not constitute a system; they are merely a set of things until they are organized into a system to support the agency and its mission and objectives (Evan, 1963). Some agencies and organizations in the task environment may not provide resources directly but may provide complementary services that allow the agency to achieve its objectives. The agency needs to assess and locate in its task environment resource providers and complementary services and link with them. It also needs to identity and assess its competitors for resources and domain. Resource providers, complementary services, and competitors can be classified as:

1. funding sources (i.e., agencies, individuals) and providers of fiscal resources);

2. client sources (i.e., referral sources including client self-referrals);

3. legitimation and authority sources that provide the agency with sanctions and mandates (i.e., accrediting agencies, legislatures, the media);

4. complementary service providers, whether formal or informal, that enable the agency to complete its service package to its clients;

5. consumers of the agency's products (i.e., resources for client placements, program graduates and employers); and

6. competing organizations, that is agencies seeking the same domain, the reduction or elimination of the agency's domain, and some or all of the agency's resources.

The relationship between an agency and the other agencies in its task environment is a dynamic rather than a static one. An agency can participate in numerous diversified networks and systems at the same time or at different times to obtain resources and to establish, maintain, or protect its domain. Other units in the task environment also can belong to many networks and to a progression of networks, as illustrated in the cases presented in Chapter 1. Agencies can be complementary as well as competitive. For example, two agencies may link and coordinate their services at the same time that they compete for public and private funding.

The domain and task environment definitions and determinations are interactional. The task environment is demarcated by the agency's service mission and domain. The domain determination, the mission and objectives, are influenced by the opportunities, contingencies, and constraints of the task environment. The agency should seek opportunities and recognize the resources, contingencies, and constraints in establishing its mission, goals, and domain. The domain is the result, the product, of the negotiations, bargaining, interactions, and exchanges between the agency and its task environment.

Social Exchanges

Domains and networks are established and maintained by the processes of social exchanges. Social exchange theory is the basic theory underlying networking. It is fundamental to domain establishment and maintenance. *Social exchanges* are involved when agencies recognize the domains of participating agencies in a network. The agencies "trade," or exchange, domain recognition. Exchanges are present when the government exchanges resources for ideological commitments and programs ideologically compatible with the government's currently prevailing ideology. For reviews of ideological exchanges between the government and various constituencies on the social and political left and right, see Moynihan (1969), Murray (1984), and Pivan and Cloward (1971).

Social exchanges necessary to establish and sustain networks differ from strict economic exchanges in that there is often a general rather than a specific expectation of reward in the exchange. Also, unlike economic exchanges, the value of the exchanges by each partner may not be in the same measurement units such as dollars, which limits precise quid pro quo evaluations of the exchange. An example is the donation of money by a wealthy donor to a United Way campaign. The donor is giving dollars, an easily measurable unit, but receives less tangible and precise products in return. The donor does not expect to be a direct user of the services or to substitute the services for any product that the donor might buy. The donor's satisfaction or value is received in a series of largely intangible social products: a maintenance or an increase in social status, a reduction of social pressure from the fund solicitors, the opportunity to fulfill commitments to personal ideology and values, and perhaps a better, more pleasant, and more livable community. The intangible products' value is less precise and less easily compared to the value of alternative products available to the donor for the money.

The potential exchange partners for a network usually are not limited to a single partner for a bilateral exchange between two participants in complex communities. Instead, there is an *exchange set*, defined as the number of potential partners in the task environment or community. There is a field of potential exchange partners in the task environment. The number of potential partners in the exchange set determines the prevailing value of each participant's resources in likely exchanges. *Value* is the reward or gratification to the recipients of the resources or products received. The more potential exchange partners with the desired resource there are in the exchange set, the more easily realized and less costly are the exchanges for the party seeking the resource. *Costs* are the rewards, products, and resources traded and foregone in the exchange or the punishments incurred in order to obtain the desired resource. Each participant in the exchange relationship defines the value of the products received and compares this value to the cost of the products traded in the exchange.

DIMENSIONS OF NETWORKS

While networks are universal and inherent in social interaction, networks and the exchange relationships between agencies, as well as between people, differ on several related dimensions, such as the kinds of resources exchanged, the strength and direction of the exchanges, symmetry, the density of the network, the distribution of benefits to network participants, and the influence of units within the network (Mizruchi & Galaskiewicz, 1993; Woodard & Doreion, 1994). We will examine 10 of the related network dimensions.

Domain Consensus

For exchanges to occur and networks to be established, the potential social units in the network, the individuals or agencies, must be interested in making exchanges, know of and value the products and resources of the potential exchange partners, and have the capacity to make the exchange. In other words, domain recognition and some degree of domain consensus is necessary for interorganization relations and networking. *Domain consensus* is the recognition of and agreement on the agency's domain by the task environment and potential network partners. Recognition of an agency's domain by the resource providers in the task environment is needed if exchanges are to occur. Without some degree of domain recognition, domain consensus cannot occur. Domain consensus can be high or low on all or some of the domain variables. However, the higher the agreement on the wider range of variables, the more likely the agency is to survive. Some degree of domain recognition is necessary for the agency to engage in exchanges for resources with its task environment.

Size

Networks can be as small as two units or extensive, covering a high number of units like a telephone network. The network's size, including social support and mutual aid networks for clients, with the availability of contemporary communication and transportation technology, is not limited to a specific community. The parlor game of "six degrees of separation" holds that anyone in the world is separated from anyone else by no more than six people. This assumption was tested by Milgram (1967) in a field experiment. Milgram asked people in the Midwest to deliver a message to a particular Harvard Divinity School student or to someone whom they though might know the student, repeating the process until the student was contacted. The average number of links between all starters and the student was five, not six. Of course, the challenging practice

task is to identify and connect (network) the relevant five or six people between you and your target; convince them to pass back and forth, relatively unchanged, the exchanges between you and the target; and eventually shorten the chain of separation between you and your target so that your dependency on the chain can be reduced.

The larger the network, the more potential exchange partners are available. However, larger networks also require management by each unit, depending on the network's construction, and by the total network. The implications of size will be discussed in greater detail under the dimensions of "dependency and influence" and "density and complexity."

Symmetry

Each unit in the network has resources to exchange. The unit gains and loses resources in the network exchanges, although not necessarily symmetrically. Not all units gain and lose equally. The symmetry or balance of exchange is a function of the availability and distribution of resources in demand by all units in the network. If the resources in demand are fairly equally distributed, there is symmetry. If, instead, they are aggregated by a few units, the network's exchanges will be asymmetrical. Woodward and Doreion (1994), in their study of community service networks, found that fewer than half of the exchanges were symmetrical.

Dependency and Influence

Dependency and influence are functions of the symmetry of resources in the network. If one party in an exchange relationship is the sole or primary possessor of a highly desired resource by a number of other potential trading partners, the demand for the resource is likely to be high and the gains to the holder of the resource in the exchange should be

$IA/B = DB/A$, with the influence (I) of A over B equal to the dependency (D) of B on A for the needed resource. If A has a highly desired and limited resource sought by many agencies (many potential Bs), then A will have influence on all the agencies (all the Bs) in the network that are dependent on A for the resource. That is, $IA/Bn = DBn/A$, or the influence of A over all the Bs is equal to the dependency of all the Bs on A.

great. The holder of this resource will gain influence over the agencies dependent on it for resources. *Influence* occurs when one network member can alter the behavior of another network member by providing or withholding resources. The strength and vulnerability, the ability to influence or be influenced, of an agency in the exchange relationships of the network results from the agency's potential number of exchange partners for a resource desired by the agency and the number of potential exchange partners that want the agency's products. The greater the number of potential exchange partners an agency has for its products, the less dependent the agency will be on any single trading partner for resources. The fewer alternative potential trading partners an agency has for the resources desired, the more dependent the agency will be on the partners. If an agency has a scarce resource, a resources in great demand, with limited suppliers of the resource in the task environment, and if the agency has many options in the task environment for resources that it desires, the agency is in a position of strength in the exchanges. The network will be asymmetrical. However, if the converse exists, with the agency having limited resources and products that are not in demand, and its exchange partners having many alternative sources for the resources

they desire and only a few trading partners possessing the resources that the agency needs, the agency is vulnerable. The greater the dependency of agency on a single partner or entity in the task environment, the less secure and powerful is the agency in the exchange relationship. However, the increased opportunities for exchanges and the reduced dependency on a few exchange partners can increase potential obligations and network maintenance costs. These costs are mitigated, according to Knoke (1993), by keeping the networks informal and decentralized.

The units in a network need not engage in exchanges directly, or the exchanges may be regulated by a third agency with the capacity to mandate exchanges between network participants. Mandated referrals and exchanges of resources occur when a third party requires two units in a network to interact. This is often the case when a superordinate agency requires referrals or particular types of exchanges among its subordinate units. For example, with managed care in health provision, the managed care agency manages and mandates the exchanges of other units within the health care networks. The managed care agency is the superordinate agency. It maintains its superordinate position and the responsiveness of the health network agencies by controlling fiscal resources and patients.

The amount and desirability of an agency's resources are important in the network's exchanges, but according to research by Mizruchi and Galaskiewicz (1993), resource dependency as a critical variable in determining the strength of relationships often is nested in variables such as the social class of the participants in the network. The level of resources alone is less critical than how organization use the resources in the network. The agency's network influence and dependency on its network partners are explained as much by the agency's skills in the use of its resources in bargaining and exchanges with its network participants as they are by the level of resources. The level of resources is not as critical as the way the organization uses the resources in the network.

Knoke's (1993) metareview of the research on elite networks used two dimensions of power: influence and domination. An *elite network* is a network composed of structures that are horizontal to one another but that have vertical relationships to local communities. Elite networks are power and resource holders. *Influence*, as defined above, occurs when one network member provides information or resources to another member with the intention of altering the latter's actions. *Domination*, the stronger of the two dimension of power, occurs when one member controls the behavior of another member by offering or withholding some benefit or cost, the sanctions of rewards and punishments, to achieve the ends of the controlling member. The power of one agency over another is a function of the dependency on the latter agency on the former for resources. Knoke concluded that organizations, not individuals, in elite networks are the principal members. In more complex networks, organizational imperatives supersede individual and personal interests. Complex networks develop when agencies seek to reduce resource dependency on a few exchange partners and expand the potential number of exchange partners. Increased involvement and linkages with multiple networks reduces dependency on a few partners and increases the agency's access to potential resources. The elite networks tend to be informal bargaining units. "Most elite power structures are decentralized bargaining systems rather than hierarchial systems controlled by a centralized economic elites" (Knoke, 1993, p. 41).

Cohesion

Exchanges between participants in a network that produce gains for each participant compared to alternative uses of the resources facilitate network cohesion. Network cohesion encourages more exchanges among network participants. *Cohesiveness* is defined operationally as anything that attracts people to join a dyad, group, organization, or network.

Blau's (1964) exchange theory elaborates on the cohesion-building function of exchanges in networks in its reciprocation propositions:

1. Individuals who supply services viewed as rewards to another in a relationship obligate the other to reciprocate.
2. To discharge the obligation, the second party must reciprocate by furnishing a benefit to the first.

These two rather simple propositions leading to cohesion rest on a more complex set of propositions or principles dealing with rationality, reciprocity, justice, stability, power, and dependence. People are more likely to continue engaging in exchanges with those they view as fair and with whom the exchanges are satisfying and beneficial. If participants in the network view the exchanges as unfair, they are more likely to seek other exchange partners and networks. If the participants get what they want from a network and if the exchange is viewed as fair, the more likely the participants are to turn to that network rather than other networks to satisfy their needs. Conversely, if they believe that they have been treated unfairly and have not obtained what they wanted, they will be less likely to engage in exchanges with that partner, in the expectation that any future relationship will not be fair or beneficial, and they will seek other trading or exchange partners (other networks) to obtain beneficial and fair exchanges.

Exchange, however, do not always result from the rational calculations of the costs and benefits of engaging alternative trading partners. Sometimes exchange partners are used because they are the only partners available with the needed resource. Other options may not exist. The unit needing the resource is then dependent on the other unit. The unit with the resource, the functionally superordinate party, is more likely to be able to impose conditions for the exchange and extract compliance from the dependent unit, the subordinate party in the relationship. The superordinate party has more potential power in the exchange relationship if the subordinate party is to obtain the needed resource.

This dependent relationship reflects Blau's (1964) superordinate–subordinate power relationship principle. *Superordinate* and *subordinate* refer to the distribution of power and resources in the social exchange. If the relationship becomes too imbalanced, it can affect network cohesion. The theory and principle states:

> The more exchange relations between superordinate and subordinate become imbalanced, the greater is the probability of opposition to those with power.
> The more the norms of reciprocity are violated by the superordinate, the less fair the exchanges, the greater is the imbalance.

If networks are composed of many subordinates and few superordinates:

> The more subordinates experience collectively relations of imbalance with superordinates, the greater is the sense of deprivation and the greater is the probability of opposition by the subordinates to the superordinates.

In short, dependency rather than interdependency often breeds resentment. Interdependence and fair exchanges rather than dependence facilitates network cohesion and solidarity between the units.

Density and Complexity

Networks can be dense and complex or simple. *Density* is the number of actual relationships in the network compared to the possible number of relationships (Specht, 1986).

Density of Potential Network Relationships

Number of Network Units (N)	All Possible Network Relationships $[N(N-1)/2]$	All Possible Network Relationships for Any Network Unit ($N-1$)
2	$2(2-1)/2 = 1$	$2-1 = 1$
3	$3(3-1)/2 = 3$	$3-1 = 2$
4	$4(4-1)/2 = 6$	$4-1 = 3$
5	$5(5-1)/2 = 10$	$5-1 = 4$
6	$6(6-1)/2 = 15$	$6-1 = 5$
N	$N(N-1)/2 = X$	$N-1 = X$

Density and complexity are determined by the number of units in the network and the amount of interaction between the units. As the size of a network increases, its density and potential cohesion become more difficult to manage, given the large number of possible relationship between the units. The resources necessary for managing network density increase disproportionately for the network as a whole as network size and the number of potential relationships increase.

The size of the network is important because of the number of relationships to be managed. While the number of relationships to be managed by any single participant in the network is one less than the total number of participants or the total number of other participants, the aggregate number of relationships to be managed in the network increases geometrically with the addition of each new unit.

Centrality

Centrality and reachability are two critical variables related to an agency's influence in a networks. An agency has a position of *centrality* when other agencies in the network have to go through the agency for communication or to engage in their exchanges. The central agency provides a thermostatic or regulatory service for the agency.

In Figure 1, the chain network of five participants, participant 3, other things equal, has a position of greater influence, as exchanges from participants on one end of the chain to reach participants on the other end of the chain always must go through participant 3. The centrality of participants 2 and 4, while not as great as that of participant 3, is greater than that of participants 1 and 5. The capacity to influence participants is enhanced by centrality, as exchanges must pass through the more central participants.

In Figure 2, the star network, all participants must go through participant 3 to reach an exchange partner. Participant 3's influence should be greater than in Figure 2 because no exchange can be effected without 3's participation. Participant 3's centrality and influence should be reduced in Figure 3, as all network participants have direct access to all other network participants. With centrality, however, there is potentially greater network management and maintenance responsibilities.

An agency's *reachability*, which is important for achieving centrality, refers to

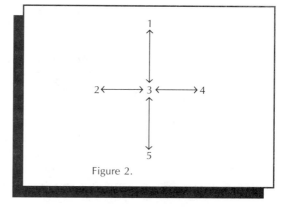

Figure 2.

whether there are paths to the agency for exchanges, that is, the structural ease or difficulty in reaching the potential exchange agency (Woodard & Doreion, 1994). The power of a network participant can be enhanced if it can achieve centrality by linking and coupling to the other network units (Knoke, 1993). Participant 3 has greater reachability to more network participants in two of the three networks than do the other participants.

Coordination and Control

Networks between agencies may first develop on a voluntary, informal basis for the purpose of acquiring resources. If successful, these immature networks evolve into sys-

1⟷2⟷3⟷4⟷5

Figure 1.

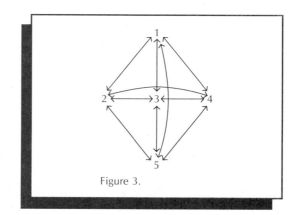

Figure 3.

tems that can reconfigure services. The degree of reconfiguration and joint action, according to Fine and Fine (1986), forms a continuum. At one end is little interaction, with member agencies having referrals of common clients but still working independently of each other much of the time and on most issues. These networks are characterized as *loosely coupled networks* (Aldrich, 1971; Weick, 1976) composed of participants loosely connected and with the capacity to act independently on most concerns but still capable of exchanges and joint actions when needed. Loosely coupled networks often reconcile the strains between autonomy and interdependence of their members.

The coordination between participants can be informal, with dominance resting with the coordinators who serve as the linchpins, as illustrated in Figures 1 and 2, or through group mechanisms, as represented by Figure 3. Group mechanisms lend themselves to more equality but suffer from the expense of maintaining multiple interactions. Group mechanisms can lead to highly interactive networks, with member organizations making joint service decisions as if for a single agency. Joint action is gained at the expense of autonomy.

As interagency cooperation and interaction becomes more dense, the network becomes more formal, with set protocols, rules, and procedures to manage the interactions. Individual discretion and variation are reduced, and the formal protocols govern the interaction. Individual agencies lose autonomy in proportion to the network's density, intensity, and control. And without management and maintenance, entropy, a characteristic of systems, begins (Hage, 1980; Van de Ven, Delbecq, & Koenig, 1976).

Agency's Member Status

The agency's networks and networking traits can vary with the participants' hierarchical level in the agency. Agencies can network on the policy and programmatic levels involving agency administrators and elites and at the operational service delivery level. Line-level staff can network as part of formal agency service plans and agreements or more informally with personal networks. Line service staff engage more often in exchanges involving client referrals, services coordination, and information exchanges for specific clients. Line service staff often are ignorant of the management networks and exchanges (Woodard & Doreion, 1994). Healy's (1991) research on service coordination by line staff found that they preferred service coordination through informal rather than formal networks. The informal networks may develop as a response to the difficulty of participating in the large, complex, and formal networks. The informal networks indicate the beginning of entropy of the formal networks.

Woodard and Doreion (1994) found that line-level staff networks were not always symmetrical but they did tend to be repetitive, with line service staff often using the same partners. The exchanges were more symmetrical with the frequently used network partners and, in general, were more symmetrical than were interagency network exchanges by management.

The agency's management level is more concerned with network exchanges of population and problem information, fiscal and material resources exchanges and management, and domain information exchanges (Woodard & Doreion, 1994).

Locus of Authority

Networks also can vary by the locus of authority, that is, where the authority for creating, maintaining, and defining the objectives and tasks resides inside or outside the network. Voluntary networks, that is, networks composed of voluntary participants, have an internal locus of authority, while mandated networks have an external locus of authority. The managed care network described earlier, and the interagency coordinating groups often required by funding sources such as the federal government or United Ways, are examples of networks with external loci of authority. The objectives, goals, structure, and rules of exchange of the network are determined not by the members but by the superordinate external authority. There is little clear evidence on the effects of the locus of authority on network performance, although Schopler (1994), after a review of the research literature, speculates on the possible associations of the loci of authority and types of tasks for which the loci might be best suited. Mandated networks with externally defined rules should be best suited for clearly defined, standardized, limited tasks. This is reasonable, as the external mandating authority usually has a reason for creating the network. Voluntary networks with an internal locus of authority should respond better to tasks requiring innovation and creativity, although they may be less efficient in operation.

DOMAIN CONFLICT AND CONSENSUS IN NETWORKS

Agencies generally seek domain consensus and a reduction of domain conflicts to obtain and maximize resources and to reduce the amount of energy and other resources expended in bargaining and negotiating to obtain resources, protect domains, and manage competition and conflict. Domain consensus promotes stability and predictability.

Domain conflicts occur whenever an agency attempts to establish itself in or obtain all or part of another agency's domain. The conflict and competition can involve any of the resources of the domain. The conflict

theorist Coser (1964) has a conception of social conflict that is applicable to the domain conflicts and competition between agencies for domains and resources. Coser's working definition of conflict is "a struggle over values and claims to scarce status, power and resources in which the aims of opponents are to neutralize, injure or eliminate the rivals" (p. 3). The injury to a social agency can be the loss of clients, fiscal resources, or public support.

Kriesberg (1982), another conflict theorist, emphasizes that competition is conflict when the parties in the competition recognize that they are seeking the same domain or resource. Without recognition of the competition, conflict does not occur. Lauer (1982) and Deutsch (1973) hold that competition is managed conflict. Competition, like most conflict, has rules of engagement or rules of the game between the competing parties. The economic marketplace has rules for national and international trade and competition. Governments devote much time and energy to developing and managing the rules. Electoral campaigns, with their own rules, represent rules of conflict for changes of government in a democracy. But the rules are followed in conflict, competition, and change only if they are seen as fair by the competing participants, if all competing participants see the others as playing fairly by the rules, and if the participants perceive that violation of the rules will produce costs that will exceed any potential gains.

An agency's domains become vulnerable to competition and conflict when it is perceived as not fulfilling its responsibilities to maintain its domain obligations and hence not allowing complementary organizations in its task environment and networks to maintain their domain obligations. Ideological differences between organizations often lead to conflict as these differences shape different perceptions of reality, domain responsibilities, and what constitutes fair exchange.

ESTABLISHING AND MAINTAINING DOMAINS

Establishing domains is facilitated by the resource richness and resource dispersion in the task environment and by the instability and weakness of existing domain agreements and networks. If there is consensus and stability among existing agencies on the inclusion of all the significant components of a domain, and if these agencies are well networked, an agency seeking to establish or expand its domain will have to engage in conflict and competition to create instability and turbulence so that a domains and resources can be claimed. It will need to break down existing networks unless there are unclaimed resources in the task environment. Conversely, once an agency has an established domain, it will seek to secure its domain by working toward stability and placidness in the task environment and a concentration of resources in its domain and networks. However, the richer the resources of the task environment, the more domains and networks can be sustained.

Task Environment Conditions That Help Agencies Establish and Maintain Domains

	Establish Domains	Maintain Domains
Task environment	Instability, turbulence, heterogeneity	Stability, placidness, homogeneity
Task environment resources	Dispersion, richness	Concentration

The 1960s and 1970s, with abundant federal funding for social agencies, a condition of resource richness, saw the creation of many new social agencies and service networks. In the 1990s and into the twenty-first century, with growing fiscal resource scarcity, social turbulence, and a decline in public support projected, the environment of social service agencies may well parallel that of the proprietary sector. This is indeed what Menefee (1994) has predicted, based on a survey of social agency executives. He has forecasted social agency consolidation, downsizing, hostile takeovers, and intense competition, with the weaker agencies driven out of the market. The surviving agencies and any new agencies will be competitive, aggressive, and entrepreneurial, according to the agencies' executive panel's predictions. These forecasts were made prior to the election of the Republican Congress in 1994.

DOMAIN CONFLICTS RESOLUTION STRATEGIES

Coser (1964) has asserted that as communities, and indeed the world, becomes more interdependent and closer, there will be greater need for rules of conflict and rules and structures for conflict resolution. Without the rules and structures, social structures can split and disintegrate. Levine and White (1961, 1963) indicate that one of functions of coordinating, planning, and joint fund-raising organizations such as the United Way is to provide a forum and structure for domain conflict resolution.

Domain conflict resolution protocols generally involve identification of the area of domain conflict and assessment of potential outcomes, such as compromise by dividing the domain to support multiple agencies or seeking exchanges of domains by the contesting parties.

One potential conflict outcome is the maintenance of the status quo; here, neither party gains or loses a domain at the end of the conflict. If the conflict concerns fundamental issues, the maintenance of the status quo is probably only a temporary solution.

Agency Domain Conflict Outcomes

Conflict Resolution	Agency A	Agency B
Status quo	No change	No change
Zero sum	+	−
	−	+
Non–zero sum	+	+

The second solution is a zero sum solution. In a zero sum (or win/lose) solution, the domain gains of one party or set of parties is commensurate with equivalent domain loses by the other party or set of parties. The distribution of the domain between the two sets is changed, but the total amount of the domain is unchanged. This solution generally involves the use of power, and the side with greater power or more skillful use of power will gain domains. The application of power can be through persuasion. Kriesberg (1982) notes that persuasion is applied when one party in a conflict tries "to convince the adversary that it should yield what is sought . . . agreement would be in the interest or in conformity to its own values" (p. 17). This solution is commensurate with Blau's (1964) superordinate–subordinate power principles discussed earlier. As previously indicated, *superordinate* and *subordinate* refer to the distribution of power and resources in the social exchange relationship. The party in the exchange relationship losing a domain will, according to the principle, likely remain in opposition to those with power and look for an opportunity to gain back the lost domain.

The more optimal solution is to cast the conflict in a non-zero-sum (win/win) game—a positive exchange relationship in which both sides make gains. This can be done by assessing the task environment for needs, resources, and other new domain possibilities, as yet unclaimed, to add to the domains of the competing parties. The assessment and division may involve direct bargaining according to rules established and agreed on to limit the conflict. Bargaining is "the process whereby two or more parties attempt to settle what each shall give and take, or perform and receive, in transactions between them" (Rubin & Brown, 1975, p. 2). The parties, at least temporarily, join together in an exchange (bargaining) relationship, regardless of any prior or future exchange relationships. The bargaining concerns (1) the division or exchange of one or more specific resources and/or (2) the resolution of one or more intangible conflicts among the parties or among those whom the parties represent. The bargaining usually involves the presentation of demands or proposals by one party and evaluation by the other party, followed by concessions and counterproposals. The activity is thus sequential rather than simultaneous (Rubin & Brown, 1975, pp. 6–18).

The bargaining rules usually adhere to the principles that seek (1) clarity of communication between the parties on areas of agreement, sharing, and precision on the disagreements; (2) compromise seeking areas of agreement, sharing, and a middle ground; and (3) mutual recognition of the legitimacy of the parties to engage in bargaining (Deutsch, 1973)).

If the parties in the conflict are unable to resolve the conflict directly, a third party is often called in to *mediate* the dispute. The third party is generally either (1) a neutral party, one perceived by both sides as fair, to mediate and negotiate if direct negotiation between the parties fails, or (2) a superordinate party with authority over the contending parties. United Ways and planning councils often serve as mediators in social agency domain disputes. Rubin and Brown (1975) claim that mediators serve as an audience and make the bargaining process more trustworthy.

> The mere presence of an audience (including the psychological presence) motivates the bargainers to seek positive, and avoid negative, evaluations—especially when the audience is salient to the bargainers. (p. 44)

Mediators and mediation can be formal or informal. Mediation helps to reduce irrationality and promote rationality among the parties, provides opportunities for face saving by the parties, facilitates communication, regulates the costs of third-party interests, and provides or explores additional resources and alternative solutions (Rubin & Brown, 1975, pp. 60–61).

The objective of mediation is to obtain the parties' compliance with the bargaining principles. The goal of mediation and of the mediator is accountability. The audience, in addition to formal mediators, may include clients and representatives of the public or other constituencies. The mediator's effectiveness rests on whether he or she is perceived as fair by all parties in the dispute. Presidents Carter and Clinton were at least partially successful in mediating disputes between Israel and Egypt and between Israel and the Palestinians. But as we saw with the 1994–95 major league baseball strike, even mediation by prestigious third parties such as the president is not always successful.

If mediation is unsuccessful, arbitration is another option before coercive action by the parties is applied. *Arbitration* is the use of a third party, who is superordinate to the contending parties for the purpose of conflict resolution, to find and dictate a solution. Arbitrators can be agencies such as the United Way, with its superordinate funding position over nonprofit agencies; a court; or other third

parties with authority over all parties to the dispute. Arbitration is dangerous to all parties in the conflict because it requires them to surrender autonomy to the arbiter.

A final task in domain conflict resolution is to establish domain boundary maintenance and protection mechanisms in order to reduce the expense of waging future domain conflicts.

The thesis is not that agencies are greedy in seeking new domains or expanding existing ones, but that in tasks environments with resource scarcity, agencies need and will seek to protect and often expand their resources and domains. In a turbulent and competitive environment, the importance and usefulness of the rules of the game, as well as the techniques, mechanisms, and structures for competition and exchanges to any agency, are generally related to whether the agency is trying to establish, maintain, or expand its domain. As social services are privatized, and as social workers move toward proprietary practice and the adoption of entrepreneurial behavior by nonprofit agencies, the skills of networking in a turbulent environment become essential.

THE CHANGING NATURE OF COMMUNITY AND NETWORKING

Social networks between social agencies and people exist in communities and are influenced by the changing nature of community institutions and organizations. Warren (1978), in his analysis of the American community, argued that one of the great changes in American society has been the movement from horizontal to vertical relationships between communities and their institutions.

Horizontal and Vertical Relationships

Organizations and institutions that share the same geographic domains, that have coterminous task environments, that exist within the same community, with similar loci of decision making, when linked, have horizontal relationships. Horizontal networks, networks comprised of agencies on the same level of community with horizontal relations, are more likely to be decentralized, informal, fluid, and, at times, competitive and marketlike (Alter, n.d.).

Vertical relationship networks are networks composed of agencies and institutions one or more of which has a domain that geographically supersedes the other agency or agencies in the network. The vertically superordinate agencies in the network extend their structures of authority and locus of decision making beyond the local community to regional, state, federal and national, and international levels. Their domains and concerns extend beyond the local community to encompass a larger community of interest. Local community agencies in a network with vertical relationships with superordinate agencies must consider and often be responsive to the superordinate agencies' extracommunity interests. Networks with vertical organizations are more likely to be rationally constructed, with an orientation to codified rules and protocols, centralized, and with formal linkage agreements.

The trend away from local human services to national agencies began in earnest with the New Deal of the 1930s, with its federal grants in aid, and expanded and accelerated with the Great Society programs such as the War on Poverty, Comprehensive Community Mental Health, and Model Cities programs of the 1960s and 1970s. The 1990s have seen a movement toward privatization but not necessarily localization. Social and health agencies, traditionally a community's mutual support agencies, are becoming increasingly privatized and part of national proprietary agencies.

The trend toward vertical relationships

between organizations and the local community is also part of other community functions, especially the economic function, with the growth of national and multinational corporations often abetted by public policy (Barlett & Steele, 1992, 1994).

The difficulty in vertical relationships between a local community, horizontal agencies within the community, and superordinate institutions is that the community bases of concern and responsibility differ. The superordinate agencies' interests, responsibilities, and accountability extend beyond the local community. The superordinate, extracommunity, vertically related agency's perception of its best interests may be different from the community's good. Local concerns simply are not a priority in the superordinate agency's decision equations.

The local community's difficulties and risks with vertical agencies are illustrated by the health care delivery systems. The Columbia/HCA Healthcare Corporation, the world's largest health care chain, in 1994 owned 311 hospitals and 125 clinics in 37 states and 2 foreign countries, up from only 30 hospitals in 1993. In some communities Columbia/HCA America owns the only community hospital (Myerson, 1994). Whether a community's hospital or clinic remains open or closes depends not on its impact on the community's health but on its impact on the corporation's economic viability and other companywide policy considerations. Columbia/HCA has purchased local, community-based, nonprofit hospitals and closed them to expand the market base for its adjoining hospitals. Destin, Florida, illustrates the point. *The New York Times* quoted the CEO of Columbia/HCA America, David T. Vandewater, after closing the community hospital in Destin, Florida: "We simply can't have a hospital on every corner" (Eckholm, 1994, p. A1). The Destin hospital, one of the corporation's 45 Florida hospitals, was

Destin's only hospital. The closing, while an economically rational action for the corporation, means that the community lost its primary health care resource, has less health care access, and has increased health risk (Eckholm, 1994).

The risks of vertical network relations are present in government programs as well. The U.S. Department of Labor (DoL) withdrew funding from a series of housing and job training programs for the homeless conducted by nonprofit agencies in 1994. Although the DoL stated that the overall program, according to a *New York Times* article, "has proven effective," it said it "wanted to revamp and consolidate the 154 employment and job training programs funded by the Department" (Kilborn, 1994, p. A14). Local programs were not closed because they were ineffectual or inefficient. Funding was withdrawn because of changes in the federal agency's policy. The DoL provided most of the local agency funding, and the dependency relationship between the DoL and the local agencies was highly asymmetrical. The local agencies were dependent on the DoL but not vice versa.

As mutual support, social welfare, and health agencies move toward more vertical relationships with local communities and privatized proprietary organizations, they will become intentionally more profit driven. Although the impact on the local community is uncertain, if these agencies follow the profit-driven decisions in the other vertically controlled and economically driven organizations, the local community's well-being will not be paramount to the extracommunity megastructures. For an extensive review of the growing importance and impact of vertically related organizations and their decisions on local communities see Bartlett and Steele (1992).

The 1980s saw a relocation of much of the industrial base of America by its corpo-

rations to offshore locations. While plant closings and policy shifts that affect the fundamental viability of a community sometimes cannot be avoided, they should not be undertaken capriciously or abruptly. The decision making and structures of national and international corporations need to be harmonized with the local community. The communitarian Etzioni (1993) argues:

> Affected communities should be accorded an opportunity to help the corporation solve its economic problems or to find buyers for the plant (including its workers), if it's to be sold rather than transferred (*i.e. in any case, sold or transferred, the community should be given opportunity to find alternative buyers to retain the plant and the company should be compelled by policy to cooperate. The social environment, the community's life, needs to be considered by policy in a plant's closing [just] as the environment impact is considered in the opening*). (p. 127)

A related argument can be made regarding a proprietary corporation's obligation to repay the community for the enticements it provided the corporation to locate there. Enticements include tax breaks, low-interest secured loans, streets and other infrastructures, and often the physical facilities, such as stadiums and arenas, provided by states and municipalities to privately owned sports teams. A similar logic should apply even more strongly to government's impact on the community due to military base closings and social program reductions. The government should be the agent of the community; the community should not become a victim of government.

PROTOCOLS FOR DEVELOPING AND MAINTAINING DOMAIN CONSENSUS

Establishing domain consensus, developing and coordinating networks, and managing networks, as discussed above, are related to the resources available in the task environment, the above dimensions, and the skills of the participants. Agencies seek to maximize their autonomy and resources. This is also the charge to social workers in client empowerment and self-determination: to maximize client autonomy. However, neither agencies nor clients operate in social isolation. Maximizing autonomy and resources require interaction with the social environment or the task environment. In establishing and maintaining networks, the task is to facilitate interdependency rather than dependency.

Social agencies have missions and objectives that relate to the environment, whether the are to increase the economic self-sufficiency of welfare mothers, the social functioning of mental patients, or the reduction of child abuse and neglect. They seek domains and resources, and generally must network with other agencies and organizations to achieve their objectives and fulfill their mission.

Protocols for determining the needed network are as follows:

1. Determine the total scope of the technology, tasks, and resources required to accomplish the objectives.

2. Determine the agency's current domain of technology, tasks, and resources.

3. Compare the agency's existing domain with the total scope of technology, tasks, and resources required to accomplish the objectives. If a gap exists, the agency will either need to expand its domain or network with resource providers, both fiscal and nonfiscal, clients, legitimizers, technology holders, and other complementary agencies, to achieve its objectives.

4. Assess the community, that is, the task environment, for the domains, the holders of the needed resources, and their exchange preferences.

5. Negotiate exchanges with the resource providers based on resource exchanges required by both agencies. In the negotiation and networking, the importance of size, complexity, dependency, cohesion, centrality, and the other dimensions of networks should be recognized.

CLIENTS AND SOCIAL SUPPORT NETWORKS

Clients exist in communities with networks and a potential range of networks beyond formal social agencies. Researchers and scholars have linked client empowerment to participation in social support networks, natural groups, and self-help groups, especially when these networks serve as mediating structures (Anderson & Shaw, 1994; Blau & Alba, 1982; Cochran, 1990; Gestan & Jason, 1987; Heller, 1990; Lee, 1988; Levine, 1988; Lewis & Ford, 1990; McCarthy & Nelson, 1991; O'Connell, 1978; Schwartz, 1986; and Whittaker; 1986, among others). Client empowerment means increasing the client's capacity to act to achieve the client's goals. Like power, it is the ability to act. Empowerment, therefore, is the cornerstone of the social work value of client self-determination. Many of the dimensions and caveats of networking explored above apply to social support networks.

Whittaker and his associates (1983) found that social support networks and professional interventions supplemented rather than replaced each other. They distinguished social support networks from the more generic concept of social networks, which can either support or detract from the individual's social functioning. Social support was defined as a set of interconnected relationships among a group of people that provide enduring patterns of nurturance (in any or all forms) and provide contingent reinforcement for efforts to cope with life on a day to day basis. (p. 5)

Schore and Atkin (1993) defined social support less precisely as "the experience of belonging to groups of people who understand, support, and value you" (p. 321).

Social support networks provide mutual support, help with living, and emotional supports, especially during times of crisis, and reduce the need for institutional and social agency help (Balgopal, 1988). A social support network to promote client empowerment is based on interdependency and reciprocity rather than dependency. Mutual helping is interdependency. Members learn skills to help themselves while they are helping others. Informal and primary groups need interdependency, as their maintenance often depends on the satisfaction they provide to their members.

The experience of Auslander and Auslander (1988) and Manzall (1986) has led them to conclude that self-help groups and volunteer networks are beneficial to agencies as well as to clients. Self-help groups and volunteers can add efficiency if they enable agencies to serve a greater number of clients, increase visibility in the client community, and link agencies with community groupings and networks. Volunteers legitimize an agency and can be effective in media relations.

Shumaker and Brownell (1984) conceive of social support as "an exchange of resources between two individuals perceived by the provider or the recipient as intended to enhance the well-being of the recipient" (p. 11). Resources can include material, specific, and instrumental resources such as money and shelter or the nonmaterial and ex-

pressive, symbolic, and emotive gratification of affiliative needs or belonging, self-identity maintenance and enhancement, and self-esteem enhancement (Shumaker & Brownell, 1984, pp. 17–25; Specht, 1986). Reciprocity or mutual obligation is inherent in social support networks, as "providing support to someone in the same network increases the probability that one's own needs will be met in the future" (Shumaker & Brownell, 1984, p. 29). The findings of Walker and his colleagues (1993) support the importance of reciprocity. Reciprocity, as expected from the propositions of exchange theory, tends to match the recipient's view of the value of the resource supports received. When reciprocity is absent, the social support network withers. Without reciprocity, according to Blau's (1964) reciprocity principles, whether the network involves individuals, agencies, governments, or communities, the network's cohesion will be reduced (Shumaker & Brownell, 1984, pp. 24–29).

The integrating and cohesive effects of social support networks can reduce social isolation and possibly alienation. Zimmerman and Rappaport (1988), in a cross-sectional study of community participation, concluded that greater involvement was positively associated with individual psychological empowerment and inversely associated with alienation. Psychological empowerment was defined as the "connection between a sense of personal competence, a desire for, and a willingness to take action in the public domain" (p. 746). Schore and Atkin (1993) reported on DoL data from the 1960s demonstrating that the incidence of depression rose from 12% among workers in workplaces with high levels of social support to 26.8% in workplaces with low levels of social support.

Caution, however, should be exercised in embracing social support networks as wholly positive. Specht (1986) insists that the concepts of social support and social support networks have not been precisely and uniformly used in the literature. Often these labels are used for different phenomena. The directions of the relationships between the social support groups and networks are imprecisely used and research results have been inconclusive, with the relationships being more associative than causative. The alternative question—Do social supports contribute to people's well-being or does greater well-being increase social support network involvement?—has not been answered.

Primary, Secondary, and Tertiary Social Supports

Clarity in the conception of social support groups and networks is needed. Social support groups and networks might reasonably be conceptualized as either primary, secondary, or tertiary. Primary social supports are those ascribed to or into which the individual is born, such as the family, kinship, and primary groups associated with family. Secondary support groups are those with broad interest in and meaning to the individual, such as informal friendship groups and more formal groupings with broad interest in the individual, such as church and religious groups, fraternal groups, unions, and other similar associations.

Tertiary groups have more focused and limited interest in the individual than the other two types. Tertiary supports include the range of therapy and formally constructed support groups, as well as special interest associations such as the Sierra Club. As Putnam (1995) says, their ties are to common ideas or issues shared by the membership but not a commitment to the people who comprise the membership. Although secondary relationships may grow out of tertiary associations, such as some members becoming close friends, the individual member does not turn to the formal association or expect it to provide a wide range of social supports. Tertiary support groups provide a forum for individuals to focus on themselves, generally for specific problems such as alcoholism or sexual abuse. Bonding between members as individuals is not required. Any group of like-minded others is sufficient. The bonding is to the group and to the idea. It is often relatively unimportant who the other members of the audience are; the audience can be transient, as long as it exists. The criticism of tertiary groups is focused not so much on what they do as on what they don't do and their restraining the individuals from turning to more encompassing primary and secondary associations (Bellah, Madsen, Sullivan, Swidler, & Tipton, 1985, 1991; Putnam, 1995). In their packaging and limiting of relationships, tertiary groups may drive out the time, energy, and effort required for the bonding and reciprocity of primary and secondary associations, hence reducing social supports and a general sense of community, which do not fall within their purview.

The exchanges between social support network participants are not always rational or intentional, and the actual effects sometimes differ from the intended ones. Parties may differ on the perception and evaluation of benefits and helpfulness, with the differences in evaluations reducing cohesion (Shumaker & Brownell, 1984, p. 21). Social supports can have harmful effects even when their intention is beneficial. The short- and long-term coping effects can differ, with beneficial effects in the short term and negative effects in the long term, especially if these social supports lead to long-term dependency, future obligations, and reciprocal claims for future resources. Shinn, Lehmann, and Wong's (1984) exploration of social support networks found that the reciprocity demands, that is, the current and future demands for resources by the provider of current resources, on the recipient can be pernicious. If the recipient fails to reciprocate because the obligations exceed the recipient's resources and capacity, this failure creates stresses on both the provider and recipient. The provider may come to view the recipient as a free rider. The recipient has the stresses of the unmet obligation and the sense of a loss of autonomy and dependency, especially if in a constant recipient role. The situational and compliant requirements to receive continuing unilateral support are harmful to the recipient's sense of self-efficacy. However, if the network is to be maintained, there must be reciprocity. If there is true reciprocity, then there must be a balancing of the provider and recipient roles.

Maton (1988) supports the importance of reciprocal roles. He reports that where social supports were essentially bidirectional, where the parties were both givers and receivers of support, there was a greater sense of well-being among the members than occurred in unidirectional networks or where the individual was only a receiver or a provider of support. Additionally, activity beyond the self-help group, where members had other involvements, was a key component of self-help group efficacy. The extragroup involvements may have lowered demands on the self-help group.

Heller's (1990) review of social support network research concluded that social networks generally helped strengthen members' capacity to deal with personal, interpersonal, and environmental stressors. However, it also found that social networks themselves can be a source of stress.

Similar to interagency networks, personal networks and social supports, including those used by clients, demand maintenance and can consume time, energy, and even money that the client cannot spare. A too tightly integrated, dense, and cohesive network can be socially isolating and limit-

ing. Barth and Schinke's (1984) examination of social supports for teenage mothers found that tight family networks may cut the mother off from other potential social supports. Nonetheless, network participation usually was associated with enhanced social and interpersonal skills, parenting skills, and efficacy.

Metaresearch by Walker, Wasserman, and Wellman (1993) supported the view that unilateral support is a myth. Social support is not a unidimensional concept. Not only can social support networks be simultaneously beneficial and detrimental, different kinds of relationships provide different kinds of support: emotional aid, material aid, information, and companionship. It is unlikely that a single social support network, especially a tertiary network, will provide all the needed forms of support.

Access to social support networks differs across societies, communities, and individuals (Walker et al., 1993, p. 75). As with social agency networks, proximity and the ability to make contact (reachability) are important for individual social support networks. Although proximity correlates with reachability, the telephone, the Internet, and modern transportation and communication technology reduce the need for physical proximity for contact and connectedness. Proximity is important for the social support of companionship, but proximity is less critical than reachability for some of the other types of social and emotional supports.

Social support networks vary in size. While the research indicates mixed findings, a midsized network is typically most supportive. Density, that is, the number of relationships or possible relationships, also affects network cohesion and integration. Again, the research results are mixed. Optimal density depends on the type of support needed, with less dense networks more conducive to emotional support.

Kelly and Kelly's (1985) research on natural helping, a form of social support, indicates that social support networks may be focused rather than generalized. They found that helpers tended to be respondent or network specific and were not "generalized helpers" helping a large number of respondents. The helpers often became helpers as reciprocity for help they had received from the respondent or others. Patterson et al. (1988) found that natural helping in rural areas also differed by gender and content. Female natural helpers were more dependent on bonding, more expressive, and more effective with friends and family than they were with neighbors and less close contacts. Male natural helpers were more effective instrumentally with neighbors and less so on personal and emotional or expressive levels than were females. Effectiveness was evaluated by professionals and by the natural helper's network.

Practice Implications

In assessing a client's social support networks, social workers should not assume uniformity across clients. Social supports will vary across clients by culture, integration into the community versus isolation from a primary community, and the richness of the client's task environment. Primary and secondary social support networks should be explored before turning to the often more accessible tertiary supports.

Volunteers and natural social support networks can link the agency, client, and resources. They can also reduce the isolation of clients, as well as the isolation of the agency from the community, and help integrate both into a social support system. Clients need to be linked with appropriate volunteers and social supports, and social agencies need to be a part of the community, with active support constituencies.

Social workers assisting clients in developing and linking with social support networks should be aware that social support and social support networks can have both beneficial and detrimental effects on clients. Not all self-help and support networks are socially helpful to the client or to the community, although the client may receive some social support from participation. The Klu Klux Klan and other ethnic supremacist groups, regardless of the ethnicity espoused as superior, may provide social and mutual support to a bigot who is a member of the group, but the group does not assist the member to develop socially, nor does it contribute to the community's well-being. The test of a social support network is whether it contributes to the client's and the community's well-being and social functioning.

Youth gangs may be a source of social support to their members. The members receive affiliative support, protection, and often material rewards for belonging to the gang and participating in its activities. However, the reciprocity requirements, both current and future, and the need to engage in violent, antisocial, and self-harming behavior makes demands on the youth that will inhibit positive current and future social functioning. Intervention requires developing for the youth alternative sources of social support.

Protocols and techniques for developing client social support networks will be discussed more fully in Chapter 13.

Information sources on actual and potential social support networks include the client, client assessment, and community assessment. Community assessment techniques, discussed in greater detail in Chapter 6, include key informants, community forums, social indicators and demographics, and field surveys. The techniques tend to be more effective when used in combination (Davenport & Davenport, 1982; Humm-Delgato & Delgado, 1986).

Social workers also need to develop their own practice and resource networks. As will be discussed in Chapter 13, individual client systems may be more useful for client empowerment than large, complex, formal, and often perfunctory efforts at social agency coordination.

References

Aldrich, H. E. (1971). Organizational boundaries and interorganizational conflict. *Human Relations, 24,* 279–281.

Alter, C. F. (n.d.). *Casebook in social service administration* (2nd ed.). Iowa City: University of Iowa School of Social Work.

Anderson, D. B., & Shaw, S. L. (1994). Starting a support group for families and partners of people with HIV/AIDS in a rural setting. *Social Work, 39,* 135–138.

Anderson, R. E., & Carter, I. (1984). *Human behavior in the social environment: A social systems approach* (3rd ed.). New York: Aldine.

Auslander, A., & Auslander, G. K. (1988). Self-help groups and the family service agency. *Social Casework, 69,* 74–80.

Balgopal, P. R. (1988). Social work and Asian Indian families. In C. Jacobs & D. D. Bowles (Eds.), *Ethnicity and race: Critical concepts in social work* (pp. 18–33). Silver Spring, MD: National Association of Social Workers.

Barlett, D., & Steele, J. B. (1992). *America: What went wrong?* Kansas City, MO: Andrews and McMeel.

Barlett, D., & Steele, J. B. (1994). *America: Who really pays the taxes?* New York: Touchstone/Simon & Schuster.

Barth, R. P., & Schinke, S. P. (1984). Enhancing the social supports of teenage mothers. *Social Casework, 65,* 523–531.

Bellah, R. N., Madsen, R., Sullivan, W. M., Swidler, A., & Tipton, S. M. (1985). *Habits of the heart: Individualism and commitment in American life.* New York: Harper & Row.

Bellah, R. N., Madsen, R., Sullivan, W. M., Swidler, A., & Tipton, S. M. (1991). *The good society.* New York: Vintage Books.

Blau, J. P., & Alba, R. D. (1982). Empowering nets of participation. *Administrative Science Quarterly, 27,* 363–379.

Blau, P. M. (1964). *Exchange and power in social life.* New York: Wiley.

Churchman, C. W. (1965). *The general systems approach.* New York: Dell.

Cochran, M. (1990). Personal social networks as a focus of support. *Prevention in Human Services, 9,* 45–67.

Coser, L. A. (1964). *The functions of social conflict.* New York: Free Press.

Davenport, J., & Davenport, J., III. (1982). Utilizing the social networks in rural communities. *Social Casework, 63,* 106–113.

Deutsch, M. (1973). *The resolution of conflict: Construction and destructive processes.* New Haven, CT: Yale University Press.

Eckholm, E. (1994, September 26). A town loses its hospital, in the name of cost control. *The New York Times,* p. A1.

Etzioni, A. (1993). *The spirit of community: Rights, responsibilities and the communitarian agenda.* New York: Crown.

Evan, W. (1963). The organizational set: Toward a theory of inter-organizational relations. In J. D. Thompson (Ed.), *Organizational design and research: Approaches to organizational design* (pp. 173–191). Pittsburgh: University of Pittsburgh Press.

Fine, S. H., & Fine, A. P. (1986). Distribution channels in marketing social work. *Social Casework, 67,* 227–233.

Galaskiewicz, J., & Wasserman, S. (1993). Social network analysis: Concepts, methodology and directions for the 1990s. *Sociological Methods and Research, 22,* 3–22.

Gestan, E. I., & Jason, L. A. (1987). Social and community interventions. *Annual Review of Psychology, 38,* 127–160.

Gouldner, A. W. (1960). The norm of reciprocity: A preliminary statement. *American Sociology Review, 25,* 161–178.

Hage, J. (1980). *Theories of organizations.* New York: Urly-Interscience.

Healy, J. (1991). Linking local services: Coordination in community centres. *Australian Social Work, 14,* 5–13.

Hearn, G. (Ed.). (1969). *The general systems approach: Contributions toward an [sic] holistic conception of social work*. New York: Council on Social Work Education.

Heller, K. (1990). Social and community intervention. *Annual Review of Psychology, 41,* 141–168.

Homan, G. C. (1958). Social behavior as exchange. *American Journal of Sociology, 63,* 597–606.

Humm-Delgado, D., & Delgado, M. (1986). Gaining community entree to assess service needs of Hispanics. *Social Casework, 67,* 80–89.

Kelly, P., & Kelly, V. R. (1985). Supporting natural helpers: A cross-cultural study. *Social Casework, 66,* 358–386.

Kilborn, P. T. (1994, April 11). Jobs program may become the casualty of its success. *The New York Times,* p. A14.

Knoke, D. (1993). Networks of elite structures and decision making. *Sociological Methods and Research, 22,* 23–45.

Kriesberg, L. (1982). *Social conflict* (2nd ed.). Englewood Cliffs, NJ: Prentice-Hall.

Lauer, R. H. (1982). *Perspectives on social change* (3rd ed.). Boston: Allyn & Bacon.

Lee, J. A. B. (1988). Group work with the poor and oppressed. *Social Work with Groups, 11,* 5–9.

Leighninger, R. B., Jr. (1978). Systems theory. *Journal of Social Work and Social Welfare, 5,* 446–466.

Levine, M. (1988). An analysis of mutual assistance. *American Journal of Community Psychology, 16,* 167–188.

Levine, S., & White, P. E. (1961). Exchange as a conceptual framework for the study of interorganizational relationships. *Administrative Science Quarterly, 5,* 583–601.

Levine, S., & White, P. E. (1963). The community of health organizations. In H. E. Freeman, S. Levine, & L. G. Reader (Eds.), *Handbook of medical sociology* (pp. 321–347). Englewood Cliffs, NJ: Prentice-Hall.

Lewis, E. A., & Ford, B. (1990). The network utilization project: Incorporating traditional strengths of African-American families into group work practice. *Social Work with Groups, 13* 7–22.

Manzall, M. (1986). Utilizing volunteers to enhance informal social networks. *Social Casework, 67,* 290–298.

Martin, Y. M., & O'Connor, G. G. (1989). *The social environment: Open systems application.* New York: Longman.

Maton, K. I. (1988). Social support, organizational characteristics, psychological well-being and group appraisal in three self-help group populations. *American Journal of Community Psychology, 16,* 53–77.

McCarthy, J., & Nelson, G. (1991). An evaluation of supportive housing for current and former psychiatric patients. *Hospital and Community Psychiatry, 42,* 1254–1256.

McIntyre, E. L. G. (1986). Social networks: Potential for practice. *Social Work, 31,* 421–426.

Menefee, D. (1994). *Entrepreneurial leadership in the human services: Trends, implications, and strategies for executive success in turbulent times.* Unpublished manuscript. University of Maryland at Baltimore, School of Social Work, Baltimore.

Milgram, S. (1967). The small world problem, *Psychology Today, 1,* 60–67.

Mizruchi, M., & Galaskiewicz, J. (1993). Networks of interorganizational relations. *Sociological Methods and Research, 22,* 46–70.

Moynihan, D. P. (1969). *Maximum feasible misunderstanding: Community action in the war on poverty.* New York: Free Press.

Murray, C. (1984). *Losing ground: American social policy 1950–1980.* New York: Basic Books.

Myerson, A. R. (1994, October 30). Now, it's the Scott health plan. *The New York Times,* pp. F1, F6.

Netting, F. E., Kettner, P. A., & McMurtry, S. L. (1993). *Social work macro practice.* New York: Longman.

O'Connell, B. (1978). From services to advocacy to empowerment. *Social Casework, 59,* 195–202.

Patterson, S., Germain, C. B., Brennan, E. M., & Memmott, J. (1988). Effectiveness of rural natural helpers. *Social Casework, 69,* 272–279.

Phillips, K. P. (1990). *The politics of rich and poor: Wealth and the American electorate in the Reagan aftermath.* New York: Random House.

Phillips, K. P. (1993). *Boiling point: Republicans, Democrats, and the decline of middle-class prosperity.* New York: Random House.

Pivan, F. F., & Cloward, R. A. (1971). *Regulating the poor: The functions of social welfare.* New York: Pantheon Books.

Powers, P. R. (n.d.). *Stirring people up: Interviews with advocates and activists.* Baltimore: School of Social Work monograph.

Putnam, R. D. (1995). Bowling alone. *The Responsive Community: Rights and Responsibilities, 5*(2), 18–33.

Rubin, J. Z., & Brown, B. R. (1975). *The social psychology of bargaining and negotiation.* New York: Academic Press.

Schopler, J. H. (1994). Interorganizational groups in human services: Environmental and interpersonal relationships. *Journal of Community Practice, 1*(1), 7–27.

Schore, L., & Atkin, J. (1993). Stress in the workplace: A response from union member assistance programs. In P. A. Kurzman & S. Akabas (Eds.), *Work and well-being: The occupational social work advantage* (pp. 316–331). Washington, DC: National Association of Social Workers.

Schwartz, B. (1986). Decide to network: A path to personal and professional empowerment. *American Mental Health Counselors Association Journal, 8,* 12–17.

Shinn, M., Lehmann, S., & Wong, N. W. (1984). Social interaction and social support. In A. Brownell & S. A. Shumaker (Eds.), *Social support: New perspectives in theory, research, and intervention* (pp. 55–76). New York: Plenum.

Shumaker, S. A., & Brownell, A. (1984). Toward a theory of social support: Closing a conceptual gap. In A. Brownell & S. A. Shoemaker (Eds.), *Social support: New perspectives in theory, research, and intervention* (pp. 11–36). New York: Plenum.

Specht, H. (1986). Social support, networks, social exchange and social work practice. *Social Service Review, 60* (2), 218–240.

Thurow, L. C. (1980). *The zero-sum society: Distribution and the possibilities for economic change.* New York: Basic Books.

Turner, J. H. (1982). *The structure of sociological theory* (3rd ed.). Homewood, IL: Dorsey Press.

Van de Ven, A., Delbecq, A. L., & Koenig, R. (1976). Determinants of coordination modes with organizations. *American Sociological Review, 41,* 322–338.

Walker, M. E., Wasserman, S., & Wellman, B. (1993). Statistical models for social support networks. *Sociological Methods and Research, 22,* 71–98.

Warren, R. L. (1967). The interorganizational field as a focus for investigation. *Administrative Science Quarterly, 12,* 396–419.

Warren, R. L. (1978). *The community in America* (3rd ed.). Chicago: Rand McNally.

Weick, K. (1976). Educational organizations as loosely coupled systems. *Administrative Science Quarterly, 21,* 1–19.

Wernet, S. P. (1994). A case study of adaptation in a nonprofit human service organization. *Journal of Community Practice, 1,* 93–112.

Whittaker, J. K. (1986). Formal and informal helping in child welfare services: Implications for management and practice. *Child Welfare, 65,* 17–25.

Whittaker, J. K., Garbarino, J., & Associates. (1983). *Social support networks: Informal helping in the human services.* New York: Aldine.

Woodard, K. L. (1994). Packaging effective community service delivery: The utility of mandates and contracts in obtaining administrative cooperation. *Administration in Social Work, 18,* 17–44.

Woodard, K. L., & Doreion, P. (1994). Utilizing and understanding community service provision networks: A report of three case studies having 583 participants. *Journal of Social Service Research, 18,* 15–16.

Zald, M. N. (1970). Political economy: A framework for comparative analysis. In M. N. Zald (Ed.), *Power in organizations* (pp. 221–261). Nashville, TN: Vanderbilt University Press.

Zimmerman, M. A., & Rappaport, J. (1988). Citizen participation, perceived control, and psychological empowerment. *American Journal of Community Psychology, 16,* 725–250.

chapter

11

Using Social Marketing

- A *New York Times* (February 23, 1993, p. B9) full-page advertisement with 2-inch boldface type screamed: **"Albany Declares War on the Aged and the Infirm."** After predicting a severe impact of Medicaid budget cuts on the state's aged population, the ad, sponsored by the Coalition of Not-For-Profit Nursing Homes, urges readers to write to New York's governor, George E. Pataki, and "tell him not to cut Medicaid funding for the aged and the infirm."

- A Family services center, after a dropoff in clients, decides to keep its office open in the evenings to better serve potential clients who work during the day.

- A private social work practitioner does pro bono work in an abuse shelter with physicians and other community professionals. In casual discussions with them, the social worker describes the scope and focus of her practice.

- A social agency establishes an advisory group of clients to advise the agency on ways to improve service delivery.

These agencies and social workers are engaged in marketing. This chapter presents an overview of social marketing and strategic marketing of social services; the definitions, operationalizations, and applications of the essential concepts and fundamental theories of marketing to social and human services; and an introduction to the practices and techniques of strategic marketing as community practice. The chapter also analyzes the characteristics of nonprofit agencies, whether voluntary or public, and of the social work profession that influence strategic marketing in social and human services.

MARKETS AND MARKETING

A *market* is a set of people who have an actual or potential interest in the exchange of goods, products, services, and satisfactions with the others in the set and the ability to complete the exchange (Enis, 1974; Fine & Fine, 1986; Kotler & Andreasen, 1987).

Markets are composed of people who have some need, desire, or preference and are willing to exchange something in order to have that need, desire, or preference met (Table 1).

Preferences and *needs* mean the same thing in this chapter. Needs, as absolutes beyond a survival level, are difficult to define and distinguish from preferences. Needs are shaped by culture, and the individual decisions in defining needs are shaped by individual and cultural preferences. In market exchanges, the concern is with social preferences and effective demand to use an economic conception. An *effective demand* occurs when people express a need or preference and are prepared to back that expression with resources and behavior (Bradshaw, 1977). Exchanges represent behavior and effective demand. The people may be called *buyers* and *sellers*, *customers* and *vendors*, *consumers* and *producers*, *service providers* such as social workers and clients or doctors and *patients*, or *fund seekers* and *fund providers*. However, in order to form a market, the people must be real, reachable by others, and interested in an exchange.

Marketing, formally defined, is the analysis, planning, implementation, and control of carefully formulated programs designed to bring about the voluntary exchange of values by one part of the market with another part of the market (the target market or mar-

kets), for the purpose of achieving the objectives on the part of the market seeking the exchange. It is the active processes of the market (Kotler & Andreasen, 1987, p. 61). Kotler (1971) defines marketing as "the set of human activities directed at facilitating and consummating exchanges" (p. 12). Enis (1974) provides an even more encompassing definition of human behavior in his conception of marketing. "Marketing is a fundamental human activity. . . . *Marketing* encompasses exchange activities conducted by individuals and organizations for the purpose of satisfying human wants" (p. 21).

Marketing is more than a set of techniques to promote exchanges. It is a philosophical perspective of providing goods or services of value to others in order to get your needs met by exchanging them for the goods or services of others. Both sides are better off, each in his or her own estimation, after the exchange.

CHALLENGES TO MARKETING IN THE SOCIAL SERVICES AND THE SOCIAL WORK PROFESSION

Markets and marketing, as exchanges and need meeting, are intrinsic to human behavior, to human services, and to social work practice. Marketing's importance to social

TABLE 11.1 A Market

Potential Exchange Partners	Resources Needed	Available Resources for Exchanges
Mental health center	Fiscal resources; mentally impaired clients in need of improved impaired social functioning	Services to improve the social functioning of mentally clients
County government	Improved social functioning for its mentally impaired citizens	Fiscal resources; mentally impaired citizens in need of improved social functioning

work in the turbulent and resource-competitive world of the 1990s is recognized by the NASW's regular feature on marketing in its monthly newspaper *NASW News*. Up to now, marketing has not been generally accepted or widely practiced by the social work profession and in nonprofit human services agencies. To engage successfully in marketing, social workers and nonprofit agencies, including public ones, must meet several challenges not faced to the same degree by proprietary agencies.

Product Orientation

Perhaps the greatest challenge is that many nonprofit agencies and social workers have a product orientation rather than a consumer and a market orientation (Andreasen, 1984; Cooper & McIlvain, 1983; Kotler & Andreasen, 1987; Lovelock & Weinberg, 1984). A *product orientation*, according to Kotler and Andreasen (1984), "holds that the major task of an organization is to put out products that it thinks would be good for the public" (p. 38). A product orientation is an inward-looking orientation and a belief by the agency and professional that they know best, that they know what is good for clients, and that their products and services are intrinsically good.

A product orientation propagates a tendency to view markets as having homogeneous preferences, with one or a few products determined by the producer as best satisfying consumers' preferences. The diversity of consumers and their preferences is ignored. To paraphrase the quote often attributed to Henry Ford with the introduction of the mass-produced automobile, "The public can have any color car it wants as long as it's black."

A product orientation is similar to a bureaucratic orientation: a preoccupation with the norms and policies of the agency and its professional orientation—the belief that the professional knows best (Rothman, Teresa, Kay, & Morningstar, 1983, pp. 62–78). Professions, including the social work profession, with their concern for autonomy and authority, are motivated to assume a product orientation even if that product is a professional service regulated by professional ethics.

Social workers and agencies will need to develop client, community, and market orientations, with the preferences of the client and market determining product and service design and delivery if they expect to survive in the turbulent future. Even for clients who are required to receive a service, such as parents accused of child abuse, client preferences regarding the time, location, and format of services should be considered to facilitate an exchange. What service design and delivery considerations will achieve the desired outcome: effective, nonabusive parenting behavior? The parents might deliver this "product" more readily if their preferences are considered.

Consumer Ignorance

The assumption of consumer ignorance is necessary to a product orientation (Andreasen, 1984, p. 133). Consumer ignorance assumes that clients do not know what they need, or what is good for them. The professional, by virtue of education, training, expertise, and experience, and the agency, which can draw on a variety of professions and professional wisdom and experience, are assumed to be in a better position to determine the client's, community's, or market's true needs and the services required to meet those needs. After all, it is on the basis of the professional's and the agency's knowledge and skills that they have received public sanction to deal with clients' needs.

Selling Is Marketing

For agencies and professionals with a product orientation, and for those who view consumers or clients as ignorant, the rational and logical approach to marketing is production and selling (Andreasen, 1984; Kotler & Andreasen, 1987, p. 39). If the product is good, the public and the clients will be better off with more of it. If the public will be better off with more of the product, the agency should produce more of it. If the agency produces more of it, the marketing task is to convince an ignorant consumer or public to use it. A *selling orientation* occurs when marketing is seen as convincing ignorant consumers that they need the agency's products. There will be an overemphasis on promotion and packaging. Communication will flow one way, from the agency and professional to the client, rather than both ways, between agency or professional and client. Marketing is narrowly viewed as selling, advertising, and persuading.

Professional Antipathy to Entrepreneurial Approaches

Professions and nonprofit human service agencies often have an antipathy to the idea of competition among professional and social agencies and an aversion to entrepreneurial approaches to meet the demands of competition (Kotler & Andreasen, 1987; Reichert, 1982; Rosenberg & Weissman, 1981; Shapiro, 1977). Marketing is viewed as unprofessional and inhumane. Adherents to this position may be repelled by the apparently self-interested nature of market transactions, the ideas of a buyer and a seller, of marketers and markets, in what should be a social welfare or altruistic activity. This may be due, as Kotler (1977) indicates, to a low level of consciousness and ignorance regarding marketing.

Government Regulations

Although politicians use marketing to develop and promote their products and ideology, local, state, and federal governments often restrict social agencies to certain marketing activities. The complexities of the 23 different categories under the Internal Revenue Code's Section 501, the section of the tax code that confers a tax-exempt status, limit the ability of nonprofits to use certain promotional strategies and engage in some political and entrepreneurial activities available to proprietary, for-profit agencies (Bryce, 1987, pp. 28–48; Cooper & McIlvain, 1983; Kotler & Andreasen, 1987, pp. 7–8, 12–17, 19–20; Lovelock & Weinberg, 1984). Many nonprofits avoid other legitimate marketing activities out of fear that they may lose their tax-exempt status (Kotler & Andreasen, 1987, p. 13).

The constraint of government regulations on nonprofits should not be overdrawn as a difference between nonprofits and proprietary agencies. The public sector has intruded into the proprietary sector with environmental, health, safety, employment, and product regulations, even though the regulations and regulators have met with political disfavor.

Social Regulation

Nonprofits face significant social regulations beyond those generally faced by proprietary enterprises and often beyond any formal governmental regulations (Cooper & McIlvain, 1983; Lovelock & Weinberg, 1984). Much of the activity of nonprofits deals with clients concerns significant and controversial behaviors, with confusion regarding the products of the agencies. Sometimes the products appear counterintuitive. Services oriented toward birth control and safe sex for adolescents, for example, are often assumed by certain segments of the public to promote promiscuity.

The use of funds donated for services and charitable purpose may be perceived as inappropriate if used for certain marketing activities, such as product advertising and promotion or market research (Kotler & Andreasen, 1987, p. 21). This position assumes a product orientation and believes that marketing is unnecessary if the services and other products are really needed. Like the product orientation, this position assumes that spending money for market research reduces the money that could be spent for services, is a waste, and should not be necessary. If the agency and the professionals are competent, they should know, probably intuitively, what their clients need. If they do not know or if their services are not used, then they are not needed. They should not try to develop new products or services to meet new needs. After all, aren't nonprofit human service agencies and professional social workers trying to work themselves out of a job? Of course, none of these arguments are applied to proprietary enterprises that are entering the human services marketplace. The arguments are losing ground with the expansion of propriety agencies into the human services, as both types of agencies struggle for resources.

Another reason that the public feels more at ease in regulating nonprofits is that nonprofit agencies operate as public trusts. There are no owners who bear the risk, nor are revenues always dependent on satisfying the preferences of consumers. Boards of directors act not for owners or even for users of the agency's services. They are stewards acting for the public and for the public's good (Anthony & Young, 1988, pp. 59–60). Public sector agencies are viewed as belonging to the public. And if nonprofit and public sector agencies are owned by everyone, every-

one often sees themselves as having a say in the operations.

Difficulty in Measuring Success

Proprietary enterprises generally have two clear criteria that are useful in measuring success: profit or return on the investment and share of the market. Nonprofits differ from for-profit agencies in that nonprofits do not have clear measurements, such as profit and market share as benchmarks of success. There is no direct imposed "market discipline," that is, survival does not depend on product demand and the ability to satisfy that demand as well as or better than competitors (Bryce, 1987, pp. 92–114; Cooper & McIlvain, 1983; Kotler & Andreasen, 1987, pp. 13–24; Lovelock & Weinberg, 1984).

Profit and market share are both goals and measurements for the profit organizations. Proprietary firms seek to improve life for their customers and markets through their services. The ultimate measurements of how well the profit agency has done this are market share and profits. The users of the products and the exchange partners in an economically competitive market determine if the products improve their quality of life by exchanging their resources (money) with the profit organization, the seller. If the buyers judge the products of a particular producer superior in meeting their needs and preferences over alternative products available to them in the marketplace, the more the buyers will turn to that producer's products. As demand increases, the producer will attempt to make more of the products for the potential buyers, both to meet the demand and to charge more for the product to balance that demand. The higher prices for the preferred products result in higher profits for the producers. When certain products meet consumer preferences, more consumers will want them. If the producer can produce more of these products, the producer will gain a bigger share of the market, raise prices, or both. This way, market share and profit represent measurements of success in meeting consumers' preferences in a consumer-driven market.

The nonprofit agency is more limited in its ability to use market measures to judge success. First, as discussed earlier in this text, coordination and market restrictions to prevent service duplication are valued more than competitive markets by public and nonprofit agencies. Without competition, market share is unimportant as a measure of success in meeting clients' preferences. An agency's counseling service that is only marginally satisfying or helpful to clients will be used if the agency has a community monopoly over counseling. The agency, as a monopoly, has 100% of that market. A public assistance agency may have almost 100% of the market for financial assistance to the poor, regardless of the degree of compassion or sensitivity shown to the poor or the ability to meet clients' preferences. Poor people do not have many alternative financial or income vendors in the public assistance marketplace. Their option is to find other, nonwelfare income exchanges, such as legal or illegal employment, or perhaps to leave the community.

Measurements and judgments of success for both profit and nonprofit agencies are difficult when these agencies operate as monopolies in which consumers and other constituencies have no or few other options, a product orientation prevails, consumer ignorance is assumed, and agencies and service vendors limit their view of marketing to persuasion.

Multiple Goals

A challenge to nonprofit agencies expressed by some authorities (Lovelock & Weinberg, 1984; Shapiro, 1977) is the nature of their products. Nonprofit agencies generally produce services and intangible products rather than physical commodities. The quality and even the quantity of services and other intangible products are generally harder to measure than the quantity and quality of tangible physical products. With services, the measurements tend to assess the characteristics of the service providers; their education and credentials; or the effects of the services on the users. The actual services dispensed and the interactions between service providers and recipients often are hidden from observation and measurement. Judgments of quality generally rely on the effects of the services on the recipients, the average amount of time spent with the recipients, and the staff/recipient ratios. The number of service hours provided, the number of clients, or similar measurements are most often used to quantify service units.

Public welfare agencies, typical of most nonprofit agencies, generally have multiple and often conflicting goals. Is the public assistance agency successful if the rolls are reduced, if the recurring pregnancy rates of mothers receiving Aid to Families with Dependent Children (AFDC) go down, if the length of time on assistance is reduced, if the families raise socially productive children, if the poverty of children is ameliorated, or if public spending for public assistance is reduced? Is the agency successful if it meets some goals but not others? And does meeting some of the goals preclude meeting other goals? Raising socially productive children may be counterindicative to reducing the public assistance rolls and the length of time on welfare. Welfare rolls can be reduced by restricting eligibility for 2 or fewer years for mothers and their children, not providing aid directly to teenage mothers, and making children conceived and born while on welfare ineligible for welfare or by "capping the grant," but will these approaches contribute to raising socially productive children or lower the community's poverty level? The public's representatives—the federal and state legislative and executive branches—are starting to clarify the goal of the public assistance system as redicomg welfare rolls by decreasing the length of time a mother and her family are eligible, raising the age required to be an eligible mother, and generally curtailing services (Anderson, 1995; Gillespie & Schellhas, 1994; Gingrich, Armey, & the House Republicans, 1994).

The distinction between nonprofit agencies providing intangible products and proprietary and for-profit agencies producing tangible commodities is becoming more hazy and was never that clear. With increased government contracting for services from the proprietary sector, called *privatization*, for everything from transportation services to education and corrections and with the growth of the proprietary sector in publicly funded health and mental health, the distinction is archaic. Governments are fulfilling more of their responsibilities through contracts with the private sector. For-profit and proprietary enterprises, medical doctors in private practice, and doctors in practice within health care corporations have long been the major providers of health care services. The proprietaries and the profit sector provide services, often intangible, ranging from mental health services to recreation and entertainment to financial and personal advice and management. Many nonprofit agencies are beginning to sell tangible products to support their nonprofit service activities. Distinctions between the for-profit and nonprofit sectors appear to reside more in ownership, mission, accountability, and views on competition than in any significant differences in the products produced.

Multiple Publics

Nonprofit agencies have multiple publics or target market segments (Andreasen, 1984; Lovelock & Weinberg, 1984). There is generally a separation of clients and service recipients from the sources of revenue for the agency. The nonprofit agency's product–revenue relationship is often indirect. Consumers or users of the services may not and generally do not provide the major source of revenue for the agency's services and products. AFDC recipients do not provide the revenue for public assistance or the services offered by the public assistance agency.

Multiple publics for nonprofit agencies go beyond the clients and funding sources to include a range of constituencies and publics in the task environment relevant and critical to the agency, such as professional associations, public and professional regulators, licensing and accrediting bodies, legislatures, employee associations and groupings, collaborating and complementary agencies serving as sources or recipients of client referrals, and volunteers, to name only a few (Holmes & Riecken, 1980).

The reality of multiple publics also is becoming more characteristic of proprietary businesses with the growth of government regulations and regulators, consumer advocate groups, environmental advocates, employee unions and associations, and so forth. However, proprietary businesses do not have as many segments as nonprofit agencies.

Lack of Market Data

The challenges, especially the product orientation and the assumption of consumer ignorance, have often resulted in nonprofits suffering from a lack of sophisticated data on the market's preferences, wants, and needs and from a lack of the social characteristics required to facilitate product development and exchanges to thrive in today's turbulent task environment. For example, if an agency believes that its product is inherently good, then the agency will assume that it is unnecessary to develop information on the preferences of clients. Similarly, the agency will not develop information on the preferences of the resource providers if the agency's choice of services or products is ideologically driven. With this orientation, the agency will view market research as a waste of resources that could better be used to generate more of the agency's product.

A MARKET ORIENTATION FOR THE PROFESSION

While the orientation and socialization of the social work profession presents challenges to marketing, marketing is compatible with professional functioning and values. A market orientation is compatible with the social work values and ethics of client self-determination and empowerment.

Although nonprofits face some challenges not always encountered by the proprietary agency, this does not mean that marketing is incompatible with social work, nonprofit agencies, and the social services. To the contrary, the challenges underscore the necessity of effective marketing by social workers in an increasingly competitive and turbulent task environment. The "consumerism movement" in human services, emphasizing client rights and responsibilities, reflects the market nature of human services (Perlman, 1975). Tower (1994), perhaps exaggerating to make a point, states that "Fundamentally, clients of the human services are consumers in the same way as are customers who acquire the products and services of a grocery store" (p. 192).

A concern for clients' views of their needs, the term *consumer*, the emphasis on consumer and client satisfaction and preferences, and accounting for these preferences in program design and service delivery are moves toward a market philosophy. Warfield and Maloney (1981) state:

> Prerequisites for consideration of consumer participation include a belief by providers of a service that consumers have something important to say, a desire to accept the feedback, and a willingness and ability to improve program operations and service delivery based on the feedback received. (p. 155)

Social work as a profession and the human services industry should be equipped by training, if not by philosophy, to practice marketing constructively in order to benefit their publics and themselves. Marketing requires a knowledge of the behavioral and social sciences in order to assess, understand, reach, and engage people for exchanges. Winston (1986b), an observer of and participant in human services marketing, writing about mental health professionals in terms applicable to all social workers, asserts that "The mental health professional is educationally suited to use marketing effectively since the background of marketing is consumer behavior" (p. vii). People are the market and the consumers (Bliss, 1970; Winston, 1986b).

There is no question that social workers, the human services, and the nonprofit sector are marketing. Markets exist. Social workers and human services are marketing whenever they try to facilitate exchanges with their task environments with formal and informal information and referral networks, fund-raising and solicitation networks, outreach efforts, needs and satisfaction studies, advisory groups, public information efforts, and adapting office hours to meet clients' preferences. The appropriate query is not "Should we market?" or "Are we marketing?" but rather "How can we market to design and deliver services effectively in an increasingly competitive and turbulent task environment?"

MARKETING AND COMMUNITY PRACTICE

A market, as discussed earlier in this chapter, is a set of people who have an actual or a potential interest in the exchange of tangible or intangible goods, products, services, and satisfactions with others and the ability to complete the exchange. The determining feature of a market is that the sets of people must be actually or potentially in an exchange relationship. This requires that the people be real, interested in making exchanges, and capable of making exchanges with potential trading partners.

Marketing is a continuing, planned process. The American Marketing Association emphasizes the deliberate process of marketing in its definition: "the process of planning and executing the conception, pricing, promotion and distribution of ideas, goods, and services to create exchanges that satisfy individual and organizational objectives" (Fine, 1992, p. 47). Marketing is the "development and management of exchange relationships through purposeful benefit configuration, communication, facilitation, and evaluation processes.... As such, marketing is compatible with basic ideologies and methods of social action" (p. 47). Marketing is concerned with transactions or exchanges between people in the market. It involves how transactions are created, stimulated, facilitated, valued, and completed (Kotler, 1977, p. 22). Marketing is appropriate for all organizations that have publics, not just consumers, with whom they make exchanges.

Marketing involves voluntary rather than coercive exchange. Good marketing rests on the ability of potential trading partners to choose whether or not to engage in the exchange. The capacity of one party to impose or force its will on the other party, according to Fine (1992, pp. 23–24), is not marketing but coercion.

Marketing is advocacy. It is not merely the advocacy, or promotion, of particular products but rather the commitment that the target market segment (the particular clients, customers, and other exchange partners) will get their preferences met.

Axioms of Marketing

Kotler (1977, pp. 22–25) proposes several axioms for marketing:

1. There must be two or more social units— individuals, groups, organizations, communities, or nations. The units need not be balanced; any unit can engage in exchanges with any other unit as an individual with any group, organization, or community.

2. At least one of the social units wants a specific response from one or more of the other units. The social unit seeking the response is the marketer, and the social unit from which a response is sought is the market. The response sought from the market is valued by the marketer. It can consist of acceptance, in the short or long run, of the marketer's product, service, organization, person, place or idea. The marketer wants the market to respond by exchanging the resources sought by the marketer.

3. Marketing assumes that the marketer can alter the market's response. Marketing is a process by which the marketer alters the market's responses. The marketer wants to produce a desired, voluntary response by creating and offering desired products with value to the market.

4. The indispensable activity is the marketer's creation and offering of value as defined by the market. Effective marketing consists of actions that are calculated to produce the desired response from the market.

Let us illustrate these axioms with a case example:

> A community mental health agency (the marketer) is trying to develop and implement a counseling service for adults who were abused as children and who are suffering from anxiety as a result. These adults constitute potential clients (the market). The agency has examined the research on various forms of therapy and the findings of a small focus group from the market to determine the most effective service. The projected service (product) is a combination of individual counseling, offered in 30 sessions of 50 minutes once a week in a given calendar year, combined with social support groups and networks. The sessions will be offered in the evenings and on weekends, as most of the adults are employed. The number of sessions is limited by the requirements of the third-party payers. The agency has to respond to two sets of actors in the community: the potential clients and the third-party payers.

The agency is seeking specific responses from the potential clients and the third-party payers; for potential clients to become clients, for the clients to reduce and effectively manage their anxiety, and for the third-party payers to pay for the service.

The potential clients' responses are not fixed; they may or may not become clients. The agency (the marketer) wants them to become clients and tries to achieve this by offering the therapy at convenient times. The likelihood that the potential clients will become actual clients can be altered by the agency's actions in terms of outreach, public information, recruitment, and referral net-working; by ensuring that the design, location, and timing of the service meet the potential clients' preferences; and by ensuring that the service is effective. However, service effectiveness—the ability of counseling and support to reduce the anxiety of these persons—is relevant only if the potential clients use the service.

Using continuous marketing, the agency will try to design its products to meet the needs and preferences of the potential clients, give value to potential clients, and demonstrate to them how the products will help them. The responses of the potential clients (the market) are voluntary; they are neither obliged nor coerced to become clients. They will engage in exchange with the agency, that is, become clients, because the agency's services meet their needs better than other options available to them.

SOCIAL MARKETING

Social marketing is a specialized form of marketing in that the commodities offered generally involve intangible social ideas. *Social marketing* is the promotion and adoption of social ideas that will produce a range of social behaviors sought by the marketer. Fox and Kotler (1987) define social marketing as social cause–oriented marketing. Social marketing is "the design, implementation, and control of programs calculated to influence the acceptability of social ideas" (p. 15). Social marketing is the application of marketing concepts, theory, and techniques to social ideas rather than physical commodities and services, although the label has been used for almost any marketing activity by nonprofit organizations. The "Save the Bay" advertisement appearing in several publications over the past decade illustrates social marketing by promoting the Chesa-

> **Save the Bay**
>
> That's been our cry since the beginning. Won't you help?
>
> The Chesapeake Bay is in serious trouble. . . .
>
> You can help by becoming a member the Chesapeake Bay Foundation. . . .

peake Bay Foundation with the social idea of saving the Chesapeake Bay.

Social marketing is not limited to non-profit organizations. It pertains to the product as a social idea, not to the auspices or even the motives of the marketer. Social marketing has been and is used by a range of proprietary, for-profit organizations to promote social ideas compatible with the proprietary agency's profit-oriented concerns. During the 1994 national health coverage debates, health insurance companies opposed national health care, claiming that their opposition was rooted in the American value of freedom of choice rather than in their desire for profits.

The tobacco companies have equated governmental limitations on their promotion of smoking and the use of other tobacco products as an infringement not only on the consumer's freedom of choice but also on the basic freedom of Americans from unwarranted government intrusion. "The smell of cigarette smoke annoys me. But not nearly as much as the government telling me what to do" says a purported nonsmoker in an R. J. Reynolds Tobacco Company full-page ad in the July 26, 1994, *New York Times* (p. A11). And if the government is allowed to regulate tobacco, perhaps alcohol, caffeine, and even high-fat foods will be taken from us next by government, admonishes another R. J.

Reynolds ad (*New York Times*, June 24, 1994, p. A11). The tobacco companies equate respect for a smoker's right to smoke with respect for other forms of social diversity.

Sometimes social marketing precedes or accompanies the promotion of tangible products. While the advertisement promotes a so-

> Our position, word by word.
>
> **Courtesy**
>
> . . . At Philip Morris, we believe that common courtesy and mutual respect are still the best ways for people to resolve their differences.
>
> By respecting each other's rights and preferences, both groups can easily work things out.

cial idea such as courtesy or freedom of choice, the application of these ideas is compatible with the marketer's physical products. The freedom to choose whether to smoke or not is essential to a tobacco company's ability to sell tobacco products. Nonprofits might promote the social idea of conservation with membership in particular organizations, such as the Nature Conservancy or the Sierra Club; of children's rights; or of mental health as a prelude to marketing more tangible services such as parent training and mental health counseling. The advertisement cited at the beginning of this chapter was sponsored by the Coalition of Not-for-Profit Homes. Continued budgetary support of the elderly is in the sponsor's financial interest.

Often social marketing takes the form of marketing social ideas to counter other social ideas. The tobacco and alcoholic beverage companies' promotion of the social idea of freedom of choice or "courtesy" is done to counter the social marketing of antismoking and antidrinking messages. In both marketing and countermarketing, the hope is that the market accepts the social ideas that will produce certain behaviors by the market beneficial to the marketer's cause. Political campaigns based on issues other than the personal traits of the candidates represent social marketing and often countermarketing.

Social marketing can also improve a marketer's image and social position with potential exchange partners. GTE, an electronics firm, sponsors collegiate academic All-Americans; this helps to promote acceptance of the firm's other products. A social worker who visibly promotes the social idea of women's rights may obtain female clients.

Social marketing's products are the social ideas and the value received by the market as satisfaction in upholding the social ideas, such as respect for the environment, concern for future generations and money savings in energy conservation, and the preferred behaviors and satisfaction the social ideas allow the market to pursue and receive (Fox & Kotler, 1987, p. 17). While other incentives may be added to manipulate the market's response and increase satisfaction, such as national public radio and public television stations giving coffee mugs and tote bags in their fund raising, the social idea is the basic product. In public radio, for example, the programs essentially are free goods to the individual listener; that is, the programs can be listened to regardless of the listener's contributions to the radio station. The programs are free to the individual listener. The fund appeals generally address listeners' values in the social ideas promoted by public radio and television; the specific "commercial-free" programs; and the provision of more tangible products such as records, tote bags, and coffee mugs to encourage the mar-

ginally committed listener to donate. The tangible items also have value in conveying the user's public image of concern and providing free publicity to the marketer, especially if they have appropriate logos, as well as any user utility of the record, tote bag, or cup.

EXCHANGE THEORY

Exchange theory (Blau, 1963, pp. 88–114; Homan, 1958; Specht, 1986; Turner, 1982, pp. 242–273), as discussed previously, is basic to community and interorganizational practice and is the explicit theory underlying marketing. To review briefly, exchange theory's central proposition is that people act in their own interest as they define it, whether economic, social, or psychological. Exchange is the act of obtaining a desired product from someone by offering something valued by the other party in return. The products can be tangible or intangible, and the exchanges do not have to consist of the same types of products. Products exchanged can include counseling and community organization services for money, adoration and praise for compliant behavior, information for status, political influence for political action committee donations, and so forth. The exchanges can involve tangible products for intangible products and social behavior. Whether exchange actually take place depends on whether the two parties can arrive at the terms of exchange that will leave each of them better off or at least not worse off, in their own estimation, after the exchange compared to alternative exchanges possible and available to them.

While an exchange is an act, it is an act dependent on a process. For exchanges to occur, information is required by and for all parties in the exchange. Information is necessary on the products, services, or ideas to be exchanged, the times and places for the exchange, the respective prices for products, and the exchange mechanisms.

Social exchange differs from strictly economic exchange in that there is often a general rather than a specific expectation of reward. Also, unlike economic exchanges, the value of the exchanges by the partners may not be in the same measurement units, which limits the capacity for precise quid pro quo evaluations. An example used earlier is the donation of money to a United Way campaign. The donor is giving dollars, an easily measurable unit. The donor receives a series of products in return: social status, reduction of social pressure, capacity to implement ideas, and a better community, measured by less precise and less easily compared measurements to alternative uses by the donor for the money exchanged.

Another example is a contribution to a homeless shelter. The donor makes a monetary donation to receive intangible products. The donor does not expect to use the shelter but expects to receive good feelings for doing a generous deed and perhaps expects a more humane social environment. The marketer, that is, the homeless shelter, competes with all other alternative uses by the donor of the money that might provide the donor with the satisfaction of contributing to the donor's good feelings and a more humane social environment.

Structure of Exchanges in the Market

In order for exchanges to occur, there must be exchange partners. These partners and potential partners constitute the market. A market requires the following:

1. Two or more parties must be present.
2. Benefits are perceived as available by each party; that is each party is perceived as being able to offer the other a benefit. A ben-

efit is a reward, a satisfier of preferences, gained through the exchange.
3. Each party is perceived by the other as capable of delivering the benefit.
4. Each party communicates the ability to deliver the benefit to the other.
5. Each party can accept or reject the benefit or exchange, although if they forgo the benefit, they may pay a cost.
6. In exchanges, both parties gain and both parties pay. The value of the exchange or profit is determined by the value of the benefit received less the cost of the resource exchange for the benefit in the estimation of each party.

STRATEGIC MARKETING AND MARKET MANAGEMENT

Successful marketing requires developing and implementing a market strategy. Lauffer (1986) defines *strategic marketing* as

a comprehensive and systematic way of developing the resources you need to provide the services that others need. By responding to the needs of the consumers, providers [of resources], and suppliers, it becomes possible to minimize some of the disruptions in supply and demand that otherwise play havoc with agency programs. (p. 31)

Effective strategic marketing involves an "outside-inside" marketing approach. This marketing strategy begins with the consumer's or target market's needs and preferences (the outside), not with the organization's product (the inside). The product is developed to meet the preferences of the consumers, clients, and targets of the proposed exchange.

Stoner (1986) asserts that strategic marketing is a planning strategy that involves developing answers to the questions "Where are we?" "Where do we want to be", and "How do we get there?" Strategic planning and implementation of the plan answers these questions. Strategic planning is a social planning model similar to social work's generic problem-solving model, reviewed in Chapter 1. The essential tasks are to determine the primary markets, those central to the agency's core functions and achievement of its mission, and the secondary markets, those important but not essential to the agency's mission. The primary and secondary markets include all the social entities in the task environment: the individuals, groups, and organizations from which resources and exchanges are sought. Target markets for social agencies, in addition to clients, include client referral sources, fiscal resource providers, nonfiscal resource providers, and sources of legitimation.

The determination and location of primary and secondary markets is market positioning. *Market positioning* consists of the processes by which an agency selects its markets. It involves determining the market's location, assessing its preferences, estimating the competition for the market, and appraising the potential for exchanges (Lauffer, 1986, p. 37). The processes of determining primary and secondary markets and market positioning will be discussed below under "Purchasers," addressing the development of target market segmentations and exchange partners.

The marketing literature (Fine, 1992; Kotler & Andreasen, 1987; Winston, 1986c) presents the components of a strategic marketing plan with varying precision by a series of related "P's". Although the number and conceptualization of the Ps vary with the authority, we will use the following six:

Probing: the market research to determine the preferences and needs of relevant publics or market segments.

Purchasers: the target market segment, the relevant publics or the exchange partner sought.
Products: the goods and services offered to the purchasers and market segment.
Price: the cost of the products to the purchasers and market segment.
Place: the locations for exchanges with the purchasers and market segments and the paths by which the segments get to the places for exchange.
Promotion: the communication of the anticipated values and prices of the products and places for exchange to the purchaser and market segment.

Fine (1992, pp. 4–5) designates an addition "P," indicating "Producer," for the source of the promotional message and products. Winston (1986c, p. 15) uses "People" for all people involved in the organization, including volunteers, if they affect the exchange. Fine's producer and Winston's people are marketers. Moore (1993) separates "path" from "place," with path being the processes the exchange partners (purchasers, clients, or customers) use to get to the place of the exchange.

Probing

Probing is the generic "P" for market research. *Market research* is the formal and informal processes and methods used to determine the target market segments, the potential and actual exchange partners, their preferences, and how these preferences can be met. The market segment's needs and preferences are the outside of strategic marketing, and developing products to meet these preferences is the inside.

A market research task is to segment primary markets and any additional secondary markets. Functional segmentation of the market will be discussed under "Purchasers."

In market research, the purpose of the outside-inside approach, and of determining and segmenting primary and secondary markets, is to establish the desired competitive market position with the resource providers (the purchasers) based on their preferences (Lauffer, 1986). At the conclusion of market research, the marketer should have answers to the key questions listed below (Winston, 1986c, pp. 9–12). Direct service practitioners, whether independent or agency based, can use the same set of questions to study their markets by substituting themselves for the organization. Clients often are used here as the illustrative exchange partner or target market segment. However, as will be discussed below, a target market segment is any part of the task environment, any potential partner, with whom an exchange is sought. Other potential exchange partners, such as potential funding sources, referral sources, or volunteers, can be substituted.

1. What is the organization's mission and purpose? What does our organization want to achieve with what parts of its task environment?

2. What are the potential exchange partners and target market segments? What parts of the community (task environment) form the target market segments? What are their social, behavioral, and demographic characteristics that can or will affect the exchanges?

3. What are the target market segment's preferences and needs, as defined by that segment? Is there a difference between a means to achieve those needs, which may be the organization's products and services, and the preferences themselves, which equal the value to the target market segment? A family services agency offers family therapy to families suffering from discord. Family therapy is the agency's product. The segment's preference, however, is a reduction of family discord and not therapy. The therapy is a means to achieve the preference.

4. What are the organization's strengths and competencies? Has it built from or can it build from its strengths and competencies, with what it knows best, in designing new products to meet target market segment preferences? Strengths and competencies are those things that can be used to build or assist in exchanges for needed resources with a target market segment.

5. What are the organization's weaknesses that require attention? Such weaknesses are deficiencies that will interfere with exchanges or place the organization at a competitive disadvantage with the target market segment's resources use.

6. Who are the competitors? What other organizations and entities are trying to meet the target market segment's preferences? A competitor is any alternative way the target market segment can use its resources that the organization is seeking.

7. What are the optimal marketing approaches to communicate and facilitate exchanges with the target market segment? How can the value and price of the products and the place for exchanges be best communicated to the target market segment? What things interfere with effective communication?

8. What prices of products and places for exchanges will best facilitate exchanges with the target market segment? How can the price be kept below the value to the target market segment and above the cost to the agency?

Market Study and Market Audit Methodologies

Market research's methodologies and techniques are similar to those of community assessment discussed in Chapters 5 and 6. The first step is market segmentation, discussed under "Purchasers" below. The market research and audit should be completed before the marketing plans are developed. Some of the methodologies of market research are as follows:

1. *Case studies* (Lovelock & Weinberg, 1984; Yin, 1986) of similar marketing efforts by the agency or other agencies. Case studies look at how successful marketers design, develop, and deliver services that meet the preferences of the target market segment or similar market segments, with the intent of replicating the successful efforts. Unsuccessful cases also should be scrutinized to avoid their failures.

2. *Surveys* of particular target market segments for their needs, preferences, and capacity and willingness to make the exchanges—pay the price—and preferences for the location of exchanges can be done by client exit interviews or other opinionaires and evaluations; surveys of target market segments such as consumer and client satisfaction surveys; or surveys of potential donors. Surveying the target market segments reveals why the segment uses or would use the agency, makes a donation, becomes a volunteer, accepts the social idea, and so forth.

Surveys (Rubin & Babbie, 1993, esp. pp. 182–212, 218–260, and 332–356), while a potentially powerful assessment tool, have several limitations. Not the least are the costs of developing, pretesting, distributing, and administering them and analyzing the results. Meaningful surveys of the target market segment require a representative sample, that is, a sample containing all the important traits and characteristics related to the market segment's preferences for products, prices, and places. If the people who respond to the survey do not represent the target market segment, the survey's results will not reveal the true preferences of the target market segment and will not be helpful in the design and delivery of the products.

3. *Focus groups* are a less costly approach to market research now widely used. A focus group (Bernard, 1994; Greenbaum, 1987; Kreuger, 1988; Morgan, 1988) is a relatively homogeneous group that addresses, or focuses on, providing information about what appeals and does not appeal to them about messages, ideas, and products. A carefully constructed focus group representing a specific target market segment can provide much information on the segment's preferences. The group should have from 6 to 12 members, with 8 being the most popular size, and should be reasonably homogeneous. The crucial issues are whether the focus group truly represents the target market segment, whether the members of the group believe they can reveal their true preferences in the group situation, and the agency's willingness to be open and candid with the focus group about its plans. If the members do not know each other in other roles and are socially similar, communication is enhanced. Diversity of group members, which may represent different target market segments, may inhibit communication. For different target market segments, different focus groups should be used.

The focus group leader should be a skilled group leader with the ability to lead but not direct the group, prevent one or two members from dominating, and keep the group focused on the question or concern without being judgmental about the group's response.

Advisory boards and panels can provide information similar to that of focus groups by sharing their opinions on product design, service delivery, and similar agency concerns. However, advisory groups differ from focus groups in that they often represent diverse constituencies or target market segments, include members who have social relations outside of the group, and have internal structures that allow the domination of one or a few members.

4. *Mall surveys*, using quota and purposive sampling techniques, are frequently used in market research. The mall survey takes its name from the market researcher's practice of going to a shopping mall and asking shoppers what they look for in products and places to shop. The data are analyzed according to a predetermined profile of consumer characteristics. The social service agency or practitioner can use similar techniques in other areas, where samples of its target market are located. If an agency is interested in developing a program for hard-to-reach adolescents, it can locate and send someone to the places where they congregate. In this example, it may indeed be the mall.

The mall survey is relatively inexpensive and easy to conduct. Its weaknesses are the weaknesses of all surveys, especially those conducted with samples of convenience: whether the participants are representative of the target population, their willingness to participate in the survey, and the truthfulness of their responses. As with the focus group, participants in a mall survey are not truly anonymous, although their responses may be kept confidential, and this may inhibit their response.

5. The *market audit* is the most complete and powerful approach to market research. This technique incorporates most of the above methodologies. It is distinguished from them by its comprehensiveness. Market audits collect information on the agency's task environment, including competitors for resources, the agency itself, and the Ps of the purchasers (target market segments), product, price, place, and promotion. The audit should help the marketer learn its weaknesses and deficiencies, its strengths, and

where it is dominant and deals most effectively with its competition. The audit report should contain recommendations and proposals to improve the organization's market access and share. A sample audit guide is included at the end of this chapter.

6. A *market matrix* is a simple approach to market research and analysis. In filling the cells, the market researcher has to specify for relevant target market segments the product, price, place, and promotion. The market matrix addresses the Ps of purchasers (target market segment), product, price, place, and promotion. The sixth P, probing, is the research and analysis necessary to complete the matrix's cells (Table 11.2).

Of course, each target market segment indicated above will require greater segmentation. Rarely are clients, funders, political influencers, legitimizers, or volunteers internally homogeneous groupings.

Purchasers

When we discuss target market segments, we discuss purchasers. The purchasers are those parts of the task environment that control or represent resources necessary for the agency to achieve its objectives. Purchasers include all the types of resource suppliers indicated above. Market segmentation, which determines and establishes the target market segments, is essential to effective product development and marketing.

MARKET SEGMENTATION
The objective of market segmentation is to obtain the precision necessary to facilitate exchanges by developing product, price, place, and promotion strategies for each segment. For-profit businesses have different market segments for different product lines. A cereal company may produce a variety of breakfast cereals to meet fairly specific pref-

TABLE 11.2 A Market Matrix

Target market segments (purchasers) Describe each target market segment, such as:	What is the product desired by and for the segment?	What is the price of each the product for the segment?	What is the place of Exchange with each segment?	What is the promotion needed with each segment?
Client segments Fiscal resource suppliers Political influencers Volunteers Providers of legitimacy Other segments				

erences of different target market segments. An automobile manufacturer develops and sells several models to meet specific target market preferences. Nonprofit agencies should recognize that they may have different target market segments with different preferences rather than attempt to have one product line for all. The mental health agency that has only one form of therapy, formatted in the same way, offered during the same hours in the same places to all potential clients, regardless of demographics or other conditions, probably is not meeting the preferences of all potential market segments. The agency may therefore lose clients.

A product line can mean different things to different constituencies (clients, funding sources and so forth) and therefore, in effect, represents different products. The nonprofit agency's perception of its products delivered may differ from the perceptions of these products by different constituencies. Nonprofit agencies need to recognize how the products, even in the same product line, are perceived by different market segments.

These perceptions may be very different from those of the agency.

The degree of market segmentation is based on (1) the specificity of resource exchanges that the marketer wants from the task environment (i.e., whether the resource de-

---

Guidelines for Target Market Segmentation:

I. Resource Desired from the Task Environment:
  1. Homogeneous and general, or
  2. Diverse and specific.
II. Number of the Potential Trading Partners:
  1. Many potential trading partners
  2. Few potential trading partners.
III. Nature of the Potential Trading Partners:
  1. Homogeneous
  2. Diverse.
IV. Products Desired by the Potential Trading Partners from the Marketer:
  1. Uniform
  2. Diverse.

sired is homogeneous and general or diverse and specific); (2) the nature of the potential trading partners (homogeneous or diverse); (3) the distribution of the resources sought (concentrated in a few trading partners or widely distributed in the task environment); and (4) the products desired by the potential trading partners (uniform or diverse).

As a guideline, the variables can be summed using the numbers 1 or 2 proceeding the subvariables. The higher the sum, the greater the need for market segmentation. If the resource desired is homogeneous (I.1), there are many potential trading partners who have the resource (II.1), the potential trading partners are similar on important traits (III.1), and their product preferences are uniform (IV.1), the summed score is 4 and little segmentation appears necessary. By contrast, if the resources desired are specific and diverse (I.2), held by a few potential trading partners (II.2), who have diverse characteristics (III.2) and desire diverse products in exchange for their resources (IV.2), the summed score of 8 represents a complex market and the need for greater segmentation to facilitate exchanges.

In market segmentation, physical, psychological, attitude, demographic, economic, and other social diversity, use patterns, cost efficiencies of segmenting, neglected segments, and preference differences should be considered. Each segment should have relatively homogeneous traits in terms of its product response. If part of the segment responds differently to the product, it probably represents another target market segment. The final target market segmentation represents a balance of the market's diversity and the economy or the affordability of more finite segmentation. Segments should be large enough to be served with a product economically and specific enough to allow the product to be differentiated and individualized.

Product

Products are tangible goods such as food, services such as counseling, and ideas such as nondiscrimination or conservation developed by the agency or the professional (the marketer) and offered in exchange for the resources needed from the target market segment (Fine, 1992). Product development presumes product mutability rather than immutability. Product *mutability* means that products can be designed and adjusted to accommodate the preferences of specific target market segments. The target market segment is not forced to fit the product, but rather the reverse. This is marketing's outside-inside philosophy, discussed earlier.

The product, as discussed earlier, may be an intangible, such as an opportunity for the target market segment to fulfill a certain ideology or value. The aim of the promoter of the idea, such as conservation or good parenting behavior, is the adoption not only of the idea but also of the behaviors resulting from it. The product for the target market is the end results of the behaviors flowing from the idea—a better environment or safer, healthier children (Kotler & Roberto, 1989, p. 140). Even more tangible products, such as counseling services, training, or case management, are designed to produce behaviors from the target market segment. For nonprofit human services agencies, the product sought by both sides in the exchange is often the behavior. However, as has been constantly emphasized, the primary consideration of product design is the product's capacity to provide value to the target market segment, as judged by that segment.

PRODUCT MANAGEMENT

After market segmentation, the agency or professional must engage in *product management*. This entails selecting the criteria by which target segments and consumers will be selected, designing the products, positioning the products in the market, and providing an appropriate mix of products for different segments.

The product design component should consider and balance the following criteria (Fine, 1992, pp. 40–41):

1. *Specificity:* products are designed to meet the needs and preferences of a specific target market segment. The use of generic product labels such as "counseling" or "psychotherapy" may be too broad and assumes little differentiation in the target market segment's needs and preferences.

2. *Flexibility:* products should be designed to be adaptable to changing markets and target market segments' preferences.

3. *Attainability:* products should be designed within the limits of the agency's or professional's capacity, resources, and competencies and should be build on the strengths of the agency or professional's strengths.

4. *Competitive advantage:* products should be built on the strengths of the agency or professional and should emphasize the marketer's qualities not possessed by the competitors.

In product development, care must be exercised to avoid the product orientation discussed earlier. If we become enamored of our products at the expense of consumers' preferences, we may not gain the resources desired from the target market segment. A product orientation leads marketers to ignore and be ignorant of generic competition, concentrate on the products delivered, and blind them to the actual values received by the target market segment. A product orientation does not consider ways that the preferences of the client or consumer may be met other than by the agency and professional's ser-

vices and products. A marketer should develop consumer orientations and be aware of what the consumer prefers and is receiving. This may differ from the products it produces and delivers or those it believes it is delivering. An example is an agency dealing with the unruly behavior of students. The agency may believe that the product is counseling and therapy to provide the student with insight into the unruly behavior. However, the product received by the student is rooted in its satisfaction and value to the student. If the student neither seeks nor receives insight, the product received by the student is different from the one the agency seeks to deliver. The product received by the student may be an hour out of the classroom or playground spent with the counselor. The student will appraise this hour compared to alternative uses and costs of the time.

An agency may believe it is delivering job skills training to AFDC clients. But if the clients do not want a job or the job skills, don't believe they will have the required job skills for employment at the end of the training, or believe they will have jobs at the end of the training, the products they receive may be different from those the agency thinks it is delivering. The products received by the clients may be entertainment, structure to life by getting out of the house and doing something during the day, a way to stay eligible for AFDC benefits, an opportunity to socialize with others in the training program, and a way to maintain or reciprocate for the cash benefits (Reid, 1972). The agency's training program is competing with other products that can provide the client with entertainment, structure, and socialization preferences. Client participation in the training may be motivated by the need to maintain eligibility and reciprocate for cash benefits if the other preferences can be met more effectively and efficiently in other ways. Participation, the client's expenditure of energy and time, may be curtailed to the level the client views as a fair exchange. If the client does not perceive that participation is necessary to remain eligible for cash benefits or has no need to reciprocate, the client will not participate. If coerced to participate in the training program, the client may perceive the product received as punishment for being on AFDC, with its demands for training time and energy. The exchange of resources by the client of motivation, energy, and effort will be minimal, occurring only at a level necessary to avoid punishment.

The product delivered relates to the views of the providers; the product received relates to the preferences of, use of, and value to the recipient. In the case of mandatory therapy for spouse abusers, the court, the agency, and the professional therapist may view the product delivered as therapy to help abusers alter their behavior. However, the abusers may view the product received, especially if they do not want to alter their behavior, as a way to avoid imprisonment and meet any requirements set by the court to continue a relationship with their spouses. These spouse abusers will expend only enough resources to achieve their preferences.

PRODUCT POSITIONING

Product positioning is the location, or position, the marketer seeks for its products in terms of the target market segments: intended consumers, clients, or users. The market position is the niche the product occupies in satisfying some segment of the range of potential target market segments. The community mental health agency, discussed earlier, that is trying to develop and implement a therapeutic service to adults who were abused as children and are now suffering from anxiety as a result, is positioning itself in the market. It is pursuing a particular target market segment and has designed a par-

ticular service to meet the preferences of this segment. The design of its services and the hours offered will not meet the preferences of all adults or even of all adults who want mental health services, but it should meet the preferences of the particular target market segment.

The target market segment's image of the product and the marketer (the producer), then, is an important ingredient in market position. *Image* is the way the product is viewed by the target market segment in meeting its preferences. A marketer may view the product as meeting certain needs, but if the segment does not share that image, there will be no exchanges. An agency may believe its counseling is helpful and nonstigmatizing, but what is critical image is whether the target market segment (potential clients) view it similarly. Their view, or product image, will determine the exchange (Stern, 1990). (See Table 11.3.)

MARKET MIX

The *marketing mix* is the number and kinds of products matched to the number and kinds of target market segments and to the prices charged the target market segments. Weinberg (1984) describes the marketing mix for nonprofit agencies as the *"maximization of the amount of products or services which are consumed or utilized*, subject to the amount of *revenues and donations* being at least equal to the cost of providing the service"* (p. 269). The marketing mix results from determining the product preferences of the selected target market segments, designing the products, and pricing them appropriately.

Price

Price is a significant factor in product management. *Price* is the total contribution of the target market segment in money, time,

TABLE 11.3 Product Image and Position

Questions for the Target Market Segment	Agency Image	Product Image
1. How would you like each to be seen by the target market segment?		
2. How is each seen by the target market segment?		
3. How the image held by the target market segment determined?		
4. How satisfied are you with the image held by the target market segment?		
5. How does the image held by the target market segment promote exchanges?		
6. What factors help or hinder changes in the image held by the target market segment?		
7. What are the strategies for changing the image held by the target market segment?		

energy, effort, psychic costs, and lifestyle changes to the marketer in exchange for the product and its benefits. The price needs to be competitive with the prices of alternative products available to the target market segment. Although the marketer determines to a degree the components of the price, the target market segment, not the marketer, decides the value received. *Value received*, the satisfaction, relative to price and to alternative commodities and their value relative to price, will guide the target market segment in its product selection. The marketer must, in the long run, set the price equal to or above the costs of producing, promoting, and distributing the products, but it is the value the target market segment receives that ultimately will regulate product exchange and use. Value must generally equal or exceed price, at least in comparison to alternative uses of the price by the target market segment.

Pricing is a critical component in regulating demand. For example, a long waiting list may indicate underpricing for the agency's service, while idle time for the services providers may indicate overpricing. Once a pricing policy is established, it is generally easier to lower the price than to raise it, especially in a competitive market. Fine (1992) states, "The key to pricing is to build in value into the product and price it accordingly" (p. 42).

Nonprofit social agencies and their staffs often tend to view their products (services) as "free goods" to their clients if the clients do not pay a monetary price. Donors or the government rather than clients customarily pay the monetary costs of the agency's services. However, the clients pay a social price. A *social price* is the nonmonetary price paid by the purchasers (the clients). Social prices are common in the use of social agency and professional services and products even when there are no direct monetary costs, and the marketer should consider them in developing a pricing policy. There are four common types of social price: time, energy or effort, lifestyle, and psyche (Fine, 1992).

TYPES OF SOCIAL PRICES

Time prices. These include the time the user spends in receiving, using, and obtaining the benefits from the product. It is the time the purchaser devotes to making the exchange and receiving the product's value. There are four elements of time price:

1. *Direct time price,* or the time spent going to and from the place of the exchange and the time spent there waiting to make the exchange. Examples of direct time price in a counseling situation include the time spent in the counseling, getting to the counselor's office and, once there, waiting for the counselor.

2. Beyond the direct times price, such as the time spent in counseling or training, there is the *performance time,* the time required to learn and carry out the desired social behavior. This might include stress reduction exercises or other behaviors that are part of the intervention.

3. Another element of time price is the *flexibility/fixity of time,* or whether the exchange and the behavior can be carried out when the client prefers or must be done on a fixed schedule. Other aspects of flexibility/fixity relate to frequency (how often the social behavior must be performed to be effective), the regularity of the social behavior required, and how long it must be performed.

4. The last factor is *disruption/simultaneity,* or to what extent the social behavior requires the target market segment to rearrange its current time preferences. Can it be done at the same time as other behaviors or in conjunction with other behaviors? How much will it disrupt other behaviors?

Services and products that have little time flexibility and high time demand compared to alternative uses of time and alternative products carry a higher price and may not be used by clients. This is especially true if the clients, such as those in a particular form of therapy, perceive that little value is received from the time investment compared to alternative uses of time in meeting their preferences. The time price of therapy to a client includes the time spent in therapy, the time to get to and from the therapist's office, the time spent waiting there, the rigidity of the therapy hours, how convenient the sessions are for the client's schedule, and the time demands outside the therapy to receive its benefits. The client's evaluation of benefits compared to price will include the time price. We make other exchange decisions, such as the selection of our bank or grocery store, based partially on time price. It is reasonable to assume that clients consider time in their evaluation of social work interventions.

Effort and energy prices. These prices include the effort, both physical and emotional, required by the target market segment to obtain value and benefit from the products compared to alternative available products, including doing nothing. For a client in therapy, the investment includes the effort and energy spent in the therapy, getting to and from the therapist's office, and energy demands outside the therapy to receive its benefits. The client's evaluation of benefits compared to price will include the energy price.

For those of us in poor physical shape, our physical condition generally is not a result of ignorance of how to get into shape or its potential physical and emotional benefits. It is not a function of money. It depends on our willingness to devote time and energy to getting into shape and making certain lifestyle changes. We remain flaccid and lethargic because it is less expensive, at least in the short run; it has a lower price in time, effort, and energy.

If the target market segment or the individual exchange partner can obtain the same results, the same or equivalent value as they perceive it, with little energy expenditure, exchange theory indicates that the more energy-saving alternative will be used. If an AFDC recipient believes he or she will be unemployed at the conclusion of a training program or perceives no greater benefits from employment than from unemployment, the client probably will not pay the price of time and energy to succeed in the training program unless coerced. The expected value (no job) is similar for the client whether the client participates with a high or low expenditure of time and energy. Rationality urges the client to save the time and energy.

Lifestyle prices. These prices are the changes the target market segment must make in lifestyle to use and receive value from the products. Lifestyle price recognizes that in the exchange, the target market segment is required to give up certain aspects of life that are rewarding in order to use the product and produce the desired effects. Their willingness to pay the lifestyle price is related to the value they place on the gains received by using the product or engaging in the service and their belief that the product or services will produce these gains. Older persons returning to college for a graduate social work degree must alter their lives when they reenter school. They must give up time with family and friends for classes and study, and often must lower their standard of living as they cut back on work to allow class and study time and pay for tuition and books. Their willingness to do so is predicated on the belief that this is the price they must pay to receive the future benefits of a master's in social work degree. Clients often

must make lifestyle changes that may represent costs to them in order to receive benefits from the intervention. Their willingness to pay the price is a function of their valuation of the current or future benefits received from the lifestyle change.

Psyche price. This is the emotional cost in self-esteem and self-image the target market segment pays in using the products. The older social work graduate student is now back in a student role after perhaps having been a competent professional, perhaps a supervisor or administrator, a parent, and a mature, responsible adult. This return to the student role may impose psyche costs. To take another example, if a client believes that mental illness is a weakness and a stigma, and that mental health treatment is a public recognition or assignment of the stigma, the use of treatment carries a psyche price and will be considered in the client's valuation of the treatment. It is the client's valuation that determines the psyche price, not the agency's or the public's. If the client perceives no greater stigma with treatment than she or he currently suffers, there is no increase in psyche price.

An agency that wishes to increase the demand for its products can look for ways to reduce the social prices. Conversely, an increase in social prices will reduce demand and clients' use of a service. This is occurring in federal and state efforts to increase the stigma of being an AFDC recipient.

In general, service or product demand and use can be managed by regulating the price, including the social price. Price, other things equal, is the converse of value in that if the price can be reduced, the value of the product will increase relative to its previous price and value. This is what sales are all about. Additionally, users are more likely to pay higher prices for services they value or if the services' or products' value to users can be increased. Service demand and use can be reduced by making the service more costly to clients in time, effort, lifestyle changes, and psyche energy.

The concept of social price needs to be distinguished from social cost and public price. The *social cost* is the cost imposed on the community by the product and the exchange. It is the externalities of the exchange beyond the costs and benefits to the marketer and the exchange partner. A homeless shelter or drug treatment center may be perceived by the surrounding neighborhood as having a social cost that the neighborhood rather than the center, its staff and clients, pay. The *public price* is the price paid by the public for the product.

A Market Segmentation Approach to Social Pricing

A market segmentation approach to social pricing consists of the following steps:

1. Identify relevant publics or target market segments, such as clients, funders, and legitimizers. This involves market research and probing.

2. Identify social exchange approaches and mechanisms to bring about social exchanges and social change (the products) for the target market segment.

3. Assess the perceived prices, including the social prices of time, energy, lifestyle, and psyche, paid by the target market segment using market research.

4. Construct a segmentation matrix of product, price, place, and promotion for the target market segment.

5. Rank the target market segment on its acceptance of the price using market research.

6. Examine possible ways to reduce the perceived price and increase the value of the product to the target market segment by altering the product to meet the segment's preferences, reduce time demands, increase time flexibility, and reduce effort, lifestyle, and psyche costs.

7. Determine specific pricing programs and strategies to encourage the target market segment to replace its present behavior or products with the agency's products.

Place

A successful market strategy, including pricing, requires the development of viable mechanisms and places for exchanges to occur. *Place* includes both characteristics and the physical location where the exchanges occur, along with the associated social prices, convenience, credibility, and legitimacy of the place to the target market segment (Shapiro, 1977, p. 110). The physical facilities, immediate environment, and, as Moore (1993) indicates, the paths and routes consumers and exchange partners take to get to the products, access services, and make exchanges are factors associated with place. Winston (1986c) states, "The place component . . . consists of the characteristics of service distribution, modes of delivery, location, transportation, availability, hours and days opened, appointment (requirements), parking, waiting time, and other access considerations" (p. 15).

Place is intimately related to price, especially social price, and to promotion. The marketer (agency or professional) should try to facilitate exchanges by making the place for exchange—the physical facility and its environment, its ease of access, and its comfort level—compatible to the exchange partner and target market segment. Does it add to the target market segment's financial, time, effort, lifestyle, or psyche prices or to the sense of benefits received? Can the prices associated with place be reduced? A central location can make exchange easier; a more remote one can effect client flow. The place for exchange can be either convenient to the parties in the exchange or intrusive to the potential purchaser if the latter is not interested in an exchange. The psyche costs of the intrusion may offset any time or price reductions.

Place, when possible, should add to rather than distract from the product's value. The place also communicates to the potential exchange partner the marketer's evaluation of the partner. Dingy waiting rooms where clients' confidentiality is not respected and where clients are kept waiting for hours add to the product's price. The value of the product has to be increased to compensate for the price of place.

Promotion

Promotion, the last marketing P task, is the communication of information by the agency or professional to the appropriate target market segments, of (1) the product, (2) how the product will meet the market segment's preferences, (3) its price, (4) the place or places, and (5) the processes of exchange. Promotion is often equated with advertising, but, as implied above, promotion goes far beyond advertising. Promotion includes *all* messages the agency and the professional communicate to the target market segment regarding their views of the market segment, the value of the market segment to the agency and professional, the products, and the products' capacity to meet the target market segment's preferences.

Effective promotion motivates its target "to take specific action and promises a desirable benefit if they do" (Stern, 1990, p. 74). An agency's or professional's office and waiting room, behavior toward and respect for clients when they arrive, and the demeanor of all those in contact with clients all communicate the value that the agency or professional assigns to the clients, the agency's

products, and the products' capacity to meet clients' preferences.

Different target market segments require different communications and venues shaped to carry the desired message to each market segment. Rothman and his colleagues (Rothman, 1980; Rothman, Teresa, Kay, & Morningstar, 1983) consider the need for differences in communication and promotion in their discussion of the diffusion of the results of social research and development (Social R and D). Diffusion, in Rothman's Social R and D model, is basically promotion and dissemination of the products—the findings of the social R and D—such as new knowledge or skills in ways that the consumer can evaluate and use. Social R and D itself is an outside-inside marketing strategy, as it starts with a client's problem or need.

Promotion can be mass promotion with low or high intensity. An example of low-intensity diffusion and promotion is advertising to a general, unsegmented target market. High-intensity promotion is targeted, individualized, personalized, and often with direct contact with the recipients of the communication. In all promotion, the marketer needs to determine the targets and their method of obtaining information—whether the targets are centralized or decentralized, have weakly or strongly controlled communication and information channels, are homogeneous or heterogeneous, what reference groups are used by the target market segment, and what environmental constraints and controls on information exists. The product, the information, and the messages need to be converted into the target market segment's language, whether lay, professional, or scientific. This requires knowledge of the target consumers. For example, messages may be translated into another language or shifted from generalizations to specific applications sought by the target consumers.

Communication strategies and techniques used to reach potential clients include feeding information into client networks and support systems, providing key informants with information and using other word-of-mouth techniques, and holding community forums and special events for target client groups. The promotional techniques should specify the benefits and prices of the products, the behavioral responses sought from the target market segment, how the exchange can be made, and how information can be obtained by the target market segment. Once clients or other target market segments begin the exchange process, communication is generally high in intensity.

Public Relations and Public Information

Any time the agency or professional (the marketer) deals with any actual or potential target market segments, it is engaging in public relations. The publics can be clients, prospective staff, donors, potential or current supporters of the agency, legitimation sources, and potential volunteers. Kotler and Andreasen (1987) define public relations as the image-building function that

> evaluates the attitudes of important publics, identifies the policies and procedures of an individual or organization with the public interest, and executes a program of activities to earn understanding and acceptance by these publics. Sometimes a short definition is given, which says that PR stands for *performance* (P) plus *recognition* (R). (pp. 576–577)

While recognizing the overlap between the concepts, Brawley (1983) distinguishes public relations from public education. Public relations are "efforts intended to interpret the characteristics, functions, and activities of human service workers to the general public or particular segments of it" (p. 12). Public education, as Brawley uses the concept, has less precise targets and is more

akin to social marketing, general image building, and educating on general social condition.

> Public education is . . . the provision of information to the general public or a given audience about social issues, social problems, categories of people with special needs, appropriate and inappropriate collective or individual responses to particular problems or needs, the functions of specific human service programs, and needs for new or changed social policies or programs. (p. 12)

Developing and Assessing Communication

In developing and assessing a public relations, information, and promotion program the following questions should be answered:

1. What is the specific public or target market segment with which the agency or professional wants to develop a relationship? Are there any special circumstances and traits—location, demographic characteristics, boundaries, other factors—that inhibit communication?

2. What is the intended purpose of the relationship? What is the exchange—the benefits offered to and responses sought from the target market segment? What specific actions or responses are sought from the target market segment?

3. How does the target market segment obtain its information? What sources of information and venues for the information—specific print media, television (specific programs and times), word of mouth, information and opinion leaders, networks—are used by the target market segment? What level of information is sought or required in order to make an exchange? What is the comprehension capacity of the segment? What are the barriers to and facilitating conditions for information exchange?

4. What type of information is needed by the target market segment to make a decision to engage in the exchange? What specific information is needed by the target market segment to understand the phenomena, perform the desired behavior, and engage in the exchange? What are the specific benefits to the target market segment? What is the price to the target market segment?

5. How will the agency or professional know that an exchange has occurred, that is, that the target market segment has received the desired product and the agency has received the desired resources in return? What are the feedback mechanisms?

Public relations and education are exercises in communication. As with all communication, the tasks for the message sender are to determine: (1) Has the message reached the intended target (2) in the manner intended, (3) in a way that the target can understand and respond in the way the sender intended, (4) to produce the outcome behavior desired by the sender, and (5) that will allow the sender to know that the desired outcome behavior by the target has occurred? The communication management task is to have the message reach the target in a timely fashion in the manner intended with the content intended.

Good formal communication as part of promotion has the following characteristics: (1) brevity—it is only as long as needed; (2) appeal—it focuses on the possible positive outcome in the exchange; and (3) honesty—it provides honest information about the product, price, and place. Messages and communication, to reemphasize the earlier discussion, go beyond advertisements and formal communication to include all the interactions between the target market segment and the agency or marketer.

A challenge in developing written and verbal messages for target market segments is assessing the educational level required to understand the message and developing appropriate messages. Assessing educational appropriateness is important if the message is to convey meaning. There are several ways to do this. Perhaps the best way is to field test the message with a representative sample of the target audience. Another method is to test the message with a focus group selected from the target population. Both of these methods suffer from the expense of developing the inventory of the target population, constructing the sample or focus group, field testing the message, and repeating the process until the appropriate message level is developed.

There are many computer software programs that will test the readability level of written messages. This is done by entering the message into the software, which will then assess the message for the readability grade level necessary to comprehend it.

A less expensive and quick (though with suspect validity) method is the SMOG Readability Formula (Office of Cancer Communication, 1992, p. 77), which is used to calculate the reading grade level necessary to comprehend the written material. SMOG's application steps are as follows:

1. Take the beginning, approximate middle, and last 10 sentences of the message, for a total of 30 sentences, and count the number of polysyllabic words. A sentence occurs when the phrase ends in a period, question mark, or exclamation mark even though it may not be a complete sentence. A polysyllabic word is a word with three or more syllables. The intent is to obtain a representation of the total message. Random sampling to obtain the 30 sentences from all of the sentences could be done, although this is probably spurious precision.

2. Numbers, whether written or numeric, abbreviations such as "etc.," and hyphenated words have the number of syllables that they have when spoken. For example, "192" has five syllables and "etc." has four syllables. Hyphenated words are counted as one word.

3. Compute the square root of the number of polysyllabic words in the 30 sentences to the nearest whole square root. For example, the square root of 193 is 13.89 and the nearest whole square root is 14. The square root and nearest whole square root of 9 is 3. The square root of 10 is 3.16, and the nearest whole square root is 3.

4. Add a constant of 3 to the square root, and the sum is the minimum educational level, within ±1.5 grade levels, necessary to understand the message. The ±1.5 grade levels is the possible error range.

For example, if the 30 sentences contain 60 polysyllabic words, the computation of the readability level is as follows:

TABLE 11.4 Readability Test Calculation Steps

Total number of polysyllabic words	60
Square root	7.75
Nearest whole squarer root	8
Addition of constant	3
Approximate minimum grade level	11
Approximately appropriate grade level range (± 1.5 grade levels)	9.5–12.5

The message should be appropriate for someone with an 11th grade reading level, although the error range indicates that it might be readable by someone with as low as a 9.5 grade reading level or perhaps require 12.5 years or graduation from high school. If the target market segment has a general reading level of 10 years, given the error range, the marketer probably should

lower the readability level. This can be done by lowering the number and ratio of polysyllabic words per sentence.

Messages with fewer than 30 sentences can be converted into a format appropriate to SMOG by using the adjustment process described in the accompanying insert.

Adjustment Procedures for Messages of Fewer Than 30 Sentences

Total number of polysyllabic words in the communication/total number of sentences in the communication × 30 = adjusted total number of polysyllabic words.

The adjusted product is entered into cell 1 of Table 11.4, and the remaining steps are completed. For example, if a communication has 15 polysyllabic words in eight sentences, the readability level is:

$$\text{Total number of polysyllabic words}$$
$$\text{to be used} = 15/8 = 1.875 \times 30$$
$$= 56.25 \text{ adjusted polysyllabic words}$$

The adjusted total number of polysyllabic words is entered into the computation procedures.

SMOG provides a rough approximation of readability level. It does not deal directly with complexities beyond the message's individual words. Indirectly it does, however, since 10 long, complex sentences are more likely to contain more polysyllabic words than 10 short, declarative sentences. SMOG's methodology is similar to that employed by the software program. If a message yields a score above the minimum educational level targeted, it probably is a good idea to rework it.

SMOG's advantage is that it requires little time and expense compared to the alternative methods. No representative panels of

TABLE 11.5 Readability Test Calculation Steps

Total number of polysyllabic words	56.25
Square root	7.5
Nearest whole square root	8
Addition of constant	3
Approximate minimum grade level	11
Approximately appropriate grade level range (± 1.5)	9.5–12.5

the target market segment are required. The time and expense of field testing are eliminated. No computers, software, or computer expertise are required. The costs for this assessment method are the costs of a calculator to compute the square roots (less than $10) and the time needed to count the sentences and polysyllabic words. SMOG's disadvantage is that it provides only a crude approximation of the readability grade level.

THE USE OF MEDIA

Target market segments are often reached through the media, although the particular venue and media may be different for each segment. When the media are used they become exchange partners, and their needs, preferences, and operating procedures must be considered. As with all exchanges, the marketer should seek ways to increase the value and decrease the price for the exchange partner. The media respond to promotional efforts when they see gains. In using a particular venue, the wants, needs, and format of the venue should be considered.

The previously discussed general communication issues apply to the use of media. Communications should be focused, brief, and honest. The journalistic criteria of the "five W's"—who, what, when, where, and why—and sometimes the "H" of how, should be reflected in the message and media releases (Rose, 1995): (1) Who are you and who is interested in the information (the target market segment)? (2) What is the newsworthy event or occurrence of interest? What will be expected of the target market segment? What will be their benefits? (3) When will or has the event occurred? (4) Where will or did the event occur? (5) Why is the event important to the target market segment? (5) How did the event come about?

Articles should be written in a manner that involves the least work and cost to the venue. Venues should be surveyed and relationships developed with the appropriate editors and reporters to discover the preferred length, timing, style, and format. The marketer should be available to the venue to answer follow-up questions for a fuller story, as well as for additional follow-up and other stories that the venue may be seeking.

The social agency or social work marketer can expedite the use of the media with a media information file (Rose, 1994). This file, computerized or manual in a file box or Rolodex, should contain the following information:

1. The names, addresses, and telephone numbers, including fax numbers and E-mail addresses, if any, of the main media outlets and contacts within each outlet. If contacts can be personalized, exchanges are helped.

2. The names, addresses, and telephone numbers, including fax numbers and E-mail addresses, if any, of the media outlets' decision makers as the editors and producers. Again, contacts within each outlet should be personalized to facilitate exchanges.

3. Specific information about each outlet's news, information, and entertainment interests, special features, target audience, and which of the marketer's target market

segments this audience reaches, both for print media when they are published and circulated and for radio and television when the particular relevant programs are aired, as well as the geographic audience radius.

4. Deadlines for media and for venues within the media as news stories, feature stories, and columns in the print media and differing program types in radio and television.

5. A brief analysis of the successes and failures for each contact and venue.

Information on the media can be obtained from the White Pages and Yellow Pages of the telephone directory and media directories. Many outlets provide media kits to promote their use. Rose (1994), *NASW News*'s columnist on marketing, emphasizes the use of smaller media outlets, "such as local weekly papers or community radio or television stations or programs. These are usually in need of material and may use just about anything you send them. They reach a smaller audience, but the coverage is free . . . this way is gravy" (p. 5). It is also often beneficial to hold media events such as press conferences, if there is significant timely news, and media receptions. However, the success of media use is measured not by the amount of coverage but by whether the coverage communicates the intended message to the intended target audience.

MEDIA OUTLETS

The following five media outlets are most useful:

1. *Print media:* op-ed pieces, press releases, letters to the editor, feature stories, and information contacts with reporters and columnists. Human interest and case studies that grab readers' attention and tell a compelling story are often preferred over statistics, although statistics may supplement the story. Magazines are often useful outlets for feature stories. Multiple letters to the editor by different writers stressing the same subject and message have a better chance of being published than a single letter. Most newspapers and magazines publish only a small fraction of the letters they receive. *The New York Times*, for instance, publishes less than 5% of the letters it receives (Zane 1995).

2. *Television:* talk and interview shows, tabloids shows, cable and public access TV, news shows with visuals and sound bites, and public service announcements.

3. *Radio:* call-in and talk shows, public service announcements, interview shows, buying time or having a regular show on a problem area (all it takes is a sponsor), news shows, and sound bites. Multiple calls and callers will probably be required for the call-in and talk shows, as these generally screen calls and limit repeat callers within a given time period.

4. *Electronic Bulletin Boards and Networks:* these are emerging venues and currently have more potential than experience. However, they may be useful in the future in reaching particular target audiences when Internet and Web surfing becomes more user-friendly, more widespread, and less costly.

5. *Volunteers:* Volunteers, in addition to providing resources, are a promotion mechanism. They link the agency to a range of networks, as well as providing the agency with personnel resources. Sources of volunteers include business firms, service clubs, "helping hand" programs in schools, and student internship programs in college departments such as business, journalism, and communications, as well as social work. These volunteers carry into

and talk about positive and negative experiences in other aspects and networks of their lives. A popular Baltimore radio columnist and commentator on business investments and financial matters regularly volunteers at a homeless meals center. He often talks about his volunteer experiences on his radio show. After his radio talks, donations and volunteers to the center increase for a short time. This is valuable free promotion for the center.

MARKETING: A SUMMARY

Marketing is a philosophy and strategy of service development and delivery and an approach to expediting exchanges. Marketing starts and ends with the target market segments and attempts to promote exchanges by meeting the preferences of these segments. Marketing is compatible with the social work ethics and values of client self-determination, starting where the client is, and client advocacy. Marketing can be used with any exchange partner or target market segment. The steps of the marketing philosophy and strategy can be summarized in the following questions:

1. What resources are necessary to complete the mission and achieve the objectives?
2. From whom are the resources sought (the target market segment)?
3. What are the benefits (products) to be offered to the target market segment for its resources?
4. What is the value of the benefits to the target market segment? How will the resources meet their preferences? How was this determined?
5. What is the price to the target market segment? What are the social price components? How does the price compare to the value as determined by the target market segment?
6. What are the places and processes of exchange with the target market segment? Does the place contribute to the value or price of the benefits to the target market segment?
7. What are the best methods of communicating to the target market segment the product's capacity to provide benefits and meet preferences, as well as its price and place of exchange?

THE MARKETING AUDIT GUIDE[1]

1. *Mission Review*

Does the organization have a written mission statement or bylaws that detail the mission? What are the mission and objectives? Are objectives stated in outcome terms regarding clients and other target market segments? If no written mission statement and objectives exist, how does the agency convey its mission and objectives to staff and other relevant publics? How does the organization determine success?

2. *Task Environment*

Has the agency determined what resources it needs from its task environment to achieve its mission and objectives? What are the target market segments that have the necessary resources

---

[1]For a complete market audit form, questions, process, and discussion see Rubright & MacDonald, 1981, pp. 84–97 and passim.

(publics, groups, organizations, agencies, and others)?

3. New Markets

Are new target market segments needed to help the agency achieve or expand its mission? What are they? How might the agency locate and assess these target market segments for resources and preferences? Have other communitywide surveys been conducted by either the agency or some other group that can be used to assess the market?

4. Communication

How does the agency communicate with each target market segment? List the publics or markets that have know barriers to effective communication. What are those barriers? How are the needs and preferences of each target market segment assessed by the agency? What is the agency's image with each target market segment? Is the image the one desired by the agency?

5. Referral Sources

List all organizations or individuals that refer patients/clients to the agency, starting with those that refer most often. Is the agency satisfied with its communication and with the results of the referral network? How does the agency provide feedback to referral sources? Are they satisfied with the feedback? What is the annual turnover, if any, of referral sources? Are the reasons for this turnover known? What changes or shifts in clients/patients have affected referrals?

6. Clients[2]

What are the products for each client target market segment? What are the services, broken down into the smallest complete components? What is their value to the target market segment? What

client preferences do they meet? What is the price to the target market segment? What do the client target market segments exchange for the products? How does the agency obtain its information on the target market segment? What does the agency do information it receives from clients or patients? Is the agency satisfied with its communication with clients and potential clients? What is the agency's image with clients? Is the image different from the agency's intended image?

Which current services and products bring the agency the most income and other resources? The least? How do the resources exchanged by the client target market segment help the agency meet its objectives?

7. Competition

List all known and potential competitors of the agency by resources sought, include size of staff, ownership, services, service area, fees, caseload, size, and annual growth rate. Describe the one agency or group that is thought to be the chief competitor. How can this competition be met? Compare the agency's fees and other social prices to those of similar organizations; are they comparable and competitive, higher or lower?

8. Market Management

Does the agency have a spokesperson? If yes, who is that person and what is the position's title? Is there an agency public relations director or a person responsible for public relations? Is there an agency marketing director or a person responsible for marketing? Do all agency staff members understand their functions as agency representatives, spokespeople, and marketers? Is there a board public relations committee and a marketing committee? Do all board members understand their functions as agency representatives, spokespeople, and marketers? If the agency has not had marketing research or planning, how has it deter-

---

[2]This section and subsequent sections can be modified for the other significant target market segments: referral sources, financial providers, complementary agencies, volunteers and nonfinancial providers, and providers of legitimation and sanction.

mined the needs of users in order to expand existing services or add new ones?

9. Promotional and Public Information Strategies

Does the agency have a written press relations policy? Where is it located and how is it used? Do all agency members understand it? How has the policy benefited the organization in the last 2 years? How were benefits determined? Does the agency have a brochure or other written information for distribution that explains the agency's mission, objectives, and services? When was the material last revised? Which target market segments get the material? Is it adapted to meet the needs, interests, and preferences of the specific target market segments that get the brochure? Does the agency have an internal newsletter or publication, an external newsletter or publication, direct-mail operations for fund-raising and information distribution, a regular news release program, a newspaper clipping service, a radio or television news recording service, radio and television public service announcements (PSAs)? Which benefits and products are covered in the radio and television PSAs? To which publics are the radio and TV PSAs directed? Are representatives of any target market segments consulted while preparing the public information program? Which target market segments are consulted and why?

Does the agency have policies and protocols for press releases? Which of the following do press releases address: new personnel (particularly managers or department heads), new services, new equipment, revised policies, procedures, special events, recruitment of employees and volunteers, financial and statistical data/information, and feature and human interest stories promoting the successes of the agency and its clients? How does the agency determine how well its purposes, objectives, problems mission, and new distribution policy are understood by the news media?

Are annual reports published? If not, how does the agency direct the flow of information that normally is found in the annual report?

Does the agency have a speaker's bureau? Which publics are addressed in activities or promotion of the bureau? Which main messages are the agency's speakers conveying to audiences? What and who determines the subject matter of speeches? Does the agency hold community seminars, symposia, or lectures? Are volunteers, board members, and other auxiliary personnel used in community relations? Has the agency benefited from their activities? What benefits does the agency derive from each of the public information and public relations activities? How are benefits determined?

Does the agency use print, radio, and television advertising? To which target market segments are these messages addressed? Do the ads bring the agency new clients or patients or other new markets? How is this determined?

Are all staff members involved in or have the opportunity to participate in promotion and make suggestions for improvement? Does management consider the suggestions?

10. Locating New Markets

How does the agency find new target market segments—clients, fiscal and nonfiscal resource providers, other sources? Who is (are) designated to find new clients, referral sources, employees, and sources of funding? Is case finding an agency practice? Do auxiliary members or volunteers perform community relations, resource location, and case-finding functions for the agency? Does the organization attract or encourage walk-in users? If yes, how do such users discover the organization?

11. Agency Fees

Does the agency have a fee structure? How do clients characterize the fee structure (acceptable, unacceptable, no opinion)? How is this

THE MARKETING AUDIT GUIDE (Continued)

determined? How is the fee structure communicated to current and potential clients? Does the agency convey an image that it can provide more free or reduced-fee care than it actually can deliver? How is this determined? What questions about fees do referral network representatives ask? How does the agency communicate the main points of its fees to its key target market segments? How often in the last 2 years has the agency raised its fees? How was this received by the key target market segments in their exchanges with the agency? Was increased value to the target market segments perceived by the segments?

References

In addition to the marketing references indicated below, readers may want to review the burgeoning literature in social services, human services, and professional marketing. Some additional references include the *Journal of Health Care Marketing, Health Care Marketing Quarterly, Journal of Marketing for Mental Health, Praeger Series in Public and Nonprofit Sector Marketing,* and the *Journal of Professional Marketing,* to name only a few.

Altman, D. L., & Piotrow, P. T. (1980). Social marketing: Does it work? *Population Reports, 8,* J393–J434.

Anderson, E. (1995). Welfare by waiver: A response. *Public Welfare, 53*(2), 44–49, 50–51.

Andreasen, A. P. (1984). Nonprofits: Check your attention to customers. In C. H. Lovelock & C. B. Weinberg (Eds.), *Public and nonprofit marketing: Cases and readings* (pp. 131–135). Palo Alto, CA: Scientific Press.

Anthony, R. N., & Young, D. W. (1988). *Management control in nonprofit organizations* (4th ed.). Homewood, IL: Richard D. Irwin.

Bernard, H. R. (1994). *Research methods in anthropology: Qualitative and quantitative approaches,* (2nd ed.). Thousand Oaks, CA: Sage.

Blau, P. M. (1963). *Exchange and power in social life.* New York: Wiley.

Bliss, P. (1970). *Marketing management and the behavioral environment.* Englewood Cliffs, NJ: Prentice-Hall.

Bradshaw, J. (1977). The concept of social need. In N. Gilbert & H. Specht (Eds.), *Planning for social welfare* (pp. 290–296). Englewood Cliffs, NJ: Prentice-Hall.

Brawley, E. A. (1983). *Mass media and human services: Getting the message across.* Beverly Hills, CA: Sage.

Bryce, H. J., Jr. (1987). *Financial management for nonprofit organizations.* (Englewood Cliffs, NJ: Prentice-Hall.

Coalition of Not-For-Profit Nursing Homes. (1995, February 23). Albany declares war on the aged and the infirm. *The New York Times,* p. B9.

Cooper, P., & McIlvain, G. E. (1983). Factors influencing marketing's ability to assist non-profit organizations. In P. Kotler, O. C. Ferrell, & C. W. Lamb (Eds.), *Cases and readings for marketing for nonprofit organizations* (pp. 10–18). Englewood Cliffs, NJ: Prentice-Hall.

DiGiulio, J. F. (1984). Marketing social services. *Social Casework, 65,* 227–234.

Enis, B. M. (1974). *Marketing principles: The management process.* Pacific Palisades, CA: Goodyear.

Fine, S. H. (1992). *Marketing the public sector: Promoting the causes of public and nonprofit agencies,* New Brunswick, NJ: Transaction.

Fine, S. H., & Fine, A. P. (1986). Distribution channels in marketing social work. *Social Casework, 67,* 227–233.

Fox, K. A., & Kotler, P., (1987). The marketing of social causes: The first ten years. In P. Kotler, O. C. Ferrell, & C. W. Lamb (Eds.), *Strategic marketing for nonprofit organizations: Cases and readings* (3rd ed., pp. 14–29). Englewood Cliffs, NJ: Prentice-Hall.

Genkins, M. (1985). Strategic planning for social work marketing." *Administration in Social Work, 9*, 35–43.

Gillespie, E., & Schellhas, B. (Eds.). (1994). *Contract with America: The bold plan by Representative Newt Gingrich, Representative Dick Armey, and the House Republicans to change the nation.* New York: Time Books.

Gingrich, N., Armey, D., & the House Republicans. (1994). *Contract with America.* New York: Time Books/Random House.

Greenbaum, T. L. (1987). *The practical handbook and guide to focus group research.* Lexington, MA: D. C. Heath.

Holmes, J., & Riecken, G. (1980). Using business marketing concepts to view the private, nonprofit social service agency. *Administration in Social Work, 4*, 43–53.

Homan, G. C. (1958). Social behavior as exchange. *American Journal of Sociology, 63*, 597–606.

Kotler, P. (1971). *Marketing management* (2nd ed.). Englewood Cliffs, NJ: Prentice-Hall.

Kotler, P. (1977). A generic concept of marketing. In R. M. Gaedeke (Ed.), *Marketing in private and public nonprofit organizations: Perspectives and illustrations* (pp. 18–33). Santa Maria, CA: Goodyear.

Kotler, P., & Andreasen, A. R. (1987). *Strategic marketing for nonprofit organizations* (3rd ed.). Englewood Cliffs, NJ: Prentice-Hall.

Kotler, P., & Roberto, E. L. (Eds.). (1989). *Social marketing: Strategies for changing public behavior.* New York: Free Press.

Kreuger, R. A. (1988). *Focus groups: A practical guide for applied research.* Newbury Park, CA: Sage.

Lauffer, A. (1984). *Strategic marketing for not-for-profit organizations: Program and resource development.* New York: Free Press.

Lauffer, A. (1986). To market, to market: A nuts and bolts approach to strategic planning in human service organizations. *Administration in Social Work, 10*, 31–39.

Lohmann, R. A. (1980). *Breaking even: Financial management in human service organizations.* Philadelphia: Temple University Press.

Lord, J. G. (January–February 1981). Marketing nonprofits. *The Grantsmanship Center News,* 54–59.

Lovelock, C. H., & Weinberg, C. B. (1984). Public and nonprofit marketing comes of age. In C. H. Lovelock & C. B. Weinberg (Eds.), *Public and nonprofit marketing: Cases and readings* (pp. 33–42). Palo Alto, CA: Scientific Press.

Manoff, R. K. (1985). *Social marketing: New imperative for public health.* New York: Praeger.

McDermott, D. R. (1986). Market research applied to charitable services: A regional case study of the United Way. *Journal of Marketing for Mental Health, 1*, 55–65.

Moore, S. T. (1993). Goal-directed change in service utilization. *Social Work, 38*, 221–226.

Morgan, D. L. (1988). *Successful focus groups.* Newbury Park, CA: Sage.

Office of Cancer Communication, National Cancer Institute. (1992). *Making health communication programs work: A planner's guide.* (NIH Publication No. 92-1493. Washington, DC: U.S. Department of Health and Human Services.

Perlman, R. (1975). *Consumers and social services.* New York: Wiley.

Reichert, K. (1982). Human services and the market system. *Health and Social Work, 7*, 173–182.

Reid, W. J. (Ed.). (1972). *Decision-making in the Work Incentive Program.* Final report submitted to the Office of Research and Development, Manpower Administration, U.S. Department of Labor, Report Nos. DLMA 51-15-69-08, DLMA 51-37-6911, DLMA 51-24-6910. Chicago: School of Social Service Administration, University of Chicago.

Rose, R. (1994, October). Marketing: To build clientele, build a media file. *NASW News, 39*, 5.

Rose, R. (1995, February). Marketing: Hook editors with a pro-caliber release. *NASW News, 40*, 5.

Rosenberg, G., & Weissman, A. (1981). Marketing social services in health care facilities. *Health and Social Work, 6*, 13–20.

Rothman, J. (1980). *Social R & D: Research and development in the human services.* Englewood Cliffs, NJ: Prentice-Hall.

Rothman, J., Teresa, J. C., Kay, T. L., & Morningstar, G. C. (1983). *Marketing human service innovations.* Beverly Hills, CA: Sage.

Rubin, A., & Babbie, E. (1993). *Research methods for social work* (2nd. ed.). Pacific Grove, CA: Brooks/Cole.

Rubright, R., & MacDonald, D. (1981). *Marketing health and human services.* Rockville, MD: Aspens Systems Corp.

Seltz, D. D. (1981). *Handbook of innovative marketing techniques.* Reading, MA: Addison-Wesley.

Shapiro, B. P. (1977). Marketing for nonprofit organizations. In R. M. Gaedeke (Ed.), *Marketing in private and public nonprofit organizations: Perspectives and illustrations* (pp. 103–115). Santa Maria, CA: Goodyear.

Specht, H. (1986). Social support, social networks, social exchange and social work practice. *Social Service Review, 60,* 218–240.

Stern, G. J. (1990). *Marketing workbook for nonprofit organizations.* St. Paul, MN: Amherst H. Wilder Foundation.

Stoner, M. R. (1986). Marketing of social services gains prominence in practice. *Administration in Social Work, 10,* 41–52.

Sweeney, R. E., Berl, R. L., & Winston, W. J. (Eds.). (1989). *Cases and select readings in health care marketing.* New York: Haworth.

Tower, K. D. (1994). Consumer-centered social work practice: Restoring client self-determination. *Social Work, 39,* 191–196.

Turner, J. H. (1982). *The structure of sociological theory* (3rd. ed.). Homewood, IL: Dorsey Press.

Warfield, D. J., & Maloney, D. (1981). Consumer feedback in human service programs. *Social Work, 26,* 151–156.

Weinberg, C. B. (1984). Marketing mix decisions for nonprofit organizations: An analytical approach. In C. H. Lovelock & C. B. Weinberg (Eds.), *Public and nonprofit marketing: Cases and readings* (pp. 261–269). Palo Alto, CA: Scientific Press.

Winston, W. J. (1984). *Marketing for mental health services.* New York: Haworth.

Winston, W. J. (Ed.). (1985a). *Health marketing and consumer behavior: A guide to basic linkages,* New York: Haworth.

Winston, W. J. (Ed.). (1985b). *Marketing strategies for human and social service agencies.* New York: Haworth.

Winston, W. J. (Ed.). (1986a). *Advertising handbook for health care services.* New York: Haworth.

Winston, W. J. (1986b). Preface and introduction to journal articles. *Journal of Marketing for Mental Health, 1,* vii–xii.

Winston, W. J. (1986c). Basic marketing principles for mental health professionals. *Journal of Marketing for Mental Health, 1,* 9–20.

Yin, R. K. (1986). *Case study research: Design and method.* Beverly Hills, CA: Sage.

Zane, J. P. (1995, June 19). A rivalry in rabble-rousing as letter writers keep count. *The New York Times,* p. D5.

chapter
12
Using the Advocacy Spectrum

[E]conomic goods are not the only kind of goods that are subject to considerations of justice; a minimal amount of a wide variety of social and psychological goods are also owed to each member of society as a matter of justice.

J. C. WAKEFIELD (1994, P. 48)

Change *never* ever, ever comes from the top down.

B. MIKULSKI (1982, P. 22)

MAKING CHANGE HAPPEN

As agents for change, we need to explore where we want to go and how to get there. Therefore, this chapter will cover three social change modes that affect our practice and discuss traditional community change models. As practitioners, we want to become effective advocates for our clients as individuals. Although the chapter begins with an introduction to social change, it is primarily concerned with the different types of advocacy available to practitioners. Advocacy and action have been conceptualized here in a variety of ways to illustrate the far-reaching nature and flexibility of these practice tools. Empowerment is a secondary focus. Another purpose of the chapter is to facilitate better communication between micro and macro practitioners by spotlighting language and leaders of importance to change agents.

Values

The four cornerstones of social work, according to Saleebey (1990, p. 37), are *indignation, inquiry, compassion and caring*, and *social justice*. Social workers whose indignation as well as compassion quotients run high are primed for professional advocacy. Hearing about situations like this, we want to do something!

> Overcrowding . . . is a constant feature of schools that serve the poorest. . . . 11 classes in one school don't even have the luxury of classrooms. They share an auditorium in which they occupy adjacent sections of the stage and backstage areas. . . . "I'm housed in a coat room," says a reading teacher at another school. . . . "I teach," says a music teacher, "in a storage room. . . ." The crowding of children into insufficient, often squalid spaces seems . . . inexplicable. . . . Images of spaciousness . . . fill our . . . music . . . [children] sing of "good" and "brotherhood" "from sea to shining sea." It is a betrayal of the things that we value when poor children are obliged to sing these songs in storerooms and coat closets. (Kozol, 1991, pp. 158–160)

There are numerous ways in which inequities of this type can be addressed by caring social workers, especially those dedicated to justice (Wakefield, 1988). As Andrews and Brenden (1993) say:

> Social work may occur within the sphere of individual services (care) with a value base in compassion and benevolence; it may broaden and deepen into environmental intervention with an emphasis on community or self-protection (cure); or . . . social reform and reconstruction (prevention). (p. 24)

Thus, it is a sense of compassion that makes us want to work with the schoolchildren who have missed so much education (care). It is a sense of indignation that makes us want to completely remodel the school buildings, encourage strong parental involvement, and develop corporate or university and public school partnerships (cure). It is a willingness to question the status quo and our sense of social justice that make us want to increase the already diminished financial allocations at the county and state levels, as well as ensure that no further cuts will be made (prevention).

Key Terms and Preliminary Definitions

SOCIAL CHANGE AS AN END

Within individuals and society, there is a desire for continuity as well as change, but we want to avoid getting stuck. In 1970, Freire addressed how social workers figure into larger change. " 'The social worker,' Freire wrote, 'has a moment of decision. Either he picks the side of change . . . or else he is left in the position of favoring stagnation' " (Kozol, 1990, p. 137). Social change goals can embrace better circumstances for service users, amelioration of particular oppression, or a more egalitarian society. These are progressive in that they aim to improve the lot of the disadvantaged and are carried out in a manner consistent with democratic values (Bombyk, 1995). When we set out to make changes (Abramovitz, 1993; Mandell, 1992), that process is known as *directed, purposive,* or *intentional* change (Warren, 1977). Change *strategies* vary widely and can include "nonviolent direct action, advocacy, political action, and conscientization [raising of consciousness]" (Reeser & Leighninger, 1990, p. 75). Checkoway (1995) describes six strategies—each with its own "practice pattern"—in connection with community change: mass mobilization, social action, citizen participation, public advocacy, popular education, and local services development (p. 2).

Relationship Between Advocacy and Social Action

Advocacy and *social action* are strategies or means to an end. These concepts are similar. The list in Table 12.1, compiled by Panitch (1974) and Hepworth and Larsen (1993), suggests the variety of techniques used by social workers engaged in advocacy and reform. This list also shows that "not all advocacy is militant" (Rothman, 1995, p. 32) and that "large-scale intervention" is "doable" (Huber & Orlando, 1993, p. 21).

Differences in advocacy and action include size variations in the societal unit normally worked with (task group vs. a larger population), adherence to norms, and typical interventions. Let us consider them.

Advocacy as a Means

Definitions. Advocacy, whether individual or systemic, case or class, means championing or speaking for the interest of clients or citizens (NASW, 1969). Social work managers, for example, often promote their clients' causes with officials and decision

TABLE 12.1 Techniques of Advocacy and Social Action

1. Conferring with other agencies
2. Appealing to review boards
3. Initiating legal action
4. Forming interagency committees
5. Providing expert testimony
6. Gathering information through studies and surveys
7. Educating relevant segments of the community
8. Contacting public officials and legislators
9. Forming agency coalitions
10. Organizing client groups
11. Developing petitions
12. Making persistent demands

Source: Hepworth and Larsen (1993), pp. 506–507.

makers (Menefee & Thompson, 1994, p. 18). Advocacy has a role in transforming "private troubles" into "public issues" (Wagner, 1990, p. 185) or "personal problems" into "social issues" (Doress-Worters & Siegel, 1994, p. 431). It has a role in challenging "inhumane conditions" (Wood & Middleman, 1989, p. 141) at a micro or macro level. Social workers also advocate within our field for a particular mission (Wakefield, 1988), program, or course of action (Simon, Altstein, & Melli, 1994). In direct-service work, advocacy is often part of client support and representation and, if possible, involves client self-advocacy. *Case advocacy* emphasizes ensuring service delivery in one's field of practice and securing resources and services for particular clients in one's caseload (Grosser, 1976; Hepworth & Larsen 1993; Jackson, 1991; Johnson, 1995). *Cause advocacy* involves groups, institutions, and modification of social conditions (Johnson, 1995).

Scope. Wood and Middleman (1989, chap. 8) show how advocacy arising naturally out of professional social work involves four spheres of activity, each with a different task focus. They also distinguish direct from indirect advocacy with individuals or a class of persons, as the following examples indicate:

- Advocate provides information of consequence to a client regarding transportation. (direct advocacy)
- Advocate argues with others, in transportation program, on behalf of client. (indirect advocacy)
- Advocate organizes, mobilizes clients into group action on transportation problem. (direct advocacy)
- Advocate influences policy makers to aid citizens needing transportation. (indirect advocacy)

Thus, advocacy can be used at any intervention level, collectively or separately, and by a professional of any title, even though it is commonly thought of as an activity in which one person goes to bat for another.

History. The advocacy tradition evolved from the legal field out of attempts to implement the Bill of Rights and humanitarian reform. Early *cause advocates* called the attention of those in office or high places to the predicament of certain exploited or ignored sectors of society. Examples include Dorothea Dix, who inspected and reported on prisons and insane asylums, and Reginald Heber Smith, who implored attorneys to provide legal aid for the poor. Social work literature separates advocacy from social movements (Sosin & Caulum, 1983) but sometimes views cause or class advocacy as the same as social action (Hepworth & Larsen, 1993). The primary distinction is that most forms of advocacy stay within established employer guidelines and procedures and traditional political processes.

SOCIAL ACTION AS A MEANS

Definition. *Social action* is a collective endeavor to promote a cause or make a progressive change in the face of opposition. It often involves "organizing the disadvantaged or aggrieved" (Fisher, 1995, p. 327) and "direct action." If necessary, agitation or "disruption" may be used (Specht, 1969). It builds on the self-advocacy of the affected part of the population by mobilizing them (J. Gamson, 1991).

Scope. Compared with advocacy, the goal is broader. *In direct-service work, social action often means tackling "cumulative problem situations and issues"* (Staub-Bernasconi, 1991, p. 36). Romanyshyn (1971) defined it as "ef-

forts at systemic intervention designed to prevent problems, expand opportunities and enhance the quality of life" and believed that such efforts "may be seen as a quest for community and a better polity [body politic]" (p. 153). Activities can entail changing the agency from within, working with mobilized populations (Kling & Posner, 1990), serving as whistle blowers (Galper, 1975), or conducting community-controlled participatory action research (Glugoski, Reisch, & Rivera, 1994; Wagner, 1991).

A distinguishing feature of social action is its emphasis on internal change through consciousness raising (Ryan, 1992) and changing (Ash, 1972). Certain thought patterns discourage our involvement—for example, believing critics who say we are going too fast or too far. In contrast, William Gamson has analyzed what facilitates involvement. He describes three collective action frames—injustice, agency, and identity—used by the mind to justify action. The *injustice* component is the "moral indignation" that can be summoned as part of political consciousness. The *agency* component refers to the sense that we can do something—"alter conditions or policies through collective action." The *identity* component creates a mental adversary, a "they"—human agents who can be affected or turned around (W. A. Gamson, 1992, p. 7).

History. Concerned with power holders and challenging groups, social action comes out of "insurgency," movement, reform, and third-party traditions against the so-called evils of life. It often involves "the collective struggle of oppressed people acting in their own behalf to improve conditions affecting their lives" (Burghardt, 1987, p. 298). For a model of collective struggle, numerous organizers have drawn from the philosophy and tactics of Saul Alinsky (Bradshaw, Soifer, & Gutierrez, 1994). Today social action manifests itself in media events, in ambitious city-wide and statewide campaigns for all manner of reforms, in the years of organizing on both sides of the abortion issue, and in "issue networks" (Burghardt, 1987, p. 292) that begin with information sharing and swell into action coalitions.

Change Modalities Relevant to Direct Service

Advocacy and action have been successfully melded in three contemporary forms of change:

- Ensuring individual rights: pursuing actual delivery of what it is assumed everyone should have.
- Public interest advocacy: participating in society's decisions and sharing benefits, power, and responsibilities.
- Transformation: perceiving the possibility of a better, and profoundly different, society and moving to bring it about.

All three manifestations of change make invisible groups more visible, address social misery and disenfranchisement, link individuals, and presuppose the advocate's optimism or *hope* (Simon, 1994).

ENSURING INDIVIDUAL RIGHTS

Fairness may require the continuous creation of new rights for designated groups and for those eligible for certain entitlements (Wood & Middleman, 1989). "Getting one's rights" adherents aim to ensure delivery of rights and services that society has pledged to everyone. They believe individuals and groups that fight for their own rights contribute to other members of society by creating a level playing field. For instance, citizens have used the courts to obtain equal protection under the law when an immutable trait (such as gender or race) has kept them from receiving what they should have had all along—fair access to jobs, apartments, or voting. Advocates are also needed. For example, right-to-shelter battles are fought on behalf of diverse individuals (in burdensome circumstances such as homelessness) and large families (fair housing).

This mode of change influences our practice in many ways. Social workers sometimes help secure or create new rights—such as the right to treatment or to die—and often help implement or enforce such rights.[1] We also mediate when there are competing claims—for example, between family members (Bentley, 1993; NASW, 1969; Rosenson, 1993). We can be criticized when our agency is perceived as interfering with the rights of those in a category, such as adoptees or adopters; clashing with a particular group, such as recipients; or ignoring a group, such as those caught up in the court system (Lynch & Mitchell, 1995).

The rights under discussion fall into three categories: (1) due process (a concept of fairness) or procedural rights, (2) substantive rights, and (3) basic human rights (Higham, 1993). The first two flow from the Bill of Rights, the Constitution, legislative directives, or court orders. Due process rights can involve such things as the right to a fair hearing before being removed from school or public housing or the right to receive timely and specific notice (Donaldson, 1976; Handler, 1979, p. 36). Substantive rights can inure or accrue to everyone (free speech); to those in a category (right to Medicare benefits if criteria are met); or to a particular group (e.g., due to past discrimination). Some are remedial; nursing home residents now can enjoy the same things as the general public, such as the right to open their own mail (Horn & Griesel, 1977). Basic human rights like those promoted by the United Nations include freedom from arbitrary government restrictions and the right to food.

Immigrants lacking citizenship rights have humanitarian appeals made on their behalf. To this, our profession would add client rights such as self-determination (Tower, 1994) and participation (O'Donnell, 1993).

Rights may be won at a societal level on behalf of a *class*, such as AFDC recipients, but "can be enjoyed only on an individual level" where advocates can help implement them (Grosser, 1976, p. 276). Social work practitioners aid *individuals* by informing them of their rights and monitoring to see whether they are respected in the course of receiving services (Brieland & Lemmon 1985). Simon (1994) warns that it "would be a grave error to assume, without inquiring, that one's client has good knowledge of his or her rights as a citizen and as a consumer of services" since few of us know our own "rights and entitlements" (p. 20).

Those who seek process rights, such as adequate representation at trial, also care about ultimate outcomes, such as the disproportionate number of African-Americans on death row.

PUBLIC INTEREST ADVOCACY

The second mode of change involves societal responsibility and a determination to "get a place at the table," to participate in decisions. "Citizen-civic action" and "democratic policy-making" are associated with public interest advocacy (Dalton, 1993; Isaac, 1992). This approach uses:

- social/legal reform to promote pluralism and entree to government by strengthening outsider groups (Handler, 1978, p. 4);
- access and investigative methods to force accountability in the private and public sectors (Cunningham, Roisman, Rich, Beatley, & Barry, 1977; Powers, 1977); and
- community education to develop "life skills" (Nader, 1977) and "civic skills" in

the populace (Boyte, 1980; Grosser, 1976; Handler, 1978; Mondros & Wilson, 1994).

This advocacy—for classes of citizens who can rarely defend their own interests—relies on citizen evaluation, expertise, awareness of pressure points, freedom of information statutes, and media.

Giving "voice to the voiceless" entails representation of *general* and *dispersed*, often disorganized, *interests* (in contrast to concentrated special interests) and of *underrepresented views*. Those with an interest in keeping public schools strong are dispersed, compared with parents of children in private school who argue collectively for vouchers. Middle-class taxpayers seeking tax relief are dispersed, in contrast to the organized business community that secures tax loopholes. Low-income people, who have particular interests but lack resources to push a claim on their own behalf, are counted among the underrepresented. Promoting pro bono (for the public good) work and legal access for indigents are thus important, along with test-case law reform. Public interest advocacy tries to "strengthen the position of weak, poorly organized, or unarticulated interests in society" (Handler, 1978, p. 4).

Unlike the rights approach, where an individual may be part of an *observable* protected class (based on gender, race, etc.), many who benefit from public advocacy are *indistinguishable* (renters, etc.). These might be actual or potential consumers. For example, a critique regarding what community mental health centers might have been was written on behalf of those who *potentially* could have benefited from innovative services and meaningful community involvement (Chu & Trotter, 1974; Spector & Kitsuse, 1987, chapter 6). It has been said that an advocate of this type is "the champion we never knew we needed against an enemy we never suspected was there" (Frost, 1994, quoting

Life magazine). Thus, efforts to protect the environment epitomize public interest advocacy (Rogge, 1993; Weisbrod, Handler, & Komesar, 1978). Moreover, policy reform's beneficiaries are faceless—seldom those who directly solicited the help—but the impetus for reform often stems from observation of the plight of a significant number of individuals (Powers, 1984).

Lack of knowledge disadvantages people. Williams (1978) says, "Given the complexities of life today, finding out how things work is a full-time job" (p. 9). In this change mode, investigative reporters, public interest lawyers, librarians, and social workers can join to assist citizens who feel that everything is out of their control due to little understood forces or legalities (Lynch & Mitchell, 1995). Through exposé and explanation, we can show "how to deal with these forces . . . and how power is exercised" (Williams, 1978, p. 5). Public interest advocacy says to social work: "We have to be public citizens and wherever there is a need we must work to meet it" (Mikulski, 1982, p. 18).

TRANSFORMATION

Structural change is more fundamental in terms of ends and more concerned with vision than the first two change modalities (Fabricant & Burghardt, 1992; Leonard, 1975; Specht & Courtney, 1994; Wagner, 1990; Walz & Groze, 1991).[2] It is supported by sundry groups, including faith-oriented networks that work to change the structural causes of poverty and injustice. Those who would transform themselves and their environment must be able to perceive how society really is and could be. There must be what some feminists colloquially call a "click" experience, as well as a willingness to "color outside the lines." A well-known example of the latter occurred when youth Commissioner Jerome Miller, D.S.W., shut down Massachusetts's isolated, custodial-oriented institutions for delinquents. His "abandonment of gradualism as a reform tactic was intended to force the development of community alternatives" (Bakal, 1973). Transformative change results in profound alteration or "revitalization" of society, although overthrow of an existing government or economy is not required (Wallace 1956). Alinsky (1972) says:

> History is a relay of revolutions; the torch of idealism is carried by the revolutionary group until this group becomes an establishment, and then quietly the torch is put down to wait until a new revolutionary group picks it up for the next leg. . . . (p. 22)

Such change within social welfare spotlights contesting ideologies of service and justice (Davis, Hagen, & Early, 1994; Lawson & Rhode, 1993; Van Soest, 1994).

There are numerous examples of how those on the service front lines can play a role. Hyde (1994) believes clinical and social action approaches can be blended since the "caseworker is in an ideal position to help a client begin to consider new life goals. As part of that exploration, the possibility of participation in a macro change effort should be included" (p. 61). Wood and Middleman (1991) urge "consciousness raising" for clients and workers (pp. 54–55). Walz and Groze call for a new breed of *clinical activists* who might also serve as advocacy researchers. Such clinicians would gather data, analyze connections between individual situations and social forces, and measure their success through "multiples" who had been helped (Walz & Groze, 1991, p. 503). Moreau (1990) singles out "unmasking power relations" (p. 56) as pertinent to direct practice, that is, being open with clients about power relationships (Hartman, 1993; Sherman &

Wenocur, 1983). The worker will promote individual awareness and a belief in human agency or instrumentality. Workers and clients, as "*co*-investigators," can explore reality, critical thinking, and liberating action (Freire, 1971, p. 97; Reisch, Wenocur, & Sherman, 1981; Simon, 1990, 1994). This Freire style of dialogue involves "reducing unnecessary social distance between worker and client ... sharing information and demystifying techniques and skills used to help," according to Moreau; it means that clients can see their files and that no "case conferences concerning them are held without their presence" (1990, pp. 56–57). Many believe that numerous individual transformations contribute to a collective metamorphosis.

PRACTICE IMPLICATIONS

At a macro level, social justice often results when all three modes of change are combined. Social workers take social change from an ideological to a programmatic level (Lord & Kennedy, 1992). At a micro level, the practitioner's orientation toward change will influence interactions with clients. Box 12.1 presents a simplified example of how social workers might respond to a question from a service user in accordance with all three philosophies of change. Conservatives might argue that the responses reinforce the excuses of welfare parasites who want reasons to take more. Practitioners operating out of any change mode must be able to respond to these critics.

BOX 12.1	**OPTIONAL RESPONSES**

Client: *Why aren't benefits higher? Our income is way below the poverty level.*

Conventional responses:

It'd be nice if they were higher. Can we make a list of your expenses to see if I might have any suggestions to help you make ends meet with the check you receive?

I wish I could get you more money, but we have to work with what we've got—given the cutbacks and today's politics.

(Goal: to avoid being personally blamed, and to express empathy. The social worker may be thinking "Benefits are low because society doesn't give a damn about you" but obviously does not say this because of the value placed on her or his job and the client's feelings)

Rights-oriented response: Perhaps you aren't receiving all you are entitled to. Want me to review your finances with you? Maybe we can appeal.

(Goal: to secure rights collaboratively)

Public interest advocacy response: A coalition is trying to influence the governor to supplement the amount the feds provide. Do you want some information about this fight to raise benefits?

(Goal: To involve the client, increase civic skills, and secure the client as a witness or letter writer)

Transformation or critical consciousness responses:

What do *you* think the reason is?

If a family with more money traded places with yours for a week, what would they learn?

Does it ever make you angry?

Who, in your opinion, decides who gets government benefits?

(Goal: to start a dialogue and raise consciousness about income and power distribution, sociopolitical and economic forces)

ADVOCACY SPECTRUM: SPANNING PEOPLE AND POLICY

Multiple Options

Advocacy aims to bring about change in order to benefit people in many circumstances. The advocacy spectrum represents the whole advocacy family. Advocacy work ranges from helping oneself or another individual to helping a group or class of people change an institution in very basic ways. It can be carried out *directly* with a client or *indirectly* on behalf of a client or group or for the public good. One advocate can operate at different points along the advocacy spectrum, or problems can be addressed simultaneously by people working in different areas of the same field.

As professionals, we have no reason to limit our intervention to the domain where we receive it. "The way the problem is defined is of major importance in determining what type of advocacy, if any, is to be attempted and what the target system will be," says Grosser (1976, p. 270). If a young child playing with a cigarette lighter starts a fire that destroys a house and kills his brother, this situation is likely to be received in the individual sphere, where a social worker might help the family by advocating for material help. Some service agencies might also treat the death as a family counseling matter. Yet, the fire is not simply an individual matter. Poorly designed lighters caused enough fires and deaths that federal regulations had to be written to require childproof lighters. In a service-only or family therapy intervention, a "bad" child is left with guilt; in moving to political intervention, this "normal, curious" child provides evidence of the need for product redesign, regulation, and enforcement.

Since the level of intervention influences the methods and skills of intervention (individual to institutional), the spectrum of ad-vocacy possibilities combines level and modality variables. The different points on the spectrum are as follows:

1. *Self-advocacy:* A practitioner who wants to start a client group must convince the boss of the project's worth.

2. *Individual advocacy:* A practitioner helps a client take steps to collect unpaid child support.

3. *Group advocacy:* A practitioner speaks on behalf of clients at a hearing on monitoring home health aides (or personal care attendants).

4. *Community advocacy:* A practitioner helps neighbors get the police commissioner to introduce a new community policing program.

5. *Political or policy advocacy:* A practitioner is asked to serve on a panel that is recommending human service reforms at a hearing.

6. *Advocacy for systems change:* A practitioner convinces a school system to commit resources to cut the dropout rate in half.

The actions taken usually will be determined by the involved organizations' standard mode of operation (although advocates sometimes get organizations to change standard practices), by the worker's skills, and by strategic decisions concerning the most effective and efficient interventions.

MULTIPLE ISSUES AND APPLICATIONS

Advocates may need to consider multiple strategies for addressing an individual or social problem. For instance, resolving a problem when a long-term care home misuses a resident's personal needs allowance (money for tissues, cigarettes, stamps, etc.), part of their Social Security or SSI check, involves advocacy on behalf of an individual.

But suppose advocates learn during their investigation that, despite a state obligation to review facilities, no agency regularly monitors personal needs allowance accounts; that the facility's record keeping is inadequate; and that other residents have similar complaints? In this situation, advocates must determine the appropriate avenue(s) of relief. *Any or all parts of the spectrum could fit*:

1. Residents (or families) could be individually empowered to straighten out their own accounts. (*self-advocacy*)

2. The advocate could represent the resident by approaching the administrator, filing a complaint with a regulatory agency, referring the matter for criminal or civil action, or any combination of these steps. (*individual advocacy*)

3. The advocate might represent a group of residents with the administrator or assert the group's interests in regulatory oversight (one advocacy avenue is to make the state do what it is supposed to do). (*group advocacy*)

4. A community education course or handout materials might be prepared and presented to alert the residents and their families to their rights. Churches or advocacy groups could get involved in assisting residents with their finances. (*community-level advocacy*)

5. The advocates and community groups might push for legislation or regulations to define facility responsibilities more clearly in managing personal funds. (*political/policy advocacy*)

6. Residents rights councils in given facilities could contract with an outside, nonprofit accountant to manage the funds independently of the facility. If this idea spreads, systems change is underway. (*systems advocacy*)

To return to our early example of the crowded schools, we can think of *many types of advocacy with which to address the problem.* The parents could advocate for themselves as taxpayers on behalf of their children. A social worker could write a letter to the board of education or lobby an influential alumnus to call for improvements. A worker could take the concerns of parents from several schools to the media and help the parents conduct interviews. A worker could organize a campaign to get local firms to forego their annual holiday parties one year in order to buy textbooks, or could organize parents and neighborhood churches to boycott school until demands for improvement are met. A worker could drive a group of parents to meet with their legislator regarding equity in education. A worker could build a coalition to overturn property tax–based school funding.

With an ongoing and complex issue, it is common—though not always necessary—to begin with individual advocacy and progress to institutional change. Consider an addictions worker who counsels individuals and then becomes involved with Mothers Against Drunk Driving (MADD). Initially, the worker helps support the members' personal feelings and provides community education, and later engages in joint efforts with the organization to secure tough yet humane sentencing. This advocacy finally leads the worker to oppose the advertising of alcohol. Activities along the spectrum can be conducted consecutively or simultaneously.

Parts of the spectrum interrelate and the process, even for a single advocate, is dynamic. An advocate may not consciously weigh options or points of entry for involvement, and yet aspects of the spectrum can be manifest in work activities, as the following brief example illustrates. Gregory monitors legislative, regulatory, administrative, and judicial developments in the federal disability benefits program and assists individuals. Derrick, who is eligible, hears about the program and, using self-advocacy, applies for benefits. A year later, after receiving a letter stating that he no longer qualifies, Derrick asks Gregory for help. Gregory is aware of revisions secured by national advocates that are in Derrick's favor, and he assists Derrick in an administrative hearing. (Note, here that systems change preceded and affected individual advocacy.) Gregory realizes that some of his other clients will be similarly affected and gets the group to approach the Legal Aid Society for help.

These examples presuppose that the worker is comfortable considering an advocacy approach on any scale and supports the advocacy endeavors of others.

LEVELS AND FORMS OF ADVOCACY

Self-Advocacy

As social workers, we must learn to advocate on our own behalf as well as for our clients (Braverman, 1986; Reisch et al., 1981). Much of the advocacy exercised on behalf of clients and oppressed groups, however, is undertaken by clients and group members who decide to make changes in their lives or to demand redress (Miller, 1986, p. 118; Murase, 1992).

Maggie Kuhn's story exemplifies this process. Until recently, men retired at age 65 with a gold watch; some women, including Kuhn, were given sewing machines. Today forced retirement is usually illegal. Workers "let go" a few years before their pensions are available need to be shown the age discrimination law in writing; told where in the company to complain and where outside the company to go for help; and encouraged to move forward to get the job back. In 1970, Kuhn had no recourse.

In the first month after I was ordered to retire, I felt dazed and suspended. I was hurt and then, as time passed, outraged. . . . Something clicked in my mind and I saw that my problem was not mine alone. Instead of sinking into despair, I did what came most naturally to me: I telephoned some friends and called a meeting. Six of us, all professional women associated with nonprofit social and religious groups, met for lunch. . . . My office at work was next to a Xerox machine, so it was easy to slip over there and whip out copies of a notice for a [large] meeting. . . . We agreed we should all band together to form a new social action organization. (1991, pp. 130–131)

Kuhn headed the Gray Panthers for 25 years (until her death in 1995). Her story epitomizes Gutierrez's point: empowerment can transform stressful life events through

increasing self-efficacy;
developing a critical consciousness;
developing skills; and
involvement with similar others. (1994, pp. 204–205)

Self-advocacy in social work includes self-help and helping others to help themselves (Mackelprang & Salsgiver, 1996). Workers can provide the knowledge and encouragement that clients need to act personally and collectively on their own behalf. When citizens are on the move, we can facilitate their personal and organizational development. This can be done through *administrative* and *technical assistance*, such as clerical and volunteer help and providing meeting rooms. More important, we help by *encouragement and acknowledgment* of the worth of the endeavor, that is, by giving it legitimacy. Another vital support is to provide *information sharing* for people concerned with the same issue. (Regarding mutual assistance and "horizontal supports," see Rose, 1990, p. 50).

This expanding self-advocacy also occurs in low-income groups. Box 12.2 features a person who started a soup kitchen in her house and now feeds thousands of people each Thanksgiving. Her first step, however, was advocacy for her own family. We can learn from self-advocates with organizational skills. We want to be on the lookout not only for indigenous leaders, but for clients who make progress in self-advocacy in a less public way—perhaps by successfully following through on our suggestions.

Challenges arise in working with clients who have circumstances that restrain their desire or ability to act (Brooks, 1991), but these can be met. For instance, a Client Support and Representation program for people coping with psychiatric problems stresses self-determination and client control. "Advocacy in this context becomes a form of personal self-assistance, based on self-identified needs, that unfolds within the context of a very supportive interpersonal relationship with an advocate (Moxley & Freddolino, 1994, p. 96). Although clients receive "knowledge, assertiveness, and problem-solving skills" from advocates in the roles of "mentor, coach, supporter, and representative" (p.

98) and assistance with environmental challenges, they must take action, for example, to express a disagreement and ask for a hearing to resolve it (p. 96).

Individual Advocacy

Those knowledgeable about dealing with the system, whether BSWs or community workers, often guide beneficiaries through housing assistance and other governmental mazes. The situation may get complicated before an attorney or an MSW gets involved. Even lay advocates—a family friend or someone from church—sometimes help with the initial steps. This may not matter, though, since many of those requiring advocacy (e.g., low-power groups, the unsophisticated or institutionalized) need a tenacious advocate more than a highly credentialed one (Shapiro, 1993).

For a social worker, starting an advocacy relationship is not too different from starting a therapeutic relationship. The presenting problem itself may call for advocacy, or we may engage in conventional direct service activities out of which a need for advocacy arises. The client directs us as much as pos-

---

| BOX 12.2 | THE START OF A COMMUNITY RESOURCE |

I said, "There's three stores here. Let's go to each store . . . and see if they will give us some food." Everybody stood in their doorways. They laughed at me. . . . I was scared, but I said, "I'm going 'cause . . . I need food for me and my children to eat. . . ." I went to my church and asked the pastor would he loan me the big garbage can on wheels. I got up the courage. I went to this store and said, "Mister, would you please give me food you're going to throw away tonight, so we can eat it tomorrow?" He said, "What did you say?" And I repeated it. 'Cause, you know you can't run out

of the store. You're not going to back out of the store, you're just going to say it again. So I said it. And he said, "Yes I will." He filled up that garbage can in his store. [After visiting the other two stores, she ended up with three garbage cans of food and a long line at her door.] And I said, "Ain't no stopping now! . . . what I'm gonna do is open up an emergency center." 'Cause I've asked God to show me how to feed me and my children first and then I will help others."

Source: *Bea Gaddy, who feeds the inner-city poor* (Challenging).[3]

sible. In turn, we try to demystify aspects of society about which we are knowledgeable.

ADVOCACY AS AN INFLUENCE PROCESS INVOLVING ACTION

Individual and family-level advocacy often involves attempting to influence organizational or institutional decisions or policies on behalf of a third party, as the example in Box 12.3 illustrates.

Once we agree to serve as an advocate, we cannot countenance or condone having our clients demeaned, whether or not they are in our presence. While this principle seems basic, it is not easy to follow because so many clients interact with an array of "officials" who make a practice of belittling them or treating them as objects (See Box 12.4).

WORKING WITH INSTEAD OF FOR

In cases where clients are jailed or ill and unable to act for themselves, such as the one illustrated by Box 12.4, the advocate honors their expressed wishes and acts on their behalf. Even people who are healthy and at liberty are not always able to advocate for themselves or to participate jointly. In most cases, though, advocates must guard against taking a "benefactor" or "liberator" role (Simon, 1994, p. 7). The benefactor role is related to the Lady Bountiful charity role, as well as to the interpersonal rescuer role warned against in human potential literature (Steiner, 1974, p. 176). We want to create situations in which individuals can develop into their own heroes rather than being dependent on a human services worker. Self-advocacy is preferred.

Advocacy for an individual arises naturally out of a trusting relationship. A request may seem trivial, yet the stakes can be high; minor incidents can turn into violent episodes. For instance, a 17-year-old Latino boy has trouble in school and needs someone to believe him. Since his mother is afraid to call the school and demand to know what was happening, the boy turns to a youth worker, who accompanies him to a meeting

---

| BOX 12.3 | THE ORDER WAS: CHANGE CURTAINS! |

Situation: The Melios, a low-income family, are happy in their new Section 8 apartment; they use thrift shops and flea markets to decorate. One day the city coordinator of subsidized housing arrives unannounced. Barlow, infamous for white-glove inspections, finds little to criticize but orders Mrs. Melios to get fingerprints off the refrigerator and replace the plastic kitchen curtains with cloth ones, "to blend into the neighborhood better." Mrs. Melio calls her worker to ask if Barlow can make her take down curtains that she likes and paid for just because they are plastic.

Analysis (based on principles presented by Sosin and Caulum 1983, p. 13): The worker reads the regulations and finds that the only taboo for window covering is newspaper or cardboard. (If the regulations confirm Barlow's demand, there probably would be no chance for success in a negotiation.) Calling the housing coordinator as an advocate, the worker will try to influence an individual to reverse a decision on behalf of a third party—the resident who waited years for this apartment and has less clout than the coordinator, who can remove the family. The worker does not want to place the resident family in danger. The worker may already know Barlow and, by doing the calling, may be protecting Mrs. Melio, who is angry. Options that could be discussed include requesting more time to comply, asking the manager to pay for the new curtains, arguing that the regulations do not require cloth curtains, asking about appeal procedures, and warning Barlow that he has no right to walk in on a tenant unless he suspects a serious infraction of rules.

BOX 12.4	GET ME OUT OF HERE!

A mother declared her teenage daughter incorrigible and in need of protection by juvenile services. Since the emergency shelter was full, Theresa was placed at a holding facility in a room where unfortunate youngsters stayed until foster homes were available. The matron soon had Theresa babysitting for 10 young children housed at the facility. When the teenager rebelled after a week and refused to babysit, she was locked up behind bars. Her worker was stunned when she came to visit, for there had been no hearing, nor had she or Theresa's family been contacted. The worker was so indignant that she told her supervisor she wanted to write a letter to the judge in charge of Theresa's case. The supervisor expressed doubt that anything would be done but agreed to humor his young supervisee. The worker wrote a letter to the judge requesting Theresa's release. The teenager was released from her cell the day the judge received it.

with the head of the school. In our earlier example, although the advocate gets her client out of jail, the system is not magically reformed. Neither is this school. Nevertheless, one benefit of advocacy is that individuals, families, or groups who are usually undervalued experience being supported and feeling worthy of attention.

Box 12.5 illustrates this surrogate strength. A woman of modest means tries to find out what has happened to her brother-in-law's welfare check. Mentally ill, Barney was hospitalized for 13 years before coming to live with June and her husband. The incident is related by a neighbor. Were the narrator to continue in this role or go to the office without June, he could obtain a signed form authorizing him to be her representative. Still, even this informal partnership with June highlights three goals of individual advocacy: influence the decision of the power person, support the individual, and teach—leading to self-advocacy.

Group Advocacy

Group advocacy often arises with a particular reform and may not be part of an on-

BOX 12.5	AN ADVOCATE BY REQUEST

Barney's welfare check failed to arrive; and when June called to find out why, a social worker told her Barney was no longer eligible. . . . After June received the same response on two more calls to the social services bureau, I suggested she go down to the welfare agency herself and volunteered to go with her. . . . [W]e finally got to see a social worker, who informed us that since Barney Moseby's file was missing, the social services department had assumed he was no longer eligible for public assistance. When we explained that his situation was the same as before, the worker apologetically agreed to have him reinstated, admitting that it was not the first time a file had been lost. June was convinced that had I not been along, dressed in my respectable gray suit and carrying an empty brief case, nothing would have happened. "It was because somebody was there who looked like somebody, that's why they treated us like people," she said. "If you come in looking stupid like you don't know anything, then they don't pay you no mind." The next month Barney's check came on time.

Source: Howell (1973), pp. 180–181.

going community organization and development process or a social movement. A group can clearly advocate for itself and "regain a sense of control" (Toseland, 1990, p. 167). For instance, parents of children who are both physically and mentally challenged and thus cannot use existing group homes might band together to get facilities modified or built to meet their children's needs. They could make demands of an individual worker or of a county or state agency. In our classification scheme, this would be an instance of self-advocacy. However, when the advocate is not a member of a particular victimized group (such as Latino high school students)—even if the advocate shares characteristics with the larger group (e.g., is Latino himself)—and is acting on the group's behalf, we consider this a case of group advocacy.

Jaime Escalante, a teacher-advocate, is one well-known example; his story was told in the film *Stand and Deliver* (Menendez, 1988). An East Los Angeles math instructor, Escalante was finally able to overcome low expectations within his high school to prove that students who resided in low-income neighborhoods could learn calculus. From the school system he secured the support his class needed to pass national calculus achievement examinations. When the students performed much better than expected of Chicanos, Escalante had to defend them against a charge of cheating. In brief, internal advocacy (in the school) and external advocacy (in the community) were required to provide students with the same higher education opportunities afforded to students living in wealthier areas.

In discovering the group nature of a problem, we may start with individuals and end up advocating for a group. A social worker might be troubled that a boy in speech therapy is being teased by his classmates about his stuttering and might talk to his teacher. This same concern, writ large, might lead that ad-vocate to write to a television show that pokes fun at a character who stutters. A worker who has a mentally ill client in jail, as a result not of a crime but of his symptoms, should tend to that person's needs but can also note other inmates who are clearly ill. The worker can then try to find out what is happening and how to aid such prisoners.

Part of an advocate's role is to ensure that maximum benefits are delivered to the greatest number of clients—not at the expense of the original client's position but in furtherance of it. Bringing together many persons who have been harmed in the same way or who seek the same remedy to a common problem helps define the parameters of a problem. Having more people involved increases the availability of information and provides documentation of a pattern of abuse. Evidence that 10 apartment building tenants are without heat and hot water is more credible than a similar complaint on behalf of one resident.

The group may already exist, such as a tenants organization, or may form after the advocate starts with one individual and finds others. In either case, the advocate must get to know each member of the group, understand the group dynamics as the process unfolds, and be accountable to the group, which is equally true in the next situation. Practitioners often work with members of a group who cannot communicate their concerns easily. Therefore, the advocate has to work through ethical issues and authority issues in this regard. When representing inarticulate, perhaps bedridden or confined clients, all the various subinterests within the group must be considered; otherwise, only members who are present and articulate will prevail. When members want to organize for self-government or to fight discrimination or hardship, the advocate must inform the group of potential risks but should follow the group's lead.

Sometimes we work on behalf of people who are scattered and are never seen by each other or the worker. This can happen because workers regularly move beyond an individual's particular plight (Wood & Middleman, 1989, p. 22). Box 12.6 shows how. In the example in Box 12.6, the social worker is moving from individual to political advocacy with the purpose of helping an invisible group; her primary role remains direct service.

Community Advocacy and Action

Community advocacy/action includes community education, development, organizing, and representation (Mizrahi & Morrison, 1993). Earlier, we sketched three ways that change unfolds at the societal level. We turn now to professional social work ways of challenging the status quo at the local level through community practice. While advocacy is utilized by many professions, community organization is particularly utilized by the social work profession.[4] Everyone in our field needs to know a few basics, so we also present simple ways that people go about organizing.

EXAMPLES OF ORGANIZING AND COALITION BUILDING

A classic social work example of advocacy took place in the early 1900s on behalf of a neighborhood in Chicago (see Box 12.7). It highlights the necessity of undertaking a wide array of tasks.

Jane Addams involved neighbors but also recognized the differences between herself and many community residents. Today we may be working in "communities of color" (Bradshaw, Soifer, & Gutierrez, 1994) or in a barrio that, again, calls for "culturally appropriate interactions for community work" (Salcido, 1993). Our knowledge of the culture, however, must be matched with *competence* in working for changes. Community organizer Fred Ross recalls how effective Cesar Chavez was in recruiting four couples during the early days of developing the Farm Workers Association. Chavez simply passed "around some self-addressed three-by-five cards with lines on the back for the name and address of the workers" and asked a plain question—"what the workers considered a just hourly wage." Ross said the method of surveying farm workers was "an instant hit"—because these workers were being "consulted" for the first time. As one worker said, "It's like letting us vote . . . on what we think" (Levy, 1975, xxi).

MODELS OF COMMUNITY INTERVENTION

Jack Rothman (1987, 1995) has delineated and compared three orientations to purposeful change at the community level, a

---

BOX 12.6	CONCERN ABOUT A SET OF PERSONS AT RISK

Consuella conducts home visits to frail elderly people living alone. Several women were burned recently in cooking accidents because their bathrobe sleeves caught fire. She attempts to locate safer nightwear for them, but there is nothing on the market for adults. Curious, she explores the issue of manufacturers' obligations regarding flammable fabrics and is directed to a federal agency. Personnel there are interested in Consuella's local cases, and she, in turn, learns more about regulations. Although she simply wanted to prevent more injury, in the process of repeating her story she engaged in advocacy and navigated corporate and governmental systems. She used her direct-service knowledge to help similarly situated individuals.

| BOX 12.7 | ALLEY CONDITIONS IMPROVED BY ADVOCACY |

... [W]e began a systematic investigation of the city system of garbage collection ... and its possible connection with the death rate in the various wards of the city.... Twelve [Woman's Club members] undertook in connection with the residents, to carefully investigate the condition of the alleys. During August and September the substantiated reports of violations of the law sent in from Hull-House to the health department were one thousand and thirty-seven.... In sheer desperation, the following spring when the city contracts were awarded for the removal of garbage, with the backing of two well-known business men, I put in a bid for the garbage removal of the nineteenth ward. My paper was thrown out on a technicality but the incident induced the mayor to appoint me the garbage inspector of the ward.... Perhaps our greatest achievement was the discovery of a pavement eighteen inches under the surface of a narrow street [after the removal of eight inches of garbage]....

... Many of the foreign-born women of the ward were much shocked by this abrupt departure into the ways of men, and it took a great deal of explanation to convey the idea even remotely that if it were a womanly task to go about in tenement houses in order to nurse the sick, it might be quite as womanly to go through the same district in order to prevent the breeding of so-called "filth diseases."

... The careful inspection, combined with other causes, brought about a great improvement in the cleanliness and comfort of the neighborhood and one happy day, when the death rate of our ward was found to have dropped from third to seventh in the list of city-wards and was so reported to our Woman's Club, the applause which followed recorded the genuine sense of participation in the result, and a public spirit which had "made good."

Source: *Addams (1910), pp. 200–205.*

conceptual scheme that has been widely used (see Chapter 1). The three ideal types are *locality or community development* (an enabling style similar to VISTA or the Peace Corps), *social planning* (a task-oriented style, such as that of the United Way and housing authorities), and *social action* (an adversarial style exemplified by MADD and other citizen coalitions). In practice, these intervention modes may overlap.

LOCALITY DEVELOPMENT

Locality or community development seeks to pull together diverse elements of an area in order to build on the strengths of individuals/organizations and to improve social and economic conditions. Rothman (1987) turns to pioneer Arthur Dunham for development *themes*—"democratic procedures, voluntary cooperation, self-help,

development of indigenous leadership, and educational objectives" (p. 5). Locality developers, then, emphasize community building (Brager & Specht, 1973), with the assumption that there is a common good that people working together can realize.

SOCIAL PLANNING

Social planning looks objectively at past, present, and future scenarios, using available data or collecting new data, to consolidate and meet service and civic needs and to address social conditions efficiently and systematically. This approach emphasizes mastering the complexity of bureaucracy in order to fill service gaps in addition to designing and implementing plans. Today planners also must be conversant with information management systems. Activities involve behind-the-scenes planning, often resulting in noninflammatory position papers full of incontrovertible information or options papers. The approach emphasizes rationality and technical expertise to achieve social goals.

An additional angle to social planning involves participation in decision-making and human service plans. To ensure that a cross section of the public is involved in the planning, community meetings and hearings must be held and representatives from different sectors secured. This means that the "out-front" planner plays the roles of facilitator, outreach worker, interpreter of regulations and policies, translator between groups with different knowledge bases, and consciousness raiser for groups not initially interested in the needs of the target population. (Guskin and Ross [1979, p. 312] use the terms "liaison-contact person" and "advocate planner.")

SOCIAL ACTION

Social action confronts—in different degrees and with a variety of tactics—hierarchical power relationships within a community and uses strategies—such as organizing large numbers of people—to force the powerful to stop or start activities in order to benefit the powerless or a societally marginal population. The aim can be to make "basic changes in major institutions or community practices" (Rothman, 1987, p. 6) or in "the policies of formal organizations" (p. 18) or to redistribute power, resources, and decision making. There will be resistance since social action involves a struggle for power. Broad participation is another emphasis.

A MORE DETAILED EXAMINATION

Rothman outlined the three styles of community intervention in 1968. He and Tropman later enhanced the typology with macro-practice discussions of linkages (1987, p. 268n), "policy practice," and "administrative practice." They underscored that no one

approach is superior, as use depends on the situation. Moreover, these various forms of community intervention each draw on social work values, although different ones (Rothman, 1995, pp. 58–59). Most recently, Rothman has accentuated combinations, "composite bimodal forms," that occur in actual organizations (1995, p. 47). Thus, the conceptual types harmonize better with real-world distinctions and organizing experiences (see below), past and present.

Composite Form	Examples
Development/action	Feminist organizations, Freire's grass-roots groups
Action/planning	Nader groups, Children's Defense Fund
Planning/development	Enterprise/ empowerment zones

RELATION TO DIRECT PRACTICE

Practitioners can use their skills in linking people and assisting them to make connections through friendships and shared tasks (Amado, 1993). They can similarly encourage participation in the process when a need arises to engage in community intervention. Mondros and Wilson (1994) make explicit the tie between organizing techniques and direct practice tasks:

[A] clinician who works with a group of homeless mothers used these techniques to help them organize for repairs and police protection in a park where they frequently took their children. She saw this work as a natural extension of her clinical work with her group. (p. xvii)

(This clinician probably encouraged assertiveness as well; see Chapter 7.) Burghardt (1982) has illustrated how intertwined the skills are in clinical and macro-practice.

Bringing various parties together for a case conference is similar to bringing block leaders together for an issue strategy session. Like a counseling relationship, a community project has a beginning, a middle, and an end.

Practitioners can bring people together in numerous ways—block parties, day camps, health fairs, holiday parties for a disadvantaged group, recycling, and single-issue support groups. Planning arrangements convenient for clients or neighborhood residents are imperative to make ahead of time. Participants in community education/support group meetings (with topics such as "incontinence" or "giving up the secret of adult children with AIDS") will benefit from the privacy of a living room setting. Convenience and privacy for participants are obviously reasons to meet in a home, but practitioners can also learn something new— for example, about the conditions that asthma patients must contend with in their home environment and how these conditions can be modified. Once there, the social worker can tune in to the larger environment as well, perhaps by smelling a burning dumping ground and checking on its legality. That same worker, or a macro-practitioner colleague, could then hold meetings with neighbors to discuss the problems connected with the dump. This same format can be used in other settings, such as shelters. One organizer encourages discussions "in a variety of situations—a member's living room, on a lunchbreak in an office or factory. It's applicable to unions, church groups, women's circles, or social agency staff and to all issues" (National Public Law Training Center, 1983).

Strategies and tactics in community practice can be based on cooperation or on polarization and confrontation (regarding the selection of tactics, see Netting et al., 1993). Residents can advocate on their own behalf (a form of self-advocacy) or others can advocate on the community's behalf. Advocacy that happens at the community level can have the beneficial effect of bringing different groups together around common values. This happened in Washington, D.C., when Gallaudet students successfully advocated against appointment of yet another "hearing" President for the university. They wanted a leader who shared their personal experience. Americans like to see people stand up for themselves. Different income and ethnic groups "bonded," savoring the victory and resulting pride of the deaf community. We should encourage and celebrate such linkage.

Political and Policy Advocacy

DEFINITIONS AND ROLES

Like the *Encyclopedia of Social Work*, we have separated *policy and political advocacy*— what Checkoway (1995) would call "public advocacy"—from community-based social action and mass-based community organizing. Political/policy advocacy in the legislative, regulatory, administrative, and judicial arenas to achieve social and political welfare can take many forms (Class, 1974; Richan, 1991). For instance, in the section on "Group Advocacy," we saw that Consuella's search led her to a federal regulatory agency. Like Consuella, direct service practitioners sometimes drift into political action; infrequently, they enter electoral politics. We often represent our agencies in coalitions and may be asked to bring a busload of supporters to a rally in the state capital. We may also be asked to find individuals or families in a certain category who are willing to appear at governmental hearings, as both the media and decision makers often seek an individual, family, or situation that epitomizes the problem or the solution (Ross, 1993). We can sometimes participate in a combination of law and social reform, as when "the law is 'mobilized' in the service of social change" (Singer, 1992, p. 11). Social workers work in many governmental jobs that involve full-time advocacy, including county commissions, state staff positions, or even as legislative directors in the U.S. Senate. Finally, some participate in media and political campaigns.[5]

There is a perception and a regret, in many quarters, that social workers in general are rarely active in the political-policy realm, apart from certain public policy issues (Jansson, 1990). One clinician turned legislator put it this way:

> I've spent a lot of time with the clinical social workers the last couple of years, trying to get them to shape up, form a lobby, form a PAC—the whole works.... [After all, many clients] can't help themselves, especially if they're clinically depressed or they've got severe problems where they're not going to be able to fight the system.... If social workers are going to serve as true helping professionals, they've got to get off their couches. (Thomas in *Challenging*)[6]

We should view this perception of a lack of professional political activity as an opportunity, not a barrier—a sign that there are unfilled niches open to us or places where an argument from a new direction could reach an apparently rigid decision maker. Social workers can enter the policy-making process part-time and succeed (Dear & Patti, 1981; Haynes & Mickelson, 1991; Mahaffey & Hanks, 1982; Patti & Dear, 1975). Richan (1991) provides guidance for beginners.

LEGISLATIVE ADVOCACY

Legislative advocacy usually involves proposing or stopping a particular piece of legislation (Pertschuk, 1986). More formally, Patti and Dear (1975) define it as something performed by "any individual, agency, or organization who attempts to influence the course of a bill or other legislative measure" (p. 108). The lobbying part of that activity means asking decision makers to help in the effort or to make some commitment, usually in exchange for votes or other support. "Multifaceted activity is needed to pass a law that might rectify a political ill," says McFarland (1984, p. 108) about Common Cause. This citizen organization uses publicity (including publicity on legislators' positions), research, litigation, campaigns for public commitments, and a field organization that helps generate mail, arrange meetings between members and elected officials, and network with friends of elected officials (1984, chapter 6). Lappe and DuBois (1994) also discuss lobbying in broader terms and remind us that it is "one thing to get policy passed and quite another to see it happen" (p. 181). In their view, citizen lobbying means "citizens learning how to influence decision making and hold others accountable" (p. 179). Some laws help build community services (Allen, Bonner, & Greenan, 1988); others foster rights (Box 12.8).

Despite many complexities in the political process, there are victories like the one described in Box 12.8, which took 6 months of "swift, concerted" effort. For other examples and legislative terminology, see Haynes and Mickelson (1991).

BUILDING CREDIBILITY

We cannot assume credibility because we are professionals, but our expertise is welcomed. To illustrate, one day "DeAnn" was on the telephone with a colleague critiquing a draft of a proposed state bill on end-of-life directives. By the next day, she had been invited to join a lobbying coalition that was ultimately successful in redrafting the bill.

Local political activists stress that familiarity breeds respect. One social worker described his early activist days this way: "I re-

BOX 12.8	POLICY CHANGES THROUGH POLITICAL ADVOCACY

The Washington State legislature has passed a groundbreaking bill extending the national nursing home reform law's residents' rights provisions to settings offering lesser levels of care. . . . [T]he Universal Residents' Rights bill applies to people living in licensed board and care homes, which in Washington State encompass assisted living facilities, adult group homes for people with developmental disabilities, and settings offering substance-abuse therapy. The bill also extends to veterans' homes and residents receiving personal or nursing services in adult family homes. . . . The new bill, indeed, affords all long-term care residents the same rights available to people in nursing homes, including the right to share a room with a spouse, to enjoy a homelike environment, and to receive information from ombudsmen.

Source: *National Citizens Coalition for Nursing Home Reform (1994), p. 1.*

call going down to the election board trying to get some voter information and being treated [like] 'who do you think you are?'" He gained experience in political work, making presentations at hearings and sharing information with elected officials. He found that decision makers want help in thinking things through.

> You can come in and sound off . . . but if you never get beyond that, then people tune you out. It's the business of bringing information to the people who make decisions. . . . I can recall while I was there in Omaha, going into City Council sessions, not even asking to be on the agenda and having the president look up and say, "Mr. Evans, do you have anything you want to say on this?" By that time I had been there enough and spoken enough, he felt I probably had something to say.[7]

Using Clients as Witnesses

Of all the actors in the political arena, it is the direct service practitioner who is most likely to provide examples of suffering that has been or will be caused by cutbacks or policy decisions or to find examples of overcoming or successfully "coping with barriers" (Chapin, 1995, p. 511). Finding clear-cut examples quickly can be surprisingly hard to do. Few of us can describe our personal situations in a concise and intriguing manner, and those we serve are no exception. Many might be nontelegenic or unconvincing at hearings. Being able to identify an appropriate *problem exemplar* and to prepare him or her to address the media or a decision-making body is a vital task for caseworkers and front-line practitioners. Advocates at the national and state levels make many calls to local offices to obtain anecdotes that make the news, appear in speeches, and humanize funding appeals. If someone's privacy is protected with a pseudonym during the initial publicity, advocates must be able to prove the person exists, has the problem in question, and/or will be affected positively or negatively. Reporters check out such stories.

Protecting Clients and Citizens

It is unethical and unwise to thrust already vulnerable individuals into the public view without first having their trust and permission because they are likely to say anything under stress. We must advise clients of the risks inherent in *any* type of advocacy, including testifying; such risks could include retaliation, reduction of benefits, or the anger of family members. Social workers can also protect witnesses by accompanying them and handling the technical aspects of testifying allowing them to simply tell their stories, without intimidation or exaggeration. Both expert and human interest testimony are often prepared for the same hearing. Witnesses should dictate or write their own statements, letting the advocate type and smooth out the final manuscript. If advocates compose testimony, a witness may be unable to read it or unfamiliar with subtleties, creating potential embarrassment. The facts must be within the grasp of the witness for easy oral recitation.

Systems Advocacy and Change

Institutional change implies "widespread and basic alteration" despite strong resistance (Brager, 1967, p. 61). *Many systems affect our clients and society in general, and we want to be able to influence them.* Individual, state, and national economic investment is one example of an effective tool. For instance, socially responsible (domestic) investments can help develop grass-roots, community-oriented, and self-help organizations (Brill & Reder, 1992). Their power as a source of leverage was shown in the campaign of the 1980s spearheaded by Randall Robinson to end apartheid by withholding U.S. investment from South Africa. As part of the advocacy spectrum, we have already discussed the political system. But the average American is also affected by the insurance system, the medical system, and an employment system (that sanctions, even requires, unemployment and merely takes note of capital flight). We are also shaped or limited by the media as an institution (Gitlin, 1980).

Many challenges have been made to various societal systems, even overarching systems such as capitalism and patriarchy (Gamson, 1990), and challenges continue to

be made (Goldberg, 1991; Ryan, 1992). While a given community or neighborhood might be organized in a year or two, major challenges to the social order play out over decades. Many recent studies of large-scale movements employ a resource mobilization framework (McCarthy & Zald, 1987) that emphasizes social movement organizations rather than individuals. However, in the activist rather than the analysis aspect of change, individual actions count, along with group and collective action. Some examples: Mother Jones started organizing coal miners at age 47 and continued for 40 years (Gilbert, 1993; Jones, 1980); George Wiley gave up a career as a celebrated chemistry professor at age 33 to fight for the down and out in civil rights and welfare rights struggles (Kotz & Kotz 1977); James Chaney, Andrew Goodman, and Michael Schwerner gave their lives in the Mississippi Freedom Summer of 1964; Cesar Chavez organized the supposedly unorganizable migrant farm workers. The first social workers, and early ones such as Harry Hopkins and Frances Perkins, were involved in many progressive battles for change, such as workers' rights, honest government, and Social Security (Andrews, 1990; Kahn, 1991; Lee, 1994; Lynd, 1961). These leaders united others.

Most people never achieve national recognition, but they still derive benefit from participation in actions to express their values. Kansas farmers and other ordinary citizens tried to change banking, monetary, and trade institutions 100 years ago. Writing about these Populists, Goodwyn (1978) captures what is important about social movements and change endeavors to the rural or urban people who are part of them (Box 12.9). (These words describe the aims of many of today's movements and embryo political parties. Voters and protestors resist the latest version of a giant industrial engine.)

| BOX 12.9 | THE HOPE OF CONCERTED ACTION |

[Populism] was, first and most centrally, a cooperative movement that imparted a sense of self-worth to individual people and provided them with the instruments of self-education about the world they lived in. The movement gave them hope—a shared hope—that they were not impersonal victims of a gigantic industrial engine ruled by others but that they were, instead, people who could perform specific political acts of self-determination. . . . [T]he men and women of the agrarian movement [were] encouraged and enhanced by the sheer drama and power of their massive parades, their huge summer encampments, their far-flung lecturing system. . . . Populism was, at bottom, a movement of ordinary Americans to gain control over their own lives and futures, a massive democratic effort to gain that most central component of human freedom—dignity.

Source: *Goodwyn (1978), pp. 196–197.*

Large-scale social change endeavors often have tendrils reaching into community advocacy/action, political/policy advocacy, and institutional/systems change. The civil rights and women's movements are good examples (Hahn, 1994, 114; Ryan, 1992). After working for years to achieve political change through suffrage and the Equal Rights Amendment (a failed constitutional amendment), women turned back to their communities and outward to larger systems, seeking other types of equality—in jobs, in education, in insurance rates, and even public sanction regarding the sharing of domestic chores. After winning important gains in the judicial and legislative areas for years, African-Americans have experienced community setbacks tied to street crime and institutional setbacks tied to standardized testing (Beardsley, 1995). In short, progress can be undercut in insidious ways or occur in unexpected ways; both the attack and the defense interweave multiple advocacy approaches.

Yet victories continue. The South has elected numerous African-Americans to public office. Today thousands of citizens are registering to vote at social welfare agencies rather than having to go to the courthouse or a special place because, after several decades, concerted action to make voting easier for the nonregistered produced legislative victories. The Motor Voter Act of 1993 requires states to provide voter registration at motor vehicle centers and public assistance offices and by mail; millions have registered in these new ways. Thus, today local social workers can help implement yesterday's victory with an eye to tomorrow's elections—an excellent example of how direct service and macro practitioners can join hands for change.

RELEVANCE TO DIRECT PRACTICE

The interconnections between various types of advocacy are clear. Past struggles influence much about our lives today—our work, our legacy. Our professional work frequently pertains to rights and programs that were won earlier through systems reform, which indicates that there truly is "give" in the system. In response to events such as elections, we often feel under siege from those opposed to what we value. Perhaps, though, reading history, we can more appropriately say to ourselves, "Let us celebrate" because so much has been won by and for social work. If there is ever any question as to whether we have allies or as to the existence of a flourishing spectrum in action, all we need do is find a national list of advocacy groups (Walls, 1993).

CLIENT ADVOCATE AND OTHER PRACTICE ROLES

Advocacy and Action Roles

The modus operandi of client advocacy extends from supportive personal advocacy to showdowns to help clients. Box 12.10 reminds us that advocacy can transpire in ways other than heated controversy.

This section seeks to clarify the terminology and challenges surrounding client advocacy. It discusses advocacy obligations, nuances involved, and (often overlapping) roles. What Henderson and Thomas (1987) say about neighborhood work is true of client advocacy: "The worker often has to handle [varied] situations within a short space of time, and he or she is therefore always working with different audiences and constituencies from varied role positions" (p. 19).

Caseworker, clinician, client home visitor, therapist, job coach, and group worker are some of the roles in micro-practice. Roles in macro-practice are, if anything, even more wide-ranging—including paid roles such as community liaison, program planner, community educator, community organizer, and unpaid roles such as communitywide advisory group member. They may include such work as identifying, training, and utilizing indigenous grass-roots leadership; developing and coordinating a program to reintegrate clients into the community following hospitalization; and fund-raising. Those who advocate as part of their work soon realize that the advocacy realm is complex and requires cognizance of the possibilities and pitfalls. As needs are discovered and services rendered, the full scope of advocacy roles and requirements comes into view (Wood & Middleman, 1991).

Job Descriptions and Advocacy Postures

Some workers who undertake an advocacy task are hired for that purpose as client advocates, lobbyists, or change agents, while others have job descriptions that emphasize service provision or counseling. In a clinical position, however, the need or the desire for advocacy may still crop up. As one social worker commented in discussing a mistreated patient, "I was developing a pretty strong hankering to do some serious advocacy work here, even though it is 'not my job' as a 'clinician' " (SocWork computer transmittal, 1995). Hybrid jobs that combine service and advocacy, advocacy and complaint handling, advocacy and organizing, or administration and lobbying are common. As social workers, we need not always act as ad-

---

BOX 12.10   NOT A RANCOROUS ROLE

[B]asic tenets of effective advocacy are sensitivity, caring and a commitment to other persons who, either out of incapacity or inexperience, cannot resolve a problem without assistance from others. . . . Advocacy involves confronting opposition, but seldom should result in hostility. An effective advocate uses an honest, constructive and steadfast approach. An opponent may be intensely challenged or displeased by an advocate but ultimately should be able to recognize, and perhaps acknowledge the advocate's thoughtfulness and fairness. This is important because the objective of advocacy is to end with favorable, beneficial changes (behavioral, environmental, program or policy changes and problem solutions) which can be understood and upheld.

Source: Elma Holder, Encyclopedia of Aging (1995), p. 28. © Springer Publishing. Used by permission.

vocates ourselves if we can steer the person to an effective complaint handler, such as a fraud department or media outlet specializing in solving complaints.

ADVOCATE AND OMBUDSPERSON[8]

Definitions. The advocacy role and the ombudsperson role are frequently confused. Both are helpers, but an advocate is a partisan, while an ombudsperson is more neutral. An *advocate* pushes a point of view. An *ombudsperson* often serves as a go-between, an interpreter, and a problem solver, untangling various points of view. However, an ombudsperson is not a conventional mediator or alternative dispute resolution player (Singer, 1979; Wood & Middleman, 1989) but rather an effective criticizer who tries to "set right" the government system that is "out of gear" (Davis, 1975, p. 286). An advocate often works outside government, while an ombudsperson frequently works as a grievance handler and red-tape cutter for government agencies. Some states, universities, and newspapers have hired ombudspersons who, although on their payrolls, work for citizens/consumers, not management. Tower (1994) argues that client-centered social service agencies should similarly "establish ombudsmen or other client assistance programs to resolve conflicts between the agency and its consumers" (p. 196).

The ombudsperson's powers are "to investigate, criticize, recommend, and publicize" (Davis, 1975, p. 286). Such ombudspersons often have license to constructively critique their employer, even publicly, although they usually function quietly, providing information, referral, and complaint resolution. Advocates vary in their license to criticize.

There is a 50-state system of paid long-term-care ombudspersons and volunteer assistants; state units are usually located in departments of aging. To ensure independence, none are employed by the institutions they monitor. As would be expected, the ombudspersons act as *intermediaries* and resolve disputes between facilities and residents. Surprisingly, they primarily *advocate* for residents; their activities include reporting violations. They help the facilities too—for example, to get paid when a resident's finances are in disarray. Social workers and these ombudspersons are "resources" for each other (Netting, Huber, Paton & Kautz, 1995, p. 355).

Others in human services, such as patient advocates in hospitals, also creatively combine the seemingly incompatible roles of ombudsperson and advocate. The important thing is to have adequate authority, since the job involves questioning professionals about their actions or inactions and ruffling feathers.

INTERNAL AND EXTERNAL ADVOCATES

Definitions. Advocacy can ensue inside or outside of the agency. Internal advocates are those looking inward to their organization (*intra*organizational effort), and external advocates are those facing outward (*inter*organizational effort) as they advocate because "professionals have the responsibility to look inward to change their organizations, as well as outward to change community conditions" (Rothman, Erlich, & Tropman, 1995, pp. xi, xii). (see Chapter 8.)

An *internal advocate* makes changes for the client through vigilance and intervention inside the agency, using decision-making channels, where possible, and informal influence systems. One advocate says:

> We can do things systemically to help an individual or group of clients. I've done this on the clinical and administrative levels— bringing about equity that impacts a particular client. . . . I've worked in instances

where it's my own *system* that's decided to interpret a regulation or policy in a rigid manner that constricts the client's ability to have an opportunity for change or growth . . . you have to begin with your own . . . system. The success from that frequently gives us data, information, and even self-confidence to move outside of an organization. (Griffin in *Challenging*)[9]

Mounting a major change effort in a system that serves as one's employer is obviously a challenge.

Internal advocacy is pertinent for those who work for large city, county, or state agencies. One state child welfare administrator sees internal advocacy and working the system effectively as synonymous.

[M]ake the system work for you. At this level of administration, which is the macro level, you're not doing anything different in terms of skills. The same insight you needed to understand a family system, you need to understand this system. In the same way you want to make changes in that family, well, I want to make changes in this system. So I need to look at it and understand how it works, so I can make the change that I want to happen. (Heisner in *Challenging*)[10]

Such systems have to work for the advocate and for those being served. Otherwise, workers within a system may be targets of advocacy by workers outside it.

An *external advocate*, paid by an outside source, tries to hold an agency accountable by using different tactics. How might a social worker become an external advocate? The parent of a learning-disabled child assigned to a special education class might come to a child welfare worker, employed outside the school system, desiring a due process hearing. A food stamp recipient wanting to appeal a reduction in aid might ask an advocate employed not in the public

benefits office but in the community for assistance. Public schools and the food stamp programs have rules that advocates can use to (1) help individuals[11] and (2) hold the agencies responsible for these programs accountable. Agencies must comply with their own regulations and rules, as well as with rulings on court cases that guarantee certain rights.

Internal and external advocates can work together or separately on the same issue. For instance, the internal advocate could be a city social services worker who is trying to reform a lamentable foster-care children's program by holding high-level administrative meetings, organizing mass meetings for staff to promote solidarity, and leaking information to outside allies. The external advocate could be an indignant social worker who works with families that have children literally lost in the system. Box 12.11 describes two internal advocates (Spolar, 1991).

This example features the ethical and professional aspects of internal advocacy. Since it is easy to fear retaliation, it is notable that the careers of the internal advocates (featured in Box 12.11) did not ultimately suffer from their decision to stick to their principles. Bureaucracies are often too big and preoccupied to destroy individual staffers, and advocates frequently advance to more responsible positions. However, advocacy does not guarantee success. Some improvements were made, but the agency described in Box 12.11 went into receivership. The internal advocates had reason for hope, though, because the receiver appointed by the court to straighten out the child welfare system was reformer Jerome Miller, mentioned earlier.

Complexities. We are, with a few exceptions, expected to direct our advocacy attention to situations outside the agency. A social worker trying to obtain health care for the homeless is expected to do external bat-

| BOX 12.11 | TWO WHO DARED TO TAKE THE STAND |

D.C. Foster Care Workers Told of Crying Children, Broken Promises

Social workers Chainie Scott and Thomas C. "Tommy" Wells say they were just doing their jobs when they told their tales of children twice forgotten, once by their own parents and then again by the District foster care agency.

"If all you do is go home and complain, you're not being a good social worker," said Wells, one of two D.C. Department of Human Services employees whose testimony, in part, moved U.S. District Judge Thomas F. Hogan to issue a memorandum yesterday calling foster care in the nation's capital "a travesty."

The judge's decision vindicated Scott and Wells, the only Human Services workers who agreed to take the stand to point out dangerous deficiencies.

"There was a lot of hesitancy on my part" about testifying, Scott said. "I thought: Why should I put my job, my career as it is, on the line? But then I thought: It's not fair to the children and it's not fair to me. . . . The comments I made and the testimony I gave is really quite mild compared to what you would hear in casual conversations in our hallways." Wells, 34, and Scott, 31, employees of the department's Child and Family Services Division, testified during a three-week trial of a law-suit brought against the city by the American Civil Liberties Union. It alleged that the city violated federal and local laws and the rights of the 2,200 foster children by failing to reunite families or help abandoned children find adoptive homes.

Scott, who holds an undergraduate degree from Penn State University and a master's degree in social work from Howard University, has worked for the department for four years. Wells graduated from the University of Alabama and received a master's in social work from the University of Minnesota before joining the city six years ago.

During their hours on the stand, each told of on-the-job predicaments that tore the social service division's safety net. Scott said she had a caseload of 251 children, many more than she could effectively handle, and told of times her office was filled with crying children with nowhere else to sleep.

Wells said he and other workers were never trained on the city computer system that is supposed to monitor children in District custody, and he recounted the time that Mayor Marion Barry promised him and 50 colleagues that 32 new caseworkers would be hired immediately. They weren't.

"My only reason for speaking was to get out the social workers' perspective," said Wells, who attends law school at night at Catholic University. "The agency is bitter about the lawsuit; the social workers are not."

Wells and Scott say they were taken aback by the reaction to their testimony in the halls of 609 H St. NE, the offices for child services. "The line workers were very supportive," Scott said. "I kept hearing the word 'courage' being thrown around, and I kept thinking: But this is no big deal. This is just the truth."

What about her supervisors?

"The testimony [from department officials] was the same nonsense we deal with everyday," she said.

Human Services Director Vincent C. Gray said yesterday that the two had not jeopardized their jobs by speaking out. "I think they were expressing their concerns and they are dedicated people," he said.

Wells said, "We might not get promotions. We're probably not in the best favor with our supervisors. But," he added wryly, "we're young."

tle on behalf of the homeless with various health bureaucracies. Similarly, the professional working with a battered woman's shelter is expected to be an external advocate with the police concerning protective orders. Even so, some problems may also be internal, especially in key government agencies. In any instrumental organization, we will be asked to intervene in-house on behalf of those working elsewhere.

Organizational culture. Within the first weeks on a job, it is important to figure out who is likely to support or resist action taken internally or externally. A supervisor who encourages "pulling out all the stops" externally may not want employees to "rock the boat" on internal issues. For example, an employee assistance program director may encourage us to advocate for employees with substance abuse problems, to ensure that their bosses will not fire them without giving them a chance to enter a program, yet may not want us to bring up internal problems such as inadequate or inappropriate office space with the host agency. In contrast, a supervisor may encourage testing and prodding the internal bureaucracy but may be wary and cautious about dealing with the media, city hall, or any other external institution. A hospital discharge planner who is positioned to spot problems in places where patients are being sent may want to report these problems to a licensing agency, only to be told to keep quiet and not risk losing a placement.

Advocacy involves sizing up situations. We need to determine if our supervisor views service and advocacy as compatible. We want to know what language is most acceptable—is "representation" or "negotiation" preferred over "advocacy"? Since managers also act as advocates, social workers new to an agency might observe their style as they go about their work—"representing the agency, expressing management's viewpoint to staff and vice versa, lobbying at the local, state, and national level, testifying, and establishing contact with legislators and government administrators" (Menefee & Thompson, 1994, p. 18). This may reveal agency traditions or norms regarding internal and external advocacy.

More than supervisors' temperaments, the organizational culture may dictate con-

straints. Tower (1994) urges administrators who care about the clientele to

> support and enhance the advocacy efforts of their frontline workers. After all, they are the ones most acutely aware of the client's unmet needs. It is likely that the main reason that more practitioners are not currently involved in consumer movements is fear of repercussion, primarily from their employers. (p. 196).

Realistically, certain positions constrain needed advocacy. Even though a particular employee assistance program may be improving employee productivity and thus is on good terms with employers, a consultant may hesitate to advocate with them about the causes of job stress problems (Ramanathan, 1992). Examples can also be found in correction systems, where social workers must advocate for inmates and staff but where complete allegiance to either inmates or the institution may be naive (Severson, 1994). We must think about our auspices and weigh the pluses and minuses of our particular slot or job requirements for success in advocacy.

Views of Empowerment and Advocacy

EMPOWERMENT AS A JOINT PROCESS WITH CLIENTS

Definitions. Employed early on by social workers such as Solomon (1976), the term *empowerment* is used to describe both the process of getting stronger and the result. As Lee (1994) says, "Empowerment is both the journey and the destination" (p. 207). One robust definition of empowerment, provided by Simon (1990), views it "as a series of attacks on subordination of every description—psychic, physical, cultural, sexual, legal, political, economic, and technological" (p. 28). Hepworth and Larsen (1993) see the goal of empowerment as assisting "clients who manifest powerlessness to develop their latent powers and to exert these powers to obtain needed resources" (p. 495).[12] Critical here is the notion of people developing and using skills to get needed resources or to influence decisions affecting their lives. Gutierrez (1990) suggests techniques for assisting with this; Ruffolo and Miller (1994) describe how to use empowerment in community relations.

Many "interventive tools" are used to enhance client empowerment, according to Simon (1994), including social investigation, humane policy and program development, and organizational innovation (p. 190). Vehicles differ as we work with clients in various social categories (Cox & Parsons, 1994) and in each case. Lee (1994) gives an example of a mother with AIDS who empowered herself by writing a journal (at the worker's suggestion) that she could share with her children and leave as a "legacy" (p. 206).

Ackerson and colleagues (1995) studied the meanings of empowerment to clinicians and found that they usually thought of it in conjunction with enablement and self-determination—useful on a personal level when clients "feel they are not in control of their lives" (p. 10). This is consistent with the previous example of the mother with AIDS. However, several of the social workers interviewed had not found it easy to engage in empowerment as a joint process with clients due to perceived client limitations, setting or program constraints, and control (even liability) issues (Ackerson et al., 1995, p. 8). Those with mentally ill clients were most conflicted. [As Lee (1994) says, "No phase of the empowerment process can be done well without the worker having a raised consciousness" (p. 14).] A number of the social workers interviewed did not associate empowerment with groups, social systems, and larger processes, but some were conscious of tensions surrounding empowerment and paternalism (Ackerson et al., p. 11).

EMPOWERMENT AS A JOINT PROCESS WITH ADVOCACY

Although recently advocacy and empowerment have been distinguished from each other, they once were viewed as facets of the "change agent" role. Messinger (1982), a social worker and city official, nicely illustrates both. Describing the ways in which she provides constituent services, she pinpoints individual advocacy, then empowerment, then community advocacy:

> Many people . . . [contact a] politician because they need something done. . . . I or my staff . . . give them an address, make a phone call, track down a check, do whatever is necessary, but we try, always, to notify the people we assist about whom we are calling, what the most useful telephone number is, how they might do the same thing for themselves, and what to do if they do not get help.
>
> Sometimes, too, it is necessary for my staff to intervene to rescue individuals from becoming victims of the system. We recognize that it takes a mass effort by many people to make systems work better, but we do not . . . turn every problem with the bureaucracy into a cause. Nevertheless, we look for patterns in this work with constituents and for areas in which it is of mutual advantage to organize a lobbying and advocacy force rather than just to give help. (p. 216)

Advocacy is appropriate in some situations, empowerment in others. Wood and Middleman (1989) make an interesting point in regard to obtaining benefits for an entitled client:

> [W]e value the positive experience which people can have as they work together and take action in their own behalf, even if they do not succeed. . . . But when [rights] are at stake, we do not value the psychological experience above task accomplishment. . . . [W]e believe that the positive feelings associated with accordance of one's rights are more real and more lasting, irrespective of

the extent to which one has obtained it through one's own efforts. (p. 145)

Pressing needs may not wait for empowerment, and the social worker will have to make this judgment call. For instance, one could still do advocacy on behalf of involuntary clients who resist mutuality and empowerment measures.

Not every client can be empowered; clients include babies as well as brain-damaged or comatose patients. Nor can every client be empowered by every experience. Within an advocacy framework, there are many roles still to be played. Lawyers argue on behalf of the families of people killed or people unable to speak for themselves due to accidents. The hospital social worker faced with a critically ill, comatose patient without a living will may be reluctant to leave all decision making to doctors and relatives. Working with a medical ethicist, that advocate could research patterns of decision making in the patient's earlier life, the patient's past expression of values, and any orally expressed preferences about dying and end-of-life treatment. Although not a legal document, such research does give the patient a "voice," but it is stretching the term to say that the person is being empowered. Moreover, the worker will need to advocate for permission to do the research and to present it to the physician and the patient's family.

Best Interests of Client versus Stated Wishes

Professional interpretations. Lawyers and social workers agree that advocacy requires being partial (Grosser, 1965) and in tune with the desires of those requesting advocacy. Differences between professionals arise when the lawyer seizes on the currently stated wishes of the client, while the social worker believes that the government has an

obligation to protect the young, helpless, or incompetent. Consider the case of a 10-year-old boy (an involuntary client) who was physically abused by his parents and removed from their custody. Decisions are being made about his future. The boy says he definitely wants to go home. Lawyers for the child (or his family) will do all they can to get the judge to honor his request. Social workers (from the agency acting as his guardian) might wonder if he realizes that other options may be preferable, even though their unfamiliarity makes them a frightening choice.

Compared to a lawyer, and in programs such as family preservation, it may be less clear whether the worker's client is the child or the family and whether ultimate allegiance is to the child, the agency, or society as a whole. Attorneys find this discomforting:

> Employment by an agency is seen as compromising the social worker's effectiveness as an advocate for the client. The agency is a force for social control. The social worker has divided loyalties: to society, the agency, and the client. Only the social worker in private practice is hired directly by the client. Even lawyers paid a salary in legal assistance programs see themselves as the client's representative just as if the client had hired them. (Brieland & Lemmon, 1995, p. 13)

Those who urge self-advocacy by clients or work with people who have disabilities sometimes warn against the "best interests" approach (Moxley & Freddolino, 1994, p. 99). To ascertain children's wishes and desires, guardian ad litem and court-appointed special advocates (CASA) programs provide the child with a personal advocate and friend (Courter, 1995).

The case of the senior citizen who wants to be left alone may sharpen these issues. Suppose neighbors report that a 75-year-old recluse is feeding herself and 11 dogs on a meager income and that several rooms of her house are filled with waste. The health department and social services start to intervene when the woman asks for help to stay in her home with her pets. The lawyer will insist that she meet all city and humane society regulations, but will defend her right to live as she chooses and fight institutionalization. The social worker will think about resources such as homemaker service, SSI, and possible guardianship. Coordination between the two professions would result in the best advocacy in such situations (Clouser, 1990).

Conciliatory versus Adversarial Strategies

A second issue involves how long to cooperate, coerce, or compromise before becoming adversarial. Wood and Middleman warn against escalating too soon on behalf of powerless clients, who, unlike the worker, will suffer the consequences if the action fails. They insist that the roles of broker and mediator must be tried first (1989, p. 142; Kolb, 1994; Parsons, 1991). On the other hand, Patti and Resnick (1972) urge workers who want to change their *agencies* to consider both collaborative and adversarial strategies, depending on circumstances. One consideration should be whether or not the target of change is "rational, open to new ideas, and acting in good faith" (p. 224). We must strategize with colleagues to decide whether a combative or a facilitative stance will be most productive for each situation (see Chapter 8).

The Legitimation of Advocacy

Advocacy for various population groups has been institutionalized by government through a number of acts—Older Americans, Rehabilitation, Americans with Disabilities, and so on. This has been done through institutions or offices such as the Legal Services Corporation (federal) and the Office of the Public Advocate (New Jersey), as well as through programs or advocacy systems such as the Protection and Advocacy Systems for the Developmentally Disabled, the Client Assistance Project in vocational rehabilitation, and mental health advocacy programs.

Employees in such systems are advocates for a class of people who seek "full community membership," not client advocates. They may focus on revised research about the population, organizational interventions, or work with nonprofit organizations statewide and client organizations such as the National Alliance for the Mentally Ill (Rapp, Shera, & Kisthardt 1993, p. 728). Such workers may think of themselves as programmatic advocates, government or systems advocates, political advocates, or issue-oriented advocates. In bringing about reforms leading to "greater consumer involvement in other spheres of systems change," for example, they may take action such as getting the mentally disabled on planning boards and councils that oversee their own programs (Segal, Silverman, & Temkin, 1993, p. 710).

ADVOCACY PROCESSES AND SKILLS

Advocacy Processes

Earlier, we discussed how macro problem-solving and community assessment processes (Chapters 1, 6) can probe to discover opportunities for influence and intervention. Problem solving and assessment are similarly involved with case or client advocacy. For example, Moxley and Freddolino (1994, pp. 100–103) provide an outline to remind advocates of their task, process, and interaction objectives. The fourth point listed is important, as it reminds client advocates to retain an ongoing relationship with their clients throughout the action cycle or event.

1. Engagement;
2. Assessment of advocacy needs;
3. Setting objectives and identifying tasks;
4. Maintaining relationships across time and space;
5. Problem solving and ongoing needs;
6. Monitoring of problem resolution; and
7. Evaluation of the outcome.

We also want to have closure with the client after the process is complete. One part of the process often forgotten is getting back to all those who helped make advocacy successful, to report the results and give thanks.

Key Advocacy Skills

Persuasion

Persuasion is a key interpersonal skill used in both micro and macro interchanges. It involves promoting, marketing, working for favorable interpretations for a client or a cause, and changing minds (Mondros & Wilson, 1994). Persuasion is part of many practice situations, as for example, during program development (Amezcua, McAlister, Ramirez, & Espinoza 1990, p. 273), case conferences, discharge planning, and many others. It is a pivotal skill in policy situations, which require knowing the pressure points and how to use them (Flynn, 1985). In addition, having personal persuasiveness (Burghardt, 1982) and projecting "personal authoritativeness" (Jansson, 1990, p. 201) with a solid command of the facts can be compelling.

Rules of thumb for persuading others are as follows:

Know what you want;
Know the facts and have them available;
Understand your source of power;
Rehearse;

Dress conventionally and comfortably;
Use clear, simple, graphic images;
Appeal to emotions *and* logic; and
Make eye contact.

Representation

As societal transactions grow increasingly complex, it becomes more difficult for individuals to have the knowledge and capacity to conduct all of their affairs on their own behalf. Consequently, most of us need an experienced person to lead us through certain areas. Just as we turn to instructors to teach us first aid or how to drive a car, others request our help to obtain public housing, credit counseling, or job protection during pregnancy.

Representation begins when one person asks another, the second person agrees to become a spokesperson, and the two of them define the nature of their relationship. To represent someone is to take that person's view (or to work out a "meeting of the minds" together) while being forthright about chances, prospects, and when nothing can be done. Adeptness is required in communication, finding out the client's real wants and needs—not our picture of them—and educating and motivating the client to assist in the process.

Rules of thumb for representation include the following:

Establish whether someone besides the affected party needs to be involved;
Share what you know with the client;
Discover and check out what your client wants;
Lay out options and let client decide which ones are desirable and their order of importance;
Investigate the particular situation;
Determine the level of formality of the process;
Coordinate with each other;

Guard against divide-and-conquer tactics; and
Allow the client to "hire" and "fire" you.

Interacting with Authority Figures[13]

There is an entire representation–persuasion–advocacy–bargaining–negotiation
continuum with concomitant skills. Yet, developing one particular ability usually makes
an advocate effective. An advocate must
know *how to contend, how to insist*. This means
defending and protecting an individual, getting those who hold power to change their
minds or behavior, and holding one's ground
with intimidating people. The skill we are
discussing lacks a formal name. It is not an
"in your face" attitude or "mau-mauing flak
catchers" (Brager & Specht 1973, p. 332). It is
knowing what to do and doing it in the face
of opposition. In most cases, advocates confront sources of resistance.

THOSE IN KEY POSITIONS

Authority is the power to influence or
command thought, opinion, or behavior, and
an authority figure is a person in command
who has legitimate power to make decisions.
Social workers have different views than
clients, citizens, and service users on who is
an authority figure. Therefore, let us think of
an *authority figure* as a person who holds or
is perceived to hold power and influence in
the situation at hand. The need to dispute or
correct such a person is difficult for novices,
yet any professional who wants to help others or make changes in a community must
deal with authority figures. The way such
persons are dealt with can be a major deter-
minant of the results. We must learn what
rules and policies a given authority figure is
subject to or must abide by, as well as those
that she or he controls.

To students, field supervisors are authority figures. To service users, the person who

collects a deposit before a telephone can be installed is in a position to help or hurt them and
is thus in a position of authority. There may
be nothing sinister or malevolent about authority figures, but they can exercise discretion
and may be intimidating in their bearing, demeanor, or tone of voice. Social workers may
be perceived as authority figures, based on
knowledge or status, on their control over a
client's family, and on formal and informal determinations they make, such as whether to report certain behavior to a court.

Advocates constantly bump up against
people with different positions, people who
dislike clients singly or en mass, and people
who can change a client's present situation
or future. Over thirty years ago, Grosser
(1965) argued that advocacy was necessary
because arbitrariness and discretion can create an uneven playing field:

> Often the institutions with which local res-
> idents must deal are not even neutral, much
> less positively motivated, toward handling
> the issues brought to them by community
> groups. In fact, they are frequently overtly
> negative and hostile, often concealing or dis-
> torting information about rules, procedures,
> and office hours. By their own partisanship
> . . . they create an atmosphere that demands
> advocacy on behalf of the poor. . . . If the
> community worker is to facilitate productive
> interaction between residents and institu-
> tions, it is necessary . . . to provide leadership
> and resources directed toward eliciting in-
> formation, arguing the correctness of a posi-
> tion, and challenging the stance of the insti-
> tution. (p. 18).

These words are equally relevant today, yet
confrontation is not inevitable. Many situations are resolved amicably. It is important
for advocates to be aware that those in key
positions view their reputations or jobs as being on the line, much as we feel about our
clients and our jobs. We should respond to
antagonism with firmness (see Chapter 7).

Social conflict can be uncomfortable. Examples of situations where we may experience difficulty or discomfort when we must—as an ethical or professional obligation—challenge an authority could include the following:

- informing an employer of his or her responsibilities on behalf of your client population (whether day laborers, teenagers, displaced homemakers, or persons who have seizures);
- arguing the merits of a group or halfway house before a hostile zoning board; or
- contradicting an elected official who has wrongfully maligned your program in the press.

"The impulse to obey authority and the reluctance to confront it are deeply ingrained in the human psyche" (Bell, 1994, p. 136). Transactional analysts might say that many of us overadapt. We may become passive-aggressive. Workers and clients are likely to react similarly to those who have the power to influence outcomes—with awe, avoidance, and anger. As professionals, those who make themselves interact anyway go on to become effective advocates.

PREREQUISITES FOR FACING AUTHORITY FIGURES

There are certain hints for approaching and, if necessary, challenging a person who is in a position to grant or deny a request or to control someone's future.

Rules of thumb for dealing with authority include the following:

Know the system you are up against;
Know your facts;
Be ready to demonstrate that you have done your part;
Know what you want (but also what you will take);

Consider all options about the time, place, and manner of engagement;
Have materials organized in serviceable fashion for use under pressure;
Speak in an even tone;
Listen carefully and take notes; and
Look for a clear decision.

ILLUSTRATING INTERACTION WITH AUTHORITIES

A common example of a task-oriented encounter involves the probable utility shut-off for a household unless negotiations with a utility company representative are successful. One of the first decisions an advocate must make regarding such a meeting is whether someone representing the household should be present. This decision will depend on deciding how that individual might fare and whether she or he wants to participate. If the service user is present, the advocate must show respect for that person (e.g., not talking over her or him) and must make sure that the authority figure shows respect; Simon (1994) entreats us to "interrupt contempt" (p. 189). However, the advocate must anticipate a variety of responses from the authority figures involved because each company representative has a different personality. In addition, the advocate should not presume prematurely that the other person is an adversary (Wood & Middleman, 1989, p. 142).

An advocate without preexisting relationships with utility customers might need to bring them along to provide information. Emergencies call for interventions before the facts can be studied. If a client's history with the utility company is unknown, the advocate might still represent her or him because of a commitment to low-income people or consumers in general. However, in a meeting with the company, the advocate might play a mediating rather than an advocacy role. Even if the client's history is known, a mediation style allows the advocate to shift

BOX 12.12 ADVOCATES CONFRONT MYRIAD PROBLEMS WITH CLIENTS

Setting: Office of customer relations representative

Advocate: I am a community service worker with the Neighborhood Center. Our office provides assistance in housing and utility issues. This is Mrs. Edna Gardner. We requested an appointment because she received a telephone call stating that her service would be terminated today due to nonpayment of bills.

U. Rep: Yes, I am aware of Mrs. Gardner's bill. (To client) Mrs. Gardner, you are two months in arrears, plus the current bill for June is due. We have received no payment. You did not contact us to say when we could expect payment, so we have no alternative but to discontinue your service.

Client: Look, I have three children at home. There has to be another way. Don't turn off the gas.

U. Rep: There is another way. Pay your bills on time like any other good citizen.

Advocate: That is exactly why we are here today. To work out an arrangement so Mrs. Gardner can pay her bill. Mrs. Gardner and I have discussed the situation and feel a deferred payment plan might be a solution.

U. Rep: In some situations deferred payment is a the solution. When we feel there is a strong likelihood that individuals will live up to their obligations to make installment payments, we agree to such a plan. Quite frankly, Mrs. Gardner, you don't appear to fit into that category.

Client: (Angry) What do you mean? I have tried very hard to pay all my bills and it's not easy. Have you ever tried coping as a single parent?

Advocate: (To client) Just a minute, Mrs. Gardner. (To utility rep) Let me explain that Mrs. Gardner moved in March, so she did not receive a bill in April. Therefore, her bill in May was over $175. She did try to explain her inability to pay to your office, but unfortunately a payment agreement was not proposed at that time. Also, Mrs. Gardner had not received written notification that her service was to be terminated and did not realize how serious the situation was until today. Mrs. Gardner is prepared to make an initial payment on her bill right now.

U. Rep: Well, we require at least half of the amount in arrears, which would be approximately $85 to $90.

Advocate: We are prepared to pay $60 today.

U. Rep: I just told you we need at least half of the amount in arrears.

Advocate: I've worked with your office before, and the policy has been to accept initial payments as low as one-third of that amount.

U. Rep: $80.

Advocate: Let me check with Mrs. Gardner (talks to her quietly, then to the utility rep). $70 is the most we can pay today, but we'll assure you of three installment payments of approximately $35 to pay the rest.

U. Rep: How do you expect to make the payments if you can't even come up with $80?

Advocate: We will manage that aspect of our agreement. What we need to do now is put the terms of this agreement in writing, in Mrs. Gardner's file, and issue the stop order on the turnoff.

U. Rep: You'll pay $70 today and $35 for 3 months?

Client: Yes.

U. Rep: However, since Mrs. Gardner's service was scheduled to be turned off today, the service men are probably at the house now.

Advocate: We just mutually agreed to a plan.

U. Rep: Well, it's alright by me, and if we had entered into the plan yesterday or before the truck started on its rounds. . . . Now, once the reconnect charge is paid, our arrangement will go into effect.

Advocate: Your company policy has been not to terminate service once a payment plan has been set up. There can't be a reconnect charge either under the circumstances. You must be able to stop the shutoff.

U. Rep: You came too late. There is no way I can reach the men now.

Advocate: Someone must have contact with the service truck.

U. Rep: I don't.

Advocate: Then let me speak to your supervisor.

U. Rep: You'd like to speak with my supervisor?

Advocate: Yes, we would.

Source: *National Public Law Training Center script (edited).*

once a concession is made in order to "create a structure through which all present and future clients can obtain their entitlement" because "the aim of advocacy is always universalistic as opposed to . . . for this client at this time" (Wood & Middleman, 1989, p. 143).

In an alternative approach, an advocate might interview the client ahead of time and agree to represent the client but follow a nonpersonal approach, that is, meeting without the client and relying on knowledge of the utility appeals system. This necessitates knowing the policies and procedures of the company and its government oversight agency. Advocates must know the chain of command in any situation.

A third advocacy approach could follow a negotiating strategy. This entails premeeting strategy preparation with the client/customer to review the bargaining situation. During the meeting itself, other negotiating techniques would be used, such as putting any settlement in writing, caucusing with the client, and threatening to go to a higher level. In bureaucracies "the power of the advocate is the potential power to escalate the problem, to raise it to higher levels in the hierarchy" (Wood & Middleman, 1989, p. 142). The situation presented in Box 12.12 illustrates this. It also highlights how frequently language that is unfamiliar to the lay person is used, whether in a utility or a psychiatric case.

Note these points presented in Box 12.12. We must not let others shift the burden of responsibility on every point to us. We cannot assume that a person who has the authority to make a certain decision can decide or order anything we want. We notice the directness with which an advocate converses with a decision maker. No time and effort is wasted in making pleasant small talk, trying to appease, ingratiate or bully, or overexplaining or excusing the client's situation. The straightforwardness needed in such situations is acquired through assertiveness training (see Chapter 7).

Discussion Exercises

1. Read the works of Shapiro, Tower, or Courter (see References) and discuss the attributes of an individual advocate.

2. View the third video in the War on Poverty series if possible. The leader, George Wiley, was admired by social workers who worked with him in the welfare and civil rights movements. His belief was that he should use himself fully. His biographers describe him as

- well organized, energetic, and uninhibited;
- committed to obtaining information and data;
- able to present information clearly and powerfully;
- able to link diverse, strong-minded allies; and
- able to get others involved.

Wiley's biographers also portray him as someone who

- believed he could convince others—even foes;
- juggled myriad tasks but kept his eye on the target;
- applied heady ideas in practical ways;
- made and kept lists (e.g., resources, contacts);
- listened well;
- sought out mentors and fund-raising help; and
- wanted to achieve concrete gains.

Pick someone you know who is successful at community practice. What traits and skills does she or he have?

3. Read the *Encyclopedia of Social Work*'s article on progressive social work. Bombyk (1995) chal-

lenges us to name a social worker with a national reputation for championing the interests of underdogs: "Is there a Ralph Nader of social work?"

4. Read the *Encyclopedia of Social Work*'s article on music and social work (Lawson, 1995). What songs have you incorporated into practice? Do newer causes (disability, gay rights) use music the way the civil rights, labor, and peace movements did?

5. Divide into three groups. Decide how to organize the low-income community with the crowded schools described at the beginning of the chapter. One group can use locality development, another the social planning approach, and the third social action.

Notes

1. Regarding a secured right, see the Bentley-Rosenson debate. Regarding a right being created, the right to refuse to answer questions about treatment for emotional disorders is being established. We struggle with implementation of rights and "selective enforcement" that results in "discretionary justice" (Davis, 1975). Social work has "a commitment to equal rights and to an equitable distribution of wealth and power among all citizens" (Reeser & Leighninger, 1990, p. 71), although social justice often takes one beyond rights.

2. Regarding reforms, see Edwards and Sherraden (1994) and Bobo, Kendall, and Max (1995). Regarding borrowing from sources outside our field, see Lewis (1991), Lee (1994), and Wakefield (1988). Regarding a critic's call for reform, see Funiciello (1993).

3. Bea Gaddy of East Baltimore, a recipient of a national Caring award. Interview by Jennifer Nelson in *Challenging* (1994).

4. Many famous organizers (e.g., Alinsky, Heather Booth, Wade Rathke) and training centers, such as, the Industrial Areas Foundation (Robinson & Hanna 1994), Highlander School, and Midwest Academy, operate(d) outside social work. Some associated with those groups have an MSW, like Arnie Graf, who has worked with the Industrial Areas Foundation for 20 years. After social work, the ministry is the profession that engages most often in organizing.

5. For publicity and media advocacy tips, we can turn to NASW (Rose, 1995) and to the work of Brawley (1985–86), Ryan (1991), and Wallack and colleagues (1993).

6. Virginia M. Thomas, ACSW, state delegate. Interview by Linda Plitt in *Challenging* (1994). As with the other advocate interview excerpts, this statement or these answers to questions are oral, not written responses.

7. Jim Evans (active in NASW, the Urban League, and welfare rights), December 9, 1993, interviewed by Brenda Kunkel for an advocates project.

8. The United States borrowed the "ombuds" concept. Sweden has had an ombudsperson since 1809, Finland since 1919, and Denmark since 1955. The first Danish "ombudsmand" helped sell the concept abroad (Gellhorn, 1966, p. 5).

9. Rosalind Griffin, DSW, manager (drug dependency, mental health, cross racial-ethnic counseling expert). Interview by Rachel Schwartz in *Challenging* (1994).

10. Linda Heisner (clinical social worker turned children and family services government leader). Interview by Cathy Raab in *Challenging* (1994).

11. Nonlawyers can act as authorized representatives, if requested, by an eligible person or a recipient for federal programs including Social Security, Medicare, SSI, veterans, and public housing.

12. Operationalizing empowerment brings controversies—for example, (a) whether calling someone a client is disempowering because it "implies subordination" (Saleebey, 1994, p. 355) and (b) whether advocacy, even if helping an "immediate situation," continues a pattern of powerlessness (Kahn, 1991, p. 51). Lee (1994) uses the phrase "people called 'clients' or 'consumers of services' "

(p. xi). Such wording reminds us that "client" is a label (and a convenience for textbook writing), not a statement about personhood or capacity.

13. Some of the material on authority figures is taken from a videotape and manuals (1981, 1983) by the National Public Law Training Center (NPLTC), a former advocacy training organization. (The video was produced by Robert Hoffman and Pat Powers. George Hacker, William Fry, Barry Greever, Cathy Howell, and Pat Powers, among others, contributed to NPLTC's Advocacy Spectrum training manual.)

References

Abramovitz, M. (1993). Should all social work students be educated for social change: PRO, in Point/Counterpoint. *Journal of Social Work Education, 29*(1), 6–11.

Ackerson, B., Burson, I., Harrison, W. D., & Martin, A. (1995, March). *The paradoxical meanings of empowerment to clinicians: Results of a constant-comparative study.* Paper presented at Council on Social Work Education meeting, San Diego, CA.

Addams, J. (1910). *Twenty years at Hull House.* New York: Macmillan.

Alinsky, S. D. (1972). *Rules for radicals: A pragmatic primer for realistic radicals.* New York: Vintage Books.

Allen, M., Bonner, K., & Greenan, L. (1988). Federal legislative support for independent living. *Child Welfare, 67*(6), 515–527.

Amado, A. N. (Ed.). (1993). *Friendships and community connections between people with and without developmental disabilities.* Baltimore: Paul H. Brookes.

Amezcua, C., McAlister, A., Ramirez, A., & Espinoza, R. (1990). *A su salud*: Health promotion in a Mexican-American border community. In N. Bracht (Ed.), *Health promotion at the community level* (pp. 257–277). Newbury Park, CA: Sage.

Andrews, J., & Brenden, M. A. (1993). Leading from the left: Three prominent female social workers of the second generation. *Arete, 18*(1), 20–33.

Andrews, J. L. (1990). Female social workers in the second generation. *Affilia, 5*(2), 46–58.

Applebaum, R. P. (1970). *Theories of social change.* Chicago: Markham.

Ash, R. (1972). *Social movements in America.* Chicago: Nelson-Hall.

Bakal, Y. (1973, April). The Massachusetts experience. *Delinquency Prevention Reporter.* Washington, DC: U.S. Department of Health, Education and Welfare.

Beardsley, T. (1995, January). For whom the bell curve really tolls: A tendentious tome abuses science to promote far-right policies. *Scientific American, 272*(1), 14–17

Bell, D. A. (1994). *Confronting authority: Reflections of an ardent protester.* Boston: Beacon Press.

Bentley, K. J. (1993). The right of psychiatric patients to refuse medication: Where should social workers stand? *Social Work, 38*(1), 101–106.

Bobo, K., Kendall, J., & Max, S. (1995). Cleaning up in the nineties. In J. Rothman, J. L. Erlich, & J. E. Tropman with F. M. Cox (Eds.), *Strategies of community intervention* (5th ed., pp. 99–113). Itasca, IL: F. E. Peacock.

Bombyk, M. (1995). Progressive social work. In R. L. Edwards (Ed.-in-Chief), *Encyclopedia of social work* (19th ed., pp. 1933–1942). Washington, DC: National Association of Social Workers.

Boyte, H. C. (1980). *The backyard revolution: Understanding the new citizen movement.* Philadelphia: Temple University Press.

Bradshaw, C., Soifer, S., & Gutierrez, L. (1994). Toward a hybrid model for effective organizing in communities of color. *Journal of Community Practice, 1*(1), 25–41.

Brager, G. (1967). Institutional change: Parameters of the possible. *Social Work, 12*(1), 59–69.

Brager, G., & Specht, H. (1973). *Community Organizing.* New York: Columbia University Press.

Braverman, L. (1986). Social casework and strategic therapy. *Social Casework, 67*(4), 234–239.

Brawley, E. (1985–86, Winter). The mass media: A vital adjunct to the new community and administrative practice. *Administration in Social Work, 9,* 63–73.

Brieland, D., & Lemmon, J. A. (1985). *Social work and the law* (2nd ed.). St. Paul, MN: West.

Brill, J. A., & Reder, A. (1992). *Investing from the heart: The guide to socially responsible invest-*

ments and money management. New York: Crown.

Brooks, N. A. (1991). Self-empowerment among adults with severe physical disability: A case study. *Journal of Sociology and Social Welfare, 18*(1), 105–120.

Burghardt, S. (1982). *The other side of organizing*. Cambridge, MA: Schenkman.

Burghardt, S. (1987). Community-based social action. In A. Menahan (Ed.-in-Chief), *The encyclopedia of social work* (18th ed., pp. 292–299). Silver Spring, MD: National Association of Social Workers.

Challenging (1994). Interviews with advocates and activists. University of Maryland at Baltimore School of Social Work monograph, ed by P. Powers.

Chapin, R. K. (1995). Social policy development: The strengths perspective. *Social Work 40*(4), 506–514.

Checkoway, B. (1995). Six strategies of community change. *Community Development Journal, 30* (1), 2–20.

Chu, F. D., & Trotter, S. (1974). *The madness establishment: Ralph Nader's study group report on the National Institute of Mental Health*. New York: Grossman.

Class, N. E. (1974). *The regulatory challenge to social work: An historical essay on professional policy formulation*. Washington, DC: National Association of Social Workers.

Clouser, J. (1990). *Lawyers and social workers: The new partnership* (Vol. 360, *Aging*). Washington, DC: U.S. Department of Health and Human Services.

Courter, G. (1995). *True stories of a child advocate: I speak for this child*. New York: Crown.

Cox, E. O., & Parsons, R. J. (1994). *Empowerment-oriented social work practice with the elderly*. Pacific Grove, CA: Brooks/Cole.

Cunningham, L. E., Roisman, F., Rich, P., Beatley, P., & Barry, S. (1977). *Strengthening citizen access and governmental accountability*. Washington, DC: Exploratory Project for Economic Alternatives.

Dalton, R. J. (Ed.). (1993, July). Citizens, protest and democracy. *The Annals of the American Academy of Political and Social Sciences, 528* (entire issue). Newbury Park, CA: Sage.

Davis, K. C. (1975). *Administrative law and government*. St. Paul, MN: West.

Davis, L. V., Hagen, J. L., & Early, T. J. (1994). Social services for battered women: Are they adequate, accessible, and appropriate? *Social Work, 39*(6), 695–704.

Dear, R. B., & Patti, R. J. (1981). Legislative advocacy: Seven effective tactics. *Social Work, 26*(4), 289–96.

Donaldson, K. (1976). *Insanity inside out*. New York: Crown.

Doress-Worters, P. B., & Siegel, D. L. (1994). *Ourselves, growing older: Women aging with knowledge and power*. New York: Simon & Schuster.

Edwards, K., & Sherraden, M. (1994). *Individual development accounts: Emergence of an asset-based policy innovation*. St. Louis, MO: Washington University, Center for Social Development.

Fabricant, M., & Burghardt, S. (1992). *Welfare state crisis and the transformation of social service work*. Armonk, NY: M. E. Sharpe.

Fisher, R. (1994, Fall). Community organizing in the conservative '80s and beyond. *Social Policy, 25*(1), 11–21.

Fisher, R. (1995). Social action community organization: Proliferation, persistence, roots, and prospects. In J. Rothman, J. L. Erlich, & J. E. Tropman with F. M. Cox (Eds.), *Strategies of community organization: Macro practice* (5th ed., pp. 327–340). Itasca, IL: F. E. Peacock.

Flynn, J. P. (1985). *Social agency policy: Analysis and presentation for community practice*. Chicago: Nelson-Hall.

Freire, P. (1971). *Pedagogy of the oppressed*. New York: Herder & Herder.

Frost, D. (1994, October 21). Interview with Ralph Nader. Aired on public television.

Funiciello, T. (1993). *Tyranny of kindness: Dismantling the welfare system to end poverty in America*. New York: Atlantic Monthly.

Galper, J. H. (1975). *The politics of social services*. Englewood Cliffs, NJ: Prentice-Hall.

Gamson, J. (1991). Silence, death and the invisible enemy: AIDS activism and social movement "newness." In *Ethnography unbound* (pp. 35–57). Berkeley, CA: University of California Press.

Gamson, W. A. (1990). *The strategy of social protest* (2nd ed.). Belmont, CA: Wadsworth.

Gamson, W. A. (1992). *Talking politics*. New York: Cambridge University Press.

Gellhorn, W. (1966). *Ombudsmen and others: Citizen protectors in nine countries*. Cambridge, MA: Harvard University Press.

Gilbert, R. (1993). *Ronnie Gilbert on Mother Jones:*

Face to face with the most dangerous woman in America. Berkeley, CA: Conari.

Gitlin, T. (1980). *The whole world is watching: The making and unmaking of the new left.* Berkeley: University of California Press.

Glugoski, G., Reisch, M., & Rivera, F. G. (1994). A wholistic ethno-cultural paradigm: A new model for community organization teaching and practice. *Journal of Community Practice, 1*(1), 81–98.

Goldberg, R. A. (1991). *Grassroots resistance: Social movements in twentieth century America.* Belmont, CA: Wadsworth.

Goodwyn, L. (1978). *Democratic promise: The populist movement.* New York: Oxford University Press.

Grosser, C. F. (1965). Community development programs serving the urban poor. *Social Work, 10*(3), 15–21.

Grosser, C. F. (1976). *New directions in community organization: From enabling to advocacy* (2nd ed.). New York: Praeger.

Guskin, A. E., & Ross, R. (1979). Advocacy and democracy: The long view. In F. M. Cox, J. L. Erlich, J. Rothman, & J. E. Tropman (Eds.), *Strategies of community organization* (3rd ed., pp. 305–318). Itasca, IL: F. E. Peacock.

Gutierrez, L. M. (1990). Working with women of color: An empowerment perspective. *Social Work, 35*(2), 149–152.

Gutierrez, L. M. (1994, June). Beyond coping: An empowerment perspective on stressful life events. *Journal of Sociology and Social Welfare, 21*(3), 201–219.

Hahn, A. J. (1994). *The politics of caring: Human services at the local level.* Boulder, CO: Westview.

Handler, J. F. (1978). *Social movements and the legal system: A theory of law reform and social change.* New York: Academic Press.

Handler, J. F. (1979). *Protecting the social service client: Legal and structural controls on official discretion.* New York: Academic Press.

Hartman, A. (1993). The professional is political. *Social Work, 38*(4), 365–366.

Haynes, K., & Mickelson, J. (1991). *Affecting change: Social workers in the political arena.* New York: Longman.

Henderson, P., & Thomas, D. N. (1987). *Skills in Neighbourhood Work.* London: Allen & Unwin.

Hepworth, D. H., & Larsen. J.A. (1993). *Direct social work practice.* Pacific Grove, CA: Brooks/Cole.

Higham, J. (1993). Multiculturalism and universalism: A history and critique. *American Quarterly, 45*(2), 195–219.

Holder, E. (1995). Advocacy for nursing home reform. In G. L. Maddox (Ed.), *Encyclopedia of Aging* (2nd ed., pp 28–29). New York: Springer Publishing Co.

Horn, L., & Griesel, E. (1977). *Nursing homes: A citizens' action guide.* Boston: Beacon.

Howell, J. T. (1973). *Hard living on Clay Street: Portraits of blue collar families.* Garden City, NY: Anchor.

Huber, R., & Orlando, B. P. (1993). Macro assignment: Think big. *Journal of Social Work Education, 29*(1), 19–25.

Hyde, C. (1994). Commitment to social change: Voices from the feminist movement. *Journal of Community Practice, 1*(2), 45–64.

Isaac, K. (1992). *Civics for democracy: A journey for teachers and students.* Washington, DC: Essential Books.

Jackson, J. F. (1991). The use of psychoeducational evaluations in the clinical process: Therapists as sympathetic advocates. *Child and Adolescent Social Work Journal, 8*(6), 473–487.

Jansson, B. S. (1990). *Social welfare policy: From theory to practice.* Belmont, CA: Wadsworth.

Johnson, L. C. (1995). *Social work practice: A generalist approach* (5th ed.). Boston: Allyn & Bacon.

Jones, M. H. (1980). *The autobiography of Mother Jones.* Chicago: Charles H. Kerr.

Kahn, S. (1991). *Organizing: A guide for grassroots leaders.* Silver Spring, MD: National Association of Social Workers.

Kling, J. M., & Posner, P. S. (1990). *Dilemmas of activism: Class, community and the politics of mobilization.* Philadelphia: Temple University Press.

Kolb, D. (1994). *When talk works: profiles of mediators.* San Francisco: Jossey-Bass.

Kotz, N., & Kotz, M. L. (1977). *A passion for equality: George Wiley and the movement.* New York: W. W. Norton.

Kozol, J. (1990). *The night is dark and I am far from home* (rev. ed.). New York: Simon & Schuster.

Kozol, J. (1991). *Savage inequalities.* New York: HarperCollins.

Kuhn, M., with C. Long & L. Quinn. (1991). *No stone unturned: The life and times of Maggie Kuhn.* New York: Ballantine.

Lappe, F. M., & DuBois, P. M. (1994). *The quickening of America: Rebuilding our nation, remaking our lives.* San Francisco: Jossey-Bass.

Lawson, A., & Rhode, D. L. (Eds.). (1993). *The politics of pregnancy: Adolescent sexuality and public policy.* New Haven, CT: Yale University Press.

Lawson, T. R. (1995). Music and social work. In R. L. Edwards (Ed.-in-Chief), *Encyclopedia of Social Work* (19th ed., pp. 1736–1741). Washington, DC: National Association of Social Workers.

Lee, J. A. B. (1994). *The empowerment approach to social work practice.* New York: Columbia University Press.

Leonard, P. (1975). Towards a paradigm for radical practice. In R. Bailey & M. Brake (Eds.), *Radical social work* (pp. 46–61). New York: Pantheon.

Levy, J. (1975). *Cesar Chavez: Autobiography of la causa.* New York: W. W. Norton.

Lewis, E. (1991). Social change and citizen action: A philosophical exploration for modern social group work. *Social Action in Group Work, 14*(3/4), 23–34.

Lord, S. A., & Kennedy, E. T. (1992). Transforming a charity organization into a social justice community center. *Journal of Progressive Human Services, 3*(1), 21–37.

Lynch, R. S., & Mitchell, J. (1995). Justice system advocacy: A must for NASW and the social work community. *Social Work, 40*(1), 9–12.

Lynd, S. (1961, July). Jane Addams and the radical impulse. *Commentary, 32*(1), 54–59.

Mackelprang, R. W., & Salsgiver, R. O. (1996). People with disabilities and social work: Historical and contemporary issues. *Social Work, 41*(1), 7–14.

Mahaffey, M., & Hanks, J. (Eds.). (1982). *Practical politics: Social work and political responsibility.* Silver Spring, MD: National Association of Social Workers.

Mandell, B. R. (1992). Firing-up students for social change: Some teaching tactics for the 1990's. *Journal of Progressive Human Services, 3*(1), 53–69.

McCarthy, J. D., & Zald, M. N. (Eds.). (1987). *Social movements in organizational society: Collected essays.* New Brunswick, NJ: Transaction.

McFarland, A. S. (1984). *Common Cause: Lobbying in the public interest.* Chatham, NJ: Chatham House.

Menefee, D. T., & Thompson, J. J. (1994). Identifying and comparing competencies for social work management: A practice driven approach. *Administration in Social Work, 18*(3), 1–25.

Menendez, R. (Director). (1988). *Stand and Deliver.* [film].

Messinger, R. W. (1982). Empowerment: A social worker's politics. In M. Mahaffey & J. Hanks (Eds.), *Practical politics: Social work and political responsibility* (pp. 212–223). Silver Spring, MD: National Association of Social Workers.

Mikulski, B. A. (1982). Community empowerment and self help strategies. In *Social Welfare Forum, 1981* (pp. 11–23). New York: Columbia University Press.

Miller, J. B. (1986). *Toward a new psychology of women.* Boston: Beacon Press.

Mizrahi, T., & Morrison, J. (Eds.). (1993). *Community organization and social administration: Advances, trends, and emerging principles.* Binghamton, NY: Haworth.

Mondros, J. B., & Wilson, S. M. (1994). *Organizing for power and empowerment.* New York: Columbia University Press.

Moreau, M. J. (1990, June). Empowerment through advocacy and consciousness-raising: Implications of a structural approach to social work. *Journal of Sociology and Social Welfare, 17*(2), 53–67.

Moxley, D. P., & Freddolino, P. P. (1994). Client-driven advocacy and psychiatric disability: A model for social work practice. *Journal of Sociology and Social Welfare, 21*(2), 91–108.

Murase, K. (1992). Organizing in the Japanese-American community. In F. G. Rivera & J. L. Erlich (Eds.), *Community organizing in a diverse society* (pp. 159–180). Boston: Allyn & Bacon.

Nader, R. (1977). Introduction to J. Anderson, *For the people: A consumer action handbook.* Reading, MA: Addison-Wesley.

National Association of Social Workers Ad Hoc Committee on Advocacy. (1969, April). The social worker as advocate: Champion of social victims. *Social Work, 14,* 16–22.

National Citizens' Coalition for Nursing Home Reform. (1994, May-June). Washington state extends residents' rights across the LTC board. *Quality Care Advocate. IX* (3)

National Public Law Training Center. (1981). *The advocacy spectrum training manual.* Washington, DC: Author.

National Public Law Training Center. (1983). *Advocacy and the New Federalism.* Washington, D.C.: Author.

Netting, F. E., Huber, R., Paton, R. N., & Kautz, J. R. III. (1995). Elder rights and the long-term care ombudsman program. *Social Work, 40*(3), 351–357.

Netting, F. E., Kettner, P. M., & McMurtry, S. L.

(1993). *Social work macro practice.* White Plains, NY: Longman.

O'Donnell, S. (1993). Involving clients in welfare policy making. *Social Work, 38*(5), 629–635.

Panitch, A. (1974). Advocacy in practice. *Social Work, 19*, 326–332.

Parsons, R. J. (1991). The mediator role in social work practice. *Social Work, 36*(6), 483–487.

Patti, R. J., & Dear, R. B. (1975). Legislative advocacy: One path to social change. *Social Work, 20*(2), 108–114.

Patti, R. J., & Resnick, H. (1972). Changing the agency from within. *Social Work, 17*(4), 48–57.

Pertschuk, M. (1986). *Giant killers.* New York: W. W. Norton.

Powers, P. (1977). Social change: Nader style. *Journal of Education for Social Work, 13*(3), 63–69.

Powers, P. R. (1984). *Focused energy: A study of public interest advocates.* Unpublished doctoral dissertation, University of Maryland, College Park, MD.

Ramanathan, C. S. (1992). EAP's response to personal stress and productivity: Implications for occupational social work. *Social Work, 37*(3), 234–239.

Rapp, C. A., Shera, W., & Kisthardt, W. (1993). Research strategies for consumer empowerment of people with severe mental illness. *Social Work, 38*(6), 727–735.

Reeser, L. C., & Leighninger, L. (1990). Back to our roots: Towards a specialization in social justice. *Journal of Sociology and Social Welfare, 17*(2), 69–87.

Reisch, M., Wenocur, S., & Sherman, W. (1981). Empowerment, conscientization and animation as core social work skills. *Social Development Issues, 5*(2/3), 108–120.

Richan, W. C. (1991). *Lobbying for social change.* Binghamton, NY: Haworth.

Robinson, B., & Hanna, M. G. (1994). Lessons for academics from grassroots community organizing: A case study—The Industrial Areas Foundation. *Journal of Community Practice, 1*(4), 63–94.

Rogge, M. E. (1993). Social work, disenfranchised communities, and the natural environment: Field education opportunities. *Journal of Social Work Education, 29*(1), 111–120.

Romanyshyn, J. M. (1971). *Social welfare: Charity to justice.* New York: Random House.

Rose, R. (1995, February). Hook editors with a pro-caliber release. *NASW News*, p. 5.

Rose, S. M. (1990). Advocacy/empowerment: An approach to clinical practice for social work. *Journal of Sociology and Social Welfare, 17*(2), 41–51.

Rosenson, M. K. (1993). Social work and the right of psychiatric patients to refuse medication: A family advocate's response. *Social Work, 38*(1), 107–112.

Ross, J. W. (1993). Media messages, empathy, and social work. *Health and Social Work, 18*(3), 163–164.

Rothman, J. (1995). Approaches to community intervention. In J. Rothman, J. L. Erlich, & J. E. Tropman with F. M. Cox (Eds.), *Strategies of community intervention* (5th ed., pp. 26–63). Itasca, IL: F. E. Peacock.

Rothman, J., Erlich, J. L., & Tropman, J. E. with F. M. Cox (Eds.). (1995). *Strategies of community intervention* (5th ed.). Itasca, IL: F. E. Peacock.

Rothman, J., with J. E. Tropman. (1987). Models of community organization and macro practice: Their mixing and phasing. In F. M. Cox, J. L. Erlich, J. Rothman, & J. E. Tropman (Eds.), *Strategies of community intervention: Macro Practice* (4th ed., pp. 3–25). Itasca, IL: F. E. Peacock.

Ruffolo, M. C., & Miller, P. (1994). An advocacy/empowerment model of organizing: Developing university–agency partnerships. *Journal of Social Work Education, 30*(3), 310–316.

Ryan, B. (1992). *Feminism and the women's movement: Dynamics of change in social movement ideology and activism.* New York: Routledge.

Ryan, C. (1991). *Prime time activism: Media strategies for grassroots organizing.* Boston: South End.

Salcido, R. M. (1993, March). *A cross cultural approach for understanding Latino barrio needs: A macro practice model.* Paper presented at Council on Social Work Education meeting, New York.

Saleebey, D. (1990). Philosophical disputes in social work: Social justice denied. *Journal of Sociology and Social Welfare, 17*(2), 29–40.

Saleebey, D. (1994). Culture, theory, and narrative: The intersection of meanings in practice. *Social Work, 39*(4), 351–359.

Segal, S. P., Silverman, C., & Temkin, T. (1993). Empowerment and self-help agency practice for people with mental disabilities. *Social Work, 38*(6), 705–712.

Severson, M. M. (1994). Adapting social work values to the corrections environment. *Social Work, 39*(4), 451–456.

Shapiro, J. P. (1993). Believing in a friend: Advocating for community life. In A. N. Amado (Ed.), *Friendships and community connections with and without developmental disabilities* (pp. 181–196). Baltimore: Paul H. Brookes.

Sherman, W., & Wenocur, S. (1983). Empowering public welfare workers through mutual support. *Social Work, 28*(5), 375–379.

Simon, B. L. (1990). Rethinking empowerment. *Journal of Progressive Human Services, 1*(1), 27–39.

Simon, B. L. (1994). *The empowerment tradition in American social work: A history.* New York: Columbia University Press.

Simon, R. J., Altstein, H., & Melli, M. S. (1994). *The case for transracial adoption.* Washington, DC: American University Press.

Singer, J. (1992). *Almost heaven, West Virginia: Mobilizing a right to shelter for the homeless.* Unpublished dissertation proposal, University of Maryland at Baltimore, Baltimore, MD.

Singer, L. (1979, December). Nonjudicial dispute resolution mechanisms: The effects on justice for the poor. *Clearinghouse Review,* pp. 569–583.

SocWork. (1995). [Electronic mailing].

Solomon, B. B. (1976). *Black empowerment: Social work in oppressed communities.* New York: Columbia University Press.

Sosin, M., & Caulum, S. (1983). Advocacy: A conceptualization for social work practice. *Social Work, 28*(1), 12–17.

Specht, H. (1969). Disruptive tactics. *Social Work, 14*(2), 5–15.

Specht, H., & Courtney, M. E. (1994). *Unfaithful angels: How social work has abandoned its mission.* New York: Free Press.

Spector, M., & Kitsuse, J. I. (1987). *Constructing social problems.* New York: Aldine De Gruyter.

Spolar, C. (1991, April 19). Two who dared to take the stand: D.C. foster care workers told of crying children, broken promises. *The Washington Post,* p. A10.

Staub-Bernasconi, S. (1991). Social action, empowerment and social work: An integrative and theoretical framework for social work and social work with groups. *Social Work with Groups, 14*(3/4), 35–51.

Steiner, Claude M. (1974). *Scripts people live: Transactional analysis of life scripts.* New York: Bantam Books.

Thursz, D. (1971). The arsenal of social action strategies: Options for social workers. *Social Work, 16*(1), 27–34.

Toseland, R. W. (1990). *Group work with older adults.* New York: New York University Press.

Tower, K. D. (1994). Consumer-centered social work practice: Restoring client self-determination. *Social Work, 39*(2), 191–196.

Tropman, J. E., & Erlich, J. L. (1987). Introduction to Part three: Strategies. In F. M. Cox, J. L. Erlich, J. Rothman, & J. E. Tropman (Eds.), *Strategies of community organization: Macro practice* (4th ed., pp. 257–269). Itasca, IL: F. E. Peacock.

Van Soest, D. (1994). Strange bedfellows: A call for reordering national priorities from three social justice perspectives. *Social Work, 39*(6), 710–717.

Wagner, D. (1990). *The quest for a radical profession: Social service careers and political ideology.* Lanham, MD: University Press of America.

Wagner, D. (1991). Reviving the action research model: Combining case and cause with dislocated workers. *Social Work, 36*(6), 477–482.

Wakefield, J. C. (1988). Psychotherapy, distributive justice, and social work. Part 1: Distributive justice as a conceptual framework for social work. *Social Service Review, 62*(2), 187–210.

Wakefield, J. C. (1994, September). Debate with author of "Social Work and Social Control: A Reply to Austin." *Social Service Review, 68*(3), 48

Wallace, A. F. C. (1956, April) Revitalization movements. *American Anthropologist, 58,* 264–281.

Wallack, L., Dorfman, L., Jernigan, D., & Themba, M. (1993). *Media advocacy and public health.* Thousand Oaks, CA: Sage.

Walls, D. (1993). *The activist's almanac: The concerned citizen's guide to the leading advocacy organizations in America.* New York: Simon & Schuster.

Walz, T., & Groze, V. (1991). The mission of social work revisited: An agenda for the 1990's. *Social Work, 36*(6), 500–504.

Warren, R. L. (1977). Types of purposive social change at the community level. In R. M. Kramer & H. Specht (Eds.), *Readings in community organization practice* (pp. 134–149). Englewood Cliffs, NJ: Prentice-Hall.

Weisbrod, B. A., Handler, J. F., & Komesar, N. K. (1978). *Public interest law: An economic and institutional analysis.* Berkeley: University of California Press.

Williams, P. N. (1978). *Investigative reporting and editing.* Englewood Cliffs, NJ: Prentice-Hall.

Wood, G. G., & Middleman, R. R. (1989). *The structural approach to direct practice in social work.* New York: Columbia University Press.

Wood, G. G., & Middleman, R. R. (1991). Advocacy and social action: Key elements in the structural approach to direct practice in social work. *Social Work with Groups, 14*(3/4), 53–63.

chapter

13

Case Management as Community and Interorganizational Practice

Mrs. J, a 30-year-old white female, came to a Family Services Agency (FSA) seeking emergency help. She has been physically and emotionally abused by her husband, both now and in the past. Mrs. J dropped out of high school in her sophomore year when she became pregnant with her first child. She did not return to school or obtain a high school equivalency diploma. The child, John, is now 14 years old. Mr. J is not John's father, and this has caused discord in the family. John and Mr. J do not get along. Mr. J has repeatedly abused the boy, both physically and emotionally. John is habitually absent from school. He is a member of a loose gang of antisocial white youth who call themselves "skinheads." He often is out of Mrs. J's control.

Mrs. J's second child, Susan, age 10, is Mr. J's daughter. Mrs. J is worried that Susan is picking up "wild ways" similar to John's.

The family moved to the community about 6 months ago from another state. They moved so that Mr. J could find work. He obtained employment as an auto mechanic, his occupation, and has been working consistently since their move. He supports the family financially. John's father provides no financial support, nor does he have any contact with John.

Mrs. J does not work outside the home. She wants to find a job so that she and John will be less financially dependent on Mr. J. Her desire for a job is a source of friction between her and her husband. He believes that he should be the family's bread-winner and that Mrs. J is responsible for the children's upbringing. He tells her that she is not doing a good job raising the children and that they are both "going bad," so how does she expect to both work outside the home and bring up the children properly? She should, her husband believes, devote her energy to being a homemaker and supervising the children. He does, however, want John to get a job since John is not devoting his full attention to school.

Mrs. J has not worked outside the home for the decade of her marriage. Prior to her marriage, she worked for about 3 years as a waitress. Her mother babysat with John. Mrs. J met Mr. J at her job. She has had no other paid employment experience. She has no close friends or relatives in the new community and feels socially isolated.

Mrs. J came to the FSA on a referral from an emergency room doctor after she was apparently beaten by her husband. Mrs. J told the doctor that she fell. The doctor urged her to go to FSA in any case, as the indications were that the injuries were due to abuse. No police referral was made, as Mr. J was adamant in stating that it was not abuse.

Mrs. J, however, did tell the FSA intake social worker that she wanted to figure out a way to either end Mr. J's abusive behavior toward John and her or find a job and leave home with her children. John has told her that he will leave home if the abuse continues. For now Mrs. J feels at a loss to do anything, as she has neither close friends nor family in this community, a place to go, money of her own, or a source of income other than Mr J.

WHAT IS CASE MANAGEMENT?

Clients like Mrs. J are generally caught up in a web of social conditions that often require myriad resources and social supports, in addition to their own capacity and potential strengths, to assist them in improving their social condition and functioning. Unfortunately, while the community resources may exist, they usually are not systematically organized in ways conducive to easy access and use by clients. Individual clients like Mrs. J face a resource management challenge. Kast and Rosenzweig (cited in Wolk, Sullivan, & Hartmann, 1994, pp. 153–154) state that the purpose of management is to "convert the disorganized resources of men (i.e., people), machine, material, time, and space into a useful and effective enterprise. Essential resources are integrated into a total system for goal accomplishment." The client's tasks are similar to the manager's. The disparate and unsystematized resources of service agencies, community organizations and enterprises, and primary support groups, as well as the client's personal resources, need to be accessed, organized into a system, and managed to help the client achieve improved so-

cial functioning. Case management is a practice approach used to access, systematize, and manage the full range of potentially available resources for clients. Case management practice integrates and uses all the community and interorganizational skills presented in this book.

Case management, in its generic form, is a model of service integration that begins with a service request from a client and ends with feedback data for evaluation of client satisfaction and goals attainment. It is a consumer- or client-centered, client-level service coordination, goal-oriented approach to service integration (Chazdon, 1991). The primary case management functions are client assessment, planning, community resources assessment, networking, and negotiation with agencies for services to meet client needs, contracting, advocacy, brokerage, and marketing, monitoring, assisting the client in developing social networks and support systems, demonstrating and teaching, and evaluation. As such, case management entails *direct practice, community organization, and management skills* (Dinerman, 1992; Morrow-Howell, 1992; Rubin, 1987; Washington, Karman, & Friedlob, 1974; Wolk, Sullivan, & Hartmann, 1994).

Case management's direct service skills are client assessment, setting intervention objectives and contracting with the client, counseling and individual therapy, teaching and modeling skills to be used by the client, and evaluation with the client of goals and objectives attainment. These skills, hopefully, are common to all types of direct service practice.

The components that distinguish case management from many other direct service practice models are its management and community practice tasks. Case management is a goals-oriented approach to social intervention and emphasizes the logic of management by objectives. The fundamental management skills in case management are (1) planning; (2) organizing and managing the services system; (3) directing and controlling; (4) negotiation, brokerage; and contracting with other service providers; (5) reporting; and (6) evaluating the service system's effectiveness. The community practice skills include (1) community resources assessment; (2) networking with other service providers and with primary social supports to develop the client's social services and support system by negotiating, brokering, bargaining, and client advocacy with potential exchange partners and service providers; and (3) community resources development. The case management process starts with marketing's inside-out philosophy, beginning with assessment by discussing the client's conception and meaning of the problem and the goals. Assessment, a task involving both client and case manager, includes appraisal of the problem, the client's social condition, and the client's strengths and resources; establishing goals and objectives with the client; and determining the resources of the client and community relative to the goals and objectives (Bisman, 1994, pp. 111–176).

The crucial aspect of case management that distinguishes it from other direct ser-

vices modalities is its recognition of the social component and context of the client's condition and problems and the use of formal and informal community resources in the intervention. This is why management and community practice skills are necessary. The case manager and the client integrate the disparate array of services and social supports into a social system so that the client can achieve the objectives. Success or failure is not determined by the case manager's provision of services, or by the quantity or even the quality of the services, but by whether the services and supports obtained, organized, or developed achieve the goals and objectives.

THE RANGE OF CASE MANAGEMENT

The use of *case manager* as a concept and a job title is diverse. It ranges from a position title providing a minimal set of services, often including therapy, to providing a comprehensive array of services in which the case manager provides little direct intervention or few services, concentrating instead on system development and management tasks. Ross (1980) has divided the range of case management conceptions into three types: (1) the minimal model, (2) the coordination model, and (3) the comprehensive model. These models examine the range of services provided or arranged for by the case manager and the case manager's stress on management and community practice responsibilities. The three models, presented in Table 13.1, are conceptual modal points on the continuum rather than empirical illustrations of case management.

The minimal model is an assessment and referral service. It provides little management beyond case organizing, planning, and referral. Community practice skills relate to assessment of potential community re-

TABLE 13.1 Three Models of Case Management

Minimal Model	Coordination Model	Comprehensive Model
Outreach, client assessment Case organizing and planning Referrals to service providers	Outreach, client assessment Case organizing and planning Referral to service providers Client advocacy, brokering negotiation, contracting Direct casework Developing client support systems Reassessment evaluation	Outreach, client assessment Case organizing and planning Referral to service providers Client advocacy, brokering negotiation, contracting Direct casework Developing client support systems Reassessment evaluation Advocacy for resource development Monitoring quality Public education Crisis intervention Modeling and teaching

Source: Adapted from Ross (1980), p. 11. Similar tasks and distributions were found by Wright, Sklebar, and Heiman (1987).

sources needed by the client and interagency referrals of the client to appropriate vendors based on assessment of client needs and available community resources.

The coordination model goes beyond the outreach, assessment, and referral of the minimal model to include the use and development of a service system for the client when that system is nonexistent or inaccessible. This is reflected in the model's additional tasks of advocacy, brokering, and negotiating, as well as in the development of the client's primary, secondary, and tertiary social support systems.

The comprehensive model includes the client-centered tasks of the coordination model with the additional community practice tasks of advocacy and social activism for services and community development to translate the private troubles of individual clients into public concerns. The comprehensive model adds to casework and counseling the direct practice tasks of modeling and teaching to improve client self-efficacy and promote client empowerment (Pecukonis &

Wenocur, 1994). The intent of the case manager's modeling and teaching is to teach the knowledge and demonstrate the skills necessary for resource and support system development and management. If clients can develop and use their own social support systems, they will be able to manage their lives more effectively. They will be empowered.

Rubin (1987) does raise the concern that if social agencies focus exclusively on promoting the management and community practice components of case management—transferring resources from direct services, including therapy, to the case management's boundary-spanning and community practice functions—few services may be provided to link into the client-centered service system. This position, however, assumes that client services and resources will be provided primarily by agencies and professionals, and that the use of primary mutual supports must be secondary. Primary and mediating groups, support groups, and other social supports might be accessed and networked to reduce the client's dependence on formal agency services.

Situs is a major variable for the case manager's services. *Situs* refers to the location where the case manager works. Does the case manager manage exclusively from the office, using a telephone and fax, like a travel agent—assessing and counseling the client, arranging, advising, providing information and referral services—or does the case manager provide the services on the street, like a tour guide? Does the case manager negotiate and demonstrate to the client the community practice skills so that the client can model these skills? The distinction is critical given different conceptions of the client, the client's needs, and the client's capacity. Clients with little knowledge of or skill in the resource community or clients with underdeveloped support systems may need a tour guide more than a travel agent.

On trips to the former Soviet Union and China in the 1980s, one of the authors was struck with the need for tour guides more than for travel agents. Without language facility and knowledge of the local social terrain, an itinerary, no matter how well planned, or referrals to resources, no matter how clearly established, quickly become useless on the streets in a strange city with a different culture and language. Similarly, clients often are ignorant of the bureaucratic and professional language of service providers and of the social service terrain. Office-bound case managers can be equally ignorant of the client's social terrain and ecology. The relevance of the travel agent–tour guide analogy, hopefully, will be made clear with the application of the case management protocol below.

SOCIAL WORK CASE MANAGEMENT

Social work case management, as defined by the NASW Case Management Standards Work Group (1992), is

a method of providing services whereby a professional social worker assesses the needs of the client and the client's family, when appropriate, and arranges, coordinates, monitors, evaluates and advocates for a package of multiple services to meet the specific client's complex needs. (p. 5)

Social work case management may differ from other forms of case management provided by nonsocial workers in its emphasis on the individual's biopsychosocial status and the social systems in which the case manager and client operate. Social work intervention, while systemically and ecologically focused, is intervention and system management *for the individual client* rather than an abstract concept of system coordination. Social work case management is both micro and macro; intervention occurs at both the client and system levels (Case Management Standards Work Group, 1992, p. 5). This compels the case manager to be knowledgeable about the availability and requirements of community resources and services.

The social work case manager adheres to the profession's ethical code, as is required for all social work interventions, with its central tenets of primacy of client interests, self-determination, and confidentiality. The ethical standard of confidentiality mandates clarity of the contract with the client and the client's understanding, as well as informed consent on any limits to confidentiality and on the information to be shared in referral, brokering, advocacy, and service monitoring (Brennan & Kaplan, 1993, pp. 220–222).

Social work case management follows the social traditions of social work discussed in Chapter 1. It has its antecedents in prepsychotherapeutic social casework. Case management may help social casework rediscover its social mission and roots, albeit under a new label.

CASE MANAGEMENT PROTOCOL

Case management's tasks involve resource assessment, accumulation, development, and management to meet client goals and objectives. It is micro-system and community linking and building, developing a support system for the client and linking the client to the necessary resources and supporting and mediating community structures. Case management protocols draw on a range of theories: systems, networking, and exchange theories, among others (Morrow-Howell, 1992; Rothman, 1991).

1. Assess and Establish Goals and Objectives

The first step in the case management protocol is assessment and establishment of goals and objectives with the client. These are interdependent steps, as the viability of any goals and objectives will depend on the resources available and the strengths of the client. Assessment involves gathering information on the presenting problems and phenomena and organizing the information into a framework, a theory of the case, to understand the client's situation in order to develop a case plan. Assessment, developing the case theory, and setting objectives with the client organizes the information around the client's capacities and ecology to provide a plan for intervention (Bisman, 1994, pp. 111–121). In assessment, to clarify the client's perspective and preferences, the client should tell his or her own story, with the case manager indicating when the story is understood. Feedback should be given in the client's language. The intent is to clarify, not to challenge. Challenging should not occur until the relationship is established and belief bonding involving trust and help has occurred (Bisman, 1994, pp. 73–110; Lukus, 1993).

Assessment is a joint activity. There must be mutual understanding and agreement between case manager and client leading to shared construction of the new reality for the client reflected in the case plan. The case manager should give credence to the client's understanding of the situation and construction of reality. The client's construction should be believed until there is evidence to the contrary. As Cowger (1994) points out, there is no evidence to indicate that "people needing social work services tell untruths more than anyone else" (p. 265).

Mutual agreement on the assessment and the case plan is critical to the success of the plan. As the client's situation is both unique and complex, an overly reductionist view of cause and effect should be avoided. Since the causes of any problems lie in a range of phenomena, solutions will also probably require a range of resources appropriately coordinated and managed (Chazdon, 1991, p. x).

THE SMARRT FORMAT

Assessment is not done in a vacuum. The resources necessary to assist the client depend on the goals and objectives selected. Conversely, the resources available will expand or constrain the capacity to achieve the goals and objectives. Although the terms *goals* and *objectives* are often used interchangeably, *goals* will be used here as the broader, final objective of a case management plan. *Objectives* are events that, when completed, should lead to the next event and eventually to the goal. Subobjectives are the events that, when concluded, should lead to the next level of objective. Goals and objectives need to be set forth in a SMARRT format (adapted from *Administrative Systems for Church Management*, n.d.; Reddin, 1971).

The SMARRT format requires goals and objectives to be specified in an interrelated set of criteria that are Specific, Measurable, Acceptable, Realistic, Results Oriented, and Time Specific. The SMARRT case management plan guides the case manager and the client in resource assessment, development, coordination, and management. The goals are stated in behavioral and measurable language. At the conclusion of the assessment phase, the case manager and the client should have developed a SMARRT case management plan specifying goals, objectives, and responsibilities.

Before applying the SMARRT format to

CASE MANAGEMENT PLAN OBJECTIVE EVALUATION CHECKSHEET

Impact Objectives

The accomplishment of desired changes in the client's situation, behavior, and lifestyle together with the results of those changes. The behavior change sought is the behavior of the client and the client's ecology.

1. Specific: The goals and objectives, as well as the words and concepts used to describe them, should be precise—not vague or stated in generic language such as to "improve the condition of" unless operational meanings are given for "improve" and "condition." The specific goals and objectives need to be developed with and understandable to the client. The goals and objectives will be constrained by the mission and eligibility criteria of the case manager's agency.

2. Measurable: The goals and objectives must contain the operational and measurement criteria used to indicate their achievement. The plan needs to state how the goals and objectives will be measured. The client needs to understand both the goals and the measurements to be used. Measurement can but need not involve paper-and-pencil scales and quantitative approaches. Quantitative measurement is often reflexive and runs the risk of naive realism. *Reflexivity* occurs when the measurements used become the phenomenon of concern rather than indicating the phenomenon (Hammersley & Atkinson, 1983, pp. 14–15; Tyson, 1992). *Naive realism* is the belief held by objectivists that all people generally perceive and define the real world the same way with the same meaning, although their descriptions may differ (Spradley, 1980, p. 4).

3. Acceptable: The goals and objectives must be acceptable to the client and, ultimately, to other resource providers who will participate in the case management plan. The case manager needs to ensure that the plan, goals, and objectives have the client's informed consent.

4. Realistic: The goals and objectives should be achievable given the complexities of the case and the time frame, resources, and intervention methodologies available. However, they should not be trivial. To be considered realistic, the goals and objectives must be considered achievable by the case manager and the client. The potential costs and resources available, the client's readiness for change, and the skills of the case manager will guide the plan's realism.

5. Results Oriented: The final goals and each objectives are expressed as outcomes, events, and accomplishments by the client or the ecology in relation to the client rather than as a service event, a process, or even an output. The statement that a service will be provided does not meet this criterion. The criterion requires that the results of the service—what the service is to accomplish and how it will benefit the client—be specified. If skills training is provided, the results are not the provision of the training or the client's attendance, but the specified increase in the client's skills.

6. Time Specific: A specific time frame for accomplishing the goals and objectives should be given. The time limits are inherent in determining realism. The projected time needed to achieve the goals and objectives is based on the risks to the client of remaining in the situation and the power of the interventions and change efforts. Without a time limit, it is not possible to measure accomplishments or have accountability, as achievement can always occur in the indeterminate future. The client may remain in traumatic and socially dysfunctional situations indefinitely while ineffectual interventions are continued.

Mrs. J's case, an additional word on the danger of reflexivity in practice is needed. Essentially, measurement provides the information, data, and basis for judgments on whether the practice or intervention acts, client behaviors, or a goal have occurred. Measurement needs to capture the meaning, not just the data on a phenomena. Tyson (1992) illustrates the risk of reflexivity in her discussion of measurement and family therapy:

> when ... members of a family spent the beginning of their first session discussing the questionnaire they had filled out, which

asked them to count the frequency of their child's swearing.... [S]uch objective measures are not "unbiased" but produce data that are biased in a different way. For example, the pre-categorizing of client responses through measurement procedures is biased against the complexity that inheres naturally in the casework process.

> Even more important, practitioners recognize that such "objective" measures are in themselves interventions because they alter the nature of the casework relationship process ... [that] questionnaires are a more legitimate source of information than the client's self-determined self-description. (pp. 550–554)

Application of "SMARRT" Criteria to Mrs. J's Case

Mrs. J could have a series of related goals for her case: (1) the establishment and maintenance of a physically and emotionally safe home for herself and her family; (2) the ability to support herself and her children financially at a level approximating her current support so that she will not be dependent on her husband; and (3) for John and Susan to perform at grade level, graduate from high school, and not participate in antisocial activities.

Each of these goals can be stated in a SMARRT format that will begin to lay out a series of objectives, interventions, and behaviors by the case manager, Mrs. J, and the target and support systems to achieve the objectives. In establishing the objectives as well as the overall goals, the case manager and Mrs. J will need to assess the resources potentially available and the interventions needed to achieve each objective in sequence in order to reach the goals. If the resources and interventions are not available, the goals will have to be modified accordingly.

The first goal, to establish and maintain a physically and emotionally safe home, can be operationalized and evaluated by the SMARRT format:

1. Specific: The elimination of physically and emotionally traumatic behavior in interactions between family members is a specific goal. It is an outside-in approach focusing on the client's situation rather than a specific intervention or product offered by the case manager. "Physically and emotionally traumatic behavior" will have to be described in language meaningful to Mrs. J, her husband, and the children, with a shared understanding, if not acceptance, of its meaning. Interventions might range from a combination of family therapies to Mrs. J and the children leaving the home. However, the goals do not dictate the intervention. They act as a guide in selecting interventions most likely to achieve the goals.

2. **Measurable:** Physical and emotional trauma can be measured by the judgments of Mrs. J, the case manager, and the doctor. Care needs to be taken to avoid reflexivity. The phenomena of concern are the physically and emotionally abusive interactions experienced by the Mrs. J, John, Susan, and perhaps Mr. J. While realiability and validity in measurement are important, it is the truthfulness and meaning of the family's experiences to them that require judgment.

3. **Acceptable:** The case manger will need to determine if the absence of trauma is acceptable to Mrs. J, and if her determinations are within the legal conceptions of trauma. It will also need to be acceptable to the children. Mr. J will need to accept these determinations if he is to remain a part of the household.

4. **Realistic:** Mrs. J and the case manager must determine whether Mrs. J has the potential to establish and maintain an emotionally and physically safe home with Mr. J or to establish and maintain an alternative safe living arrangement. If Mrs. J and the case manager determine that neither of these options is achievable, this goal will need to be recast.

5. **Results oriented:** The goal is to make certain changes in Mrs. J's and Mr. J's behavior, lifestyle, and social interaction rather than the processes, treatments, and interventions used or the networks of services established. The interventions and networks are selected based on their potential to achieve the goals. The value of the agency's products and networks is determined by how well it achieves the goals. Their value does not rest on adherence to a model of the processes or techniques used.

6. **Time specific:** The case manager and Mrs. J will need to arrive at a time for the establishment of a safe home. This is based on their assessment of the potential resources, including Mrs. J's strengths and the power of the available intervention technologies. As Mrs. J is relatively new to the community, with few social supports and with low economic skills, the time target will be longer than if these supports were immediately available to her. Mrs. J and the case manager, based on their assessment, might establish a 2-year plan for this goal. The time frame can be modified, but a realistic target should be established to guide the intervention and provide a basis for reassessment. Without a time-specific goal, Mrs. J might remain in her abusive situation indefinitely while involved in the interventions.

The other two goals—for Mrs. J to support herself and her children financially at a level approximating her current support and for John and Susan to achieve grade-level school performance, graduate from high school, and not participate in antisocial activities—can also be SMARRT formatted.

The case manager's intervention plan probably will rest on the managers assumptions regarding the nature of the client and the client's problems, as well as the nature of the community and the service agencies.

The Nature of the Client

Biopsychomedical reductionist models of behavior. Theories of human behavior under this model generally hold that dysfunctional behavior results from biological and emotional pathology, whether due to genetic content or early socialization. Psychological theories such as psychoanalytic psychology fall within this category. Treatment involves altering the client's emotional content separately from the social context or helping the client adapt to the social context. Interventions applied to the intrapsychic content frequently are called *psychotherapies*.

Educational models. These models see problems in behavior, and in the management of social relations and the social environment, as learned behavior. If so, the behavior can be unlearned and appropriate behavior learned. Interventions address unlearning inappropriate behaviors and substituting appropriate ones.

Psychosocial models. Behavior and the client's management of the environment, these models hold, is a function of the individual's psychological content in interaction with the social world. Interventions involve altering the psychological content of the individual and/or the social context of the behavior to improvement environmental management.

Biopsychosocial models. Theories under this more complex model view behavior as a function of the client's biological and psychological content in a social context. As with the psychosocial model, intervention involves the context as well as the content. It can include providing education and improving management skills, as well as altering the client's environment. This model is the most comprehensive and adaptable model for case management.

Obviously this classification scheme, like the biopsychomedical reductionist models, suffers from extreme reductionism in that empirically the models rarely exist in pure form. However, the case manager's selection of a model of human behavior influences the development and use of the case management plan. The educational model requires, in addition to treatment-based social learning

theory, the demonstration of functional behaviors by the case manager. The middle models, with their strong social content and context, are more conducive to case management, and the contributions of case management are more evident. The biopsychomedical reductionist models make case management largely irrelevant. Intervention centers on the client's physiological and psychological problems. If case management is used, it is neither central nor necessary to the model's position on successful client treatment. It is a minimal model emphasizing therapy and referrals for treatment rather than social resources development and management. Treatment compliance, condition management, and the provision of services to compensate for client deficiencies are the major social interventions. The education models, including the operant models, are concerned with the social environment as it reinforces or fails to reinforce appropriate behavior and to extinguish unsuitable behavior.

The Department of Health and Human Services' Steering Committee on the Chronically Mental Ill (1980) provided an example of the application of the more complex biopsychosocial model in its conception of the chronically mental ill:

> persons who suffer certain mental or emotional disorders (organic brain syndrome, schizophrenia, recurrent depressive and manic depressive disorders, paranoid and other psychoses, plus other disorders that may become chronic) that erode or prevent the development of their functional capacity in relationship to (3 or more of) such primary aspects of daily life as personal hygiene and self care, self direction, interpersonal relationships, social transactions, learning, and recreation, and that erode or prevent the development of their economic self sufficiency. (p. 6-2)

The strength of this biopsychosocial conception is that, while recognizing the biological and psychological components of the condition and their relevance for treatment, it also specifies that chronic mental illness has social elements: poverty, substandard housing, reduced interpersonal and social skills, isolation, and alienation. The Steering Committee (1980) championed case management and defined it as "a process for assessing coordination of treatment, rehabilitation, and socially related service to a patient/client within a specific agency, or more broadly, within a community, health, or social service system" (p. 2).

If a biopsychomedical model is used by Mrs. J's case manager, social and community influences, constraints, and resources are less likely to be pursued.

The Conception of the Community, the Social Resources and the Task Environment

It is fashionable to speak of communities as systems composed of subsystems such as mental health systems, community support systems, social service systems, and so forth. Churchman (1965), similar to other system theorists (von Bertalanffy, 1967; Leighninger, 1978; Martin & O'Connor, 1989), defined a system as "a set of parts coordinated to accomplish a set of goals" (p. 29). The client's physical and social environment may be filled with a cornucopia of potential resources: social supports, service agencies, and others. Unfortunately, for an individual client, most of these systems are intellectual constructs or reifications of constructs rather than empirical entities.

The potential resources do not exist as a system for the client until they are coordinated to share and accomplish the client's goals. At best, the client faces a *set*—a group of agencies and resources that may have similar objective or potentially may serve a common cohort of clients, but whose interaction and shared intelligence in terms of a specific client are limited or absent. Each agency and resource provider has a limited interest in a specific client's life. An employment agency's concern is limited to employment and a landlord's concern to the client's ability to rent the space without damaging it. Each service vendor and resource provider can achieve its limited objective without a high degree of interaction, coordination, compatibility, or meeting the client's objectives. While the individual client may need a support system in this turbulent and complex environment, this is not crucial for the survival or functioning of any resource provider in the set. The task of the case manager and the client is to create and manage a support system from the set of sometime indifferent and often competing resources suppliers, or *units*.

For the system to be functional for clients, according to Martin and O'Connor (1989, pp. 36–38), the system needs wholeness, interdependence, and a focus on the shared purpose of the client. While these attributes need not be shared equally by all units, they need to be present. The system needs information on the actions and behaviors of the units germane to the client, as well as direction and management of the system and its units based on the desired outcomes. Halfon, Berkowitz, and Klee (1993, p. 394) concluded, after a study of case management in three northern California child welfare programs, that case management is needed in even the most user-friendly systems because of the complexity of the social environment, social agency sets, and social agencies.

Care should be taken not to reify the intellectual models representing the systems. The complexity of the client's situation, environment, communities, and potential resources and agencies requires careful management because complex phenomena tend to be counterintuitive and require information not yielded by simple models. Forrester

(1968) states that complex systems are counterintuitive in that "they give indications that suggest corrective action which will often be ineffective or even adverse in results" (p. 9).

An example of counterintuitiveness involves approaches to alter low student self-esteem. Some educators believe that low grades result in low self-esteem. Self-esteem can be enhanced if schools adopt a grading policy whereby no one fails. The results can be counterintuitive if students recognize that the grades are bogus, as they are not based on performance, and then conclude that the school views them as being unable to learn. The result may not be enhanced self-esteem but devaluation of their achievements and their grades even by students who have performed, possibly leading to further lowering of self-esteem.

Based on California research, self-esteem itself may not be a factor in many social and personal problems such as low academic skills, deviant behavior, crime, unemployment, and welfare dependency, as is often assumed. The research arm of the California Task Force on Self-Esteem and Personal and Social Responsibility (Mecca, Smelser, & Vasconcellos, 1989) concluded that "the associations between self-esteem and its expected consequences are mixed, insignificant, or absent. . . . [T]he association between self-esteem and behavior . . . is weak, [and] even less can be said of a causal relationship between the two" (pp. 15–17). The Task Force (*Toward a State of Esteem,* 1990) basically ignored the empirical findings in their own research report. Their belief that low self-esteem as the cause of personal problems and problematic behavior—child abuse and neglect, welfare dependency, sexual abuse, school failure, and so on—and a belief in improved self-esteem as a social panacea was unshakened by the counterintuitive evidence. The possibility that low self-esteem was a by-product rather than a cause of social ills was ignored, as it was contrary to their intuition.

Counterintuitiveness is more probable when case managers use an overly reductionist model of human behavior and discount the range of social variables affecting the client. The self-esteem advocates or other naive users of biopsychomedical reductionist models, who see these models as containing the primary explanatory and predictive variables, illustrate the counterintuitive nature of simplistic approaches to system model building. Both the client's and the system's behavior can be complex, with agencies and potential resources often having conflicting eligibility requirements, with stigma for the client associated with many services, and with the many other prices that clients pay for services.

The model used by the case manager to conceptual the behavior of Mrs. J and her family will guide the assessment and provide the basis for constructing the case theory. If the case manager uses a limited biopsychomedical or educational model, information gathering and assessment will focus on the family members and their interaction. Explanations of causation and projections of interventions and solutions will center on these same units. If more expansive models are used, the family members and their interactions will still be assessed, but the impact, limitations, and opportunities provided by the social environment will also be considered in developing the theory of the case and the case plan.

2. Determine Resources Needed to Achieve the Goals and Objectives

Once the goals and objectives have tentatively been established and formatted, the necessary resources must be be determined. The resources may be available within the client, in the case manager's agency, or in the client's social environment.

ASSESS THE PRIMARY RESOURCES OF THE CLIENT, THE CLIENT'S PRIMARY SUPPORT SYSTEM, AND THE CASE MANAGER RELATIVE TO THE RESOURCES REQUIRED TO ACHIEVE THE GOALS AND OBJECTIVES

The first potential source of resources, and the first with responsibility to help achieve the case plan's goals and objectives, are the client and the client's primary community. The sociologist and communitarian Amitai Etzioni (1993, p. 144) contends that "First, people have a moral responsibility to help themselves as best they can" (p. 144).

The obligation of all people, no matter how disadvantaged or handicapped, is to be responsible for themselves "as best they can" and to the maximum extent of their capacity. This is the fundamental basis of empowerment, self-efficacy and self-determination.

Etzioni continues: "The second line of responsibility lies with those closest to the person, including kin, friends, neighborhood, and other community members" (p. 144).

Self-responsibility comes first and is linked with autonomy, empowerment, self-efficacy, and self-determination. To not consider the client the primary source of strength and responsibility is to promote powerlessness and dependency. Primary group responsibility comes second. This is where reciprocity and interdependence, rather than dependence, are most balanced and the client becomes less vulnerable. Mutual support is best given and received under conditions of mutual obligation and responsibility. Community and network cohesion as well as primary group efficacy is enhanced, trust facilitated, and interdependence promoted with primary group reciprocity. The client and the case manager should seek, whenever possible, to strengthen primary structures and build or rebuild the primary network of supports. This network helps the client reintegrate into the community, reduce social and emotional isolation, and provide some protection from the stresses of larger social institutions. As the safety nets of the welfare state are eliminated or reduced, and as the social environment becomes more competitive and demanding, primary support systems become more vital to clients.

The client as the primary source of resources is captured by the current rhetoric of the strengths perspective in client assessment (Cowger, 1994; Saleeby, 1992). The *strengths perspective* is basically a reiteration of fundamental social work practice principles emphasizing client empowerment. The assessment considers the full range of potential strengths both within the client and in the client's primary systems and the community. As discussed in Chapter 10, primary and secondary social support networks and systems should be explored and developed prior to referral to tertiary systems. Primary and secondary social supports are more conducive to reciprocity and empowerment. These strengths and social supports are generally unique to each client, and the case management plan should be individualized accordingly. The client's primary system includes immediate family and other personal support networks that can be called on to assist the client in fulfilling the case plan. The case manager's resources include knowledge and skill, as well as the agency resources available.

The case manager should recognize and help Mrs. J recognize the strengths within her and her family. Mrs. J has recognized a problematic situation for herself and her family. She is seeking to change the situation. She wants to reduce her dependency on Mr. J. Although she has not worked outside the home for several years, she has worked. John does not want the abuse to continue. Mrs. J want to preserve the family, strengthen her relationship with Mr. J, and alter the nature of that relationship. All of these factors are strengths. Leaving Mr. J is the option of choice only if the abuse continues and the nature of the relationship is not changed. Even without a more thorough assessment of Mrs. J's current and potential intellectual and social capacity, it is clear that she has many strengths. By recognizing and acting on these strengths, Mrs. J will increase her sense of self-efficacy.

Mr. J's strengths should also be considered in developing the case theory. Although he has abused both Mrs. J and John, he has been a consistent provider and feels strongly about his responsibility as the breadwinner. Preliminary information provided by Mrs. J indicates that he does not want a family breakup. Like Mrs. J, he wants change, although they may disagree on the nature of the change.

ASSESS THE DIFFERENCES BETWEEN THE CLIENT, CASE MANAGER, AND AGENCY RESOURCES AVAILABLE AND THE RESOURCES REQUIRED TO ACHIEVE THE CASE PLAN'S GOALS AND OBJECTIVES

The resources are determined by the resource deficits and strengths of the client, resources of the case manager, and resources of the case manager's agency compared to those required to achieve the case plan. If the case manager and the client possess all the required resources, or if the client has case management skills, there is no need for additional resource development and networking by the case manager with other community resources. Resources deficits, on the other hand, determine what is required from the community and guides network construction. As discussed in Chapter 10, a pragmatic reason for using the client as the primary resource is that networking, system construction, and management and monitoring are time consuming and expensive. The client should share in the development and management of the networks and systems as much as possible.

If Mrs. J and her family have either the resources or the knowledge and skills to assess employment resources, to manage the socialization and education of John and Susan, to establish a social support system, and to manage Mrs. J's relations with Mr. J, there is little need for case management. However, it appears that supportive primary and agency services will be needed in addition to the family's resources.

---

3. Assess the Community, the Social Ecology, and the Task Environment to Locate Needed Resources and Their Exchange Requirements in Addition to Client and Case Manager Resources

Etzioni (1993) holds that the third imperative for support beyond the client and primary groups is the community. "As a rule every community ought to be expected to take care of its own. . . . Last but not least, *societies (which are nothing but communities of communities) must help those communities whose ability to help their members is severely limited*" (p. 146).

The need for community and societal responsibility does not absolve the client and the primary support systems. Also, community responsibility should be explored before state responsibility.

After the client and case manager have assessed the resources they and the primary groups possess relative to the case plan's goals and objectives, the additional resources must be located and their exchange requirements determined. The basic questions here are: (1) what resources are needed in addition to those possessed by the client and the client's primary groups, the case manager, and the case manager's agency? (2) where are the resources located? and (3) how can they be secured? The assessment, using community assessment, networking, and marketing methodologies discussed in preceding chapters, determines which agencies or community structures have the resources and uses market analysis to determine their social price.

The assessment, as indicated above, will be constrained and guided by the case manager's and client's selection of models, the client's problem, and the community's responsibility. If a biopsychomedical reductionist model is used, concerns about social supports (e.g., housing, employment, daily living tasks) become largely irrelevant. The community assessment for potential resources will be limited.

Even with biopsychosocial models, service providers, including social workers, are limited by their knowledge and skills in locating the task environment's resources and in systematizing and networking the environmental sets for the client. They need to know the range, location, and availability of potential services required by the client and how to induce the potential providers to engage in exchanges. Whether the case manager can reasonably act as a travel agent or a tour guide depends on the assessment of the client's strengths and capacities.

The case manager and Mrs. J will need to assess the community resources needed to achieve the case plan and their availability in the task environment. The resources will allow Mrs. J and her family to create a new social environment and community of interaction. The ability of Mrs. J to obtain the resources of agencies and organizations that provide family counseling, education, job training, and placement will be critical. Before intervening, the case manager should determine how legal aid and a possible safe haven can be established for Mrs. J and the children, if needed.

Primary social supports to integrate Mrs. J her into the community and reduce her social and emotional isolation need to be located or developed. Although Mrs. J is relatively new to the community, she shares social isolation and a lack of primary support networks with many clients. In addition, her children need tutorial assistance and alternative secondary social support groups to replace the gangs they are now using.

---

4. Evaluate the Case Plan's Goals and Objectives Relative to the Total Resources Available from the Client, the Client's Social Support Networks and Potential Networks, the Case Manager, and the Community

If the current and potential resources do not appear appropriate and adequate to meet the case plan's SMARRT goals and objectives, the goals and objectives will need to be modified. This, however, should be an incremental modification, not a wholesale discarding of the original goals and objectives. The client and case manager may wish to pursue the original goals and objectives with subsequent case plans, or the client may do so independently after the development of greater self-management skills.

Case managers should not assume that resources are unavailable simple because the case manager has no contacts with the domain (the holder) of the resources. The task, as discussed in Chapter 10, is to assess and establish the linkage between the client and case manager and the desired resources. The case manager knows the first link in the chain, the client and the case manager, and the final link, the resource holder. The remaining tasks are to assess and establish the network between the first and last links, and then to reduce the number of required links.

Under the comprehensive case management model, when resources are not available or potentially available, it is necessary to establish a perception of the need in the community and to develop the resources.

5. Negotiate Exchanges and Link the Client with the Resource Domains

After the domains and potential resource trading partners have been identified, located, and their preferences determined, the next task is to make the exchanges and obtain the resources for the client. This is the process of establishing and managing the client-centered system and network. This phase of the protocol entails marketing the client's or case manager's resources to the trading partners, brokering, negotiating, linking the client to social supports, and using the case manager's power (Dinerman, 1992; Hagen, 1994; Levine & Fleming, 1985).

Case managers need to understand and use power in their networking. Dinerman (1992, pp. 5–6) asserts that case managers potentially have the following sources of power:

1. The power to publicize;

2. Hierarchial power inherent in the case manager's control of case plan;

3. Legislative mandate if the case management model was established by a legislative action;

4. Power derived from the client as a potential resource to the trading partner in client resources such as voucher and third-party payment and the client's and/or case manager's capacity to help the trading partners achieve their goals. Both exchange and learning theory, discussed earlier, tell us that trading partners are more likely to engage in exchanges when their needs are met and the exchanges are perceived as fair.

5. Program coordination skills; and

6. Occasionally, the power to purchase services.

The case manager also should possess and use the power derived from expertise and skill in assessment, system development and management, negotiation.

Negotiation is advocacy. Although it does not necessarily involve conflict, it often involves managed conflict. Coser (1964) and others (Cox, 1980; Dahrendorf, 1959; Deutsch, 1973; Kriesberg, 1982; Oberschall, 1973) define *conflict* as involving a struggle over scarce resources or values. It is not always conflict that is problematic. Conflict may be part of any social change, including the reallocation of resources. The rules of conflict and conflict resolution may be problematic. If the struggle is viewed as a zero-sum game and pure conflict, with only one side winning, resolution tends to demand that one side dominate the other.

The case manager's negotiating and bargaining is designed to avoid zero-sum situations and to produce win-win results, if possible, by using the marketing strategies discussed in Chapter 11. *Bargaining*, as defined by Rubin and Brown (1975), is "the process whereby two or more parties attempt to settle what each shall give and take, or perform and receive, in transactions between them" (p. 2). Effective bargaining occurs when exchanges are fairly reached.

The structural and social psychological characteristics of bargaining are similar to the axioms of marketing (Rubin & Brown, 1975, pp. 6–18):

1. At least two parties are involved.
2. The parties have a conflict of interest with respect to one or more issues, means, ends, allocations of resources, effort, or responsibilities. The seller may ask more for the products than the buyer wishes to pay. They have a conflict, which is resolved by bargaining over the price.
3. The parties, at least temporarily, join together in a a bargaining relationship, regardless of any prior or future relationships.
4. The activities in this relationship concern (a) the division or exchange of one or more resources and/or (b) the resolution of one or more conflicts among the parties or among those whom the parties represent.
5. The activities usually involve the presentation of demands or proposals by one party and evaluation by the other party, followed by concessions and counter-proposals. The relationship consists of sequential offers and counteroffers rather than simultaneous behavior.

The presence of an audience (the client, publics, or other components of the support systems discussed in Chapter 1, including their psychological presence motivates the bargainers to seek positive evaluations and avoid negative ones, especially when the audience is influential to all the bargainers (Rubin & Brown, 1975, p. 44). This is the basis of accountability. Accountability should be built into the process as well as being an end result.

Advocacy, another essential case management practice skill, involves an assertive approach to help clients obtain resources. The case manager/advocate helps clients clear bureaucratic hurdles to obtaining services and resources. Advocacy has a number of intensity levels, according to Rothman (1991, p. 526), depending on the availability of resources and the resource holder's demands and resistance. Advocacy ranges from discussions of client needs through efforts to persuade, prod, and, lastly, coerce. "Typically . . . the levels of intensity are increased in a stepwise fashion as is necessary. Advocacy requires a sophisticated understanding of how organizations are structured and how they work, including an appreciation of organizational politics" (Rothman, 1991, p. 526). Coercion, it should be pointed out, can sometimes be used to get potential exchange partners to come to and remain at the bargaining table. This may be done by strikes, informational picketing, and other tactics.

The case manager/advocate, in keeping client goals and objectives central, must recognize and anticipate the potential for strains with other service providers. Mailick and Ashley (1981) state that power struggles in social and client advocacy may make collaboration with other social workers and agencies difficult. The choice of collaboration or advocacy to obtain resources depends on which is more appropriate in a particular situation. Advocacy calls for professional judgment regarding when to engage in it, and skill in using client advocacy without ending the collaborative relations with other network professionals.

Not only will the case manager need to negotiate for the needed resources, Mrs. J will need to be prepared to be a resource to the exchange partners. She can affect the quality of the services received by what she contributes to the resource provider. Mrs. J or other family members are the resources to the other units in the network if they help these units achieve their objectives. Mrs. J will need to demonstrate that she is indeed a resource and reciprocate appropriately. For example, for training agencies to be successful, they need trainable clients who can and will be employed. As Mrs. J learns what she can bring to the exchange, (how she reciprocates), her self-efficacy and sense of power should increase.

6. Monitor the Network and the Exchanges for Fairness

Networks as systems do not automatically maintain themselves (Churchman, 1965, p. 33). They require managing, monitoring and intelligence, and maintenance to ensure that the negotiated exchanges occur and that all parties in the exchange network fulfill the bargain. Without attention, the exchange network as a system will undergo entropy. *Entropy*, an enduring property of systems, according to systems theorists (Anderson & Carter, 1984, pp. 3–36; Hearn, 1969, p. 66; Martin & O'Connor, 1989, pp. 38–109), is the tendency of systems to deteriorate, becoming disorganized and random. Entropy in a client-centered system or network occurs when the network units, often including the client, no longer engage in the agreed-on resource exchanges necessary to achieve the goals and objectives.

Monitoring and evaluation by Mrs. J and the case manager will address not only the contributions of the service providers in the network but also Mrs. J's participation in the exchanges. In order for the exchanges to be fair, all the parties in the network have to uphold their part of the contract. Mrs. J will need to reciprocate appropriately.

7. Teach and Model the Networking Protocols to the Client So That the Client Can Construct and Manage the Social Support and Resource Networks, as Well as Locate and Access the Mediating Structures to Manage The Case for Client Empowerment

Client empowerment is both an ethical obligation and practice objective. A case management practice task is to teach and model the knowledge, skills, and behaviors so that clients can assess, develop, access, and manage their social support systems and mediating structures. Client empowerment is enhanced as their capacity to control their own lives is increased.

Social learning theory (Bandura, 1977; Bushell & Burgess, 1969; Kunkel, 1975; Minhauyard & Burgess, 1969; Thyer & Hudson, 1986–87) states that personal and environmental influences are bidirectional, interactional, and interdependent, and that over time they can become self-reinforcing, with less need for external stimuli and reinforcement. Involvement in developing and implementing the case plan allows the client to learn and the case manager to teach and model (Kunkel, 1975, pp. 51–76; Pecukonis & Wenocur, 1994; Weiser & Silver, 1981). As clients learn and use appropriate community practice skills—community assessment, bargaining, negotiation and self-advocacy, construction of client-centered networks and systems, systems management and monitoring—their sense of efficacy should increase

and their dependency on the case manager to implement the case plan should decrease.

Mrs. J is empowered when she recognizes what she has to exchange and when she learns how to access and negotiate with social and community resources. The resources can be job training, educational and social supports for her children, or financial support from the children's fathers. As Mrs. J's skills in assessment, bargaining, negotiation, advocacy, and management increase, the case management situs moves from tour guide to travel agent, with Mrs. J's dependency declining. Equally critical is Mrs. J's need to increase her knowledge and skills to access, negotiate, manage, and reciprocate with the range of social supports required in any healthy, functional life. The case manager should recognize that an integral part of case management is modeling and teaching these skills to Mrs. J.

EFFECTIVENESS OF CASE MANAGEMENT

The literature assessing the effectiveness and efficacy of case management generally presents a positive picture. Unfortunately, this literature is not methodologically rigorous. It often reviews the problems faced by clients, and their difficulties in handling these problems, and concludes that an often untested case management model of service integration should be effective and is critical to various service deliveries. The models generally are not fully operationalized or tested (Cheung, Stevenson, & Leung, 1991; Fiene & Taylor, 1991; Kanter, 1985, 1991; Korrs & Cloninger, 1981; Polinsky, Fred, & Ganz, 1991; Sonsel, Paradise, & Stroup, 1988; Wright, Sklebar, & Heiman, 1987).

The empirical studies are usually case studies of a single agency and a single model of case management. Case management is broadly defined as whatever was the intervention so labeled. Research on case management as the independent variable typically examines whether case managers conform to the model of choice. Clients' social functioning resulting from application of the case management model usually is not scrutinized.

Rapp and Chamberlain (1985), in a demonstration project using BSW and MSW

student case managers working with discharged mental patients with the student case managers supervised by Ph.D. students, did find support for case management effectiveness. The case managers, following the tour guide model, produced a high level of client satisfaction with the case management services: help with housing and employment (91%) and emotional support (74%). A majority of clients (91%) reported that they functioned better with the case manager's help than without it. The patients' principal therapists (84%) reported a high level of satisfaction with the case managers' assistance with social and environmental problems. None of the 19 patients were rehospitalized during a 6-month follow-up period, although 15 of them had had multiple hospitalizations in the past and all 19 were diagnosed as chronically mentally ill. The overall county hospitalization rates declined by 20% during the follow-up year compared to the preproject year.

While this study indicates some empirical support for case management effectiveness, cost factors were not considered. Student case managers had caseloads of about four clients and received intensive supervision. Nor were alternative explanations for changes in the dependent variables ruled out.

Zimmerman (1987) reported similar results in a Mississippi study of professional MSW case management, using a model similar to the coordination model, with recipients. Clients reported higher satisfaction with the quality of case management service compared to pre-case management service; favorable ratings were as follows: accessibility, 76%; empathy, 86%; caring, 78%; and friendliness, 73%. Clients generally favored the case management approach over the pre-case management approach. The longitudinal study lacked a control group and was limited to client satisfaction.

Washington and his colleagues (Washington, 1974; Washington, Karman, & Friedlob, 1974) concluded, as a result of their seminal case management social research and development work, that the model of case management used can produce outcomes beyond increased client satisfaction. The model of choice resembled the coordination model. Effectiveness was related to the case manager's ability to induce vendors to provide services. While success was based on the manager's assessment, negotiation, and brokerage skills, it was also associated with the availability of funds to purchase needed services ("hard clout"). As governments and private financial sources cut back on spending, hard clout will continue to be reduced.

Halfon and his colleagues (1993), in a descriptive comparison of case management in three children's programs, concluded that effective case management is "need driven" and links the child, family, and service array. The major case management tasks involved brokerage and coordination. Time allocations to tasks varied by program, and different client needs were clustered by program, with the determinations made at intake. The authors accepted these intake decisions as valid measures of the differences.

An empirical single-panel design with no comparison group was developed by Rife, First, Greenlee, Miller, and Feichter (1991) for the homeless mentally ill in a comprehensive case management project served by no other mental health therapy providers. The authors found that the strongest predictor of ongoing client engagement in case management was the frequency of contact. The more frequent the contact, the less likely the client was to return to a homeless condition. Keeping in touch and direct social support by the case manager were critical to preventing homelessness. Clients receiving case management services and placed in housing for at least 6 months showed a significant increase in their quality of life and residential stability, but not necessarily in social relationships or employment opportunities. Client dropout from the programs was significantly related to staff turnover. The shelters and case managers, as primary social supports, may have isolated the clients socially. Measurements consisted of client reports.

Rothman (1991) and his colleagues at the Research and Development Program, Center for Child and Family Policy, UCLA, developed an empirically based and grounded, dynamic, flexible case management model. The model is prescriptive and normative as well as descriptive, but it is still tentative pending adequate field testing. Some of their more pertinent observations of effective case management were as follows:

> Counseling typically is not highly intrapsychic—as is traditional therapy—and involves problem solving, reality testing, socialization skills, and practical help in such areas as housing, money matters, parenting, and employment. It includes consultation offered to family members, agency representatives. . . . In the research, effective counseling approaches included such things as teaching basic living skills, using role playing, and modeling desirable behavior. (p. 525)

The researchers also found that short-term therapy had more value than long-term therapy.

Rubin (1992), a longtime observer of case management, reviewed the effectiveness of eight empirical research studies of case management with mixed findings. All the studies had a small number of case managers, methodological weaknesses, and conceptual and measurement problems for both the independent variable (case management) and the outcome variables. Three studies reported no or little difference for case management; four studies indicated mixed results, with some indicators positive and no gains on others; and one study reported positive gains on all indicators. Case management was not effective in overcoming the limitations of a resource-starved task environment.

SUMMARY: A CASE MANAGEMENT MODEL

Case management as community practice rests on several assumptions regarding the client and the community:

1. The client often is beset by a range of living and environmental management problems.
2. The client's problems occur in the social environment, not in the service center, social agency, or therapist's office. The community is the context of the client's behavior, providing both opportunities and limits.
3. The client's behavior and problems are not biopsychological alone.
4. Regardless of the model used, the clients' problems are real and need to be addressed if the client is to function more effectively and obtain greater control over his or her life.

5. While clients vary in their capacity to manage their social context, all clients have some strengths that should be used.

If the client and community propositions are valid, a reasonable case management model is as follows:

1. Case management's *objectives* are to improve the client's social context and assist the client in managing the social context to improve social functioning.
   a. These objectives are defined in behavioral and measurable terms in a SMARRT format.
   b. Case management's objectives (the dependent variable) are improved client behavior and social functioning. The independent and intervening variables are the client's social environment, including the case manager, and the service delivery system.

2. Case management's strength lies in its emphasis on specified objectives, stated in behavioral and measurable terms, with clear objectives agreed to by the client, case manager, and other resource providers in the service delivery set and social support networks. A fundamental goal of case management is to integrate clients into a supportive social environment.

3. Case management's strength is also its flexibility, which allows the case manager and client to use an array of possible services to achieve objectives and goals rather than to be limited to the case manager's agency services or limited contract services. Flexibility allows the development of client-centered systems and networks.

4. Case management's service protocol flow requires the case manager to understand the client's goals and perceptions of reality and the community or social context.

It also depends on the ability to help the client perceive and define goals in realistic and objective terms within a given social context. The case manager and the client must specify attainable objectives within the contemporary state of the art and technology of case management and the resources available.

5. The case manager's use of the travel agent or tour guide approach to managing services for the client depends on the client's capacity, knowledge, and skill in functioning within the social context. The case management model used with a specific client should be based on that client's strengths, needs, and objectives, not on the situs agency's service array. If the case management process begins with the tour guide approach, it should move toward the travel agent approach as the case manager models and teaches and as the client learns the skills to manage the case.

6. Case managers, therefore, will need knowledge and skill in client assessment; community and organizational behavior; the client's social context and potential resources; negotiating, bargaining, contracting, and advocacy skills; and the capacity to model and teach the client these skills and behaviors.

7. The case manager needs the authority to develop and manage the service package. Therapy is not a case management function, although, occasionally it may be a required service. If so, therapy should be treated as part of the service array, to be used like other services to achieve objectives. It should be used under the same constraints as other services, whether provided by the situs agency or the case manager. The case manager needs hard clout and the authority and responsibility to develop and manage the case plan with the client.

8. Case management should be evaluated by the achievement of SMARRT objectives based on improved client functioning, satisfaction, and the client's capacity to manager his or her own case. Self-management is the essence of empowerment.

References

Administrative systems for church management. (n.d.). Colorado Springs, CO: Systemation, Inc.

Anderson, R. E., & Carter, I. (1984). Human behavior in the social environment: A social systems approach (3rd ed.). New York: Aldine.

Ballew, J. R., & Mink, G. (1986). Case management in human services. Springfield, IL: Charles C. Thomas.

Bandura, A. (1977). Social learning theory. Englewood Cliffs, NJ: Prentice-Hall.

Bertalanffy, L., von. (1967). Robots, men and mind. New York: Braziller.

Bisman, C. (1994). Social work practice: Cases and principles. Pacific Grove, CA: Brooks/Cole.

Brennan, J. P., & Kaplan, C. (1993). Setting standards for social work case management. Hospital and Community Psychiatry, 44, 219 –222.

Bushell, D., Jr., & Burgess, R. (Eds.). (1969). Behavioral sociology: The experimental analysis of social process. New York: Columbia University Press.

California Task Force to Promote Self-Esteem and Social Responsibility. (1990). Toward a state of esteem: The final report of the California Task Force to Promote Self-Esteem. Sacramento: Bureau of Publications, California State Department of Education.

Case Management Standards Work Group. (1992). NASW standards for social work case manage-

ment. Washington, DC: National Association of Social Workers.

Chazdon, S. (1991). *Responding to human needs: Community-based social services*. Denver, CO: National Conference of State Legislatures.

Cheung, K-F. M., Stevenson, K. M., & Leung, P. (1991). Competency-based evaluation of case management skills in child sexual abuse intervention. *Child Welfare, 70*, 425–435.

Churchman, C. W. (1965). *The systems approach*. New York: Dell.

Compher, J. V. (1987). The dance beyond the family system. *Social Work, 32*, 105–108.

Coser, L. A. (1964). *The functions of social conflict*. New York: Free Press.

Cowger, C. D. (1994). Assessing client strengths: Clinical assessment for client empowerment. *Social Work, 39*, 262–268.

Cox, A. J. (1980). Social conflict theory and community organization practice. *Journal of Humanics, 8*, 26–40.

Dahrendorf, R. (1959). *Class and class conflict in industrial society*. Stanford, CA: Stanford University Press.

Department of Health and Human Services Steering Committee on the Chronically Mentally Ill (1980). *Toward a national plan for the chronically mentally ill: Report to the secretary*. Washington, DC: U.S. Government Printing Office.

Deutsch, M. (1973). *The resolution of conflict: Constructive and destructive processes*. New Haven, CT: Yale University Press.

Dinerman, M. (1992). Managing the mazes: Case management and service delivery. *Administration in Social Work, 16*, 1–9.

Etzioni, A. (1993). *The spirit of community: Rights, responsibilities and the communitarian agenda*, New York: Crown.

Fiene, J. I., & Taylor, P. A. (1991). Serving rural families of developmentally disabled children: A case management model. *Social Work, 36*, 323–327.

Forrester, J. W. (1969). *Urban dynamics*. Cambridge, MA: MIT Press.

Hagen, J. L. (1994). JOBS and case management: Developments in 10 states. *Social Work, 39*, 197–205.

Halfon, N., Berkowitz, G., & Klee, L. (1993). Development of an integrated case management program for vulnerable children. *Child Welfare, 72*, 379–395.

Hammersley, M., & Atkinson, P. (1983), *Ethnography: Principles in practice*. New York: Tavistock.

Hearn, G. (Ed.). (1969). *The general systems approach: Contributions toward an holistic conception of social work*. New York: Council on Social Work Education.

Johnson, P. J., & Rubin, A. (1983). Case management in mental health: A social work domain. *Social Work, 28*, 49–55.

Kantor, J. S. (1985). Case management of the young adult chronic patient: A clinical perspective. *New Directions for Mental Health Service, 27*, 77–92.

Kantor, J. S. (1991). Integrating case management and psychiatric hospitalization. *Health and Social Work, 16*, 34–42.

Kerson, T. S. (1991). Progress notes: Contra Costa County AIDS case management program. *Health and Social Work, 16*, 142–143.

Korrs, W. S., & Cloninger, L. (1981). Assessing models of case management: An empirical approach. *Journal of Social Service Research, 14*, 129–146.

Kriesberg, L. (1982). *Social conflict* (2nd ed.). Englewood Cliffs, NJ: Prentice-Hall.

Kunkel, J. H. (1975). *Behavior, social problems, and change: A social learning approach*. Englewood Cliffs, NJ: Prentice-Hall.

Lamb, R. H. (1980). Therapist-case managers: More than brokers of services. *Hospitals and Community Psychiatry, 31*, 762–764.

Lanoil, J. (1980). The chronic mentally ill in the community: Case management models. *Psychosocial Rehabilitation Journal, 4*, 1–6.

Leighninger, R. B., Jr. (1978). Systems theory. *Journal of Sociology and Social Welfare, 5*, 446–466.

Levine, I. S., & Fleming, M. (1985). *Human resources development: Issues in case management*. Baltimore: Center for Rehabilitation and Manpower Services, Community Support Project, Maryland Mental Health Administration.

Lukus, S. (1993), *When to start and what to ask: An assessment handbook*. New York: W. W. Norton.

Mailick, M. D., & Ashley, A. A. (1981). Politics of interpersonal collaboration: Challenge to advocacy. *Social Casework, 62*, 131–137

Marlowe, H. A., Marlowe, J. L., & Willetts, R. (1983). The mental health counselor as case manager: Implications for working with the chronically mentally ill. *Journal of American Mental Health Counselors Association, 5*, 184–191.

Martin, P. Y., & O'Connor, G. G. (1989). *The social environment: Open systems application*. New York: Longman.

McFarland, B. H. & Beavers, D. J. (1984). Preventive strategies and program evaluation methods for chronically mentally ill/suicide attempters. *Comprehensive Psychiatry, 25,* 426–437.

Mecca, A. A., Smelser, N. J., & Vasconcellos, J. (Eds.). (1989). *The social importance of self-esteem.* Berkeley: University of California Press.

Minhauyard, D. E., & Burgess, R. L. (1969). The effects of different reinforcements contingencies in the development of social cooperation. In D. Bushnell, Jr., & R. L. Burgess (Eds.), *Behavioral sociology: The experimental analysis of social process* (pp. 81–108). New York: Columbia University Press.

Morrow-Howell, N. (1992). Clinical case management: The hallmark of gerontological social work. *Journal of Gerontological Social Work, 18,* 119–131.

Oberschall, A. (1973). *Social conflict and social movements.* Englewood Cliffs, NJ: Prentice-Hall.

Pecukonis, E. V., & Wenocur, S. (1994). Perceptions of self and collective efficacy in community organization theory and practice, *Journal of Community Practice, 1,* 5–21.

Polinsky, M. L., Fred, C., & Ganz, P. A. (1991). Quantitative and qualitative assessment of a case management program for cancer patients. *Health and Social Work, 16,* 176–183.

Rapp, C. A., & Chamberlain, R. (1985). Case management services for the chronically mentally ill. *Social Work, 30,* 417–422.

Reddin, B. A. (1971). *Effective management by objectives: The 3–d method of mbo.* New York: McGraw-Hill.

Richmond, M. E. (1917). *Social diagnosis.* New York: Russell Sage Foundation.

Richmond, M. E. (1922). *What is social casework? An introductory description.* New York: Russell Sage Foundation.

Rife, J. C., First, R. J., Greenlee, R. W., Miller, L. D., & Feichter, M. A. (1991). Case management with homeless mentally ill people. *Health and Social Work, 16,* 58–66.

Roberts-DeGennaro, M. (1987). Developing case management as a practice model. *Social Casework, 68,* 466–470.

Ross, H. (1980). *Proceedings of the conference on the evaluation of case management.* Los Angeles: Volunteer for Services to Older Persons.

Rothman, J. (1991). A model for case management: Toward empirically based practice. *Social Work, 36,* 520–528.

Rubin, A. (1984). Community based care of the mentally ill: A research review. *Health and Social Work, 9,* 165–177.

Rubin, A. (1987). Case management. In A. Minahan (Ed.), *Encyclopedia of Social Work,* Vol. I (18th. ed., pp. 212–222). Silver Spring, MD: National Association of Social Workers.

Rubin, A. (1992). Is case management effective for people with serious mental illness? A research review. *Health and Social Work, 17,* 138–150.

Rubin, J. Z., & Brown, B. R. (1975). *The social psychology of bargaining and negotiation.* New York: Academic Press.

Saleebey, D. (Ed). (1992). *The strength perspective in social work practice: Power in the people.* White Plains, NY: Longman.

Sanborn, C. J. (1983). *Case management in mental health services.* New York: Haworth Press.

Schwartz, S. R., Goldman, H. H., & Churgin, S. (1982). Case management for the chronically mentally ill. *Hospitals and Community Psychiatry, 33,* 1006–1009.

Social case work: Generic and specific, a report of the Milford Conference. (1929). New York: American Association of Social Workers.

Sonsel, G. E., Paradise, F., & Stroup, S. (1988). Case management practice in an AIDS service organization. *Social Casework, 69,* 388–397.

Specht, H., &, Courtney, M. (1994). *Unfaithful angels: How social work has abandoned its mission.* New York: Free Press.

Spradley, J. P. (1980), *Participant observation.* New York: Harcourt Brace Jovanovich.

Sullivan, J. P. (1981). Case management. In J. A. Talbott (Ed.), *The chronically mentally ill* (pp. 119–131). New York: Human Sciences Press.

Thyer, B. A., & Hudson, W. W. (1986–87). Progress in behavioral social work: An introduction. *Journal of Social Service Research, 10,* 1–6.

Tyson, K. B. (1992). A new approach to relevant scientific research for practitioners: The heuristic paradigm. *Social Work, 37,* 543–556.

Walden, T., Hamer, K., & Kurland, C. H. (1990). Case management: Planning and coordination strategies. *Administration in Social Work, 14,* 61–72.

Washington, R. O. (Ed.). (1974). *A strategy for service integration: Case management.* East Cleveland, OH: East Cleveland Community Human Service Center.

Washington, R. O., Karman, M., & Friedlob, F. (1974). *Second year evaluation: Report of the East Cleveland Community Human Service*

Center. Cleveland: Human Services Design Laboratory: School of Applied Social Sciences, Case Western Reserve University.

Weiser, S., & Silver, M. (1981). Community work and social learning theory. *Social Work, 26,* 146–150.

Wolk, J. L., Sullivan, W. P., & Hartmann, D. J. (1994). The managerial nature of case management. *Social Work, 39,* 154–159.

Wright, R. G., Sklebar, H. T., & Heiman, J. (1987). Patterns of case management activity in an intensive community support program: The first year. *Community Mental Health Journal, 23,* 53–59.

Zimmerman, J. H. (1987). Negotiating the system: Clients make a case for case management. *Public Welfare, 45,* 23–27.

chapter

14

"Being There" in Our Practice

Social workers have often relegated thinking about the community dimensions of practice to those who specialize in community organization or community work. Yet, community variables affect all fields of social work: case management, gerontology, child welfare, advocacy, and psychotherapy.

E. E. MARTINEZ-BRAWLEY (1990, P. 213)

[The specialist] is often in the position of a [person] desperately trying to replace a fuse when it is the entire community power line that has broken down.

E. H. AUERSWALD (1968, P. 207)

UNIFYING THEMES

The underlying assumption of this book is that the skills and concepts typically used by community organizers, planners, and administrators are also extremely important for direct service practitioners. Increased allegiance to community will affect our thinking, our values, our behavior, and our scope and

method of social work practice. This sentiment is repeatedly expressed in a number of *themes*, which are summarized here.

1. *All people have the capacity to improve.*

Citizens, service users, and social workers can grow, change, and build on their existing strengths. People change because they

414

want to (e.g., obtaining training) and have to (e.g., due to divorce or paralysis), and because opportunities are available. Our work is predicated on the belief that individuals and groups are responsive, amenable, and can be influenced positively. (The converse is also true, of course. People can choose not to change and can be influenced negatively.) Social workers have many basic skills in communication and interpersonal dynamics that can be used as a springboard to new capabilities for macro-practice. By developing and refining these skills, we can begin to help our clients develop some of the knowledge and skills that they need "to obtain and utilize resources to achieve individual or collective goals" (Solomon, 1976, p. 28). In effect, social workers become a resource in an environment that all too often blocks opportunities for various segments of the population, such as racial minority groups. And, in this way, we take a small step toward reducing powerlessness, both our own and our clients'.

2. *Individual lives are entwined with the social environment.*

Social context and the larger society affect every being and each relationship. We are members, not separate entities (Falck, 1988). In the ecological view, human behavior is psychosocial and entails interactions, exchanges, and engagement with the environment. Consequently, the people-in-environment (P-I-E) concept obliges social workers to help people manage their social situations and to utilize resources in their environments. Client empowerment, in part, involves generating the capacity to acquire social management skills. Equally significant, the meaning of our lives comes from both the larger and the immediate environments. There is an "umbrella civilization in our nation with different cultures embedded beneath" that creates a meeting of our minds

(think of television), and there is an immediate social environment surrounding every individual that creates a "certain way of thinking about the world" (Potok, 1983). With clients, then, social workers must be tuned in to environmental influences as well as to individual uniqueness.

3. *Social networks and organizational infrastructure affect professional practice·*

Social workers do their work through structures, processes, clusters, and paths established by institutions, others in the human service field, and informal helpers. Thus, organizational and personal linkages must be taken into consideration. There are not only customs, regulations, and standards governing our conduct that flow from this infrastructure. The rules of the service delivery system, or "game" (Cohen, 1980), are also influenced by community norms, traditions, and resources, as well as by national factors. Those who would change the rules often must become "organizational reformers" (Weissman, Epstein, & Savage, 1983).

4. *Strengthening community can solve individual and community problems.*

The more social workers can build community capacity, the more groups and families can obtain needed resources and supports and the more societal problems will be addressed. There is nothing mystical about the goal or endeavor of strengthening community. Social workers need to take planned, collaborative, and concrete steps, just as they would with individuals and families.

5. *Community is cardinal in current views of personhood and nationhood.*

Collective endeavors such as political reform, economic development, and charitable campaigns are held together and defined by their community aspect. At the present time, the idea of community is central to many different theories, practice principles, and political doctrines. For some factions, the mainstream community is of central importance because, it is argued, some larger community needs have been neglected in the process of aiding communities with particular needs. Yet, the needs of vulnerable populations, including the need for strong communities, have not disappeared. However, today this popular ideological commitment is not matched by the programmatic commitment to neighborhoods—suburban or inner city— that was evident in the 1960s.

6. *Knowledge of the larger world is empowering.*

The complexity of modern society sometimes seems overwhelming. Sometimes the only constant in our lives seems to be rapid change. It's hard to keep up. Learning how to deal with change is empowering. This means learning "pressure points" and how to access the information we need to achieve our goals and influence the decisions that affect our lives. It means putting information to effective use, and this, in turn, means connecting with people and organizations in ever-widening circles. The goal may be to build community or connect clients to others with similar concerns, problems, or dreams.

7. *Collective, as well as individual activity is of value.*

Collective action is of value because it is often more effective politically. It builds relationships, which is necessary to a caring community, and its benefits flow not only to the active but to others around them. Communitarians and progressives argue that our individualistic American society benefits from cooperative and communal endeavors, especially those linking groups that are often separate and apart from each other.

8. *At every system level, there are myriad ways to exert influence.*

Many avenues can lead to change. Since problems are not monoliths and can be approached from many angles, social workers have ample opportunities to produce an effect. Leadership in the social service and social welfare field is imperative. For good or ill, influence spreads through a web of relationships. Once learned, change strategies can be passed on to others. One purpose of social work advocacy is to channel energy and direction within systems of all sizes.

THE IMPORTANCE OF COMMUNITY PRACTICE SKILLS FOR DIRECT SERVICE PRACTITIONERS

Many social workers regularly deal with P-I-E problems that require a mix of micro and macro skills. These social workers may be working in school systems, medical settings, family agencies, protective services, public health settings, community centers, community rehabilitation settings, residential treatment settings, and more. Although these settings often require specialized knowledge related to a particular age group, such as the elderly, or to a social problem area, such as child welfare or homelessness, or even to an institutional structure and culture such as a school system or a hospital, methods of intervention that social workers use draw on a mix of micro and macro skills. We think of these social workers as "method generalists." In the words of Rothman, Erlich, and Tropman (1995):

> The interrelationship of individualized (micro) and community (macro) practice is

best reflected in the generalist practice school, also identified by the terms integrated, unitary, generic, holistic, and multirole practice. All of these convey the notion of using both micro and macro practice together in ways that are mutually supplementing and reinforcing. The practitioner starts with a broad assessment of the problem and develops an intervention approach that draws on the full range of practice options, often employing combinations of practice initiatives as appropriate. (p. 21)

The recent growth of a variety of community-based or community-centered models of social work practice speaks to this generalist perspective (Adams & Krauth, 1995; Dore, 1993; Hodges & Blythe, 1992; Indyk, Belville, Lachapelle, Gordon, & Dewart, 1993; Tracy, Whittaker, Pugh, Kapp, et al., 1994). Family support programs, for example, may be neighborhood based or community connected (Lightburn & Kemp, 1994). Many of these models have been developed in the context of family preservation programs, where social workers provide intensive assistance in the home to families at risk of having a child removed by the courts due to abuse or neglect. These approaches often involve the provision of support and nurturing to needy parents or the provision of concrete services, such as obtaining a new bed for a child who has none, as well as teaching child management skills. Other approaches have aimed more broadly at strengthening families and neighborhoods, such as with the patch program that originated in England. The patch approach deploys teams of human service workers to neighborhood-sized geographic catchment areas or "patches," where they "support(s) and build(s) on the resources of informal networks of kin and neighbors" and join with other local organizations and institutions "to solve both individual and community problems" (Adams & Krauth, 1995, p. 89; Adams & Nelson, 1995).

Built on earlier ideas of social work practice in settlement houses and charity organization societies (Brieland, 1990; Hancock & Pelton, 1989; Richmond, 1917; Wasik, Bryant, & Lyons, 1990), community-based models seem applicable to a great variety of practice settings. Some of the main features of these models are as follows:

1. Services are provided in the client's natural environs—home, neighborhood—in a sense, truly starting where the client is.

2. The stance of the worker entails a balanced power relationship and reciprocal learning. The worker has knowledge and skills to share with clients, but at the same time, the clients have much to teach the worker about life and culture in their environment, and more. The aim is to develop a true working partnership in which clients become more efficacious.

3. Concern for fostering client empowerment is customary. Attention is paid to the inequities of the systems that affect the client, and skill in negotiating and influencing these systems is a goal (Cowger, 1994; Gutierrez, 1990; Simon, 1994).

4. This requires that workers operate from a strengths perspective, that is, from an assessment of client and community strengths that can be engaged and further developed, rather than from the perspective of problems and dysfunctions that require remediation (Chapin, 1995; DeJong & Miller, 1995; Saleebey, 1992).

5. Workers are therefore engaged in constructing and activating a variety of helping networks that will promote personal and social development. Workers typically see themselves as collaborators with other helpers rather than as solo practitioners.

Community-based practice, to the extent that it includes the features mentioned above, draws on the skills and knowledge that we have tried to identify in this book. Social workers need to be able to go out into communities where clients live and work in order to provide services effectively. They also need to understand how community comes into play emotionally, in the hearts and minds of their clients, as well as practically in the opportunities and blocks it may present. This means developing skills in entering communities safely and unobtrusively, and with sensitivity to culture.

In terms of assessment, community-based practice requires the understanding and use of information and observations obtained in the surroundings and context most familiar to the client. It also means tuning in to the systemic aspects of problems beyond the individual and family, hence community and organizational analyses. In terms of relationship building, it means reaching out and starting where the client is, and its success depends heavily on good listening, observational, and communication skills.

Helping interventions require the ability to discover and establish a variety of helping networks, as well as the capacity to communicate and collaborate with community leaders, public and nonprofit human service workers, church and school officials, and many other potential helpers. Workers will often have to organize and chair meetings of various kinds—teams, planning groups, action groups. As attention is paid to client empowerment and systemic problems, workers will need to model assertiveness and advocacy and impart those skills to clients. A more complete range of helping interventions could require social problem assessments, needs assessments, and assessments of the structures and dynamics of power that impact on clients' lives. Workers will need planning, organizing, marketing, and management skills.

A WORD ABOUT COMMUNITY PRACTICE AND SOCIAL WORK CAREERS

Although *community* is important in all social work practice in terms of context, sanction, funding and other support, and purpose, a given practitioner's involvement in *community practice* may be continual, intermittent, or supplemental. Community organizers and developers, and various advocates, have a continual involvement with their communities and larger political systems. Generalists and many direct service practitioners integrate knowledge of community and work in the community into their practice with individuals, groups, families, and service networks. Clinicians and those in private practice must still understand the communities that clients carry with them in their heads (thinking, values, culture, behavior) into the counseling relationship.

While this textbook emphasizes the integration of community work into direct service practice, another pattern is prevalent in our field as well. During their careers, many social work practitioners *move back and forth* between positions labeled as direct service, clinical, or micro-practice and positions labeled as community intervention, management, or macro-practice. Some jobs could fall under either rubric. The professional experience from a resume of a successful social work practitioner—with clinical, administrative, institutional, and community experience—illustrates these points.

- Case work—licensed foster, adoptive, and daycare homes.
- Supervisor, Family Services Unit—state Department of Children and Family Services. Child abuse and neglect emphsis.
- Developed and directed a public resource center for a village that had no library previously.
- Director, Community Resource and Infant Stimulation Program, Association for

Retarded Citizens (county). Program development, grant writing. A second position emphasized coordination, respite care program.

- Hospital social work (surgery, maternal and child health, and adolescent medicine units). Publications on geriatric use of emergency departments and interagency relationships.
- Demonstration Project by university for inner city community. Engaged in aggressive outreach, case management, supportive services, and advocacy with families who did not meet tougher requirements to stay on the Aid to Families with Dependent Children program.

Finally, regarding work patterns, while the majority of those becoming social workers envision themselves providing direct personal service or therapy, the jobs actually held throughout one's career are affected by many factors, including national funding shifts, geographic moves, and shifts in personal interest. Thus better understanding of community enhances (1) integration into clinical work, (2) success in either community or clinically oriented jobs, and (3) being well positioned for future career changes.

This text is intended to prepare practitioners who spend full time, part time, or some time during their careers concentrating on building communities and serving residents. It is also intended to help all social workers integrate community practice into their social work practice, no matter what their specialization or approach.

What unifies social work practice that builds on community is a philosophy of "being there" for people that goes beyond psychological support. A commitment to community means being available to any group in the community, hearing what all citizens want, and providing for those most in need. It means choosing locations, hours, and staff that will make service users experience us as

being there for them, available to them. It means providing the political support needed for programs to survive and thrive and to protect the vulnerable and marginalized. As just described, helping practitioners can contribute to the community in different ways at different points in their careers, so long as they stay open to community needs, demands, and desires.

This type of work is valued by the larger society. A number of organizations (such as the MacArthur Foundation) give awards to those making outstanding contributions to the public good. For example, Box 14.1 describes the work of several of the first nine recipients of the American Achievement Awards sponsored by a national news magazine. They epitomize the work of those "who are quietly making a difference in communities across the country" (*Newsweek*, 1995, p. 26). These social workers and the other award recipients were honored with a ceremony at the Kennedy Center.

THE NEED TO REVITALIZE COMMUNITIES

As we look at some of the changes occurring in the American political economy, we see an increasing emphasis on devolving responsibility for human services on smaller, more local units of government and to private for-profit and nonprofit organizations. Health care, mental health services, nursing care, services to the elderly, education, social work services, and many other types of human services are concerned with local service alliances, maintaining clients or patients in the community, and maintaining local control that will be more accountable to ordinary citizens. At the same time, private enterprise seems to be moving toward corporate mergers to create megastructures and a global economy. The creation of a worldwide communication web has already occurred. One

BOX 14.1   **EXEMPLARY PRACTICE IN OUR COMMUNITIES**

REHABBING BROKEN HOMES—AND SPIRITS

The Phoenix Group

Archie Roberts needed serious help. He was homeless, living on friends' couches when he was lucky and in shelters when he wasn't. Because of an "anger problem" and a cocaine habit, he hadn't held a steady job in years. He didn't know where his five children were. At the age of 40, he had nothing to show for himself except a bad back, a case of diabetes and $68. "It was like, the end of my life," says Roberts. That's when he met The Phoenix Group.

The group was founded in 1991 by Chuck Beattie and Bret Byfield, two Minneapolis social workers who shared a growing anger at the way government helps—or fails to help—street people like Roberts. Throwing money at them doesn't work, Byfield and Beattie believed, at least not for long. The key is helping them find jobs, a community and a sense of purpose for themselves. Armed with a few grants from private donors and foundations as well as a healthy dose of optimism, they began buying run-down houses on Minneapolis's shabby south side and fixing them up. They not only hired and trained people like Roberts to do the construction and maintenance; they also moved the homeless workers in, so they could benefit from what they'd built. "It's the most hopeful activity I've seen in a long time," says former Minnesota Human Services commissioner Sandra Gardebring.

It didn't stop there. Phoenix now houses more than 300 tenants in 39 properties, all run by Steve Wash. And as its successes multiplied, the group has started other operations to employ its residents. It opened an upholstery shop, a supermarket, an art gallery—11 businesses in all, and all hiring people who couldn't get work elsewhere. Some, like the People's Garage auto shop, turn a tidy profit. Most, like the Wall Art Gallery and the Phoenix Cafe, about break even. But profits are beside the point. "I don't make a lot of money, but I feel like I'm a king," says Roberts, who earns $290 a month as a Phoenix property manager. He also owns a Phoenix-rebuilt home and spends the summers with his kids, who visit him in Minneapolis. "Nothing can stop me."

"SHE MAKES US FEEL WONDERFUL"

Anita Septimus

When Anita Septimus started as a social worker for HIV-infected children in 1985, she did not know how emotionally draining the job would be. In her first few months she watched three of her tiny clients die—and the despair began to overwhelm her. She turned for advice to Dr. Arye Rubinstein, head of the Pediatric AIDS Center at New York's Albert Einstein College of Medicine. What was the point? How could she help these children? Rubinstein persuaded her to give it three more months, and Septimus did some soul-searching. She remembered a classmate in social-work school who complained about working in poor areas. "My teacher said, 'Well, my friend, you have not chosen a pretty profession.' Those words were ringing in my head."

That was 10 years ago. The clinic has since grown to become the Family Comprehensive AIDS Center, and Septimus now heads its social-work department. She and her staff look after more than 300 families with AIDS-infected children—going to their homes, teaching infection prevention and helping parents plan for the future. They also give their young clients a semblance of childhood, with trips to the zoo, the circus and summer camps. "She makes us feel wonderful about ourselves," says Petra Berrios, the mother of a child with AIDS who is HIV-positive herself.

That, Septimus says, is her job—helping families make the most of the lives they have. Happily, that time is expanding for some of them. One AIDS baby at the center wasn't expected to see her first birthday. Now she's 10 years old. Such "long term" clients give Septimus something in return—what she calls an "indestructible sense of hope." As she puts it, "You don't choose the day you enter the world and you don't choose the day you leave. It's what you do in between that makes all the difference.

trend pushes toward strengthening local communities, the other toward looser, less rooted, more fragmented relationships. How do we reconcile these trends?

While there is no easy answer and no either/or solution, a fundamental axiom of this book, presented in Chapter 1, is that vigorous, fit communities are necessary for healthy and empowered individuals. People live in local communities; they want and need real relationships, not just virtual relationships. We have to be able to build the social infrastructures that enable us to take care of each other. We need strong communities to deal with the forces pressing toward dislocation. Fragmented, atomistic communities will spawn insecure, vulnerable, and suspicious individuals. A robust sense of community is fundamental to mutual support. A fit community is an important contributor to our individual and collective mental health (Doherty, 1995). Social workers have an important part to play in fostering healthy communities.

DETERIORATION OF COMMUNITY

The shift in the American community over the past several decades from locality-focused communities stressing primary, holistic relationships and responsibilities to vertical communities based on more explicit social contracts, divisions of labor, and secondary relationships have led to an estrangement of people from one another. The horizontal community, the locality-focused community where people live, get their needs met, and learn the skills of social participation, is in danger of antiquation as community functions become increasingly specialized. Community complexity and fragmentation have resulted in a growing sense of individual isolation, social organization around limited special interests, "lifestyle" enclaves within local and national communities, increasing normlessness

and loss of community values to guide behavior, loss of local control, and lack of congruence among the community functions (see Chapter 4) within a locality (Bellah, Sullivan, Swidler, & Tipton, 1985, 1992; Corlett, 1989).

Today some community functions (especially production and distribution) are carried out nationally and often globally. Decisions are made regarding one community function without considering its effects on other community functions. Community functions generally do not correspond geographically or socially. Decision making is more remote from the individual. As Nisbet (1953) asserted almost a half century ago, "for more and more individuals the primary social relationships [of community] have lost much of their historic function of mediation between man and the larger ends of our civilization" (p. 52). Without strong local communities, citizens will become mere accessories of the state and the global economy rather than these being the servants of the people and the community.

For many years, mediating and integrating community structures in American society, such as the family, the neighborhood, and the civic association, have grown weaker. Now, for example, political and civic participation has declined to an almost negligible level for the poor, the working class, and much of the middle class (Bureau of the Census, 1995, pp. 286–287; Doherty & Etzioni, 1994–95; "Portrait of the Electorate," 1994). There is less parental involvement in schools and PTAs; less regular churchgoing and participation, even though organized religious affiliation levels are up; and lower union, fraternal, and civic association membership. From 1967 to 1993, group memberships have fallen for college-educated individuals from 2.8 to 2.0 per person, for high school graduates, from 1.8 to 1.2, and for those with less than a high school education from 1.4 to 1.1 (Putnam, 1995, p. 27).

Primary and secondary groups are where people learn the skills of social interaction, civic participation, and individual and collective efficacy. However, secondary associations and involvement are being replaced by more impersonal tertiary relations, interaction, and organizations (Putnam, 1995). Bureaucratic structures have filled some of the void, although dissatisfaction has been rapidly mounting. The radio and television talk show has replaced the give-and-take of face-to-face social and political debate on community issues. Television and videos have replaced recreational social engagements. Leisure has become more solitary due to technology. Virtual reality is touted as an acceptable alternative to physical reality.

Tertiary mass membership groups like the National Rifle Association and the American Association of Retired Persons have also evolved with the help of new mass communication technologies. These tertiary associations often have political clout, but they also lack internal social connectiveness. Membership is tied together by ideology and leaders, but members are not solidly bonded by social interaction. Members' interest in each other is often limited.

A wide array of specialized support and therapy groups are replacing many primary and secondary social support groups and networks. The tertiary support and therapy groups now emerging on the electronic networks and "webs," while perhaps valuable, limit member involvement, sharing, and bonding, and hence are constrained in their capacity to serve a general mediating function for their members.

In the political arena, the town meeting, formal and informal face to face discussion and debate, consensus building, and traditional modes of interacting have been replaced by representative government, nominal political parties, and PACs. The number of people who vote in elections is down, and seems to be giving way to voting by public opinion polls and impersonal talk shows where discussion to decide "how things ought to be" is isolated and anonymous.

Civic participation is essential for a healthy community. *It is essential to participatory democracy.* In the words of Hollenbach (1994–95), "democratic life and the exercise of true freedom . . . depends on the strength of the communal relationships that give persons a measure of real power to shape their environment, including their political environment. . . . [D]emocracy . . . requires the virtues of mutual cooperation [and] mutual responsibility" (p. 20).

Not surprisingly, with the decline of civic participation of the poor, the working class, and the middle class since the 1980s and especially in the 1990s, we have seen diminished government interest in and support for these strata of the community. National social policymakers are abandoning welfare functions to the economic marketplace or to economically hard-pressed state and local political jurisdictions. Without revitalized social and civic participation, this barren trend will continue. Phillips (1990) postulates that the state's interests are largely a reflection of who controls the government. "Since the American Revolution the distribution of American wealth has depended significantly on *who controlled the federal government, for what policies, and in behalf of which constituencies*" (p. xiv). Although lower-income and less educated populations tend to favor a more communitarian and mutual support ideology, they vote at lower proportions than higher-income segments of the community. Without greater political participation, government and community decision makers will not consider the interests of low-income and minority group members.

REVITALIZATION OF COMMUNITY

Communities need to be revitalized because such communities will be better places for us all to live and to work. Observers from de Tocqueville to those of the present day have observed that the quality of public life and the performance of social institutions are powerfully influenced by the quality and quantity of civic participation (Putnam, 1995, p. 18). Schools perform better with strong parental and community involvement. Government is more responsive and efficient. Neighborhoods are safer. And, most critically, the capacity for mutual support and helping is enhanced. Mutual support is one of the features that distinguishes community from a simple aggregate of people.

Healthy communities and social environments do not just occur; they need to be developed. Their development is an obligation of all social workers, not just of community organizers and developers. In their rebuilding, we will need to spend much effort looking for shared concerns, shared values, and common resources while still finding ways to value cultural diversity and draw strength from it (Chafetz, 1993–94). This is a challenging task when you consider that the social variance within gender and ethnic groups is probably as great as any variance between the groups.

Essential in the revitalization of community is the reinforcement of public morality. Communitarians such as Etzioni maintain that there are, or need to be, common values for the community into which all members are socialized. A viable community, says Etzioni (1993) requires

a set of dos and don'ts, a set of moral values, that guides people toward what is decent and encourages them to avoid that which is not. . . . *We need to return to a society in which certain actions are viewed as beyond the pale*, things that upright people would not do

or even consider: to walk out on children, file false insurance claims, cheat on tests. . . . (p. 24)

While these values need not reflect a particular religious base, they would reflect a common ideology. They would address the moral responsibility of people to help themselves as best they can and would emphasize that citizenship and membership in the community carry responsibilities and obligations as well as rights, that children are not a right that come without responsibilities, that human life is to be respected, and that differences not harmful to others are to be tolerated.

Jim Wallis, cofounder and pastor of Sojourners Community in Washington, D.C., writes (1992) that community concerns such as helping the poor and the distressed, restoring a safe environment, maintaining the physical infrastructure, and reinvigorating healthy families

can be achieved only by a combination of solid moral values and sound social policy. This requires a number of fundamental shifts in perspective—from unlimited growth to a sustainable society; from endless consumer goods to re-prioritizing of social good; from the habit of self-protection to an ethic of community; from viewing life as an acquisitive venture to restoring the sacred values of our relationship with our neighbor and our environment. These shifts will not be easy, nor will they come without costs. The only thing more costly is not to change. (p. 15)

Without strong socialization to a congruent set of values, there is no internal control of behavior. The result is a greater need for the external imposition of social control of behavior by the community or the state.

Community revitalization also will require the establishment of a foundation of trust. Trust, the ability to feel secure with another, is essential if mutual support, caring, and sharing are to occur. If we view others as exploiters or free riders, and ourselves as victims or suckers, then mutual support, mutual identity and caring and sharing are difficult to accomplish (de Jasay, 1989). If our clients are not perceived as participants in community life, as communally responsible, and as fulfilling a public or common good, then, in the eyes of the public, *they* are free riders and *we*, the rest of the community, must be suckers.

Trust is diminishing among Americans and apparently has been for several years. David Brinkley (1993), the news commentator and observer of the American scene in the 1960s, related a report of two British college students traveling in the United States. The students spent a summer hitchhiking in the United States and kept a record of their experience. They traveled through almost every state and reported that they had been met always with friendliness and courtesy. They obtained rides by holding up a cardboard sign stating "We are British." Their records indicated that they received 916 rides by 916 different Americans. Ninety-two percent of the people who gave them rides "sooner or later in conversation said something like this: "If you were American, I would not have picked you up" (p. 20). The hitchhikers' interpretation of this response was that it went beyond curiosity about foreigners to a lack of trust between Americans "because they [Americans] were afraid of them [Americans] or did not trust them [Americans]" (p. 20). The proportion of Americans who say that most people can be trusted declined from 58% in 1960 to 35% in 1994 (Putnam, 1995, p. 28). Trust is a necessary ingredient of community building. Trusting people are more optimistic, altruistic, and willing to work on community and shared problems (Putnam, 1995, p. 29). Trust will, however, require a shared set of moral values, as discussed earlier, as well as an emphasis on our similarities. There needs to be a sense of "we-ness."

In a State of the Union Address, President Clinton stated: "Our civil life is suffering in America today. Citizens are working together less and shouting at each other more. The common bonds of community which have been the great strength of our country from its very beginning are badly frayed" (January 24, 1995). We share these concerns and have tried to respond to them in this book. Direct service practitioners are being called back to the community by fellow social work professionals (Martinez-Brawley, 1990; Specht & Courtney, 1994), and those in the empowerment tradition see a key role for social workers—if we would just play it (Simon, 1994). Basic principles of community organization—community control, participation in decision making—are being restated in new ways, and sometimes in older, more familiar ones. These include rebuilding local activist organizations from the bottom up, as well as registering to vote (Piven & Cloward, 1988) so as to be more able to influence the decisions that affect our lives. In the words of Lappe and DuBois (1994), "Living democracy is about creating real power, not just temporarily alleviating misery" (p. 163).

GOING BACK TO THE FUTURE

As we move toward the 21st century, it is hard to avoid comparisons with American society and social work in the early 20th century. While society has obviously changed in many ways since 1900, especially in astounding new technologies, in other respects, today's Americans are struggling with many of the same social, political, and economic issues. During the late 19th and early 20th centuries, America experienced an enormous transformation from a rural to an industrial, urbanized, corporate economy, just as in the late 20th century we have been changing from an industrial to a postindustrial, high-technology, service-based economy. In both periods, these changes have produced a very uneven pattern of social and economic development. "In 1900 a relatively small number of families and corporations owned most of the nation's wealth, while much of the worst poverty was concentrated in the newest and least powerful groups: industrial workers, immigrants, and rural Southern blacks" (Wenocur & Reisch, 1989, p. 22). Today the disparity in wealth is just as great, and southern and northern blacks, immigrants, and unemployed industrial workers carry the heaviest burdens of poverty. Granted, current immigrant groups are not coming primarily from Europe; still, attitudes toward immigrants are also just as negative. In 1880, a leading charity in New York wrote, "Our city, operating like a sieve, lets through the enterprising and industrious, while it retains the indolent, the aged and the infirm . . . to become a burden and often because of their vices, a nuisance to the community" (Association for the Improvement of the Conditions of the Poor, 1880, p. 1, as quoted in Wenocur & Reisch, 1989, p. 23). Today we have legislation aimed at preventing legal and illegal immigrants from receiving welfare and other public benefits and services. In addition, we have experienced a massive degree of corporate and white flight from cities to suburbs, leaving behind an impoverished population of unskilled, unemployed, and underemployed men and women, disproportionately made up of minority group members, including immigrants, and the elderly.

With respect to urban and rural social problems, some older ones are still with us—poverty, inadequate health care, hunger, illiteracy, and poor schools, to name a few; some that we thought had been eradicated are coming back, like tuberculosis; and new problems have surfaced to replace some of the older ones—child abuse replacing child labor, for example. Finally, there are new problems—substance abuse, violence, and AIDS, perhaps like nothing ever seen before in their form and prevalence.

What about the government's response then and now? In 1995, a Republican Congress was making plans to go back to the pre-1930 era by transferring responsibility for basic social protections from the federal government to state and local entities and to for-profit and nonprofit organizations, that is, privatization. Even popular welfare state programs and entitlements like Social Security, Medicare, and Medicaid are in jeopardy. At the same time, in the name of encouraging prosperity, conservative Republicans and Democrats are pushing for tax relief for the wealthy by reducing capital gains taxes, and a variety of new, nonprogressive tax strategies, as well as loosening of restraints on corporations through deregulation of banking, occupational safety, and environmental laws, among others. These "reforms" sound much like President Harding's post–World War I recipe's for a "return to normalcy," which included a repeal of progressive taxes on income, inheritance, and profits, subsidizing industries, and a hands-off approach to antitrust laws. On the social front, the 1920s also fostered racism and intolerance, with attacks on unions and labor leaders, socialists, immigrants, and blacks. For example, the Ku Klux Klan, promoting white supremacy, had 4.5 million members by 1924 (Wenocur & Reisch, 1989), not unlike the growing militia movement of the 1990s, while in the same year Congress established quotas on immigration. If America in the millennium returns to pre-1930s social, political, and economic policies and practices, is it possible that we will also have to relive the Great Depression of the 1930s in the 2030s?

Whether or not America experiences a new Great Depression, the conservative social policies and programs now in the offing will place a great deal of stress on local communities. Neighborhoods and cities, whose resources are already stretched thin, will be challenged to draw on some deeper reservoir of community good will, concern, and mutual support to deal humanely with increased levels of social distress. Social workers will inevitably be drawn into community-based social work to provide direct services; to bear witness and testify to inhumane social conditions, just as settlement workers did in the late 1920s and early 1930s; and to help communities organize themselves to obtain resources and challenge regressive social policies. Social work researchers will also be drawn back to a focus on the community to help "track the effects of policy changes as they occur" and "to contribute to the development of a modernized version of community social work practice" (Coulton, 1995, p. 439). As Claudia Coulton asked in a recent *Social Work* editorial (1995):

> Does social work practice today have ways of connecting workers in poor communities to training and labor markets, creating networks to meet family needs, building communities' internal controls, generating community-supported emergency and other types of assistance, and restoring communities as climates for economic opportunity? That is what a community social worker will need to do, not alone, of course, but collaboratively with leaders and residents. Practice research must support the development and enhancement of social work methods that can be embedded in and use the strengths of the community context. (p. 439)

With the millennium approaching, it is clear that, from many quarters, our profession is being asked to have even more of a face-to-face connection with community groups. We must do the work of the world together.

CONCLUSION: "ON THE GROUND" SOCIAL WORK

Our profession must make many decisions on how to be most relevant and effective in a changing world. In the meantime, practitioners must get out there and do what needs to be done now to support community and to respond to what community residents seek. One professional put it this way:

> I set out to stay involved with issues on the ground in everyday life, people's struggles in their everyday life, to find a way, by working at the intersections between theory and practice, of doing that while still keeping my eye on the bigger picture. . . . (Forester, 1994, p. 333)

Something needs doing. Community policing, community health, community service by high school students—in all cases, the idea is to get people out of buildings and into the world, *into the field*, as some would put it, or into the fray, or *"on the ground,"* as journalists now say when they mean having an *engaged and immediate presence*. Being present is an idea used in many ways for example, "Once our staff member was on the ground in Costa Rica we had a much better handle on what was really going on." On the ground contrasts with in a car, in the air, in a command center away from the action. It also contrasts with *office bound*.

"On the ground" is a phrase originally used—by broadcasters and print reporters—in international aid and military contexts to describe the role taken by those deployed literally on the ground, in contrast to those providing air support, gathering intelligence, or operating ham radios from within the zone. In a war context (and perhaps our inner cities are exploding and imploding), "on the ground" means viewing circumstances from the beleaguered participant's point of view, no matter how gritty or uncomfortable this may be. In a crisis, "on the ground" suggests a concrete response. For instance, "Three weeks from now, there will be 4,000 Americans on the ground in Zaire, Uganda, Kenya and probably Rwanda" (*Newsweek,* August 1, 1994, p. 28).

Perhaps even more to our purposes, journalists have taken to using the phrase metaphorically as well to denote where action is taking place, where help is clearly needed and one has to be there with the people to provide it, and where the white gloves come off and one hits the ground running. Others use the phrase in the sense of "from the ground up," real life, or being out there. For instance, a review on the back of *Checkerboard Square* commends it as "an excellent on-the-ground ethnography of the human content of homelessness" (Wagner, 1993). Others use it (as in the Forester quote above) to mean staying in touch with current realities of ordinary people's lives. Most uses of the phrase presuppose increased involvement at the local or community level and increased insight.

Being there for others, being present with others, is a physical and psychological commitment. This war-crisis metaphor signifies compassion, action, results, and courage. It suggests that if we are not out there in the middle of things, we can't be effective. Professionally, we see on-the-ground commitment from individuals who enter medical school at a time when their peers avoid it due to fear of HIV, national health insurance, or malpractice suits; from lawyers who provide legal aid in all corners of town with a goal of achieving social justice; and

from social workers who work daily with those without homes, those living with AIDS, those being physically abused—emotionally draining situations. Besides tuning in and being responsive, on-the-ground commitment also means taking an *active* stance, vigorously addressing problems alongside fellow citizens.

Perhaps Marge Piercy had something like this in mind when she wrote "To Be of Use" (1994). We end with her poem.[1]

The people I love the best
jump into work head first
without dallying in the shadows
and swim off with sure strokes almost out
  of sight.
They seem to become natives of that element,
the black sleek heads of seals
bouncing like half-submerged balls.

I love people who harness themselves, an ox to
  a heavy cart,
who pull like water buffalo, with massive patience,
who strain in the mud and the muck to move
  things forward,
who do what has to be done, again and again.

I want to be with people who submerge
in the task, who go into the fields to harvest
and work in a row and pass the bags along,
who are not parlor generals and field desert-
  ers
but move in a common rhythm
when the food must come in or the fire be put
  out.

The work of the world is common as mud.
Botched, it smears the hands, crumbles to dust.
But the thing worth doing well
has a shape that satisfies, clean and evident.
Greek amphoras for wine or oil,
Hopi vases that held corn, are put in museums
but you know they were made to be used.
The pitcher cries for water to carry
and a person for work that is real.

Note

1. "To Be of Use" by Marge Piercy. From CIRCLES ON THE WATER by Marge Piercy. Copyright © 1982 by Marge Piercy.

References

Adams, P., & Krauth, K. (1995). Working with families and communities: The patch approach. In P. Adams & K. Nelson (Eds.), *Reinventing human services: Community and family-centered practice* (pp. 87–108). New York: Aldine de Gruyter.

Adams, P., & Nelson, K. (Eds.). (1995). *Reinventing human services: Community and family-centered practice.* New York: Aldine de Gruyter.

Auerswald, E. H. (1968). Interdisciplinary versus ecological approach. *Family Process, 7,* 202–215.

Bellah, R. N., Sullivan, W. M., Swidler, A., & Tipton, S. M. (1985). *Habits of the heart: Individualism and commitment in American life.* New York: Harper & Row.

Bellah, R. N., Sullivan, W. M., Swidler, A., & Tipton, S. M. (1992). *The good society.* New York: Vintage Books.

Berger, P. L., & Neuhaus, R. J. (1977). *To empower people: The role of mediating structures in public policy.* Washington, DC: American Enterprise Institute.

Brieland, D. (1990). The Hull House tradition and the contemporary social worker: Was Jane Addams really a social worker? *Social Work, 35*(2), 134–138.

Brinkley, D. (1993). Public services and private trust. *Public Welfare, 51*(1), 19–20.

Bureau of the Census. (1995). *Statistical abstract of the United States; 1994* (114th ed.). Washington, DC: U.S. Government Printing Office.

Chafetz, J. S. (1993–94). Minorities, gender, mythologies, and moderation. *The Responsive Community: Rights and Responsibilities, 4*(1), 40–46.

Chapin, R. K. (1995). Social policy development: The strengths perspective. *Social Work, 40*(4), 506–514.

Cohen, B. J. (1980). Coordination strategies in complex service delivery systems. *Administration in Social Work, 4*(3), 83–87.

Corlett, W. (1989). *Community without unity: A politics of Derridian extravagance.* Durham, NC: Duke University Press.

Coulton, C. J. (1995). Riding the pendulum of the 1990s: Building a community context for social work research. *Social Work, 40*(4), 437–439.

Cowger, C. D. (1994). Assessing client strengths: Clinical assessment for client empowerment. *Social Work, 39*(3), 262–267.

de Jasay, A. (1989). *Social contract, free rides: A study of the public goods problem.* New York: Oxford University Press.

De Jong, P., & Miller, S. D. (1995). How to interview for client strengths. *Social Work, 40*(6), 729–736.

Doherty, D., & Etzioni, A. (1994–95). The commitment gap. *The Responsive Community: Rights and Responsibilities, 5*(1), 75–77.

Doherty, W. (1995). Community considerations in psychotherapy. *The Responsive Community: Rights and Responsibilities, 5*(2), 45–53.

Dore, M. N. (1993, November). Family preservation and poor families: When "homebuilders" is not enough. *Families in Society: The Journal of Contemporary Human Services, 73*(9), 545–553

Etzioni, A. (1993). *The spirit of community: Rights, responsibilities and the communitarian agenda.* New York: Crown Books.

Everyday heroes: A tribute to Americans who care. (1995, May 29). *Newsweek,* pp. 28–29.

Falck, H. (1988). *Social work: The membership perspective.* New York: Springer.

Forester, J. (1994). Lawrence Susskind: Activist mediation and public disputes. In D. M. Kolb (Ed.), *When talk works: Profiles of mediators* (pp. 309–354). San Francisco: Jossey-Bass.

Fullinwider, R. K. (1988). Citizenship and welfare. In A. Gutman (Ed.), *Democracy and the welfare* state (pp. 261–278). Princeton, NJ: Princeton University Press.

Gutierrez, L. (1990). Working with women of color: An empowerment perspective, *Social Work*, 35(2), 149–153.

Hancock, B. L. & Pelton, L. H. (1989). Home visits: History and functions. *Social Casework*, 70(1), 21–27.

Hodges, V., & Blythe, B. J. (1992). Improving service delivery to high risk families: Home-based practice. *Families in Society: The Journal of Contemporary Human Services*, 73(5), 259–265.

Hollenbach, D. (1994–95). Beyond the public–private dichotomy. *The Responsive Community: Rights and Responsibilities*, 5(1), 15–23.

Indyk, D., Belville, R., Lachapelle, S., Gordon, G., & Dewart, T. (1993). A community-based approach to HIV case management. *Social Work*, 38(4), 380–387.

Lappe, F. M., & DuBois, P. M. (1994). *The quickening of America: Rebuilding our nation, reworking our lives*, San Francisco: Jossey-Bass.

Lightburn, A., & Kemp, S. P. (1994). Family-support programs: Opportunities for community-based practice. *Families in Society: The Journal of Contemporary Human Services*, 75(1), 16–22.

Martinez-Brawley, E. E. (1990). *Perspectives on the small community: Humanistic views for practitioners*. Washington, DC. National Association of Social Workers.

Mayer, S. E. (1991, November 6). The assets model of community development. Remarks made at a conference on "Maximizing Returns on Community Development," Denver, CO.

McCollough, T. E. (1991). *The moral imagination and public life: Raising the ethical question*. Chatham, NJ: Chatham House.

Nisbet, R. (1953). *The quest for community: A study in the ethics of order and freedom*. New York: Oxford University Press.

Phillips, K. P. (1990). *The politics of rich and poor: Wealth and the American electorate in the Reagan aftermath*. New York: Random House.

Piercy, M. (1994). In circles on the water. *Selected poems of Marge Piercey* (p. 106). New York: Alfred A. Knopf.

Piven, F. F., & Cloward, R. A. (1988). *Why Americans don't vote*. New York: Pantheon.

Portrait of the electorate: Who voted for whom in the House. (1994, November 13). *The New York Times*, p. 24.

Potok, C. (1983). *Cultural confrontation in urban America: A writer's beginnings*. Unpublished paper presented at the Urban Experience Conference, Rutgers University [on video].

Putnam, R. D. (1995). Bowling alone. *The Responsive Community: Rights and Responsibilities*, 5(2), 18–33.

A race with death. (1994, August 1). *Newsweek*, pp. 26–31.

Richmond, M. E. (1917). *Social diagnosis*. New York: Russell Sage Foundation.

Rothman, J., Erlich, J., & Tropman, J. E. (Eds.). (1995). *Strategies of community intervention*. Itasca, IL: F. E. Peacock.

Saleebey, D. (Ed.). (1992). *The strengths perspective in social work practice*. White Plains, New York: Longman.

Simon, B. L. (1994). *The empowerment tradition in American social work: A history*. New York: Columbia University Press.

Solomon, B. B. (1976). *Black empowerment: Social work in oppressed communities*. New York: Columbia University Press.

Specht, H., & Courtney, M. (1994). *Unfaithful angels: How social work has abandoned its mission*. New York: Free Press.

The 1994 elections. (1994, November 9). *The New York Times*, p. B4.

Tracy, E. M., Whittaker, J. K., Pugh, A., Kapp, S. N., & Overstreet, E. J. (1994). Support networks of primary caregivers receiving family preservation services: An exploratory study. *Families in Society: The Journal of Contemporary Human Services*, 75(8), 481–489.

Wagner, D. (1993). *Checkerboard square: Culture and resistance in a homeless community*. Boulder: CO: Westview.

Wallis, J. (1992). Violence, poverty, and separation: No one really expects the children of the inner cities to enter the economic mainstream. *Public Welfare*, 50(4), 14–15.

Warren, R. L. (1978). *The community in America* (3rd ed.). Chicago: Rand McNally.

Wasik, B. H., Bryant, D. M., & Lyons, C. M. (1990). *Home visiting*. Newbury Park, CA: Sage.

Weissman, H., Epstein, I., & Savage, A. (1983). *Agency-based social work: Neglected aspects of clinical practice*. Philadelphia: Temple University Press.

Wenocur, S., & Reisch, M. (1989). *From charity to enterprise: The development of American social work in a market economy*. Urbana: University of Illinois Press

Author Index

431

Subject Index